The Linguistics of Hu

The Linguistics of Humor

An Introduction

SALVATORE ATTARDO

OXFORD
UNIVERSITY PRESS

OXFORD
UNIVERSITY PRESS

Great Clarendon Street, Oxford, OX2 6DP,
United Kingdom

Oxford University Press is a department of the University of Oxford.
It furthers the University's objective of excellence in research, scholarship,
and education by publishing worldwide. Oxford is a registered trade mark of
Oxford University Press in the UK and in certain other countries

© Salvatore Attardo 2020

The moral rights of the author have been asserted

First Edition published in 2020

Impression: 3

All rights reserved. No part of this publication may be reproduced, stored in
a retrieval system, or transmitted, in any form or by any means, without the
prior permission in writing of Oxford University Press, or as expressly permitted
by law, by licence or under terms agreed with the appropriate reprographics
rights organization. Enquiries concerning reproduction outside the scope of the
above should be sent to the Rights Department, Oxford University Press, at the
address above

You must not circulate this work in any other form
and you must impose this same condition on any acquirer

Published in the United States of America by Oxford University Press
198 Madison Avenue, New York, NY 10016, United States of America

British Library Cataloguing in Publication Data

Data available

Library of Congress Control Number: 2019942517

ISBN 978–0–19–879127–0 (hbk.)
ISBN 978–0–19–879128–7 (pbk.)

Printed and bound by
CPI Group (UK) Ltd, Croydon, CR0 4YY

Links to third party websites are provided by Oxford in good faith and
for information only. Oxford disclaims any responsibility for the materials
contained in any third party website referenced in this work.

Contents

Preface — xiii
List of figures — xix
List of tables — xxi

PART I. Humor Studies

1. Humor studies: a few definitions — 3

- 1.1 Terminology — 4
  - 1.1.1 The characters — 4
  - 1.1.2 Humor as umbrella term — 7
  - 1.1.3 Joke — 14
  - 1.1.4 Mirth, humor, laughter — 17
- 1.2 A brief overview of humor studies — 18
  - 1.2.1 Why do we need a field of study? — 23
- 1.3 A few basic distinctions — 25
  - 1.3.1 Linguistic humor vs. verbal humor — 25
  - 1.3.2 Humor and meta-humor — 26
- 1.4 Further readings — 29

2. Methodological preliminaries — 30

- 2.1 Competence and performance — 31
  - 2.1.1 Application of the principle of commutation to humor — 34
  - 2.1.2 Other methodologies — 36
- 2.2 Identifying humor — 38
  - 2.2.1 Humor, mirth, and smiling/laughter — 39
  - 2.2.2 Smiling — 40
  - 2.2.3 Laughter — 41
- 2.3 Mirthful vs. non-mirthful laughter — 42
  - 2.3.1 On the lack of direct linear correlation between humor and mirth displays — 44
  - 2.3.2 Recognition vs. appreciation — 46
  - 2.3.3 Confusion between humor and humor appreciation — 49

2.4 Keying — 50
2.4.1 Playful mode — 51
2.4.2 Surprise — 53
2.4.3 Unintentional humor — 53
2.5 Identifying humor: the triangulation approach — 54
2.6 Further readings — 56

3. Theories of humor and their levels — 57
3.1 Explanation, reductionism, essentialism — 57
3.2 The three major theories of humor — 59
3.3 Humor as release — 60
3.3.1 Humor as play — 61
3.3.2 Are release and play theories essentialist? — 63
3.4 Humor as incongruity — 64
3.5 Humor as aggression — 64
3.6 Other theories — 67
3.6.1 Neurolinguistics of humor — 68
3.6.2 Evolutionary theories — 69
3.6.3 Anti-essentialist theories — 69
3.6.4 Mixed, partial, and no-theory-theories — 70
3.7 Complementarity of the theories of humor — 71
3.7.1 Evaluation of theories — 73
3.7.2 Bisociation theory — 73
3.7.3 Evaluation of the theories — 74
3.8 Further readings — 77

4. Incongruity and resolution — 78
4.1 Incongruity — 79
4.1.1 Enter semantics — 81
4.2 Resolution — 82
4.2.1 The history of resolution — 83
4.2.2 Full vs. partial resolution — 87
4.2.3 Foregrounded vs. backgrounded incongruities — 88
4.3 Linear organization of the joke — 90
4.3.1 The isotopy–disjunction model — 91

4.4 Conclusions	93
4.5 Further readings	94

5. Semiotics of humor — 95

5.1 Humor and semiotics	96
5.1.1 Communication and semiosis	96
5.1.2 Connotative semiotics	97
5.1.3 Perlocutionary definition of humor	98
5.1.4 Defunctionalization of the sign	99
5.1.5 Semantics vs. semiotics of humor	103
5.2 Conclusions	108
5.3 Further readings	109

PART II. Humor Competence

6. The semantics of humor — 113

6.1 The Semantic Script Theory	113
6.1.1 Origins	114
6.1.2 The notion of script	116
6.1.3 Dynamic scripts	123
6.1.4 Combinatorial explosion	126
6.2 The Semantic Script Theory of Humor's two conditions	127
6.2.1 Oppositeness	128
6.2.2 Overlapping	128
6.2.3 The exemplar doctor's wife joke	129
6.2.4 Methodological issues	131
6.3 Non-bona-fide	133
6.4 The Ontological Semantics Theory of Humor	134
6.5 Conclusions	134
6.6 Further readings	135

7. The General Theory of Verbal Humor — 136

7.1 The knowledge resources	137
7.1.1 Language	138
7.1.2 Narrative Strategy	141
7.1.3 Target	144

7.1.4 Situation	147
7.1.5 Logical Mechanism	149
7.1.6 Script Opposition	150
7.2 Further issues with the General Theory of Verbal Humor	152
7.2.1 Broadening the Theory?	152
7.2.2 The application of the General Theory of Verbal Humor to longer texts	153
7.2.3 A small methodological note on cherry-picking	154
7.3 Conclusions	156
7.4 Further readings	156

8. Pragmatics of humor — 157

8.1 Pragmatic principles	158
8.1.1 Speech acts	158
8.1.2 Cooperation and implicatures	159
8.1.3 Implicature	161
8.1.4 Humor and the implicit	163
8.2 Nature of the violation of the CP	163
8.2.1 Is humor a flout?	163
8.2.2 The LDP	166
8.3 Irony and humor	168
8.4 All humor is intentional	170
8.5 Conclusions	175
8.6 Further readings	175

9. Verbal humor — 176

9.1 Defining puns	177
9.2 Classifying puns	180
9.3 Ways to bring about two meanings in a text	181
9.3.1 Ambiguity	181
9.3.2 Syntagmatic placement	186
9.3.3 Paronymy and phonetic distance	188
9.3.4 Connectors and disjunctors	190
9.4 The fate of the interpretation	191

9.5 Cratylism: resolution in puns	192
9.5.1 Evidence for the Cratylistic folk-theory	194
9.6 The psycholinguistics of puns	196
9.7 Conclusions	197
9.8 Further readings	198

PART III. Humor Performance

10. The performance of humor — 201

10.1 A little history never hurt anyone	202
10.1.1 Early studies on the social context of humor	203
10.1.2 Carrell's performance theory	203
10.1.3 Stand-up performance	204
10.1.4 Performance of canned jokes	206
10.1.5 GTVH and performance	207
10.1.6 Sociolinguistic approaches	208
10.2 The Hymes-Gumperz sociolinguistic model	211
10.2.1 Linguistic repertoires	213
10.2.2 Speech acts and speech events	215
10.2.3 Genres	221
10.2.4 Contextualization cues	226
10.3 Empirical studies on markers of humor performance	227
10.4 Further readings	234

11. Conversation analysis: humor in conversation I — 235

11.1 Conversation and discourse analysis	236
11.1.1 Bracketing	236
11.2 CA of laughter	239
11.2.1 Laughter is indexical	239
11.2.2 The definition(s) of laughable	241
11.3 The canonical CA joke analysis	246
11.3.1 Sacks on jokes	246
11.4 Issues in CA of humor	252
11.4.1 Is humor–laughter an adjacency pair?	252
11.4.2 Humorous and non-humorous laughter in conversation	253

CONTENTS

      11.4.3 Is humor a test of understanding?   258
      11.4.4 Tellability   259
  11.5 Conclusions   261
  11.6 Further readings   262

12. Discourse analysis: humor in conversation II   263
  12.1 Functional DA   264
      12.1.1 Tannen's Thanksgiving dinner   266
      12.1.2 Catherine Davies' joint construction of humor   267
      12.1.3 Priego-Valverde's dialogic model   269
      12.1.4 Functions of humor in conversation   273
  12.2 Conversational humor in various settings   280
      12.2.1 Conversation among friends   280
      12.2.2 Medical   281
      12.2.3 Workplace   283
  12.3 Corpus-based discourse analysis   286
  12.4 Some issues in the DA of humor   289
      12.4.1 Establishing the humorous intention   289
      12.4.2 How do speakers identify humor?   291
      12.4.3 Failed humor   293
      12.4.4 Sustained humor turns   295
  12.5 Conclusions   297
  12.6 Further readings   298

13. Sociolinguistics of humor   299
  13.1 Universality of humor   299
  13.2 Variationist humor theory   304
      13.2.1 Humor and gender   304
      13.2.2 Social class   306
      13.2.3 Age   308
      13.2.4 Dialects as humorous languages   309
  13.3 The social construction of humor   313
  13.4 Conclusions   315
  13.5 Further readings   315

PART IV. Applications

14. Humor in literature — 319
- 14.1 Script-based theory of humorous texts — 321
  - 14.1.1 The expansionist approach — 322
  - 14.1.2 Chłopicki — 322
  - 14.1.3 Holcomb — 323
  - 14.1.4 The revisionist approach — 324
- 14.2 Other approaches — 328
- 14.3 Narratology — 330
- 14.4 Stylistics — 332
  - 14.4.1 Register humor — 334
- 14.5 Some examples of literary constructs — 336
- 14.6 Further readings — 339

15. Humor and translation — 340
- 15.1 A few definitions — 343
  - 15.1.1 Source text and target text language — 343
  - 15.1.2 Intra- and inter-semiotic translation — 344
- 15.2 Theories of humor translation — 344
  - 15.2.1 Faithfulness — 344
  - 15.2.2 Literal vs. functional translation — 346
  - 15.2.3 Zabalbeascoa's priority scales and solution types — 347
  - 15.2.4 Eco's translation-as-negotiation — 351
  - 15.2.5 Skopos theory — 351
  - 15.2.6 Relevance Theoretic approaches — 353
- 15.3 Audiovisual translation — 355
  - 15.3.1 Dubbing — 356
  - 15.3.2 Subtitling — 357
  - 15.3.3 Interpreting — 358
- 15.4 Translating puns — 359
  - 15.4.1 Are puns untranslatable? — 360
  - 15.4.2 The practice of translating puns — 363
- 15.5 Conclusions — 365
- 15.6 Further readings — 366

16. Humor in the classroom — 367

    16.1 The pioneers — 368

    16.2 The apologists — 371

    16.3 The realists — 372

    16.4 Classroom discourse analysis — 377

        16.4.1 How much humor do teachers produce in class? — 378

    16.5 Conclusions — 379

    16.6 Further readings — 380

17. Conclusion — 381

Glossary — 385
References — 393
Author index — 441
Subject index — 453

Preface

For a long time, the working title of this book was *Lessons on the Language of Humor*. The original project was to collect a number of lessons on the linguistics of humor. I meant and mean the term "lesson" quite literally: the main goal of this book is pedagogical. The project slowly evolved into an introduction to the study of the linguistics of humor for the novice to humor research.[1] The reason for doing so is that many humor scholars and newcomers to linguistics are interested in the substantial contribution that linguistics has brought to humor research, but are kept at bay by the somewhat unfriendly nature of the discipline (as several students and colleagues have admitted to me in conversation).

I have taught occasionally workshops, classes, and courses on some aspects of the linguistics of humor using some version of parts of these chapters for the past 20 years or so. The book in its present form was started in the summer of 2000 and slowly developed into extensive sets of notes on various topics in the linguistics of humor. The primary motivation for drafting the first version of parts of this textbook as lectures was the fact that a colleague needed materials to teach a last-minute assignment class on the linguistics of humor, at Georgia State University, in 2006. I wrote a few lectures that I would send to her a few days before the class. Long story short, we married in 2012. So, in a very real sense, this book has been quite successful already, for me at least. If it also helps some young scholar to learn about the linguistics of humor, it's gravy!

This book cannot hope to also be an introduction to linguistics; there are excellent ones on the market.[2] In what follows, I will assume that the reader either has had a chance to familiarize him/herself with one such introduction or will do so as they encounter various basic concepts in linguistics. Occasionally, I will provide some background information when I cannot assume it is common knowledge. For example, while every self-respecting introduction to linguistics will define the concept

---

[1] Gelotology (Apte, 1988) never really caught on.
[2] In fact, I coauthored one such book myself: Brown and Attardo (2000), although modesty prevents me from vouching for its excellence.

of morpheme, I cannot assume that knowledge for *isotopy* or even *script*. The glossary defines all technical terms and should be helpful for newcomers to the field, but again it does not define terms such as phoneme or morpheme.

This book aims at being a simple, straightforward description of the results achieved by linguistics in humor research, as well as the methodologies used to achieve such results. The goal is that by mapping the cutting edge of the field and engaging with it, the reader will be in a position to contribute to the linguistics of humor, both theoretical and applied.

This is the first book on the linguistics of humor that attempts an integrated approach encompassing all the fields of linguistics, both theoretical and applied, on an equal footing. I am aware of the originality of such a stance, so much so that I had to develop an approach to do so. In particular, Chapters 10–12 develop an ethnomethodological perspective that encompasses discourse analysis and variationist sociolinguistics in the first-ever cohesive discussion of the performance of humor (as opposed to the competence of humor). Obviously I did not develop the whole approach out of thin air. In fact, it was the realization that the ethnomethodological approach developed by Gumperz and Hymes (and Goffman and Bateson, and many others) had so much to say about humor in its original formulation, that led me to the decision (foolhardy, I am sure) to organize the third part of the book around that theoretical backbone and integrating the research on conversation, discourse, and sociolinguistics within it.

This book is meant for an advanced undergraduate course or a graduate seminar on humor or for scholars from other fields, with limited familiarity with linguistics, who are interested in the contribution of linguistics to humor studies. As such it is a systematic but not exhaustive presentation of the field. It is organized in 16 chapters, so as to be useable within a standard academic semester in American universities, but of course there is no reason one should not proceed at a slower or faster pace. I do however recommend reading the chapters in the order they are presented, at least until Chapter 13, after which the linearity of the presentation is less relevant. The other exception to the recommendation of following the linearity of the argument is Chapter 1. Some readers may find some of the theoretical and methodological hairsplitting less than captivating. If they are willing to take my word for the usefulness of the conventions I adopt in the book, then they can safely move on to the rest of the chapters. If they are not, as they are fully entitled to be, then they should read on and see why I made those decisions.

In the age of tweets and hypertext, the presence of an argument that takes ten or more chapters to elaborate may surprise or even put off readers, but *à la guerre comme à la guerre*, as they say in France, or to quote one of my favorite philosophers, it is what it is.

The presentation of the material is cyclical: a central topic such as the incongruity–resolution model is first approached in the general context of the three major theories of humor, then taken up again in a separate chapter, and then taken up again in specific linguistic terms in the chapters on the Semantic Script Theory of Humor (incongruity) and the General Theory of Verbal Humor (resolution, a.k.a. the Logical Mechanism). Likewise the significance of the competence/performance distinction is first discussed in Chapter 2 and then resurfaces repeatedly, for example in Chapter 6 on the Semantic Script Theory of Humor, in Chapter 15 on translation, etc. This is done to facilitate the pedagogical goal of the book.

Phonetic transcriptions are in (simplified) IPA. I occasionally will use symbols common in American linguistics, such as [y] to indicate a glide (IPA [j]) or [D] to indicate a flap (IPA [ɾ]). As usual, phonemes and morphemes are represented between slashes and allophones and allomorphs between square brackets. Syntactic trees use an "Aspects" notation (Chomsky, 1965), for readability. Scripts are indicated in SMALL CAPS. I have tried to respect the different annotation styles of conversation and discourse analysts, but I occasionally had to simplify or modify the transcription for practical reasons. Those are indicated in the text. I have tried deliberately to keep logical symbols and formalisms out of the text.

The fact that I need a disclaimer about the non-exhaustive nature of the references is a very good indicator of the progress the field of the linguistics of humor has made in the past quarter century. In 1994, when I published my first book on the linguistics of humor, on which I had worked for ten years, the attempt to be all-inclusive was foolhardy but not obviously absurd. Today, most of the topics covered in the chapters to follow have bibliographies that include several monographs. To attempt a broad comprehensive coverage would be virtually impossible, as new works appear constantly, in a variety of journals. The coverage of the bibliography is thus representative and selective.

With the advent of the internet, it is now possible to locate and often retrieve with minimal effort hundred of "scholarly" articles on any topic. A researcher's work is thus both easier (just a mere 20 years ago it would have required years of expensive research to gather such a list of sources) and more complicated: many of these sources are substandard and do not meet basic criteria for scholarship, being riddled with fundamental errors, misinterpretations, unverified second-hand citations, etc. So, to a certain extent, the work of today's scholar consists in some part in discarding sources unworthy of other scholars' attention. This creates a problem of interpretation: prior to the age of the internet research, if a serious scholar did not quote scholar X, there were two possible interpretations: 1) an omission in error (i.e., the scholar was not aware of the existence of the source but had he/she been aware of it he/she would have quoted/discussed it), or 2) a deliberate omission either a) due to the low quality of the work, b) to the need to be selective, c) the impossibility of reading every source. Today, 1) is unlikely, precisely because with the internet we can find almost anything, but 2) remains as relevant as it ever was, if not more. I cannot guarantee that all omissions are deliberate and due to the need to be selective, whereby only the most significant or representative works are discussed, or are a gesture of mercy toward subpar scholarship, which should be allowed to fade off into oblivion, but I have done my best in that sense.

I would like to thank the following friends and colleagues for their help in the writing of this book: Delia Chiaro, Greg Dean, Margherita Dore, Elisa Gironzetti, Christian "Kiki" Hempelmann, Alan Partington, Béatrice Priego-Valverde, Victor Raskin, Willibald Ruch, Willy Tsakona, Manuela Wagner, and Patrick Zabalbeascoa. I also would like to thank all the scholars who sent me copies of their articles, too many to name them all, but this show of collegiality is always heartwarming. I also would like to thank the librarians and the interlibrary loan staff at Gee library, at Texas A&M University-Commerce. Truly, without their help this book would not have been possible. I would also like to thank, without any hint of irony, the reviewers and editorial team: thank to their help the book is truly a better, if unfortunately less funny, work.

I feel like I should apologize to those who may have bought the book thinking it will be funny. For them, I have an anecdote: more than 20 years ago, at the ISHS humor conference masterfully organized by Amy Carrell at U. of Central Oklahoma, I found myself in a car with Victor Raskin, Elliott Oring, and Christie Davies. We had gone off to find a sushi restaurant (I know, don't ask) and were rejoining the rest of the conference at a local comedy club, for an evening of standup comedy. We arrived at the place, which was pretty big, and asked at the bar where the Humor Conference people were seated. The bartender told us not to worry, "You'll find them in no time. They are the ones not laughing."[3]

Finally, I would like to thank Tempest and Blue, our two rescue mutts, Xena, our rescue cat, Dani, the non-rescue horse, Arnie, the armadillo that lives in the bushes in our front yard, the families of swallows literally living under our roof, and the various turtles, snakes, lizards, frogs, herons, cardinals, hummingbirds, and assorted other fauna that share our property, and my wife Lucy Pickering, who contributed a picture of a paratone, saved countless frogs, and made me fall in love with her again every day.

The Middle of Nowhere Ranch, near Lone Oak, Texas, 2020

---

[3] Script opposition: laughter/no laughter; Logical mechanism: reversal (humor scholars have no sense of humor); Target: humor scholars; Situation: comedy club; Narrative Strategy: conversational one liner; Language: irrelevant.

List of figures

1.1	The irony–sarcasm continuum	10
1.2	The relationship between humor, mirth, and laughter	17
1.3	Semiotic humor hierarchy	26
2.1	Venn diagram of the intersection between humor and laughter	43
5.1	Denotative (bottom left) and connotative (top row) semiotics	97
6.1	A very simplified semantic graph for CAT; the links are labeled after the semantic connection	119
6.2	The lexical script for DOCTOR in Raskin, 1985	120
6.3	Simple, macro-, and complex scripts	121
7.1	Hierarchical organization of the knowledge resources	138
7.2	Orientations and targets of humor as a function of aggression	146
9.1	The first interpretation of the sentence "I shot an elephant in my pajamas"	183
9.2	The second interpretation of the sentence "I shot an elephant in my pajamas"	183
9.3	The two interpretations of the sentence "Squad helps dog bite victim"	183
10.1	A paratone, at the end of the performance of one of the jokes. "That's cool" is the punch line. Note the declination, indicated by the continuous line. The dotted lines indicate the approximate resets of each tone unit.	230
11.1	Hay's presuppositional scale of hearer's reactions to humor	250

List of tables

2.1	Relationships between humor and laughter	43
2.2	The interplay of humorous keying and text	52
3.1	Attardo's three families of theories chart	60
6.1	Combinatorics for two scripts	127
10.1	The abstract–concrete continuum exemplified by the article "the"	212
11.1	Notation for transcription, based on Jefferson's	238
11.2	Sequential organization of joke telling	247

Part I
Humor Studies

This book is divided into four parts. The first is foundational and aims at providing general and background information which is necessary for properly understanding the discussions in the next three parts. The second part is dedicated to humor competence and the third part to the performance of humor. The fourth part consists of applications to various disciplines of the results discussed in the first three parts. The parts should be read sequentially.

The first part of the book starts out by introducing, in Chapter 1, some basic terminology, which should go a long way in helping offset the constant terminological issues that have plagued the field. The rest of the chapter is dedicated to providing a very short overview of the field of humor studies, to which the linguistics of humor belongs. Needless to say, a real introduction to humor studies would require a much broader treatment, along the lines of the *Encyclopedia of Humor Studies* (Attardo, 2014). Chapter 2 tackles the competence vs. performance distinction and various meta-theoretical issues. Primarily these issues manifests themselves in the conflation of humor and laughter/smiling, along the lines of a naive implicit stimulus–response model. Once the equation humor–laughter is dispatched, there arises the question of how to identify humor. The third chapter describes the various theories of humor that have informed the field of humor studies, focusing particularly on the three major theories: release, incongruity, and aggression. Chapters 4 and 5 introduce the incongruity–resolution theory and the semiotics of humor.

The purpose of this part is to prepare the reader for the actual discussion of the linguistics of humor, which will take up Parts II and III of the book. For linguistics to provide its unique set of contributions to humor studies it is essential that linguists understand where humor studies is coming from and what the questions and issue it handles are.

1
Humor studies: a few definitions

1.1 Terminology 4
1.2 A brief overview of humor studies 18
1.3 A few basic distinctions 25
1.4 Further readings 29

This chapter introduces some necessary terminology and presents the field of humor studies, primarily from a historical perspective, to help the reader situate where the linguistics of humor fits in within the broader humor studies field. Thus, much of it is preliminary in nature and probably quite dry. One may in fact wonder whether it is really necessary to have all this set of terms and definitions. In a sense, if the reader is willing to take me on faith and accept that we will use 1) *speaker*, *hearer*, and *text* as umbrella terms for the prototypical roles of the humorous exchange, and 2) the term *humor* as an umbrella term for the stimulus (without any further attempts at differentiation between sub terms, such as comic and ridicule or irony and sarcasm), 3) the term *mirth* for the emotional response, and 4) the terms *laughter* and *smiling* for the overt, physical responses typically associated with humor, then the reader may just skip the next section and start reading about the history of the field and why I think having one is important.

However, I believe it is important to clarify what it is we are talking about when we say "humor" or "laughter." There has been a lot of confusion in the field from using terminology inconsistently, especially in the early days of humor studies. That the field has moved away from terminological free-for-all is a testament to the work of many humor scholars who have carefully defined their terms.

1.1 Terminology

1.1.1 The characters

Let us start from a non-controversial humor situation: someone says something and someone else reacts laughing. We would describe this situation as someone said something funny, humorous, amusing, droll, or the like, and that made the other person laugh. This is the prototypical case of humor situation. Let us call the first person the *speaker*, the second person the *hearer* and whatever was said the *text*. For a large number of situations, this will be enough.

Consider the following example:

(1) In a reply to a post by my daughter on Facebook, in which my grandson tells a little story in which one character is a nose, I jokingly criticized my daughter for having him read Gogol at age four and a half. The post reads "I don't want to challenge your educational practices, but having the child read Gogol's masterpiece The Nose at 4 seems premature."

In this situation, I am the speaker and my daughter is the hearer, even though of course the exchange took place in writing, and the text is my post above. So far, so good. However, since this was posted on Facebook, all of our friends and family members can see the exchange and one of them in fact responded to it. Was the unintended response also from a hearer? Dos it matter that I meant the joke only as a response to my daughter's post? Does it matter that several people, including my daughter, "liked" the post by using little icons of a thumbs up or a little red heart? Probably yes.

So we see that things can be much more complex than the little situation we started from: there can be multiple hearers, there can be different kinds of hearers and of course there can be many different kinds of texts. Just like in a non-humorous situation we can distinguish between hearers and over-hearers: the latter are not directly addressed by the speaker—although they may be the real intended recipients of what the speaker says. In example (1), does the family member who was not an intended participant qualify as an over-hearer? Probably yes.

Also the situation is complicated in further ways: for example both speakers conveys the text in writing, and speaker and hearer are not in the same place at the same time. This is significant, because being face-to-face is one of the defining features of speech. Things can get even more complex. However, I think that the prototypical situation above, in its simplicity, is a good starting point, if for nothing else, at least to establish some terminology.

We will then speak generally of "speaker," "hearer," and "text," regardless of the fact that the speaker may not speak, the text may be spoken, or written, or conveyed in any modality[1] (visual, e.g., cartoons, auditory, e.g., music, kinesic, e.g., mime, etc.), and the hearer may be in fact a television audience, or read the text (and thus not actually "hear" anything at all), etc.

Needless to say, when necessary we may differentiate: so if we were investigating humor in the deaf/hearing community (see for example Sutton-Spence & Napoli, 2012) we would refer to signed jokes, or if investigating the differences between written and spoken forms of jokes and say, internet memes, we would refer to oral, written, and multimodal texts.

When we move away from speech, we need to consider that other media (writing, printed press, television, film, social media, etc.) may involve exceedingly complex (and usually hidden) chains of "co-authors": a TV show may put a certain joke in the mouth of a character, but besides the person who wrote the script, the "author" of the text, the director of the show, the producers, the TV network executives, the cable channel that broadcast/rebroadcast it, etc. may be held accountable or become relevant is some cases: for example, suppose that the executives of a TV network were to censor parts of the jokes or less dramatically, would need to apologize for them or distance themselves from them. In those situations, the "author" (speaker in our terminology) ceases to be a unified figure and dissolves in a chain of co-authors, with different agendas, ideologies, and constituencies they need to keep happy.

Furthermore we need to consider that speaker, hearer, and text, may diverge significantly from the prototypical terms in social/interactional aspects. For example, the distinctions between ratified (official, openly acknowledged) and unratified participants and addressed (i.e., the utterance is directed to them) and unaddressed listeners (Goffman, 1981, pp. 131–133) may be particularly relevant. It has been claimed, e.g., Bubel (2008) that in a TV show, for example, the audience consists

---

[1] Hence the term "multimodal" to indicate texts such as films which incorporate both visual and auditory signs.

of overhearers. One then would need to distinguish the hearers in the show and the overhearers in the audience. This is the case with so-called dramatic irony. Dramatic irony is generally defined as a situation in which the audience, of a play, for example, knows something that the character(s) in the play do not, which causes them to interpret the actions and words of the characters differently. Thus for example, in *Oedipus Rex*, the audience is aware of whom Oedipus killed long before he does. Likewise, Iago's deception is known to the audience before it is to Othello. Clearly the status of the audience is different than that of the characters on stage. The audience is probably best classified as unaddressed listeners, for the perspective of the characters (who of course are not supposed to be aware of their presence at all). So in the case of dramatic irony or of similar situations, the different status of various hearers is relevant and hence should be addressed. Consider the following joke: Freud (1905, pp. 183–184) which is analyzed in Chapter 8 as example (81) from a slightly different standpoint.

(2) Two children are performing in front of their family a play they themselves wrote. The plot revolves around a fisherman who leaves his wife to go in search of fortune. In the second act, set several years later, the fisherman returns with a huge fortune. His wife greets him by saying: "I too have not been idle." "And thereupon she opens the door of the[ir] hut and reveals to his eyes twelve large dolls lying asleep on the floor... At this point in the drama the actors were interrupted by a storm of laughter from the audience, which they were unable to understand." (Freud, 1905, p.184)

In this example the difference between what the children know and what the adults know is crucial to understand why the adults find the situation funny and the children do not. We might describe it as a discrepancy between the addressed hearer imagined by the children and the actual hearers, who in the children's eyes would be overhearers. However, and this is my point, in most other cases, there is no need to distinguish between hearers and overhearers, addressed and unaddressed participants. For example, in examples (7) and (10) below, there are just two speakers and thus no need for further theoretical apparatus.

All this may seem complex and confusing. My argument however is that, unless necessary, we can simplify the matter greatly and speak of a speaker, telling a text to a hearer. If the situation requires it, we can bring in a more sophisticated understanding of the situation, but unless we need it, we will shelve the unnecessarily complex apparatus. The same argument holds for my use the term humor as generic designation for the subject of inquiry of humor studies.

1.1.2 Humor as umbrella term

As is well known, there are many terms that have been used to designate what happens in the situation above: humor, comic, funny, laughable, droll, wit, amusing, etc. Scholars have tried, vainly, to distinguish between, say, humor and ridicule, or between irony and sarcasm, and the likes. The situation is even worse when we try to translate these categories from one language into another. This is probably due to the fact that all of these terms are folk-terminologies, that work well in some prototypical cases, but fail lamentably when we try to apply them to difficult, borderline instances. So, clearly humor is less aggressive than ridicule, but where would one draw the line? The same can be said, after accounting for any differences, for irony and sarcasm, farce and comedy, etc.

Ultimately, the fact that twenty-five hundred years of discussion have failed to yield clear-cut internal categories is a witness to the fact that it seems to be impossible to do so. Recently, within the field of humor research, a consensus seems to have emerged, whereby *humor* is being used as the umbrella term to indicate the complex of humorous phenomena, with further differentiation being left for future research or just abandoned.[2]

This is not to say that we cannot differentiate between a joke and a funny play, or between comedy and irony. In oder to understand the issues at stake, we need to consider terminology in more detail. The point of having terminology is to facilitate the scientific process. An effective terminology has, among others, the following features; it is clear and precise: there is no doubt as to whether any given entity is or is not described by a given term;[3] it is unique, i.e., each concept has one term describing it (to put it differently, it is not ambiguous); it is stable,

---

[2] See for example the titles of Raskin (1985), Morreall (1987), Attardo (1994), Ruch (1998), and the name of the oldest journal of the field *HUMOR: International Journal of Humor Research*.

[3] Ideally, it is formal, i.e. there is an algorithm that can make the determination without human input.

i.e., it does not change;[4] it should cover all the phenomena one needs to cover, i.e., it should not leave aspects of the phenomenon undescribed; relatedly, it should group all the phenomena that are related into one category (or related ones); and, last but not least, it should not lead to confusion by using terminology already used in a different sense, in the same or related fields. Little harm is done by using the term isotopy which is a technical term in chemistry (isotope) but if we wanted to redefine "allophone" we'd be asking for trouble. Finally, it should be kept to a minimum: there is no reason to coin a new term if there is a perfectly good one already.

In my experience, within humor studies, the most frequent problems one encounters with definitions are: 1) they are insufficiently precise to be useful, and 2) they are not mutually exclusive. Let us consider both problems in that order. If I define a joke as a short narrative text with a punch line at the end, I am essentially listing the features of the joke: 1) a linguistic text; 2) narrative (this excludes dramatic/dialogic texts); 3) short; and 4) having a punch line located at the end. There is nothing wrong with this definition, but it will struggle operationally when confronted with Renaissance *facezie*, which can be quite long. Clearly, we can arbitrarily define a threshold, of say, 50 words and stipulate that anything longer than 50 words is not a joke, but this is theoretically useless. If you have a 51 words text, are you willing to say that that is no longer a joke but it is now a short story, or novella, or whatever other terminology you have for a longish text with a punch line at the end?[5] Consider that a synonym of "narrative" is "story" and a short story is not very different from a short narrative text. Moreover, what about jokes in non-linguistic form, for example, cartoons with a caption or with text in a balloon? What about jokes that are made only of dialogue, such as question and answer jokes, or riddles? What about very short dramatic plays not meant to be performed, such as Achille Campanile's *Tragedie in due battute* [Tragedies in two lines]? I translate[6] one of my favorites in what follows:

---

[4] For an example of the problems inherent in a changing definition of a concept, see the discussion of the term "isotopy" in Attardo (1994).

[5] These texts do exist: Katherine Mansfield's short story *Feuille d'album* ends on a punch line. See Attardo (2001, p. 93) for a discussion.

[6] Literally and without any attempt at recreating the artistry of the text, evident in the choice of the names.

(3) INTRODUCTION.
Characters: MR. PERICLE FISCHIETTI
THE OTHER GENTLEMAN

At the opening of the curtain, MR. PERICLE FISCHIETTI approaches THE OTHER GENTLEMAN

MR. PERICLE FISCHIETTI (Introducing himself to the other gentleman) May I? I am Mr. Pericle Fischietti. And how about yourself?
THE OTHER GENTLEMAN I am not. (curtain)

So the only value of this sort of definition is to give us a list of features that (some of) the texts we are focusing on share. By the time we've broadened it enough not to produce any false negatives (i.e., failing to include texts that are jokes) it becomes virtually useless: A humorous text with a punch line at the end. Note how this will not differentiate between jokes, short stories, or even novels.

The mutual exclusiveness issue is even worse: consider satire, irony, and puns. Any given text could be all three at the same time, regardless of what your definition of any of the three terms are. All you have to do is find an instance of a pun that creates an ironical opposition and make sure that that opposition is critical of someone/something. If someone were trying to code a text for these features they would end up with a hopelessly tangled mess.

Now, let's go back to the mini-definition of joke. We can make this definition more useful if we compare it to the definition of the anecdote, as a short humorous text, without a punch line at the end. Now the distinguishing feature is whether there is punch line at the end of the text. Of course, it will still be complex to define operationally "end" (The last word? Last morpheme? Last phrase? Last sentence?) and you will also need a definition of punch line. However, this definition is now operationally sound: you can make predictions (any text without a punch line at the end will be an anecdote), you can analyze texts, test your analyses against others' and so get an inter-rater reliability score, etc.

Anyone can define things in such a way that they will convince themselves that their definitions are useful and mutually exclusive. For example, Aubouin (1948), who is an otherwise much overlooked genius in the field, insists on a difference between humor (*le comique*) and ridicule, the latter being aggressive. Predictably, it is not a convincing argument. Consider the Larack Tobama meme, widely circulated on the internet in 2016.

(4) An image of President Barack Obama, with an obviously fake mustache. The caption reads: "Independent party announces new candidate coming late into the election, Larack Tobama." https://me.me/i/independent-party-announces-new-candidate-coming-late-into-the-election-2852592

Is this comic or ridicule? Some elements of distortion (the mustache, the changed name) are present, but they do not seem to be openly aggressive or mocking. However, is there really no aggression or tendentiousness? Isn't there a criticism, implicit to be sure, of the other candidates? Would a Republican or a Democrat categorize the joke the same way? How about a white supremacist?

A similar problem with definition is exemplified with the distinction between irony and sarcasm. There is a general consensus that irony is less aggressive than sarcasm, as can be evinced from the etymology of the word "sarcasm" which comes from Greek "sarkazein," i.e., to rip pieces of flesh. Thus, presented with the following two examples:

(5) Nice weather! (It is raining.)

and

(6) Great idea to invest all of our lifelong savings in Enron stock!

most people would probably agree that the former is ironical and the latter sarcastic, given the knowledge that the Enron bankruptcy in 2001 caused its stock to fall from a valuation of $90 to essentially zero. Many of the employees who had invested their retirement in Enron stock lost their savings.

The problem is the in-between cases. We can conceptualize the irony–sarcasm divide as a continuum, with irony at one end and sarcasm at the other end; see Figure 1.1. The clear-cut cases, such as those above, will be handled without problems, whereas those cases that fall somewhere in between will be harder to classify.

Figure 1.1 The irony–sarcasm continuum.

Thus for example, imagine a different context than the standard default one (something along the lines of the two speakers are indoor watching the rain) for the first example, namely that "Nice weather!" is being uttered by the owner of a company who scheduled, on the advice of the interlocutor who assured him/her that the weather would be great, an outdoor picnic for the entire company, at great expense, and whose costly suit has been ruined by the storm. Where would the utterance of "Nice weather!" fall in the continuum? The term of art here is "a grey area" which makes the point nicely: it is difficult to differentiate in the grey area. In fact, Figure 1.1 considerably simplifies the real-life problem, insofar as it is easy with a ruler to measure where the middle of the gradient falls. In real life, of course, we have no idea where the ends of the continuum lie and therefore we cannot estimate where the half-point lies. Summing up, binary distinctions on a continuum are possible, but are only reliable for the prototypical, extreme cases at the opposite ends of the continuum. The in-between cases, which are the most interesting, where a theory through its terminology should help distinguish the data, are precisely those in which the distinction will fail. This severely limits the usefulness of such distinctions.

Another problem is unnecessary redefinitions. Consider the example of irony. Since ancient times there have been definitions of irony as, simplifying drastically, saying one thing and meaning another. Furthermore, irony was divided between negative irony (i.e., critical) and positive (i.e., praising) The latter is known as "asteism." An example would be introducing a famous speaker at a conference, say Noam Chomsky, as "our speaker has published a few books that have had some small impact on the field of linguistics and politics," meaning to imply ironically that one means the opposite, and namely that he has published many very influential books. Enter Garmendia (2010, p. 402), who claims that all irony is negative ("critical"). When confronted with positive (non-critical) irony, she denies that it is irony and claims it is something else (a joke, Garmendia, 2010, p. 410, or "banter" (Leech, 1983, p. 144). It is clear that such re-definitions do nothing to advance our knowledge of the field. We had a distinction: positive vs. negative irony and we replace it with another distinction: irony vs. joking or banter. All we have here, theoretically speaking, is rearranging the socks in the drawer, with the added inconvenience that now we have phenomena that are identical in terms of semantic-pragmatic mechanisms, by Garmendia's own admission (p. 410), but have completely different and unrelated terms to describe them (even worse, the term "joke" has a completely different much more salient meaning and "banter" is in its general sense, something entirely different, i.e., teasing).

Finally, one more distinction, which has lately cropped up increasingly frequently: within politeness theory, for example, researchers distinguish between first- and second-order constructs: first-order theories are folk-theories, whereas second-order theories are "scientific" (i.e., they are proposed by scholars).[7] Here we need to be careful: notoriously, the speakers' metalinguistic judgements are unreliable. So, asking speakers: "Is this ironical?" or worse, "is what you just said ironical?" will lead to all sorts of distortions (just imagine asking the speakers if what they just did is aggressive or not; obvious social barriers exist that will prevent the speakers from answering reliably). Likewise, asking speakers if something is humorous or not, if it is ironical or sarcastic, or parodic, etc. requires all sorts of experimental techniques to avoid biasing the results, including the problem of knowing what the speakers think such terms as "ironical," "sarcastic," etc. mean. The terms "irony" and "sarcasm" provide again a striking example. In British English and in American English, "irony" used to mean, as we pointed out above, roughly "saying something and meaning something else, generally critical." However, in the 1990s, at least in some populations in the US, a semantic shift occurred, exemplified by the song Ironic, by Alanis Morrisette, in the album *Jagged Little Pill* (1995). Nunberg (2001, pp. 91–93) sums the situation up as "irony" is now used to indicate something bad or upsetting. Concurrently, the semantic space of "sarcastic" broadened to include what would have previously been described as "ironical." Morrisette was widely ridiculed for not knowing what the word ironical meant, whereas it is clear that Morrisette's (and her age cohort) first-order definition of "irony" and "sarcasm" is different from that of older generations (and other languages; to the best of my knowledge this semantic shift did not take place in other languages or in British English). Nelms (2001) for example purports to describe the use of sarcasm in higher education classroom discourse, but her examples include irony as well. The responsible scholar needs then to be alert to

---

[7] A term often used in this context is the etic vs. emic distinction, used in anthropology, for example, where an emic description is from the point of view of the subjects and an etic description is from the point of view of the researchers. I prefer to avoid this terminology due to the possible confusion with the suffixes used to indicate the phonetic and phonemic levels in linguistic theory, for example, where they have a different meaning.

the fact that his/her subjects may very well have a different first-order definition of irony and sarcasm than his/her (hopefully) second-order definition. Thus he/she needs to make sure that this difference does not interfere with his/her analysis. It is impossible to be specific on how exactly to do this, since it depends on what the research questions are; however, keeping a strong distinction between first- and second-order concepts is the necessary presupposition to avoid embarrassing pitfalls. Likewise, if gathering a corpus of utterances labeled as "ironical" by speakers (say, by using emoticons), it is crucial to have access to demographic information relative to their age and language variety (in this case American vs. British English) in order to discriminate the data appropriately.[8] One more consideration: I am using these cases merely for the purpose of exemplifying the issues. I do not claim that these are full discussions of the concepts and that the definitions I am discussing here are either what I believe to be correct and/or the best we can do.

Clearly, as we said, there are some well-established categories, such as irony, farce, the burlesque, etc., but in a sense, humor research investigates what all these categories have in common, first, and only after it has established what the general category of humor consists of, it attempts further classification. Concretely, these distinctions represent more the historical remnants of discipline-specific taxonomies than seriously considered scientific classifications: the concept of irony, for example, originally comes from rhetorics. It is ultimately unclear what its relationship to humor is.[9] Many of the literary terms (comedy, farce, burlesque, carnival, etc.) are the result of Renaissance reinterpretation of classical models. To be honest, most of the terminology in humor studies comes from the various disciplines. Thus, for example, the idea of "script" comes from psychology, via artificial intelligence, and linguistics, which ultimately introduced it in humor studies.

Very few terms have been created specifically for humor studies: take "gelotophobia" (the fear of being laughed at) for example. The term "gelotophobia" was introduced by Michael Titze (Titze, 1996), a German psychotherapist, who had encountered the pathology in his practice. It was then taken up by Ruch and his team and a formidable set of

---

[8] It is true that second-degree theories are always inevitably influenced by first-degree theories. The problem is to keep them apart as far as possible. Both theories have their place, but confusing them will lead researchers to error.

[9] See Downing & Recuero (2008) and Attardo (2001b) for some discussion.

studies was produced, resulting, among others, in a special double issue of *HUMOR* in 2009, guest edited by Ruch. Part of the work was to define precisely what counts as gelotophobia and whether it manifests itself across cultures.

In conclusion, in what follows we will be using the generic umbrella term *humor* to indicate the general category, as is common usage in the field. Any further differentiation will be introduced and motivated in the text. In particular, in the chapter on literary humor, we will examine more closely some of the distinctions mentioned above.

1.1.3 Joke

The term "joke" also deserves some discussion, because of the outsized importance it has acquired, almost by happenstance. I have mentioned the "joke" in the previous section repeatedly, with a rough definition of a short (narrative) text ending in a punch line. As I mentioned, there is nothing wrong with this definition, per se. However, we need to distinguish between canned and conversational jokes. Canned jokes are relatively decontextualized: they are built as small narratives that can be reused. Conversely, conversational jokes exist and are produced in context only, i.e., as part of a conversation. Conversational jokes tend *not* to have a narrative introduction. One can think of it as the context of the conversation playing the part of the setup of the joke (the introduction) and the humorous remark being the punch line.

Consider the following extract from a dyadic (two speakers) conversation recorded over computer chat, in which two students are talking to each other. The setup was such that one student was in my office, while the other was in my friend and colleague, Steve Brown's. Steve kept his office very tidy and orderly, whereas mine was a mess of papers and books. Marina (M) delivers a joke on line 162, but as is very clear it consists of just one turn "This looks like Sal's" and relies on the previous conversation for its context, for the setup of the opposition (the "clean" office vs. the "dirty" messy office) and the other half of the opposition.

```
(7) 146 C // there's lots of BOOKS [243][66] in
        here//
    147 1.57
    148 M //yeah I'm LOOKin [250][68] around at
        all these PApers [188][64]//
    149 0.34
```

```
150 M //hangin on the WALLS [172][65] //
151 0.52
152 M //this OFfice [198][71] is really DIRty
    [182][67]//
153 0.64 ((smack))
154 C // this OFfice [294-279][67] is really
    CLEAN [222][62] //
155 0.44
156 C //i THINK [334][63] it's Steve BROWN's
    [206][58]//
157 0.92
158 M //AHH. [172][68]//
159 0.52
160 C //yeah//
161 0.883
162 M //this looks like SAL's [179][72]//
163 0.21
164 M ((laughs))
```

Zajdman (1991) has shown that the difference lies on a continuum of contextualization and that a conversational joke can be turned into a canned one and vice versa (joke recycling): canned jokes may in some cases originate from conversational jokes that have been decontextualized. Conversely, canned jokes may be contextually adapted to the point that a canned joke may be presented in a manner indistinguishable from a spontaneous joke.

Consider the following joke:

(8) Mrs. de Gaulle enters a room where her husband is waiting. She trips on the rug and involuntarily mutters "Mon Dieu!" He replies: "How many times must I remind you? It is quite sufficient to say "Mon général."

which appears in Yvonne de Gaulle's *New York Times* obituary, by Frank J. Prial (Nov. 9, 1979, p. 4). One day, a student walked in my office to retrieve an exam I had returned in class. I handed her her exam, which had earned a 98% score (I was famous for being a tough grader in my early days). She was surprised and exclaimed "My God!" to which I replied, "You can call me Dr. Attardo." The student was amused and, of course, I did not tell her that all I had done was contextualize the joke to her present situation. She probably thinks to this day I am very witty, but indeed very little effort was involved in recontextualizing the canned joke.

The following is another example, from the same set of recordings as above, in which Carmen recontextualizes a well-known joke

(9) What do you call someone who speaks two languages? A bilingual. How about someone who speaks three languages? Trilingual. How about someone who speaks only one language? An American.

using Marina's modesty in saying that she does not speak any language besides English (at least fluently) as the setup and delivering the punch line recontextualized to apply to Marina "*you are* (an) American."

```
(10)   276 C // do you speak any OTher [225][62]
           languages besides ENGlish[242][60]? //
       277 1.11
       278 M // NOPE [251][71] //
       279 0.42
       280 M // nothin FLUently [216][59] //
       281 0.12
       282 M // little bit a this n THAT [210][60] n //
       283 1.26
       284 M // k OTher [185][73] thing //
       285 0.66
       286 M // you KNOW [147][65] = //
       287 C // =you're aMERican [227][60] //
       288 1.03
       289 ((both laugh))
```

Thus "joke" is an ambiguous term. It can refer to narrative texts and to single turn witticisms. What accounts for its popularity in humor studies, then? In Attardo and Chabanne (1992), we reviewed several reasons for the popularity of the term and the subject, in humor research:

1. jokes are short and therefore can be used freely without using too much space;
2. they are easily available, especially on the internet;
3. they tend to be self-contained, and hence can be used without much explanation/contextualization;
4. they come with a built-in guarantee that they are instances of humor, unlike a novel or a conversation in which the humorous passages are not somehow marked for the analyst;
5. they have been the subject of extensive research.

In particular, we should mention the doctor's wife joke[10] which has assumed in the linguistics of humor the role of an exemplar (Kuhn, 1962) i.e., a solved problem (as in "textbook problem") used by beginners and experts alike as an example or model of how to "do" science. Part of theoretical linguistics training, for example, consists in solving phonology and morphology problems that simulate field linguistics problems (such as identifying minimal pairs or determining the phonemic or morphemic status of a given allophone or allomorph). The doctor's wife joke will be discussed in Chapter 6.

Finally, and this has caused much consternation among those who study discourse, in popular parlance we speak of "joking" and "telling a joke" for the delivery of any kind of humor in conversation, be that prepared or prepackaged (canned) or extemporaneous (conversational) humor. So, one should always be careful to specify what kind of joking one means. Of course, we mustn't forget that stand-up comedy and scripted humor will often masquerade as improvised humor. So, when relevant, that dimension should also be considered as well.

1.1.4 Mirth, humor, laughter

Another significant distinction is that between the cognitive stimulus, which we agreed to call humor, its emotional effect, which is referred to as *mirth* and the physical manifestation of the emotion: laughter and smiling. See Figure 1.2.

Ruch (1993) proposed the term "exhilaration" to indicate the underlying emotion of laughter/smiling caused (among other things) by humor. Martin (2007) rejects the proposal because "exhilaration" has an excitement component to its meaning, and prefers "mirth": "Mirth (...) is the distinctive emotion that is elicited by the perception of humor" (p. 8). Both terms are used widely. I have preferred "mirth" in this book

Cognitive stimulus	Emotional response	Physical manifestation
• Humor	• Mirth Exhilaration	• Laughter Smiling

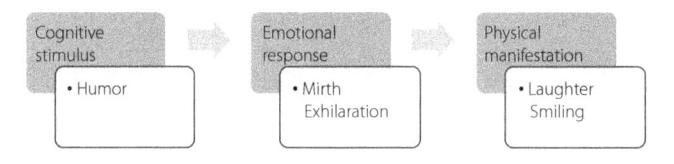

Figure 1.2 The relationship between humor, mirth, and laughter.

---

[10] Raskin (2017a) jokingly calls it "the" joke.

only because compounds such as "mirthful laughter," are simpler than "exhilaration laughter."

Finally, the emotion caused by the cognitive stimulus may manifest itself physically, typically in laughter or smiling. Note the all-important qualification "may." One may experience mirth and not show any visible signs thereof. There are many issues at stake around these concepts: for example, is smiling an attenuated form of laughter, or are they independent phenomena? The question is beyond the scope of this book.

It should also be pointed out that laughter and smiling may occur without any accompanying emotion of mirth or exhilaration. For example, many cultures have a laughter of embarrassment. Furthermore, mirth or exhilaration may occur without humor. Conversely, as we saw, humor may occur without mirth, exhilaration, laughter, or smiling. So, there is no one-to-one correlation between humor and laughter and/or smiling. There is at best a general association between the two, but it would be a serious error to assume that because you observe either of the two items the other must be present as well. We will return to this issue in some of the next chapters.

Within humor studies it is not uncommon to see significant confusion on the use of this terminology. First, there may be confusion among the three levels: for example, one often sees claims that getting (as in understanding) a joke results in laughter. This is true, only insofar as it is taken to be an oversimplification of "getting a joke results in exhilaration or mirth, which then is manifested as laughter." Second, one may confuse the levels. A good example of this is Bergson's (1901) titled "Laughter" which does in fact study comedy.

1.2 A brief overview of humor studies

The study of humor goes back to ancient times. Attention to humor dates from the Egyptians (2600 BC) and the Sumerian (2200 BC), who both documented humor in the form of jokes or humorous texts. However, the Greeks are the first to consider the subject theoretically. One can trace the origins of some of the modern theories of humor (see Chapter 3) back to Plato and Aristotle (third century BC). I did so myself in Attardo (1994, ch. 1). Besides philosophy, literary criticism takes a front stage with Aristotle's *Poetics* and Theophrastus' *Moral Characters* (third century BC). Rhetorics likewise has taken up the problem of humor, often with surprisingly modern insights and formulations, see for example Cicero's distinction (first century BC) between verbal and referential humor (Attardo 1994: 26–29), which we will examine below. Quintilian has the distinction, in his *Institutio Oratoria*, of having the first coherent treatise on humor, if we except the lost second part of Aristotle's *Poetics* (Janko, 1984).

All this, however, is ultimately mostly of historical significance: for example, a scholar may be interested in finding out where a given theory comes from, what the earliest mention of, say, incongruity or superiority is, or who was the first thinker to realize that surprise is an important factor of humor. However, and this is an important point, all of these theories have been supplanted by more recent, more specific, and far more detailed, in short, more scientific, formulations. In what follows, then, we will review how modern theories of humor got to be what they are and when the field of humor studies, as a field of study, emerged. The review is short and flippant. For dead-serious reviews see Attardo (1994, pp. 14–59) or Larkin-Galiñanes (2017).

The Middle Ages were a dark period (pun intended): the Catholic Church engaged in a prolonged and losing battle against laughter and the rest of the people were too busy dying of the Black Plague and being killed by marauders and barbarians to worry about the definition of humor. We have to wait for the Italian Renaissance (1300–1400) to see significant humorous texts being written and distributed and the rebirth of literary criticism concerning humor. France, Germany, and England eventually catch up with the Renaissance, and we get Erasmus' *Praise of Folly* (1511), Rabelais' *Gargantua et Pantagruel* (1532), and eventually Shakespeare. The theory of humor is not limited to the literary theorists: in 1579, Laurent Joubert writes his *Traité du ris* (Treatise on Laughter), which has the distinction of being the first extended treatment of humor in a vulgar language (i.e., not in Latin, until then the vehicle for science) and the first explanation of the physiology of laughter.

In 1598, Ben Johnson writes *Every Man in His Humor* which is the first major use of the term humor in its modern sense. To be fair, the first actual use of humor as comedy, is *An Humorous Day's Mirth* a comedy by one George Chapman, produced in 1597. Both Johnson and Chapman are still using "humor" in the theory of humors sense: dating back to Hippocrates (4th century BC), the idea was that one's temperament was determined by the proportion of four humors (i.e., bodily fluids):

blood, bile (yellow and black), and phlegm. We still get a relic of this conception in expressions such as a "sanguine" (=blood) temperament" or a "phlegmatic" character. However, the association with comedy and humor in the modern sense is there as well. On the four temperaments and humor theory, see Hempelmann (2017).

In 1649, René Descartes writes *Les passions de l'âme* (The Passions of the Soul) in which he presents a psycho-physiological explanation of joy and laughter. Descartes connects psychological concepts, such as surprise, physiological concepts, such as facial expressions and increased blood flow, to the expression of joy (we would say exhilaration or mirth). Descartes considers laughter to be the result of a mixture of emotions, such as indignation against an evil, surprise, and joy, since the evil is harmless (Descartes, 1649, Article 197).[11]

In 1651, Thomas Hobbes writes *Leviathan* which is the grandfather of the aggression theories of humor, which he defines as "sudden glory," i.e., the triumph over an adversary. Needless to say, the idea of laughter as aggression or superiority is already present in the Greeks. In 1695, Congreve, followed, in the first half of the eighteenth century, by the Earl of Shaftesbury (1709), Addison (1711), and Hutcheson (1750), publishes essays on laughter and humor. Despite all these contributions, there is still no sense of a coherent body of research.

Bain, the founder of the journal *Mind* in 1859, in *The Emotions and the Will* discusses humor, followed by Spencer's *The Physiology of Laughter* (1860), and Darwin's discussion of laughter (1872) in *The Expression of the Emotions in Man and Animals*, which is still used in the field. Hall, the founder of the *American Psychological Association*, publishes *The Psychology of Tickling, Laughing, and the Comic* (1987), and Sully, the founder of the *British Psychological Association*, *An Essay on Laughter* (1902). With these publications, we certainly witness the first steps within humor of the discipline that will eventually dominate the field, psychology. Yet, while we definitely have a discipline in the modern sense of the term, we still do not have a field, despite the influence of Kant's philosophical theory, and the connections to literary criticism. See Simon (1985) for a broader and fascinating discussion, which I am simplifying significantly. In particular, the mutual influences of the psychologists and literary scholars are fascinating.

---

[11] This definition eerily reminds one of the so-called benign violation theory of humor (McGraw & Warren, 2010).

1.2 A BRIEF OVERVIEW OF HUMOR STUDIES

At the beginning of the twentieth century, we have a remarkable convergence, when three major intellectual figures publish books on humor within a ten-year frame: Bergson (1899; in book form 1901), Freud (1905), and Pirandello (1908). It is tempting to see the beginning of humor studies in this trifecta, especially given that all three scholars respond to a series of works on humor, within their disciplines. Freud, for example, is influenced by Groos' work (Simon, 1985). Yet, these works, however significant, do not form a "critical mass" for an academic discipline.

Where is linguistics, you might ask? Well, not really in the picture. Until 1916, linguistics was part of philosophy, literary criticism, history, or perhaps anthropology. For many linguists, linguistics was a historical science. Linguistics does not come into its own until after 1916, after the posthumous publication of Saussure's *Cours de Linguistique Générale*. Even then, linguistics has very little to contribute to humor studies, except for the study of puns, which was considered the province of the linguistics of humor. We will have to wait until the 1980s and Raskin's work (see ch. 6) for linguistics to take a central role in humor studies.

Isolated scholars elaborate sophisticated, even brilliant theories; however, that does not make a field of study. The main defining characteristics of humor studies is that it is an interdisciplinary field. Interdisciplinarity requires that more than one discipline be used as the source of both the problems (the questions) and the methodologies (the tools) used to address them. If the problems come from one discipline and the methodologies from another, all you get is an applied field (for example, forensic linguistics, which seeks to answer questions from forensic science using linguistic tools: e.g., is the person making this threatening phone call the same person in these other recordings?). What defines interdisciplinarity is that both the questions and the methodologies come from a variety of disciplines.

In this sense, humor studies as a field, is born around the mid-1970s, after Goldstein and McGhee (1972) book appeared, with the first humor conference, held in Cardiff, Wales, in 1976, by Anthony Chapman and Hugh Foot. The conference was followed by another one in 1979, in Los Angeles, and then in 1982, in Washington, DC, in 1984, in Tel Aviv, and, in 1985, in Cork, Ireland. The other significant event was that in 1982 Don and Alleen Nilsen at the University of Arizona, started the World Humor and Irony Membership (WHIM), which held annual meetings until 1987. In 1988 the last WHIM was held at Purdue university.

The year before the International Society of Humor Studies (ISHS) was created, which replaced WHIM. The ISHS has held a yearly conference since 1988.

WHIM published extended abstracts, in a soft-bound book format, called the WHIM Serial Yearbook (WHIMSY). This was the first periodical humor research publication. It published yearly volumes from 1982 until 1989. Together, the WHIM conferences and the WHIMSY proceedings established a reliable forum for scholars wishing to research humor-related topics and helped establish the viability of a humor-related journal.

In 1988, *HUMOR: International Journal of Humor Research* started publication, with Victor Raskin as editor-in-chief. The role of HUMOR in legitimizing the field by offering a high-quality outlet to humor research should be clear, since it constituted the only respectable, reliable forum to publish humor research, at least for the first 20 years of publication. HUMOR is still being published currently, but now other journals specializing in humor exist: the *Israeli Journal of Humor Research: An International Journal* which started publication in 2012, the *European Journal of Humour Research* which started in 2013, and the *Rivista Internazionale di Studi sull'Umorismo*, based in Italy,[12] which started publication in 2017. In the Francophone world, CORHUM (the Centre de Recherche sur le Comique et l'Humour) has also been publishing a journal since 1988. In 1994 the *Humor Research* book series, with Mouton the Gruyter, was launched, followed by Transaction Publishers (now with Routledge), Wayne State University Press, Gordon and Breach, Benjamins, and others. Moreover, numerous articles on humor appear regularly in many relevant journals such as the *Journal of Pragmatics*, *Discourse Processes*, and many others. Finally, the publication of such reference works as the *Encyclopedia of Humor Studies* (2015) and the *Handbook of Language and Humor* (2017), no doubt also helped establish humor studies as a field, and within it the linguistics of humor. So, in conclusion, I think it is fair to say that today, the field of humor studies has established itself as a legitimate field of academic research.

Another way to look at the birth of the field is to track the emergence of university courses on humor. Wycoff (1999) is, to the best of my knowledge, the only attempt at charting the rise of the teaching of humor

---

[12] *International Journal of Humor Studies*; the acronym RISU is the ablative case of Latin *risus*, meaning roughly "with or through laughter."

as an academic subject. He reports that the first pioneering courses were taught in the sixties and that by the 1970s the field begun to emerge as a credible field. The earliest course documented in Wycoff was taught in 1966, at Michigan State. Wycoff reports that by 1999 there were in excess of 100 humor courses being taught.

1.2.1 Why do we need a field of study?

The reason I wish to establish the origins of the field of humor studies is that its presence is a mutual guarantee of quality for the scholars that engage in research within it and it allows the recruiting of young scholars and the establishment of the research on a sound basis. Consider a potential objection: one might question the significance of trying to establish when humor studies "came together" as a field. After all, one may reason, research is ultimately done by individuals and works of genius advance knowledge, regardless of whether there is a group of people who support it. One may use as an example, Wittgenstein, who, notwithstanding his early ties to the Neopositivists, developed his work in splendid isolation.[13]

Now, setting aside what we know about the history of science, which tells us that this idea of the lone wolf author is deeply mistaken, there is another reason for needing a community of scholars. Kuhn (1962) identifies "normal science" as what scientists do most of the time: they move within an established paradigm, that tells them what methodologies are and are not acceptable, what kinds of observations are good and what are not, what kinds of experiments are acceptable, even what kinds of arguments are valid, and so on.

Let us consider an example: within linguistics itself there is a sharp difference on the status of intuitive data: for some linguists, if I think about it and come to the conclusion that I would never say the sentence "very banana I love much," that counts as a bit of evidence (a datum). Put together a lot of those and you get data. For many other linguists, this kind of data is deeply suspect. These other linguists object that they are not naturally occurring data. They want their data to come from a corpus of language facts that occurred independently of the observer, the larger the better. Other linguists also object that the data are not

---

[13] I do not claim that this is a valid description of the genesis of Wittgenstein's oeuvre, but his work is definitely less embedded in a tradition, than, say, Bertrand Russell's.

naturally occurring, but would like their data to come from a small set of interactions (conversations, primarily, albeit not limited to spoken data, so they would include online chats, etc.) and preferably with the involvement of the researcher, which gives him/her access to the inner dynamics of the exchange. The naturally occurring data linguists mock the first linguists as "armchair" linguists and decry the "artificial" nature of the data. Needless to say, the armchair linguists mock the inherent limitations of finite corpora and restricted samples.

The point of the previous paragraph is not to uncover the seedy underbelly of the profession but rather to point out the fact that even what counts as data is determined by the paradigm one does science within.[14] Where and how to find one's data is not the only purview of a paradigm: a paradigm determines how scientists go about their business of generating hypotheses, arguing for them, what counts as a valid argument, and so on. My overall point then is that the existence of a field gives us the paradigm from which we can determine the value of the research. The existence of a scientific society that holds periodical conferences, the existence of publications (journals, yearbooks, book series, etc.), which vouch for the quality of their contents, are all elements that contribute to the emergence of a scientific field of study. Needless to say, the interactions between the scholars themselves, collaborations, tips, references, discussions, etc. are also significant, but I believe that the paradigmatic elements, in Kuhn's sense, are most important due to one last factor: academic respectability.

In order to be viable, a field of study must be accepted as a respectable area of research in which one may dissertate and/or find a job. These may seem crass considerations, but realistically speaking, a field thrives when young scholars with an interest in it are encouraged to pursue their interest. However, responsible advisors must warn their students if their choice of dissertation topic may prevent them from getting desirable positions in academe. If humor is a "questionable" topic, it will be hard for young scholars to enter the field. It was no coincidence that at the beginning of humor studies their proponents were all established academics with significant credentials in non-humor-areas. The same

---

[14] Technically, the differences between linguists approaches are not paradigms, because the differences between the various "schools" are not significant enough. There is also the small matter that in some ways linguistics is not yet a mature science. In Kuhn's sense, it is pre-paradigmatic: there are competing approaches, without a dominant paradigm. These distinctions are significant, but need not concern us in this context.

problems have been reported, at their respective beginnings, for such fields as sexology, film studies, etc. Generally speaking, the reasoning seems to be that, if the topic is fun, the research on it cannot be serious and/or respectable.[15]

Occasionally, other academics or members of the public ask me if humor studies is fun. My reply is to offer to read them a few pages of Attardo (1994). No-one has ever taken me up on that offer. I will admit, however, that data collection when one is looking at memes online or at comedians performing is less personally difficult than perusing letters from the Holocaust (one of my colleague's field of study was genocide—now *that* is a serious field of study).

1.3 A few basic distinctions

We can wrap up this introductory chapter with two more distinctions which are general enough so as not to fit clearly in any of the next chapters and yet important enough that they need to be introduced early.

1.3.1 Linguistic humor vs. verbal humor

Linguistic humor is humor expressed through language, spoken or written. Another term used to refer to linguistic humor in this sense is "verbally expressed humor" as opposed to visually expressed humor, in film/television studies.

Linguistic humor is a subclass of semiotic humor (see Chapter 5). Other types of semiotic humor are visual humor, musical humor, multimodal humor (humor expressed in media that involve more than one communicative modality, such as television, cinema, theater, video games, etc.). Physical humor (e.g., slapstick, clowning) also falls under semiotic humor. This is represented visually in Figure 1.3. The examples under each category are not meant to be exhaustive. They just represent the kind of humor that would be classified under that category.

Linguistic humor should not be confused with verbal humor, as opposed to referential humor. Simplifying quite a bit, verbal humor consists of puns (ch. 9), i.e., humor which relies significantly on semantics

---

[15] In this respect, my personal hero is Dolf Zillmann, who after studying humor, went on to study pornography!

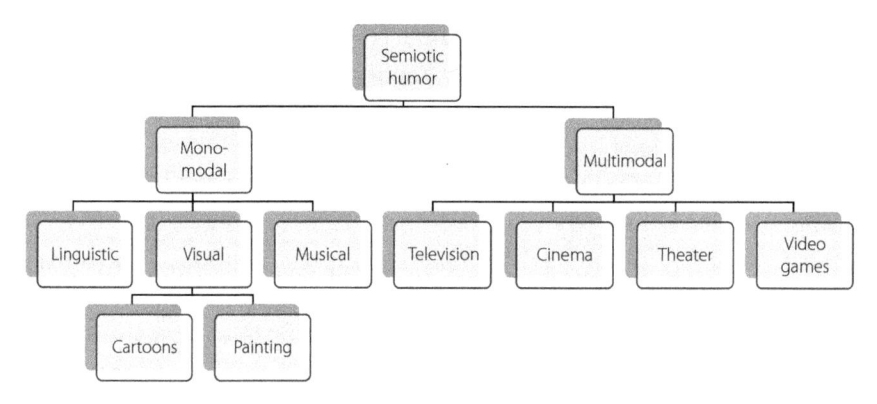

Figure 1.3 Semiotic humor hierarchy.

(meaning) and similarity or identity of two linguistic forms: phonemic (sounds) or graphemic (spellings) whereas referential humor is just based on semantics. To reiterate, referential humor relies only on meaning. Verbal humor also relies on meaning, but not exclusively. Needless to say, what kind of meanings we are talking about is a significant issue, which will be tackled in the chapters to follow.

The distinction is not unique to linguistic humor. For example, there exist visual puns (Lessard, 1991; Hempelmann and Samson, 2007; Mitchell, 2007; Tsakona, 2009). Berger (1993, p. 45) provides a duly broad definition of semiotic pun as "a signifier that stands for two signifieds." Turner (2005, pp. 204–205) discusses several examples, as well.

1.3.2 Humor and meta-humor

The next distinction we need to address is that between humor and meta-humor. The reason for doing so is that, as we will see, meta-humor can be seen as an exception to the fundamental definitions of humor as incongruity. So we need to be very clear about this category.

To put it simply, meta-humor is humor about humor. The term has been used widely, along with other terms, such as anti-humor, second-degree humor, self-referential humor. Attardo (1988) reviewed the (scant) literature.

We will begin by defining our terms. Intuitively, meta-humor comes from meta-language, a technical term within logic for a language used to talk about another language (the object language). The idea of metalanguage is closely related to Russell's theory of types (Russell, 1908; Copi, 2011) which he elaborated to solve the paradox he had found in Frege's set theory. Without getting too technical, the set of all dogs consists of all the entities in the world that are dogs, so the set of all dogs does not contain itself. Conversely, a set of sets would contain itself (since it is a set). Consider now the set of all sets that do not contain themselves. Should it contain itself? If we say yes, we are violating its definition (it is the set of sets that do *not* contain themselves), and if we say no, it meets the requirements for belonging in the set and so *should* be in it. Russell developed his theory of types which we can describe as essentially forbidding the kind of cross-level definition we have used. Popular versions of this paradox exist, such as the barber of the village who shaves only those who do not shave themselves. Should he shave himself? Interestingly, Bateson's (1972) theory of schizophrenia as the result of a "double bind" is based on the same principle. Bateson will figure prominently in the definition of play, in the next chapters.[16]

Jakobson (1960) introduced metalanguage to linguistics in his famous model of communication, which distinguishes six functions of language, which include the metalingual (metalinguistic) function. So, in a natural language (i.e., a language spoken by people, as opposed to a formal language such as logic, or a computer language, such as COBOL or Java), a metalinguistic statement is a statement about (some part of) the language itself. Metalanguage should not be confused with self-referentiality. The sentence

(11) The first sentence of Moby Dick is "Call me Ishmael"

is metalinguistic but *not* self-referential, whereas

(12) This sentence consists of six words.

is self-referential. All self-referential sentences are metalinguistic, but not all metalinguistic sentences are self-referential. For example, the sentence

(13) All self-referential sentences are metalinguistic, but not all metalinguistic sentences are self-referential.

---

[16] Surprisingly, Russell dealt with meta-humor. Russell's discussion of the hierarchy of jokes can be found online at http://www.gutenberg.org/files/38430/38430-h/38430-h.htm. Blackwell (2011) provides some background information on this little known aspect of Russell's thought.

is metalinguistic but not self referential. Whereas

(14)   I am lying.

is both metalinguistic and self-referential.[17]

So, what is meta-humor then? Any humor about humor would qualify. So for example, making fun of someone for not telling a joke properly would be meta-humor. It is clear that self-referential meta-humor is the more interesting category. The infamous joke

(15)   Why did the chicken cross the road? To get to the other side.

is a self-referential meta-joke because it refers implicitly to the form of jokes, in particular to the presence of a punch line at the end of the text, and fails to deliver it, thereby violating incongruously the expectations set up by the stereotypical joke introduction (a riddle in this case). The shaggy-dog jokes I examined in Attardo (1988) are precisely long-winded jokes that do not deliver a punch line at the end (see also Fry, 1963, p. 148; Suls, 1983, p. 53; Lefort, 1986, p. 191).

The reason self-referential meta-humor is significant for humor theory is that it works by violating the rules of the genres of humor. Therefore it will always be an apparent exception to any generalization about humor. As we will see in Chapter 4, a punch line occurs in all jokes at the end of the text. In meta-jokes the punch line is that there is no punch line. This sounds paradoxical, but using Russell's theory of types, the paradox is dispatched easily: there is no level 1 punch line, which creates a level 2 punch line. A related reason, is that joke-cycles, such as the light-bulb jokes, start out as level 1 jokes but soon develop jokes of level 2 that are based on knowing the format of the joke and then incongruously *not* delivering it. Quite literally so, in the following example,

(16)   How many feminists does it take to screw in a lightbulb?
       That's not funny!

I examine joke cycles in these terms in Attardo (2001, pp. 69–78).

Suls (1983) discusses meta-humor as one "problem" of the incongruity/resolution model. His answer is right on target: "they provide enjoyment by playing off the fact that they pretend to be humor but do

---

[17] Epimenides' paradox famously consists in saying that all Cretans are liars and the speaker is Cretan.

not possess all of the requisite features" (p. 53). Indeed, this is correct: meta-humor is the fly in the theoretical ointment of humor theory because meta-humor will invalidate any generalization about humor or any of its genres, because meta-humor plays with the expectations about humor and its forms. Because of the relative sophistication of jokes using meta-humor each generation rediscovers them, which may help explain their popularity.[18] However, the exception is only illusory, as far as the incongruity theory goes: there *is* an incongruity in the chicken crossing the road joke or in the shaggy-dog joke: it is precisely that there is *no* incongruity where we expected one.

1.4 Further readings

There is no comprehensive history of humor studies. The web site of the International Society for Humor Studies (http://www.humorstudies.org) provides some helpful resources, including a listing of all humor research conferences organized by the society. The preface to McGhee & Goldstein (1983); Derks (1996), which is the introduction to the second edition by Transaction of the classic Chapman & Foot (1976); Carrell (2008); and Goldstein & Ruch (2018), which is the preface to a Festschrift for Paul McGhee, in HUMOR, are all good places to gather information about the history of humor studies.

Further discussion of the terminology of humor studies can be found in Hempelmann's (2017) chapter of the *Handbook of Humor Studies*. Attardo (1994, pp. 3–5) offers a review of some of the attempts at internal subcategorization. The discussion between referential and verbal humor is discussed in some depth in Attardo (1994). There is no comprehensive treatment of meta-humor, beyond the texts indicated in the chapter.

---

[18] The Wikipedia page for the chicken crossing the road joke reports a version dating back to 1845. https://en.wikipedia.org/wiki/Why_did_the_chicken_cross_the_road

2
Methodological preliminaries

2.1 Competence and performance	31
2.2 Identifying humor	38
2.3 Mirthful vs. non-mirthful laughter	42
2.4 Keying	50
2.5 Identifying humor: the triangulation approach	54
2.6 Further readings	56

This chapter starts out by setting the background for the rest of the work. Thus, it is fairly dry and abstract. The reader may consider it a necessary evil but should not bypass it, as the points discussed in this chapter are truly foundational. Broadly speaking, we are concerned with methodology. When students ask me why methodology is so important, I explain that it is how you avoid making a fool of yourself.[1] We start out by discussing the competence–performance opposition, which underlies most of the book and the principle of commutation, which underlies the theoretical approaches to the linguistics of humor. We briefly consider other methodologies (quantitative, qualitative, etc.) to show that, whatever one's methodology, there are rules and warrants that must be followed. The second part of the chapter deals with the all-important methodological question of how do we know that a given text is humorous. The de-facto criteria of identification (laughter and smiling) are discussed and problematized. Finally, we conclude by proposing a triangulation approach which ecumenically gathers all sources of information about the text to make the determination.

---

[1] Surprisingly, so is etiquette. Food for thought.

The Linguistics of Humor: An Introduction. Salvatore Attardo, Oxford University Press (2020). © Salvatore Attardo.
DOI: 10.1093/oso/9780198791270.001.0001

2.1 Competence and performance

It is perhaps peculiar that we will begin by discussing a meta-theoretical problem (i.e., an issue concerning the theory of theories), rather than by—say—defining our object of study, humor. The reasons is that "humor," as we saw, is a folk-concept, i.e., it exists pre-theoretically. What does that mean? Simply that the fact that people refer to something as "humor" does not mean that they know exactly what that thing is, where its boundaries lie, how to tell it apart from other similar things, etc. Think for example of whales: for centuries people thought that whales were a kind of fish, only because they live in water and look like a large fish. However, when the pre-theoretical conception of the whale-as-fish came under scientific scrutiny it was abandoned for the current theory of the whale-as-mammal.[2]

A good way to begin is to ask the question: "what should a humor researcher study?" Should we study actual texts? The exchanges in which instances of humor occur? The psychological motivations of the jokers and/or their audience? The unconscious motivations of either? Their goals and/or responses in/for joking? The electrical impulses in the brain of the person hearing a joke?

The answer is, clearly, all of the above, since they interest one or the other discipline. Moreover, those I listed above are not, by any means, the only topics worth studying, they are just a sampler of questions. Can we narrow down things a little, if we take a linguistic standpoint? Clearly, some aspects of the problem become foregrounded (for example the types of texts, the genres, so to speak, of humor) but still there are a plethora of approaches to the, as yet undefined, object of study. At this point, we must turn to theoretical linguistics for insight on the definition of one's object. Saussure's fundamental *langue* vs. *parole* distinction,

---

[2] Let us note that the disciplinary standpoint one assumes largely (pre-)determines the object of inquiry. This meta-theoretical point is of some interest, if for nothing else in that it prevents one from beginning one's inquiry by defining one's object of investigation. One must first determine one's (sub-)discipline and *then* one's object. Objects of research do not preexist theories. This should not be construed as a relativistic position, let alone as a social-constructivist one. Reality preexists any of its conceptualizations. The fact that science is a social enterprise should not be confused with the claim that reality is one as well. The point of this note is merely that theoretical linguistics will approach humor differently than sociolinguists, who will approach it differently than psycholinguists, etc. And naturally, one is free to take a multidisciplinary stand, as I will, and look at humor from different perspectives. However, one will see different things.

later echoed[3] in Chomsky's "competence" and "performance," provided linguists with the general "object" that the discipline had lacked, up to that point. Linguistics must study the system (the *langue*), the abstract set of relationships that convey meaning, while other disciplines, such as stylistics, will study the *parole*, the concrete, actual realizations of the abstract possibilities of the system.

We need not pursue this issue any further. The significant aspect, from our point of view, is that theoretical linguists distinguish between two levels, or two approaches to language: an abstract one (competence) and a concrete one (performance). Seen from this perspective, it becomes clear that we need to develop a theory of humor competence *and* a theory of humor performance, in keeping with the assumption that the former founds (i.e., precedes logically) the latter.

What are the advantages to this approach? By adopting this distinction, we neatly distinguish between the essential[4] factors (i.e., the necessary and sufficient conditions for a text to be funny) and the accidental factors (e.g., who happens to have told a given joke, when, where, etc).[5] Furthermore, by defining the necessary and sufficient conditions for a text to be funny, we will have a falsifiable, scientific theory, since any counterexample would falsify the theory: it would merely require that one produce a text that meets the necessary and sufficient conditions and is *not* funny or that one produce a text that *is* funny and lacks any of the supposedly necessary and sufficient conditions. Not to mention that by avoiding those factors that are not essential we will not be led astray by facts which, however interesting, are ultimately irrelevant to the definition we are seeking.

Needless to say, the claim that we should build both a theory of competence and of performance is not a mere condescending nod towards applied linguistics. Many have—and rightfully so—objected to the devaluation of performance, implicit in Saussure and explicit in Chomsky. Even better, starting with Bally (a student of Saussure, and

---

[3] Chomsky's competence is in this respect identical to Saussure's *langue*, except that Chomsky locates competence in the genetic make-up of humans, whereas Saussure located competence in the social (i.e., it is a social phenomenon), after Durkheim. There are some differences between the two conceptions, most notably in the role of syntax. These need not detain us in this context.

[4] Recall the definition of "essence": what makes a given thing that thing.

[5] Of course, if you are interested in who tells jokes to whom, then *those* become the essential factors that your theory will focus on and the content of the jokes become accidental. Each perspective determines its object of study.

editor of the *Cours*), many have theorized (and practiced) a linguistics of the parole/performance. We will return to the performance aspect of humor below and in Chapter 10.

How does one go about reaching the competence level? After all, we have only access to performance data. Different disciplines and fields have different ways of approaching the issue of idealization, or, to put it differently, to insure that their results are not contaminated by any number of methodological problems. For example, in psychology, sociology, etc. the use of large pools of subjects protects (by the law of averages) the conclusions drawn by the researchers against the vagaries of individual variation. For example, there is always the possibility that a subject has "seen through" the test he/she is being administered and that he/she decides to answer in a deliberately nonsensical way merely to irritate the test administrator. However, the possibility that a majority of subjects did is close to zero and thus in a sufficiently large sample that the aberrant behavior of that lone subejct is eliminated. Thus, the larger and more representative the sample, the more secure the conclusions drawn from it.

So, how does theoretical linguistics reach the competence level? Linguists use a process of idealization quite different from those of statistics, because quantitative data are basically irrelevant from that point of view. The likelihood that the sentence

(17) My pink elephant loves to dance the tango.

has ever been uttered is pretty low, whereas the following sentence (or at least sentences built on the schema) is fairly common:

(18) Me Tarzan, you Jane.

but nonetheless (17) is grammatical and (18) is not.[6] In fact, one of the most significant points that Chomsky uses to justify his generative approach to language is that language makes infinite use of a finite set of elements. Therefore, no sample may, in principle, ever guarantee that it is exhaustive (i.e., it contains all the relevant facts).

Grammaticality, meaningfulness, ambiguity, and their counterparts, ungrammaticality, semantic anomaly, and monosemy are not

---

[6] Example (18) is ungrammatical because it contains no verb and because the subject is in the accusative case. The point here is not on grammaticality of example (18) but on the fact that speakers may recognize the grammaticality of sentences they have never encountered before.

determined statistically, but rather via a theoretical elaboration based on the principle of commutation, a.k.a. distinctiveness.

2.1.1 Application of the principle of commutation to humor

At the most basic level, in phonology, two sounds are said to be different phonemically if they are distinctive, i.e., they are part of a minimal pair, such as /bɪt/ ("bit") and /bit/ ("beet"). Because changing the sound [ɪ] to [i] changes the meaning in the minimal pair, then the two sounds are functionally different, i.e., phonemes. Consider now the following joke:

(19) Harry prays to God: Dear Lord, please make me win the lottery.

The next day Harry begs the Lord again: Please make it so I win the lottery, Lord!

The next day, Harry again prays: Please, please, dear Lord, make me win the lottery!

Suddenly he hears a voice from above: Harry, would you kindly go and buy a lottery ticket. (https://short-funny.com/funniest-jokes-3.php)

Consider the following possible changes to the text:

1. Change the name from "Harry" to "Larry"
2. Change the name from "Harry" to "Mary"
3. Change the name from "Harry" to "Abramovitz"
4. Change the name from "Harry" to "Oluwakemi"

while the first change has virtually no effect on the text, the second one changes the gender of the supplicant, but has no effect on the humor. The third changes the joke into a Jewish joke, but likewise leaves the humor untouched. The fourth change makes the joke about a Yoruba person, but as before leaves the humor unchanged. So, we know, that the name and characteristics of the person doing the supplication is largely[7] irrelevant to the humor.

---

[7] But not completely: if we replace "Harry" with Jeff Bezos, the multibillionaire (note the "b") founder of Amazon, the fact that he wants to win the lottery becomes incoherent and ruins the setup of the joke.

2.1 COMPETENCE AND PERFORMANCE

Consider now another set of changes:

1. Change "beg" to "pray"
2. Change "the next day" to "the next week"
3. Change "a voice" to "the Lord's voice"
4. Change "The Lord" to "God"
5. Change "The Lord" to "Buddha"
6. Change "the lottery" to "a trip to the Bahamas"
7. Change "buy a lottery ticket" to "I already granted your wish"

Once more, the first four changes have no impact on the humor, thus showing that those are not significant details, as far as the humor goes. However, with the fifth change, the humor disappears, because Buddhism does not believe in a personal god (in fact in any kinds of god) and moreover, to the best of my knowledge, there is no tradition of asking the Buddha for personal gifts. So, in order for the joke to work we need a superhuman personal entity capable of bestowing gifts and willing to do so. So, in a sense, this is a Judeo-Christian joke at a deeper level than it is a joke about Harry. However, the next two changes are even more devastating to the humor: if Harry wants to win a trip to the Bahamas, the element of "random drawing" of the lottery is gone, hence the fact that an omnipotent god could, if they so decided, make an individual the winner of the lottery, is also gone. Compare "make me win the lottery" to "buy me a ticket to the Bahamas." The former requires a superhuman entity, the latter just someone with a few thousand dollars to spend (i.e., the cost of a ticket to the Bahamas).

Finally, the last change also eliminates the humor, by removing the explanation why god has so far not granted the wish. Note that god is quite willing to grant the wish, but, reasonably enough, points out that in order to win the lottery, one has to buy a ticket, apparently disregarding the fact that if god is capable of making someone win the lottery they could perfectly well make them magically acquire a ticket as well.

So in conclusion, we have been able, by applying the principle of commutation, to determine that the joke "works" because a) it involves a personal god character; b) it involves winning the lottery, which has a random extraction aspect to it and; c) it requires god to be willing to violate randomness but not causality. Let me add that this is just a partial[8] and informal analysis. We will see the actual application of this methodology to semantic and pragmatics in Chapters 6–7.

2.1.2 Other methodologies

We have seen that theoretical linguistics is built, methodologically speaking, on the application of the principle of commutation. Conversely, variationist linguistics (a branch of sociolinguistics), achieves idealization statistically, i.e., by evaluating the likelihood that a given result, for example that speakers laugh more frequently when in a group, could have been arrived at by chance. This is not the place to discuss the actual statistical tools used to arrive at this determination, but we will review a few basic concepts. In order for data to justify a given (theoretical) conclusion, the following conditions must be met:

- The sample must be representative of the population (i.e., all the things you want to describe).
- The variables must be controlled as much as possible. Special methodologies (such as double blinding and control groups) have been developed to ensure that no unaccounted for variables affect the data.
- Proper statistical measures must ensure that the likelihood that a given result was arrived at by chance is kept below a given threshold (usually 0.05 i.e., 5%). This is called "significance" and is *not* the same as significance in everyday parlance (for example, "this is a significant problem").

Unless these prophylactic measures are adopted, the only thing that empirical data can tell us is the tautological fact that they exist and have been observed. Corpus-based and corpus-assisted studies, in which the researcher begins by securing a (large) body of relevant data, likewise give the same level of attention to the representativeness of the corpus, because if the corpus is not representative of the population one wants to generalize to, then the study is pointless. Suppose one wants to

---

[8] In the version of the joke that I first heard, probably from Victor Raskin, in the late 1980s, the man is described as "righteous" which goes a long way to explain his entitlement to ask God for a gift. Furthermore, much was made of him being apologetic about doing so. A considerable improvement on the quality of the joke, but not a change in its "moving parts" that make the humor happen.

describe jokes that circulate among high-school students. A corpus of Facebook posts would not be a valid corpus to generalize to all high-school students, because a) many high-school students do not use Facebook, which is perceived to be for "older" people, and b) because not all jokes that circulate among the students might be posted on Facebook.

It should be noted that phenomenologically oriented approaches differ from either of these approaches I have sketched above. They will be discussed in Chapter 11. Finally, within applied linguistics, researchers speak of "warrants" for the research. Essentially warrants are "validity checks." Among the warrants are

- credibility
- replicability
- transferability
- freedom from biases.

Credibility is related to the level of validity that one's research has (valid research is credible). There are various criteria of validity (Creswell & Miller, 2000). In particular their discussion of triangulation (Creswell & Miller, 2000, pp. 126–127) will be quite relevant, particularly about the thorny problem of identifying humor in a text (see below, Section 2.5). In a nutshell, triangulation is defined as using "convergence among multiple and different sources of information" to validate a category or an interpretation. The focus is essentially on relying on more than a single form of evidence and in fact in seeking a variety of sources of evidence. Incidentally, the term "triangulation" as used in linguistics is a metaphor going back to ancient sailing techniques and does not necessarily require *three* sources. One can triangulate with four, five, or more sources of evidence.

Replicability is achieved by being as explicit as possible on one's procedure, so that other scholars may reproduce a given study and check whether they get the same results. Transferability concerns the lack of ad hoc explanation: if we have an explanation for a phenomenon that applies only to that particular phenomenon, we cannot be sure of the validity of the explanation; conversely, if we can apply the same explanation to several independent phenomena, there is a greater probability the explanation is not illusory. Freedom from biases is fairly self-explanatory: it is well known that if we go into a situation expecting that, say, women are less funny than men, we will probably observe precisely that (this is called confirmation bias).

2.2 Identifying humor

We now need to introduce another important methodological aspect of studying humor and namely finding it. How do we know that something is funny, or how do we know that a given part of a text, or a given situation, is humorous? Historically, this has not been a big problem: either scholars were operating with texts, such as jokes, that came pre-labeled as humorous, or they were working with small corpora of data they themselves had collected and thus they had a reasonable idea of what was funny and why people were laughing. When we start looking at large corpora of data collected by third parties, or at large texts, such as novels, the presumption of humorousness is no longer there and the question of whether a given turn in a conversation, or a given passage in a text is humorous or not becomes a serious issue.

Again, historically, many researchers have used a short cut: essentially, they assumed that the presence of laughter was enough to determine that there was humor. For a variety of reasons, the primary one being that video recording was very expensive and cumbersome, while audio recording was easy and cheap, smiling was pretty much ignored, until recently, despite the fact that smiling is the most frequent reaction to humor (Ruch, 2008).

In this respect, psychologists and sociologists have a much easier task: they ask a large number of people "is this stimulus funny?" or "how funny do you find this?" and then use statistics to weed out the weird and unreliable answers and then they have an answer: a given stimulus is funny, and it is moderately so, for example. A linguist is in a much more complex position: suppose he/she is analyzing a conversation, in which one of the speakers says something, and the other responds by smiling. Sure, the linguist could ask the interlocutor if they were smiling because they got the joke or appreciated its humor, but the problem is that there is only one speaker who can answer that question and so if the speaker is an outlier or confused, there is no way to ask another 100 subjects. This means that there are all sorts of possible biases, which cannot be eliminated by aggregating the responses of many subjects. Some linguists have responded to this by simply not asking and assuming that we just do not have access to the inner states of the speakers. Others argue that we can reconstruct them from their behavior. Many use the short cut and check whether either speaker is laughing or smiling. If they are, one of them experienced humor. So, most of what follows in this chapter can be read as the answer to the question: is this a legitimate short-cut?

So we need to answer the question, "Can laughter/smiling be reliably used to identify humor by themselves?" The rest of the chapter will illustrate why the answer is negative and propose more reliable ways of identifying humor.

2.2.1 Humor, mirth, and smiling/laughter

The reader will no doubt recall the fundamental distinction we introduced right at the offset of the discussion between the cause (humor) and the emotional effect (mirth) and between the mental and physiological manifestations of humor and mirth. Humor itself is a cognitive process, which takes place in the brain. Mirth or exhilaration is the emotion one feels when experiencing and appreciating humor (Martin, 2007; Ruch, 1993). Emotions have physiological correlates, so mirth straddles the mental/physiological boundary. Emotions are manifested through external (physical) manifestations. These manifestation may be intentional or unintentional, i.e., they may happen despite the intention/will of the speaker or they may be intentionally planned and executed. At the unintentional end of the continuum one finds the idea of "leakage" proposed by Ekman, who asserts that emotions "leak" through the control that the speaker exerts (Ekman & Friesen, 1969). At the other end is the idea of emotions as social displays, i.e., the manifestations of emotion are meant to send a message to our audience (the people around us) (Fridlund, 1994). Needless to say, intermediate positions are also found, such as Buck (1980; 1994) who thinks that facial expressions are both internal and social manifestations.

Both smiling and laughter may occur spontaneously, in which case they are called "felt" or "spontaneous," or they may be deliberate and are then referred to as "volitional" or "voluntary" smiles/laughter. The prototypical involuntary laughter is often described as "cracking up" or "breaking up," further emphasizing the lack of agency of the speaker and his/her powerlessness in refraining from laughter. Attempts to suppress laughter, for social constraints, such as funerals, formal ceremonies, etc., may in fact make it even more difficult to refrain from laughing (Goffman, 1974, pp. 351–354). As we will see below, felt smiling can be differentiated from social smiling. While the facial displays and acoustic productions of laughter do not allow the differentiation of felt and volitional laughter, they activate different areas of the brain and so in principle may be discriminated. So, can we use felt smiling/laughter to identify humor? Let us consider them separately, first.

2.2.2 Smiling

Ruch reports that there are about 20 types of smile (2008, p. 21). They result from the combination of the activation of different muscles in the face. Ruch lists the following five: zygomatic major, zygomatic minor, risorius, levator anguli oris, buccinator (1995/2005, p. 113). He notes that only the zygomatic major is involved in the smile of enjoyment.

Felt smiling is marked by the so-called Duchenne display which involves the flexing of the zygomatic major muscles, which raise the corners of the mouth, and of the orbicularis oculi, which cause the wrinkling of the corner of the eyes. Volitional smiles do not involve the orbicularis oculi and/or are asymmetrical. A full discussion of the muscles activated in smiling can be found in Platt & Ruch (2014). The primary difference investigated in psychology is whether the smile is felt (genuine) or social (deliberate, contrived). The Duchenne display is considered to be the test of the felt enjoyment smile.[9] However, recent research has challenged the validity of the Duchenne display test of spontaneity (cf. Gironzetti, 2017a, p. 32, for a discussion). Other emotions which produce facial expressions may also be mixed in, such as embarrassment, negative emotions, flirting, etc. (Ruch, 2008, p. 22). These other emotions may cause other muscles to be activated.[10]

Ruch (2008, p. 21) reports that, in experimental settings, smiling is the most frequent response to humor. The subjects are five times more

---

[9] The situation is more complex: Ruch (1995/2005) notes: "Voluntary smiles are more frequently unilateral (present in one half of the face only) or asymmetrical (stronger in one half of the face); their onset is abrupt or otherwise irregular but not smooth; they are more frequently too short (less than half of a second) or too long (more than 4 sec); and they are more frequently asynchronous (i.e., the zygomatic major and orbicularis oculi muscles do not reach their apex at the same time)" (p. 114).

[10] Smiling, laughter, and other facial expressions are commonly studied using the Facial Action Coding System (FACS) elaborated by Ekman & Friesen (1978). Essentially, each muscle in the face is examined for its degree of activation, on a 1–5 scale, ranging between minimal activation to maximum activation.

likely to smile than to laugh at a humor stimulus. Despite this fact, as Ruch notes, laughter remains the response most strongly associated with humor (p. 23). Of course, from the standpoint of identifying humor, smiling presents two related problems: a) people smile (even felt smiles) for positive reasons other than mirth, such as happiness or pleasure (Frank & Ekman, 1993, p. 10), and b) one may experience mirth or recognize humor and still not smile. Ruch (1995/2005) reports that in a meta analysis of studies on reactions to humor, anywhere between 5% and 39% of subjects "showed no facial response at all" (1995/2005, p. 131). Most of those who showed no response were introverts.

2.2.3 Laughter

There are many different kinds of laughter, acoustically and phonologically, in terms of syllables, aspiration, rhythm, volume, etc. (Chafe, 2007, pp. 25–40; Trouvain & Truong, 2017, pp. 344–345). Laughter may occur on its own or interspersed in speech (Chafe, 2007, pp. 41–49). Speakers may laugh alone or jointly (antiphonal laughter; Smoski & Bachorowski, 2003). Generally speaking, laughter is associated with a more intense response to humor (Ruch, 2008, p. 23); also "different intensities of smiling reflect different degrees of exhilaration" (Ruch, 1995/2005, p. 110). Chafe (2007) notes that smiling has been described as "the mildest form of laughter" (p. 52), for example by Darwin (1872), but ends up questioning the idea of smiling and laughter lying on a continuum because smiling has many social uses and is not limited to the expression of mirth. Platt & Ruch (2014, p. 704) flatly deny that a "graduate series" (i.e., a continuum) could be applied, if the emotions are different.

Laughter can be spontaneous (irrepressible) or intentionally produced (voluntary; contrived); to put it differently, one can laugh without intending to do so or deliberately: "[C]ontrived and spontaneous laughter within a person are strikingly similar with respect to the respirational pattern" (Ruch & Ekman, 2001, p. 428); therefore, it may be difficult or impossible to differentiate between them on acoustic or other observational grounds, even though they do activate different areas of the brain. This would mean that unless one knows that the speaker intended to laugh (for example, because one happens to be the speaker, and thus has access through introspection to one's intentions), one could not tell whether the laughter was voluntary or not. This is not the case with smiling, where, as we saw, a spontaneous smile (Duchenne smile) manifests different facial muscular patterns than a deliberate smile.

Much like smiling, therefore, laughter cannot be used uncritically to identify humor because a) people experiencing mirth do not always laugh, and b) people laugh for other reasons than mirth. As we have seen, both smiling and laughter exceed the boundaries of mirth and mirth is not necessarily expressed by laughter. More damningly for the idea of identifying humor through the presence of laughter and/or smiling, both smiles and laughter may be volitional and fully social or contrived. If either can be produced deliberately, for whatever communicative purpose, then the assumption that laughter, and secondarily smiling, are effective markers of the presence of humor is seriously called into question. Frank et al. (1993/2005) argue that there are observable differences, at least as far as smiling goes, between genuine and contrived displays and that "these differences are observable and influence subjective impressions" (p. 234). However, they acknowledge that while their study shows that genuine, felt, "enjoyment" smiles "can have social signal value," i.e., be recognized by their audience as such, that does not necessarily mean that speakers engaging in conversation will treat them differently.

There exists, as we have hinted at, an imbalance between the significant amount of research dedicated to laughter and the much smaller amount of research on smiling, at least within linguistics. In what follows, we will pursue the discussion of the possibility of using laughter to identify humor a little deeper. Most of the argument carries over to smiling as well.

2.3 Mirthful vs. non-mirthful laughter

Indeed, the field of humor studies has long known that laughter is not coextensive with humor (see Attardo 1994, pp. 11–13 for a review of the literature). This is a fancy way of saying that we may have laughter without humor (as in pretend laughter, laughter of embarrassment, tickling, or laughing gas), humor without laughter (as one who reacts to humor smiling or with a nod of understanding, saying "I heard that one before," or saying "that's not funny!"), and clearly humor with laughter (Ruch, 2008, p. 23; Chafe, 2007; Trouvain & Truong, 2017).

2.3 MIRTHFUL VS. NON-MIRTHFUL LAUGHTER

Table 2.1 Relationships between humor and laughter

	Humor	No humor
Laughter	Mirthful laughter	Embarrassment laughter
No laughter	Non-laugh response	Serious exchange

In order to avoid confusion, we will introduce the term "mirthful laughter" when discussion the differences between laughter related to humor and laughter that is not related to humor. A good way to conceptualize mirthful laughter is a Venn diagram, describing "mirthful laughter" as the intersection of the "laughter" and the "humor" categories. (See Figure 2.1.)

Figure 2.1 Venn diagram of the intersection between humor and laughter.

There is extensive literature on the distinction between mirthful laughter and other types of laughter. Giles and Oxford (1970) list seven kinds of laughter: humorous, social, ignorance, anxiety, derision, apologetic, and laughter as a reaction to tickling. Ziv (1979a, p. 16), Poyatos (2002), Chafe (2007), and others have a more extensive list of different types and functions, which could probably be pared down significantly, but are still emblematic of the fact that "laughter" is not a uniform monolithic construct.

Aubouin (1948) and Olbrechts-Tyteca (1974) had already pointed out that one could not use reliably laughter as a one-to-one marker of humor because "laughter largely exceeds humor" (Olbrechts-Tyteca, 1974, p. 14). Poyatos (2002) contains a long list of laughter types, most of which are non-humorous. Chafe (2007, pp. 73–85) also has a list of non-humorous causes of laughter. Glenn and Holt (2013) stated that "Much laughter occurs without anything noticeably humorous nearby, and much that people think of as humorous occurs without laughter" (p. 2). Trouvain and Truong (2017, p. 340) also have a list of non-humorous sources of laughter.

While it is certainly true that spontaneous uproarious genuine laughter is probably the most overt indicator of humor, the claim that laughter is the most common indicator of humor is in error: smiling is probably the most frequent one, as we saw. More importantly, displays of mirth (laughter and smiling) and humor have a complex relationship that make the use of either or both as the sole criterion to determine the presence of humor inappropriate. Unfortunately, at least some areas of humor studies have yet to fully digest the falsity of the equation "humor equals laughter and vice versa."

2.3.1 On the lack of direct linear correlation between humor and mirth displays

Despite the fact that genuine enjoyment smiling and laughter occur frequently with humor, the two are not coextensive. In the previous section we have looked at how some mirth may not occur with smiling and/or laughter and how non-mirthful laughter exists. Now we turn to a different argument. Essentially, we will consider the fact that mirthful displays are mediated socially, which makes the possibility of a direct correlation between mirth display and humor unlikely.

Consider now a hypothetical simple direct correlation model, which assumes a direct linear[11] correlation between intensity of the reaction (laughter/smiling) and humor stimulus appreciation. Basically, the more a speaker enjoyed a humorous stimulus, the more intensely they would react (with a mirth display). Unfortunately for this direct correlation hypothesis, psychological and sociological studies show that the relationship is not direct, but rather mediated culturally.

The difference between humor (stimulus) and laughter (response) is a well-known fact in psychology and in the social sciences, thus for example, it is an established result that subjects laugh more at a joke when they are in a group than if they are alone (Leventhal & Cupchik, 1976; Chapman, 1976; Malpass & Fitzpatrick, 1959;[12] Young & Frye, 1966; Butcher & Wissell, 1984; Fridlund, 1991; Pollio & Swanson 1995; Devereux & Ginsburg 2001). Even the size of the audience (Morrison, 1940) and the crowdedness of the room (Stokols et al., 1973) may affect

---

[11] A linear correlation is one in which each increase or decrease in one value is met by a correspondingly large change in the other value.
[12] But not for cartoons, where Malpass & Fitzpatrick find that the opposite is true.

the intensity of laughter or its enjoyment (Aiello et al., 1983). On the effect of the audience on reactions to humor, see Section 10.1.1.

The fact that socialization enhances humor appreciation holds true for children (Chapman & Chapman, 1974, Chapman & Wright, 1976), and regardless of the actual presence of others (i.e., even an imagined group increases laughter). People also laugh more if the other people are friends (Murphy & Pollio, 1975; Pollio & Swanson, 1995), regardless of age (Foot, Chapman, and Smith, 1977). Women smile/laugh much more in reaction to cartoons and caricatures, in the presence of friends than strangers (Wagner & Smith, 1991). Mixed gender groups laugh significantly less when they are made up of strangers (Pollio & Swanson, 1995).

Similarly, it is a well established fact that accompanying laughter (laugh track) will increase laughter (e.g., Martin and Gray, 1996; Lawson et al., 1998; Platow et al., 2005) and that being observed (videotaped) will decrease it (Dale et al., 1991; Martin, Sadler, Barrett, & Beaven, 2008). The size of the audience is also a relevant factor: generally speaking, the larger the audience, the greater the laughter (Morrison, 1940; Andrus, 1946; Prerost, 1977; Aiello et al., 1983). For more discussion of the audience effects on laughter, see Chapter 10.

Thus, even if we wanted to establish a correlation between humor and laughter, doing so would prove practically impossible (or at least very hard). For example, we would not know whether we should measure the laughter of a given subject alone, or in a group, with strangers or friends, with or without a laugh track, etc.

These are not the only problems one would encounter. If we present several stimuli in an experimental environment, or if in a conversation several humorous turns occur in a row, the repeated presence of humor affects its perception. Gavanski (1986) notes that "cartoon repetition did reduce amusement" (p. 211), whereas "ratings of cartoons on a 'funniness' scale (...) were totally insensitive to reduction in amusement" (p. 212). The same result was found in Deckers et al. (1989). On repetition see also Forabosco (1994) on seriality.

Even more damaging for our hopes of a linear correlation between humor and laughter, is Brown et al.'s (1982) finding that when presented with unfunny stimuli but in the presence of confederates who have been instructed to laugh, subjects will laugh. Fridlund (1991) shows that subjects who merely imagined a companion smiled more whereas they did not report increased emotional response. He comes to the conclusion that smiling may be more related to the social context than to the emotional setting. These results would of course make the use of laughter or smiling as indicators of humor extremely problematic.

Finally, there is a significant literature, within the field of discourse analysis, which has shown that there are numerous situations in which laughter occurs without any mirth or exhilaration. These include embarrassment at the discussion of sensitive topics, displays of resiliency in trouble-talk (i.e., non-humorous descriptions of one's problems), complaints, and as a coping mechanism in aphasia. The literature is discussed in some detail in Section 11.4.2. The other contribution of discourse analysis to the discussion of whether laughter can be used to identify humor comes from another strong result in the field, which goes back to Jefferson (1979), i.e., the use of laughter to prime a laughter response (and hence the first use of laughter is not a response to the humorous stimulus). More broadly speaking, discourse analysis puts to rest the idea that laughter is a univocal reaction to humor: laughter may or may not be a reaction to humor and laughter may or may not be an expression of, or even associated with, mirth.

So, in conclusion, it is not methodologically sound to claim that something is humorous just because someone laughs (or smiles) immediately before, during, of after. This is not to say that one cannot or should not study laughter. On the contrary, as we will see, one of the central results of the discourse analysis of humor has been precisely that speakers signal by initiating laughter the humorous nature of their utterance. However, one should not confuse the study of laughter with the study of humor, as some have.

2.3.2 Recognition vs. appreciation

What mechanisms allow us to decouple the perception of a humorous stimulus from having a mirthful reaction? One of the reasons is that the recognition of the humorous nature of a text is independent of its appreciation. To recognize the humorous nature of a text requires only the activation of some cognitive mechanisms (which will be examined in Chapter 6 and following) that can be roughly described as the recognition of an incongruity. The appreciation of humor, whatever its nature, logically requires the recognition of humor, plus a set of other mechanisms (since one cannot appreciate what one does not know is there!).

2.3 MIRTHFUL VS. NON-MIRTHFUL LAUGHTER

Hay (2000) has introduced a four-level hierarchy to describe the attitudes of the hearer when faced with a humorous remark or text. Hay's taxonomy was elaborated within the context of face-to-face conversational joking, but it can be expanded intuitively to all texts.

1. Recognition: at this level, the hearer merely recognizes the intention on the speaker's part to produce a humorous text without necessarily understanding the humor of the text.
2. Understanding: at this level, the hearer recognizes the intention of the speaker and understands the humorous import of the text.
3. Appreciation: at this level, the hearer manifests in some way his/her enjoyment or displeasure with the contents of the joke and/or the fact that the joke has been uttered.
4. Participation: at this level, the hearer actually engages with the speaker in the creation of further humor.

Hay's most significant point, however, is that the latter levels presuppose (in the logical sense) the former. What this means is that in order to react to a joke, the hearer must first realize that the joke has occurred and then understand what the joke is. This means that there are several "failure" points from the hearer's point of view since he/she may a) fail to recognize that the joke is being delivered; b) fail to understand the joke; c) fail to react to the joke; and d) fail to participate in the joking situation. We return in more detail to Hay's hierarchy in Section 11.3.1.2.

The distinction between recognition and appreciation is well established in psychology: for example, Leventhal & Mace (1970), Leventhal & Cupchik (1976), and Gavanski (1986) distinguish between cognitive and affective responses to humor: "the cognitive component is the evaluation of the humor stimuli in terms of their perceived humor content; the affective component is the subjective feeling of enjoyment produced by the humor stimuli" (Gavanski, 1986, p. 209).

There is even neurological evidence for the distinction between recognition and appreciation (Goel & Dolan, 2001; Moran et al., 2004). In Goel and Dolan's work, "semantic comprehension of jokes was associated with increased activation in the left and right posterior middle temporal gyrus. By contrast, activity in ventromedial prefrontal cortex correlated with subjects' explicit ratings of how funny they found each joke" (Moran et al., 2004, p. 1055). In the case of right hemisphere damage patients, Shammi and Stuss (1999) report a dissociation between the cognitive and affective responses to the humorous stimuli whereby the patients appear to understand the joke, and they rate the joke as funny, but they do not respond with smiles or laughter, unlike their normal controls and patients with lesions in other locations.

This observation is a central foundation in the establishment of a pragmatics of humor in the sense of a theory of the audience. When observing an audience's reaction to a given joke we, as observers, are faced with a problem. Given a joke utterance, the audience's reaction may be a) laughing or b) not laughing (let us ignore, for the time being, intermediate reactions such as snickering, smiling, etc.). If the audience laughs we do not know whether they are laughing because they a) recognize but do not understand the joke, b) recognize and understand the joke. If the audience does not laugh, we do not know whether they a) did not recognize the joke, b) did not understand the joke, or c) did not believe that it was appropriate to show appreciation of the joke or otherwise decided to suppress observable reactions. In other words, our audience may be laughing not because of the humor (false positive), or may be not laughing while fully cognizant of the fact that a humorous event just took place (false negative). False negatives are common in humor research: the "that's not funny" retort clearly belies its own force since it implies that the speaker knows that the event was funny but that he/she believes that appreciation should be withheld.

As can be seen, if one wants to investigate humor appreciation or in general wants to construct a theory of humor audience/reception, one must address these issues that would otherwise nullify any effort at such an endeavor. The only examples of such controlled studies come from the psychological disciplines where to a certain degree, joke appreciation is measured not through self-reports but via physiological correlates (e.g., heart rate, vasco-dilation, electromagnetic activity in the cortex). Needless to say, even these empirical measurements are not 100% effective as the "truth machine" (polygraph) has demonstrated.

When considering self-reports, humor researchers should be aware of the fact that these are necessarily filtered via one's societal and emotional biases, i.e., that subjects will tend, for example, to underreport amusement at offensive or otherwise problematic stimuli. Another related issue is the presence of other subjects within the perception of the individual subject. It is a common phenomenon to laugh at a joke that one has not understood simply because those around him/her are laughing at the joke. This makes the study of group appreciation of humor dauntingly complex as there is virtually no way of having access to the relevant information. Recall that studies have shown that subjects laugh more when they are in a group and that they will laugh to a non-funny stimulus if the rest of the group laughs at it (this is investigated experimentally using compères who are in on the experiment (Brown et al., 1982)).

In short, neither direct behavioral observation nor self-reports are self-evident clues of either understanding or appreciation of humor.

2.3.3 Confusion between humor and humor appreciation

A common confusion, which also needs to be dispelled, is that between humor and humor appreciation. It has been claimed that a text is not funny unless it is funny to someone. While this has a certain ring of truth, further examination reveals this position to be in error. Specifically, it confuses humor competence and humor performance. Consider the following situation:

A tells B a joke. B is upset, or hungry, or in pain and does not want to hear the joke. Therefore B does not laugh and in fact says to A. "It's not funny." However, a few minutes later, after B's emotional problems, hunger or pain have been taken care of, B remembers the joke and says "That was funny."

Would we want to say that the text was not funny at time t_0 and was then funny at time t_1? It seems much more natural to say that the joke was funny all along and that B was not in the right state of mind to appreciate it. Indeed, since the text has not changed, what could possibly have changed, if not B's condition?

One could argue that a text only exists in context and therefore that only pairs text/context can be funny. But this argument does not carry through, because once more the text can be an invariant, whereas the situations will inevitably change and the reason why certain texts will tend to be identified as funny or provoke a certain kind of reaction would remain. In conclusion, humor is a property of the stimulus, the text (competence level). Humor appreciation is a property of the situation (which includes a specific speaker and hearer, the context in which the humor is produced, etc., i.e., is the performance level).

2.4 Keying

A stimulus may have all the necessary and sufficient conditions for the text to be classified as humor, but still not be perceived as humor, because of a performance issue. These conditions are essentially a special type of incongruity, as we saw before and will discuss more fully in the next chapters. The question then is not "why do certain incongruities not trigger humor experience?" but rather "what performance factors are necessary for a text that is humorous at the competence level to be perceived as humorous in a given situation, by a given individual or group, etc., i.e., in performance?" We know that some incongruities may be perceived as threatening or scary. For example, cognitive dissonance (Festinger, 1957; see Harmon-Jones, 1999; Cooper, 2007 for a synthesis of current research) can be described as the perception of an incongruity that is unpleasant. Cognitive dissonance is defined as follows:

> the possession at one and the same time of cognitive elements (knowledges) having psychologically opposite implications generates an unpleasant state of tension, or dissonance, within the individual which then motivates him[/her] to attempt to reduce dissonance by altering his[/her] cognitions. (Berkowitz, 1969, p. 97)

Relatedly, Berlyne (1960) suggested that there was an inverted-U shaped curve describing the relationship between complexity of the stimulus and humor response (or to put it differently, that very hard or very easy incongruities are not funny). Hence, incongruities that are threatening or too complex to process will not be perceived as humorous. These are, of course, only two of numerous factors that may inhibit the humorous appreciation of the incongruity.

We can then safely say that, all other things being equal, a humorous text will be perceived as humorous if the incongruity is

- non-threatening
- not too complex or too simple
- based on available scripts/knowledge
- unexpected, surprising
- occurring in playful mode (see Section 2.4.1)
- sudden (see Section 2.4.2)

The above list is indicative and not meant to be exhaustive and, in fact, it is not possible to address the entire list in this context. Some of the issues mentioned have a significant literature (e.g., cognitive dissonance). I will examine briefly the playful and surprising aspects which have received relatively little attention.

2.4.1 Playful mode

We saw that for humor to be successful the situation must be framed or keyed as humor, in the sense of Goffman's "frames" (Goffman, 1974, pp. 43–44) and Hymes' "keys" (Hymes, 1972, p. 62); a discussion of these concepts, within the sociolinguistic framework, will be found in Chapter 10. Particularly, it should reflect suspension of disbelief on the factuality of information (fictionality). We will deal more fully with fictionality and play in Section 3.3.1.

A possible argument against the essential nature of incongruity is that an incongruity may not be perceived as funny if the situation is not keyed to humor. This is true, but it turns out not to be an argument against the incongruity–resolution theory of humor; see Chapters 3–4. First of all, let us note that keying is a dynamic phenomenon: a situation may start out keyed for humor or may evolve or change its keying to humor. This shows that keying and humor are not causally connected, since neither can exist without the other: we can have un-keyed humor, i.e., humor that occurs without warning or signaling in an otherwise serious situation (deadpan humor); similarly, we can have serious content keyed to playfulness, for example, the Schoolhouse Rock videos in the US presented serious academic material using songs and playful cartoons. Naturally, when humor is recognized its presence keys a posteriori any situation as "funny" in the intentions of the speaker who produced the humor (the audience may still refuse the keying, for example using the formula "That's not funny").

Summing up: if a situation is not keyed for humor, i.e., playful, cheerful, upbeat mood, the occurrence of humor may rekey the situation toward humor or the attempt at humor may fail. Conversely, if a situation is keyed for humor, for example, by the prior occurrence of humor, humor may occur or not. If the situation is keyed for humor and humor occurs, the likelihood that both speaker and hearer will assess the situation as 'something humorous was uttered' is highest. If the situation is not keyed for humor, but humor occurs, they may or may not assess the utterance as humorous. If the situation is keyed for humor but no humor occurs (for example, the speaker fails to deliver a properly

Table 2.2 The interplay of humorous keying and text

	Humorous keying	Serious keying
Humorous text	High likelihood of humor assessment	Medium-high likelihood of humor assessment
Serious text	Medium-low likelihood of humor assessment	Low likelihood of humor assessment

formed humorous text) they, once more, may not assess the situation as humorous. If the situation is not keyed for humor and no humor occurs, the likelihood of speaker and hearer assessing the situation as humorous is very low (but not impossible). The situation is summarized in Table 2.2. Note the difference in likelihood of humorous assessment in the two cases of mismatched keying/text, which follows from my assumption that the nature of the text takes precedence on the key.

It should also be noted that humor shares the non-serious keying with fiction, where the distinction is usually conceptualized as "fiction" vs. "factuality." This is not the place to go into the details, but see Attardo (2008a, 2009).

Finally, it should also be noted that keying of humor is a woefully under-studied issue: there are situations that are keyed by default to humor (comedy routines, late night talk shows, friendly banter, etc.) and there are others that are not (war declaration, judicial sentencing, discussion of divorce among spouses, etc.). For example, how the type of situation and the production of humor interact has not really been addressed, nor has the fact that the use of humor may influence the way the situation is keyed (or re-keyed). From a different psychological perspective, the issue can be framed as the need for the speakers to be in the right frame of mind, called the humor mindset (Ford, 2014). The serious normal mindset is called "reality assimilation" whereas humor is part of "fantasy assimilation" (McGhee, 1972). Ford explains that

> Reality assimilation is the default process that occurs when encountering discrepancies between our cognitive schemas and actual events. In contrast, when in the fantasy assimilation mode, people do not require a realistic resolution of incongruous events. Therefore, they do not attempt to adjust their cognitive schemas to fit unexpected events. They simply disregard the requirement of literal congruity that characterizes reality assimilation. (2014, p. 361)

2.4.2 Surprise

The two aspects of the incongruity should be perceived simultaneously, i.e., should be active at the same time, cognitively speaking. This seems related to another factor in humor perception: the surprising or unexpected aspect of the humorous stimulus. Punch lines are usually unexpected. Humor tends to be surprising. Conversely, for example, Catholic theologians commonly discuss the incongruous idea that God is one and three persons, at the same time, at least since the third century. While the conditions of humor (incongruity and co-presence, as we will see in Chapter 6) are clearly fulfilled, which may lead us to expect that the idea may be funny, the situation is hardly surprising and definitely not keyed for humor. A related example comes from physics which sees light as both a wave and a particle. The two descriptions are incompatible and so the description is incongruous, but discussions of optics are not usually keyed for humor, nor are they surprising (i.e., the information is presented upfront).

Finally, not all unpredictable and surprising things are funny. For example, in mysteries, the identity of the killer is unexpected, and if the author did a good job, unpredictable, but that a killer would be found is expected. Generally, mysteries are not keyed for humor (with some exceptions, Janet Evanovitch and Pierre Dard come to mind) but even when they are, usually the revelation of the identity of the culprit is not sudden. So, in part some unpredictability is predicted and in part the delivery of the unpredictable element is not sudden enough to be surprising. There are more factors (having to do with the resolution of the incongruity) which will be taken up in Chapter 4.

2.4.3 Unintentional humor

Finally we need to mention briefly the phenomenon of unintentional humor, which shows that the keying for humor is crucial in recognizing the presence of potential humor. The idea of voluntary and involuntary humor (e.g., Ziv, 1984, p. 83) is straightforward: either one intends to amuse someone else or one does not. Nonetheless, the idea of "unintentional humor" is a good example of possible confusion. In the prototypical situation, the speaker says something he/she intends to be perceived as humorous. But what if the speaker says something that he/she did not intend to be perceived as humorous and yet has all the prerequisite semantic/pragmatic trappings of competence-level humor (i.e., is potentially humorous)? In that case the hearer is faced with a choice: he/she can realize that the intention of the speaker was not to produce humor and therefore ignore the potential humor or he/she can choose to treat the non-humorously intended utterances *as if* it had been intended for humor. Needless to say, this choice is not a conscious one (at least not always). This is why I have claimed that there is no such thing as unintentional humor, since either the speaker or the hearer has to intend the interpretation of what was said as meant humorously (in other words, someone is always intending the potential humor as humorous, if they react to it as such). But what if neither the speakers nor the hearer realize that the speaker's utterance is potentially humorous? Then, while the potential humor is objectively there, there is no humor perception. Needless to say, the possibility of people laughing without anything to laugh at is also there (as we saw, in the experiments described above, in which laughter increases if other people are laughing). A fuller discussion of the concept of unintentional humor will be found in Section 8.4.

2.5 Identifying humor: the triangulation approach

This brings up again the issue of how a researcher goes about identifying humor in a text. The answer is that it depends largely on the type of text. Some texts, such as novels or written jokes, have no extra-textual markers, such as those that, for example, sitcoms have (e.g., the laugh track).[13] In that case, only semantic/pragmatic analysis can be used. If there are markers of humor (such as laugh tracks, or real laughter, or smiling, etc.), then one can use a triangulation approach, that is use of several cues to the humorous nature of the intention, such as the semantic analysis to identify the humor, checking the locations where the conversation participants laugh and/or smile. In some cases, for example, some corpora such as transcriptions of legal discourse, markers such as "[laughter]" are introduced. In the case of conversational data, when access to the participants is possible, stimulated recall interviews after the data collection itself, revisiting the data, may help.

---

[13] They may have paratextual cues, such as a title along the lines of "5000 jokes" of a subtitle "a comedy in 3 acts." Other paratextual cues can be inclusion in a series of humorous books, or a cover depicting a man slipping on a banana peel, etc.

2.5 IDENTIFYING HUMOR: THE TRIANGULATION APPROACH

In the case of multiple participants, consensus of interpretation may also be useful. There exist sophisticated statistical techniques to assess the degree of agreement of judges or raters (inter-rater reliability).

As we saw previously, triangulation is not limited to three cues to the humorous nature. If more clues are available (say, interviews with the speakers, facial expressions, judges ratings, etc.), then more than three points of triangulation may be used. One may object to the use of the term *tri*angulation, since we admit more than three kinds of evidence, but the word "n-sided polygonization" does not exactly roll off the tongue. Triangulation is very useful, as it allows to double check one's analyses and thus to reduce the possibility of biases. Researchers should be extremely careful not to fall for the mistake of using laugh tracks or non-theoretically grounded transcriptions (i.e., transcriptions that are not made for research purposes) as the sole determinant of what to analyze. For example, the choice of looking at only those instances of humor in a sitcom at which laugh tracks occurs exposes one to the risk of both false positives and false negatives: a false positive would be a laugh track where no humor is actually found, and a false negative would be an instance of humor for which no laugh track was provided. This is closely related to the issue of "failed humor," i.e., humor that fails to be interpreted as such by the audience. By definition, failed humor is not usually followed by laughter or smiling. Thus using the occurrence of laughter and/or smiling as the sole criterion for deciding if a piece of text is humor or not, will inevitably lead to false negatives (i.e., missing all failed humor). On failed humor, see Section 12.4.3.

Finally, one could ask, why not rely on the researcher's intuition? After all, much like linguists in the 1960s and 1970s relied on native speaker intuition to determine the grammaticality of a sentence, couldn't we rely on the speaker's intuition to identify humor? The answer to that is that people are appallingly bad at it and the worst performers are almost entirely unaware of how bad their performance is (Kruger & Dunning, 1999, pp. 1123–1124). So using an untrained judge is a recipe for disaster. Using a battery of judges and testing inter-rater reliability solve this problem and bring us in the domain of experimental psychology or the social sciences.

So, generally speaking, a triangulation method to the identification of humor is the best way to proceed. By cross-referencing any sources of information about the potential humorous nature of the text in question, the researcher increases the reliability of their study by avoiding both false positives (i.e., finding humor where there is none) and false negatives (missing humor that is there). The sources should not be ranked equally: objective information should be considered more reliable than subjective considerations. Multiple judges are more reliable than a single, potentially biased, judge.

Within theoretical linguistics, studies have largely relied on metatextual information (for example, if the text you are looking at comes from a published collection of jokes, the likelihood of it being a joke is extremely high; if moreover it contains a punch line, you can safely assume it is one) and historical records (for example, if you are considering Shakespeare's *Merry Wives of Windsor*, the historical record tells us that it is a comedy). Other fields, such as discourse analysis, have used other methodologies, such as participant observers, which will be discussed in the relevant chapters. For a more formal discussion of the triangulation approach, see Section 12.4.2.

2.6 Further readings

On the differences between humor and laughter, see a review and references in Attardo (1994, pp. 10–13). On mirth, see Martin (2007); on exhilaration, see Ruch (1993). Chafe (2007) and Trouvain & Truong (2017) are excellent descriptions of laughter and its phonetics. On smiling, see Platt & Ruch (2014).

On the application of the principle of commutation to humor studies, see Attardo & Raskin (2017). On warrants in applied linguistics, see Edge & Richards (1998). Any introductory textbook of statistics will deal with sampling and validity issues. On the implicatural hierarchy of understanding, appreciation, etc., see Hay (2000). The discussion of keying is developed more broadly in Attardo (2009) and in Chapter 10.

3

Theories of humor and their levels

3.1 Explanation, reductionism, essentialism — 57
3.2 The three major theories of humor — 59
3.3 Humor as release — 60
3.4 Humor as incongruity — 64
3.5 Humor as aggression — 64
3.6 Other theories — 67
3.7 Complementarity of the theories of humor — 71
3.8 Further readings — 77

This chapter begins by discussing briefly the concept of reductionism and more generally of "explanation." It also very briefly argues in favor of reductionist/essentialist theories of humor, before launching a survey of humor theories from different areas of research which range broadly from the neurological level, taken as the point of higher determinism (or conversely as the lowest possible reduction), to the macro-sociological theories that see humor as a societal phenomenon. A final section deals with the evaluation of theories of humor.

3.1 Explanation, reductionism, essentialism

What does it mean to present the explanation of a phenomenon? Generally, it means that given a phenomenon, such as humor, we can describe its causes, the contexts in which it takes place, the effects it has, etc.

The Linguistics of Humor: An Introduction. Salvatore Attardo, Oxford University Press (2020). © Salvatore Attardo.
DOI: 10.1093/oso/9780198791270.001.0001

It also means that we "understand" the phenomenon, i.e., we know what causes it, and often that we can replicate it. Generally, we want to explain a phenomenon in terms of simpler causes/phenomena. This stance is called reductionism. For example, explaining rain as the interplay of water vapor, condensation, and gravity would be a typical reductionist explanation. An essentialist explanation is a reductionist explanation which claims that there is one or more core features that "makes the phenomenon what it is" i.e., is its essence. The essence of a thing (thing should be understood in a very general sense here, as "entity") is what makes it be such, for example, the essence of a fork is that it has "teeth" (tines) and a handle. Among the non-essential (accidental) features of forks are that they are made of metal (since there can be plastic or wooden forks) but also the number of tines, which may range from two to four, or more.[1] The opposition of essence and accidence goes back to Aristotle. Theoretical linguistics is mostly reductionist and essentialist as it seeks to reduce linguistic behavior to a small set of rules. Seeking the necessary and sufficient features that cause a phenomenon is a characteristic essentialist stance. Other approaches to linguistics are less interested in finding the essence of the phenomena but lean toward functionalism, i.e., what do speakers "do" with the phenomena at hand, what is their function in discourse? Yet other approaches, such as cognitive linguistics, espouse a prototypical approach to categorization, which means that there may not be a single individual essence of a phenomenon, but rather the phenomena may be classified in "families" of concepts. For the time being, we need not concern ourselves with these philosophical subtleties (those interested can start with Scholz et al., 2016). We will instead turn to the three major theories of humor and examine them from a reductionist and essentialist standpoint.[2]

---

[1] It's actually slightly more complex: the number of tines on a fork is a range from 2 to 5 or 6 maximum. A fork with only one tine is a spear and one with 40 or 50 is a comb.

[2] Here a caveat is necessary: in many circles, "essentialist" is basically an insult. This is because in some fields essentialism is associated, for example, with biological determinism. For example, in gender studies, this would be the idea that the presence of a penis or a vagina would be the essence of masculinity/femininity. In cultural studies, essentialism is associated with the idea that an entire culture (say, Western culture) has an essence. Needless to say, seeking essentialist reductions of phenomena does not imply embracing rigid determinism nor that all phenomena *must* have an essence at a level of generalization that makes it interesting/useful. For example, in trying to find the essence of "game" or "food" one will most likely end up with very high level generalizations, such as "an activity that one engages in for pleasure" or "any substance ingested for sustenance" which will not be helpful if your goal is creating a new game or you are a nutritionist. Likewise a social constructivist perspective is *not* incompatible with an essentialist view. No-one said that the

3.2 The three major theories of humor

There are very many theories of humor. Piddington (1933) listed 49 authors; Bergler (1956) listed 80; Smuts (n.d. 2006) claims that there are more than 100. One of the best reviews is Keith-Spiegel (1972) who distinguished 8 types of theories:

1. Biological, Instinct, and Evolution
2. Superiority
3. Incongruity
4. Surprise
5. Ambivalence
6. Release and Relief
7. Configurational
8. Psychoanalytic

"New" theories emerge all the time, as a quick glance at the internet will reveal: a Google search of "theories of humor" returned a staggering 17.5 *million* hits. Amazon.com lists 8000 books under the "theory of humor."[3] However, most "new" theories often turn out to be restatements in a different terminology of old ideas, or just a different mix of known factors.

To make sense of this abundance of data, the theories of humor are commonly classified into three groups:

- incongruity theories (a.k.a. contrast) (Raskin, 1985, pp. 31–36),
- hostility theories/disparagement (a.k.a. aggression, superiority, triumph, derision) (pp. 36–38), and
- release theories (a.k.a. sublimation, liberation) (pp. 38-40).

(See Table 3.1, adapted from Attardo (1994, p. 47); after Raskin (1985), Ziv (1979a) and Monro (1951); for details about the theories, see the text.)

---

essence of a phenomenon may not be socially constructed. The novice may be well advised to avoid actively advertising his/her essentialist stance, while quietly pursuing reductionist explanations which is, as far as I can tell, what most scholars do, including most of those who denounce essentialism.

[3] Granted that a quick glance at the results reveals that Amazon has a lot of work to do about filtering its results (what do calendars and novels have to do with theories of humor?); nonetheless, the point stands: that's a lot of books.

Table 3.1 Attardo's three families of theories chart

Cognitive	Social	Psychological
Incongruity	Hostility	Release
Contrast	Aggression	Sublimation
Saliency	Superiority	Liberation
Bisociation	Triumph	Economy
Catastrophe	Derision	Benign violation
	Disparagement	
	Disposition	

3.3 Humor as release

Release theories, as the name implies, are based on the idea that humor "releases" the "pressure" of mental energy. The idea of "energy" flowing in the mind is a metaphor, introduced by Spencer in his "The Physiology of Laughter" essay (1860). The best known proponent of a release theory is Freud (1905). Martin (2007, p. 58) characterizes release theories as the "hydraulic theory" of the nervous system. The theory was based on the steam engine, then the prominent new technology. This metaphor was replaced by the "mind as computer" newer metaphor (see for example Hurley et al., 2011). In other words, there seems to be a tendency for people to compare humor to the most current and salient technology at the time. The problem is that metaphorical theories may be useful, insofar as they allow us to map some properties of a phenomenon, such as humor, onto a better understood mechanism, but up to a point. A metaphor is only a metaphor and all analogies eventually break down. Spencer's and Freud's metaphorical hydraulic theory is nowadays discredited: no-one believes that there is actual mental pressure that needs relieving.

Nonetheless, Freud's theory deserves special mention because he paid a lot of attention to the linguistic mechanisms of humor: the first part of his book on humor is dedicated to these mechanisms. However, subsequent research has shown that none of the mechanisms located by Freud were unique to humor, but that in fact he had rediscovered some of the mechanisms present in any linguistic form (Attardo, 1994, p. 55).

In terms of linguistic behavior, the significance of release theories comes from the fact that they account for the so-called "liberation" from the rules of language, for example in puns and word-play more generally. The metalinguistic nature of puns and word-play account for this liberation, to the extent that it is a fact (one could easily argue that no real freedom from the rules of language is found in puns, for example).

Release theories can also be seen as accounting for the violations of the Principle of Cooperation (Grice, 1975; 1989) in humor (see Chapter 8). Essentially, the idea is that one is freed of the constraints of having to follow the Priciple of Cooperation. This is closely related to the "defunctionalization" of language in humor (Guiraud, 1979, pp. 111–119; see Chapter 12). Contemporary researchers such as Fry (1963) and Mindess (1971) have also proposed release theories.

3.3.1 Humor as play

Play can also be seen as a release from the goal-oriented nature of "serious" life.[4] A playful mindset is a significant component of the humorous experience. Bateson (1955/1972) has shown that playful, and humorous, behavior carries (either explicitly or implicitly) a metamessage roughly paraphrased as "this is play."

Bateson starts from the definition of metalanguage in Russell (see Section 1.3.2) and introduces the idea of meta-communicative language, i.e., discourse in which the subject is "the relationship between the speakers" (1972, p. 67). While observing monkeys playing at a zoo, Bateson realized that the very idea of play "could only occur if the participant organisms were capable of some degree of metacommunication, i.e., of exchanging signals which would carry the message 'this is play'" (p. 68).

Bateson notes that the metamessage "this is play" has the logical form of a paradox: "These actions, in which we now engage, do not denote what would be denoted by those actions which these actions denote. The playful nip [of the playing monkeys] denotes the bite, but it does not denote what would be denoted by the bite" (p. 69). Finally, Bateson observes that since much play is fictional, not only is the metamessage "this is play" paradoxical, in its concurrent claim of being something and not-being something, but it is also about non-existent entities (p. 70).

From our perspective, the important aspect of Bateson's contribution is the "this is play" metamessage. One the one hand, in itself,

---

[4] One can classify play theories of humor as a separate category of humor theories, as Smuts (n.d.) does.

it becomes the foundation of the idea of keying/framing humor (see Section 10.2.2.2) and of markers of humor (contextualization cues; see Section 10.2.4); on the other hand, it is the source of the defunctionalization aspect of humor, which plays a major role in the functional analysis of humor in discourse, see Section 12.1.4.

Fry (1963) was directly influenced by Bateson, with whom he worked. Fry builds a complete model of humor based on the notion of paradox, explicitly starting from the self-referential paradoxes identified by Russell and in particular Epimenides' paradox (see Section 1.3.2). According to Fry, the metamessage "this is play" or "this is not real" is paradoxical, because if I broadcast this metalinguistic framing message then the metalinguistic framing is itself part of the non-reality, which triggers the paradoxes identified by Russell and Bateson. Fry uses the terminology "play frame" (p. 138) and mentions as "things people do to indicate fantasy" (p. 138), such as voice quality, body movements, posture, lifting of the eyebrows (p. 138) and more broadly "non-verbal communication devices" (p. 139). However, Fry goes on to note, humor is not just paradoxical. Humor has a punch line, in the technical sense used in humor studies, i.e., a climax of the narrative which reveals the heretofore implicit incongruous element. Fry argues that the punch line brings in another paradox, this time not at the level of the overall communicative situation (the "this is play" paradox), but an "internal" (p. 153) paradox "*which [...] specifically concerns the humor content rather than the total situation*" (p. 149; emphasis in the original). He likens this to the figure-ground reversal introduced by Gestalt psychology (pp. 154–155).[5]

Among the markers or indicators of the play frame, is the so-called "play-face" in primates (see Martin 2007, pp. 3–4, 128, 165–166, for discussion and an image), which as expected for a marker of play, does not occur in aggressive situations:

Ethological studies of the silent bared-teeth display and the relaxed open-mouth (play face) display in apes, which are viewed as primate homologues of human smiling and laughter, respectively, reveal that these facial displays occur exclusively in the context of friendly social and play activities, and not in the context of aggression.

(Martin, 2007, p. 54)

---

[5] The connection with the logical mechanisms of humor (see Section 7.1.5) was already noted by Forabosco in his commentary incorporated in the Attardo & Raskin article (1991, p. 337).

3.3 HUMOR AS RELEASE

Apter's "para-telic" (non-goal-oriented; from the Greek "telos" goal) mode is also a variety of humor-as-play theory (1982, 1989). Reversal theory, as Apter's theory is called, posits that an incongruity will be experienced as humorous in a safe, non-threatening, playful environment. Further, reversal theory claims that the target of the incongruity must be "diminished" (i.e., reversal theory is a variant of the superiority theories, in this respect). If the target is enhanced the incongruity would be perceived as something else, such as art.

3.3.1.1 Willing suspension of disbelief

As part of the playful nature of humor, we should consider another aspect of playfulness, and namely the willing suspension of disbelief in which the hearers must engage in order to appreciate the text. To put it differently, if the hearer does not play along, he/she locks him/herself out of the fun. In fiction, hearers must routinely suspend disbelief about the fictional nature of what they are being told. If one were to argue that since there was no Sherlock Holmes, Conan Doyle was just a liar, and one was not willing to waste one's time listening to falsehood, then one is unlikely to experience pleasure reading about Holmes' adventures.

Perlmutter (2002) argues that in jokes "the listener's sacrifice is more than merely the ordinary suspension of disbelief; he or she is prepared to suspend a wide variety of every day prerogatives." Perlmutter (2002) mentions tolerating "egregious violations" of the principle of cooperation (p. 157; on violations of Grice's principle of cooperation, see Chapter 8), the "suspension of critical assessment" (p. 159) and of avoiding "detailed analysis" (p. 163).

3.3.2 Are release and play theories essentialist?

Release and play theories focus on the release humor provides. As such, they do not lend themselves as readily to essentialist claims, since they do not really look "under the hood" so to speak. Whereas one can make a plausible claim that humor is essentially incongruity processing or that it is more or less disguised aggression, it is a lot harder to claim that humor is essentially release or play. This may explain why most of the theories that include release or play do so concurrently with other components (see for example Freud's and Apter's theories, reviewed above). In light of the stance of complementarity that I take below (Section 3.7) this is actually a strength of the release and play theories.

3.4 Humor as incongruity

The best known theory of humor is probably the incongruity theory. Incongruity is basically defined as divergence from expectations: "*if it differs, it is perceived as incongruous*" (Forabosco, 1992, 54). This is consistent with the ordinary meaning of the word "incongruous" indicating the opposite of "the quality or state of agreeing, coinciding, or being congruent" (Merriam-Webster).

Within humor research, incongruity theories are primarily associated with psychology. A common contemporary conceptualization in psychology is to view *incongruity–resolution* (IR) models as "two stage" (Suls, 1972) models.

> In the first stage, the perceiver finds his[/her] expectations about the text disconfirmed by the ending of the joke (...) In other words, the recipient encounters an incongruity— the punch line. In the second stage, the perceiver engages in a form of problem solving to find a cognitive rule which makes the punch line follow from the main part of the joke and reconciles the incongruous parts. (Suls 1972, p. 82)

The two stages involve giving the text a first interpretation which is then rejected in favor of a second interpretation. Note that the two interpretations must coexist, at least to the extent that they are to be judged incongruous.[6]

Incongruity and incongruity–resolution theories are most clearly essentialist: they claim that the essence of humor is the perception of the incongruity and its resolution, or merely the unresolved perception of incongruity. Since a more detailed discussion of incongruity and resolution, including its criticisms, will be found in Chapter 4, we can leave this short introduction of incongruity and resolution and move on to the darker view of humor as a form of aggression.

3.5 Humor as aggression

One of the oldest and most widely held theories of humor sees it as an essentially aggressive or disparaging phenomenon. This theory has been couched under many terms starting from Aristotle and Hobbes

---

[6] See also Shultz' definition as "a biphasic sequence involving first the discovery of the incongruity followed by a resolution of the incongruity" (1976, pp.12–13).

all the way to Gruner's work (1978, 1997) or Zillmann (1983). As we saw, Apter's reversal theory (1982), which is primarily a play and incongruity theory, also contains a disparagement (diminishing) component. Recently, Billig (2005) has argued in favor of aggression as an explanatory variable in humor. Essentially the humor-as-aggression theory boils down to the claim that humor can be explained at least at some level as the pleasure/satisfaction or plain enjoyment of an enemy's discomfiture at our "triumph" over him/her. The dispositional theories of aggression (Zillman, 1983) do not require an "enemy" but merely someone whom one is negatively disposed toward. The idea is that we tend to find more humorous things that we are negatively disposed toward and conversely that we find less humorous things that we are positively disposed toward. Thus for example, a conservative should find humor directed at progressive targets funnier than the other way around. There is some evidence that disposition theory may predict correctly appreciation of humor based on political affiliation (Becker, 2014).

The most blatant counterexample to the aggression theory is of course innocent or non-tendentious humor (Freud, 1905). Let us consider again example (15), not from Freud's repertoire incidentally, and here repeated for convenience

(20) Why did the chicken cross the road?
To get to the other side.

Who or what would be the target of the aggression in this joke? The chicken? The road? It is clear that the joke does not target any of its characters, props, etc.; however, an aggression theorist might reply that the joke does aggress someone, namely its hearer, i.e., the person who has been told the joke and has therefore been exposed to a (presumably small) dose of aggression connected to the fact that he/she has been presented with an unsolvable riddle and has therefore been exposed to a mild degree of ridicule. Therefore the aggression theory posits two levels of potential aggression:

- aggression towards characters within the text;
- aggression towards participants to the joke telling exchange

It follows from this subdivision that a joke may or may not be aggressive at either level. Therefore, a joke need not logically be aggressive at either level, i.e., a joke may be aggressive at the internal level or at the exchange level which means that it is clear that either level of aggression is separate and independent of the other. In other words, we can conceive of a joke that is aggressive at both the contents level and at the interaction level but by the same reasoning it follows logically that we can conceive of a joke that is aggressive at neither. So, in order to work, an essentialist aggression theory needs to specify that there has to be an aggression at either level, which is somewhat circular.

In fact, the claim of the aggression theories examined before, while plausible in the context of unsolvable riddles and in some cases of mildly disguised aggression, for example, in children's humor some riddles are just an excuse to physically hit the dupe, is clearly untenable in the case of puns and other "innocent" humor. For example, there are cycles of charming jokes about elephants, such as

(21)   How did you know elephants have been in your fridge?
       Footprints in the butter.

that clearly have no aggressive component[7] and one need only pick up a collection of jokes for children under the age of six to find plenty more of examples.

Clearly, as an essentialist theory, the aggression theory fails to provide a complete theory of humor. Nonetheless, this does not mean that in fact, a large number of jokes aren't aggressive, and indeed, any theory of humor that failed to address this very significant facet of the humorous phenomenon would be remiss. Humor can be used deliberately or unconsciously as an aggressive tool and this can be done as we saw above both within the text and within the humorous exchange situation. In this respect, humor does not differ significantly from any other kind of text. The only difference that humor has with respect to other forms of aggression is its deniability which comes from the pragmatic aspect of the text; see Chapter 12 on the functions of humor and Chapter 8 on the violation of the cooperative principle that affords the deniability. As we will see in Chapter 12, humor is often used in interaction as a tool to probe the audience's views and attitudes, precisely because of its deniability embodied in the well-known expression "I was only joking."

---

[7] One needs to be a Freudian to see anything else than playful incongruity here. To assume, as Dundes (1987) does, that the elephant stands for African-American men's sexuality, is, well, Freudian.

Some authors use aggression (or variants such as "subversion") as essentially metaphorical constructs to indicate any criticism or even merely playing with of any idea. Criticism need not be aggressive and play is certainly not. This is not to say that some play may not degenerate into aggression, but the very idea of the metamessage "this is play," as per Bateson (1972), denies the possibility of real aggression being part of play. The danger of conflating aggression with criticism or play is that we lose the useful category of aggression: if all humor is aggressive, then the two jokes below would both be considered aggressive

(22) A guy walks into a bar and says: "Ouch!"

and

(23) A lawyer and a priest are flying in a small plane with a group of children. Suddenly the plane's engines start smoking. The captain comes into the back of the plane and says: "There are only a few parachutes. I think we should give them to the children." "Fuck the children!" says the lawyer and the priest replies: "Do you think there's enough time?"

It seems to me that (23) is an aggressive joke which expresses hostility toward priests by accusing them of being pedophiles and lawyers by accusing them of being morally reprehensible. Conversely, I have a hard time believing that (22) expresses hostility toward either guys, bars, or the hearer. Be that as it may, I believe it would be useful to keep the label *hostile* or *aggressive* for jokes such as (23) in order to distinguish them from jokes such as (22).

More sophisticated versions of the aggression theory state that humor is not simply aggressive but involves a sense of superiority or ridiculing. However, it is easy to see that the same criticism levied against aggression theories applies to superiority and disparagement (ridicule). While certainly lots and perhaps most of humor is aggressive, superiority-based, and disparaging/ridiculing, not all humor is so.

3.6 Other theories

After reviewing the "classical" theories of humor, we are reminded that all classifications are to some extent arbitrary and that many approaches do not fit clearly into the categories above.

3.6.1 Neurolinguistics of humor

Neurolinguistics deserves particular mention because it is the most extremely reductionist approach to explaining humor. Reducing psychology to neurology, i.e., explaining cognitive phenomena as activation of neurons, and/or other electro-chemical events in the brain cells, is the most reductive explanation possible of cognitive phenomena (on the topic see, e.g., Bickle, 2006).

Besides the neurolinguistic work on the distinction between appreciation and response to humor considered in Section 2.3.2 recent work in neurolinguistics has yielded some interesting results about the nature of humor, which are generally consonant with the incongruity theory. Derks et al. (1997) showed that a "negative-going cortical activity at 400 milliseconds" (N400) is associated with what humor theory has described as the incongruity of humor. Derks et al. describe the N400 as "occurring when categorization, usually semantic, is relatively unsuccessful and a search is initiated for better alternatives" (p. 287); see also Coulson and Kutas (1998, 2001). Coulson (2001) not only find evidence for the N400 response, but also for the second phase of the joke processing process, i.e., the resolution of the incongruity (i.e., the activation of a new frame/script). The suggestion that incongruity perception and resolution may be concurrent, rather than sequential is very interesting and dovetails with recent work on irony.[8] Other studies of neural activity that are consistent with the incongruity/resolution include Ozawa et al. (2000), Iwase et al. (2002), and Mobbs et al. (2003).

Goel and Dolan (2001) have shown, using MRIs, that different areas are involved in the processing of verbal and referential jokes.[9] This is significant, because it shows that the distinction between verbal and referential humor has a neuroanatomical foundation. They also distinguish between areas involved in the processing of the semantic and phonological material of the texts (for example, puns activate Broca's area) and the "affective" components of humor (i.e., the perception of funniness). For a broader discussion of the neurolinguistics of humor and an emphasis

---

[8] Incidentally, the fact that processing of jokes requires backtracking and longer reading times clearly militates against any "direct access" interpretation of humor. On the direct access theories of irony, see Colston (2017).

[9] Semantic and phonological jokes in their terminology; all humor is semantic, needless to say, so their terminology may be confusing.

on the distinction between the cognitive and the affective aspects of humor perception/appreciation, see Chen et al. (2017).

There exists considerable (highly technical) discussion of the lateralization of humor processing, which seems to show that the right hemisphere of the brain is crucial to humor processing. Derks et al. (1997), Coulson and Kutas (1998, 2001), and Goel and Dolan (2001) all show that this approach may be in need of some revision. There exists some literature on the neuro-anatomy of laughter, which is outside the scope of this discussion, but see Vaid and Kobler (2000).

3.6.2 Evolutionary theories

Other less common theories include attempts at seeing an evolutionary advantage to humor. The most developed linguistic approach along these lines is Chafe's (1987) disabling theory. He sees humor as evolutionarily advantageous in disabling the speaker when he/she begins to pursue lines of thought that lead to absurdities, contradictions, etc. The disabling theory is expanded in a full-fledged theory of humor and laughter in Chafe (2007). On the evolutionary theories of humor, including Chafe's, see Vaid (1999, 2002) and Porteous (1988). A different, non-linguistically aware, approach is to be found in Gervais and Wilson (2005).

3.6.3 Anti-essentialist theories

At a meta-theoretical level (i.e., the theory of theories), all the theories we have reviewed agree on some basic facts: one of them is that humor can be explained in an essentialist framework, or to put it differently, that there are sufficient and necessary conditions for a given "thing" to be humorous such that all humorous things share these conditions. The assumption that there is an essence of humor has been questioned, more or less fortunately. It is logically possible that humor is a concept such as that of "game" which, as shown in a famous argument by Wittgenstein (1953), does not have a set of features common to all games. Let us consider the only serious challenge to the essentialist paradigm[10]

---

[10] A "paradigm" is a complex epistemological background shared by several theories (Kuhn 1962). See the discussion in Chapter 1.

within humor research: in 1990, Ferro-Luzzi published an article claiming that a particular example of alliterative humor in Tamil did not involve incongruity. I showed (Attardo 1994: 139) that alliteration does involve an incongruity between the expected statistical frequency of phonemes in a given stretch of text and the observed repetition of a given (set of) phoneme(s) in the text. Thus the alleged refutation of incongruity theory by the counterexample of alliteration is found to be groundless.

3.6.4 Mixed, partial, and no-theory-theories

In reality, most theories are mixed, in the sense that they take a little bit from all three categories. For example, Freud, the grand-dad of all release theories, spends a significant amount of his book on jokes developing a treatment of the mechanisms used to establish incongruity. Bergson, one of the chief exponents of the socially-oriented theories (humor as a social corrective), also developed the view of humor as "mechanical vs. living" (read, incongruity).

Partial theories are simply theories that do not attempt to provide a complete treatment of all forms of humor but limit their goals to one or more aspects of the phenomenon (for example, satirical humor, or humor in a given culture, or lexical ambiguity puns, etc.). Most theories of irony, for example, are partial theories of humor, if they acknowledge the connections between irony and humor.

Finally, there is a number of writers that deal with humor in a more or less deliberately non-theoretical manner: their writings are (sometimes) interesting, rich of intuitions, usually well exemplified, and generally devoid of generalizations or explanations that go beyond common sense. Another characteristic is that they typically refuse to engage with the cutting edge of the research on humor and instead review obsolete classics (Aristotle, Kant, Freud, etc.). I discuss two such approaches in Attardo (1994, pp. 8–10), but one could multiply examples: Nash (1985), Ross (1998), Redfern (1984), or more recently Blake (2007) and Bevis (2013). Let me be very clear: there is nothing wrong with pre-theoretical collecting of examples and considerations or with writing introductory books. Our goals here are simply different: mapping and engaging with the cutting edge of the field so as to put the reader in a position to contribute to it.

3.7 Complementarity of the theories of humor

The three families of theories of humor are not predicated at the same level of generality. In fact, rather than being opposed they are complementary.[11]

It is clear that the incongruity theories are more or indeed exclusively interested in the stimulus of the humor phenomena or even more specifically in some of the features of the stimuli (i.e., the specific kind of contrast in which the two concepts that are involved in the incongruity must find themselves in, e.g., Giora's (2003) "negation," or Raskin's (1985) "local opposition." The neurolinguistic theories are even more reductionist in that they target neuronal activity in the brain supporting these concepts (thus the N400 wave of deactivation is commonly identified with the concept of incongruity and the P600 with the concept of resolution).

Release or liberation theories consider the effect of incongruity on the psyche of the individual producing the humor. They are concerned with the feelings or attitude of the joker, so to speak, and reference social factors only insofar as the individual may have internalized social constructs, such as Freud's Super Ego.

Aggression or superiority theories are squarely concerned with the social setting of the humorous phenomena. They address exclusively the interactional aspect of humor: what speakers do with humor when dealing with other speakers. They are social theories.

Once seen in this light, it is clear that the three families of theories might really only be three aspects of a rather gigantic, broader, all-encompassing super-theory which would specify the nature of the stimulus, all the way to the neuronal activity, the relation of the stimulus to the individual psyche, and the interplay of the individual and its society. Needless to say, no such *Über-Theorie* has been proposed.[12] Consider an example:

(24) One day, as I was withdrawing some money, the cashier at the bank asked me: "Do you want me to take it out of your checking?" I answered, "No, take it out of someone else's checking."

---

[11] I owe the general observation on which this section is based to Donald Casadonte. The elaboration of the basic idea is however mine.
[12] But see the conclusion of this book, for a shot at it.

At the stimulus level, we have clearly an opposition between the normal, received way of withdrawing money in a bank, supported by a complex network of scripts about depositing and withdrawing money, interests, etc., and an abnormal way. Clearly there are connotations being activated, since taking the money from someone else's account would leave it in mine (a good thing) but would constitute theft (a bad thing). So it is a complex opposition. The resolution aspect is merely the ambiguity of the expression "take it out of your checking [account]" which may have (among others) two different figure/ground articulations: the one intended by the cashier, where the figure is "checking" (as opposed to "savings" account) and the one I deliberately (and uncooperatively) chose with the figure on "your" as opposed to "someone else's" account.

At the individual personal level, I was clearly in a playful mood. I enjoyed showing off my capacity to detect an ambiguity where there was none (contextual pressure rules it out as a bona-fide ambiguity) and possibly I released any tension I might have had.

At the social level, I engaged the cashier in a personal, non-work, playful exchange, acknowledging her as being a person before being an employee of the bank. Hence I engaged her in an in-group solidarity building exchange. Potentially, one could argue that my remark also expressed an anti-capitalist stance close to Proudhon, since by rejecting the principle of personal property (hence the request to withdraw funds from another account) I would undermine the whole economic system, needless to say if one took it seriously. Hence one could categorize my remark as subversive and hence aggressive.

As this sketchy analysis of an example[13] has shown, there is nothing incompatible about the various "explanations" provided by the three families of theories. Of course, the theories cannot claim to be complete explanations of the humor phenomenon. They highlight different aspects of the same phenomenon, much like in the parable of the elephant and the blind men (see Berger, 1995).

---

[13] The example was first analyzed in Hamrick (2007) as an example of "trumping" (Veale et al., 2006). Trumping is a form of forced reinterpretation that plays on the distribution of saliency in the text. Further analysis of the example can be found in Section 9.3.1.3.

3.7 COMPLEMENTARITY OF THE THEORIES OF HUMOR

3.7.1 Evaluation of theories

After having discussed the ways in which theories which appear to be opposed are in fact complementary, we are now in a position to discuss a related matter, namely the evaluation of competing theories at the same level of abstraction. As a case study, we will investigate the success (undeserved, as we shall argue) of Koestler's bisociation theory, compared with the incongruity theories, and two linguistic theories of humor (the Semantic Script Theory of Humor and the Isotopy Disjunction Model).

3.7.2 Bisociation theory

The bisociation theory was introduced in Koestler's book (1964) about creativity and has been very influential. Koestler defines bisociation as

the perceiving of a situation or idea (...) in two self-consistent but habitually incompatible frames of reference (...) The event (...), in which the two intersect, is made to vibrate simultaneously on two different wavelengths, as it were. While this unusual situation lasts, [the event] is not merely linked to one associative context, but bisociated with two. (1964, p. 35)

The source of Koestler's insight is Maier (1932), a Gestalt psychologist, who pointed out that insight and humor shared some traits, summarized as follows by Lòpez and Vaid, "the experience of humor (like that of insight) involves a sudden and unexpected restructuring of the elements of a configuration leading to clarity and a solution. In other words, humor can lead to discovery" (Lòpez & Vaid, 2017, p. 270).

As I noted in Attardo (1994, p. 175) bisociation is a cognitive theory, and, clearly, a type of incongruity theory. The definition of bisociation is metaphorical (more on this below), and roughly coextensive with the notion of isotopy disjunction (see Section 4.3.1) and of script opposition and overlap (see Chapter 6). It is endowed, however, neither with the same degree of formal definition nor with the heuristic procedures for determining which script/isotopy is being activated. This is the defining features that characterizes linguistic theories: they provide the researcher with (rather elaborate) procedures for identifying the scripts or isotopies being activated by the text.

Basically, the issue boils down to this: Koestler's formulation is entirely metaphorical and no description (algorithmic or not) of how to identify the planes of bisociation is given. On the contrary, incongruity theories have at least independently motivated conceptual bases that are not metaphorical and are (at least in part) based on interpersonal assessments of stimuli. Linguistic theories, finally, have independently motivated,[14] non-metaphorical conceptualizations, with algorithmic (semi-) formal procedures for analysis. Therefore, linguistic theories are better theories because they are more formalized, while preserving the same degree of descriptive adequacy, and because they provide explanations that are not ad hoc, i.e., they are based on concepts introduced independently of humor.[15]

From a linguistic point of view, in fact bisociation is thus only a notational variant of the isotopy disjunction theory, or the script theory, with the further flaw that bisociation/incongruity etc. had already been identified since the Greeks as the central mechanism of humor. Hence, bisociation is not even a novel theory. What changes are not the underlying conceptualizations, but the metaphors used to describe them, and, of course, the degree of formalization/replicability of the theory.

3.7.3 Evaluation of the theories

How does one evaluate a theory? There are some more or less accepted scientific metrics for theories. They include:

- coverage and comprehensiveness (your theory must account for all the facts)
- verifiability (falsifiability) and intersubjective verification (i.e., others must be able to replicate your results)
- simplicity (all other things being equal, the simplest theory is to be preferred); read "simple" as 1) have less axioms,[16] 2) having less theorems/rules, etc.

---

[14] The reader will recall the warrant of transferability, i.e., independent motivation, from the discussion in Section 2.1.2.

[15] Chomsky (1965) distinguishes various levels of adequacy for a grammar (but the reasoning may be extended to theories). Descriptive adequacy means that the theory handles the data: it accounts for all the data. Explanatory adequacy "explains" the data in terms of underlying principles. Linguistic theories strive for explanatory adequacy.

[16] An axiom is an unprovable fact (from within the theory) that is taken as the starting point of the theory. For example, in Chapter 5 we will take that humor happens within a semiotic-inferential system as axiomatic.

3.7 COMPLEMENTARITY OF THE THEORIES OF HUMOR

- reductive (i.e., it should explain things in terms of simpler, better understood other[17] things; in other words, you cannot use a similarly or (even worse) more complex concept to explain a simpler one, e.g., defining humor in terms of "the ridiculous," or vice versa).
- formality (i.e., the theory must be statable in a way such that it needs no recourse to the reader's intuition, or to put it differently, it must be algorithmic, i.e., it should be, in principle, implementable in a computer program).

Using these criteria we may venture in a difficult, but extremely important avenue: explaining some of the theoretical choices made both by the field at large and by the present writer.

First, by definition no-theory theories and partial theories are ruled out as non-scientific or non-comprehensive, respectively. While the latter may still be scientifically interesting, for example if they are used as material for the construction of a comprehensive theory, the former are by definition uninteresting scientifically. What these publications are doing may be stimulating, entertaining, at times even helpful if they present good or memorable examples, or if they spark the interest of young researchers, but it is not science and should not be confused with it.

Second, by the principle of simplicity, it follows that an essentialist theory should be preferred, if available, to any other theory. Essentialist theories, if formalized enough, are very easily testable (falsifiable) since it is only[18] necessary to find a serious counterexample to the theory to falsify it.

From within incongruity–resolution theories, we have several candidates to choose from. In Attardo (1997), I pointed out the obvious fact that incongruity is a semantic concept. It follows that a linguistic (or philosophical) definition of incongruity is at an advantage over an anthropological or psychological definition, as both linguistic and (to a lesser degree) philosophical semantics have developed (more or less) scientific accounts of meaning. From within linguistics, two

---

[17] Note the importance of the "other" here, otherwise a theory would fall under the dreaded "circularity" pitfall.

[18] Not really: theories are not discarded in toto if any of their predictions turn out to be unsupported by data. Most commonly they are modified as little as necessary to account for the data. Needless to say, sometimes the data are declared to be irrelevant or outside the purview of the theory, and correspondingly the focus of the theory is changed. This is dangerous business, however, as it may reduce the comprehensiveness of the theory.

full-blown theories[19] have been developed, a script-based one, and an isotopy-based one. The problems with the isotopy-based model are such (Attardo, 1994, pp. 61–81)[20] that it is not a serious contender as a comprehensive theory (although it does have an interesting advantage for the conceptualization of the linear ordering of the joke, see Section 4.3.1). This leaves the script-based theory as the sole contender.[21]

Because the incongruity theories are essentialist (i.e., the attempt to pinpoint what makes humor funny), linguistics has tended to side (largely unwittingly) with this kind of theory. However linguists have show some interest for hostility theories (see for example the concept of "target" in the General Theory of Verbal Humor, below) and release theories. For example, the idea of defunctionalization (Guiraud, 1979) of language in puns fits in very nicely with the liberation approach, since it frees the speaker from the constraints of the linguistic code. Similarly, the idea of retractability in discourse of humor and irony frees the speaker from the consequences of his/her actions. These connections with humor theory have not been pursued in any systematic fashion.

From a different perspective, namely the performance side of humor, the picture is much different. Essentialist theories are more or less sidelined, in favor of a discursive, ethnomethodological stance (see Chapter 10 for discussion) which strongly favors comprehensiveness and intersubjective verification and more or less abandons any attempt at formalization. Perhaps because of the reductionist stance of the three major humor theories, or perhaps because of the focus on the positive aspects of humor, which go against the aggression theories of humor, the discursive and ethnomethodological approaches have developed more or less apart from humor studies. See the conclusion of the book for an argument on why they should be brought back together.

---

[19] There are other approaches, cognitive, relevance-based, corpus-based, etc. but none has presented a developed theory. See Brône et al. (2015) and Yus (2017) for examples of cognitive and relevance-based approaches. Corpus-based approaches are discussed in Section 12.3.

[20] I hate to have to say this, but the discussion is not for the faint of heart, or those without some linguistics background. They may read pages 61–62, in Attardo (1994), take my word for it, and miss very little from the humor point of view. Professional linguists will have to bite the bullet, so to speak.

[21] I assumed, wrongly, that this point was obvious. Some reviewers of Attardo (1994) took me to task for my "favoritism" towards the script-based theory. If there is only one theory that does what one needs done, one has to embrace it, warts and all. The fact that two entire chapters (and many other sections) in the said book were dedicated to developing aspects neglected by the script-based theory, not to mention that I had published in 1991 a serious revision thereof, apparently did not suffice to establish my (attempts at) objectivity.

3.8 Further readings

Surveys of humor theories can be found in Piddington (1933), Monro (1951), Bergler (1956), Keith-Speigel (1972), Raskin (1985), Morreall (1987), Attardo (1994), Smuts (n.d.). Martin (2007) now in a second edition co-authored with Thomas Ford (2018) provides an outstanding survey of the three classes of theories of humor from the standpoint of psychology.

Forabosco's (1992) treatment of incongruity in cognitive terms remains fundamental. The history of the incongruity theory can be explored in Morreall (1987) and Attardo (1994, 1997). Other incongruity-based theories are Koestler's (1964) bisociation theory, Paulos' (1980) catastrophe-theory model, and Hofstadter and Gabora's (1989) model. On bisociation, see Krikmann (2014).

Non-essentialist theories of humor have been presented by Ferro-Luzzi (1990) and Latta (1998). An example of the synchretistic approach to humor theory is M. S. Davis (1993, p. 7). For a discussion of mixed, partial, and no-theory theories, see Attardo (1994).

On the neurolinguistics of humor, see Vrticka et al. (2013), Chen et al. (2017), and Rodden (2018). On the evaluation of theories in the linguistics of humor, see Attardo and Raskin (2017).

4
Incongruity and resolution

4.1	Incongruity	79
4.2	Resolution	82
4.3	Linear organization of the joke	90
4.4	Conclusions	93
4.5	Further readings	94

This chapter deals more specifically with the cognitive processes that underlie humor. We turn first to the incongruity aspect, leaving the resolution issues for the second part of the chapter.

Concepts eerily similar to the modern incongruity and resolution model can be traced back to Aristotle. In the *Rhetorics*, he points out that in many witticisms and puns "the speaker says something unexpected, the truth of which is recognized" and "In all these jokes, whether a word is used in a second sense or metaphorically, the joke is good if it fits the facts" (III, 11 1412b). We already have, in a nutshell, the modern theories: the unexpected nature of the incongruity, the presence of two senses (often one of them being figurative), and the resolution phase: recognizing the "truth" of the witticism or its "fit" with the facts. Quintilian, a Latin rhetorician, in his *Institutio Oratoria*, also anticipates modern definitions of incongruity: in reviewing three kinds of humor: directed against others, ourselves, and neutral (i.e., not directed at anyone in particular), he notes that the third kind consists of the "thwarting of expectations, taking differently the things said." (VI-3-24).

Whether incongruity theories date back to the Greek and Latins, or as is more commonly assumed, to Kant and Schopenhauer (see Morreall, 1987) is ultimately irrelevant. In their modern form, incongruity and resolution theories originate in psychology, with the work of Sigmund Freud, whose 1905 book on humor contains a very significant discussion of the mechanisms of humor, which is unrelated to his sexual-oriented model of the psyche. Freud is probably also the unacknowledged source of the isotopy–disjunction model (Attardo, 1994, pp. 63–64). Incongruity–resolution theories were among the first theories to be conceptualized and tested in humor studies (e.g., Suls, 1972), and have seen a more recent resurgence as one of the three dimensions in Ruch's 3WD theory (Ruch, 1992), as INC-RES (the other two dimensions being sex and nonsense). An excellent review of the psychological theories of incongruity/resolution and the debate of whether both are necessary can be found in Forabosco (1992).

We saw that incongruity theories are one of the three major theories of humor. We now take the time to examine in depth what exactly incongruity is and will later subject the concept of resolution to the same treatment. The last section of the chapter deals with the linear organization of jokes, i.e., the isotopy–disjunction model.

4.1 Incongruity

Incongruity is a semantic concept. So, in this sense, incongruity theories are semantic theories, as I argued in Attardo (1997). This logical primacy of semantics vis-à-vis incongruity theories should not be (and has not been) taken too seriously. In fact, most humor scholars tend to think that semantic theories (usually the Semantic-Script Theory of Humor and the General Theory of Verbal Humor, but one could make the same argument for the isotopy–disjunction model) are incongruity theories. This is because, as we have seen, incongruity is one of the major classes of theories of humor (in fact, the major one, one could argue). However, the point remains. Incongruity is defined, implicitly most of the time, semantically. Let us go back to the pellucid definition proposed by Forabosco, and already mentioned in the previous chapter: "*if it differs, it is perceived as incongruous*" (Forabosco 1992: 54). This definition has the distinct advantage of emphasizing that the definition of incongruity is based on expectations.

In one of the classic experiments in humor studies, Nerhardt (1970, 1975) conducted a study in which subjects, under the guise of comparing them to a standard, lifted weights of increasing heaviness until one of the weights was significantly lighter than the previous ones. Upon lifting the unexpectedly lighter weight, the participants smiled or laughed more than if they weight series was congruent (i.e., increased). The experiment was widely replicated (see Gerber & Routh, 1975; Deckers & Kizer, 1975; Deckers & Winters, 1986; Deckers, 1993; Martin, 2007, pp. 68–70). What is most interesting, in our perspective, is that it is the clearest and simplest operationalization of the idea of incongruity, in the sense of violation of expectations.[1] The weights experiment is widely assumed to demonstrate that incongruity alone can be responsible for the production of mirth. We will return to this in Section 7.1.5.

For now, we focus on the expectation: the fact that in all the designs of the experiment that subjects first lift the standard weight and then after a varying number of judgements, ranging from zero to 22, they were given a "target" weight that was either much heavier, much lighter, or weighed the same. When the weights matched or after no other judgements, there were no mirth reactions, or virtually none. Conversely, after 7, 11, or more judgements, significant mirthful responses were observed. This result is interpreted as showing that the first few comparisons establish an expectation (e.g., slow increase of the weight) and that that expectation is then violated by the unexpected, and thus incongruous, weight. This argument will re-emerge in different form in the discussion of narrative strategies (Section 7.1.2), in which in the telling of a joke a regularity is established by two occurrences, only to be broken in the third instance.

It should be noted that the definition of incongruity discussed above is essentially the same as that of surprise. Surprise can be considered the emotional response to incongruity. While most scholars see surprise as an emotion (e.g., Ekman et al., 1983), others see it as a cognitive phenomenon (e.g., Lorini & Castelfranchi, 2007). In humor studies, one occasionally encounters the idea that incongruity needs to be sudden or surprising (e.g., Eysenck, 1942, p. 306). So, if the basic definition of incongruity and surprise are the same, how can there be non-sudden incongruity? The reader will recall the discussion (in Section 2.4.2) of how the presentation and the keying of incongruous items eliminate the surprise effect. Another way of conceptualizing this is that incongruity

---

[1] Not entirely free of external factors: for example, when Nerhardt originally tried the experiment with suitcases in a train station, he failed to elicit a mirth response, probably because the participants were not in a playful frame of mind (Martin, 2007, p. 70).

is a competence category and surprise is a performance-level category (i.e., it is an experience, an effect of an incongruous stimulus). Incongruity conceptualizes the mismatch of expectations at a systemic, static level, whereas surprise conceptualizes it in a dynamic, experiential way. Another concept related to incongruity is cognitive dissonance (see Section 2.4), which can be conceptualized as the non-playful, unpleasant reaction to an incongruity.

4.1.1 Enter semantics

As soon as we introduced the idea of expectations, we also implicitly introduce the idea of semantics. If we say that we "expect" A to follow B, then producing intentionally B comes to *mean* A. It is in this sense that expectations imply meaning.[2] Here, we must thread carefully. Surely, one may object, linguistics has nothing to do with expectations of weights. First, meaning is a semantic issue and not a linguistic one. Meaning (semantics) exceeds language.[3] This is just a fancy way of saying that there is meaning within language (let's say words and sentences, to simplify) and there is meaning that is extra-linguistic, because very simply, it is conveyed using a non-linguistic system of communication (think of flags between ships, of road signs, of pictures, of clothing, especially uniforms, etc.).[4] So, the claim that expectations are semantic has nothing to do with linguistics (yet). Second, even psychologists recognize the logical primacy of semantics; see for example, Deckers and Winters (1986) who frame the issue in terms of "schemata":[5] "A schema is an abstract mental representation of environmental and behavioral

---

[2] This is the foundation of Grice's Meaning$_{NN}$, incidentally. This definition is tied significantly to the Principle of Cooperation, which will play a significant role in the pragmatics of humor; see Chapter 8.

[3] Here one may object that semantics is a branch of linguistics. While it is true that linguistics has a branch called semantics, it is limited to "linguistic semantics" (i.e., meaning conveyed via language). Philosophers would be ready to point out that model theoretic semantics, just to name one, is independent of language. Computer languages have their own semantics as well, which are also completely independent, and very different, from linguistic semantics.

[4] If we wanted to be picky, we could observe that even these non-linguistic systems of communication, rely on language in some form of another: for example, the meaning of the roads signs are explained in a handbook which every driver needs to memorize in order to pass an exam. Lotman, defines language as the primary modeling system of a culture, from which all secondary systems are derived (Lotman, 1975).

[5] The plural of "schema" is "schemata." "Schemas" is also acceptable, but indicates a lesser degree of sophistication in the speaker.

regularities. Discrepancy or incongruity refers to a stimulus feature that does not match the abstracted value of that feature in the schema" (p. 57). As we will see in Chapter 6, "schemata" is another term for scripts or frames, which are all semantic objects.

So, in conclusion, incongruity is a semantic (but perhaps not necessarily a linguistic) concept, because it presupposes the attribution of meaning to a regularity in the observed world. The field that deals with meaning in all its manifestations, linguistic and not, is of course semiotics. We will take up the semiotics of humor in Chapter 5.

There are plenty of incongruity-based theories of humor. In fact, most theories of humor, at least covertly, include an incongruity aspect, such as Aristotle, commonly considered to be the proponent of a superiority theory of humor, or Freud, associated with a psychoanalytical theory and Bergson's mechanical/living opposition. See Attardo (1994), for discussion of these examples. Among the most quoted incongruity theories are Kant, often credited with coming up with the idea, Schopenhauer, Koestler's (1964) bisociation theory, and Paulos' (1980) catastrophe-theory model.

Incongruity is mostly a non-controversial, generally accepted idea, as claimed, for example, by Perlmutter (2002, p. 155) "the observation that some form of incongruity is an essential condition for humor, is universally accepted in every serious analysis of the subject." There have been, however, some claims to the contrary, such as Ferro-Luzzi (1990), Latta (1998), and Veale (2004). Ferro-Luzzi is refuted in Attardo (1994). Latta is reviewed negatively by Oring (1999) and not even mentioned in Martin (2007). Veale's objections are addressed by De Mey (2005, p. 74).

4.2 Resolution

The second part of the incongruity–resolution formula is probably the most misunderstood concept of humor studies. The most common mistake is to take the label "resolution" too literally and to expect that the resolution of the incongruity of a joke completely remove the incongruity. We will first work our way through some major contributions to the subject: Sigmund Freud, Elie Aubouin, a French psychologist, Avner Ziv, an Israeli psychologist and one of the founding fathers of humor studies, Giovannantonio Forabosco, an Italian psychologist, and Elliott Oring, an American folklorist. We will then introduce the concept of logical mechanisms, which is the present-day most in-depth treatment of the subject. After that we will address the issue of full and partial resolution of incongruity and whether incongruity is foregrounded or backgrounded in the text.

4.2.1 The history of resolution

4.2.1.1 Freud

Freud's theory of humor as economy of mental energy is well known and needs not detain us any further beyond the fact that his theory is implicitly an incongruity theory (see Attardo, 1994, p. 56). In this context what is relevant is his use of the concept of "sense in nonsense" (Freud 1905; I am quoting from the 1916 translation, p. 10) which is borrowed from Lipps (1898):

> A saying appears witty when we ascribe to it a meaning through psychological necessity and, while so doing, retract it. It may thus have many meanings. We lend a meaning to an expression knowing that logically it does not belong to it. We find in it a truth, however, which later we fail to find because it is foreign to our laws of experience or usual modes of thinking. We endow it with a logical or practical inference which transcends its true content, only to contradict this inference as soon as we finally grasp the nature of the expression itself. The psychological process evoked in us by the witty expression which gives rise to the sense of the comic depends in every case on the immediate transition from the borrowed feeling of truth and conviction to the impression or consciousness of relative nullity.
> (Lipps, 1898, p. 85; translated by A.A Brill, 1916)

Freud may have been the one to invent the catchy expression "sense in nonsense." Maier (1932), whom we have encountered previously as a source of Koestler, speaks of a "limited" logic that holds only temporarily.

4.2.1.2 Aubouin

Aubouin (1948) introduced the term "*justification*" in the same sense in which we currently use "resolution": the second phase of the humorous cognitive process. His term for the incongruity phase was *inconciliabilité*, "irreconciliability." Aubouin argues that two incongruous, irreconcilable objects are not perceived as humorous, per se. For humor to be triggered the two object have to be "accepted" simultaneously by the hearer. Acceptance is the hearer-side behavior; justification is the neutral-situation-side view of the phenomenon.

Aubouin stresses that the acceptance is *not* a real, full-fledged belief. It is brief, "superficial," merely "masking for an instant the absurdity of the judgement" (Aubouin, 1948, p. 95). Aubouin contrasts the acceptance of humor to that of a mathematical proof (p. 94): a mathematical proof is fully and permanently accepted. The acceptance of the incongruity of a joke is fleeting.

According to Aubouin, the acceptance of humor, the *justification*, involves an actual error of judgement, or at least the possibility of one. I believe that this part of Aubouin's explanation is itself in error (ironically enough) as I have shown in Attardo (1994, pp. 146–147), since there is no need to postulate an actual error. In some cases, the hearer will be really misled, for example when the context strongly primes one interpretation, which is then revealed to be wrong, as in the following example, from Attardo & Raskin (1991, pp. 305–306):

(25) George Bush has a short one. Gorbachev has a longer one. The Pope has it, but does not use it, Madonna does not have it. What is it? A last name.

which reveals its age from the fact that some of the readers will need to google who these people are. Conversely, in many jokes the hearer has to deliberately play along with the joke, as in

(26) Q: What do you get when you cross a cow and a lawnmower?
A: A lawnmooer.

where at no point in time the hearer believes that one can actually cross a cow with an inanimate object[6] or that a lawnmooer can actually exist or what it would actually be. All that the hearer is aware of is that "lawnmooer" and "lawnmower" sound similar.

The value of Aubouin's contribution resides in the fact that his was the first in-depth, and so far the most significant, discussion of the resolution of the incongruity of humor. His relative lack of recognition is probably due to the fact that he published in French, and his output seems limited to two books and a couple of articles.

---

[6] Cyborg cows are beyond the imagination of most people, but apparently not beyond that of engineers, who are inserting bio-monitors under the cows' skin; see Metz (2018). For the opposite side of the debate, see the prescient song Cows with Guns by Dana Lyons (1996).

4.2.1.3 Ziv

Ziv coined the term "local-logic" (Ziv, 1984, p. 77) by analogy with "local patriotism" which corresponds to the Italian term "campanilismo" (which means the bragging about the height of one's village's bell-tower). The point here is not the bragging part, or the attachment to one's land, but the association with small villages, with the "locality" of the matter. In local patriotism, the focus of one's positive affect is deliberately restricted to a very small domain. So, analogically, local logic is a logic that is valid only in a very small domain, for a very short amount of time. "Like local patriotism, local logic is appropriate only in certain places" (p. 90).

Local logic "brings some kind of explanation" to the incongruity. It must provide an explanation "with a certain suitability" (p. 90). Ziv analyzes the following example:

A young man looking for a wife went to a computerized marriage agency. Filling out the form, he wrote, "I'd like someone who likes lots of company, water sports, and formal dress, and is preferably rather short." The agency sent him a penguin. (p. 88)

Being sent a penguin for your mate is certainly surprising and incongruous. However, it has "suitability" (p. 90) as a comparison revels: if the agency had sent a horse it would have been equally surprising and incongruous, or perhaps even more so, but it would have lacked the local logic suitability of the penguin. The suitability comes of course, from the fact that penguins are short, live in large colonies (in some species, of tens of thousands of birds), are aquatic, and for some species their plumage resembles formal wear (for example, emperor penguins).

Local logic must be taken in a playful way: it "is very amusing if we are willing to play along, but not" if we stick to normal logic/knowledge. In the penguin example, Ziv notes that local logic will not work if "we say crossly that marriage bureaus do not send penguins to their clients" (p. 90).

Finally, Ziv argues that local logic "occupies a middle position between logical and pathological thinking" (p. 98). In logical thinking, logic is in control of thinking, whereas in pathological thinking, "fantasy and the absurd are in control and are perceived as reality" (p. 98). On the contrary, in local logic thinking "uses and enjoys both logic and fantasy without confusing them" (p. 98). In short, it involves willing suspension of disbelief (see Section 2.4.1). The analogy with pathological thinking is quite apt as Arieti (1967) had shown in his discussion of paleo-logic in schizophrenia. Ziv uses the term "pararational" to describe local logic (p. 107) which of course brings to mind Apter's (1982, 1989) "paratelic" mode of communication.

4.2.1.4 Forabosco

As we saw, Forabosco defines incongruity as follows: "a stimulus is incongruous when it differs from the cognitive model of reference" (1992, p. 54) and stresses the importance of including the perceiving subject in the definition (using the term "model" which presupposes someone doing the modeling). Forabosco then considers that one may define resolution as a "problem-solving" activity that finds a rule which "reconciles the incongruous parts" or, following McGhee (1979) as "cognitive mastery" (i.e., the cognitive capacity to understand that if something unexpected occurs, this is because it goes against "how things should be"; McGhee, 1979, p. 38).

Forabosco then argues that there are two ways to interpret "resolution." The first one is "a cognitive rule [...] that reconciles the incongruous parts" (p. 57). The second one, is a "congruence criterion" (p. 58), i.e., any element relating to the stimulus on the basis of which the stimulus, at least in that specific respect, is congruous" (p. 57). Forabosco does not say this, but I think we can reach the conclusion that the first is a complete resolution (elimination) of the incongruity, whereas the second is a partial resolution. A congruence criterion allows cognitive mastery. The example that Forabosco provides is a child seeing a distorted face (caricature) and realizing that "it is just a drawing and not a real face" (p. 57). Forabosco notes that in the case of the congruence criterion it co-occurs with the incongruity (it is "contemporaneous") and below the threshold of consciousness.

Most significantly, Forabosco notes that "Resolving the incongruity does not mean eliminating it. It means having, at the end of the process, an incongruity 'that makes sense'" (p. 59) or a "*congruent incongruity*" (p. 59; emphasis in the original). The "residual incongruity represents [...] the margin of inadequacy of the cognitive rule and tends to be ignored" (p. 59).

4.2.1.5 Oring's appropriate incongruity

Elliott Oring is a folklorist (and as a non-psychologist in this section, he automatically gets bonus points). He has long maintained that the resolution of jokes is "the perception of an appropriate relationship between categories that would ordinarily be regarded as incongruous" (Oring, 2003, p. 1). Oring argues that his approach is not homologous to the incongruity–resolution theories insofar as no actual dissolution of the incongruity is assumed: "the incongruity remains, even though points of connection between the incongruous categories are discovered" (p. 2). Further, his approach is not committed to a processing order, implicit in the incongruity-then-resolution terminology of the incongruity–resolution theories. He then adds that either the incongruity or the appropriateness must be "illegitimate" or spurious (p. 6). Whether appropriate spurious incongruity is really different than all formulations of the incongruity–resolution theories is not a topic that can be addressed presently. We will return to the issue of full or partial resolution below.

4.2.1.6 The GTVH on resolution

The General Theory of Verbal Humor (Attardo and Raskin 1991) was the first linguistic theory to address the issue of the resolution of the humor, although we did not word it that way in the original 1991 paper. We spoke instead of the "logical mechanism" to describe the "crudely approximate logic of a paralogism" (p. 304), the "semblance of logic" which included "faulty or cheating inferential processes" which would not "withstand any close scrutiny" and "paralogisms instead of correct syllogisms" (p. 304) and concluded that "a joke must provide a logical or paralogical explanation of the absurdity or irreality it postulates" (p. 307), while also noting that this was not a novel problem, but one that has not been fully addressed, despite some of the discussions seen above.

The Logical Mechanisms went on to be the most controversial of the components of the General Theory of Verbal Humor. We will turn to that in Chapter 7. Instead here we will consider a few studies that have investigated the general nature of the resolution, rather than its specific mechanisms.

4.2.2 Full vs. partial resolution

In Hempelmann and Attardo (2011), we tackled the issue of full and partial resolution. Based on Oring's (2003) appropriate incongruity, we argued that humor only partially resolves incongruities. The reader will recall that Oring claims that humor only partially resolves incongruities and does so spuriously, at that. Whereas metaphors find real legitimate connections between disparate (incongruous) objects (and have some explanatory power because of that) jokes find spurious, illegitimate connections. Oring then argues that the difference between jokes and riddles is that in a riddle the incongruity is fully resolved, i.e., there is a solution (2003, p. 6), whereas in a joke (or a joking riddle, a.k.a. a pseudo-riddle) there is no full resolution. Attardo (2009) applied the same line of reasoning to mystery stories arguing that once we find out "who done it" (in other words, the incongruity in the text is resolved) the incongruity is fully eliminated: consider the "locked-room" sub-genre of mysteries: a crime is committed in a room or other location in which only a restricted group of people are present or have access to, but they *all* have an alibi. Once we find out that the butler or the husband did it, and how he managed to do it while apparently also having an alibi, the resolution is complete and the incongruity truly and fully resolved. Once we know that the murders in rue Morgue were committed by an orangutan, there is no mystery left.[7]

The idea of partial resolution is operationalized as "residual incongruity" with a view toward quantification in Hempelmann & Ruch (2005), as follows: "how much incongruity remains un(re)solved; how much new incongruity has the LM introduced; how puzzled are you still at the end of the joke" (p. 364). Their analysis of a sample of cartoons showed that nonsensical cartoons contain significantly more residual incongruity (p. 368), as one would expect. Samson et al. (2009, p. 1029) shows significant differences in brain activation between the two categories of jokes.

4.2.3 Foregrounded vs. backgrounded incongruities

Rothbart and Pien argued that (1977, pp. 37–38) a humorous text may contain multiple incongruities and moreover the resolution of the punch line itself may introduce new incongruities. Tsakona (2003) established that many jokes have more than one punch line. The technical details of the analysis are reviewed in Section 7.1.6. What matters presently is that this perforce means that there will be multiple, independent script oppositions within a joke. This is not to say that *all* jokes

---

[7] One of the earliest example of the genre is E. A. Poe, *The Murders in the Rue Morgue* (1841).

have multiple script oppositions, but only that *some* do. Specifically, in her corpus, about 25% did not have multiple punch lines (p. 320).

Tsakona notes that the idea that jokes contain several "implausibilities" or (background) incongruities is not novel, having been stated in Sacks (1978, p. 258)) and discussed by Mulkay (1988, pp. 130–133), Attardo (1994, pp. 304–307), and Attardo et al. (2002). Tsakona argues that these implausibilities, do not go "unnoticed" as Sacks had argued, but in fact help frame the joke as non-bona-fide communication, i.e., as being told in a humorous key. Finally, she notes, and this is very significant, that "*the script opposition introduced in the punch line of the narrative joke is always different from (all) the other(s) that may appear in the joke-text*" (Tsakona, 2003, p. 326; emphasis in the original). It should be noted that Raskin (1985, pp. 132–134) had already noted that there are complex jokes, with more than one script opposition.

In Attardo et al. (2002) we suggested distinguishing between *focal* and *background* incongruities. The focal incongruity is the one involved in the punch line and in its resolution. In Hempelmann and Attardo (2011)[8] we consider the following variants of a joke:

(27)   **a.** How does an elephant hide in a cherry tree? It paints its toenails red (Hempelmann & Attardo, 2011, p. 132).
     b. How does a monkey hide in a cherry tree? It paints its toenails red (p. 133).
     c. How does a monkey hide in a cherry tree? It paints its toenails blue (p. 134).
     d. How does an elephant hide in a lime tree? It paints its toenails red (Oring, 1992, p. 22).[9]

and note that (27.a) contains an incongruity which (27.b) does not, and namely that a very large, non-arboreal animal might have climbed a relatively small tree and not crushed it under its weight. Both (27.a) and (27.b) partially (very partially!) resolve the incongruity by an incongruous means, i.e., painting their toenails to simulate the color of the

---

[8] The paper was in fact written much earlier, around 2005, but due to the significant backlog in *HUMOR* at the time and due to my desire not to appear partial to a former student and to my own work, since I was then the editor-in-chief, there was a considerable delay in the publication.

[9] Oring does not actually present the joke per se, but notes that "the absurdity is rule-governed (...) it would not do to answer that elephants paint their toenails red to hide in lime trees."

fruit of a cherry tree and thus achieve some camouflage. This is very much fantasy assimilation and suspension of disbelief. (27.c) removes the color match which supposedly helps with the camouflage and thus eliminates the resolution, as does (27.d) but by changing the type of tree and hence the color of the fruit. Our point was that in (27.a) there is a massive incongruity that is not addressed by the text, which chooses to address a very marginal incongruity (the color of the toenails). So, we would say that the fact that the elephant is in the tree is a backgrounded incongruity, and as such can be removed from the jokes, as we did in (27.b), whereas the coloring of the nails (using very large nail polish brushes?) is the foregrounded incongruity. Finally, we argued that there is an intermediate type of incongruity, which can be removed and does not change the nature of the joke, as our change in (27.b) did. A full discussion can be found in Hempelmann and Attardo (2011, p. 135–137).

Samson and Hempelmann (2011) tested empirically Tsakona's (2003), Hempelmann & Ruch's (2005), and Hempelmann & Attardo's (2011) claims that backgrounded incongruities affect both processing and appreciation. They found that, as anticipated, backgrounded incongruities especially affect the funniness rating: stimuli with backgrounded incongruities were considered funnier (p. 173). "The presence of a backgrounded incongruity [...] leads to more unresolved incongruity and contributes to the perception that the cartoons are more nonsensical" (p. 180). Samson and Hempelmann hypothesize that the increase of perception of nonsense which parallels the increase of backgrounded incongruities may possibly be due to the fact that "some of the backgrounded incongruities remain unresolved but contribute essentially to the emotional response" (p. 181).

4.3 Linear organization of the joke

The incongruity–resolution model has an interesting aspect which we have not considered in detail yet, namely the fact that the idea of introducing an incongruity and then resolving it presupposes a temporal linearity, as mentioned by Oring (see above, Section 4.2.1.5). The isotopy–disjunction model has provided the most compelling analysis of this aspect of humor and so we will discuss the linearity of humor using the isotopy–disjunction model of jokes as an example.

4.3.1 The isotopy–disjunction model

At its core the isotopy–disjunction model is the implementation of a basic, and very interesting observation, namely that among the various polysemic lexical items of a coherent sentence, there emerges a shared thread of meanings that work with one another, while other meanings, also potentially available in the lexical items, are not functional in that given interpretation. This is of course the phenomenon known as *disambiguation*. Greimas called this "thread" of compatible meanings an "isotopy" (Greimas, 1966) and argued that a special type of semantic features was responsible for its establishment. He labeled these *classemes* and opposed them to the more specific *semes*. The history and difficulties of establishing the boundary between semes and classemes are detailed in Attardo (1994) and are not relevant in this context, beyond the conclusion that the distinction was in fact untenable and that an isotopy could be established merely by the repetition of any semantic feature.

An example will clarify. Consider the following sentence:

(28) John poured the coffee in the cup.

It is clear that, whatever the polysemic nature of the various lexical items in the sentence, the noun *coffee* has at least two possible senses: 1) coffee beans and 2) a liquid obtained by infusing ground coffee beans in hot water. It would be too complex to run a full feature analysis of the two meanings, but we can simplify the analysis by saying that meaning (1) will have a feature [+ solid] while meaning (2) will have a feature [+ liquid].[10] Greimas' insight is that the occurrence of the feature [+ liquid] in "pour" selects the meaning of "coffee" which also shares the [+ liquid] feature. Presumably one could also have a feature analysis of "cup" sophisticated enough to note that containers may hold liquids.

Greimas was never interested in humor per se and only analyzed a joke to show how the setup of the text presented one isotopy which was then replaced by a second one in the punch line. He introduced the terms of connector (a polysemous term in which both isotopies could occur simultaneously) and of disjunctor (the lexical item which forced the separation of the two isotopies).

---

[10] Any reader smart enough to note that we really only needed one feature [+/− solid], for example, should also be smart enough to understand the pedagogical reasons why we did not do so. Moreover, ground coffee is [− solid] and [− liquid]. Feature analysis is fun!

Greimas' model of jokes was adopted and developed by various European scholars, primarily by Violette Morin (Morin, 1966), who added a three-part division in narrative functions, inspired by Propp's work (1928) on the subject in folk tales. Because of considerable variation in the terminology, in Attardo (1994, p. 87), I introduced a simple numbering of the functions: F1, the introduction, F2, the setup, and F3, the punch line. The Greimas/Propp/Morin isotopy model was quite successful in Europe in the 1970s and 1980s and then faded away.

The success can be explained by two factors: 1) the formalization of the concept of incongruity in the isotopy model, and 2) the focus on the linear development of the text. The model ultimately failed to remain productive due to several issues: first and foremost, feature analysis was shown to be incapable of dealing with the full semantic analysis of the lexicon. Once taken outside of subdomains such as kinship terms or kitchen utensils, the methodology starts generating too many features and any explanatory gains are nullified by the proliferation of features. Whereas the phonetic inventory of a language could be reduced to a few handfuls of features, the semantic inventory of a language would require the same order of magnitude[11] of features as of lexical items. Second, the analysis in narrative features was shown to be common to all narrative forms and not specific to jokes. Third, the definitional problems of the concept of "isotopy" weakened the formalization advantage. Finally, the appearance of semantic models that were both more sophisticated, in that they adopted the concept of semantic scripts/frames, and more elaborated, led scholars away from the isotopy model.

The specific focus on the linearity of the text was not taken up by the script/frame-based models and this explains why Bucaria (2004) still managed to make a very meaningful contribution on the typology of the connector/disjunctor placement using the isotopy model. Logically, we expect the connector to precede the disjunctor or to coincide with it.[12] Consider this headline, from Bucaria's data (p. 298):

---

[11] You can think of orders of magnitude as zeroes that follow a number: so 50 and 70 have the same order of magnitude, as do 53 and 84, but 300, 999, and 157 have one order of magnitude more, 1000 has two more, etc.

[12] In the case of coinciding connector/disjunctor, we could also say that the connector is absent and we just have a disjunctor.

(29) MARCH PLANNED FOR NEXT AUGUST

the lexeme "March" is ambiguous (the name of the month vs. walking). It is the connector. Assume that due to saliency the month interpretation is preferred. When we reach the end of the headline, we encounter the disjunctor ("August") which forces the reinterpretation from "month" to "walking." Consider now the next example, also from her data,

(30) DRUNK GETS NINE MONTHS IN VIOLIN CASE

Here the connector co-occurs with the disjunctor as they both are revealed in the word "case" (legal action vs. box for the safekeeping of an instrument). Bucaria found examples in which the disjunctor ("lingerie") precedes the connector ("slip"), as in the following:

(31) LINGERIE SHIPMENT HIJACKED – THIEF GIVES POLICE THE SLIP

The significance of this is that it contradicts Attardo et al. (1994) in which we speculated that such a configuration was impossible. Bucaria instead established that the order of presentation of the elements of the joke is free.

4.3.1.1 The three functions

Tsakona (2003) showed that while the final position of the punch line in jokes holds true, other incongruities may occur in the texts (backgrounded incongruities). These may appear as non-final punch lines, or jab lines; see Chapter 7. Tsakona (2003) has provided several significant insights in the organization of the text of the joke. First, she showed that F2 is significantly longer than F1, by a ratio of 3:1 in her sample. The distribution of the jab lines in the text of the jokes is the same. Second, and more significantly, the script opposition introduced in the punch line is always different from those in the jab lines. It is a novel opposition that cannot appear in either F1 or F2, although it will involve, as one of the polarities, a script introduced in F1 or F2.

4.4 Conclusions

We have examined the incongruity and resolution theory of humor, with a particular emphasis on the semantic nature of the concept of incongruity. We also emphasized the partial nature of the resolution and its ludic, local, illegitimate aspect. We then focused on the linear organization of the presentation of the incongruity and its subsequent resolution, instantiated in the disjunctor and (optional) connector. Having established that the incongruity theories are based on a semantic concept, we will move on to the properly linguistic treatment of the semantics and pragmatics of humor in the second and following parts of the book, but not before dealing with one last foundational issue, the semiotics of humor, in Chapter 5.

4.5 Further readings

The historical roots of the incongruity–resolution theory can be further explored in Morreall (1987) and Attardo (1994). On modern treatments of incongruity, see Forabosco (1992). The rest of the discussion on incongruity and especially resolution is technical and there are no general sources, beyond those quoted in the text. Oring (2003, ch. 1) is very accessible. Martin (2007) can be useful for the psychological side of the discussion. On the isotopy–disjunction model, see Attardo 1994, Chapter 2. For an update, see Aljared (2017).

5
Semiotics of humor

5.1 Humor and semiotics   96
5.2 Conclusions   108
5.3 Further readings   109

This chapter consists of a discussion of the semiotics of humor. Semiotics can be conceptualized as the science of how communication takes place in general, within any system of communication, i.e., not limited to language.

We start from the assumption, unspoken so far, that humor is a communicative event.[1] In other words, humor takes place within a situation in which one speaker is communicating with another speaker. The reader will recall the basic humor situation we introduced in Chapter 1.

Of course much of humor is not expressed or communicated linguistically. The prototypical humorous situation of a man slipping on a banana peel has no linguistic component of note.[2] Since the realm of communication is much broader than language (e.g. non-verbal communication, kinesics, proxemics, etc.) a broader approach becomes necessary and will have to be provided within semiotics, i.e., the general science that encompasses all forms of communication (intentional and unintentional, linguistic, visual, musical, etc.).

---

[1] Morreall (2009, p. 70) presents examples of humor that would not involve communication, such as oddly shaped rocks. I will not discuss these cases here, but I believe they can be reduced to communicative situations anyway. We are taking the communicative nature of humor as axiomatic, in other words. See Section 3.7.3 for a discussion of axioms.

[2] One could argue, with Lotman, see Section 4.1.1, that since language is the primary modeling system of a culture, we see the man slip *through* language, so to speak.

From a linguistic/semiotic standpoint one can start from two approaches at a definition of humor: a semantic (structural) definition and a pragmatic (functional/contextual) definition. These will be developed more fully in Parts 2 and 3 of the book, respectively. Here, we will be satisfied with providing a general outline of how the definitions work. Our goal is to show that the argument we propose is not limited to language but in fact applies to any communicative situation.

5.1 Humor and semiotics

This chapter sets out to combine several strands of research to achieve a general explanation of how the structural features of humor determine its manifestations and usages. This objective is based on the generalization that *the semantic and pragmatic mechanisms of humor are the determining factors of the unique features of humorous communication.* In order to arrive at this conclusion, we must start by providing a few definitions of semiotics. Furthermore, in order to investigate the particular nature of humorous communication we need to introduce some concepts, derived from semiotics and from linguistics, as well as some theoretical approaches to humorous phenomena. The following sections will provide these necessary background materials.

5.1.1 Communication and semiosis

Communication presupposes a system through which the exchange of information is achieved, i.e. a semiotic system. All communication is (a form of) semiosis. Semiosis is here defined as the exchange of information through a semiotic system.[3] It should be noted that there can be exchange of information *without* a semiotic system, for example by answering the question "What do you have in your briefcase?" by opening it and showing the contents to the inquirer (this is what Wittgenstein called "ostensive" communication). From the opposite angle, there can be use of a semiotic system, without transmission of information (cf. below "defunctionalization").

---

[3] It should be noted that we do *not* claim that all that is needed for communication is a semiotic system. In order to communicate, you also need a pragmatics, in its broadest sense.

5.1 HUMOR AND SEMIOTICS

5.1.2 Connotative semiotics

Saussure's (1916) definition of the sign as the indissoluble unity of a *signifié* and a *signifiant* (signified/signifier) was not meant to hold for linguistic signs alone, but was meant to be extended to all semiotic systems. The signifier of a sign is the mental representation of the physical support of the sign (sounds, graphical elements, bodily movements, etc.), while the signified is the mental representation of the concept (the idea, the meaning) conveyed by the sign.

Hjelmslev (1953) defines any system of signs as a semiotics. A denotative semiotics is a system of signs in which neither the signifier nor the signified are semiotics; hence languages are denotative semiotics, since their signifiers are (mental representations of) sounds, and their signifieds are (mental representations of) concepts. A connotative semiotics, on the other hand, is a semiotics in which the signifier is a semiotics. If a semiotics has as its signified another semiotics it is a metasemiotics (i.e., it is a semiotics of another semiotics; an example would be the metalanguage of linguistic description). But if a semiotics has as its signifier another semiotics it is a connotative semiotics. As an example consider a person speaking in Italian saying "Mamma mia." This is a semiotic sign, made up of a signifier [mam:amiya] and a signified "Oh my!" (literally: "mother mine"). However, this entire semiotic fact can become the signifier of another semiotic fact, that is the entire situation connotes "Italian." Schematically, we have the representation in Figure 5.1.

This fact has some very important consequences for the study of humor, which will appear in full in the rest of the discussion. For the time being, let us be satisfied with the observation that since the signifier of a semiotics does not carry any "meaning" in and of itself, the original meaning of "mamma mia" is lost, and only the meaning of "Italian" survives the establishment of the connotative semiotics (just as

Connotative Semiotics

Expression "Mamma mia !"		Content "Italian"
Expression: [mam:amiya]	Content : "oh, my !"	

Denotative semiotics

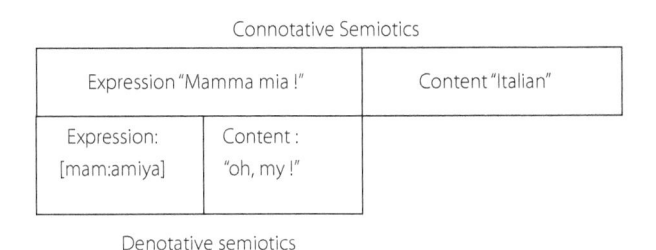

Figure 5.1 Denotative (bottom left) and connotative (top row) semiotics.

for any non-Italian-speaking speaker of English the string [mam:amiya] is meaningless, with the exception of its identification of the speaker as Italian). In other words, when a sign is used as the signifier of a connotative semiotics, its primary meaning as a sign is lost, and the connotative semiotics acquires a secondary meaning, proper to the connotative semiotics, and independent from the primary meaning.

5.1.3 Perlocutionary definition of humor

The only definition of a humorous text[4] general enough to apply to all humor is that of a text whose perlocutionary[5] goal is to be perceived as humorous. This definition (Attardo & Chabanne, 1992) stresses the intentions of the speaker and/or the hearer. More to the point, a definition of humor based on its goal implies that the text will use all its resources to achieve the perlocutionary goal of the speakers, to the detriment of any other purposes the text may have had beyond that of being perceived as humorous. In this perspective, the only thing that matters for the speaker is to achieve his/her goal, and the text will be shaped accordingly.

This fact is grounded in the analysis of humor as a connotative semiotics: the humorous text can be shaped in any way, as long as the perlocutionary goal is attained, just as any string of Italian words would have worked as expression of the signified "Italian." Since any Italian words would have worked to convey the meaning "Italian" even the following sentences would convey the meaning "Italian," as long as the audience can reliably identify them as being spoken in Italian:

(32) "Non sono italiano" (I am not Italian)
      "Scusi, sa dov'é il bagno?" (Excuse me, do you know where the bathroom is?)

From this it follows that the original content of the semiotics (i.e., the text in the humor situation) is backgrounded, just as the theory of connotative semiotics would predict. In the case of humorous texts, this means that the actual contents of a joke may be completely irrelevant to the context in which they occur, as long as the humorous text itself is pertinent to the context: a joke may be about chickens crossing the

---

[4] In the generic sense established in Chapter 1.
[5] This term will be better defined in Section 8.1.1. For the time being, "a goal of the speaker" is a sufficient definition.

road, elephants in trees, or whatever, but the joke must occur in a given context, following certain rules, etc. Consider again example (10), in Chapter 1, in which Carmen recontextualizes an old joke (What do you call someone who speaks only one language? An American.) to playfully tease Marina. Carmen could just as well have asked if she spoke Greek or Chinese, so that the conversation could have gone as follows:

(33)   Carmen: Do you speak any other languages, besides English?
       Marina: Nope, nothing fluently, a little bit of that and...
       Carmen: (Ironically) You don't speak Greek, or Chinese?

In other words, a different joke, which is pertinent to the context and achieves the same perlocutionary goals of the speaker, could have replaced the original joke. However, crucially, the joke needs to be delivered as a response to Marina's modest turn in which she admits, somewhat hesitantly, to monolingualism.

This explains, among other things, why non-sense and absurdities are tolerated within humorous texts: the absurdities are at the level of the expression of the connotative semiotics, and not at the level of the contents of the connotative semiotics, where they would not be tolerated. Carmen could not mock Marina's monolingualism at the beginning of the conversation, for example, because this would violate the relevance of the turn (humor must be à propos). The humorous text can take any form, that is including breaking the rules of communication (non-sense, absurd), as long as the result is perceived as humorous; if the result is not perceived as humorous the absurdities are not "redeemed" by their functional use within the joke text. If Carmen started the conversation mocking Marina's monolingualism, the conversational move would be perceived as extremely aggressive and thus unfunny.

Likewise, Carmen need not be seriously committed to the claim that monolingualism is a flaw at all and that it is particularly common among Americans. Once more, one can assert propositions one does not believe to be true, thus violating several rules of communication, for the perlocutionary purpose of being humorous.

5.1.4 Defunctionalization of the sign

The fact that humor is a connotative semiotics does not imply that the humorous text does not have any feature beyond its perlocutionary goal. In order to discuss this issue it is necessary to first consider the semantic mechanisms at work in humor. The reader should bear in mind that the following is a cursory presentation, which introduces only the essentials required to understand the discussion of the relationship between semantics and semiotics of humor. A full presentation will be undertaken in Chapter 6.

5.1.4.1 The semantics of humor

One of the most theoretically significant contributions of linguistics to humor theory has been establishing the fact that the necessary and sufficient conditions for humor are semantic (see Chapter 6). The semantic theory of humor begins by distinguishing between humor *competence*, an abstract highly idealized model of humor, and the actual *performance* of a given humorous text by given speakers, in a given situation, context, etc. (see Chapter 1). Humor competence abstracts away from all individual idiosyncrasies, such as the fact that a speaker may consider certain types of humor offensive, or that a speaker has had a bad day, and is in a bad mood, etc. By abstracting away from all performance considerations, the semantic theory of humor is capable of reducing all humor to a relational function (opposition between overlapping scripts) with minimal positive semantic weight, but with well defined requirements, namely the relation of opposition of the scripts involved in the joke. In other words, any two scripts which are opposed (in a technical sense), and overlap in a text (i.e., the text is compatible with both scripts, at least in part), can *potentially* generate humor. Whether the overlap of two opposed scripts will be perceived as humorous by a given audience in a given situation, at a given time, etc. is not a concern for the *semantic* theory of humor (competence), but becomes one for any *socio-pragmatic* theory of humor. For a full discussion of the competence/performance opposition see Section 2.1.

5.1.4.2 Semantics and defunctionalization of humor

As noted above, the semantic theory of humor has very little to say about the contents of the script opposition, since it is a relational concept, and not a substantial one. While this may seem a paradoxical or idiosyncratic conclusion, it is mirrored by another important conclusion reached in humor research, and namely the loss of meaning of the signs used in humorous texts. This fact has been noted across the literature in the field, although not always in as clear terms as Guiraud's (1979) "defunctionalization" of the sign. Guiraud's point was made in the context of the discussion of puns, but the reasoning behind it allows its generalization to all humor. When we communicate we use language according to its primary function, i.e., the transmission of information. When this primary function of language is abandoned in view of some other non-linguistic goal such as play, or aesthetic purposes, we have a defunctionalization of the medium (language). Jakobson's (1960/1987) definition of the aesthetic function of language as centered on language itself[6] also fits the definition of defunctionalization. In other words, any time that the linguistic medium is used for purposes other than the transmission of information (and possibly other non-communicative mental processes, such as thought) we can speak of defunctionalization.

In the context of humor, the idea of defunctionalization is particularly interesting, since it is a well-known fact that humor is considered "non-serious" or otherwise devoid of commitment to any utility principle, beyond the fulfillment of the humorous purpose of the text. For example, nobody takes seriously the information, provided in the following joke

(34) How do you fit four elephants in a compact car?
      Two in front and two in the back.

All theories of humor, even the more committed to the "seriousness" and the social and/or interpersonal relevance of humor have to grant that humor has an element of playfulness, of lack of practical goals.[7] This defunctionalization is reflected in the "semiotic" nature of the humorous text. The important issue, from the point of view of the participants in the joke exchange is not the contents of the joke text, but whether the text is funny. In other words, jokes are defunctionalized texts. The joke text exhausts its function in its perlocutionary goal (trying to make the hearer laugh as a result of the feeling of mirth).

Composed of a signifier and a signified, like any other text, the humorous text transcends both, and connotes only "humor" beyond the primary meaning of the signs used in the text, since as we have said, the primary goal of the text is not to convey information, but to amuse. In simple terms, it doesn't matter much about the chicken and the road, what matters is that it is funny.

---

[6] Jakobson's definition is: "The poetic function projects the principle of equivalence from the axis of selection into the axis of combination" (Jakobson, 1960, p. 71), i.e., that the combination of linguistic elements to form sentences is ruled by the similarities of the various linguistic items, rather than their meaning, as is usual.

[7] Cf. the definition of humor as a "paratelic" mode (Apter, 1989).

This is not to say that the joke communicates *only* its own humorousness. The "reuse" of the semiotics is hardly "transparent": consider making a joke about a political figure. Especially if the joke ridicules or mocks the politician, the choice of what politician to mock, what to make fun of, etc. will be hardly irrelevant. One's choices will be dictated by one's opinions, attitudes, likes, dislikes, etc. In other words, the choice of a given subject matter becomes part of the joke's potential meaning/communicative import. We will return to this issue below, but for the time being let us set it aside, and return to the consequences of the defunctionalization of humorous texts.

5.1.4.3 Metamessages and metasemiotics

Compare now the situation of defunctionalization described above with the definition of connotative semiotics, also given above, and it appears that the humorous text[8] is a connotative semiotics, whose signified is "this text is funny" and whose signifier is the text of the joke (which in turn is made of a given signifier and signified). In other words, a humorous text is a connotative semiotics, connoting humorousness.

This ties in with Bateson's remarks about the metamessage "this is play" present in play, discussed in Section 3.3.1. The various disclaimers and exploratory introductory turns studied in conversation analysis (see Chapter 11) perform the same function of marking in discourse. The issue of "markers" of humor will be taken up in Part III of the book.

Bateson's original observation can be expanded to the social setting of the interaction in which the joke text is produced. By uttering a joke, say at a social gathering, one not only expresses the metamessage "this is play" (regardless of explicitly doing so), but also a number of inferences can be drawn: thus "this is play" implies "I think it is appropriate to joke here, now, about this subject," "I am in the mood to joke," etc. Thus, the utterance of a joke will inform its audience about the teller, his/her perception of the context, etc. Even in the case of printed jokes[9] the text will reveal that the author or editor considers these texts funny, appropriate for printing, etc. Imagine the differences between

---

[8] The reader will recall that by the definition in Chapter 1 a text is anything used to convey meaning regardless of its semiotic modality (spoken language, image, gesture, music, etc.).

[9] Printed collections of jokes are the "zero degree" of context for jokes, as no contextual information beyond the title of the book, the author's name, the publisher, and the date of publication, is available.

5.1 HUMOR AND SEMIOTICS

a collection of jokes edited by a Baptist minister, and a collection of neo-Nazi jokes on the 4chan bulletin board.

Since humor is a form of play, it is logical to extend the idea of the presence of metamessages to humor. These metamessages will alert the speakers that the humorous exchange is "play/humor." These considerations set the necessary background for all the issues of suspension of the rules (linguistic, semiotic, social), since, as we know from the theory of metalanguages, metasemiotic status guarantees the suspension of the rules of the object-semiotics. This accounts for a number of facts we know about humor: humor carries metamessages saying "this is humor," humor violates semantic and pragmatic rules (see Chapter 8) but this fact does not cause the communicative situation to be destroyed (Attardo, 1993). Most importantly, it accounts for the baffling fact that humor can "mean" different things to different people. In fact, beyond "this is humor," the signified (i.e., the meaning) of the metasemiotics is empty; it is only the meanings of the primary semiotics which may "surface" in the final overall communicative import of the text and thus give an effect of meaningfulness, apropos, etc., to jokes.

5.1.5 Semantics vs. semiotics of humor

The previous sections have established the fact that humor is a connotative semiotics, and have pointed out the direct consequences of this fact: the defunctionalization of the humorous text and the metamessages that a humorous utterance carries. It is now possible to explore another facet of the relationship between the semantics and the semiotics of humor.

From semiotics, we know that we have to deal with any number of systems based on the signifier/signified opposition. The linguistic semiotic system is just one among many (however primary it may be) and therefore we have to create a model where there are as many different signifiers, which are, however, all opposed to one signified, since by the principle of intersemiotic translation (Jakobson 1960), we can vary the signifier and keep the signified constant. Or in other words, as we can "translate" the signified "beautiful" across languages (*beau, bello, schön*),[10] we can also, and with the same ease, translate the signified into a drawing, a motion-picture, gestures, etc. The relationship form/expression in a humorous text will then look like this:

---

[10] Albeit with a certain variation in the exact correspondences between the terms.

$$\left.\begin{array}{l}\text{verbal}\\ \text{figurative}\\ \text{musical}\\ \text{etc.}\end{array}\right\} \quad \text{signifier} \quad / \quad \text{humorous signified}$$

From this fact it follows that, since the semantics of the humorous text remain unchanged through all the translations across semiotic systems, the semantic requirements should be applicable, with all due changes, to all semiotic humor. The analysis of the following examples will address this issue.

Let us consider two non-verbal examples: a clown's oversized shoes, and a well-known 3-frame cartoon by Gary Larson showing four cows standing on their hind legs by the side of the road, one of which is shouting "Car!" in the first frame, a car with two people aboard going by the cows who are now standing on their four legs, in the second, and the cows standing again on their hind legs in the third and final frame. There is no caption, and the details of the landscape/setting are bare and minimal.

I think that it is uncontroversial that the first example has no verbal element whatsoever, while the second example use of language is marginal, and does not seem to be the source of the humor of the cartoon. A fair paraphrase (intersemiotic translation) of the first example would be: "The clown is wearing shoes that are way too big for his/her feet." A semantic theory of humor would account for the humorous potential of the example by pointing out that the script (i.e., what we know[11]) for "shoes" prescribes a) that they should fit the feet of the wearer within reasonable standards, and b) that no shoes are made beyond a certain foot-size (this may be seen as an inference derivable from a) and the script for "foot"). Thus what we see is incompatible with our script for shoes, and yet we see it used as if they were normal shoes (i.e., they are worn, and the clown walks around, etc.). In other words, the script SHOES is both incompatible and overlapping with the script CLOWN SHOES or its actualization in that specific pair of shoes. This is a very primitive form of humor, and in fact it may be that some of its constituents are missing, namely we have located an incongruity (size) between the script SHOES and the actual shoes we see, but we cannot

---

[11] A full definition of script is found in Chapter 6.

find a resolution of this incongruity, which many researchers consider an important part of the humorous experience.

Let us turn to the second example, which is more complex. A paraphrase of the cartoon might be: there are some cows that are standing on their hind legs, and one of them shouts "car!"; they stand on their four legs while the car goes by, and when the car is gone they resume their standing position.

The first thing that strikes the reader, even before he/she starts processing the cartoon, is that the cows are anthropomorphized: they speak and they stand. Here we already have the basic opposition between the normal script COW and what we see represented in the cartoon HUMAN-ACTING-COW. But the cartoon also provides the "local logic" (4.2), i.e., the resolution of the incongruity.

Two inferences are central to the perception of the humor of the cartoon. Why is the cow in the first frame shouting "Car!"? Shouting may be caused by a number of causes, fear, rage, emotion, etc., but also by the desire of being heard at a great distance. From the features of the drawing there seems to be no particular emotional involvement from the cow's part (these would be represented by large round eyes, lines on the face representing tension of the muscles, etc.) and hence we can draw the conclusion that the cow is shouting in order for the other cows to be aware that the car is coming, or in other words, that the cow warns the others of an approaching car. We may also note that the four cows in the drawing are not all standing together: the cow that shouts is standing by itself, somewhat distant from the other three who are looking at the shouting cow. This may mean that the cow is "on the look out," but the drawings do not provide enough evidence to argue this point definitely. Nevertheless, if someone, not just a cow, warns someone else of something this means that at least one of them is interested in that something. The drawing does not give any direct hint at why the first cow may feel the need to alert the other cows of the presence of the car, but if we look at the two other frames we quickly realize that when the humans are in the picture (quite literally) the cows act like the script COW, and that when the cows are alone, they act in the script HUMAN-ACTING-COW. Here we may apply a general rule: if someone acts in a given way only when in front of someone else he/she is adapting his/her behavior to the person in question (note that this is not a necessary conclusion, it is an abductive, probabilistic step, which may or may not turn out to be correct). Why would then cows that act like humans not act like humans when humans are around? Here again we can jump to the conclusion that they are trying to hide from the humans their behavior.

In conclusion: by a rather complex, and largely abductive process of inference we conclude that the cows are hiding from humans that they can talk and stand: this explains why the cow in the first frame is shouting "car!" and why the cows change their posture in the second frame. Thus we have provided a resolution of the incongruity: the reason we have never seen a cow speaking and standing on its hind legs is because the cows are purposely hiding these feats from us!

What is remarkable about this process of progressive inference making is how closely it resembles and parallels the processing of verbalized jokes. Certainly there are differences, the most significant being that texts are processed with rigid linearity, whereas the processing of a figurative sign is entirely different, and governed by complex rules based in part on the nature of the sign itself. Shapes and masses in a picture will "guide" the scanning of the image by the observer, as well as the expectations of the viewer. Our perception of the stimulus may be altered by the stimulus itself, to take an extreme example. This is the case with the well-known optical illusions of Mueller-Lyer.[12] Furthermore, different semiotic systems vary in terms of analyticity and adeptness at dealing with some types of information. Language is very good at dealing with abstract entities, whereas it handles rather poorly such *Gestalten* as facial expressions, which drawings or pictures can reproduce more easily (it is no coincidence that we talk of a "Gioconda smile"). A puzzled expression can be expressed much more effectively by a few lines in a drawing than by the hopelessly underdetermined phrase "puzzled expression."

However great the differences between the various semiotic systems (we have only considered two, fashion and graphical, but the considerations could be expanded without theoretical problems to other systems, though not to all, see below), there are important parallels: in order to process a humorous text[13] we must perceive the presence of two opposed scripts in the text, and somehow resolve the contrast between the two scripts, even if in playful local logic terms.[14] Naturally, the farther away

---

[12] In this example, two lines of the same length appear to be of different lengths because of other lines which touch them.

[13] Once more, "text" here refers to any cluster of semiotic signs, independently of their nature, and not limited to linguistic signs in any way, as we saw in Chapter 1.

[14] The reader should keep in mind that some humor, such as absurd or nonsense humor, may not have any resolution at all.

from linguistic signs we move, the more strained the extension of the concept of script becomes, without however, losing the specificity of a baggage of information that the speaker carries about something (be it a lexical item, a proxemic perception, or a figurative element).

The considerations above lead us to the formulation of a significant generalization: *all humor in whatever semiotic manifestation is based on a semantic mechanism, i.e., all humor is semantic.*

The semantic hard-core of all humorous facts does not mean that issues at the level of the signifier are irrelevant to a semiotics of humor. In fact the contrary is quite true. Most of the available materials on the semiotics of humor deal with mechanisms of the signifier, although they all are based (implicitly, to be sure) on the assumption of a semantic base for humor. We will turn now to some of these issues, in order to gather further evidence of common humorous mechanisms across semiotic systems.

In fact the concept of "semiotic pun" has been elaborated, and is central to the research of Lessard (1991, and references therein). Lessard shows very convincingly that the same mechanisms that apply to verbal puns apply to visual puns. Thus Lessard analyzes graphical text in which one graphical element is taken to refer to two different things *at the same time* and he correctly analyzes this fact as the graphical analog of the lexical ambiguity pun. Lessard's example is a drawing showing on the top left part a man marooned on a small island with concentric circular waves, which become on the right bottom part of the drawing the furrows in the field of a puzzled looking farmer. If we consider now a linguistic example, the old pun:

(35) Why did the cookie cry?
Its mother had been a wafer so long [a wafer/away for]

based on the equivalence of the two strings 'away for' and 'a wafer' in pronounciation, we can draw the following proportion:

furrows : waves :: a wafer : away for

which shows plainly that the same mechanisms are at stake. As in the linguistic pun we take one string of sounds to stand for another meaning than the one intended in the text at first, in the semiotic pun we take one semiotic element to stand for another meaning than the one intended in the semiotic "text" at first.

If we consider the issue from a linguistic standpoint, we will see that all semantic differences in the system can be exploited for humor. For example, in Chapter 9, we spend some significant effort cataloguing the various levels at which a semantic ambiguity may occur: phonological (puns), morphological, lexical, syntactic, and even pragmatic. This can be stated as another significant generalization: *All meaningful aspects of language may be exploited for humorous purposes.* To put it differently, if it's meaningful, we can use it for humor.[15]

However meaningful and convincing these successes of the cross-semiotic analysis of humor are, they should not give the impression that the task left to researchers is a mere cataloging. In fact, entire semiotic systems elude this kind of taxonomy. Take the example of music, too abstract to have a referent in the sense linguistic signs have a referent, and therefore impossible to account for in terms of scripts, or worse in terms of ambiguity. Yet, we have musical humor, even if it takes particular forms and manifests itself mainly by surprise or allusion (i.e., intertextual reference). Thus the *Andante* movement Haydn's Symphony No. 94 in G Major contains a sudden isolated chord (in the 16th measure) in the middle of a passage where the instruments had been quite soft for the previous six measures. This is then an example of the humorous use of surprise; see Scher (1991: 116) for the relevant score and some comments. Mozart's famous parodic piece *Ein Musikalischer Spass* [K 522] mocks the fashionable music of the time, by quoting and distorting it (an example of humor achieved though parody or allusion).[16]

5.2 Conclusions

This chapter has reached several important conclusions: the mechanisms of humor are the same in linguistic and non-linguistic communication. In all cases, humor is based on an incongruity (violation of expectations) and its resolution (albeit within the limits discussed

---

[15] Incidentally, this is why taxonomic approaches to humor are doomed to failure: because language, due to its creativity, always exceeds any taxonomy.

[16] An interesting passage from Sadie (1965: 118) confirms the claims in the text:

Much of the broad humor of the *Musical Joke* is lost today, except perhaps on musicologists who know what bad eighteenth-century is like or on teachers of composition who know the elementary faults. To the normal music-lover, the joke is likely to misfire.

above). The meaning of the humorous expression is backgrounded, in favor of the connotative semiotic's meaning "this is humor." The normal rules of communication no longer apply within a connotative semiotics; in particular, the signs are defunctionalized, i.e., they are no longer used for communicative purposes. This in turn has the effect of making humor "retractable," i.e., it explains all the pragmatic uses of humor as politeness, as a testing mechanism, and as a way to state something without committing to its truth or functional value. Furthermore, humor contains the meta-message "this is play," which reinforces the defunctionalization and suspension of the normal rules of communication.

5.3 Further readings

There are no introductory treatments of the semiotics of humor. Attardo (1994) remains, despite the years, the best place to get started. On visual puns, Hempelmann and Samson's work (2007, 2008) is accessible. On musical humor, see the entries on music and humor in Attardo (2014). Intersemiotic translation is taken up again in Chapter 15.

Part II
Humor Competence

The second part of the book is dedicated to the theory of humor competence. As we have seen, competence is defined as an abstract set of necessary and sufficient conditions for humor to exist and be potentially perceived as such by an audience. The actualization of the potentiality will be taken up in Part III of the book, dedicated to humor performance. Another way of conceptualizing the differences between what the second and third part of the book contain is to think of it as the theoretical linguistics of humor (Part II) and the applied linguistics (Part III but also Part IV). Yet another, different way of looking at Part II is that, after considering the methodology of humor studies and of linguistics' parent discipline, semiotics, the field of humor studies and the theories of humor studies, finally we get to the linguistics of humor per se. The observant reader will have noticed that I have not considered a semantics vs. pragmatics opposition, despite the fact that some conceptualizations of pragmatics are broad enough to encompass all of Part III of the book. This is because the competence of humor is not only semantic, it is also pragmatic, and indeed Part II includes a chapter on the pragmatics of humor. The chapter consists of the exposition of Raskin's Semantic Script Theory of Humor, of its expansion in the General Theory of Verbal Humor (Attardo and Raskin, 1991), of a chapter on the pragmatics of humor, which expands on work initially also developed by Raskin (1985), and of a chapter on puns, which have a distinct set of issues that are best treated separately.

6

The semantics of humor

6.1	The Semantic Script Theory	113
6.2	The Semantic Script Theory of Humor's two conditions	127
6.3	Non-bona-fide	133
6.4	The Ontological Semantics Theory of Humor	134
6.5	Conclusions	134
6.6	Further readings	135

In a certain sense, seen in Chapter 5, the essence of humor is semantic. Therefore this chapter is quite central, in a way that other chapters are not. This chapter will explain and motivate this claim.

Historically, most of the research on humor in linguistics did not focus on the semantics of humor, but rather primarily on phonology, morphology, and marginally on syntax. This attitude is well represented in Pepicello and Weisberg (1983) which presents a largely non-semantic synthesis of the "linguistics" of humor. Needless to say, other approaches, especially in the incongruity/resolution tradition (see Chapter 4), were much closer to the semantics of humor. For example Koestler's theory, discussed in Section 3.7.2.

6.1 The Semantic Script Theory

The Semantic-Script Theory of Humor is widely recognized to have been one of the most successful theories of humor, since its introduction. Consider the begrudging acknowledgments of some of its *critics*: "The General Theory of Verbal Humor (GTVH) has dominated the

The Linguistics of Humor: An Introduction. Salvatore Attardo, Oxford University Press (2020). © Salvatore Attardo.
DOI: 10.1093/oso/9780198791270.001.0001

discussion of humor theory for more than thirty years" (Oring, 2018); "Raskin's Semantic Mechanism of Humor (1985), which develops a General Theory of Verbal Humor (GTVH), has been the most influential work in humor research in its recent history" (Rutter, 1997, p. 21); the "two most influential linguistic humor theories of the last two decades, the Semantic Script Theory of Humor and the [General Theory of Verbal Humor]" (Brône et al., 2006, p. 203); "the most influential approach to humor at present is that represented by the semantic theories of Victor Raskin (1985)" (Smith, 2009, pp. 10–11).[1]

This is not the place to investigate the reasons for it success, which would require a study in the sociology of science, and since the 1985 book in which Raskin presents it in detail[2] is quite accessible, we will content ourselves with restating the two conditions that must obtain for a text to be humorous and then focus primarily on the discussion of various issues that are often overlooked and misunderstandings of the theory.

The Semantic Script Theory of Humor's stated goal is to provide the necessary and sufficient conditions for a text to be humorous. This makes the theory essentialist. The Semantic Script Theory of Humor is reductionist as well, as we will see below.

6.1.1 Origins

As its name makes patently clear, the Semantic Script Theory of Humor is based on semantic scripts. The script-based approach to semantics originated in psychology, with Bartlett's views on memory (1932) and the Gestalt psychologists (cf. Anderson & Pearson 1984). It was later taken up in Artificial Intelligence (AI) (Minsky, 1974; Schank, 1975; Schank & Abelson, 1977), and eventually arrived into linguistics (Chafe, 1975; Raskin, 1981, 1985; Fillmore, 1982, 1985). Within linguistics some connections between frame/script semantics and other areas of linguistics emerge forcefully: field semantics, a.k.a. lexical field semantics (going back to Trier's work in 1931; Lehrer, 1974; Lehrer & Kittay, 1992) has some interesting correlations with frame/script semantics, as does case grammar (unsurprisingly, since Fillmore was largely responsible for

---

[1] With enemies likes these, who needs friends?
[2] For the historically minded, the Semantic Script Theory of Humor was first presented in 1979 in a Berkeley Linguistics Society paper and in 1986 in a *Psychology Today* article, which contributed significantly to its popularity.

it as well), and of course the psychological work on prototype theory (Rosch & Mervis, 1975) which will later be one of the principal sources of the cognitive linguistics approach.

An important point that bears being made explicitly is that because of their foundations in psychology, script/frame theories have an important stake in psychological reality. This is not the place for a review of the literature on the psycholinguistics of text processing and reading which makes heavy use of script/frame theories. Such a review would require a separate monograph. However, let us note, for example, that Rumelhart's influential (1980) model comprises the simultaneous processing of semantic, syntactic and pragmatic information, as does Just and Carpenter's (1980). In Attardo (2001a) I also noted the parallels and mutual support of current psycholinguistic theories of text processing (e.g., Kintsch 1998). Both major approaches to script/frame semantics evolved in a formal/computational direction: script-based semantics (Raskin, 1985) eventually led to ontological semantics (Nirenburg & Raskin, 2004); frame semantics evolved into FrameNet (Ruppenhofer et al., 2016).

This diversity of disciplinary sources is reflected in the wide terminological variety (frames, scripts, schemata, scenes, memory organization packets (MOP), etc.) used in the field. The reaction has been to generalize and standardize around a single term (Fillmore's (1985) "frame," Raskin's (1981) "script"), leaving open the possibility of further differentiation. The terminological discussion can be found in Andor (1985: 212–213) and Fillmore (1985: 223n).[3] By and large, frame semantics has been the more successful term in semantics and the study of reading, whereas script semantics has been the default term in humor research. The two terms, as defined by Fillmore and Raskin, are synonymous.

In the context of humor research we will primarily deal with the script-based semantics of Raskin, because, as we mentioned, it was the most successful semantic model in the linguistics of humor, and it is the most developed and the broadest of all the linguistic approaches.

---

[3] A very common misunderstanding is that there is a difference between, say, a script and a frame: since both Fillmore and Raskin argue for the use of the respective term as an umbrella term, by definition, the two are synonymous. Special terminological conventions may be adopted by individual scholars, but they do not apply to Fillmore and/or Raskin.

6.1.2 The notion of script

A script is defined as a related, organized cluster of nodes and their connections in the semantic network[4] that represents the global web of knowledge of the speakers of a language. Raskin's exact words are "a limited domain of the continuous semantic graph" (1985, p. 84); elsewhere he describes it as "a large chunk of semantic information surrounding the word or evoked by it" (p. 81) and, technically, as the domain in the semantic graph "around the word in question as the central node of the domain" (p. 81).

All the scripts of a language are connected to one another and form a "a single continuous graph" (p. 81) which represents the sum total of knowledge of the speakers of a language. A good way to conceptualize this is to imagine the Oxford English Dictionary as a graph, with each word linked to the words that make up the definition and each word in the definition linked up to the words that make up their definition, and so on. To use a different metaphor, in the age of the internet, each script can be considered the equivalent of a web page. Each web page is connected to other web pages (albeit haphazardly, whereas in the semantic graph the connections are systematic and meaningful). The organization of knowledge as a semantic network was prefigured by Peirce (1931–36; see Eco, 1979, pp. 26–49) and introduced into AI by Quillian (1967). The endless nature of the semiotic relation (whereby a sign's meaning is represented within the network by other signs, ad infinitum) has been dubbed "unlimited semiosis" (Eco, 1979, pp. 44–46) or "infinite semiosis" (Atkin, 2013).

Despite the technical terminology it should not escape our attention that scripts are, setting aside the technical definitions, essentially ideas, thoughts, or meanings. There has been a certain tendency to reify the concept, as if it did have an objective nature, external to the minds of those who think the thoughts. However, this is not the case. Meanings exist as parts of signs; the other side of signs is of course the signifiers. A sign is a social fact for Saussure, following Durkheim. Hence, even if indirectly, the meanings (signifieds) exist in the minds of the speakers who constitute the social group that legitimizes the social fact. So, in conclusion, scripts are concepts, ideas, thoughts. These exist because there is a social group that thinks the same thoughts (i.e., they are social

---

[4] The technical mathematical term for this is "graph."

facts), as can be evinced by the fact that they function as a social group: if they did not share the same thoughts they could not function as a group (cf. Davidson, 1984, p. 153).

6.1.2.1 Analysis of the definition

Let us consider in more detail each of the elements of the definition of script above. Needless to say, this is a very quick, informal review. Each of the topics that we will take up below could be developed much more, but this is only an introductory treatment. The interested reader should consult Raskin (1985) and references therein. Occasionally, I elaborate on a concept beyond Raskin's original definition. For those, see Attardo (2020).

6.1.2.1.1 Nodes Each node corresponds to a concept that has been lexicalized in a given language. In other words, we are considering in this definition only lexical scripts.[5] There are larger scripts which can represent sentences, paragraphs, and even larger texts; those will be discussed below. Furthermore, scripts can be activated without a lexematic handle, i.e., inferentially. We discuss this in Section 6.1.3.1, below.

6.1.2.1.2 Connections Links among nodes correspond to the kind of connections found among lexemes such as

1. synonymy, antonymy
2. hyponymy (ISA hierarchies, see below), hyperonymy (superordinate)
3. partonomy/partonymy (a.k.a. meronymy), i.e., the parts of an object
4. homophony, homography, homonymy
5. lexical functions (Mel'čuk, 1981).

Lexical functions may not be familiar to the beginning reader, so we will exemplify. A lexical function is a systematic relationship between two sets of lexical items. For example, the function "magn" indicates a

---

[5] Grammaticalized concepts can also be seen as scripts, albeit more abstract ones. Whereas lexical scripts have 'handles' (so to speak), i.e., are associated to and directly activable by a lexeme, grammatical scripts would be activated by any of the allomorphs of the given grammatical morpheme. Lexical scripts rarely have allomorphs, hence they are more concrete than grammatical scripts.

great degree of intensity. So the following pairs of words are connected by the lexical function "magn."

(36) speak // shout
      eat // devour
      punch // pummell

Hence, "shout" is a high degree of intensity "speak," etc. The function "son" indicates the typical sound produced by an entity, so again, the following pairs of words are connected by the lexical function "son":

(37) leaves // rustle
      dog // bark
      thunder // rumble

In other words, the typical sound of leaves is rustling, dogs bark, and thunder rumbles. Many lexical functions are quite similar to better known lexical relations, such as antonymy and synonymy, but the breadth of Mel'čuk's functions, which catalog over 50 relationships, make them an important part of semantic description.[6]

6.1.2.1.3 Semantic network The sum total of the connections among nodes is the semantic network that represents the sum of the semantic knowledge of the speakers of a given language. The semantic network can be traversed in infinite ways, while being itself finite. The reader will recall the concept of infinite/unlimited semiosis introduced above. One can visualize traversing all the links connected to a given node as gathering the meaning of that node (i.e., its connections to other meanings).

For example, in Figure 6.1 we see a few of the adjacent nodes (FELINE, TAIL, etc.) to the script CAT, with two examples of "immediate neighbor" nodes in the graph in a hierarchical organization: the hyponyms, labeled as is customary as the ISA relationship (see below), and the partonyms (has-parts). The unlabeled link (MOUSE) is a script that is probably highly associated with CAT (as in "cat and mouse") without being in a specific relation to it. The immediate neighbor nodes will become important when we consider spreading activation, below. Needless to say, the above is a purely pedagogical presentation and should not be misconstrued as a full description of the semantics of CAT.

---

[6] See Raskin (1985, p. 84) for a methodological difference between Mel'čuk's (1981) functions and Raskin's links.

6.1 THE SEMANTIC SCRIPT THEORY

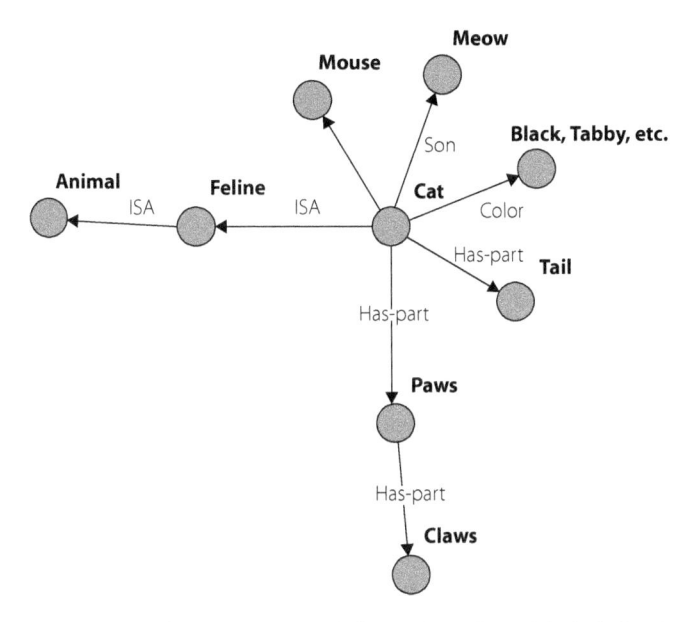

Figure 6.1 A very simplified semantic graph for CAT; the links are labeled after the semantic connection.

6.1.2.1.4 Related nodes The nodes are not a set of nodes selected randomly. There needs to be a relationship between them. Each link defines the specifics of the relationship. In mathematical terms, this makes them "labeled" links. Technically they are directed labeled nodes, i.e., there is a direction in which they must be traversed. So, for example, the ISA link, one of the most common relationships in a semantic network and in ontologies (see below), which corresponds to the hyponymy linguistic relationship must be traversed from the hyperonym to the hyponym (for example, from "fruit" to "apple") and not the other way around. So APPLE (ISA FRUIT) would be a basic semantic bit of information. In artificial intelligence and frame semantics it is very common to use a slot-filler notation, as I just did above. Essentially information is represented as a pair, in which the first part indicates the kind of information (slot) and the second indicates the specific information (filler). So, the ISA slot could be filled with FLUFFY (ISA DOG) or BOB (ISA HUMAN) or CAR (ISA VEHICLE). ISA of course stands for "is a" (a car is a kind of vehicle). Other slots are created as needed. Standard ones are location, time, has-parts, color, size, etc.

6.1.2.1.5 Organized cluster It should be noted that the definition that I am employing here is slightly different from the canonical ones, which

```
Subject:  [+Human]   [+Adult]
Activity: > Study medicine
     = Receive patients: patient comes or doctor visits
                         doctor listens to complaints
                         doctor examines patient
     = Cure disease: doctor diagnoses disease
                     doctor prescribes treatment
     = (Take patient's money)
Place:   > Medical School
         = Hospital or doctor's office
Time:    > Many years
         = Every day
         = Immediately
Condition: Physical contact
```

Figure 6.2 The lexical script for DOCTOR in Raskin, 1985. Note that ">" stands for "in the past," and " = " for "in the present."

do not as a rule emphasize the connections among scripts as part of a given script. However, careful consideration will reveal that each filler of a given slot (and for that matter, each slot) is itself another node. Therefore, a script is properly merely a special section of the global network. Furthermore, the cluster is organized in the sense that there exist specific relations between the nodes and that (sub)scripts may occur as parts of scripts (i.e., as nodes).

Figure 6.2 is an example of script, in the original notation used in Raskin (1985, p. 85). The notational conventions are different than those used in this book and in later versions of the theory, which are influenced by LISP[7] pseudocode. No particular meaning should be attributed to the notation.

6.1.2.2 Fractal nature of scripts

Raskin (1985) introduced the notions of complex script and macro-script, which matched similar distinctions in the field: for example, frames may have sub-frames (Petruck, 1996; Mandler, 1984, p. 15)

In Raskin's definition, the difference between scripts, complex scripts, and macro-scripts is primarily one of level: a script is the simplex form; a macro-script is a group of scripts organized chronologically, what some authors would call a script, as opposed to a frame or schema; a complex script is a script made of other scripts but without chronological

---

[7] LISP (LISt Processor) is a computer language, originally invented in 1958, which became popular in artificial intelligence. The first formalizations of Raskin's scripts were written in LISP, around 1989–1990.

6.1 THE SEMANTIC SCRIPT THEORY

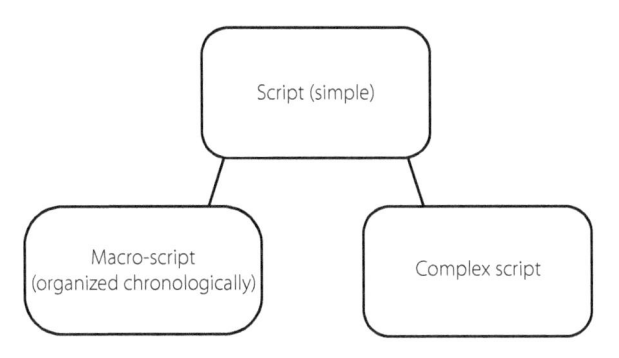

Figure 6.3 Simple, macro-, and complex scripts.

organization. The classification of scripts is presented graphically in Figure 6.3.

The RESTAURANT script in Schank and Abelson (1977) would be an example of macro-script: it consists of several other scripts linked chronologically (DRIVE UP TO THE RESTAURANT, BE SEATED, ORDER FOOD, etc.), while a complex script would be WAR, which presupposes other scripts such as ARMY, ENEMY, VICTORY, DEFEAT, WEAPON, etc. Needless to say, no hard distinctions between complex and macro-scripts are tenable: even a complex script as WAR has some chronological organization: imagine a war that started with an armistice, whereas the RESTAURANT script has many events that may occur in no particular order (for example, go to the restroom, chat with the other dinner guests) or are only loosely organized (for example, asking for the check must occur toward the end of the meal, but need not occur at the absolute end of the meal—it is perfectly acceptable to ask for the check and for coffee). Chłopicki's character frames are complex scripts, whereas the representation of the development of the story in the text as a vector (text-world representation; Attardo, 2001a) is a macro-script; see Chapter 14. The organization of scripts in a nesting hierarchy of larger units is a common assumption, cf. Mandler (1984, p. 15) and references therein.

We can further generalize the notion of complex script, by noting that the filler of any slot in a script may be another script (most often a link via the lexical handle of the script). Another way of putting it is saying that scripts are fractal. In a script, you will find the same kind of constructs, regardless of the level of generality. The geometrical figures known as fractals are generated by recursion (much like embedded structures in sentences can be recursive in language, so that, one can have a NP inside a NP, ad infinitum, for example). Many fractals, but not all, also have the feature of being "self-similar," i.e., invariant at scale (Mandelbrot, 1977, p. 18), or to put it more simply, they have the same shape at different levels of magnification: if you zoom in on a detail of a fractal, you will find the same shapes. In Attardo (2001a, p. 48), I spoke of scripts "nested into one another." The present formulation is more precise. Note that the fractal recursive nature of scripts is consonant with the primeless nature of the semantic network described by Raskin and can be usefully connected to Peirce's and Eco's concept of "unlimited semiosis." While scripts may be more or less abstract, they are equally complex as they all consist of links to other scripts.

6.1.2.3 Operational definition of scripts

In Attardo (2001a, p. 6), I described the procedure of building a script as an hypothesis on the semantic content of a given lexeme[8] which is disproved if we encounter a bit of information not included in the script. If we encounter a bit of information currently not in the script, the script is revised and the revised version then takes the place of the original hypothesis, only to be further tested by new texts. If the script is viable, after a few revisions it will become stable, i.e., few if any changes will be required. Consider a reader who encounter for the first time the term "crypto-currency." Let us assume, for the sake of simplicity, that the first encounter is in an opaque context, such as "Mary worked as a crypto-currency expert" which only tells us that "crypto-currency" is a subject one can become an expert of and that this makes you employable. Our frame or script for CRYPTO-CURRENCY is pretty sparse, looking more or less like this:

```
(crypto-currency
    (ISA currency)
    (object-of BE EXPERT))
```

Note that the (ISA currency) is a guess based on the assumption of non-arbitrary morphology. If it were to turn out that crypto-currency is a kind of cake, our guess would have been wrong.

Suppose now that the we encounter the information that crypto-currency is transacted online. This would confirm the (ISA currency) guess and would add the information that CRYPTO-CURRENCY con-

---

[8] The same applies to those scripts that lack a lexematic handle, see below.

tains an (object-of FINANCIAL TRANSACTION) slot, with a sub-slot (location currency-exchange).

```
(crypto-currency
     (ISA currency)
     (object-of BE EXPERT)
     (object-of ((FINANCIAL-TRANSACTION
                         (location exchange))))
```

A more sophisticated bit of information might be added if a detailed explanation of how crypto-currencies are based on solving complex cryptographic problems, using computers. Further information might appear, such as the fact that one of the currency-exchanges in which crypto-currencies are bought and sold is called *Coinbase*, which would then be added to the frame, making it more detailed and complex. Again, further information, when available, would be added to the frame, until no further information appears. At this point, one's CRYPTO-CURRENCY frame would be "complete" (at least, this writer's is).

However, as we know from Popperian epistemology, this does not *prove* that the script is complete, but it is merely the best available construct that matches the available evidence. While this may seem to be problematic, since it is tantamount to claiming that scripts are open-ended, in fact it is evidence of the falsifiability of the definition.

Essentially, one can never know that a given script is complete, since the next sentence one processes may include a new bit of information that was previously unavailable to the system. It is simple to imagine a dynamic system which updates its knowledge banks whenever it encounters a bit of information it was not aware of (and which is consistent with its prior knowledge). This is, in fact, what humans do: faced with a new bit of information they revise their scripts. An interesting aspect of this process is that when faced with conflicting information (say, two incompatible fillers for one slot) humans tend to react with cognitive dissonance (see Section 2.4) and this they resolve it by either compartmentalizing the information or by eliminating some of the information.

6.1.3 Dynamic scripts

The idea of building up scripts as we accumulate information and of updating the scripts as information changes, prefigures the dynamic view of scripts I introduced in Attardo (2001a). In a nutshell, I was interested in how readers build up a representation of the text they are reading,[9] which preserves the plot (in a non-technical sense), information about the characters, and other aspects of the setting, without necessarily preserving the surface structure of the text (the lexical choices, for example). To do so, I introduced the idea of a "storage area" which stores the most current and up-to-date information on the story, in a macro-script built around sentences and paragraphs. This corresponds to a dynamic view of scripts, see for example the following definition:

> schemas came to be thought of, not as fixed structures to be pulled from memory on demand, but as recipes for generating organizational structures in a particular task context. (Kintsch, 1998, p. 37)

The reader would activate a storage area (which I called the text world representation) as an empty sentential script, which will be filled by the lexical and inferential scripts (see Section 6.1.3.1) activated by the text:

> the model of text processing that I am outlining, consists in activating sequentially scripts, until the main script of a text is determined, and then the entire text is interpreted as an instance of that script, filled with the actual details of the text instantiating the script. (Attardo, 2001a, pp. 56–57)

In Attardo (2001a) I also review the considerable evidence for the psychological reality of this approach, e.g., Kintsch (1998).

6.1.3.1 Implicit activation

We now turn to the activation of scripts without a lexical handle. Consider the following example

(38) "I drove to Dallas"

The utterance of sentence (38) activates a number of scripts, beyond those activated by the lexical handles "I," "drive," "to," and "Dallas." In Attardo (2001a) I spoke of inferentially activated scripts. I would now like to distinguish more specifically between presuppositionally activated scripts, inferentially activated scripts, and scripts activated by implicatures. Consider that "drive" activates the script for "car" or, rather, less specifically "vehicle" (I could have driven to Dallas in my truck, for

---

[9] Needless to say, this applies also to people hearing a story, watching a movie, etc.

example). This is a necessary inference from (38): if I drove to Dallas it follows necessarily that I did so using some vehicle. Note also that if I utter (39)

(39) "I did not drive to Dallas"

it also follows that I did not do so using some kind of vehicle (so I could have walked to Dallas, or ridden a bus to Dallas). The resistance to negation is a clear indication that the inference that I went to Dallas (regardless of mode of transportation) is a presupposition.

Now, (38) also activates personal scripts for SHOPPING (I occasionally go to Dallas to shop) or SYMPHONY (I occasionally go to the symphony at the Meyerson Symphony Center). So, upon hearing (38) my friends could reasonably say

(40) "Oh, what was playing at the Meyerson?"

or

(41) "Went shopping, eh?"

The fact that these inferences are entirely probabilistic (I could have gone to Dallas for another reason than shopping or going to the symphony) and would not resist negation (either (40) or (41) would be absurd following (39)) tells us that these are inferences, and more specifically, implicatures. Along the same lines, we could have inferences that activate scripts (they follow necessarily from the utterance, but do not resist the negation test). For example,

(42) I drove to Dallas with my wife.

would dis-activate the BACHELOR script (assuming it had been active, of course).

The conclusion then is that "inferential activation" as I used it in 2001a, is a generic term that covers all three kinds of inferences: presuppositions, inferences, and implicatures. All three can activate a script. Since all three are implicit forms of information, I speak of implicit activation of scripts.

There is another way to activate a script, by "spreading activation." Spreading activation is a term from cognitive-psychology: when a node is activated, its immediate neighbors are also activated, but at a much lower level. The neighbors of the latter nodes are also activated, but at at an even lower level, and so on, until the activation falls below the threshold of activation.

Consider now a situation in which a set of adjacent nodes (because they are all related to a given concept) is activated, while the node they all are related to is not directly activated. Despite not having been explicitly activated (by being mentioned in the text), the node that is related to the others will receive enough spreading activation to become activated as well. Petruck (1996, p. 3) has a good example:

consider the sentence *Julia will open her presents after blowing out the candles and eating some cake*. Although there is no mention of a birthday party, interpreters sharing the requisite cultural background invoke a birthday party scene.

While BIRTHDAY PARTY has not been lexically activated by being mentioned in the text, it becomes activated by spreading activation because enough activation "spills over" from the lexically activated scripts for PRESENT, CAKE, BLOW OUT CANDLES to activate the script for BIRTHDAY PARTY, at least within a culture that celebrates birthdays with cakes with candles, etc.

6.1.4 Combinatorial explosion

As we have seen, scripts can be activated lexically, by spreading activation, and inferentially. It is not clear whether there is a distinction between the last two modalities of activation. How is the sentence meaning arrived at? Plainly by combining all the lexical and implicit activation into a macro-script. This immediately presents a problem, described in Attardo (2001a) as a combinatorial explosion. Indeed, if one considers all the possible meanings of all the scripts activated in a text, the combinations among them reach the hundreds of thousands even for relatively short texts.

The combinatorial proliferation is kept in check by disambiguation, which eliminates most alternative meanings as incompatible with the script being activated but also by strictly pragmatic factors such as relevance and appropriateness. This explains why the storage area does not run out of space.

The combination of the various meanings is technically called "unification." Unification is an "information-combining operation" (Shieber, 2003, p. 9). For example, the words "she" and "loves" both have

6.2 THE SEMANTIC SCRIPT THEORY OF HUMOR'S TWO CONDITIONS

Table 6.1 Combinatorics for two scripts

	unmarried	academic title	knight	seal
disease	paralyzed unmarried	paralyzed BA	paralyzed knight	paralyzed seal
moral	indecisive unmarried	indecisive BA	indecisive knight	indecisive seal

the features [3rd person] and [singular] (*she* [3rd person], [singular]; *loves* [3rd person], [singular]) and thus they can be unified, yielding *she loves* [3rd person], [singular]). In its most abstract notation, unification can be represented as aa = a.

What this all boils down to is that if one of the possible meanings of the script is incompatible with another, their unification fails (i.e., they are not combined) and another meaning is tried. Raskin represents this as a matrix of combinations among the numbered senses of the scripts (1985, p. 86). For example, "paralyzed" has a DISEASE meaning and a MORAL meaning (as in unable to act); "bachelor" is famously analyzed by Katz and Fodor as 4-way ambiguous: 1 MARRIAGE (as in un-married); 2 ACADEMIC TITLE (as in bachelor of art); 3 KNIGHT, and 4 SEAL (without a mate). This yields potentially 8 combinations listed in Table 6.1 above. Contextual pressure would then select among these combinations to reduce the acceptable meanings to one (ideally) or a few more.

We have now reviewed all the technical information about script-based semantics necessary to understand the original formulation of the script-based semantic theory of humor, to which we turn next.

6.2 The Semantic Script Theory of Humor's two conditions

Let us repeat here Raskin's formulation of the Semantic Script Theory of Humor's central hypothesis:

(43) A text can be characterized as a single-joke-carrying-text if both of the [following] conditions are satisfied:
   i) The text is compatible, fully or in part, with two different scripts.
   ii) The two scripts with which the text is compatible are opposite (. . .). The two scripts with which some text is compatible are said to overlap fully or in part in this text (Raskin, 1985, p. 99).

6.2.1 Oppositeness

The concept of oppositeness was examined in some detail in Attardo (1997). The following is the operational definition I proposed as the synthesis of previous research:

> It should be clear from the highlighted sections that incongruity is essentially defined as divergence from expectations, in a way consistent with its ordinary meaning indicating the opposite of "the quality or state of agreeing, coinciding, or being congruent" (Merriam-Webster). (Attardo, 1997, p. 398)

Raskin's definition of opposition is as follows:

> [the opposed scripts are] local antonyms, i.e., two linguistic entities whose meanings are opposite only within a particular discourse and solely for the purpose of this discourse.
> (1985, p. 108)

As I noted in Attardo (1997), Lyons' definition of antonymy is of no use here, despite being quoted by Raskin, because Raskin is rejecting that definition. I proceeded to provide a definition of local antonymy, that borrows from Lyons, but that avoids Raskin's criticism:

> the locality requirement of the Semantic Script Theory of Humor is to be interpreted as constructing a context in which being a doctor is the opposite of (i.e., is *not*) being a lover.

while the antonymy is to be interpreted simply as the logical negation of the script (i.e., any other script).[10] Tinholt (2007, p. 50) further refines the definition proposing that

> two words are antonyms when they have all characteristics in common, except for one

where characteristics are defined as nodes and links. Essentially, antonymic scripts would differ in one node and/or link, whereas the rest of the activated nodes and links would overlap.

6.2.2 Overlapping

The definition of "overlapping" is simpler: two scripts are said to be overlapping in a text if the text overall is, or parts of it are compatible with

---

[10] In Attardo (1997), I also carry out an attempt at redefining opposition in terms of accessibility and informativeness. This is not the place to discuss that hypothesis.

6.2 THE SEMANTIC SCRIPT THEORY OF HUMOR'S TWO CONDITIONS

both scripts. Thus, putting on one's cowboy boots, hat, and bandanna, are compatible both with the scripts BRONCO BUSTING *and* HONKY-TONK DANCING. In Raskin's infamous doctor's wife joke (44), the knocking on the door of the patient, the breathy voice, and the inquiry as to whether the doctor is home are compatible both with the script for PATIENT VISITING THE DOCTOR and MAN VISITING HIS LOVER.

6.2.3 The exemplar doctor's wife joke

As mentioned in Chapter 1, the doctor's wife joke, analyzed by Raskin (1985, pp. 117–127) has become an exemplar text for the linguistics of humor. It should be emphasized that Raskin chose the joke not because it is a good joke, as in aesthetically pleasing or interesting, but on the contrary, because it is a simple, clear joke, with a single opposition, and no special complications. Below is the text:

(44) "Is the doctor at home?" the patient asked in his bronchial whisper. "No," the doctor's young and pretty wife whispered in reply. "Come right in."

The exposition of the analysis is going to be non-technical, as a full blown analysis would require extensive discussion, mostly repetitive in nature (see Raskin, 1985, pp. 117–127; Attardo, 2001a, pp. 10–16, for examples).

The reader will activate the lexical scripts for DOCTOR, PATIENT and BRONCHI, even assuming that the latter script is minimal and includes only vague information such as links with MEDICAL and possibly LUNGS. Inferentially, the script for MEDICAL VISIT is activated. Here the joke shows its age as today doctors rarely if ever receive patients at home. However, one will probably be familiar (i.e., have as part of their script for DOCTOR) with the fact that in the past, they used to have their office in a room of their home, at least in smaller villages.[11] So far, so good. We have activated a macro-script DOCTOR VISIT in which the patient is the man asking if the doctor is at home. His whispering is compatible with the script, as respiratory track illnesses often affect breathing and speaking patterns, for example by making speaking painful.

However, the second sentence complicates things: first, the speaker is the doctor's wife, who informs the man that the doctor is not home.

---

[11] I can attest visiting my childhood doctor in his office at his home.

From the script for DOCTOR we know that physical presence is a prerequisite for a visit[12] and hence the reader can extrapolate that the man's purpose having been defeated he will leave (perhaps to return later, when the doctor will be home). Second, the text informs the reader that the wife is young and pretty. This information is irrelevant to the man's goal of seeing the doctor, thus it is odd with what has been presented. Third, the wife is also whispering. It is possible that the wife is also ill: maybe an epidemic of respiratory illnesses has struck the village. However, this is again an odd bit of information, which a well-behaved text would topicalize. Fourth, the wife invites the man to enter the house. This last detail, which is incompatible with the first script entirely, forces the reader to stop trying to patch up the first hypothesis and to try to come up with a different hypothesis. Here, the wife's youth and beauty become potentially relevant (as presumably, young people have more sex than older people), but the whispering is compatible with a SECRECY script (people who want to keep something secret often whisper it rather that speaking in a full voice for fear of being overheard), and the invitation to come in the absence of the doctor/husband is compatible with an ADULTERY script (one tends to commit adultery when one's spouse is not present, as spouses tend to react negatively to their partner's adultery).[13] So, if we reinterpret the text as a secret (hence the whispering) meeting between lovers in the absence of the husband, the second part of the text makes sense and the behavior of the wife is explained.

Thus the text is compatible in part with two scripts: DOCTOR and LOVER (Raskin, 1985, p. 117) or to be more precise MEDICAL VISIT and ADULTERY. Note that the overlap is not full: in the first sentence the man is described as a "patient" thus negating the ADULTERY script. Clearly a different wording of the text could have produced a fully overlapping text. The two scripts are opposed, for the purposes of the text: either the man is there to see the doctor or he is there to see his wife.[14] Hence the Semantic Script Theory of Humor concludes that the

---

[12] Again, the quaintness of the text is apparent, as in today's age, telemedicine would fix that problem.

[13] There exist sexual perversions in which spouses actively encourage adultery. If this were the case, the text would have focalized this detail. Since it did not we can safely assume that the doctor would be upset if he found out his wife is sleeping with a patient.

[14] I guess it is possible that the lover of the doctor's wife is ill that day and goes to the doctor opportunistically thinking that he either will get cured or will have sex with the wife. However, we are now writing another story.

text in question has all the necessary and sufficient characteristics to be potentially humorous.

6.2.4 Methodological issues

The Semantic Script Theory of Humor is essentialist, that is it provides the necessary and sufficient conditions for a text to be humorous, and reductivist, i.e., it reduces its object of study to simpler, better known phenomena. Specifically, it reduces humor to three simpler concepts: scripts and the overlap and opposition thereof. As we saw, it is also an essentialist theory, since it provides us with the necessary and sufficient conditions for a text to be funny, potentially. This brings about the next topic: the Semantic Script Theory of Humor is a theory of humor competence.

6.2.4.1 The Semantic Script Theory of Humor is a theory of humor competence

Probably the biggest misunderstanding about the Semantic Script Theory of Humor is that it is a theory of humor competence, not of humor performance. As such it has nothing to say about whether a given text is perceived as humorous (performance). So to be precise, we should state the goal of the theory as presenting the necessary and sufficient conditions for a text to be potentially perceived as humorous. Whether this is *actually* humorous to a given audience, etc. is the subject of the third part of the volume.

6.2.4.2 The Semantic Script Theory of Humor is a theory of jokes

This too has been seriously misunderstood. The Semantic Script Theory of Humor is elaborated on the basis of a corpus of jokes for a simple and very effective methodological reason: jokes are simpler forms of humor, in the sense that they tend to be limited to one source of humor at a time. Other texts are hyperdetermined (Attardo, 1994), i.e., have multiple concurrent sources of humor. When elaborating a theory one should start from the simpler cases and then build up the theory to account also for the more complex cases. Indeed, pre-theoretically, one would not even know how to isolate the various sources of humor from a hyperdetermined text.

6.2.4.3 Relational nature of the Semantic Script Theory of Humor

Let us focus our attention on the fact that this semantic definition of humor has in fact very little to say about the "content" of humor. Raskin (1985, pp. 111–114; 126–127) has some more specific considerations, but they are contingent, and in fact extraneous to the theory itself (Raskin, p.c.). Let us consider an example: Raskin (1985, p. 127) lists the following basic oppositions on which all the numerous jokes analyzed in his book are based:

good / bad
life / death
sex / no sex
money / no money
high status / low status[15]

While indeed the list has a very broad coverage we note that the oppositions

excrement / non-excrement
physical handicap / non-physical handicap

are missing although a large segment of humor is based precisely on those. It should be emphasized again that this is not an inadequacy of the semantic theory of humor, but merely an indication of breadth of coverage of the corpus used to develop it. While the readers may be quite familiar with excretory jokes, jokes on physical handicaps are an absolute social taboo in our society today. Yet, during a period ranging from the Middle Ages to the Renaissance court jesters were often persons afflicted by some physical handicap.

Moreover, different cultures may have different sets of scripts available for humor. In the Middle Ages, people affected by dwarfism and by other deformities (hunchbacks) were considered perfectly acceptable targets for pranks and humor. In fact, they sometimes became jesters. Today, laughing at someone's physical deformity is considered beyond the pale, at least in polite society. Likewise, blackface minstrel shows are now considered offensive, but between 1850 and 1950 they were quite popular and taken to be funny in the US. Another example, about mocking a blind man, considered humorous in an African culture, is analyzed in Section 13.1. Phallophoric processions were common in

---

[15] I am slightly altering the wording of the oppositions for clarity.

ancient Greece and still are in contemporary Japan, but are unheard of in contemporary Western society. One could multiply the examples.

While the historical and cultural changes of what counts as appropriate for humorous exchanges are a fascinating subject of inquiry, the entire issue is irrelevant from the point of view of the semantics of humor: what matters is that all humor can be accounted for in terms of overlapping and opposed scripts, regardless of the fact that a given society, group or individual will or will not consider a given combination of scripts a fitting subject for humor. In other words, the semantic theory of humor is a relational or functional description of humor, in which what matters are the interrelations of the various scripts, and not their substance (i.e., what specific scripts are involved).

6.3 Non-bona-fide

The Semantic Script Theory of Humor has another facet, seldom discussed in conjunction with the overlap and opposition hypothesis discussed above, namely that humor is a non-bona-fide mode of communication. Non-bona-fide is defined as an utterance that does not follow Grice's principle of cooperation (Raskin, 1985, p. 100); bona-fide (Latin: "in good faith") communication are utterances that follow the principle of cooperation. We discuss in full the violation of Grice's principle of cooperation and its maxims in Chapter 8, so a discussion of this aspect of Raskin's theory will be found there.

Here we must however address another common misconception, namely the idea that the Semantic Script Theory of Humor does not include a pragmatic component. While one must admit that the name of the theory may be misleading in that respect[16] even a superficial reading of Raskin's text immediately reveals that the Semantic Script Theory of Humor contains a significant pragmatic component at two levels:

1. script-based semantics incorporates a lot of what has been called encyclopedic information (world knowledge), as opposed to lexical information (word meaning); encyclopedic information lies on the pragmatic end of the semantics-pragmatics continuum.

---

[16] After all it is called the Semantic Script Theory of Humor, not the Pragmatic and Semantic Script Theory of Humor.

For example, the differences between "spinster" and "bachelorette" are exclusively encyclopedic, because their lexical meaning ([+human][+/−female][+adult][−married]) is identical.

2. the theory directly addresses the non-bona-fide nature of humor, going so far as to propose (admittedly, tongue-in-cheek) a set of maxims for non-bona-fide communication joke telling.

It is Raskin's contention that semantics cannot fruitfully be separated from pragmatics. One cannot do semantics properly without pragmatics. Pragmatics is part of semantics, in other words. So, in conclusion, the Semantic Script Theory of Humor is in fact a Semantic Script and Pragmatic Theory of Humor in fact if not in name.

6.4 The Ontological Semantics Theory of Humor

Script-based semantics, much like frame-based semantics, has evolved in a computational direction: having started out as semantic/pragmatic theories of meaning, both theories have been implemented in computational applications. Raskin's script-based semantics work was one of the foundations of ontological semantics (Nirenburg & Raskin, 2004) which was later a major influence on the work on ontologies that swept computational linguistics and computer science at large and is at the base of the semantic web and related initiatives (see for example Huang et al., 2010; Poli et al., 2010).

Raskin, Taylor and Hempelmann have developed the Ontological Semantic Theory of Humor, a fully computational theory of humor, which embodies the Semantic Script Theory of Humor principles in a fully computational development. For a discussion, see Raskin (2017b). Because in order to understand properly the position of the Ontological Semantic Theory of Humor vis-à-vis other approaches to computational humor would require an understanding of the non-semantic (or marginally semantic) other approaches, we will not undertake this task in this context.

6.5 Conclusions

This chapter reviewed briefly the Semantic Script Theory of Humor, which is the favored semantic theory of humor competence. The theory consists of a central hypothesis, which provides the necessary and sufficient conditions for a text to be potentially humorous: the text must be compatible with two scripts (overlap) and the two scripts must be opposed, in a technical sense (opposition). Pragmatically, the Semantic Script Theory of Humor maintains that humor is a non-bona-fide mode of communication, i.e., one in which the principle of cooperation and its maxims are violated, i.e., the speaker does not speak in earnest. Since the Semantic Script Theory of Humor reduces humor to the presence of overlapping and opposed scripts in a text, under certain pragmatic conditions (non-bona-fide) it is a reductionist and essentialist theory. These are positive qualities, as explained in Chapter 3.

6.6 Further readings

Probably because the foundational text of the Semantic Script Theory of Humor is easily accessible, there have been no definitive introductory treatments of the subject. Someone interested in going deeper should just read Raskin (1985). Attardo (1994, 2001a, 2008) review the theory and some of its offshoots.

There exists no comprehensive treatment of frame or script semantics that surveys the entirety of the literature. Useful surveys are Andor (1985), Raskin (1985 ch. 3), Attardo (2001a ch. 3), and Attardo (2020). Collections of papers were edited by Raskin (1985, 1986) and Lehrer and Kittay (1992). On Fillmore's frame semantics, see Petruck (1996). On the evolution of Raskin's work into ontological semantics, see Raskin et al. (2009); Taylor & Raskin (2012); Raskin (2017b).

7
The General Theory of Verbal Humor

7.1 The knowledge resources 137
7.2 Further issues with the General Theory of Verbal Humor 152
7.3 Conclusions 156
7.4 Further readings 156

The General Theory of Verbal Humor was born out of the observation that the Semantic Script Theory of Humor, despite its advantages over other linguistic theories of humor, was not a complete theory. This claim was motivated by two facts. First, the Semantic Script Theory of Humor does not differentiate between verbal and referential humor (simplifying, between puns and non-puns, respectively). This is correct, as far as the Semantic Script Theory of Humor goes, since both verbal and referential jokes have the same script opposition and overlap, but verbal jokes may be characterized by their recourse to specific patterns of the signifier (the phonological form of the utterance). These patterns do not occur in referential jokes. Hence, the Semantic Script Theory of Humor misses a potential generalization. Second, there exist a relationship of similarity among jokes, such that two jokes will be perceived as more or less similar to another joke. For example, the following pair of jokes is more similar to each other, than to the Doctor's wife joke, example (44).

(45) Q: What do you get when you cross a cow and a lawnmower?
A: A lawnmooer.

Q: What do you get when you cross a lemon and a cat?
A: A sourpuss. (http://www.funology.com/mix-match-jokes/)

The Linguistics of Humor: An Introduction. Salvatore Attardo, Oxford University Press (2020). © Salvatore Attardo.
DOI: 10.1093/oso/9780198791270.001.0001

Once more, then, the Semantic Script Theory of Humor misses a potential generalization. The General Theory of Verbal Humor was created to address these two issues, with a heavy emphasis on the second one. In a sense, much of the impetus behind the General Theory of Verbal Humor is to answer the question, when are two jokes the same joke?

The answer was found to be tied to the introduction of five other parameters, which along with the script opposition rounded up the six knowledge resources. That the knowledge resources should be six and not, say, nine, was a purely empirical matter. Quite simply, we found that we only needed six resources to account for the similarity of jokes, and for the differences between puns and non-puns.

So, the main claim of the General Theory of Verbal Humor is that jokes may resemble each other along the lines of six parameters. These parameters are the resources upon which someone wishing to construct a joke from scratch would have to draw from. For this reason they were called Knowledge Resources. We noted that while some of these were already quite elaborate, others were more or less new, or required the contribution of other disciplines.

Attardo and Raskin (1991) is somewhat notorious due to its length and relative complexity. Much of that length and complexity come from the observation that the knowledge resources are not an unordered set, but are in fact organized hierarchically and linearly and that to the order in the hierarchy corresponds the degree of similarity perceived by the speakers. This was confirmed empirically by Ruch et al. (1993).[1] Figure 7.1 presents the list of the knowledge resources and their hierarchical organization.

7.1 The knowledge resources

In the following sections, we will review the knowledge resources. We will follow a bottom-up direction, starting with language and working

---

[1] The Logical Mechanisms parameter is a little off in that it performs less closely to the linear and hierarchical assumptions made in the paper. The subjects perceived the jokes differing by the Logical Mechanisms as less different than those differing by Situation, but the difference is not significant. Jokes differing by Logical Mechanism are still perceived as more different than all the other knowledge resources, except the script opposition, as predicted by the model. In short, the divergence from the anticipated results is not that major (Ruch et al., 1993, p. 131).

Script Opposition
↓
Logical Mechanism
↓
Situation
↓
Target
↓
Narrative Strategy
↓
Language

Figure 7.1 Hierarchical organization of the knowledge resources.

our way up to script-opposition. I will not justify the hierarchical ordering of the knowledge resources in this context. Those interested in the detail may consult Attardo & Raskin (1991). The best way to conceptualize the knowledge resources is a toolbox, in which each partition of the toolbox has tools specific to a task: if you want to inflate your tires, you need air chucks (the metal connectors that attach to the valves on the tires themselves), nozzles, and a gauge; if you want to change your spark plugs, you will need a spark plug socket, and if you want to drill a hole you will need drill bits or a hole saw (and of course a drill). Likewise if you want to examine the targets of a joke, you will need tools to do so, and they will probably be different from those used to analyze the narrative strategy (organization of the text). In some cases you can get by with general purpose tools (you *can* remove a spark plug using an adjustable wrench, I just would not recommend it) but by and large, each aspect of the joke needs a different treatment. So, each knowledge resource can be thought of as a collection of tools to analyze an aspect of the joke.

However, the tools themselves are generally not specifically designed for the purpose of analyzing jokes. So, the analogy falls apart on that respect: humor makes extraordinary use of ordinary linguistic devices. There are no humor-specific constructs in the Semantic Script Theory of Humor or in the General Theory of Verbal Humor: both theories are relational: it is special combinations of features that acquire humorous potential. Scripts, oppositions, targets, situations, etc. are not specific to humor. They become so only in specific combinations.

7.1.1 Language

In its original formulation (Attardo & Raskin 1991), the Language Knowledge Resource deals with the verbalization of the text. It can be thought of as all the possible paraphrases of the text. It contains a phonological, morphological, syntactic and lexical description of the text. It also contains information about the basic frequency of occurrence of these units in general texts as well as information connecting this sort of formal features of texts to registers and stylistic codes. Moreover it contains formal information pertinent to various textual genres, including most notably the final position of the punch line.

The need for a phonological description is obviously motivated by puns, as argued above, so that if a text, such as (46) includes a string of sounds [aweyfer] the knowledge resource needs to be able to describe this fact but also that the string may be analyzed as [a+weyfer] and/or [awey+fer] and that these two parses of the string correspond to the lexical items "a wafer" and "away for."

(46) Why did the cookie cry? Its mother had been away for/a wafer too long.

Homophony and homonymy are not the only types of ambiguity exploited for humor. Some puns rely on morphological ambiguities, such as the following headline:

(47) Dealers will hear car talk at noon (Bucaria 2005, p 292)

which relies on the categorical ambiguity between "talk" as a noun and as a verb (the incongruous meaning being the verbal one, in which the cars are talking).

Likewise, jokes may hinge on syntactic ambiguity, such as the following example

(48) Captain Spaulding (Groucho): One morning I shot an elephant in my pajamas. How he got in my pajamas I don't know (Animal Crackers; 1930)

analyzed in Chapter 9. There are many more cases of ambiguity that are accounted for on the Language Knowledge Resource, for which see Chapter 9 and references therein.

The requirement that the Language Knowledge Resource contain a statistical distribution of phonemes and morphemes originates in the need to account for alliterative humor, such as the following example

(49) You remember Sunset Strip – where the unneat meet to bleat! (Attardo et al., 1994, p. 35)

also analyzed in Chapter 9. In a nutshell, the occurrence of three instances of the /i/ phoneme in four syllables is statistically improbable and hence notable.

Stylistic issues are also handled in the Language Knowledge Resource. A significant proposal to broaden the Language Knowledge Resource by making it aware of different ways of working an expression, for example to include "idiomaticity," or constructions, was proposed by Antonopoulou (2002) and Antonopoulou and Nikiforidou (2009). Essentially this would be a sort of intermediate level between verbal humor (based on the signifier) and referential humor (based on the signified). The proposals are reviewed in more detail in section (14.4). In Attardo (2017b), I provide an example of sophisticated stylistic humorous allusion (p. 129) but of course there are many more examples of stylistic humor in which the incongruity is between the register used to describe them and the facts, known as register humor (Simpson and Bousfield, 2017; Alexander, 1997; Attardo, 1994, pp. 230–253). This is taken up in more detail in Chapter 14. Another stylistic aspect is the use of obscene or scatological terms/registers (e.g., Seizer, 2011). The socio-cultural salience and significance of obscenity and taboo words is obvious enough. The connections to humor theory (e.g., Freud) are also clear.

The Language Knowledge Resource is also responsible for determining the actual placement of the punch line. As work by Attardo et al. (1994) showed, the vast majority of the punch lines (92% to be precise) occurred in the last phrase of the last sentence of the text. Moreover, even on the few instances in which there was linguistic material after the punch line, it tended to be semantically empty, such as repetitions of the punch line, interjections, expletives, identifications of the speaker, and in a few cases unnecessary explanations of the punch line. An example of unnecessary identification of the speaker is the following joke, from Attardo et al. (1994, p. 45):

(50) One Monday morning at breakfast a man said to his wife, "I think this is the first time in five or six years that I have remembered a special date. Thursday will be your birthday. How times [sic] flies. You'll be 40 years old. What would you like most?" "Not to be reminded of it," was her quick reply.

where in keeping with the unnecessary wordiness of the setup, the material after the punch line is not really needed, as it is clear who the speaker is.

The syntactic structure of the language and the valences of the verb of the clause in which the punch line occurs will determine the exact position of the punch line itself. For example, English adverbials may occur sentence finally, and so in a few cases they did occur after the punch line. The language knowledge resource needs to have prosodic information. Prosodic information, such as stress placement, is significant for the performance of humor; see Chapter 10.

Finally, an important issue is the name of the knowledge resource, which is (confusingly) "Language" but should really be "Semiotic Strategy." The reasons for our choice of the term in 1991 should be clear: we were presenting a linguistic theory. However, in retrospect, I wish we had used "Semiotic Strategy" rather than "Language," because there has been a certain perception that the General Theory of Verbal Humor was limited to linguistically expressed humor, despite numerous examples of analyses of non-linguistic or multimodal texts (e.g., Paolillo, 1998, and Tsakona, 2009, which analyze cartoons, and Attardo, 1998, which analyzes a sitcom episode, including visual gags).

7.1.2 Narrative Strategy

The Narrative Strategy is concerned with the organization of the text, not in the syntactic sense (which belongs to the Language Knowledge Resource), but in the narrative sense. A story can be told in many ways. Jokes are prototypically very short stories (similar in this to anecdotes, the main difference being that jokes end in a punch line; Oring, 1989; Attardo, 1994). For example, many jokes consist of a narrative closed by a dialogical part, which contains the punch line. In some cases, jokes consist only of the dialogical part, and so strictly speaking, do not have any narrative aspect, unless we want to argue that the narrative is implicit. Consider the old joke:

(51) Can you take shorthand?
       Yes, but it takes me longer.

in which the script for SECRETARY, before the 1980s, when the widespread availability of dictation machines made shorthand unnecessary, allows us to fill in the gaps and assume that the first speaker is the boss and the second speaker the secretary, thus activating the background script OFFICE WORK (a.k.a. the Situation, in General Theory of Verbal Humor terminology) which provides us then with the (implicit) narrative: the boss calls his (new) secretary and asks her, etc. Note that the recent hire of the secretary is implied by the question: if the secretary had been in the employ of the boss for a long time he/she would know the answer to the question.

Regardless of how convincing the analysis of dialogical jokes as implicit narratives may be, it is clear that not all jokes are narratives. There are plenty of examples of jokes that are not prototypical: one liners have extremely compressed or implicit stories; riddles have a question/answer structure; top-ten lists are precisely that: lists; memes and cartoons rely on the interplay of a verbal and a visual component; etc. It is somewhat of a stretch to claim that a meme has a narrative and, while one may defend that idea, we do not need to: the General Theory of Verbal Humor simply stipulated that the term Narrative Strategy covers all the forms of textual organization, as exemplified above.[2]

The discussion of the narrative strategy within Attardo and Raskin (1991) was fairly simplistic: the kinds of example we used were a question/answer format (riddle, pseudo-riddle) or the three-step sequence frequently used in jokes because it is the smallest number of repetitions necessary to set a pattern of expectations and breaking it. The three step sequence may have another function as well: as Atkinson (1984) noted, three-part lists are used by speakers to invite applause, given the predictability of the occurrence of the third item. The three-step sequence may likewise signal the arrival of the punch line. The fellatio joke analyzed in Sacks (1978, p. 251) is an excellent example of this organization (see example (112), in Chapter 11). Another example of the structure is example (60) below.

Rozin et al. (2006) investigated the AAB pattern (i.e., the three-step sequence) and found that the three-step sequence is more frequent and considered funnier by speakers, with a four-step sequence (AAAB) significantly less frequent and less funny, and the AB sequence (simple opposition) slightly more frequent than the AAAB pattern, but considered the least funny. On the three-step sequence, see also Loewenstein and Heath (2009) and Loewenstein et al. (2011) who dub the phenomenon "repetition break." Other more complex narrative strategies may involve scripted sections, involving two speakers, such as the

---

[2] I toyed with the idea of replacing the term Narrative Strategy with Textual Organization, which gets rid of the distracting mention of "narrative," but it seemed unwise to change the terminology of the General Theory of Verbal Humor so long after the original proposal.

knock-knock joke, which follows the following elaborate construction (A and B are the two speakers)

(52) A: Knock-knock.
B: Who's there?
A: X
B: X who?
A: punch line

or are tricks to get the audience to say something incongruous:

(53) Q. How do you pronounce M,A,C (pause), M, I, L, L, A, N?
A. MacMillan.
Q. How about M,A,C (pause), H, E, N, R, Y?
A. MacHenry.
Q. And how about M,A,C (pause), H, I, N, E, R, Y? (Hockett, 1973/1977, p. 279)

where automatism should lead the responded to answer MacHinery, rather than [maʃɪnərɪ]. Often the word(s) the teller is trying to elicit are embarrassing or obscene. The following is an example of plain tricking:

(54) A: I bet I could make you say black!
B: Okay
A: What color is my [something red]?
B: Red
A: What color is my [something white]?
B: White
A: What color is my [something yellow]?
B: Yellow
A: Hah! I made you say yellow!
B: Wasn't I supposed to say black?

while the following is an example of getting the audience to say something obscene

(55) A: "You're a dickfor."
B: "What's a dick for?"

While the last four examples have all been very simple (and target younger children, at least in my experience) other types of narrative strategies can be very elaborate, such as the Limerick, a five line stanza with a rhyme scheme AABBA, and an elaborate metrical system, and a nonsensical type of humor, or the Chastushka, described by Raskin (1985) which involves obscene humor. At this upper end of sophistication and formalization, narrative strategies end up approaching literary genres and forms.

A very important aspect of jokes, and namely the functional position of the punch line belongs properly to this knowledge resource, since for example, Oring (1989) has claimed that the absence of a punch line in final position in the text is the defining difference between jokes and anecdotes.[3]

In the subsequent versions of the General Theory of Verbal Humor, beginning with Attardo 2001, I introduced several concepts that also pertained to narrative strategy: the distinction between jab and punch lines, the distribution of the humor along the textual vector, and the typology of humorous texts based on the presence or absence of a narrative disruption and the presence of a humorous central complication. Further discussion of these issues will be found in Attardo (2001) and in Chapter 14.

Finally, other issues handled by the narrative strategy knowledge resource involve the role of narratives in conversation. Narratives, being produced as single turns, disrupt the turn-based flow of conversation. Studies have focused on ways to negotiate and secure the floor for the extended narrative turn as well as the reactions to it. Analyses of conversational humor based on the General Theory of Verbal Humor should take this into account. Discussion of these issue will be found in Chapters 11 and 12.

7.1.3 Target

The target knowledge resources is probably the least sophisticated one and the easier to understand. Essentially it addresses the fact that many and perhaps most jokes are aggressive and the aggression has a target. This is know in common parlance as the "butt" of the joke. Targets generally are human or related to human activity (institutions, practices, beliefs, etc.).

---

[3] Strictly speaking the actual position of the punch line in the text is of course a matter of language, and thus best handled by the Language knowledge resource (see Section 7.1.1 above). Narrative strategy is interested only in the functional position and not in the actual placement.

Significantly, the target is an optional knowledge resource, in the sense that it may be empty if the joke happens to be what Freud would call a "non-tendentious" joke, or more simply a non-aggressive joke. For example, in this joke, repeated from above

(56) Q: What do you get when you cross a cow and a lawnmower?
A: A lawnmooer.

it is hard to imagine what the target of the joke could even be: cows? Lawnmowers? People who mow the lawn? It is a far more reasonable hypothesis that the joke is non-aggressive and that the humor is associated with coincidental resemblance between the "son" lexical function in the script for COW (i.e., the sound cows make) enriched by the derivative morpheme -er ("moo" + "er" = [mʊ + ər]) and the lexeme "mower" [moʊər].

While people are the prototypical targets of jokes there exist other kinds of targets. Ideological targets (Karman, 1998) are institutions or groups without a clear constituency (compare the National Rifle Association, which is a clearly defined group, as one has to pay membership dues to belong, to the "establishment" which is an amorphous group, or even more abstract notions such as "marriage" or "romantic love." In Attardo (2001) I speculated that these groups are associated with human activities or beliefs and that, these groups, however vaguely identified, could therefore be targeted with aggression (p. 21).

While that may be true, it remains that it is unclear that there is any aggression toward lawnmowers or cows, or people who mow lawns or own cows, in the joke above. In recent work, Priego-Valverde et al. (2018) show that humor is always oriented toward a participant of the interaction: Speaker, Hearer, or a third-person/object, or possibly the setting or situation. However this does not imply aggression toward the focus of the orientation (which would make them a target). Priego-Valverde et al. (2018) use the terms "speaker/hearer/other-oriented humor." Orientation of the humor is not part of the original General Theory of Verbal Humor and thus introducing this distinction is an extension of the General Theory of Verbal Humor, which has the advantage that it no longer requires the knowledge resource to be optional, in case of lack of aggression.

First-person orientation is self-deprecating humor (Rodney Dangerfield was the master of this form: "I told my psychiatrist that everyone hates me. He said I was being ridiculous, everyone hasn't met me yet."). An example of non deprecating first-person orientation is the following joke, which I used to tell people: "modesty is one of my greatest virtues." Second-person orientation is humor directed at the hearer. A good example is Carmen making fun of Marina's monolingualism, in example (10) which may or may not be seen as aggressive and hence is ambiguous as to whether it is a target or just an orientation. The reader will recall the example of aggressive joke (23) in Chapter 3, which is openly aggressive against lawyers and priests, depicted as uncaring (the former) and sexual predators (the latter). That joke displays a third-party orientation (assuming neither the teller or hearer happen to be the lawyer or priest in the joke). The following example, from Priego-Valverde et al. (2018) illustrates a third-party orientation (the situation), but no aggression, as the participants jokingly compare their being in the anechoic room to being eggs in an egg carton. The symbol @ represents a laughter pulse.

(57)   CL 46   t'as pas l'imp
                Don't you have the imp
        CL 47   @@pression d'être dans une@@ boite d'œufs
                @@pression@@ of being in a@@ egg box
        JS 42   @
        CL 48   @
        CL 49   @
        JS 43   @@avec les petits@@
                @@with the small@@
        JS 44   @@*@@
        CL 50   @

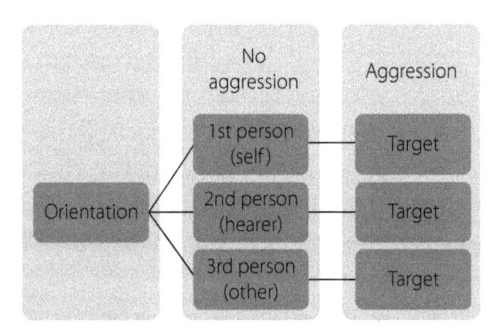

Figure 7.2 Orientations and targets of humor as a function of aggression.

We can thus summarize the situation in Figure 7.2. If there is aggression, the orientation turns into a target; if no aggression is present, then the joke is simply oriented toward the person but does not target it.

Finally, let us point out that the targets need to have relevant scripts attached to them in the encyclopedia (for example, the Scots' stinginess or the Belgians' love of fries) which mark them both as stereotypically humorous and as such available for humor. The work of Christie Davies (e.g., 1990) is the principal source for a review of these stereotypes and their sociological origins.

Other work on targets includes Scogin & Pollio (1980) who found that laughter-producing remarks could be coded into whether the remark did or did not have a specifiable target. After recording humorous events in six different natural settings involving over 1,300 events, targeted remarks varied from 36% to 79%, with an overall average of 66%. So, roughly speaking, two thirds of humor would be targeted and about a third would be non-directed (i.e., not have a target). They find significant differences among groups and that transient, short lived-groups have less targeted humor.

7.1.4 Situation

The Situation is essentially the background script that describes the environment in which the events of the joke take place. Because of its generality it is probably best described as a macro-script.

The activation of the background script may be completely inferential. Consider the joke (51) again. All the scripts that the text activates directly are SHORTHAND and LONG.[4] Everything else has to be triggered inferentially. Yet most readers will conjure a boss and a secretary, will assign them stereotypical genders, and will probably date the scene between the 1950s and the 1980s, when cheap recording devices rendered shorthand obsolete. It is worth noting that these inferences all belong to a stereotypical frame/script for SECRETARY. In a sense, these inferences activate a minimal character frame for the boss and the secretary (see Section 14.1.2).

---

[4] The text also activates scripts for CAPACITY, for the lexeme "take" in the "take shorthand" context, and so on. I am simplifying.

The activation of the script for BUSINESS OFFICE, still inferentially from BOSS and secretary explains why we could easily "beef up" the narrative along the lines of:

(58) The boss called his new secretary on the intercom: "Miss Smith, can you take shorthand?" "Yes, replied the young and pretty woman, but it takes me longer."

The presence of the intercom in an office setting does not surprise us, because it is part of the script for BUSINESS OFFICE. Conversely, if the boss called his secretary on a walkie-talkie this would be odd, and if he used a megaphone, completely out of the ordinary and perhaps even incongruous/funny. Likewise the youth and good looks of the secretary do not surprise us because they fit in the stereotype of the lecherous boss who hires his staff based on looks and not on skill. In Attardo (2017b, p. 132), another example is analyzed, along the same lines. The joke is

(59) A skeleton walks into a bar and says, "I'll have a beer and a mop."

where the script PATRONIZING A BAR is evoked, among others.

Of particular note is the fact that the humorousness of (51) and (58) is identical or perhaps lesser in the "expanded" version. This is because the Script Opposition and the Logical Mechanism of the joke are unchanged. The only (very minor) difference lies in the explicitation of some of the inferentially activated scripts, which by lowering the mental processing required to "get" the joke, may negatively affect its funniness.

This is significant, because backgrounded incongruities "reside" in the Situation. Hempelmann and Attardo (2011) introduce the notion of backgrounded incongruity (i.e., an incongruity that is not addressed and not resolved in the text). Because they are assumed to be part of the Situation, or to put it differently, they are built in into the text-world or the mental space opened by the narrative, these incongruities are not "active" so to speak, and are suppressed ("willing suspension of disbelief") in the processing of the text. Examples of backgrounded incongruities are talking animals, very common in folklore and in many jokes, all the stereotypical ethnic traits (the stupid Poles/Belgians/Newfoundlanders, etc.; the stingy Scots; the oversexed French, etc.), and even idiosyncratic entities such as the walking, talking, drinking skeleton in joke (59). Note how, while we are supposed to ignore that a skeleton cannot either walk, talk, or drink, we need to notice that, if the skeleton drank, since it does not have a stomach, the beer would spill on the floor. This latter incongruity is focalized, whereas the previous ones are backgrounded.

Needless to say, a normally backgrounded incongruity may be focalized in a given joke, witness one of my favorite jokes, in which the punch line has precisely to do with a talking animal:

(60) A guy in a bar bets drinks with the bartender claiming his dog can speak. "OK, says the bartender, prove it." "What's on top of a house?" says the patron to his dog. "Roof!" says the dog. "That's cute, says the bartender, "but that's not talking." "How about this?" says the guy, and to the dog "What is on the side of a tree?" "Bark!" "You're messin' with me," says the bartender getting angry. "No, no," says the guy, "Look: who's the greatest baseball player?" And the dog: "Ruth!" The bartender is enraged and throws the guy and his dog out. The guy and the dog dust themselves off and then the dog says: "Should I have said DiMaggio?"

The Situation of the joke is directly related to what Clark and van der Wege call "imagination" in a narrative (2015), i.e., the fact that the hearers of a story visualize mentally (imagine) the events of the narrative by constructing a mental model of the narrated events, using their prior knowledge (scripts), simulations (in which they explores "what if" branches of the story), while engaging in the co-construction of a "joint pretense" in which they willingly suspend disbelief for the backgrounded incongruities and of the contrived nature of the story-telling (for example, the narrator may do different "voices" for different characters, but no-one would be fooled into thinking that someone else is speaking). So, summing up we could call the Situation of a joke the mental space built for it by the narrator and the narratees.

7.1.5 Logical Mechanism

The Logical Mechanism is the part of the General Theory of Verbal Humor that accounts for the resolution of the incongruity (script opposition and overlap). The resolution is not complete and/or real. It is a partial, playful, non-serious resolution. In fact, the Logical Mechanism may introduce other incongruities itself. Furthermore, the Logical Mechanism is the other knowledge resource that is optional. The reader will recall from Section 4.1 that in the famous Nerhardt (1970) weights experiment, the mere presence of a unexpectedly heavier weight in a series of weights triggered smiling and laughter. Hence the idea that incongruity alone is sufficient to produce humor. Furthermore, absurd humor is usually regarded as having no resolution. Hence, the claim that the Logical Mechanism is probably optional.

In simple terms, the Logical Mechanism is the attempt by the text to explain away the incongruity by justifying it (once more, playfully and non-seriously). Consider the following joke:

(61) Three kids are bragging about their fathers. "My father is the fastest, says the first kid, he can run a mile in 4 minutes."
"That's nothing, says the second, my father can run a mile in 3 minutes."
"You don't understand what fast means, says the third one, my father's work ends at five and he's home by 3:45."

Here the Logical Mechanism works as follows: if shorter times mean faster speed, then negative times mean even faster speeds, therefore, since the third kid's father is home an hour and 15 minutes before quitting time, he must be extremely fast. Needless to say, another inferential path is also possible and namely that the third kid's father is home before quitting time because he does not work hard and cheats his employer out of one hour and 15 minutes of work time. Note how the resolution (shorter times mean faster speed *hence* negative time is even faster) is partial and non-serious.

More work on Logical Mechanism, including a list of all logical mechanisms known so far[5] and an attempt at classification, can be found in Attardo et al. (2002) and Hempelmann and Attardo (2011); see also Section 4.2.1.6.

7.1.6 Script Opposition

The concept of Script Opposition and overlap was of course defined and exemplified in detail in Raskin (1985). Attardo and Raskin (1991) did not change the original definition in any way. Script Opposition was discussed in detail in (6.2.1). In Attardo (1994, pp. 203–205), I pointed

---

[5] In one of the most frustrating misconceptions about the General Theory of Verbal Humor there have been several claims in print that the list is the "complete" list of Logical Mechanisms, despite the fact that we say explicitly that it is merely the list of *known* Logical Mechanisms and that a *complete* list is probably impossible to produce.

out that simple oppositeness of two scripts and/or simple overlap of two scripts in a text does not result in humor. Both conditions must hold simultaneously. All that needs to be added to this discussion is a short discussion of the various levels of generality of the Script Opposition.

Raskin (1985) reduces all Script Oppositions to three extremely high level (abstract) oppositions: good/bad, normal/abnormal, and actual/non-actual. Many researchers get confused because they try to identify the very abstract Script Opposition, without first identifying the text-specific script opposition. Each text instantiates these high-level script oppositions into text-specific local oppositions. Di Maio (2000) unpublished PhD dissertation, which was used in Attardo et al. (2002) introduced a third (intermediate) level of abstraction (e.g., sex/no sex, excrement/non-excrement), which we found useful to bridge the step from the concrete instantiation in the text and the very abstract opposition.

For example, consider the following joke,

(62) One day three women went for a job interview. The man interviewing them posed all three the same question. What would you do if you found an extra €50 in your paycheck that you shouldn't have received? The first one said, "I'd give it back as it wasn't mine and I wasn't entitled to it." When he asked the second one she replied, "I'd give it to Charity." When he asked the third one, she was more honest and she said, "I'd keep it for myself and go out for a drink." Which one of the three women got the job? The one with the biggest tits!

which was the "joke of the day" on April 20, 2018 on the web site http://www.laughfactory.com/jokes/joke-of-the-day

The script opposition here is sex/no sex, but the specific instantiation is much more complex since all the way until the last (fragmentary) sentence, the text is ostensibly a narrative about an elaborate test of personality in a business hiring situation. So the script JOB INTERVIEW explicitly activated in the first sentence turns out to be an instantiation of the much more abstract no-sex category. Metaphorically speaking, the joke is a garden-path construct, since it leads the reader to believe that the story is about finding out the character of the women interviewing for the job presumably to determine who is the most suited for the position. Intermediate scripts activated are also BUSINESS PRACTICES and HIRING, but also upon reading the punch line, MALE versus

FEMALE, since the logical mechanism here is the stereotypical behavior of the male interviewer (the "lecherous boss" mentioned above). Notice that the fact that the three applicants for the job are women becomes significant only after the punch line is reached and the script opposition is triggered. Among the backgrounded oppositions let us note that the presence of only three applicants and that they are all females may be perceived as anomalous, under certain circumstances (for example within current hiring practices in the US).

Summing up, each humorous text will instantiate one very abstract Script Opposition in a very concrete text-specific opposition, which will generally require at least one of the scripts in the opposition to be explicitly stated in the text and the other to be directly or at least easily retrievable inferentially/abductively from the text. There may be any number of intermediate scripts, increasingly abstract, bridging the distance between the scripts occurring in the text and the very abstract oppositions identified by Raskin.

In the prototypical examples of Script Opposition in jokes there is only one Script Opposition, which makes the text incongruous. However, this is not always the case. Tsakona (2003) showed that many jokes do not just have a final punch line, but in fact there are other Script Oppositions along the body of the text (jab lines). This is not an issue for the expanded version of the General Theory of Verbal Humor which incorporates multiple instances of humor in the text (jab lines and punch lines). Norrick (2010) documents jokes with multiple punch lines (Hockett, 1977, p. 261, "compound jokes") and with jab lines, as well as numerous examples of laughter within the body of the joke text, triggered by various aspects of the performance of the joke (see (10)). Hempelmann and Attardo (2011) discuss backgrounded incongruity, which is assumed as part of the situation of the text; see (4.2.3). Backgrounded incongruities overlap with the multiple jab lines of jokes described by Tsakona and Norrick.

7.2 Further issues with the General Theory of Verbal Humor

7.2.1 Broadening the Theory?

There has been some discussion as to whether more knowledge resources are needed and/or should be added. All the proposals in that sense focus on performance issues, therefore they will be discussed in Part 3 of this book. For discussion, see Section 10.1.5.

Relatedly, there has been some discussion about dropping the Logical Mechanism (e.g., Davies, 2004). In a nutshell, Davies argues that while one can make generalizations on bona-fide discourse, non-bona-fide discourse is essentially un-generalizable, or rather that one can find generalizations but they are pointless. According to Davies, evidence of this would be found in the lack of testable hypotheses that could be generated from studying logical mechanisms (2004, p. 379). In Hempelmann and Attardo (2011), we listed some hypotheses, derived from the logical mechanisms, that have been tested empirically. Since then, more evidence has emerged showing that the distinctions within the logical mechanisms are psychologically real and even have neurological correlates (see a review in Chen et al., 2017). A further list of criticisms of the General Theory of Verbal Humor, with some responses, can be found in Attardo (2017b).

7.2.2 The application of the General Theory of Verbal Humor to longer texts

As is well known, the Semantic Script Theory of Humor, and the General Theory of Verbal Humor after it, were developed using jokes, for the methodological caution of starting by analyzing relatively simpler phenomena. Almost immediately, though, the theories were applied to other types of texts. However, the broadening of the scope of a theory comports a potential issue, which is that significant additional conceptual apparatus may need to be added to handle the new phenomena that now fall under its purview. As discussed in Attardo (1994, pp. 221–222), two approaches emerged: the expansionist approach, which assumes that other types of texts are more-or-less essentially similar to jokes and that so a simple expansion of the theory can include other types of texts under its purview, using the same conceptual apparatus. Conversely, the revisionist approach takes it that it is necessary to develop a new set of tools to handle the new materials. Both of these approaches will be discussed in Chapter 14.

The GTVH has been applied to a variety of materials, such as telephone calls (Antonopoulou & Sifianou, 2003), Greek young men conversations (Archakis & Tsakona 2005), Jordanian joke telling

(Al-Khatib, 1999), conversational irony (Alvarado Ortega, 2013), cartoons (Paolillo, 1998; El-Arousy, 2007; Tsakona, 2009), Polish sketch comedy (Brzozowska, 2009), Latin satire (Vincent, 2010), and of course translation (see Chapter 15).

7.2.3 A small methodological note on cherry-picking

As I noted in Attardo (2017b), the methodology underlying the expansion of the General Theory of Verbal Humor to longer text included a proviso of great significance. I have referred to this by a motto of "no cherry-picking of data." Let us briefly examine what this means and the significance of this admonition.

Let us start by imagining a graduate student, let's call him Bob, who wants to test his theory of the genetic foundation of fetching behavior in dogs. He gathers as many dogs as he can, borrowing dogs from his friends and neighbors, and starts throwing sticks at them in a very controlled, double-blind setup (the dog is behind a fence). After a few frustrating days, he finds that all of the dogs fetch, except one named "Blue."[6] In frustration, the graduate student decides to drop Blue from the experiment. That is very bad behavior, science-wise. By excluding those observations that do not confirm his theory our graduate student has essentially falsified the data. This is an instance of cherry-picking (ignoring data that go against your theory). Another way to cherry-pick is to only consider the data that support the theory: suppose that about a quarter of the dogs refused to fetch; if our graduate student writes a paper on fetching behavior without mentioning that 25% of the dogs did not fetch, he has again cherry-picked the data (considering only data that support the theory).

The above examples are semi-facetious in the sense that no researcher would be that bad. Unfortunately, there are subtler ways of cherry-picking the data. Suppose that our student wants to investigate how loudly speakers deliver punch lines. He collects 20 recordings of speakers delivering a given joke, using a good microphone, making sure he has 10 males and 10 females and taking every care not to bias his sample. He then proceeds to measure very precisely the volume of the punch lines. He finds that the average punch line is delivered at 70 decibels, accounting for male/female differences. The problem here is

[6] Any resemblance to dogs in our household is purely coincidental.

7.2 FURTHER ISSUES WITH THE GENERAL THEORY OF VERBAL HUMOR

that this measurement, however accurate and unbiased, is not meaningful: in order to be meaningful the student needs to compare it to the non-punch line language. In other words, he needs to determine a baseline volume in parts of the recordings that are not punch lines and then he can compare this to the punch lines. This too is a form of cherry-picking the data: by analyzing only what you are interested in, you lose track of the big picture. Humorous language is *also* language. If we are interested in determining what makes it humorous we must contrast it with non-humorous language. It is not enough to say that such-and-such a feature, phenomenon, etc. occurs in our data. It could be occurring outside the data as well making the observation pointless, as far as understanding humor is concerned.

Disgusted by his results, Bob leaves academe and becomes an entrepreneur opening a dog-sitting business that earns him a small fortune. Another graduate student decides to take up humor research. She[7] collects a large corpus of naturally occurring conversations and is struck by the fact that in several of the conversations, one speaker reacts with obscenity to most instances of humor. She transcribes all the conversations and analyzes in painstaking detail the behavior of the speaker. It becomes clear that there is a quasi-systematic correlation between the presence of an instance of humor and an obscenity. The student becomes intrigued, does some research, and she discovers that the speaker is a Tourette syndrome sufferer and that he manifests his anxiety in delivering the punch line of a joke or a jab line by producing an obscenity. Thus she comes to the conclusion that, while the obscenities and the humor are connected, there is no causal correlation between them as there is an intervening variable that explains the correlation. The student publishes a case study on the phenomenon, but then goes back to her data and looks at many more speakers. Eventually she becomes a successful academic.

The second student's experience illustrates yet another cherry-picking problem: given a sufficiently large corpus of data, one will find some exceptional instances within it that will be very interesting, but not necessarily representative of the data. The only way to avoid this problem is to examine *all* the data or a representative[8] subset of the data. This is the reason why the General Theory of Verbal Humor argues that one

---

[7] This one is a woman. Her name is Mary.
[8] I.e., such that it reflects all the characteristics of the data. You make sure that this is the case by selecting the subset randomly.

needs to examine all the instances of humor in a given text, or at least a representative subset thereof. Failure to do so will necessarily introduce unconscious biases in the selection process.

7.3 Conclusions

In this chapter, we examined the reasons for the creation of the General Theory of Verbal Humor and the six knowledge resources that comprise it. The General Theory of Verbal Humor is a less abstract theory than the Semantic Script Theory of Humor, insofar as it deals with the implementation of the script opposition at a textual level. It is, however, still on the competence-side of the continuum. Applications of the General Theory of Verbal Humor to the performance side will be examined in the third part of the book.

7.4 Further readings

Attardo & Raskin (1991) is technical and best approached with a general understanding of how the theory works, which can be gathered from any of the many presentations of the General Theory of Verbal Humor, such as Attardo (1994; 2008; 2017b). The work by Attardo et al. (2002) has shown that more formal versions of the General Theory of Verbal Humor can be produced relatively easily. It is, however, more technical. The applications of the General Theory of Verbal Humor to various fields and problems are ongoing. This is not the place to review them, but see Attardo (2017) for a start.

8
Pragmatics of humor

8.1	Pragmatic principles	158
8.2	Nature of the violation of the CP	163
8.3	Irony and humor	168
8.4	All humor is intentional	170
8.5	Conclusions	175
8.6	Further readings	175

We've seen in Chapter 5 that we can arrive at two significant generalizations about humor and namely that all meaning differences may be used for the creation of humor and that all humor is semantically based. This is not to say, however, that humor is purely a semantic phenomenon. It is clear that humor has a significant pragmatic component.[1]

We can now introduce a third generalization about humor: humor may arise from the violation of pragmatic rules alone. Note that this does not contradict the first two generalizations: pragmatic rules are meaningful, albeit at a different level than semantic rules.

---

[1] As we saw, the Semantic-Script Theory of Humor (and therefore the General Theory of Verbal Humor) incorporate pragmatics *within* semantics and that therefore the argument of whether humor is a semantic or pragmatic phenomenon is moot. It should be noted that while it is true that pragmatic factors enter in the construction of the sense of a text, it is also true that the text has a relationship with its context and that the overall meaning of the text is given by the interplay of the semantically-and-pragmatically-arrived-at meaning and the context.

8.1 Pragmatic principles

The material in this chapter may require some linguistic background that goes beyond what a typical introductory course in linguistics will provide. Therefore, we will first introduce some pragmatic principles that underlie communication, starting with speech act theory.

8.1.1 Speech acts

J. L. Austin and John Searle are the founders of speech act theory. As the name of the theory indicates, speaking is performing a kind of action. Speech act theory begins by distinguishing three different acts in each utterance:

- Locutionary act: what we say literally.
- Illocutionary act: the commitment made by saying the locutionary content. Examples are betting, promising, swearing, baptizing, and naming. This is the force of the sentence; the activity the speaker is trying to accomplish with it.
- Perlocutionary act: the effect or intended effect the utterance has on the hearer.[2] Surprising someone, scaring them, or amusing them would be perlocutionary effects of an utterance.

Attardo and Chabanne (1992) defined a humorous utterance as one whose perlocutionary goal is to amuse its audience or at least evoke the recognition of the intention on the part of the speaker to amuse his/her audience. This definition, far from being circular, emphasizes the dependence of the humorous nature of the text on its context, and the intentions of the speaker/hearer. Defining the humorous text as a text whose perlocutionary goal is to be perceived as humorous is a strictly functional definition, but it also ties the definition to the intended perception of the text by an audience, i.e., the effect that the speaker thinks his/her text will have on the hearer(s). In what follows, we will expand slightly this definition, to highlight the potential role the audience plays in defining something as humorous.

---

[2] Recall that "hearer" is used as a technical term, meaning not just a lone hearer, but possibly a wider audience, including overhearers.

8.1.2 Cooperation and implicatures

There are some special preconditions that are common to all sentences of all languages and not just to speech acts. One such precondition is that we assume that other speakers are telling the truth. Naturally, we know that this is not always the case, and that speakers lie, on occasion. However, as a general rule, we assume that speakers are truthful and are not trying to deceive us. If we didn't, communicating would be impossible, since we could not trust anything said by other speakers. Another assumption is that speakers are sticking to the point. Suppose that someone asks you "What do you think of hip hop?" The answer, "My sister just graduated from college" is not to the point and so irrelevant to the question. In conversation, this would be considered a non-sequitur. Thus, if we want to communicate, we must stick to the point of what is being said. These assumptions are some of the rules that govern conversations. These are general rules or principles that all speakers follow unconsciously. They are not prescriptive rules. They are more like good advice, along the lines of:

(63)   Avoid Highway 635 in Dallas at rush hour.

You are free to go there, of course, but you'd better not if you don't want to get stuck in traffic.

Paul Grice, a British philosopher transplanted to Berkeley, codified these general expectations as the co-operative principle (CP). The CP consists of four maxims (in a nod to Kant, who states parts of his moral philosophy as maxims). Taken together, the four maxims and their sub-maxims form the principle of cooperation, which states roughly that a speaker's conversation should be as effective and cooperative as possible. Grice's original formulation is worth quoting:

> Make your conversational contribution such as is required, at the stage at which it occurs, by the accepted purpose or direction of the talk exchange in which you are engaged.   (Grice, 1989, p. 26)

The following are the four maxims:

1. The maxim of quality
   - Do not say what you believe to be false.
   - Do not say that for which you lack adequate evidence.
2. The maxim of relevance—Be relevant!

3. The maxim of quantity
   - Make your contribution as informative as is required.
   - Do not make your contribution more informative than is required.
4. The maxim of manner
   - Avoid obscurity of expression.
   - Avoid ambiguity.
   - Be brief.
   - Be orderly.

What happens if speakers do not follow the CP? There are several cases. The simplest one is that communication breaks down. The speakers become confused, do not understand each other and need to resort to forms of repair, or abandon communication entirely. For example, consider the following passage from Heidegger:

(64) Will we see the lightning-flash of Being in the essence of technology? The flash that comes out of stillness, as stillness itself? Stillness stills. What does it still? It stills being into the coming to presence of world. (Heidegger, M. (1977) *The question concerning technology and other essays*. New York, NY: Harper and Row. p. 49)

Example (64) clearly violates the maxim of manner and specifically the submaxim warning to avoid obscurity of expression. It may violate other maxims as well, but since I, for one, have no idea what Heidegger is saying, it is hard to determine whether it is relevant in the context in which it is said, etc.

Other options are giving up entirely on the communicative exchange: socially codified forms of doing so are the expressions "no comment" and "I cannot say more." Non-socially ratified forms are simply abandoning the conversation entirely (i.e., stopping speaking, or changing the topic entirely).

There are some modes of communication that allow violations of the CP, under specific constraints. So fiction writing, playacting, and any forms of creative uses of language have a certain amount of leeway. One may freely make up events and circumstances and even invent entire universes within fiction.[3] The need to maintain suspense in a work of

---

[3] The existence of genres such as the memoir, in which real-life stories are fictionalized, is an ambiguous area. For its problems, and in general for the non-cooperative aspects of fiction, see Attardo (2008).

fiction will require the author to withhold crucial information from the reader/viewer (a violation of the maxim of quantity), such as the identity of the assassin. Humor and jokes fall under this category, both because they are mostly fictional and because they violate the CP in specific ways.

Other modes of communication, such as lying and deceiving are based on the assumption that one's violation of the CP will remain undetected, at least long enough for one's goals to be achieved. For example, some rules of politeness require one to lie to avoid offending ("How do you like my new haircut?"). It should be noted that white lies, such as the surgeon lying about the health of his parents to the injured child whose parents perished in the same accident, are plain violations of the CP but done for purposes that society approves of (helping a child, not hurting someone's feelings). Regular lies are violations of the CP done for personal gain. The distinction is ethical, not semantic/pragmatic.

In other situations the maxims may clash: thus one may want to be truthful but lack adequate evidence for what one wants to say. Clashes are problematic for the speakers, because there are generally no easy solutions to the clash and the speaker may need to violate one maxim in order to follow another one. Often the cause of a clash is politeness, a principle not included in Grice's original formulation, but that Leech (1983) has argued should be given the same status. Thus one may think a friend's outfit to be hideous, but politeness will prevent him/her from telling the truth. There exists one last case of violation, with special properties, to which we turn next.

8.1.3 Implicature

Implicatures are violation of the CP that are obvious ("blatant"), where there is no clash with another maxim or intention to mislead. Grice labels these "exploitations" of the maxims. These exploitations are violations that are redeemed by the fact that, if we make the assumption that the violation is deliberate and intended to be perceived as such, since it is obvious and thus cannot be seen as intending deception, on the part of the speaker, the hearer can work out another intended (implied) meaning which can be inferred from the context of the communicative exchange. Context, broadly defined, includes the co-text (the other words in the text), the situation in which the utterance takes place, as well as background information, and awareness of the CP itself. This implied meaning is called an implicature. Implicatures have been used to explain metaphors, irony, and other tropes (understatement, hyperbole, etc.). They are generally believed to be crucial to explaining figurative and generally non-literal uses of language.

Implicatures can be usefully contrasted to logical inferences, which follow from the meaning of a sentence: thus from the meaning of

(65) John is a doctor.

it follows logically and necessarily that

(66) John has a doctoral degree.

Inferences are necessary and undefeasible, witness the anomaly of

(67) * John is a doctor but he does not have a PhD, EdD, or MD.

Since we cannot say that John is a doctor *and* he does not have a PhD, it follows that the inference is undefeasible. Contrast this with implicatures: implicatures are probabilistic (i.e., probable, not certain) and defeasible without contradiction. Contrast the following example:

(68) Mary and John are married, but do not love each other

which may be sad but is perfectly well formed, in which that two people who are married should love each other is an implicature (and hence defeasible) to

(69) Mary is single, but is married to John.

in which being single implies necessarily and undefeasibly that one is not married. Note that it would be a logical contradiction to say that Mary is single and not single.

A special class of inferences are presuppositions, which are inferences that hold simultaneously for a sentence and its negation. So, considering again (65), and its negation

(70) John is not a doctor.

from both (65) and (70) it still follows that there exists someone whose name is John. Note how the existence of John is presupposed by both (65) *and* (70) and that this is a necessary inference, witness the anomaly of

(71) * John is a doctor but there is no-one called John.

8.1.4 Humor and the implicit

Implicatures, inferences and presuppositions are all implicit, in the sense that they are part of what the text does not say literally and explicitly. In this respect, they are crucial to addressing an heretofore seriously neglected aspect of humor, and namely its connection with the implicit of a text. The topic of humor and the implicit is in dire need of research (see Attardo, 1994, pp. 289–290 for a review). Guagnano (2013) shows that the difference between jokes and humorous anecdotes lies, among other things, in the fact that whereas jokes keep implicit both the second script and the resolution of the incongruity it brings about, humorous narratives present both scripts and the resolution more or less explicitly within the text.

8.2 Nature of the violation of the CP

There exists an extensive literature that regards humor as a violation of the CP. As we saw, Raskin (1985) classifies humor as a non-bona-fide mode (bona-fide communication follows the CP).

There have been a few attempts to claim that humor is not a "real" violation of the CP, either by claiming that the violation is merely mentioned, or attributed to a character in the text, or otherwise normalized, for example, by turning it into an implicature (Klungervik-Greenall, 2003; Dynel, 2009b; Goatly, 2012). Mooney (2004, p. 915) claims that humor is a non-successful violation and that therefore implicatures follow from it. There are serious problems with these views, some of which are refuted in Attardo (1994, 2017c). We address the idea that the violation of the CP in humor leads to a flout below.

8.2.1 Is humor a flout?

Recently, an interesting proposal has been presented by Goatly (2012: 235) to see humor as a short-term violation (or as he has it "a flout delayed by violation"). Goatly explain that "the breaking [=violation] of the maxims must be recognized almost immediately, at least within the next couple of turns of the discourse for the joke to work" (235). There is a problem with this idea, which Goatly acknowledges in a footnote, and namely that these flouts would behave differently from all other flouts. For starters, they are not defeasible and they do not generate implicatures. More importantly, the violation is not meant to be recognized immediately, at the time of the first processing of the text, as it is in flouts.

Let us consider the following joke

(72) My wife accused me of being immature. I told her to get out of my fort.

From the first sentence we recover the following relevant inferences: the speaker is male and the speaker is married.[4] From the script for MARRIAGE we also derive the inference that the speaker is of legal age to be married (hence at least 18 or 16 with parental consent, in Texas) and the implicature that the speaker is probably at least in their mid-twenties (only about 7% of men marry before 20, according to the US census data). The second sentence however conflicts with the script we have constructed so far (MARRIED MAN OLDER THAN 20) since the lexeme *fort* activates the script FORT which itself activates GAME and CHILD (children play in make-pretend forts). The incongruity of why a married man is playing a children's game is not resolved, but there is a minor resolution aspect in the fact that the speaker of the text (another presupposition: from "my" and "I" we know the text is in the first person) considers the response of expelling his wife from his play-fort an appropriate answer to the accusation of immaturity.

How does the text violate the CP? First, the text is fictional. There is no evidence that this exchange might actually have taken place, at any time. To put it bluntly, this is not a true story. Hence, this is a violation of quality.

Second, the text withholds significant information in the first sentence. The text does not focalize the age of the speaker nor the degree of maturity of the speaker until the second sentence, which contains the punch line "my fort" (the last phrase of the last sentence of the text). Consider that a fully informative text should have been shaped as follows:

(73) A man who still engages in games inappropriate for his age says: "My wife accused me of being immature. I told her to get out of my fort."

---

[4] Gay marriage is still uncommon enough that it would have been topicalized if this had been the situation.

Third, since no explanation is provided within the text for the incongruity between the presumptive age of the speaker and his behavior, it is difficult to assess the relevance of the second sentence to the challenge presented by the wife to the husband. Presumably, a self-defeating response is not a good argumentative move and so it may be considered irrelevant, since a relevant response should have addressed the wife's allegation of immaturity, not confirmed it.

In light of this analysis, the text is clearly non-cooperative (non-bona-fide). However, we can agree with Goatly that the recognition of the violation occurs very soon after it occurs. From psycholinguistic studies, we know that incongruity is detected about 400 milliseconds after it occurs and resolved about 200 milliseconds later. However, from the second and the third violation, it is hard to see what the implicatures triggered by the flouts would be (we easily derive an inference "the speaker is immature", but this does not lead us to a coherent train of thought, what Grice calls "working it out"). Instead it takes us to an interpretive cul-de-sac: the text is contradicting itself. The speaker is both immature and old enough to contract marriage (which would probabilistically implicate maturity). Moreover, the "implicature" (let us treat it as such for the sake of the argument) is not defeasible as witness by:

(74) The man is immature, despite his age, but he is not immature.

In a normal implicature, the speaker flouts the CP trying to get the hearer to work out an intended meaning. In humor, some of the violations lead to no intended meaning at all, only contradiction and incongruity. Note, in passing, that trying to claim that the perception of humor or the triggering of laughter is the intended "meaning" that the speaker is trying to convey, changes irresponsibly the definition of implicature (which is now broadened to include perlocutionary goals).

So, in conclusion, while Goatly is correct that the violation of the CP in jokes lasts for a very short time, in contrast with lies, for example, whose duration is indeterminate, it seems difficult to categorize the violation as a flout. Simply put, humorous violations of the CP do not generate implicatures, or if they do, they are not the same kinds of implicatures that flouts generate outside of humor.

In conclusion, humor is non-cooperative (non-bona-fide). It shares this characteristic with other modes, such as fiction. However, we should not assume that humor is therefore nefarious. There are different kinds of non-cooperation: some are antisocial (such as deception) and some are pro-social (humor and fiction would fall under this category). Speakers are quite willing[5] to engage in pro-social non-bona-fide modes, for example for the purpose of entertainment (fiction, humor). We cannot pursue the discussion of anti-social lies and other fully and partially non-cooperative forms of communication (propaganda, advertising, sales talk, for example) but we will look briefly at the way speakers handle non-cooperation.

8.2.2 The LDP

Violations of the CP are not random; they follow certain rules. As a first approximation, the Least Disruption Principle (LDP) has been proposed (Attardo, 1999, Eisterhold et al., 2006). The LDP's wording is as follows: Super-maxim: Minimize your violation of the CP;

1. limit your violation of the CP to the smallest possible conversational unit (one utterance, one conversational turn, one speech exchange);[6]
2. try to link the entire CP-violating unit to the rest of the interaction, for example by finding a certain appropriateness to the CP-violating unit;
3. limit your violation of the CP to the smallest possible distance from its requirements;
4. if you must violate a maxim do so in the direction that is expected by your audience (i.e., say what your audience wants to hear).

The LDP is in part a set of advice of how to effectively violate the CP, or in other words how to effectively make as if one were producing a bona-fide speech act, while in fact one is not. Some of the maxims of the LDP concern the degree of the violation (smaller violations are less likely to be detected), and the direction of the violation (tell your audience what they want to hear); clearly, they are instructions on how to lie, obfuscate and/or inveigle.

[5] As Coleridge aptly stated, it is a "willing suspension of disbelief."
[6] Conversational demands, such as preferred and dispreferred responses may require longer stretches of discourse than a single turn. For example, in Southern Italian culture, while at the dinner table, one should refuse offers of seconds for food at least twice before accepting. In order to non-cooperatively refuse food, one then needs at the very least 6 turns (3 for each speaker).

Others maxims of the LDP concern the interplay between the violation and the non-violating environment. So, if the speaker wants the hearer to be aware of his/her violation of the CP, it is better to keep the violation short, because if the violation is prolonged, the hearer may lose the motivation to engage in the interaction (why waste resources processing known non-bona-fide messages, from which no implicatures can be drawn?). Needless to say, if the speaker does not want the hearer to be aware of the non-bona-fide nature of the exchange, then no such need to minimize the length of the violation exists. This second aspect of the LDP is predicated on the fact that even when violating some of the most central norms of social interaction, agents are still within the scope of their social bonds. There are sanctions for those who engage in inappropriate violations (more or less formalized, ranging from prosecution for perjury to social shunning).

Empirical evidence in favor or against of the LDP is hard to come by. Much has been made about the existence of long stretches of humorous banter in which speakers either support one another's humor or top it (i.e., produce more or better humor), e.g., Kotthoff (2007). However, even these extended periods of joking never exceed 15 turns (the longest documented one is 13 turns) and need to be continuously keyed (Hymes, 1972, p. 62) or framed (Goffman, 1974, pp. 43–44) (marked) as humorous (e.g., Zhang and Attardo, 2015). Framing or keying for humor can be achieved in many different ways. One is to produce humor support (Hay, 2001) such as producing more humor; see Chapter 10. Other strategies include laughter, and changes in eye contact and smiling patterns (extended, more intense smiling; see Section 10.3).

Recent results corroborating the idea that speakers return to the serious mode as soon as possible include Tsakona (2011), who found that the ironical turns in a Greek parliament discussion did not exceed three utterances, and only two instances were cases of mode adoption (i.e., the hearer continuing the speaker's irony) and Ruiz Gurillo (2009) who found that 48.5% of her corpus of ironical conversational exchanges consisted of single turns and 68.5% consisted of three or less turns. Holmes and Marra (2002) report that single-turn humor in workplace conversations never accounted for less than about 40% of humorous turns and in one setting (factory floor) single-turn humor outnumbered two-or-more-turns humor. Nuolijärvi & Tiittula (2011) in an analysis of Finnish television debates find that,

The recipient [of the irony] usually treats the irony-implicative utterance as literal (...) the recipient overtly bypasses the ironic meaning and ignores the negative evaluation in it, but simultaneously ironises the original ironist or his/her talk. Thereafter, the original ironist in turn responds literally, so that the conversation shifts back to the serious, non-mocking mode. In other words, the original ironist continues as if he or she had not been ironic at all.   (p. 584)

To paraphrase, the Speaker is ironical, the Hearer responds to the literal meaning, but mode adopts, i.e. responds with irony to irony (see Section 11.3.1.3), to save face. The original Speaker responds also literally, hence completing the return to the serious mode. In this case, return to the serious mode is delayed by one turn to save face (essentially an ironical tit-for-tat).

8.3 Irony and humor

There is a common misconception that irony is saying the opposite of what one thinks. In fact, irony is a much broader phenomenon. In pragmatic terms, saying the opposite of what one thinks corresponds to a violation of the maxim of quality. However, convincing evidence has shown that the violation of any maxim may generate irony. Good examples are understatements and exaggerations: for example, in torrential rain, one might say,

(75)   It seems to be drizzling.

Clearly, these are violations of the maxim of quantity, not of quality; after all there is some precipitation. It is the intensity of the precipitation that is inappropriate. Importantly, ironical violations of the maxims are meant to be recognized as such and thus generate implicatures, unlike the violations of jokes, which are not meant to be recognized at the same time that they are first processed.

The theories of irony are fairly complex and many require fairly sophisticated psycholinguistic apparatus, which is beyond this treatment (see Giora, 2003 for a synthesis of the debates). So we will limit ourselves to a few observations that will place irony within the context if humor research.

The difference between irony and sarcasm, which has elicited significant discussion, is actually fairly simple to describe: in the classical model, sarcasm is a particularly aggressive form of irony, whereas irony is a gentler, less critical type of discourse move. Unfortunately, semantic shift took place in the USA in the 1990s and the meaning of "sarcasm" took over the entire semantic field of irony/sarcasm, with "irony" being relegated to the meaning of an annoying coincidence (see Section 1.1.2). Practically speaking, this means that one needs to be very careful, when reading studies on irony/sarcasm, concerning the age and geographical location of the subjects, as they may have different understandings of the folk-terminology *irony* and *sarcasm*.

Irony is not necessarily critical of its target. Irony can be used to convey a positive evaluation of the target. For example,

(76) J. K. Rowling published a few moderately successful novels.

This example of positive irony draws attention to the fact that Rowling's Harry Potter novels were very successful. Another example, which Alan Partington drew my attention to, comes from Wodehouse:

(77) "Shakespeare said some rather good things."
      "I understand that he has given uniform satisfaction, sir.[...]
      (P. G. Wodehouse. *Jeeves and the Tie that Binds*. New York: Simon and Schuster. 2000. p. 53.)

In (77), the description of Shakespeare's work as having given "uniform satisfaction" is of course inappropriate, as Shakespeare is widely considered the greatest English writer. Since the text is using a characterization of Shakespeare's success that is worse than the reality, it is a negative utterance. However, since it implies a positive evaluation it is a positive irony.

There is a consensus that irony comes from a contrast, in a sense close to the idea of opposition in humor. This is clearly correct, for example, in the torrential rain vs. drizzle example there is a clear contrast or opposition between the two ideas. However, contrast is not enough to generate irony ("I don't like beans, but I like tomatoes" also includes a contrast, but is patently not ironical). I have suggested (Attardo, 2000a) that in order to be perceived as ironical, a contrast has to be both relevant and inappropriate. Let us examine both aspects.

It is clear that irony is a flout in Gricean terms. The speaker says X, while intending something else (Y). Y is arrived at using the maxim of relevance as a heuristic. When looking for a possible interpretation of an utterance, the maxim of relevance is one's default tool, as the assumption that the speaker is meaning something relevant will guide one's search. For example, suppose that the speaker says "It's drizzling" the hearer would be well served by looking for weather-related items in the immediate context: for example, he/she may look outside a window to check the weather, or turn on the weather channel, or look at a thermometer, etc. Checking for the presence of tomato cans in the pantry would make no sense, because tomato cans are not relevant to the weather. Let us suppose, for the sake of the argument, that the hearer can locate a window in the immediate context and look outside where there is a torrential outpour. The hearer may then infer that the speaker is trying to communicate something else than the literal statement "it is drizzling."

This is a flout, first, because the speaker is clearly trying to convey something else than what he/she literally said, but also because the utterance is inappropriate[7] in this context (it is raining and the speaker says it is drizzling). If I assume that the speaker is being deliberately inappropriate but also relevant (i.e., the reference to the drizzle is related to what he/she intends), then I can conclude that the speaker is trying to convey ironically that he/she feels the rain is annoying, or unexpected, or perhaps that someone had predicted only a small amount or rain (this is called echoic irony, because it echoes critically someone's words). Notice how a simple flout of the maxim of quantity (drizzle vs. rain) is not ironical per se. If it were drizzling and the speaker exaggerated saying "it's raining," there would be no perception of irony. In order to be ironical, what is said to generate the flout has also to be inappropriate. This extra inappropriateness is what I have called "residual violation" (because it persists after the flout has been resolved; Attardo, 2001a, p. 111) which causes irony to be often perceived as humorous.

8.4 All humor is intentional

This section argues that all forms of humor must be either uttered or interpreted as intentional distortions of normal, serious, bona-fide communicative practices. A direct corollary of this thesis is that the category of "unintentional humor" turns out to be have potentially confusing effects, and should be avoided in the discussion of humor.

---

[7] Inappropriateness is defined as a mismatch in presuppositions (Attardo, 2000a). Note that the presuppositions of "it's drizzling" are calculated based on that sentence, and on "it's not drizzling," as we saw above.

The theory of involuntary humor is mainly implicit, i.e., it is assumed as self-evident without discussion. For example, Freud (1905: 182) notes that "naive" humor is "found" and not "made" and leaves it at that. A problematic aspect of the folk-theory of involuntary or unintentional humor is that of distinguishing humor from all sorts of errors and other phenomena such as slips of the tongue, spelling errors, typing mistakes, typographical errors, etc. Not all ambiguous sentences are puns.

Consider the following example (from Sherzer, 1978):

(78) In a course in Linguistics there's a lot to cover.

This sentence appears quite straightforward, and its meaning is largely unambiguous. However, example (79) shows that in fact there is a hidden ambiguity in the lexeme "cover" which can be exploited for punning:

(79) In a course in Human Sexuality there's a lot to cover.

Note that the ambiguity of the lexeme "cover" is also present in (78). One can therefore ask the question: "Why isn't (78) also funny?" The structural requirements for a pun are all there (ambiguous element, opposed and overlapping scripts HIDE and EXAMINE, as in "peruse"), so what is missing? The missing element in (78) is the intention of the hearer/reader to make a pun. Suppose to read (79) in any situation where the contextual clues about the speaker are abolished. There is no telling whether the inscription is meant as a joke, or is the weary comment of a Human Sexuality teacher. What will lead the audience to opt for the HIDE script, rather than for the EXAMINE script? Clearly nothing in the structure of the text itself, as the option did not present itself in (78). Inevitably one must reach the conclusion that the audience is alerted to the ambiguity of "cover" by the activation of the default SEX humorous script. In other words, the audience (the reader/hearer) will see the second meaning of "cover" because it "is on the look out" for hidden meanings. In fact, even (78) can become as much of a pun as (79): suppose that a given teacher of linguistics considers some influential trend in linguistics a dangerous influence for his/her students, and he/she wants to shelter them from this influence, then (78) becomes (suddenly) a reasonably good pun. (79) can lose all its humorous potential in the right situation: consider the case in which (79) is uttered by an untenured junior faculty member who has failed to cover significant parts of the syllabus in his/her Human Sexuality class, and who has solicited a meeting with his/her Department Head in a desperate plea not to be fired. In conclusion, it is safe to say that an ambiguous sentence becomes a pun depending on the context and on how the hearer is disposed towards the communicative situation.

Consider this example:

(80) This writer, a non-native speaker, was once in need to discuss a delicate situation with a female faculty member. So I asked as a favor of my advisor if he could "feel up" the faculty member about that issue.

The above error (lexical replacement) was easily corrected ("feel up/feel out") and therefore the hearer could very easily determine what the intended meaning was, and proceed accordingly, disregarding the parasitic sexual meaning. It should be noted that whenever the conditions of communication are sub-optimal (e.g., noisy background, physical illness, etc.) the hearer goes to a lot more trouble to reestablish the speaker's intended meaning. If the hearer wants the communicative exchange to succeed he/she must attempt to reconstruct as far as possible, the speaker's intention. Clearly, by choosing to disregard the fact that in example (80) the speaker did not intend to evoke a sexual script, the hearer is leaving the realm of cooperation and violating the principle of Charity, which would enjoin the hearer to assume that the speaker is making sense. "Feel out" makes much more sense than "feel up" in this context.[8]

In other words, it is up to the hearer to decide whether he/she will respect the cooperative principle or will deliberately misinterpret the text by refusing to reconstruct the speaker's intention. It should be added, to ward off a possible objection, that most sentences are potentially ambiguous, and thus almost all sentences can be deliberately misinterpreted as containing hidden sexual references (sex being the default script for humor).

Consider finally the following classical example, borrowed from Freud (1905, pp. 183–184) and here summarized:

---

[8] There are numerous formulations of the principle of Charity. For our goals, we will adopt the definition that requires the speakers to maximize the number of true sentences uttered by each other. In other words, the speakers should try to interpret what each other says assuming that the other speakers are trying to make sense as much as they are.

(81) Two children are performing in front of their family a play they themselves wrote. The plot revolves around a fisherman who leaves his wife to go in search of fortune. In the second act, set several years later, the fisherman returns with a huge fortune. His wife greets him by saying: "I too have not been idle." "And thereupon she opens the door of the[ir] hut and reveals to his eyes twelve large dolls lying asleep on the floor... At this point in the drama the actors were interrupted by a storm of laughter from the audience, *which they were unable to understand*." (Freud, 1905, p. 184) [my emphasis, SA]

Normally adults cut some slack to children, and assume that they cannot really mean the sexual overtones that an adult would see in a given situation. So the question becomes "why the adults in Freud's story find it amusing, and do not dismiss it as a child's error?" The only hypothesis that seems plausible is that the adults are projecting their own thought patterns on the children, thinking, as it were, that the situation would be very funny, if the sentence had been uttered by someone who would be aware of the implicatures of the situation (namely, adultery). If the adults processed seriously the situation the inferential paths would be (greatly simplifying): she shows twelve children she had while her husband was away; however, in her knowledge of the world children have nothing to do with sex (say, they are brought by the stork), therefore no sexual innuendo is meant, and the implication of the situation is that she has been busy too. Yet, the adults choose to process the situation as if the child were aware of the fact that having children presupposes sexual relations, a fact for which they have (or presume to have) evidence that it is false. Therefore, the adults are being non-cooperative and uncharitable.

Let us assume, for the sake of the argument, that any of the examples above were not intentionally mis-intepreted but erroneously: in other words that the hearer interprets the children's utterance erroneously as intending the sexual implicature. In this case, the hearer should experience surprise, dismay, and perhaps even concern that such young children would be aware of sexual matters. To react with laughter implies that the hearer is at some level aware of the fact that the children cannot mean what they have just implied.[9] Still, we could argue that in the case

[9] I am using "mean" here in the folk meaning, not as a technical term in Gricean pragmatics.

of an honest mistake, the hearer laughs because he/she is surprised by the incongruous situation (for example, of a student asking his advisor to feel up a colleague). Needless to say, this is not the case in reality, because upon correction of the misapprehension, the hearer should apologize to the speaker, along the lines of "I am sorry, I misunderstood you, I thought you were saying that X" and I am not aware of any claims that this happens habitually after cases of unintentional humor (although I am not saying that it cannot happen).

The crucial aspect of unintentional humor lies not in the intention of the speaker or the text being uttered, but in the way the audience interprets the utterance. And since it has been shown that the audience interprets the utterance either erroneously or not along the lines of Grice's cooperative mode, but rather along a non-cooperative mode for humor (non-bona-fide), it appears that the audience is responsible from the humorous interpretation of the text. Two corollaries follow from this conclusion: 1) If the audience is aware of the fact that they decide to move to the non-bona-fide mode of communication, they intentionally interpret the utterance in a humorous way; if the audience is not aware that they misinterpreted the utterance, they are nonetheless aware (or at least they act as if they were so—I make no claim for the fact that the audience is in fact consciously aware of anything) that they are interpreting uncharitably the utterance, by the very fact that they find it ridiculous.[10] 2) the interpretation is in fact a misinterpretation (either deliberate or not) since, as it has been shown of Freud's example above, the communicative intention of the speaker is (deliberately) altered by the hearer/audience. From these corollaries it follows naturally that no text that is perceived as humorous is unintentionally such: either the speaker or the hearer are always aware that the principle of cooperation is being violated. They may not both be aware of the fact at the same time, but one always is. When the hearer finds humorous a text not meant to be funny he/she is intentionally misreading it as being funny, whereas at best the text can be faulted for being ambiguous (as is often the case with "funny" headlines, typos, etc.) or somehow inappropriate. Thus we can formulate a fourth significant generalization about humor.

All humor is intentional, either in the intention of the speaker, the hearer, the audience, or any combination thereof.

---

[10] A charitable interpretation of the children example in Freud would of course be that they cannot possibly mean what they are saying, etc.

8.5 Conclusions

All humor involves a violation of the principle of cooperation and of other principles such as appropriateness and charity. These violations are real, if short lived. They are not flouts or otherwise pretend violations. There is some evidence that the speakers tend to contain the violations of pragmatic principles, along the lines of the Least Disruption Principle. The interpretation of the humor is guided by the maxim (or principle) of Relevance. Some or most irony is humorous. Irony is a flout, but that does not make irony humorous. There needs to be more of a violation for irony to be humorous. Finally we added two significant generalizations: humor may arise from a pragmatic violation and all humor is intentional, either on the speaker or the hearer's side, i.e., someone has to intend (key/frame) the situation as humorous.

8.6 Further readings

There are many introductions to pragmatics, but Austin (1962) and Searle (1969) are clear and worth reading in full. Grice's (1989) collection of his work published during is lifetime is only for the advanced student. A discussion of the violation of the maxims and the CP in humor is found in Attardo (1994, Chapter 9). Leech's (1983) discussion of politeness is also accessible. On humor and relevance, see Yus (2017). There is no accessible discussion of the principle of charity but I found Jackman's (2003) quite useful. The least disruption principle is discussed in some detail in Eisterhold et al. (2006). The discussion of irony as relevance and inappropriateness is discussed in more detail in Attardo (2000a). A good advanced book on irony is Gibbs and Colston (eds.) (2007). The connection between humor and irony is complex and goes beyond an elementary treatment. See Hidalgo Downing and Iglesias Recuero (2008) for a good discussion. The section on intentionality follows closely Attardo (2003), which is however only available in Russian translation.

9

Verbal humor

9.1	Defining puns	177
9.2	Classifying puns	180
9.3	Ways to bring about two meanings in a text	181
9.4	The fate of the interpretation	191
9.5	Cratylism: resolution in puns	192
9.6	The psycholinguistics of puns	196
9.7	Conclusions	197
9.8	Further readings	198

In this chapter we deal primarily with puns, but not exclusively. The title "verbal humor" may be confusing due to the use of the other term "verbalized humor," primarily in translation studies. Verbalized humor is simply all humor expressed through language, as opposed to through facial expressions, gestures, etc. In multimedia studies which deal with multimodal humor (e.g., video, television, film, theater, etc.) likewise, verbalized humor may usefully distinguish linguistic humor from slapstick or visual humor. Verbal humor, conversely, is humor that is crucially focused on the signifier, the phonemic support of language.[1] It is opposed to referential humor, i.e., humor that does not require a special attention to the linguistic form. The nature and modalities of the "focus" on linguistic form for verbal humor will be one of our primary concerns in this chapter.

---

[1] There is also verbal humor focused on orthography and on the shape of signs in sign language and in ideographic languages, such as Chinese. We will ignore these in this context.

However, before we jump into the treatment of the subject matter of this chapter we need to make a very important clarification: verbal humor, puns and all the other forms of verbal humor we will explore, is always without exception, semantic humor. Verbal humor has an incongruity and a resolution, exactly like referential humor. In fact, as we saw, Raskin's SSTH does not distinguish between verbal and referential humor and treats them identically (i.e., finds a script overlap and opposition). The focus in the literature on the taxonomies, often based on the form of the signifier, and on other phonetic/phonemic aspects (for example the phonemic threshold of difference between paronyms, see below) has obscured this fundamental fact which may mislead one into thinking that verbal humor is just a phonological issue. That would be wrong indeed, since we've seen that there can be humor only if there is a semantic opposition.[2]

Another significant distinction is that not all language play is verbal humor. Play is one of the important factors of humor, as we saw in Section 3.3.1, but of course not all play is humorous; just think of competitive sports. Some authors use "wordplay" as a synonym of "puns" or what I have termed "verbal humor," whereas others use wordplay as a broader concept subsuming puns. Humorous language play would definitely be the same thing as verbal humor. Regattin (2015) suggests using wordplay for puns and word games for non-humorous language games.

Playing Scrabble, doing crossword puzzles, or anagrams are all metalinguistic games based on orthography and while they constitute examples of language play they are not, or are only marginally, humorous. Moreover, they are "artificial" in the sense that they require training, have special rules, etc. whereas verbal humor is done by all speakers of languages without any special training. There is nothing wrong with language play but it falls outside the purview of this book (except insofar as it is used alongside humor in classroom activities; see Chapter 16, on humor and teaching)

9.1 Defining puns

In Attardo (2018) I provided a definition of puns, here slightly altered for clarity:

[2] A pragmatic one will do too, to be fair. Of course, it's all meaning anyway.

A pun is a textual occurrence in which a sequence of sounds must be interpreted with a formal reference to a second sequence of sounds, which may, but need not, be identical to the first sequence, for the full meaning of the text to be accessed. The perlocutionary goal or effect of the pun is to generate the perception of mirth or of the intention to do so.

This is dense prose indeed, so let's unpack it in what follows. Puns occur in a text, i.e., in a linguistic event, which takes place in a context, has a speaker and hearer, etc. In this respect, they are like any other linguistic phenomenon. The next part is more important: puns are defined in terms of a sequence of sounds. First, note that it is sounds, nor letters (graphemes); puns are by and large spoken language phenomena. Second, it is a sequence of sounds (not a string, in which the sound have to be contiguous, to be technical), so what we mean is that the sounds in question may be scattered in the utterance. By "interpreted," we mean the usual processing of language to make sense of an utterance. The next step is more complex: the interpretation of the utterance must refer (take into account) formally to a second sequence of sounds to get the "full" meaning of the text. Incidentally, the word "formal" in the definition specifies the nature of the reference to clarify that in puns we refer to similarity or identity in signifier only, and not to the similarity or identity of words/sentences (as in paraphrase, for example).

Let me add that I do not mean to imply that this is an original definition or even that it is much of an improvement on previous definitions. In fact, Delabastita's (1996, p. 2) definition of wordplay (puns) is as follows:

Wordplay is the general name for the various *textual* phenomena in which *structural features* of the language(s) used are exploited in order to bring about a *communicatively significant confrontation* of two (or more) linguistic structures with *more or less similar forms* and *more or less different meanings*. [emphasis in the original, SA]

and the reader can easily see that there is not much of a difference between the two.

Puns have a duality of meaning. What does this mean? Assume you get a first meaning out of a text. If you miss the second meaning you still get a text, with a meaning, perhaps a perfectly valid one, or perhaps nonsense, but you do get a meaning. Unfortunately, you missed the second one and with that the humor. This is crucial, so let's work it out in more detail. Consider the following example:

(82)   When is a door not a door? When it's a jar.

assume that you do not see the "ajar" meaning, but only the "a jar" meaning. The text is nonsensical (a door is not a jar) but it can stand alone as nonsense. Consider now the following excerpt from a conversation (Hay, 1994, p. 46):

(83) Meena: I'm the only person in this room who freestyled at nationals and came second in the women's division
Dan: let's face it Meena always comes second
Meena: yeah i know that's cause Sue Willis always beats me (.) except at distance
Dan: we were actually making sexual innuendos well I was

Here the pun on "comes" (arrives vs. has an orgasm) provides two perfectly meaningful senses, so much so that the target of the joke (Meena) does not get it, i.e., misses the pun, and addresses the only meaning she is aware of. So, this is the nature of the "presence" in the text of the two meanings.

The next step is the caveat that the sequences may be identical (as in the two examples above) but need not to be so. When the sequences are identical we have homophones or homographs (homonyms), whereas when the sequences are different, we have paronyms. The following is a pun based on a paronym, which we already encountered as (45) in Chapter 7:

(84) Q: What do you get when you cross a cow and a lawnmower?
A: A lawnmooer.

The two strings [ˈlɔnmoʊər] vs. [ˈlɔnmʊər] differ by one phonemes. We will return to this aspect in more detail below.

Finally, the definition calls for the perlocutionary goal (or effect) of any of the participants in the exchange to be either to generate the experience of mirth (amusement) or the have the intention to do so recognized.[3]

The distinction between perlocutionary goal and effect is necessary because involuntary puns may be detected and interpreted as humorous only by some member of the audience, not necessarily the speaker or the addressee, and no intention to amuse may be present in the speaker.

---

[3] Some readers will recognize a nod to the Gricean M-intention (Grice 1957, 1989, p. 105), later dubbed reflexive intention by Searle (1969, p. 47). Those that don't should not feel bad: that is seriously technical stuff, best left to a pragmatics book. Suffice it to say that the intention of the recognition of the intention and not just having the intention is important: for the text to be funny to you I have to want you to be aware of my intention.

Finally, why do we talk about strings or sequences of sounds and not words? Quite simply because, even though many puns are based on words (as are the examples above), not all of them are. Compare the following:

(85) Be alert! Britain needs more lerts.

which dates back to World War 2 England (Pollack, 2012, pp. 138–139) and is based on the reanalysis of the word "alert" in two strings a+lert, neither of which is a morpheme, let alone a word, in that context. On the other side of the morpho-lexical continuum some puns operate on multi-word units, cf. the title of Pollack (2012)

(86) The pun also rises

where the relevant unit is the phrase "The sun also rises" (the title of a novel by Hemingway).

So, going back to the distinction between referential and verbal humor, the necessary and sufficient condition of a text to be humorous is the presence of a script opposition and overlap. The necessary conditions for a text to be a pun are a) the presence of a script opposition and overlap, and b) the reference to a string of sounds, in the sense discussed above.

9.2 Classifying puns

Most of the literature on puns is taken up by a classificatory frenzy unseen in any other field of humor studies. The interested reader may consult Attardo (1994, pp. 112–128) for a review of the main taxonomies. Attardo produced a taxonomy of taxonomies of puns, which follows:

- based on linguistic phenomena (e.g., homophony, homography, paronymy, etc.)
- systematic (based on linguistic categories; e.g., syntagmatic, paradigmatic, etc.)
- based on surface structure (e.g., the phonetic distance between the two phonetic strings punned upon)
- eclectic (i.e., they pick and choose any criteria)

However, the whole operation is ultimately disappointing because however detailed and comprehensive one's linguistically-based taxonomy is, it is ultimately defeated by the richness of language. Another strategy is to go for very broad categories: paradigmatic vs. syntagmatic, for example, i.e., things that co-occur in the string (syntagmatic) or things that might occur in a given slot (paradigmatic).

There is another drawback: all taxonomies presuppose a theory; a theory of language, or a theory of puns, or a theory of psychology, and so forth. The authors of taxonomies are not always explicit on what their underlying theory is. Taxonomies find what they expect to occur. As such what they exclude tells us a lot about what their proponents used as data to build the taxonomy and what their (implicit) theory is. Needless to say, explicit theories are better than implicit ones. The problem is that taxonomies cannot replace theory building, if for no other reason that taxonomies do not have explanatory power, beyond the (implicit) theory they are built on.

9.3 Ways to bring about two meanings in a text

As we saw, one of the necessary but not sufficient conditions for a pun is the presence in the text of (at least) two senses. Yet this is no different from non-punning humor (referential humor). The difference is that in puns the surface structure of the text (its form) is affected and not only its meaning. In this section, we will look at some of the ways to bring about the duality of meaning.

9.3.1 Ambiguity

Ambiguity is one of the most salient among the many ways of bringing about the presence of two different senses in the text. While it has received a lot (possibly most) of the attention, it should be clarified that it is not the only way to do so. Not all ambiguity is humorous of course. William Empson dedicated his entire book (1930) to seven different types of ambiguity that generate esthetic effects and very little of it is humorous.

The most extensive and detailed study of verbal ambiguity in English is Oaks (2010), which dedicates a lot of attention to humor. The most natural classification of ambiguity is between lexical and structural ambiguity. There are other forms of ambiguity, of course. Referential ambiguity is properly semantic ambiguity. Of course, pragmatic ambiguity is also possible. It should be noted that the so-called "phonological ambiguity" (Seewoester, 2009) is subsumed by the string-based definition of puns used in this chapter.

9.3.1.1 Lexical ambiguity

Lexical ambiguity is found whenever a string has two meanings associated with it. Often strings coincided with lexical items (lexical ambiguity), but it does not need to be this way, as example (85) demonstrates, since it operates on the string "lert" which is not a lexical item or even a morpheme (those with etymological knowledge would analyze it as Italian *alla+erta* "all'erta" = to the watch spot).

9.3.1.2 Syntactic ambiguity

In syntactic ambiguity, two different syntactic structures may be connected to the same surface structure.[4]

The standard example is an old joke from the Marx Brothers:

(87) Captain Spaulding (Groucho): One morning I shot an elephant in my pajamas. How he got in my pajamas I don't know (Animal Crackers; 1930)

The ambiguity comes from the PP attachment: "in my pajamas" could modify (be attached to) the direct object "an elephant" or to the VP "shot" (see Figures 9.1–9.2). Semantic knowledge disambiguates toward the interpretation that the shooting took place while the speaker was still wearing his pajamas (Figure 9.1), but the occurrence of the disjunctor ("How he got in my pajamas") forces a second reading, in which the pajamas modify the elephant (Figure 9.2).

Another form of syntactic ambiguity is categorical ambiguity, doubly exemplified in Figure 9.3.

(88) Squad helps dog bite victim

(Bucaria, 2004, p. 292) where the syntactic role of the word "bite" (as the verb of an embedded clause "dog bite victim" or as a modifier of "victim," itself modified by "dog;" in parallel, the syntactic role of "dog"

---

[4] We assume a circa-1965 default Chomskian syntactic representation for simplicity.

9.3 WAYS TO BRING ABOUT TWO MEANINGS IN A TEXT

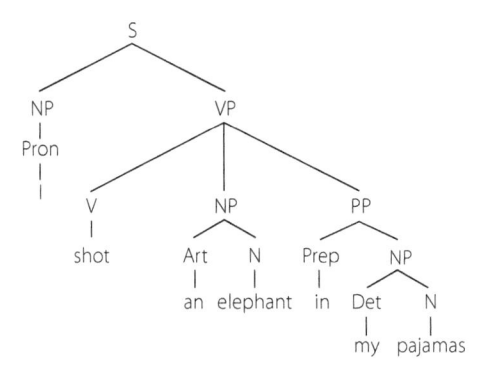

Figure 9.1 The first interpretation of the sentence "I shot an elephant in my pajamas."

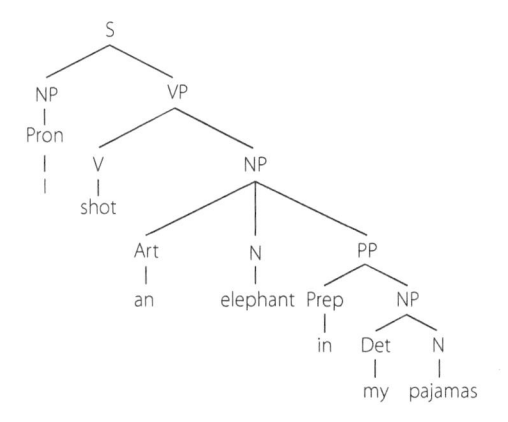

Figure 9.2 The second interpretation of the sentence "I shot an elephant in my pajamas."

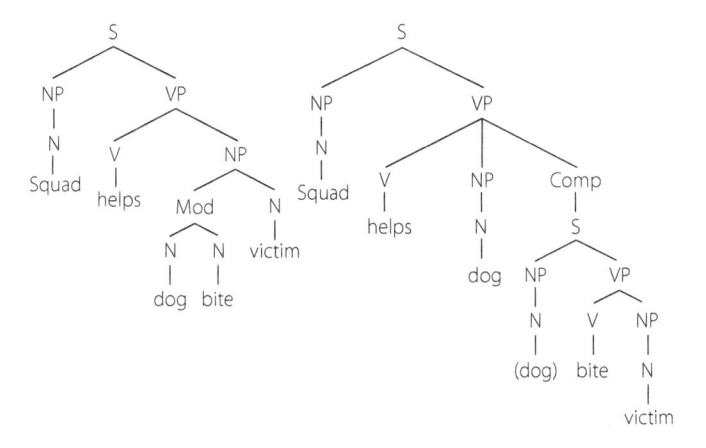

Figure 9.3 The two interpretations of the sentence "Squad helps dog bite victim."

is demoted from the subject of the subordinate clause to a modifier of "bite."

9.3.1.3 Other forms of ambiguity

The ambiguity between the literal and figurative senses of a metaphor[5] is a very common way of triggering the incongruity (Goatly, 2012, pp. 180–181). A short example is

(89) How's your plumbing business going? We're flush. (Oring, 2003, p. 120)

Whether this is considered a semantic or pragmatic ambiguity depends on the theory of metaphor one subscribes to, so I will let it rest, but will note in passing that not all taxonomies of puns would classify this phenomenon as a pun.

Referential ambiguity may bring about the second sense, as in the following example:

(90) John sleeps with his wife once a week. So does Paul.

in which the ambiguity is between the referential attribution of the pronoun "his" in the ellipsed constituent "sleeps with his wife once a week." In other words, there are two possible interpretations: 1) John sleeps with his [=John's] wife; Paul sleeps with his [=Paul's] wife; and 2) John sleeps with his [=John's] wife; Paul sleeps with his [=John's] wife. Note that this is no syntactic ambiguity as the structure of the sentence remains the same for both interpretations.

---

[5] One may question whether the ambiguity between the meanings of flush (as in skin engorged with blood, hence metaphorically a rush or any fluid, hence water in a toilet, and by further metaphorical extension, plentiful; here, having plenty of business) is indeed metaphorical or the meanings have separated in unrelated lexical items, which would then lead one to classify this example as homonymy. However, dictionaries list the senses as part of the same meaning. For those readers still unconvinced, a different example might help in which there can be no doubt of the metaphorical nature of the relationship between the two senses, as one is expressed visually: in the movie *Harold & Kumar Go to White Castle* (2004) there is a scene (available online at https://www.youtube.com/watch?v=D_ZlnWQbCeE) in which Kumar notices a bag of marijuana and his attraction toward it is visualized as a montage sequence in which the stereotypical phases of a love story between two people are revisited as the interactions between the Kumar character and an anthropomorphic human-sized bag of marijuana. This is an extended example of literalization of a metaphor "to love something," with humorous effects.

9.3 WAYS TO BRING ABOUT TWO MEANINGS IN A TEXT

Finally, a generally neglected form of ambiguity is pragmatic ambiguity.[6] Consider again joke (24), from Chapter 3, repeated here for convenience.

(91) One day, as I was withdrawing some money, the cashier at the bank asked me: "Do you want me to take it out of your checking?" I answered, "No, take it out of someone else's checking."

When the cashier asks me if I want to take the money out of my checking account, the sentence is unambiguous: the ambiguity of the lexical items has been resolved by the context. "take out" for example means "withdraw" and not "purchase food to eat outside of an establishment" or "accompany for a walk" (as in "take out the dog"); the syntax is likewise unambiguous: it is the direct object (anaphorically referring to the money), "take out" is the verb, which has undergone "particle hopping"[7] and collocates with "of something" (in our case, my checking account). Here pragmatic enrichment tells us that the question is in fact a dual option: checking or savings (this being a small credit union, there were only two kinds of accounts; no fancy high-yield accounts, or bonds, etc.). Thus the pragmatic force of the utterance is a yes/no question, should the withdrawal come from my checking account or from my savings. The two possible answers are thus: yes, take it out of my checking account, or no, take it out of my savings account.

By forcing a reinterpretation of the theme/rheme organization of the sentence (which will be reflected in the intonation of the utterance) I force a new marked pragmatic interpretation in which the question remains a yes/no dual question, but the focus shifts on the modifier of account "mine" ("your" with direct speech referential shift), which would turn the question in "do you want the money withdrawn from your checking account or from someone else's account?" By deliberately choosing the second, less likely interpretation, I forced the marked reading onto the text. Below the two intonations of the utterance are reproduced (caps mark the prominent syllable):

---

[6] "Pragmatic homonymy (ambiguity) is the phenomenon by which [speakers] use the same linguistic devices to achieve different ends." Tannen (1979, p. 31).

[7] Cf. "Take out the money" vs. "*take out it" and "take the money out" vs. "take it out." Particle hopping is obligatory if the DO is a pronoun.

VERBAL HUMOR

(92) Original: "Do you want me to take it out of your CHECKing?"
Reinterpretation: "Do you want me to take it out of YOUR checking?"

Once again, it should be noted that the ambiguity is here completely pragmatic: the lexical items, the syntax, the semantic referents of the anaphors, etc. have been satisfactorily disambiguated, so that in context there is no functional ambiguity left.[8] The ambiguity that is exploited in the text is a pragmatic one.

Let me be open about the fact that few people would label the above example a pun, even though it meets the standards of the definition given above, as it is based on two meanings co-existing in one string (the entire sentence). Indeed, it is not a prototypical pun. I have included this phenomenon here for completeness of the discussion on ambiguity-generated humor.

9.3.2 Syntagmatic placement

As we have seen, a lot of verbal humor utilizes ambiguity. However, not all verbal humor is based on the exploitation of a duality of meaning contained in the text. For example, (93) below is not based on any ambiguous string

(93) Mind your till and till your mind (Milner, 1972, p. 20)

since both the two instances of the word "mind" and "till" have distinct disambiguated meanings and their syntagmatic copresence in the text is what reminds the reader of the fact that the two pairs of strings are in fact homophonic.

This example may not be convincing, because after all, one could argue that while it is true that the first instance of "mind" is a verb, meaning "pay attention" and the second one is the noun, both words "mind" are ambiguous. Consider then the next example,

(94) Genius is 1% inspiration and 99% perspiration (Milner, 1972, p. 17)

---

[8] We can always find ambiguities if we want to: "you" could be referring to someone else than me, etc. This is normal. The point is that for the purposes of the exchange (withdrawing money), there were no ambiguities left.

186

where there is no ambiguity whatsoever: both inspiration and perspiration mean their own separate unambiguous meanings. The source of the punning resolution (see (9.5) below) comes from the co-presence in the text of the string "spiration" repeated twice.

So, in conclusion, we can formulate the syntagmatic triggering of puns as follows: the repetition of strings in the text can generate incongruity, if different meanings are associated to the strings, but the strings resemble each other sufficiently. Identity is of course the limit case of similarity.

Alliterative humor falls clearly under verbal humor under this definition. Alliterative puns consists of the repetition of sounds, or groups of sounds, within the text. The following example (discussed in Attardo, 1994, p. 139)

(95) Today's tabloid biography: High chair, high school, high stool, high finance, high hat— hi, warden! (Meiers and Knapp, 1980, p. 21)

is typical: the repetition of the dyphthong [ai] eight times[9] is clearly recognizable. Is it incongruous? Yes, because we have unconscious expectations for how often sounds repeat in normal, unmarked contexts: here the string [ai] repeats 8 times in 19 syllables, which is clearly out of the ordinary, not to mention that in the last part of the text, the placement of the [ai] syllables is very salient, and follows a pattern [ai] - X(x), where X(x) represents a random syllable, possibly followed by an unstressed syllable, repeated six times, which continues until the end of the text, where the pattern ends, with a second incongruity between the "normal" development of the life trajectory and the unexpected ending in jail. It should be noted that the alliterative pun is independent from the "life story unexpected ending" incongruity.

The following example is a pure alliterative pun, with a lower number of repetitions:

(96) You remember Sunset Strip – where the unneat meet to bleat! (Attardo et al., 1994, p. 35)

where the repetition of the [it] string in the last three prominent syllables is still highly noticeable.

---

[9] If the reader is counting only seven [ai] there is another [ai] in "biography."

Finally, within syntagmatic puns, the presence of the two strings may be explicit, as in all the examples above, or implicit (i.e., it has to be reconstructed inferentially). When the activation is implicit the puns are labeled "paradigmatic." Many examples are obscene, playing precisely in the opportunity to suggest an obscene meaning without having to state is explicitly. The following is typical and is based on a chiastic reversal (Attardo, 1994, pp. 116–117) of the [s] and [f] phonemes of "sucks" and "fingers":

(97) What's the difference between a baby and the conductor of a women's choir? One sucks his fingers... http://allowe.com/laughs/book/What%27s%20the%20Difference.htm

A non-obscene example is

(98) Diplomacy: The noble duty of lying for one's country. (Milner, 1972, p. 17)

with the inferentially activated "dying for one's country."

9.3.3 Paronymy and phonetic distance

In the definition of verbal humor above, we emphasized that the two strings "may, but need not, be identical." It is time to unpack this aspect of the definition more thoroughly. Hempelmann and Miller (2017) standardize the terminology so that puns in which the two strings are identical are called homonymic (or perfect); conversely, if the two strings are different, the pun is said to be heterophonic (or imperfect). Heterophonic puns correspond to paronymic puns, in Attardo (1994).

So, one way to characterize puns is to take homonymic puns and assume they are the limit case in the direction of similarity, i.e., they are puns that differ in zero sounds. Heteronymic puns then can be arranged on a scale of increasing difference. Let us consider some examples:

(99) Context: on a birthday card there is a picture of a beautiful woman holding a birthday cake. The legend reads:
"You can't have your cake and Edith [eat it] too." (Attardo, 1994, p. 149)

The pun, loosely transcribed as [ˈiDɪθ] vs. [ˈiDɪt] (the "D" symbol indicates a flap in American English) is based on the two strings of phonemes differing in one phoneme ([θ] vs. [t]).[10]

Hausmann (1974, p. 66) provides us with an example where the pun differs in two phonemes:

(100)   Vatican vs. vaticancan (with an allusion to the Parisian dance)

where the difference is the two phonemes "can" [kã] (the tilda indicates the nasalization of the vowel in French). Obviously we can get three, four and more differences. However, the problem of looking at the difference between two strings is that several factors start to come into play: just to use an example, is the difference between replacing a sound with another in the same position, the same as deleting it (both differ by one morpheme, but is the difference perceptually similar)? How about replacing a sound in a different position of the string, since we know that beginning and ends of words are more salient? To obviate these problems, Hempelmann and others have turned to Optimality Theory, with good results, but let us just say that they are very technical, as they rely on the ranking of various constraints which are then responsible for weighing each phonetic, morphological, intonational, etc. choice. Overall the main conclusion that Hempelmann and Miller reach is that the proper way to describe heteronomy is "psychoacoustic" i.e., sound-based but considering also the position of the sound in the syllable and word, and the context in which it is located.

Hemplemann and Miller (2017) list some "general consensus" on these metrics:

the quality of vowels is more violable than that of consonants, with vowel substitutes usually having similar height and backness. There is an overwhelming preference to maintain the number of syllables, and in light of phonotactic constraints on syllable structure, this makes vowels resistant to both insertion and deletion. Any change in lexical stress is extremely rare. Contrasting segments are most likely to be found at or near the pun's extremities, with a slight preference for the beginning. Among consonants, stops have the highest interchangeability, followed by stops and fricatives

---

[10] The normally unstressed pronoun "it" would be stressed, in this context, due to its prominence. Intervocalic [t] is voiced and becomes a flap, in American English. [ˈit ɪt] becomes [ˈiDɪt].

sharing the same place of articulation. In both English and Japanese puns, voicing is often substitutable in otherwise identical consonants; changing the place or manner of articulation incurs a greater cost.   (Hempelmann & Miller, 2017, p. 106)

The preference of puns for the "extremities" corresponds to the bath-tub effect, noted in Attardo (1994, p. 123).

This is one of the most exciting and open-ended areas of research in the linguistics of humor. For example, one important question that remains unanswered is how far can two strings differ and still be recognized as a pun? Attardo (1994, pp. 120–126) provides a history of the research and some discussion. Hempelmann (2003) formalized the discussion in terms of Optimality Theory and Hempelmann and Miller (2017) update the discussion. Guidi (2012a/b), building on Hempelmann's work, applies the metric to several families of languages and arrives at a rough estimate of five phonemes. She shows that the results hold for many languages outside of English and may be universal. The claim of the universality of puns and of its mechanisms is not new, see for example, the references in Henry (2003, p. 106), but all the prior claims have been theoretical, i.e., based on the nature of language, its rules, etc. Guidi's claim is empirical and hence notable. Furthermore, Guidi notes that the mechanisms used by puns are the same mechanisms used by phonological processes: addition, deletion, substitution, and inversion (Guidi, 2012a, pp. 90–91; Hempelmann, 2003).

9.3.4 Connectors and disjunctors

As we saw in Section 4.3.1, the string (usually it is a word, but as we saw above, it does not have to be), that is either ambiguous or that is similar to another string and by so being allows that co-presence of the two senses in the text is called a *connector*. So in example (82), the connector is the NP "a jar," whereas in example (83), the connector is "comes." The connector may occur anywhere in the text of a joke, provided that the speaker will remember it by the time the second sense comes about, so when we are dealing with longer texts (short stories, for example), we probably should have a more stringent definition. I know of no research on this metric.

The *disjunctor* is the element of the text that forces to the surface the presence of the second sense. This is meant fairly literally: when a hearer processes the senses of a word those that are not found to fit in with the current interpretation of the text are suppressed, i.e., their presence is not part of the consciousness of the speaker, even though initially (> 200 ms) there may have been activation of all the senses of a word. For strings this is even more clear, since random strings do not activate lexical processing:[11] for example, most readers will be somewhat surprised to find out that "luminescence" contains the string "mine," if for no other reason than the pronunciation is different, due to stress placement. In example, (85) "lert" is the disjunctor and "alert" is clearly the connector.

Connector and disjunctor may occur separately, as in example (85) above, or they may coincide, as in example (86). In the former case they are called "distinct" and in the latter "non-distinct." Distinct disjunctors may occur before or after that connector. The position *after* the connector is easy enough to see, as exemplified in example (85) above. Bucaria (2004) documented the existence of disjunctors that occur *before* the connector.[12] See Section 4.3.1, for some examples.

9.4 The fate of the interpretation

What happens to the senses of the pun, after they have been brought together? Guiraud (1979) examined the question in depth and we will follow his presentation. For the sake of this discussion, assume that the hearer or reader of a joke constructs a first interpretation of the text, whereby he/she attributes to the connector a given sense. We label this sense S_1. In example (83) above, Meena, the swimmer, clearly attributes to the word "comes" the sense of "arrive" (as in come first, second, third, etc.). However, Dan, her punster friend, forces a second sense "have an orgasm." We label this second sense S_2. The incongruity is brought about in the text when we (and Meena) become aware of the presence of both S_1 and S_2 in the text.

In this example, as far as Dan is concerned, the sexual innuendo (S_2) is the sense that should prevail. In other cases both senses may coexist, or S_1 may be the dominant one. The question that this section addresses is, what happens to the senses in the joke *after* the punch line/disjunctor?

---

[11] There is neurological evidence for this: Jessen et al. (1999) show that the activation in the brain is different for random strings than for words.

[12] Correcting my own claim to the contrary (Attardo, 1994, p. 105).

The following example, attributed to French poet Paul Valéry (Landheer, 1989, p. 37), is an example in which S_1 remains dominant:

(101)   Entre deux mots il faut toujours choisir le moindre. [between two words/evils one should always choose the lesser]

The pun plays on the homophony of the French word [mɔ] ("mots" = words or "maux" = evils). When the disjunctor "moindre" is reached, which is incompatible with the semantics of "words" which does not afford a ready scalar meaning (in what sense are words less or more?), whereas the reading as "evils" affords very easily a scalar reading (bad things are easily classified on scale of badness: think about spilling coffee on your pants vs. being run over by a car), the second meaning (evils) is brought to consciousness. However, S_1 persists and takes on the connotations carried by S_2: words can be evil/bad.

In the following example on the contrary, both senses S_1 and S_2 are compatible with the text which makes sense either way:

(102)   Bassompierre was a prisoner at the Bastille. While reading, he flipped the pages of his book hastily. The warden asked him what he was looking for, and Bassompierre replied: "I am looking for a passage, but I cannot find it."

The word "passage" is ambiguous: a passage may be a spot in the text or an exit (from the prison). Coincidentally, this works both in the original French and in English. It is easy to see that both interpretations of the text make perfect sense in isolation, but that when activated jointly, we get the pun to trigger. Needless to say, in this case, either sense could be labeled S_1 or S_2, as we have no way of knowing, barring experimental evidence on brain activation, which sense gets activated first. The significance of the order of activation is mostly apparent in the field of psycholinguistics in which the presence (or absence) of the senses and the order in which they are accessed is significant. I was first made aware of this by Rachel Giora.

9.5 Cratylism: resolution in puns

As seen in Chapter 4 the incongruity in humor, and hence in puns, is often "resolved" in the technical sense already discussed. Furthermore, within the General Theory of Verbal Humor, the resolution is handled

9.5 CRATYLISM: RESOLUTION IN PUNS

by the Logical Mechanism Knowledge Resource (Chapter 7). Puns have a particular Logical Mechanism, which may be summed up by the concept of a Cratylistic folk-theory of language, i.e., a theory of language in which form and meaning are not arbitrary, but are motivated and therefore, similar sounds convey similar meanings. Homonyms (homophones and homographs) are the extreme case, i.e., identical sounds or graphemes convey identical meanings.

Before proceeding to a quick review of the evidence for the Cratylistic folk-theory, it is important to stress a few points, which have often proven confusing.

1. The Cratylistic folk-theory is not scientific, it is factually wrong and not supported by science. These are akin to superstitious beliefs, such as jinxing the result of an event, casting the evil eye, or the existence of ghosts.
2. The Cratylistic folk-theory was refuted roundly in Saussure's (1916) arbitrariness of the sign doctrine. It goes against the tenets of most linguistic theory. Even those who espouse views in which iconicity and sound symbolism play a part, do not advocate a motivated (i.e., Cratylistic) view of the sign.
3. Nonetheless, speakers believe subconsciously these things and/or act in accordance to them.
4. The "resolution" of the incongruity is not a real resolution that eliminates the incongruity. In puns, this is particularly evident as the Cratylistic resolution is mostly subconscious and can be documented only indirectly.

The Cratylistic folk-theory of language is named after Cratylus, the character in the Platonic dialogue named after him. Hermogenes, Cratylus' opponent in the dialogue, summarizes Cratylus position right at the beginning of the discussion with Socrates:

Hermogenes: Cratylus, whom you see here, Socrates, says that everything has a right name of its own, which comes by nature, and that a name is not whatever people call a thing by agreement, just a piece of their own voice applied to the thing, but that there is a kind of inherent correctness in names, which is the same for all men.[13]

---

[13] http://data.perseus.org/citations/urn:cts:greekLit:tlg0059.tlg005.perseus-eng1:383a

9.5.1 Evidence for the Cratylistic folk-theory

As mentioned above, most of the evidence for the Cratylistic beliefs held by speakers is indirect. In Attardo (1994, pp. 149–170), I list a long series of phenomena which provide evidence that the speakers hold Cratylistic beliefs. Here, I will limit myself to paretymology, rhyme, and sound-based lexical associations. These should suffice to establish that speakers do indeed hold these beliefs. The interested reader may consult directly the full discussion, which is not overly technical.

9.5.1.1 Paretymology

Historical linguistics has long known that in some cases the etymology of words reveals sound/meaning associative patterns. When traveling in North-West France, I always make sure to eat a *choucroute garnie*, a delicious sauerkraut-based dish. The etymology is quite interesting, as the German word "sauerkraut" was imported into French and there reanalyzed according to similarities with French words as "chou" (= cabbage) and "croûte" (= crust). Along the same lines, the word "hamburger" (German "Hamburg" (the name of the town) + [-er] a derivative suffix), which signified a ground beef patty made in the fashion of Hamburg (in Italian it is know as a Swiss steak), was reanalyzed as "ham" + "burger" (as evidenced by the existence of the words "cheese-burger," "veggie-burger," etc.).

What makes these reanalyses interesting from our perspective is that the reinterpretation of the word in the borrowing language is done on the basis of the sounds forming the word and not of its semantics (there is no ham in hamburgers, nor crust in choucroute) which shows that the speakers of the borrowing langauge must be reasoning along the lines of "if it sounds like the word "croute" then it must mean "croute" (it does in fact mean cabbage) and if "sauer" sounds like "chou" it must mean "chou" (cabbage; while it does actually mean "sour").

9.5.1.2 Rhyme

It is a well-known fact that the strength of the rhyming effect is affected by semantic factors. This is unexpected, since, in poetry, rhyme is defined as the repetition of sounds at the end of two words, usually in different lines of a poem. Nonetheless, words that have unrelated meanings have a very strong rhyming effect, as in Italian "marmellata"

(= jam) and "martellata" (= hammer blow).[14] In English similar examples would be "telephone" and "scone." Conversely, words with similar meanings have much weaker rhyming effect: Wessex and Essex barely rhyme. Telephone and sousaphone likewise are not good rhymes, because a word does not rhyme with itself (which is the extreme case of semantic similarity) and the etymological origin of the words, both derived from the Greek "phonē" (= voice), is apparent enough to nullify the rhyme. These effects are only explained by an association of sound and meaning in the mind of the speakers, who are pleasantly "surprised" to find that similar sounds are associated with different meanings.

Another semantic effect of rhyming has been investigated as well in aphorisms and advertising slogans. McGlone and Tofighbakhsh (1999) postulate a "Keats' heuristic":[15] "the aesthetic qualities of a message are equated with its truth" (McGlone & Tofighbakhsh, 1999, p. 240), in the context of aphorisms. The phenomenon is not limited to aphorisms: "The rhyme-as-reason effect occurs not only in evaluation of existing aphorisms, but applies also to perception and evaluation of advertising slogans" (Filkuková & Klempe, 2013). This asseverative effect (i.e., forcefully stating the truth) of rhyming and generally assonance can be summed up as the belief that if it sounds good, it must be right, which is also consonant with the Cratylistic views of speakers.

9.5.1.3 Sound-based lexical associations

We know, see for example Aitchison (1987); Bybee (1998); Bybee and Moder (1983), that words are stored in the lexicon according to semantic connections but also along phonological connections (sound similarity). Meara (2009) states that "Rhyming responses, assonance, responses with the same initial sounds as the stimulus, or a similar prominent consonant cluster are a common types of clang associates" (clang associates is a technical term meaning sound-based associations). Fitzpatrick (2013) likewise summarizes the findings in the field stating that "clang responses, [...] share phonological or orthographic features with the cue, but are otherwise not related." In fact, Saussure (1916) already listed among the paradigmatic associations of words, sound-

---

[14] I owe this example to Prof. Sergio Cigada, from the first course in phonetics and phonology I ever took.
[15] "Beauty is truth, truth beauty," Keats, *Ode to a Grecian Urn*; 1819.

based ones. So, we can consider well-established that fact that words in the mental lexicon have associations that are based on sound similarity. This is probably the ultimate cause of the Cratylistic view of language evidenced by speakers.

In conclusion, we have presented some of the evidence for the Cratylistic view of language that speakers hold. If speakers hold this view of language, subconsciously of course, then it is no surprise that they would consider sound similarity or sound identity as justifications for the overlap of two different meanings in a string or word.

9.6 The psycholinguistics of puns

Among the most promising areas of research in the linguistics of humor today, I would count recent work in psycho- and neuro-linguistics which has brought about a number of studies that look at the actual processing of puns either in the brain, using FMRI or EEG scans, or using eye-tracking devices which allow scholars to plot where the attention of the reader is directed.

It would be too technical to review in detail the methodology of the various studies, so I will limit myself to summarizing the conclusions of some of the studies. Lopez and Vaid (2017) offer a broader discussion about humor, but with many relevant data concerning puns. Chen et al. (2017) provide an overview of he results in the neurolinguistics of humor, many of which are relevant to the discussion of puns. First and foremost, there is evidence that puns and referential humor are processed differently at the neurological level (e.g., Goel & Dolan 2001; Bekinschtein et al., 2011; Chan & Lavallee, 2015).

Vaid et al. (2003) show that in a joke the activation of the first meaning continues until the punch line when both meanings are active. After a longer interval (4.5 seconds) only the second meaning is still active. It would be interesting to test if the differences identified by Guiraud (1979) are reflected in the activation times, as studied by Vaid et al., especially in light of some of the results in Bekinschtein et al. (2011, p. 9670) which suggest that there is a difference between incongruity resolution and ambiguity resolution in non-humorous sentences, due to the persistence of both senses in humor.

Jared & Bainbridge (2017, p. 10) confirm the incongruity–resolution approach to puns, using eye tracking:

> readers initially notice that the presented homophone in a pun does not fit the adjacent context, (...). This momentary lack of fit of the presented homophone and the subsequent resolution of the incongruity may be needed to appreciate a pun.(...) Supporting evidence from our study regarding the importance of incongruity for humor was that puns that were later rated as funnier had longer gaze durations on the homophones. Furthermore, puns that were later rated as funnier also had shorter total fixation durations on the homophones, providing evidence that swift resolution is also important for humor.

9.7 Conclusions

We have reviewed various types of classifications of puns and the particular role played by ambiguity in puns. We also reviewed a set of issues that are specific to puns, such as the threshold between paronyms, the persistence of the interpretations of the text, and the Cratylistic resolution typical of puns. We concluded with a review of some of the psycholinguistic evidence for these phenomena.

While puns are a special category of humor, they are still based on a semantic opposition and a resolution. In this they are identical to other forms of humor that do not rely on the form of signifier. However, the way in which puns do rely on the signifier and the way in which they partially resolve the incongruity are different and to some extent unique, which justifies their separate treatment. There is some evidence that puns are universal as well and that they exploit the same general phonological mechanisms.

The treatment of puns concludes the second part of the book, which covered humor competence. Humor competence is primarily semantic and pragmatic. As we have seen, in order to account for some phenomena, such as puns, or targets, we need to move to a slightly less abstract level in which we do consider that linguistic expressions have forms (signifiers) and that jokes are about things and that sometimes the oppositions express value judgements (good vs. bad, for example) and that these value judgements may be predicated of people (targets), for example. In the next part, we will turn to humor performance, thus moving even further toward the concrete side of our theoretical stance, and we will consider audience and social interactions.

9.8 Further readings

The most recent general treatment of puns can be found in Hempelmann and Miller (2017). Hausmann (1974) is a classic, in German, but the examples are in French. Guiraud (1979) also in French is another classic text. Pepicello and Green (1984) is also interesting. My own treatment of puns in Chapters 3 and 4 of Attardo (1994) is still worth reading, especially on the Cratylistic theory. The bibliography is updated in Attardo (2018). Other essential resources are Sobkoviak (1991), Lew (1996) and Hempelmann's (2003) dissertations, Ritchie (2004: ch. 9), and Guidi (2012a), which is in Italian but helpfully summarized in (2012b) in English.

Part III
Humor Performance

In the third part of the book, we turn to the performance aspect of humor or, to put it differently, humor in context, i.e., actual uses of humor by speakers, in certain settings and circumstances, with specific goals and intentions. The organization of the third part of the book is fairly linear: we begin by presenting the ethnomethodological approach that will underlie this whole part of the book and then we examine conversation analysis, with its focus on humor in conversation, before moving on to the next chapter which deals more broadly with discourse analysis and the functions of humor in discourse. The chapter on sociolinguistic variation and humor wraps up the discussion of the performance of humor and in fact that entire presentation of the linguistics of humor per se, as the fourth part of the book deals with applications of the linguistics of humor to other areas, such as translation, pedagogy, and more.

10

The performance of humor

10.1	A little history never hurt anyone	202
10.2	The Hymes-Gumperz sociolinguistic model	211
10.3	Empirical studies on markers of humor performance	227
10.4	Further readings	234

In this chapter we begin to tackle how speakers actually produce humor, primarily in spoken discourse, i.e., how they perform humor. Another way to conceptualize the subject matter of this chapter is to think of it as humor in discourse. In order to address this subject we will need to introduce a slightly different perspective than the one we have been working under in the first part of the book. The chapter is organized as follows: the first section reviews previous attempts at providing a theory of humor performance. The second section presents the Hymes-Gumperz theory of ethnography of communication and organizes relevant research on humor performance within that framework. Since the Hymes-Gumperz framework is rather broad and, as a whole, has not been widely adopted within humor studies,[1] I will present its underpinnings in somewhat more detail than other approaches mentioned elsewhere. The third and final section presents some recent empirical studies in the performance of humor which combine discourse and instrumental analyses.

As the reader will recall from our brief discussion in Section 2.1, one of the foundational points established by Saussure (1916) is that it is crucial

---

[1] There are plenty of studies that fit *within* the framework of ethnomethodology, for example most discourse analysis, but very few studies encompass the *entire* ethnomethodological framework.

The Linguistics of Humor: An Introduction. Salvatore Attardo, Oxford University Press (2020). © Salvatore Attardo.
DOI: 10.1093/oso/9780198791270.001.0001

to distinguish two levels of analysis in the study of language: the *langue*, language, in an abstract sense, and the *parole*, speech/discourse, in a concrete sense, and including the uses of language in writing. Chomsky renamed the distinction competence and performance, respectively, with minor changes in the definition of the role of syntax, which are not relevant in this context. The title of the chapter then should be understood with "performance" in the Saussurian/Chomskian sense (i.e., as opposed to competence) and not specifically in a theatrical or cinematic sense, although we discuss stand-up comedy, which is a form of performance in the theatrical sense, and delivering a joke is, to some extent, a form of micro-performance (for example, the teller will embody characters, do "voices," or accents, etc.). Performance in the acting sense is outside the realm of this study.

The reader will recall that Chapter 6 detailed Raskin's Semantic-Script Theory of Humor, a theory of humor competence. This chapter, and the following three, on conversation and discourse analysis and sociolinguistics, deal with the performance side of humor. However, the nice parallelism ends here. While the competence side of the parallelism is fully theoretically developed, the performance of humor lacks a coherent comprehensive theory. In fact, this chapter will attempt to be a first presentation of such a theory.

One could then wonder if there is any difference between the performance of humor and the conversation/discourse analysis of humor. The performance of humor goes beyond the discourse analytic framework and encompasses it, as we will see below, in Chapters 11–12. In another sense, the difference between the conversation/discourse analytical studies we review in Chapters 11–12 is one of focus. The focus in Chapter 11 is on how humor fits in conversation and what the functions of humor are in that context (Chapter 12).

In the present chapter we will also look both at how humor is realized in conversation; however, we will do so from an empirical and instrumental perspective and using a more quantitative approach. We also consider humor analyzed in experimental settings, unlike conversation and discourse analysis.

10.1 A little history never hurt anyone

This section details a number of studies that are directly relevant to the performance of humor or that propose a theory of performance without however presenting a comprehensive theory. From a disciplinary standpoint, we have contributions from psychology and sociology, theatrical studies, rhetorics, stand-up comedy studies, conversation analysis, the General Theory of Verbal Humor, and sociolinguistics.

10.1.1 Early studies on the social context of humor

Psychologists and social scientists have long been aware that reactions to humor stimuli vary significantly in relation to the social context in which they are experienced. Summing up the literature on the subject, Pollio and Swanson (1995, p. 8) state: "reactions to humorous materials depend at least as much on the social contexts in which they are encountered as on the specific nature of the comic material itself." Research has shown that increased group size increases the appreciation of humor. For example, Morrison found that in a theater audience, the larger the audience the greater the number and duration of laughter episodes (1940, p. 183). Prerost (1977) found that increased group size facilitated humor appreciation in children and teenagers. Stokols et al. (1973) found that subjects in a crowded situation laughed more. Aiello et al. 1983 found that "high spatial density environment [= crowding] produced a considerable enhancement in subjects' enjoyment of the humor" (p. 193). Thus it is clear that one of the first topics that a full-blown theory of humor performance will need to address is the audience of humor and its size, if nothing else.

10.1.2 Carrell's performance theory

The first sustained proposal for a theory of humor performance, comes from the perspective of rhetorics (Carrell, 1993, 1997a/b). The concept of "humor community" (Carrell, 1997a) is inspired by the idea of "discourse community." A humor community is the audience of a given show (say the sitcom *Friends*): whereas the audience that watched the show when it first aired is more local, once a sitcom is syndicated (i.e., is re-broadcast on many local American TV stations and abroad) its audience becomes global (i.e., made up of several different audiences; think of the Spanish, German, Italian, etc. versions of *Friends*) and non-homogeneous (since the various audiences may be interested in different aspects of the sitcom). Carrell stresses that the concept of humor community with its global and non-homogeneous nature can be applied to many other humorous phenomena. Updating her examples, consider humorous memes on the internet which spread very quickly across a truly global community, which is however extremely ephemeral.[2] Jokes have always been known to "travel" far and wide, as they were easily translated and adapted to other cultures/countries. The work of Christie Davies is to a large extent dedicated to explicating and describing this fact (e.g., Davies, 1990).

Carrell (1997b) distinguishes between humor competence (as in Raskin's Semantic Script Theory of Humor) and joke competence, the latter being the speaker's capacity to recognize a text as a joke, without determining if the joke is funny (p. 174). Thus Carrell argues that if one wants to determine if a given joke is perceived as humorous by a given audience (i.e., performance), one has to take into account "the situation" in which the joke is told.[3] In Carrell (2008), she stresses, once more, the importance of the situation, or context, of the joking (p. 315). The slogan-like statement that "nothing is inherently humorous, or funny" (p. 314) should be understood as "nothing is inherently funny in a vacuum" i.e., all humor in actuality occurs in front of/for an audience. Humor competence (in Raskin's sense) is of course an abstraction away from performance (i.e., humor-to-an-audience).

10.1.3 Stand-up performance

Other approaches to the study of audience have included the study of the audience of stand-up comedy (Rutter, 1997, 2000, 2001). Rutter's dissertation argues for the necessity of a separate theory of performance, that is concerned not with why the jokes are funny but to how they are received as such in a given situation, by a given audience.

Rutter sees the interaction between the stand-up comedian and his/her audience as pseudo-dyadic (i.e., it apes dyadic conversation in that the audience is seen as one participant; 1997, p. 118). According to Rutter, laughter does not occur randomly, for example, when individual

---

[2] The life span of a meme is measured in months. Cf. https://www.digitaltrends.com/social-media/the-lifespan-of-a-meme/ Zhao et al. (2013) show that tweets and text messages have an even shorter life span.

[3] This is a far cry from the accusation (Meany et al., 2014, p. 9) that Carrell's "approach disenfranchises the process of production and follows the post-structuralist / post-modern logic of negating fixed meanings – nothing is inherently anything as all meaning is negotiated." Carrell's theory should be understood as a theory of humor performance.

members of the audience get a given joke, but is regulated, much as turn taking is regulated in conversation (p. 112). Rutter comes to some interesting conclusions, such as that "the transition between performers talk and audience laughter is negotiated so as to minimise overlap and during changes in turn that laughter tends to take precedence over talk" (p. 127) and so in this sense follows the "one-speaker-at-a-time" principle of conversations. Furthermore, audience laughter has a characteristic shape: it starts softly, builds up rapidly in volume, reaches a plateau which is sustained for a variable period of time, typically between 0.5 and 8 or 9 seconds, and then slowly tapers off (p. 129). Rutter notes perceptively that

In order to minimise the potential for silence after laughter comedians will start their talking before the laughter has ended but towards the end of the audience response. The ability to do this is provided by their recognition of laughter growing quieter.

(p. 131)

thus showing how performers take advantage of the nature of the pseudo-dyadic interaction to further their success on stage. Likewise, performers may use various devices to sustain the laughter once it has been initiated.

Rutter also claims that "The changes of pitch in [...] delivery [of stand-up comedians] is [sic] used [...] to signpost the completion of jokes and create an invitation to laugh" (1997, p. 232). According to Rutter, there is "a contrast in tone between the principal stress in the sentence that sets up the joke and a principal stress in the punch line" and specifically a falling intonation followed by a rise (p. 232). The example he gives is by British comedian Oliver Double, who is talking about his mother being upset by his swearing:

(103)   Double: An [sic] she [=Double's mother] goes, "Oh, Oliver (.) What have I done to deserve you?" I said, "Ya ↓fucked ↑da:d.?" (p. 233; I am simplifying the transcription and silently correcting errors in the text; SA)

Needless to say, it is not just the audience that reacts to the performer. DeCamp (2015) shows how comedians "tailor" their material to the audience, deciding on the fly what material to include and/or exclude, or including explanations and contextualizations, based on the racial make up of the audience, for example. Scarpetta & Spagnolli (2009) show that comedians use "filler" lines (semantically empty material serving the purpose to delay the next turn and to connect one joke to the next) but also "surveys" in which they check the audience's familiarity with a given experience, with the function of increasing solidarity. Another technique is expanding successful punch lines, in which the comedian add on more humor to a successful punch line (and so he/she can determine on the fly when to do so). Conversely, comedians may develop subroutines to handle jokes that "flop," for example by pretending to make a note to themselves of what material in the act is not working so well. Wells & Bull (2007) and Tsang & Wong (2004) describe various affiliative responses which include laughter and applause, but do not differentiate among them. Atkinson (1984) also describes various ways of drawing applause and other affiliative responses, including laughter and suggests that here are affinities between the two, a suggestion that Rutter (1997) endorses. The first to follow that suggestion were McIlvenny et al. (1993). They find the familiar three-part list, with the punch line in the third item, contrasting pairs, and disclaimers. more interestingly, they find that comedians often overlap on the audience's reaction, i.e., they do not wait for the laughter to die down before resuming their act. Also Bull & Wells (2002) and Bull (2006) argue that stand-up comedians use techniques similar to those studied in Atkinson (1984) but add jokes to the list of devices drawing applause. Jokes received both laughter and applause (Bull, 2006, p. 574). Seizer (2011) discusses the use of obscenity and profanity in stand-up.

10.1.4 Performance of canned jokes

One way to conceptualize the discourse analysis of humor is to see it, at least in part, as the study of the performance of canned jokes. Sacks (1974) foundational article consists of the analysis of the retelling of a canned joke. Norrick (1993, 2010) has documented many aspects of the telling of canned jokes in conversation. Norrick (2003) shows how the GTVH can be applied to conversational humor, even in its original formulation, i.e., as a theory of text and not of their performance (see also Attardo 2001a). More significantly, Norrick (2003) calls also for a description of the performance of humor in conversation and discusses the issue of timing in the delivery of humor. Norrick (2003) is also worthy of notice because it is one of the few articles that attempts a blend between conversation analysis and humor research.

10.1.5 GTVH and performance

The GTVH is unabashedly a theory of competence (Attardo, 2001a, p. 30, Attardo, 2008b). Both in Attardo (2008b) and Attardo (2017a), I show how the GTVH may be able to contribute to a theory of the performance of humor, while nonetheless maintaining that the two are very different endeavors: "a theory of competence and a theory of performance articulate mutually independent categories and therefore cannot mix in principle" (Attardo, 2017a, p. 100). In Attardo (2017a), I examine a) what a theory of performance might look like (it mostly deals with the idea of repertoire, developed below), b) what (little) the GTVH might contribute to it, and c) what I had been working on with the Applied Linguistics lab group at Texas A&M University-Commerce for the past decade (see below, Section 10.3).

It may thus come as somewhat of a surprise that there have been three proposals to expand the GTVH to include (aspects of) a theory of performance. We will briefly review them.

1. Canestrari (2010) suggests adding a "meta" knowledge resource including "the signals that refer to the speaker's intention of being humorous and to the hearer's recognition of such intention" (p. 330).
2. Tsakona (2013) proposes the addition of a "Context" Knowledge resource containing information about the sociocultural context of the humorous text and including two different but interrelated kinds of information: first, the sociocultural presuppositions for the production and interpretation of SOs, LMs, and TAs; in simple terms, what participants need to know about the sociocultural context of the text to derive meaning from it; and, second, speakers' metapragmatic stereotypes on humor: ideological assumptions and stances on whether a specific text can be considered humorous or not, why, how, when, and to whom.
3. Ruiz-Gurillo (2012, 2016), finally, proposes completing (or "modifying" 2012, p. 40) the six knowledge resources with a (meta)pragmatic component, which includes, for example, information about register, genre, (meta)pragmatic markers, etc.

Given the general reasonableness of the three proposals, why am I skeptical toward an attempt to incorporate a theory of performance in the GTVH? Consider, as an example, smiling intensity, i.e., the degree of smiling, ranging from a faint smile to a broad, open-mouth smile. The Applied Linguistics lab team has spent some significant time studying the matter (the research is outlined below, in Section 10.3). There is simply no way that I can see to get to the values of smiling intensity from the knowledge resources of the GTVH. Smiling intensity is a category of performance, which makes perfect sense, is measurable and correlates, probably, with some internal states of the speakers. The knowledge resources cannot predict or even be related to it. It would be like trying to correlate the use of fertilizer and tilling of wheat fields to the baking of good pizza. Surely, wheat is somehow related to pizza making, but not in any directly significant way. Much more important variables can be found that directly affect and effectively determine the perception of goodness (temperature of the oven, quality of the tomatoes, freshness of the mozzarella, quality of the olive oil, etc.), than the amount of fertilizer used to grow the wheat. Of course, without wheat, there's no flour and without flour no pizza, so there *is* a correlation, but it is remote and not very significant.

Likewise, the GTVH accounts for all the features of the jokes qua texts, whereas a theory of performance must account for a host of issues that are in principle not even related to the texts, such as political stance of the interactants, social and economical determinants, gender and age factors, etc. For example, a comedian may introduce a non-sexual joke using profanity and "blue" language. This does not make the joke-as-text sexual in any significant way, but may significantly affect its tellability and acceptability by a middle-class audience. So, in conclusion, I believe that since the categories that affect performance are different from those that affect competence, one is better off creating a theory of performance directly built around the categories we need for a theory of performance. The next sections of this chapter attempt to outline such theory.

10.1.6 Sociolinguistic approaches

There has been plenty of research in various areas that fall under the purview of humor performance (such as discourse analysis, or sociolinguistics) but no serious attempts have been made to organize these contributions in a coherent theory of performance. Exceptions to this are Davies' (2017) chapter for the *Routledge Handbook of Language and Humor* that gathers and systematizes the work on the sociolinguistics of humor, Gasquet-Cyrus (2004), a broad sociolinguistic analysis of humor in Marseilles (France), and my own Attardo (2015), which tries to organize the research on humor in conversation and discourse analysis. The most recent work to be considered in this respect is Chukwumah (2018), an uneven collection of essays on joke performance in Africa.

Another exception to the neglect of the theory of the audience is Smith (2009), in which the author advocates creating a theory of the audience to accommodate "unlaughter," Billig's (2005) term for the deliberate refusal to display humor support (laughter, or metalinguistic comments that are favorable to the display of humor). Billig (2005, pp. 192–193) notes that here is a difference between not laughing, because, say, one did not hear the joke, and actively signaling that one is not laughing ("a display of not laughing" p. 192).

Smith's (2009) argument is that unlaughter may be used to "higlight" differences between the joke teller[4] and the recipient and to "heighten exclusionary social boundaries" (p. 151) Smith's starting point is that the switch from the serious bona-fide mode to the non-bona-fide humorous mode is a "unilateral" move by the speaker and that it "demands" a response accepting the switch. "[T]he joker's unilateral switch into humor cannot stand alone" (Smith, 2009, p. 152). Thus responding with humor support (laughter, etc.) indicates an acceptance of the switch. As an example of unlaughter, Smith relates that Tom Cruise reacted to being squirted in the face with water by a fake reporter by pointing out, accurately enough, that the man was being "a jerk" (p. 155).

In a social situation, humor establishes an in-group and an out-group (see Attardo, 1994, pp. 322–325, for a synthesis of the research). Smith refers to these categories as "solidarity" and "difference." This dynamic becomes self-perpetuating:

---

[4] Here we need to keep in mind the point made in Section 1.1.1 that the terms speaker/teller and hearer/recipient of the joke may be used in very broad senses. Consider that in Smith's example (the Muhammad jokes controversy) the "teller" is not just the cartoonist, who drew the cartoon, but also the editors who selected the cartoon, the publisher who printed it, and ultimately the society that is comfortable with the publication, whereas the recipient is not just an individual reader of the Danish newspaper in which the cartoons were originally published, but ultimately the entire (self-defined) group of people, *who may or may not have actually seen the cartoons themselves*, who feel that they are entitled to opining on the legitimacy and acceptability of producing the text. I have argued elsewhere that the controversy was artfully provoked for political reasons, so I will not comment further on the cultural differences that the episode purports to highlight.

Shared laughter enhances solidarity, and accompanying unlaughter from those who are outsiders or marginal only magnifies this effect. Accordingly, in their boundary-setting work, well-integrated individuals sometimes do not wait for chance unlaughter but deliberately provoke it. Marginal group members may become the repeated butts of targeted jokes precisely because they are marginal. (p.161). Clearly, then, some jokes are not meant to be funny to all. That is, some humorous performances are intended to include some people in shared laughter but to exclude others.   (Smith, 2009, p. 162)

The significance of this conclusion is very important, and often neglected in humor studies: the intention of the speaker may not be that of eliciting laughter/amusement in all the hearers, in the sense that in a (practical) joke the ratified addressee (i.e., the target of the joke) is not necessarily or not at all the one supposed to find the situation funny. In aggressive, out-group building humor, the ratified addressee is supposed to find the experience distressing, while the unratified or at least unaddressed hearers are the ones supposed to find the (practical) joke funny. Ultimately, the speaker may be his/her own addressee, with the ostensible addressee merely playing the part of the target of the joke. The following is an example of precisely this situation.

(104)   Two teenagers, brother and sister. The sister is getting ready to go out on a date. She changes clothes repeatedly, walking by her brother who is reading on the couch, to get her mother's opinion on her outfit. The mother is in another room. Finally, the sister leaves, only to return a minute later, go to her room and change again. As she is leaving, the brother, who has otherwise been entirely silent, says: "It was better before." The sister slams the door and leaves in a huff. The mother, who has overheard, comes and scolds the brother. However, they are both laughing.

Here the brother is both the speaker and the (real) addressee, while the sister is the target of the joke; the mother was an unintended unaddressed overhearer.[5]

Going back to the Mohammad cartoons, Smith argues that their original publication was a deliberate test of group-belonging, as was their republication: "unlaughter was being provoked deliberately when newspapers around the world chose to republish these cartoons" (p. 164). Smith's and Billig's conclusion on unlaughter is that it is a form of failed

---

[5] No sisters were harmed in the telling of the joke. The sister is only the ostensible addressee, as there is no real intention to communicate.

humor, deliberately set up to fail, according to Smith, in the case of the Muhammad cartoons. We deal more fully with failed humor in Section 12.4.3. This concludes our review of various disciplinary approaches to the performance of humor. We now turn to outlining the Hymes-Gumperz framework we wish to adopt for the rest of the chapter.

10.2 The Hymes-Gumperz sociolinguistic model

A theory of humor performance needs a theory of performance, period. I believe that the broad framework of the Hymes-Gumperz socio-interactional model of language use (a.k.a. ethnography of communication) is a tool sufficiently broad and general to provide the theoretical support to do so. Incidentally, I would like to stress the continuity with Saussure's view of language I have espoused in this work (and elsewhere). As we saw, competence is an abstract form (but not the most abstract way of looking at language), while performance is the most concrete form. Hymes (1964, p. 11) sees the distinction as one of more or less emphasis (or primacy) on "the structure, or system, of speech (la parole), rather than that of the linguistic code (la langue)."

A theory of performance is still an abstraction, to be sure, only less so. The distinction competence/performance needs to be seen as a continuum, with different descriptions arranged on the basis of greater or lesser concreteness. The concrete token is an actual use by an individual speaker in a certain circumstance. So for example, this morning, my wife upon waking up inquired on the location of our cat by saying "where's the cat?" That actual instance of the token "the," uttered by Lucy Pickering at around 7:00 am, on May 15, 2018, in our bedroom, in my presence, without any other participants present, with all its attendant contextual factors, which include the tendency of said cat to wander off and get stuck on trees on our property, or the neighbor's, and countless other potentially relevant factors, is a concrete instance of performance. The definite article level, in English, is the morphemic level /the/. The grammatical concept of "article" in English is a more abstract concept. The class of Determiners is yet more abstract and finally the N/N notation is categorial grammar and stands for a category that applied to a Noun yields a Noun. It is an extremely abstract representation of the concept of article. Intermediate levels of abstraction are of course possible and it is possible that more abstract

Table 10.1 The abstract–concrete continuum exemplified by the article "the"

Grammatical category	N/N
Determiner	Articles, demonstratives, possessives, quantifiers
Article	a/an, the
Definite article	the
Concrete token	"the"

representations than categorical grammar exist or can be created. I am not sure what a more concrete form of an actual speech instance could be. The various levels of abstraction in the production of "the" are summed up in Table 10.1.

So in this sense, when Bally (1909) distinguishes, after Saussure, between *langue* and *parole* but introduces the *langue expressive* (expressive discourse), i.e., the "possibilities offered" by language to the speakers, he is considering intermediate levels of abstraction.[6]

Hymes' communicative competence (1972) and his SPEAKING model (see below) are a good place to start. Hymes (1964) stresses "the need to investigate directly the use of language in contexts of situation so as to discern patterns proper to speech activity" (pp. 2–3) and that the ethnographic approach "must take as context a community, investigating its communicative habits as a whole, so that any given use of channel and code takes its place as but part of the resources upon which the members of the community draw" (p. 3). Specifically, Hymes draws attention on the ancillary role of linguistics per se within the ethnographic approach:

> it is not linguistics, but ethnography – not language, but communication – which must provide the frame of reference within which the place of language in culture and society is to be described. The boundaries of the community within which communication is possible; the boundaries of the situations within which communication occurs; the means and purposes and patterns of selection, their structure and hierarchy, that constitute the communicative economy of a group, are conditioned, to be sure, by properties of the linguistic codes within the group, but are not controlled by them.
>
> (p. 3)

[6] Interestingly the more or less open hostility toward Saussurean and Chomskian linguistics one often finds in applied linguistics is *not* shared by its founders. Witness the approving comments by both Gumperz and Hymes in their 1972 opus magnum: e.g. Gumperz (1972, p. 5) or Hymes nuanced recrimination against formalism, acknowledging that "some who are formalists show more concern for the implications their notions have for behavior and the behavioral sciences than do some who are not" (1964, p. 1) or modeling of his terminology of "communicative *competence*" on Chomsky's (grammatical) competence.

Let us note in passing the stress on *resources* and on the *communicative economy* of the group, as they will shape the concept of "repertoire" (see below).

10.2.1 Linguistic repertoires

Gumperz (1964, p. 137) describes linguistic interaction as a process of "decision making, in which speakers select from a range of possible expressions." The range of choices forms a "repertoire." Gumperz defines "repertoire" as "the totality of linguistic forms regularly employed in the course of socially significant interaction." Repertoires include "a greater number of alternants, reflecting contextual and social differences in speech" (1964, p. 137). More generally, repertoires can be defined as "the totality of linguistic resources (i.e. including both invariant forms and variables) available to members of particular communities" (Gumperz, 1972, p. 20). Platt and Platt (1975, p. 35) provide another similar definition: "the range of linguistic varieties which the speaker has at his(/her) disposal."

The idea of a linguistic repertoire shared by a community of speakers is a significant step forward in the establishment of an ethnography of communication, because it subsumes variation: "The concept of linguistic repertoire is a fundamental departure from the traditional conception of one people–one homogeneous and unitary code" (Bauman & Sherzer, 1975, p. 104). For example, Bauman and Sherzer mention "Friedrich's analysis of nineteenth century Russian pronominal usage [1972]. The linguistic repertoire made available to speakers two forms for the second-person singular, ty and vy, but actual usage covaried with no fewer than ten socioexpressive factors" (Bauman & Sherzer, 1975, p. 103).

Choice within the repertoire is not unconstrained:

Every message must conform to the grammatical restraints of the verbal repertoire but it is always interpreted in accordance with social restraints. [...] This connection must be statable in terms of regular rules allocating particular sets of forms to particular kinds of interaction. [...] The power of selection is [...] limited by commonly agreed-on conventions which serve to categorize speech forms as informal, technical, vulgar, literary, *humorous*, etc. (Gumperz, 1964, p. 138; my emphasis, SA)

Hymes (1972) mentions in passing "indicating" humor "by switching from one mode of speech to another" (p. 38). Gumperz' and Hymes' casual references to humor as one of the options in the repertoire of speakers validates, to some extent, our decision to investigate humor performance within a Hymes-Gumperzian framework, as it shows that the idea is quite compatible with it. However, neither Gumperz, nor any of the interactionist work on humor attempted to define a humor repertoire, so we will turn to that task next.

10.2.1.1 Humor repertoires

In Attardo (2002d), I presented, among considerable indifference, a first outline of what a partial theory of humor performance could include. Among various topics I touched upon the gamut of possibilities open to a speaker in a specific situation: after the Speaker has uttered an Utterance and the Hearer believes the Speaker had the intention for the Utterace to be funny. The Hearer may:

1. not get the joke and laugh,
2. get the joke, but not react,
3. get the joke and smile,
4. get the joke and laugh,
5. get the joke and comment metalinguistically,
6. get the joke and change the subject,
7. not get the joke and ask for clarification,
8. etc.

We should emphasize that the list is not closed-ended: other classes of behavior may appear as well, as indicated by the *et cetera* at the end; moreover, this is a list of classes of behaviors, not of actual behaviors (so this is an intermediate level of performance, not concrete communicative events). Laughter, smiling, changing the subject may take many different forms and manifestations.

More importantly from a communicative interpersonal perspective, while the external behavior may be the same, the mental states of the participants may be significantly different: so for example, laughter may occur upon getting or not getting a joke. Smiling may likewise signify (somewhat muted) appreciation or be a cover for non-comprehension. Changing the subject may indicate that one disapproves of the humor or that one wanted to talk about something else. This is called the "indeterminacy" of humor and its markers.

Significantly, the repertoire included the failures, both of Speaker and Hearer, i.e., failure to produce a humorous turn when the intention was there and failure to recognize a humorous turn. Failed humor was at the time an unexplored domain. Since then, significant work has been developed (see Section 12.4.3). In Attardo (2017b), I pointed out that the repertoire of humor is not limited to reactions to humor, but of course must encompass the decision to produce humor and so cover the social criteria for appropriateness of humor, i.e., when and where it is socially acceptable to be facetious.

In this light, we can consider Jefferson's work on the invitation of laughter (1979) as a contribution to the analysis of the repertoire of speakers delivery of humor. Lavin & Maynard (2001, p. 465) describe the repertoire for *declining* laughter invitations (i.e., not reciprocating laughter), in the telephone interview setting: talking over it, typing, and "attending to survey question" (i.e., reverting to on task talk).

Finally, there is another aspect of the humor repertoire that should be included, i.e. the performance of humor includes also the choices in the delivery of the humor, i.e., "all the linguistic and paralinguistic choices made by the speakers as they produce the humorous utterance (ranging from the pitch and volume with which the syllables are uttered, to the font choice of the text, for example)" (Attardo, 2017a). I will address some aspects of this seriously understudied aspect in Section 10.3 below. Furthermore, the idea of repertoire figures prominently in Bell and Pomeranz' (2016, pp. 10–11) treatment of humor in the classroom; see Chapter 16. This should give a sufficient idea of the complexity of the coverage of a humor repertoire.

10.2.2 Speech acts and speech events

The reader will recall the discussion of speech acts and the work of Austin (1962) and Searle (1969) in Section 8.1.1. Within the ethnographic perspective, speech acts fit within speech events, which in turn are part of speech situations (Hymes, 1972, p. 56). The difference is primarily of size ("magnitude" p. 56):

a party (speech situation), a conversation during the party (speech event), a joke within the conversation (speech act). [. . .] the same type of speech act may recur in different types of speech event [. . .] Thus a joke (speech act) may be embedded in a private conversation, a lecture, a formal introduction.   (Hymes, 1972, p. 56)

It is clear that here Hymes means "joke" in the sense of jab line, rather than in the sense of "narrative ending in a punch line" because the latter may not occur in a formal introduction. Telling a narrative joke is more of a speech event.

Gumperz (1972, pp. 16–18) defines speech events as "communicative routines" which have the following characteristics:

1. they are viewed by members of a society "as distinct wholes,"
2. they are considered "separate from other types of discourse,"
3. they are "characterized by special rules of speech and non-verbal behavior,"
4. they often have "recognizable opening and closing sequences,"
5. they often have a "special name" (p. 17),

While Gumperz does not say so, it is fairly clear that joke telling meets all the requirements above. Stand-up comedy also clearly fits the definition of a speech event.

Speech events have a variety of components which Hymes catalogs using the famous SPEAKING mnemonics: "settings, participants, ends, act sequences, keys, instrumentalities, norms, genres" (p. 65).

10.2.2.1 Hymes' SPEAKING components

In this section we will deal quickly with some of the components of the SPEAKING model that are less relevant (but *not* irrelevant) when considering humor and the move on to the crucial concepts of humorous genres, keying and framing, and contextualization cues.

Setting The setting includes the time and place in which the speech act takes place, the "physical circumstances" of the event (1972, p. 60) but also the "scene" i.e., the "psychological setting" of the occasion, for example "formal or informal, serious to festive" (p. 60). The setting for humorous events will be informal and non-serious, generally speaking.

Participants Among the possible factors of this component, we find the speaker and hearer we are familiar with, but also an addressor, addressee (the originators of a message), spokespeople, interpreters, and the audience (a non-addressed entity). Here Goffman's distinctions between ratified and unratified participants and addressed and unaddressed listeners (think of a teacher talking to one student in front of the rest of the class about the subject of the lecture) would become relevant. (Goffman, 1981, pp. 131–133; see Chapter 1.

Ends The ends include both the goals and purposes of the act and its outcomes. In the case of humor, most unplanned improvised humor will fall under the speech act category, rather than speech events or speech situations: while "stand-up comedy" or "comedic performance" have recognized status as socially sanctioned entities, a jab line speech act in the middle of an otherwise serious occasion does not have a recognized status, except perhaps as disruption. Being facetious during a dinner conversation isn't a distinct activity like, say, dinner table conversation is. Conversational humor is expected in some situations, for example, talk among friends, but it piggybacks, so to speak, on an otherwise serious (or at least non-humorous) activity. Conversely, stand-up comedy, with its attendant "rituals" (see Rutter, 1997) or playing "the dozens" are exactly the sort of speech events envisioned by Gumperz, the purpose of stand-up comedy being to provide entertainment and diversion for its attendees, and revenue for its performer. The outcomes will be influenced by the quality of the show, the nature of the crowd, the presence of hecklers, etc.

Act sequence The act sequence regards the message form and content. The form is how the speech act is realized. Gumperz (1972, p. 59) emphasizes that the form of the message is a crucial component. With the current developments of audio and video recording and such sophisticated techniques as spectrographic sound analysis, eye tracking, gesture analysis, etc. we can account with striking accuracy with the details of how speakers deliver their utterances. The content of the message is what is being talked about, the topic of the interaction.

Key The key is the "tone, manner, or spirit in which an act is done" (p. 62). Hymes lists "mock: serious" as an example of key. We deal separately with keying below.

Instrumentalities These include the channel of the speech event: spoken language, but also writing, signaling with other codes, and we may add today, computer-mediated communication, and the likes. The second component are the forms of speech, such as dialects, varieties, registers, etc. On dialects and humor, see Section 13.2.4; on register, see Section 14.4.1.

Norms of interaction and interpretation These norms concern when and how to interrupt, allocating speech turns, what can be talked about and in what situations, what is considered rude, polite, permissible, aggressive, etc.

Genres Genres are textual types. Humor has numerous genres, which will be dealt separately below.

10.2.2.2 Keying or framing

The terms "keying" (Hymes, 1972) and "framing" (after Goffman, 1974) are used more or less interchangeably, in their original sense.[7] The fundamental idea goes back to the groundbreaking work of Gregory Bateson (1972). As we saw in Sections 3.3.1 and 2.4, the concept has close ties with humor from the beginning, in Bateson's theorizing on the metamessage "this is play."

As we saw above, Key accounts for the "tone" of the speech event. Even more explicitly, Hymes comments that when a key

is in conflict with the overt content of an act, it often overrides the latter (*as in sarcasm*). The signaling of key may be nonverbal, as with a wink, gesture, posture, style of dress, musical accompaniment [...]   (p. 62) [my emphasis, SA]

For an example of sarcastic keying of an otherwise non-humorous situation (mob conflict) through musical accompaniment, see Chapter 15. A possible keying device for stand-up comedy may be the use of profanity (Seizer, 2011), which sets squarely the discourse in the informal domain. A discussion of keying in relation to humor is found in Section 2.4 and see also below the discussion of contextualization cues.

Bauman and Sherzer offer a pellucid definition of framing in a Batesonian sense, which is worth considering in its entirety despite its length:

The notion of frame is drawn chiefly from Bateson, though the component of a speech event that Hymes labels "key" is related to frames. A frame is a metacommunicative device which signals the interpretive context within which a message is to be understood, a set of interpretive guidelines for discriminating between orders of message (Bateson [1972], pp. 177–93, 222). Examples of frames might be *joking, in*

---

[7] See Goffman himself uses "keying" in a sense similar to Hymes (1974, p. 44). Tannen (1993, p. 6) notes that the reference of the term "framing" has been expanded significantly, under the pressure of the work on frame semantics and artificial intelligence.

which the words spoken are to be interpreted as not seriously meaning what they might otherwise mean, imitation, in which the manner and/or matter of speaking is to be interpreted as being modeled after that of another person or persons, and translation, in which the words spoken are to be interpreted as the equivalent of words originally spoken in another language or code. Framing is accomplished through the employment of culturally conventionalized metacommunication, i.e. each speech community will make use of a structured set of distinctive communicative means from among its resources in culturally conventionalized and culture-specific ways to signal or key [to use Goffman's term (50)] the range of frames available to members.

(Bauman & Sherzer, 1975, p. 106)[my emphasis, SA]

Let us note several significant aspects of this discussion: first Bateson's "framing" is equivalent and an inspiration to both Hymes' and Goffman's "keying." Second, recall the discussion of Bateson's metamessage "this is play" as a fundamental component of humor (see Sections 2.4.1 and 3.3.1). Third, the other frames used as examples are "imitation" and "translation." We could add "performance of a play" and "practicing grammar rules" as other examples. What all these situations have in common is that the normal conventions of goal-oriented communication are suspended and overridden by a different set of goals. Fourth, the explicit acknowledgment of the metalinguistic nature of the framing process. It is necessary to have recourse to a meta-level (i.e., communicate about the communicative interaction) in order to settle the framing process.

What is generally not discussed, at least not in the humor studies literature, is that Goffman's own discussion of framing is directly connected to humor: when discussing "primary frameworks", i.e., the basic categories that are used to make sense of reality, such as physical events (say, the weather) and social events (events that involve agency) (Goffman, 1974, p. 22) Goffman mentions Bergson's (1901) famous definition of humor as the mechanical overlaid on the living. Goffman comments:

Bergson only fails to go on and draw the implied conclusion, namely that if individuals are ready to laugh during occurrences of ineffectively guided behavior [= mechanical], then all along they apparently must have been fully assessing the conformance of the normally behaved, finding it to be no laughing matter. (1974, p. 39)

Goffman concludes "observers actively project their frames of reference into the world" (p. 39). Immediately after this discussion, Goffman turns to "keying" and starts the discussion precisely with Bateson's essay on

"The message 'this is play"' (originally published in 1955), but also mentioning Groos (1898), which is a significant source of Freud's (1905) classic. Furthermore, Goffman quotes Fry (1968), one of the founding fathers of humor studies. So, it is fair to say that the whole idea of keying is closely related to humor. Goffman reviews Bateson's definition of play, and delves fairly extensively into the research differentiating play from the real action. Without going too deep into the discussion, I will focus on two features: 1) play is performed so that "its ordinary function is not realized" (p. 41), so that play biting cannot involve real (i.e., hurtful) biting; the "real" activity is the "pattern" on which the play form is built (so, play fighting must resemble fighting, but not be fully fighting); 2) "signs presumably are available to mark the beginning and termination of playfulness" (p. 43; see also p. 45).

Goffman then introduces the term "key" as follows: "by keeping in mind these comments on animal play" (p. 43) one can define it as

the set of conventions by which a given activity, one already meaningful in terms of some primary framework, is transformed into something patterned on this activity but seen by the participants to be something quite else. (p. 44)

If the connections to humor studies were not strong enough already, Goffman here quotes Austin's famous passage in which Austin defines speech acts performed on stage as "parasitic" or "etiolated" uses of language (1962, p. 22). Humor is one such form of "parasitic" use of language. The term "parasitic," probably because of its negative connotations, never caught on. The term *non-bona-fide* (Raskin, 1985; see Section 6.3) did. It is surprising then that Goffman never really discusses humor keying, although he does mention, in passing "not taking something seriously or making a joke of it" as "cast[ing it][...] into a playful key" (p. 82).

Goffman (1974, 87–95) returns to jokes in the category of "fabrications" (i.e., framing that involves deceit). Goffman lists different kinds of deceits, starting with "kidding" which lasts only the duration of a sentence or "a turn at talking" (p. 88),[8] leg-pulling, practical jokes, and hoaxes, which may last for extended periods of time. Note, in passing, that Goffman is very clear on the non-cooperative nature of these deceits (for their duration). Goffman then deals briefly with teasing, under the

[8] I was unaware of this detail of Goffman's work when I formulated the Least Disruption Principle; see Section 8.2.2. I now note with pleasure this convergence.

rubric of "negative experiences" and with wordplay (puns; pp. 441–443), in the "vulnerabilities of experience" chapter of his book. Puns are seen as shifts between frames. Goffman then mentions "frame disputes" and quotes Emerson (1969) on debates about whether joking is appropriate (pp. 498–499). If we also consider the numerous references to comedy in plays, film, and television routines, I think that it is more than fair to say that a serious consideration of Goffman as a humor theorist is likely to be very rewarding.

Finally, let us wrap up our discussion of framing with the mention of Norrick's work (2010, pp. 234–235) which traces the history of the idea of framing humor within the context of discourse analysis. Other scholars to explicitly mention the idea of framing or keying include Straehle (1993); Norrick (1993); and Kotthoff (1999). Canestrari and Attardo (2008) and Canestrari (2010) develop a Batesonian account of framing metacommunicative signals that the interlocutors engaged in the "language game" of the humorous exchange may or may not receive, accept, and/or reciprocate. If both speakers are on the same "wavelength" and they reciprocate the metacommunicative cues, they achieve humorous syntony. If the metacommunicative signals are not received, the humor fails, at some level (on failed humor, see Section 12.4.3).

10.2.3 Genres

The concept of genre is clearly inspired by literary theory, where genres such as the sonnet or the Elizabethan comedy have specific historical and literary meanings. As long as we keep in mind that genres in Hymes' sense are not limited to literary genres but transcend them completely and range across all linguistic usages, that characterization is not problematic. A more technical definition is provided by Bauman & Sherzer (1975, p. 105): "culturally conventionalized utterance types which can be employed in the construction of discourse. Genres are verbal forms organized at a level beyond the grammar."

There is no question that jokes are a genre[9] of humor as are anecdotes, riddles, limericks, doggerel, and now in the age of the internet,

---

[9] I have used elsewhere the term "text type" as synonymous to genre to refer to jokes (Attardo & Chabanne, 1992), based on Fillmore (1981) and DeBeaugrande & Dressler (1981). This should not be confused with Biber's (1988) definition of text type as a set of co-occuring linguistic features, as opposed to genre, which is defined externally.

memes. Kotthoff (2007) is a (non-exhaustive) review of conversational humor genres and includes: teasing, humorous stories about problems (different from the trouble talk described by Jefferson, insofar as these are actually funny stories; for example, one student relates having had to withdraw from the university after her 39th semester), joint fantasizing (joke co-construction), parody, humorous gossip. Another review of humor genres is Dynel (2009a). The most recent and comprehensive treatment of genres of humor is Tsakona (2017).

The performance of jokes, i.e., joke telling sessions, has been investigated by Sacks (1974); Norrick (1993) and many others. Norrick (1993, pp. 112–118) shows that speakers may engage in joke telling sessions, in which the purpose of the conversation becomes that of telling and hearing jokes. In those settings, i.e., when the context has been set up for the production of humor, checking whether the joke may be delivered is no longer necessary. Much can be said about joke telling, for example how speakers catenate jokes based on topical relevance and similarity (Norrick, 1993, p. 117) and how the laughter arising from such sessions can start feeding on itself (see Section 12.4.4). However, in what follows I will consider a few humorous genres that are less well known, just to attest to the wide variety of humorous genres. A secondary goal of the choice of examples below is to show that not all joking is affiliative or carries positive affect (Gruner, 1978; Attardo, 1994; Kotthoff, 1996; Boxer & Cortès-Conde, 1997; Priego-Valverde, 2003; Billig, 2005).

10.2.3.1 Sounding, a.k.a. the dozens

Labov (1972) was not the first to describe the practice of young African-American speakers to trade ritual jocular insults, but he certainly put the practice front and center of the sociolinguistic field of study by situating it within the context of his ongoing study of African-American Vernacular English and also explicitly within Hymes' ethnography of speaking (p. 305).

Below I present a selection of sounds, or dozens, targeting mothers (a favorite topic), but other targets are members of the group and other relatives.

(105)   Your mother's a duck. (p. 304)
        Your mother so old she got spider webs under her arms (p. 312)
        Your mother eat rice crispies without any milk (p. 315)

According to Labov, the sounds are "immediately evaluated" (p. 325) and "the primary mark of a positive evaluation is laughter" (p. 325). There is a competitive aspect to sounding: Labov states that some members of the group who are known to be good sounders will stop other members from initiating sounding against them, since the lesser sounders "know in advance that they will be outdone" (p. 326).

The speech act of sounding is described as consisting of a sequence of pair-wise connected sounds. The first speaker starts, usually with an insulting reference of speaker B's mother. The audience evaluates the sound, for its humorousness but also for its cleverness. Speaker B retaliates with an insult to speaker A, usually a variation on the theme introduced by A. Again the audience evaluates the sound for originality and quality of delivery. If B's performance was better than A, B has "won" the sound. A goes again. Here he/she can choose to introduce a new theme or create another variation of the original sound. The latter option is considered more virtuosic. B then responds and the process continues until one of the two is perceived to be the winner or the exchanges degenerates in actual, no longer ritual, insults. This can be seen when one of the participants reacts to

(106)   Your momma drink pee.

with

(107)   That's a lie!

rather than with the expected ritualized

(108)   Your father eat shit.

thus showing that they are taking the insult seriously (p. 335). As Labov notes, sounds are never denied (much like in improv comedy, we may add), they are reciprocated, whereas personal insults are denied, or mitigated. In other words, sounds are ritualistic insults in that the speakers must believe that they are not true/meant (p. 339), or to put it differently, they are in play mode (non-bona-fide).

There is much more to sounding that I have summarized above, as Labov's own analysis, which is much more extended, shows. Further research on sounding has questioned some of Labov's points, such as for instance that the sounds are necessarily false (Kochman, 1983), when they only need not be meant seriously (in other words, one can joke about true facts as well). Rahman (2014) shows that ritual insults are widespread, including the Anglo-Saxon world, and notes antecedents in many African cultures. For example, Kihara (2015) provides an analysis of the *mchongoano* a type of verbal dueling among the Luhya (a Bantu people primarily located in Kenya).[10]

This is a good transition then to the next genre of humor we will examine. Culpeper (1996) notes that the practice of sounding is essentially an elaborate form of banter and argues that this was quite widespread in ancient Scandinavia. Let us note also the affinity, already remarked upon by Gumperz and Hymes (1972, p. 132–133), of sounding with the verbal dueling among Turkish adolescents discussed in Dundes et al. (1970/1972) and with the verbal dueling of poets in pre-islamic Arabia (e.g., Sowayan, 1989). Dollard (1939) and Abrahams (1962) are two of the classical treatments of the dozens/sounding. They are conveniently reprinted, along with an extract from Mitchell-Kernan (1971; see also Mitchell-Kernan, 1972) and numerous other essays, all with valuable introductions by Alan Dundes, in Dundes (1973; 3rd ed. 1990).

10.2.3.2 Jocular mockery

Haugh considers "jocular mockery" (2010, 2014) as a type of teasing (Haugh, 2017b). Essentially, teasing may be framed or keyed either as playful (affiliative, non-serious) or as aggressive (disaffiliative, serious). Needless to say, the framing may be ambiguous, so that "it is not entirely clear whether the teaser really is being non-serious, or is in fact covertly serious" (Haugh, 2017b, p. 207). Jocular mockery, according to Haugh, is "a particular subset of teasing where participants are orienting to fostering solidarity, rapport or affiliation. Such teasing is invariably carried out within a marked non-serious or joking frame" (Haugh, 2010, p. 2107). A more intense form of banter is jocular abuse, which involves mock insults (Hay, 1994, 2002; Haugh & Bousfield, 2012).

Haugh does not refer to it as such, but he describes the repertoire of responses to mockery:

1. Reject the mockery (response to the criticism)
2. Accept the mockery or pretend to accept it (response to the playful frame)
3. Ignoring it

---

[10] Kihara (2015) is also significant because he explicitly bases his analysis on Hymes' SPEAKING model.

Laughter may occur both with acceptance or rejection, and in both cases marks the jocular (non-serious) reception. If the mockery is accepted, the recipient may elaborate on the mockery (self-disparaging humor) or counter it (i.e., respond in type, mode adopt) "the latter giving rise to what is commonly termed 'banter"' (Haugh, 2010, p. 2108).

There are cultural restrictions to banter. For example, Haugh and Bousfield (2012) find that some topics of mock abuse appear only in Australian data (e.g., lacking toughness), while others appear only in British data (e.g., embarrassing behavior in childhood). Haugh and Bousfield (2012) also examine the politeness status of jocular mockery and abuse. On the politeness aspect of jocular mockery, see also Section 12.1.4.2.

10.2.3.3 The Igbos' njakiri

The "njakiri" is a genre of joking among the Igbo, in South Central Nigeria. Duruaku (2015) defines the "njakiri" as "a public abuse to make fun of someone else" and lists is as one of the categories of "oral art" in the Igbo culture. It is distinct from jocular abuse, because it is more aggressive, while still being playful. Nwachukwu-Agbada (2014) defines it as a "joking relationship" similar to teasing" and as "satirical and jocular exchange meant to amuse its auditors, and probably to tease or abuse its victim(s)" (Nwachukwu-Agbada, 2006, p. 153). The critical component of the njakiri is kept under control by a set of specific criteria for choosing the target: essentially, one addresses the njakiri only to one's peers, either in terms of socio-cultural status, or education level, or gender (Nwachukwu-Agbada, 2014, p. 379).

Thus, Ebeogu (1991), whose work on njakiri remains the best available, presents a lengthy example, in which the members of a patrilineal group (hence on the same social footing) trade grotesque accusations (for example, of having gone to one's in-laws to have a newly purchased car blessed, rather than to one's own patrilinear group; pp. 30–31). Ebeougu argues that njakiri consists of "sarcasm" and "curse." Both are pretty harsh: Ebeogu notes "the satire is [...] hard-hitting" (p. 33). Much like in sounding and jocular abuse "participants in a njakiri are not expected to take offense" (p. 36).

Sounding, jocular banter, and njakiri fall under the category of verbal dueling (Rahman, 2014), which is of course a type of language play (Sherzer, 2002). The specific differences between the three seem to be tied to the level of acceptability of the playful aggression displayed.

10.2.4 Contextualization cues

Gumperz' definition of contextualization cue is as follows:

> any verbal sign which, when processed in co-occurrence with symbolic grammatical and lexical signs, serves to construct the contextual ground for situated interpretation and thereby affects how constituent messages are understood.
>
> (Gumperz, 2015, p. 315)

Examples include formulaic expressions, code switching, pronunciation, prosody, rhythm, tempo, and other suprasegmentals. Gumperz (1992, p. 231) lists the following categories:

1. Prosody
2. Paralinguistic signs (tempo, pauses, synchrony, latching, overlaps, tone of voice)
3. Code choice (from the repertoire)
4. Choice of lexical form or formulaic expressions

Features of contextualization cues are:

1. contextual; they function "in co-occurrence with symbolic grammatical and lexical signs," hence
2. non-symbolic (neither grammatical nor lexical),
3. non-semantic; they "signal meaning largely by cueing indirect inferences" (p. 316),
4. intrinsically oral, "present in talk" (p. 316),
5. specific to a culture or subculture

Note how Gumperz goes out of the way to state that contextualization cues "signal meaning" and do not directly "mean." Levinson (2003, p. 27) explains that

> the term 'cue' denotes an encoded or conventional reminder, like a knot in a handkerchief, where the content of the memo is inferentially determined. Thus the 'cue' cannot be said to encode or directly invoke the interpretative background, it's simply a nudge to the inferential process.

Gumperz (1977, p. 198) examines a conversational joke in which a man on an airplane is pretending to be a bus conductor asking for: "Tickets, please!" "spoken in higher than normal pitch, more than usual loudness, and staccato rhythm" (p. 198) and one of the two women who are traveling with him says to the other "I TOLD you to leave him at home" [caps indicate phrasal stress]. Gumperz notes that "if the statement of the man or the woman had been uttered in normal pitch and conversational intonation, the connection between them might not have been clear" (p. 198). In this case, the formulaic expressions and the prosodic features functioned as contextualization cues.

Besides the examples used by Gumperz and Hymes themselves seen above, one of the earliest explicit discussion of the uses of contextualization cues in the context of humor is Deborah Tannen's dissertation.[11]

Gumperz (1977) demonstrates that speakers signal what activity they are engaging in, i.e. the metacommunicative frame they are operating within, by use of paralinguistic and prosodic features of speech – i.e. intonation, pitch, amplitude, rhythm, and so on. Gumperz calls these features, when they are used in signaling interpretive frames, "contextualization cues."   (Tannen 1979, p. 37)

Siegel (1995) reports on code-switching (Fijian-Hindi) as the cause of humor, in Fiji. Code-switching is a contextualization device, which may indicate that "a switch to the code appropriate for humor can be a signal that the content is not serious" (Siegel, 1995, p. 101). Many linguistic communities in which two varieties coexist "conventionalize" one of them for humor (Apte, 1985, p. 190) and so the mere switch to the humorous variety may function as a contextualization cue. For a discussion of the use of dialectal varieties as humorous, see Section 13.2.4.

Kotthoff (2000, p. 64) states that "Laughter is the contextualization cue for humor par excellence." In Kotthoff (2006, p. 7) she lists a number of contextualization cues for humor, which include laughter, prosody, repetition, and much more, but no specifics are provided. Everts (2003) lists among the contextualization cues, word order, intonation, speech rate, nasalization, and facial expressions. Norrick (2004) argues that contextualization cues may help orient a story telling toward humor, rather than the newsworthiness of the story itself.

10.3 Empirical studies on markers of humor performance

There is a large literature on the markers of irony and sarcasm, which I reviewed in Attardo (2000b). A more recent and comprehensive survey

---

[11] Tannen's dissertation committee consisted of Robin Lakoff (chair), John Gumperz, and Wallace Chafe.

is found in Burgers and van Mulken (2017). Burgers and van Mulken distinguish three categories of markers:

1. utterance markers: metalinguistic, typographical, morpho-syntactic, and schematic (repetition, echo, register shifts)
2. co-textual markers, such as other humor,[12] rhetorical figures,[13] intonation, prosody, facial expressions, etc.
3. contextual markers, such as the background information about the situation contrasting with the utterance.   (p. 390)

Detailed charts are provided that list all the markers proposed in the literature, for the first two categories (the third one of course cannot be listed).

In particular, I will highlight one aspect of the research on prosodic and intonational markers, i.e., its relational (contrasting) nature. Summing up the research on prosodic and intonational marking of irony, Burgers and van Mulken (2017) note that the idea that there is a specific ironical tone of voice has come under mounting criticism. First, different features are listed across different languages, so that, for example, in English irony would be marked by a lowering of mean F0 (the fundamental frequency of the vowel), whereas in Chinese it would be marked by a raising of the F0. Second, in experiments using masked speech (i.e., speech filtered so that the actual sounds are not recognizable but the prosodic features are) speakers can recognize irony in their language but not in others. So, if there is an ironical tone of voice it is language-specific and not universal. Several studies (Attardo et al., 2003; Bryant & Fox Tree, 2005; Bryant, 2010) have claimed that "speakers adapt [...] their way of speaking to mark that something was going on in the ironic utterance. In that way, ironic intonation may not be hidden in a specific intonational pattern, but rather in a contrast with preceding utterances" (Burgers & van Mulken, 2017, p. 391).

Another area of research, albeit drawing less interest, are the markers on humor at large. Adams (2012) examined markers in computer-mediated communication. We will focus on the prosodic markers of humor, which have been investigated by a research team led by Lucy

---

[12] The presence of humor in a text indicates that the speaker of the text feels that using humor in that context is appropriate and therefore other humor may act as a marker of the potential presence of humor.

[13] For example, hyperbole and/or understatement and irony go often hand in hand.

Pickering and myself, with a number of students (some of whom are now colleagues) from the Applied Linguistics lab at Texas A&M University-Commerce.

There exists a folk-theory of humor performance, embodied primarily in books and advice for would-be comedians on how to perform humor on stage or in other situations (speeches, toasts). This folk-theory has influenced academic research, as evidenced by some of the claims found in the sparse literature. Broadly speaking, the expectation is that punch lines, since they are the climax of the story, will be delivered in a marked, emphatic way, "with bells and whistles" (Chafe, 1994). Confusingly, this general area is know as the "timing" of humor.[14] We used the existing discussions to generate a set of hypotheses that we tested empirically on 10 speakers performing two canned jokes each. The hypotheses were operationalized (Attardo & Pickering, 2011) as follows:

- there should be a significant pause (longer than 0.6 seconds) before the punch line
- punch lines should be delivered faster and in a more clipped way than the rest of the text
- there is a shift in voice quality (pitch) and volume

The results of the instrumental analysis of the performance of the jokes were unexpected. The mean length of pauses in the setup of the joke, as opposed to the punch lines was actually *longer* than the pauses immediately before the punch line. Only in very few cases there was a significant pause before the punch line and in one of those the speaker got confused and hesitated, thus producing an involuntary long pause. We found no significant difference in the speech rates of punch lines, as compared to the rest of the text, although speakers do deliver them slightly *slower* (i.e., the opposite of the prediction of the folk theory). We found a significantly *lower* pitch (i.e., the opposite of the prediction by Bauman, 1986, p. 68) and no significant differences in volume, again contrary to the predictions of the folk theory (Pickering et al., 2009; Attardo & Pickering, 2011).

How do we explain such a débacle for the folk theory? As it turns out, canned jokes are (mostly) extended narrative single turns. When

---

[14] Speech rate is the only aspect investigated in these studies that *scricto sensu* belongs to timing. Other authors, such as Norrick (2001), have a much more expansive definition of timing.

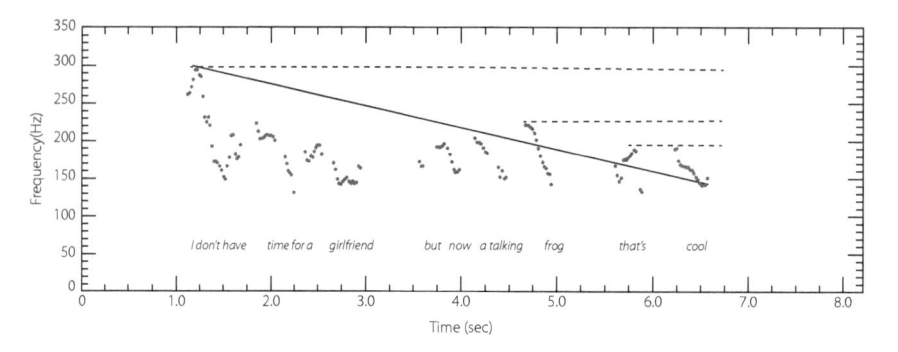

Figure 10.1 A paratone, at the end of the performance of one of the jokes. "That's cool" is the punch line. Note the declination, indicated by the continuous line. The dotted lines indicate the approximate resets of each tone unit.

speakers produce a longer turn there is a specific intonation pattern for this called a paratone. Essentially a paratone is a spoken paragraph. As can be seen from Figure 10.1 above, phonetically paratones are distinguished by a high pitch/volume reset at the beginning followed by a progressive lowering of the pitch/volume, called declination. This causes the last syllables of the paratone to have significantly lower pitch and volume. Since punch lines occur at the end of the narrative and hence of the paratone, prosody trumps any attempt at emphasizing the punch line prosodically.

We successively replicated the study using conversational data, to see whether the nature of the data (monological performance in front of a camera) might have affected our results. To do so we used data collected in four dyadic conversations (8 participants) recorded over video conferencing software. The speakers were instructed to tell one another a joke (provided by the experimenter) and then to talk freely for a few minutes. This provided us with canned jokes to compare to the Pickering et al. (2009) data, as well as a set of naturally occurring conversational humor (mostly jab lines). The results, summed up in Attardo et al. (2013), are even more damaging for the folk theory hypotheses. There are no significant differences for any of the measures (pitch, volume, speech rate, and pauses). Since most of the data are jab lines, they do not occur at the end of a paratone, and therefore we do not see the lower pitch present in the punch lines.

While we had also included laughter in our accounts (with no significant results), around this time, we also started considering smiling. In order to analyze the smiling behavior of the speakers we developed a smiling intensity scale (SIS) ranging from no smile (0) to open mouthed smile (4). The full description of the SIS can be found in the appendices of Gironzetti, Attardo and Pickering (2016) and Gironzetti et al. (2016). What we found was that speakers smile a lot in conversation. However there is a reliable correlation between smiling intensity and humor. In other words, the speakers do not necessarily smile more often when humor occurs, but they smile more broadly. Furthermore they tend to match each other's intensity of smiling (i.e., they display synchronicity). This indicates that the speakers are engaging in a negotiation of the nature (key/frame) of the situation. Curran et al. (2018) show that speakers are sensitive to differences in intensity of laughter.

The hypothesis that the speakers in face to face conversation are actively negotiating the humorous frame of the interaction is further supported by research presented in Gironzetti et al. (2016) and Gironzetti (2017) using eye tracking technology, Gironzetti shows that speakers when they engage in humor display a heightened interest in the eyes and mouth areas of the face, where the Duchenne display of felt smiles are produced. However, the relationship is far from linear: for example, irony and jokes seem to comport different gaze patterns: more attention is paid to the mouth when the humor type is irony, whereas less attention is paid when the humor is a canned joke punch line. Likewise, Spanish speakers show overall less attention to the face, thus opening the possibility of research in cultural differences of gaze patterns in humor. Other patterns including mutual gaze and gaze aversion (looking away) seem to offer promising avenues of research as well. Williams, Burns, & Harmon (2009) show that gaze aversion correlates with sarcasm, for example.

Other research on the matter includes a collection of articles (Attardo et al., 2013, originally published in 2011 as a special issue of *Pragmatics and Cognition*) in which a few other studies concerning the prosody of humor. Bird (2011/2013) is dedicated to the prosody of riddle questions, essentially the first part of a riddle, such as (109).

(109) Why'd the mouse cross the road?

Bird's findings are that

> riddle questions and conversational questions differ significantly in their pitch characteristics. Regardless of the gender of the speaker, riddle questions generally have less pitch change over the utterance due to lowered maximum pitch, less average pitch change within nuclei, and less drastic changes in pitch contour within nuclei on average.
>
> (2013, p. 99)

which is consonant with the results discussed above. Flamson et al. (2011/2013) likewise find that speakers do not mark prosodically either the punch lines of the set up of humor passages.

Not all research is consonant with the findings reported above. Wennerstrom (2011/2013) examines two kinds of joke in which "the intonation triggers the shift of the script and hence the humor" (p. 127) which could be a counterexample to the studies presented above.[15] A genuine counterexample can be found in Archakis et al. (2010) who find that the humor in Greek adolescent girls' conversations is presented with significantly higher volume, lower speech rate and pauses before and after the humor. Methodological concerns about the Greek data are discussed in Attardo et al. (2015, p. 186–187). Hoicka and Gattis (2012) found that mothers reading to infant children

> use a higher mean Fo, larger Fo standard deviation, wider Fo range, larger intensity standard deviation, wider intensity range, and slower speech rate when expressing verbal humour versus verbal sweet-sincerity. The second study also showed that humorous and sweet-sincere utterance contours were significantly different. Humorous utterances followed a rising linear contour, whereas sweet-sincere utterances did not tend to follow any specific pattern. (p. 545)

Hoicka and Butcher (2016) find that parents signal a joking frame to children using various cues that include intonation.

Fatigante and Orletti (2013) also consider smiling as a marker of affiliation, whereas they consider laughter to be either affiliative or disaffiliative. Ikeda and Bysouth (2013) mention gaze and smiling as multimodal clues. They study multi-party conversations and find three types of laughter: spectator laughter, which signals disengagement, turn-initial, stepped up laughter, which signals engagement and a willingness to take the floor, and delayed laughter, which shows a desire to set themselves apart. Ruiz-Madrid and Fortanet-Gòmez examine humor in plenary lectures using a multimodal framework. Further studies are reviewed in Gironzetti (2017). Some studies are beginning to consider the possibility of gestures as markers of humor; for example, Buján (2019) examines a variety of gestures in talk show interviews, such as facial expressions (smiling, raised eyebrows), head gestures (nods, shaking etc.), bodily gestures, such as turning toward the interviewer, etc.

---

[15] Interestingly, Wennerstrom described one of the special intonations as a L+H*, which matches Double's stand-up example quoted by Rutter, cf. example (103).

She comes to the conclusion that none of the gestures is particularly associated with humor and that the gestures when associated with humor have the same meaning than when they are not associated with humor. This contradicts Tabacaru & Lemmens' (2014) claim that raised eyebrows would be associated with sarcasm and humor at large.

Peräkylä and Ruusuvuori (2006) anticipated the frame-by-frame analysis of smiling in dyadic conversations. The authors selected assessments (evaluative statements) and analyzed only those parts of the conversations, for affective displays. They do not use FACS, but define smiling in the same terms. They find, in a case study, that facial expressions display affect and assessment and that the speakers' facial displays are coordinated (synchrony). Their most interesting finding, from our perspective, is that

> there seems to be a particular continuity in the parties' facial expression [=smiles] and the affect that it incorporates: while the verbal action and an aspect of the topic change, the affect, as displayed by the participants' faces, in this case remains the same.
>
> (p. 138)

In another study, based on the same materials, Kaukomaa et al. (2013) consider "anticipatory" smiles, which occur before the verbal turn of a speaker and find that they are all reciprocated by the interlocutor. The turn-initial smiles were associated with "a shift in emotional stance" (p. 22). Some of the smiles introduce a "humorous emotional stance" (p. 23). The interlocutor may either "join the emotional stance" of the speaker after the first speaker has "clarified the grounds" for it, or immediately, i.e., without waiting to know why the speaker is smiling (p. 27).

It is too early to draw any significant conclusions about the empirical study of humor performance, except to say that there seems to be ample evidence that the study of the markers of humor performance is shaping up as a rewarding area of research, in which much remains to be done. It seems that some results are relatively well established, such as the refutation of the folk theory of "louder, faster, and after a pause" and of a specific ironical tone of voice. Furthermore, the importance of synchronicity cannot be overstated. However, we have to be clear that research in this area is just getting started.

This concludes also our presentation of the theoretical background of the study of the performance of humor. As we anticipated, only a full theory as comprehensive as the ethnomethodological approach proposed by Hymes and Gumperz (and many others, including, Goffman, Sherzer, Tannen, etc.) can handle the complexity of a complete account of humor performance. In the next chapters we turn then to the specific details of some of these analyses, beginning with conversation and discourse analysis.

10.4 Further readings

There are many introduction to the study of discourse, in a broad sense. I find Schiffrin (1994) to be particularly good. Saville-Troike (1982) is a classic. The two-volume *Handbook of Discourse Analysis* (Tannen et al. 2015) is comprehensive and authoritative. There are no comprehensive treatments of humor performance. The relevant chapters in the *Handbook of Language and Humor* (Attardo, 2017d) are good introductions to their respective areas of coverage. Brodie (2015) is a very good introduction to stand-up comedy.

11
Conversation analysis: humor in conversation I

11.1 Conversation and discourse analysis	236
11.2 CA of laughter	239
11.3 The canonical CA joke analysis	246
11.4 Issues in CA of humor	252
11.5 Conclusions	261
11.6 Further readings	262

This chapter deals with the realization of humor in conversation, as part of the broad Hymes-Gumperz ethnomethodological interactional approach to the performance of humor. The topic here is how humor fits within the flow of conversation. We first need to examine the special methodologies used by conversation and discourse analysis, the fields that specialize in the study of conversation and discourse. As we will see, some of the underlying assumptions, such as the influence of phenomenology, are somewhat different from the previous chapters and need to be elucidated. Because conversation and discourse analysis are one of the fields of research relevant to humor in which most research has been published in the past 20 years or so, in order to keep the size of the chapter manageable, I have had to split the discussion on two parts. This chapter deals with Conversation Analysis and Chapter 12 deals with Discourse Analysis. Despite the methodological differences between the two fields, sometimes it is difficult to classify a given study as belonging clearly to either field. No special significance should be assumed in my having dealt with a given publication in this or the other chapter. Sometimes it was convenient to keep different treatments of a topic together and sometimes, despite the fact that the work is *not* conversation analysis, it fit in the discussion (see for example the discussions of humor support and mode adoption, among the reactions to humor).

11.1 Conversation and discourse analysis

Conversation analysis (CA) is used to refer to the research that originates directly in Sacks and his collaborators and that puts an emphasis on the sequential organization of conversations. Discourse analysis (DA) is also interested in conversations but broadens the scope of analysis in several directions. The most evident one is that CA, as the term "conversation" indicates, focuses on spoken multiagent (small groups) interactions, whereas discourse is more broadly defined as potentially any type of text. In our analysis we will focus primarily on the functional aspect of conversation, i.e., what speakers do with humor in conversation. Another difference is that CA of humor rejects quantitative analysis, if not outright, at least programmatically, whereas DA is more open to it, especially in the group of scholars inspired by Holmes' work. The CA stance against premature quantification is articulated in Schegloff (1993).

This is not the place to discuss phenomenology in any detail, so we will limit ourselves to noting that one of the tenets if phenomenology is the idea that the explanations provided by the research must "ring true" or be relevant to the people who are involved, not just to the scholars doing the research. Another central tenet is that the object of research must be ecologically valid, i.e., as naturally occurring and untampered by the researchers. A further idea is that of withholding preconceptions and assumed ideas and looking at the phenomena with "fresh eyes." This is called "bracketing."

11.1.1 Bracketing

The idea of "bracketing" consists in putting aside (metaphorically in brackets, hence the name) assumptions, preconceptions, biases, pre-existing beliefs, and (significantly) theories and explanations, in order to look at the data per se. In the case of conversational humor, this would mean stepping away from the idea that "someone intends to amuse their audience and so tells a joke" to consider questions such as, How do people tell jokes in conversation?, How does a turn in conversation get counted as funny?, and Who is funny and why?

The first step of bracketing in CA and DA is the data collecting and transcription. Frequently, CA analyses use participant observation, which has the advantage in the case of humor, to allow an in-group perspective, which allows the researcher to know what turns are meant as humorous, for example. Traditionally, data were collected as audio files. More recently, video and eye-tracking data have also been utilized. Also, more recently, larger corpora not collected by the researcher have been used. These studies will be addressed in Chapter 12.

The transcription is very fine grained and pays attention to overlaps, latchings, pauses, etc. that usually get "edited out" of literary dialogue. The transcription system of CA was heavily influenced by the work of Gail Jefferson. We present some of the notation used in CA studies of laughter and humor in Section 11.1.1.1, below.

Next, the conversational data are conceptualized as "turns" and not as questions, answers, arguments, or repartees. The researcher can now observe that speaker A utters a turn, consisting of, say a question, and speaker B utters a turns which consists of a statement and if speaker A treats the response he received in the turn uttered by B as an answer to this/her question, then the researcher would classify this as a question and answer sequence, rather than assuming that each response to a question is an answer. So, for example, if A says something and both A and B orient to it as an insult, then A insulted B. Note that the content of what A said, is not considered particularly relevant, if at all.

11.1.1.1 Jefferson's notation

One of the most significant contributions of classical CA to linguistics is the transcription system, devised by Gail Jefferson, which allowed scholars to capture some of the prosodic detail lost in conventional transcripts of speech, while emphasizing the sequential organization of speech, and providing the distance from the data necessary for the bracketing required by the phenomenological methodology.[1] The system is based on traditional orthography and punctuation, with several modifications

---

[1] See an example contrasting a word-by-word transcription and a CA style transcription, in Wooffitt (2005, pp. 11–12).

aimed at capturing overlapping in speech, indicated by matching square brackets and the placement of the transcript on the page, so that the overlapping turns match in position on the page, like staves in music. Some of the notation is provided in Table 11.1.

Most scholars adapt the Jefferson model for their purposes. For example, in some of the work discussed in Chapter 10 precise measurements of the length of pauses are required, and so the length of the pauses is indicated in milliseconds, whereas in Jefferson's system it is indicated in seconds. Additions have been made for specific purposes, for example, Chafe (2007) uses "☺" to indicate words ☺spoken with a smiling☺voice. For a more complete discussion, see Atkinson and Heritage (1984, 1999)

Table 11.1 Notation for transcription, based on Jefferson's

.	sentence final falling intonation
,	clause-final intonation ('more to come')
!	animated tone
?	rising intonation
italics	emphatic stress
CAPS	spoken much louder than surrounding text, or prominent syllable
°words°	spoken more quietly than surrounding text
:	after a vowel indicates elongated vowel sound
::	more elongation
/words/	in slashes indicate uncertain transcription
wo[rds	beginning of overlapping speech
[words	
=	latching
hhh	aspiration
.hhh	inhalation
HHH	aspiration/laughter while speaking
(sarcastically)	description of voice quality or non-verbal action
(…)	part of a turn (or turns) has been omitted
(.)	short pause
(7.2)	pause with length in seconds
'words'	speaker is quoting another person or adopting his/her voice
@ words @	smiling voice quality (also used for laughter pulses)

11.2 CA of laughter

and specifically on laughter Jefferson (1985) and Hepburn and Varney (2013).

11.2 CA of laughter

It is fair to say that within conversation analysis the main focus has been not on humor but on laughter. The reader will recall from Chapter 1 the discussion of the fact that humor and laughter are not coextensive. This is not controversial, including within CA, which in fact contributed a body of discussion on non-humorous uses of laughter in discourse analysis, briefly reviewed below in Section 11.4.2. Witness also Clift's claim that "Perhaps the most significant outcome of Jefferson's early work on laughter was the now well-established analytic distinction between laughter and humour (1984)" (2012, p. 1303).

Nonetheless, in conversational or discourse-oriented approaches, for various historical reasons, which will be mentioned below, laughter has been used as the indicator or marker of humor, witness the pellucid statement by Kotthoff (2000, p. 64) "Laughter is the contextualization cue for humor par excellence," or Consalvo (1989, p. 288) definition of "humorous interaction" as "communications in which at least one participant [...] laughed."

11.2.1 Laughter is indexical

CA starts from the basic assumption that laughter is indexical: "when it [= laughter] occurs, people hear it as having a referent, pointing to something in the immediate environment, typically just preceding or concurrent" (Glenn & Holt, 2013, p. 3). Glenn (2003) states also that the placement of laughter "displays precisely what the referent or laughable is, typically via placement *concurrent with or immediately following* the object" (2003, p. 49; my emphasis, SA). This idea was already found in Sacks (1974, p. 348; Sacks, 1992, p. 745) "Laughing is the sort of thing that, when it's done it will be heard as *tied to the last thing said*" (my emphasis, SA).

However, things are not that simple. Holt (2011, p. 393) also mention that the referent of laughter might be other laughter or smiling and "something external to the interaction." Günther (2003, p. 195) reports that "quantitative data on laughter position shows a relatively high proportion of laughter in *initiating moves* or turns containing an initiating move compared to response moves" (my emphasis, SA). Glen and Holt concur, "Laughter can occur before, after, or during talk" (Glenn & Holt, 2017, p. 6). So, recapping, laughter can occur before, after, or at the same time as the referent is refers to.

Laughter may constitute an entire turn. It also may occur after a pause. Laughter does not punctuate speech (Nwokah et al. 1999; Chafe 2007), contra Provine's claim (2000). The referent may be talk, other laughter, or anything else. If the laughter may occur anywhere, how can hearers identify the referent pointed to by the laugher? "Laughers will do things that mark the referent of their laughs; other participants noticeably orient to identifying what that referent is" (Glenn & Holt, 2013, p. 3). This claim is too strong, in the sense that even though it is generally true that people laugh *at* something, there are plenty of situations where the something is left unspecified, deliberately or not. We refer to this feature of humor as "indeterminacy."

Moreover, laughter may occur away from its referent. Consider the following exchange, from the same corpus used in Attardo and Pickering (2011).

(110) Dyadic conversation between classmates
    J   hhh
          //[i couldn't carry a TUNE in a BUCKet]//
    M   [hh]h
          (0.90)
    J   //wow that wa[s really CORny]   //
    M   [((clears throat))]   //yeAH hh   [h]//
    J   [heheh]

J's joke revolves around the ambiguity of "carry" as in "carry a tune" (sing following a melody) or "carry" (as in haul, physically move a load). M responds with a long pause and some muted laughter, so J assesses negatively her own joke. M concurs ("yeah") and provides again muted laughter. I would argue that in example (110) above, in the last turn, J is not joining in with M's laughter, which is asynchronous, but is in fact laughing at her own corny (by her own self-assessment) joke in the second turn of the fragment.

While it is true that laughter tends to be tied to its immediate context, it is also true that laughter per se has no specific referent, it is ambiguous (Attardo, 2002, p. 169) or as Ikeda and Bysouth put it, "equivocal with regards to its social meaning" (2013, p. 63). Assume that someone tells a joke: the hearer may laugh because they got the joke, or because they did not get the joke and are embarrassed, or because they did not get the joke and do not want to show that they did not get the joke, or they may laugh at the face made by a third party, etc. Often the situation is such that the laughter is disambiguated by context, but, and this is my point, it does not necessarily always get disambiguated.

11.2.2 The definition(s) of laughable

In CA, the concept of "humor" is considered too abstract and theoretical to be safely used. It is, according to most Conversation Analysts, a "typification (see Heritage, 1984, pp. 144–150) of events in interaction, an abstract category that is insufficiently specific" (Glenn & Holt, 2017, p. 295) to describe what is going on in interactions. To put it differently, it does *not* bracket our common knowledge that some things are funny and others are not.

Since saying that something is humorous prejudges the issue, according to CA/DA proponents, the concept of "laughable" has been introduced. Unfortunately, several definitions have been proposed and/or used, thus leading to potential confusion. As with most concepts in CA, laughable can be traced back to Sacks (1992, pp. 745–746) who notes that laughing "has to be done directly after the utterance it's laughing at" (p. 745) and "you laugh at something that happened *here*" (p. 746) and that people assume one laughs at the last utterance (if it's not the case, one will need to identify the utterance one is laughing at). Sacks uses the term "laughable" (albeit as an adjective) on p. 746. In Jefferson, Sacks, and Schegloff (1977) the term laughable is used as a noun.

Let us start our discussion with Glenn's definition, which is as follows: "any referent that draws laughter or for which I [= Glenn] can reasonably argues that it is designed to draw laughter" (2003, p. 49). Let us focus first on the first sentence in the coordinate construction. We will return to the second part below. "Drawing" laughter is synonymous with "occurring with" and so it boils down to the equating laughter and laughable.

The laughable is the referent of the laughter. This is clear and straightforward.

However, Glenn explains that "the occurrence of laughter marks its referent (usually retrospectively) as laughable – and potentially as humorous" (2003, p. 33) and thus "funniness becomes understood not as an inherent property of a message, or the internal state of a social being, but rather as a jointly negotiated communicative accomplishment" (2003, p. 33). In Glenn and Holt (2017) the connection to laughter is more explicit, but nonetheless Glenn and Holt are very clear about the fact that laughable does *not* imply humorousness, "Although *laughter is not necessarily a reaction to the presence of humor*, clearly it does have a close relationship with the (usually preceding) talk: when we laugh we laugh at something" (p. 298; my emphasis, SA). The last sentence brings up the indexical aspect of the definition of "laughable," already discussed above. So, overall, Glenn's definition is that laughter is indexical, it is a marker of a conversational item as a laughable and in some cases (potentially) of humor.

Another definition, clearly incompatible with the Glenn-Holt indexical definition, comes from Ford and Fox: "To count as a laughable, a turn (or part of a turn) must be produced with possibly laugh relevant sounds and/or bodily displays, and it must be responded to with laugh-relevant sounds or bodily displays (Ford & Fox, 2010, p. 340) Chovanec (2018), who adopts Ford and Fox's definition, is explicit: "the term [laughable] refers to a turn that both interlocutors orient to as funny" (p. 157). To be fair he immediately below problematizes the connection, thus somewhat voiding the definition.

The main difference between Ford and Fox and the Glenn and Holt definition is that Ford and Fox are much more restrictive, since they would limit "laughable" to laughter to which *both* the Speaker and the Hearer orient to it as such (for example, by laughing). This would eliminate, all laughables that are single turns (for example, in trouble talk). Regardless of whether one wants to pay this theoretical price, we already have a term for an interaction in which both speakers orient to with laughter: humor. There are other problems with the definition of laughable, to which we turn in the next section.[2]

---

[2] Within humor studies, "laughable" is a somewhat archaic term for humor; see for example the titles of Grant (1924) "The ancient rhetorical theories of the laughable: the Greek rhetoricians and Cicero" and Herrick (1949) "The theory of the laughable in the sixteenth century," so the terminology is unfortunate to begin with.

11.2.2.1 Problems with the definition of laughable

Probably the biggest problem is that there seem to be several "levels" to the definition (Glenn & Holt, 2013, p. 9). We will make this explicit in this section.

Glenn's (2003) definition with the escape clause that a laughable may be "designed to draw laughter" (2003, p. 49) introduces the speaker's intentionality in the equation. Moreover, there seems a tendency to equate laughter and humor, despite the explicit denials. This is made particularly clear by the following quote: "Many laughable turns seem far from anything humorous, for example, those that occur in tricky or delicate environments such as complaints [...] or troubles-tellings [...]" (Glenn & Holt 2017, p. 294). So, if laughter of embarrassment, for example, is part of the category of laughable, which is by definition not necessarily humorous, then why would a laughable be expected to associate with something humorous?

A purely indexical definition has its epistemological validity: while it assumes that "laughter" is a unified category, which is of course an unanswered question, as Glenn and Holt concede (2013, p. 5),[3] it has on its side simplicity and clear operationalization: if there occurs an instance of laughter in the conversation, look for the immediately preceding turn or the present turn, or a turn nearby for the referent/antecedent of the laughter. The price to be paid for this definition is that it can only accommodate cases in which laughter is present. The absence of laughter is outside the boundaries of the definition. The non-occurrence of laughter cannot have a referent, in the same sense that its occurrence does.[4] Thus, under this definition, if a speaker tells a canned joke which is followed by silence, there would have been no reason to expect laughter. One can add a theory of jokes to one's theory of laughables, but the point remains: the indexical definition of laughable can only function for present laughter/laughable pairs. Relatedly, considering smiles, or other features that make laughter "relevant" (2013, p. 9)

---

[3] The question may be unaswered in CA, but it has long been answered, in the negative, in psychology; see the discussion in Chapter 2.

[4] This is not to say that non-occurrence of laughter may not be meaningful, as we saw in "un-laughter" in Section 10.1.6. However, there is a significant difference between laughter marking a laughable, in the sense, Sacks, Glenn, etc. mean (i.e., co-occurrence), and the absence of response to a social expectation (unlaughter). The difference is of course that in unlaughter the previous turn is identified as humor and the refusal to sanction its humorous nature is what makes the unlaughter meaningful.

raises the question of why this should be so, unless laughter points at more than its referent/antecedent, i.e., carries the association with humor.

One could be picky here and point out that if we reject "humor" as an abstract category superimposed on the data (a typification), then laughter is as much of an abstract category. Glenn and Holt point out, correctly, that "laughter" is a "member's category" (i.e., it is part of the lived experience of the participants), but of course so is humor. However, we know from humor studies, primarily psychology, that laughter is not a unified category (see the discussion in Section 2.2.3). Readers will also recall from Chapter 1 that there can be humor without laughter and laughter without humor. So the only coherent definition of laughable is any turn that is preceded, accompanied, or followed by laughter.

The definition of laughable is not merely a terminological matter, as it creates a serious theoretical problem that has not been discussed in the literature, to the extent that it should have been. Here we can only touch briefly upon failed humor, which will be discussed in Section 12.4.3. A preliminary definition, which we do not endorse but that will do for the present discussion, is that failed humor is humor at which the audience does not laugh.

The logical problem raised by failed humor is that, unless the failure is remarked upon by the speakers, it can occur without any external markings. Indeed, this is the case. Consider the following example, from Hay (1994), already discussed above and here repeated for convenience

(111) Conversation among friends (Hay, 1994, p. 46)
    1 Meena: I'm the only person in this room who freestyled at nationals and came in second in the women's division
    2 Dan: let's face it Meena always comes second
    3 Meena: yeah I know that's cause Sue Willis always beats me +
        except at distance
    4 Dan: we were actually making sexual innuendos well I was.

Here turn 4, by Dan, makes it clear that he intended his turn 2 to be humorous, but, if he had not uttered turn 4, Meena, who clearly missed the sexual double entendre, would have been entirely oblivious to it. So, if Dan had not uttered turn 4, the analyst, much like Meena, would have entirely missed the presence of the failed humor.

On the contrary, if we accept Glenn's "designed to draw laughter" definition then we are within the domain of speakers' intentionality, which can only be inferred. However, this brings us back full circle to the definition of humor as a speech act whose perlocutionary goal is the perception of the intention to be humorous (Attardo & Chabanne, 1992) and therefore, from the standpoint of humor studies, the concept of laughable is redundant, one the one side, and misleading, on the other, since it is dissociated from humor and laughter is not a unified category (there are unrelated types of laughter that share no emotional or cognitive component, as we saw in Chapter 2).

Another problem are false positives: for example, there exist documented instances of laughter response to a non-laughable (i.e., the hearer laughing at something the speaker said seriously). Clift, for example, mentions the "You're kidding' response," i.e., a "response to a turn not designed to be a so-called 'laughable' (Glenn, 2003)" (Clift, 2016, p. 75). In this case the hearer incorrectly attributes the intention to draw laughter to the speaker. As we just saw, an even bigger problem are false negatives: failed humor can be considered (reductively) the failure, on the hearer's part, to orient to humor after a turn "designed to draw laughter." We will return to failed humor in Section 12.4.3.

Ultimately, as we saw, laughter is indeterminate, as Curran et al. (2018, p. 1) state, "laughter is inherently underdetermined and ambiguous, and that its interpretation is determined by the context in which it occurs." In other words, if one sees someone laugh, one still does not know what their "emotional state" is (p. 3).

In conclusion, to solve the ambiguity inherent in the definition of laughable, I will adopt the following terminology: a laughable is a referent (i.e., a part of the meaning of the text either explicitly stated or inferred by the participants as part of the common ground) about which someone laughs. A humorous laughable is one that meets the semantic/pragmatic requirements for humor (regardless of the reaction of the other speakers). Laughter is any vocalization as described in Chafe (2007) and others. Mirthful laughter is laughter whose referent is a humorous laughable, whereas non-mirthful laughter is laughter with a non-humorous referent.

11.3 The canonical CA joke analysis

The founding text of the CA analysis of humor is Harvey Sacks' analysis of the telling of a canned joke in conversation. The conversation took place among a group of teenagers. There was also an adult counselor present but he is silent. The joke itself was an old-fashioned joke even at the time of the telling (prior to 1974). The text of the joke is as follows:

(112) Three sisters marry three young men on the same day and the mother of the young women talks them into spending their first night at their home, each in a room. The mother, after everyone has retired to their respective rooms, listens at the closed doors. At the first one she hears an "Uoo-ooo," at the second door an "Yaaa," but at the third door she hears nothing. The following morning she asks the first daughter why she went "Uoo-ooo" and the daughter says "It tickled." She then asks the second daughter why she went "Yaa" and she replies "It hurt." Finally she asks the third daughter why she did not say anything. The daughter says "Well, you told me it was always impolite to talk with my mouth full." (Sacks, 1978, p. 251)

Sacks' analysis is focused on two aspects: first the organization of the telling event and second the function of the telling. We will consider both and then address some issues with them. While Sacks intended his analysis to apply to canned jokes, there is no inherent difference between canned and conversational humor, so what follows can be applied, with some reservations, to both canned and conversational humor. The reader will recall that "jokes" are a genre of humor; however, the term is often used loosely as synonymous with "instance of humor."

11.3.1 Sacks on jokes

11.3.1.1 Sequential organization of joke telling

Joke telling is interesting in several ways. First, telling a joke is an extended turn, which requires the audience to concede the floor for a period of time. Sacks identifies three parts: the preface, the telling, and the response. Table 11.2 schematizes the analysis. Patently, except for the telling of the joke, all other activities are optional, i.e., we can have jokes without a preface and without a response, but not without a telling.

11.3 THE CANONICAL CA JOKE ANALYSIS

Table 11.2 Sequential organization of joke telling

Canned joke	Teller	Hearer
Preface	disclaimers, secure floor, key humor	accept or refuse joke, key humor
Telling	text performance	interrupt
Response	signal end, incite laughter	laughter

11.3.1.1.1 Preface The main object of the preface is to secure the floor by announcing that one intends to produce a long(er) narrative. However, this is not the only function: the speaker needs also to negotiate the acceptability of the joke, for potentially offensive topics, but also for the social appropriateness of producing a joke in the particular time, situation, and broadly context. Moreover, the announcement of the intention to tell a joke orients the audience to the fact that the coming extended turn will be intended humorously so that they may frame or key the situation as humorous. Yet another function is preemptive face-saving: by warning the audience that the joke may not be very good, or offensive, or that the telling may not be very good, the speaker preempts any potential criticisms of his/her performance, potentially going so far as to dissociate themselves from the text they are about to produce. The hearer may turn down the offer of joke telling (for example, by saying: I have heard it before, or by producing the punch line, thus demonstrating that they know the joke).

Interestingly, the preface may be entirely absent, as is often the case in conversational humor. It is however also possible to produce a canned joke without preface. Absence of the preface is almost always required in irony, with some exceptions in writing, where the detection of irony may be more difficult (Jefferson, 1979; Edwards, 1984; Cashion et al., 1986).

11.3.1.1.2 Telling The telling consists essentially of one extended turn in which the speaker delivers the joke. There may be supportive interruptions, requests for clarifications, and of course disruptive interruptions, if the audience doesn't "play along." Some genres of jokes require interactive responses to be incorporated in the narrative, such as knock-knock jokes.

11.3.1.1.3 Response According to Sacks, the response part of the joke telling may consist of laughter, delayed laughter, or silence. The work on failed humor has shown that there is, in fact, a much broader range of reactions which may include verbal abuse or even actually hitting the speaker. We will consider these reactions below in Section 12.4.3 and will limit ourselves to the original three responses described by Sacks.

Sacks calls laughter the "minimal response sequence" because it is the smallest and simplest response. There is now an extensive literature on laughter in discourse, which we reviewed in Chapter 10. Here we will only briefly consider some of the results that CA has produced about it. Jefferson dedicated several studies to laughter. She notes that laughter is often associated with "termination" and "closure" of "interchanges." Laughter, unlike other verbalizations, occurs in overlap with other speech, and in fact mixed in with speech ("within-speech laughter," Chafe, 2007, ch. 3). Multi-party laughter may be in unison, "antiphonal," or the speakers may take turns, "relay" laughter (Smoski & Bachorowski, 2003).

Jefferson (1972, p. 300) notes that laughter is "regularly associated with termination of talk" and so it can "signal or attempt closure of interchanges" (p. 449n), while also signaling the uptake of the humorous intention of the speaker. However, Jefferson's most significant finding about laughter was that speakers can use it to elicit laughter from the hearer by producing it at the end of their turn ("post-utterance completion laugh particle"). This flies against the stereotype that one should not laugh at one's own humor, or at least should wait until others have started and then join in. Instead Jefferson found that speakers used laughter to incite laughter in their audience, both with utterance final laughter and with within-speech laughter. Glenn (1989) shows that in dyadic interactions, the teller frequently initiates laughter, whereas in multi-party interactions, someone other than the speaker initiates the laughter. Ikeda & Bysouth (2013, p. 52) show that speakers may laugh turn initially to secure the floor raising the intensity of the laughter gradually (stepped up laughter).

Laughter may not be produced immediately, i.e., it may be delayed. Sacks sees the delayed response as a strategic compromise, on the hearer's part, between, on the one hand, the desire to display understanding of the joke,[5] and, on the other hand, the desire to wait and see how the audience reacts. Finally, laughter may be withheld. This

---

[5] On jokes as a "test of understanding," see Section 11.4.3, below. On understanding of jokes as a status enhancer, see Graesser et al. (1989).

is a dispreferred choice as "laughings have a priority claim on a joke's completion" (Sacks, 1974, pp. 348–249). Refusal to laugh, as we saw, has a very negative connotation of displeasure ("unlaughter").

It should be stressed in this context that different situations or genres of communication afford different types of reactions. For example, stand-up comedy is quite different in the ways in which performers "manage" laughter and other reactions from the audience: for example, comedians use various techniques to signal to their audience when to laugh, applaud, or cheer, as we saw in Chapter 10. Needless to say, Sacks' was not the last word in the analysis of joke (in a broad sense) telling in conversation.

11.3.1.2 Humor support

The role of the audience is far from being passive. The audience may reject the humor, in a disaffiliative move. Conversely, the audience may provide affiliative support for the humor-producing speaker. Hay's groundbreaking work (Hay, 1994, 1995, 2000, 2001) introduced and conceptualized the analysis of humor support, to which we turn next.

Hay introduced the notion of humor support to indicate a conversational move acknowledging and supportive of the speaker who produces humor. Hay lists a number of verbal strategies, to which we can add paralinguistic support (which could also be seen as included in the "heightened" involvement category):

- contribute more humor
- repeat (part of) the previous turn
- offer sympathy or contradict self-deprecating humor
- overlap and heightened involvement in conversation
- heightened smiling intensity
- laughter
- facial expressions and gestures indicating agreement or amusement

Needless to say, non-supportive (disaffiliative) responses are also present. Hay lists two items (the first two the list below) to which we can add a few more

- withhold appreciation while showing understanding
- lack of reaction (this corresponds to Sacks' "silence")

Recognition → Understanding → Appreciation → Reaction

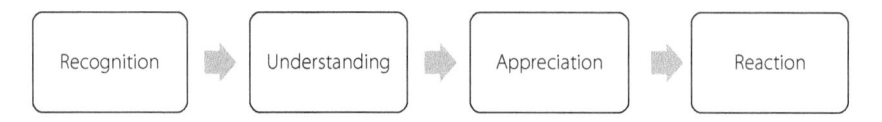

Figure 11.1 Hay's presuppositional scale of hearer's reactions to humor.

- negative remarks on the quality of the humor
- claims that the situation or setting are inappropriate for humor
- claims to know a better/different variant of the joke (typically heard at humor studies conferences)

Disaffiliative moves characterize some forms of failed humor (see below, Section 12.4.3).

Hay's further presents an extremely useful analytical tool, already seen briefly in Section 2.3.2: a presuppositional scale of Hearer's reactions (see Figure 11.1):

1. recognition of the intention to produce humor
2. understanding
3. appreciation
4. reaction (Hay, 2001)

So understanding humor presupposes that one has recognized the intention of the speaker to be funny; appreciation presupposes understanding, and reacting presupposes appreciation. This will figure crucially in Bell's analysis of failed humor.

As we saw, according to Sacks (1974, p. 348) laughter has a "priority claim" but laughter is not required. Gavioli claims laughter is a "preferred action" after telling a joke (Gavioli, 1995, p. 371). As we have seen above, there have even been claims that joke/laughter may be an adjacency pair. However, not all humor socially requires support: humor that is itself supportive does not require support. Irony likewise need not be supported.

One form of humor support is the repetition of the jab line. The repetition may be verbatim or in paraphrase. Consider the following example, which ends a longish narrative in which P tells M about his trip to Galway.

11.3 THE CANONICAL CA JOKE ANALYSIS

(113) Dyadic conversation among classmates

```
221   P    //uh taken the BUS uh into//
222        0.2
223        //into GALway was that //
224        1.3
225        //uh when I came around the CORner //
226        0.42
227        //uh there is uh you know of course the HUGE rolling//
228        0.15
229        //beautiful hillsides of Ireland and //
230        0.43
231        //there's this little dodge around the CORner
232        and you go around the corner and the first three things I
             saw were McDOnalds //
233        0.3
234        //a Pep Boys and an Aldi's GROcery store //
235        0.81
236   M    //wh:::ich [((laughs)) that's very IRISH [((laughs))] //
237        0.32
238   P    //yeah you really don't expect THAT //
239        0.3
```

The jab line begins on unit 232 and concludes in unit 234. After a pause, M acknowledges the humor by laughing and then paraphrases ironically the jab line (thus both displaying comprehension and supporting the humor) and P supports the supportive turn by the asseveration ("yeah") and another paraphrase of the jab line. Note also that by producing an ironical turn, M has mode adopted, i.e., joined in the production of a sustained humor turn (see below). Humor support is not limited to spoken interactions; for example, see Vandergriff & Fuchs (2012) on humor support in online conversations.

11.3.1.3 Mode adoption

Mode adoption can be defined as being "in essence, about adopting a broad manner of speaking, a manner that has been established via the joint involvement of the speaker and listener. This can be thought of in terms of play frames" (Whalen & Pexman, 2017, p. 377). The term "mode adoption" was introduced in Attardo (2002) and as Whalen and

Pexman (2010, 2017) note, it has been applied primarily to the ironical mode (i.e., an ironical response to an ironical statement) but in principle, it can be applied to any humorous mode, for example responding with a pun to a pun, or capping a joke with another joke. As Whalen and Pexman observe, even mere repetition of a speaker's turn can be seen as mode adoption. Pexman and Whalen have extended the study of mode adoption to children.

There is evidence that mode adoption is a highly affiliative practice, as Drew (1987) reports that very few teases are responded to with teases; instead, speakers respond seriously (po-faced) and primarily attend to the criticisms of the tease. I can report that when speakers have an extremely high level of intimacy, teasing mode adoption may occur; my daughter and I enjoyed mutual teasing for most of her childhood. Responding with a joke to a joke is the most common form of mode adoption.

The question of the frequency of mode adoption is unresolved, with estimates ranging from a high of 21–33% (Gibbs 2000) to lower percentages such as Eisterhold et al. (2006) 7% and Pexman et al. (2009) 7%–8% (conversations involving children). See Section 8.2.2 for more examples.

11.4 Issues in CA of humor

11.4.1 Is humor–laughter an adjacency pair?

The problem is discussed in Glenn and Holt (2013, pp. 12–14). Surprisingly, despite Glenn and Holt's claim, echoed by numerous other scholars, that Sacks (1974) claims that joke/laughter (or laughable/laughter) is an adjacency pair, the term "adjacency pair" does not appear in Sacks (1974). It does appear, however, in Jefferson, Sacks, and Schegloff (1977) a pragmatics microfiche characterized as a "revised draft of a paper presented" in 1973, at a seminar at the university of Pennsylvania. In this document, on p. 30, there appears the claim that "Laughable/Laughter" would be an adjacency pair, along the lines of question/answer and greeting/return greeting. The assertion is couched in the conditional mood ("the Laughable and its responsive Laughter could constitute [...] an adjacency pair [...] In this case the Pair Type is [Laughable/Laughter] and may be affiliated to a list which includes" the above mentioned adjacency pairs).[6] One may speculate that the reason for not using the term in the latter paper is that Sacks might have further developed his thinking on the subject. In the 1974 paper, Sacks makes several claims that are incompatible with the idea the laughable/laughter be an adjacency pair: laughter has a "priority claim [...] But each recipient is not obliged to laugh" (p. 348). Hearers may choose to be silent, to delay their laughter, or produce "talk directed to grading the joke and teller's wit negatively" (p. 351). Obviously if the hearers have four options (laughter, delayed laughter, silence, and negative talk) laughable/laughter is not an adjacency pair, stricto sensu.

Other authors have also claimed that humor and laughter are an adjacency pair, such as Norrick (1993) and Holcomb (1997). For example, Norrick (1993, p. 23) in the case of puns: "The appropriate initial response to a pun is, of course, laughter. Thus we can say that joking and laughter are linked as two parts of an adjacency pair." Thonus (2008, p. 334) initially quotes the definition of "laughable (humor)/laughter" as an adjacency pair, only to problematize it immediately and eventually rejects it (p. 335). Schegloff speaks of jokes "sequentially implicating" laughter and does not use the term adjacency pair (1987, p. 206).

Hay (2001) is also critical of the humor/laughter as adjacency pair idea as she presents a set of humor support strategies, as seen above, in Section 11.3.1.2. If there are a number of options, laughter cannot be a member of an adjacency pair. Hay (2001) and Sacks' own work, seem to point toward the conclusion that humor and laughter are *not* an adjacency pair and that the hearer of a humorous turn (or laughable) has a set of choices (a repertoire) with which to respond.

11.4.2 Humorous and non-humorous laughter in conversation

The purported correlation between humor (stimulus) and laughter (response) has been shown not to hold, in fact. There is extensive research in discourse analysis that documents the presence of laughter in non-humorous contexts: Potter & Hepburn (2010) sum up nicely the issue stating that laughter (broadly construed) "may have a range of interactional roles quite separate from punning, joking or humour" (p. 1544). Clift (2012) considers "laughter in non-humorous contexts"

---

[6] Capitalizations in the original.

(i.e., non-mirthful laughter) and specifically laughter that is not shared (i.e., not answered by laughter).

Jefferson (1979) showed in a groundbreaking article that the stereotype of the speaker saying something funny and the hearer responding with laughter was hopelessly mistaken. In fact, speakers often initiate the laughter *before* the hearer, to signal and invite a laughter response. In Jefferson (1984), she shows furthermore that speakers will also laugh in contexts in which there is nothing at all humorous, as in the example below (I have simplified the transcription):

(114) Dyadic conversation quoted by Jefferson (1984)
G: You don't want to go through all the ha:ssle?
S: hhhhI don't know Geri,
(.)
S: I've stopped crying uhehh-heh-heh-heh-heh,
G: Wuh were you cry::ing? (p. 346)

It is clear that S is not being facetious in his/her answer and in fact the speaker is "exhibiting that, although there is trouble, it is not getting the better of him[/her] (…) he[/she] is managing; he[/she] is in good spirits and in a position to take the trouble lightly (p. 351). As Jefferson notes, Geri responds not by joining in the laughter, which would be inappropriate, but rather by a "recognizably serious response" (p. 346). Jefferson sums up the role of the hearer in trouble-talk as "taking the trouble seriously" or being receptive to it. (p. 351). Potter and Hepburn (2010) analyze a striking example of a speaker laughing during the description of an accident that broke several of his vertebrae and caused him to be late in paying his bills. They comment with splendid understatement "this could be heard as a somewhat odd description of his own reaction to a spine crushing injury" (p. 1549) but go on to explain that the three laughter particles occurring in the middle of the words "I am very grateful" (that the injury was not any worse) mark his reaction as "insufficient or problematic." Needless to say, there is no humor in this context.[7]

Günther (2003) reports that in her corpora, in 8 instances she was unable to see a connection of laughter with humor (p. 152; 183). Edwards (2005) describes laughter in serious telephone complaints.

---

[7] In fact, Potter and Hepburn do not even use the term "laughter particle" and prefer "interpolated particles of aspiration" to avoid confusion with mirthful laughter.

11.4 ISSUES IN CA OF HUMOR

So does Clift (2013) from which we take as an example the following fragment,

(115)
```
    Robbie: my:↓God there's a lotta children in this   [(h)ss
            cla(h
    Lesley:                                            [I↓kno::w.
```

(Clift, 2013, p.231; I have simplified the transcription for clarity) in which we see two teachers complaining about class size Clift notes that the hearer (Lesley) does not orient to the laughter "infiltrating the final word" (p. 231; i.e., the two aspirations) and instead responds to the complaint by expressing solidarity. Clift notes the similarity with trouble talk and with other "delicate" subject matters. Laughter in this context serves as a mitigator, by introducing a distance between the complaint and the person producing it (p. 236), and is thus not an expression of mirth.

Another situation where non-humorous laughter occurs is doctor–patient interactions. West (1984) found that patients laugh more than doctors and interprets this as evidence of the power imbalance inherent in the situation. However, Heath (1988) and Haakana (2001, 2002) convincingly argue that it is more likely that patients are laughing because of embarrassment. Haakana (2002, p. 226) shows that numerous patient-initiated turns consist of reactions to "delicate and dispreferred" activities, such as refusals (a dispreferred choice), discussions of financial matters, etc. Fatigante & Orletti (2013) also report laughter in gynecologist examination talk in dispreferred responses (the patient contradicting the doctor). In short, when patients laugh at delicate or dispreferred choices they are not displaying mirth, rather they are embarrassed. Likewise, Zayts & Schnurr (2011, 2017) report that in prenatal counseling, both nurses and patients laugh when disagreeing or resisting the other's opinion (the nurses are trying to push prenatal testing and the patients refuse). Zayts and Schnurr interpret this as laughter mitigating the disagreement or as a "laughing off" (2017, p. 135) the dispreferred choices of the interlocutor.

Wilkinson (2007) reports that patients with language impairments will laugh during repair sequences when the repair sequence fails (i.e., they cannot successfully produce the utterance). Hearers do not respond with laughter in those cases. The following example (simplified) will illustrate the completely non-humorous nature of the situation. Paul, the aphasic speaker, is talking to his wife, Amy:

(116) Paul: that was the doctor. she's (.) trying to find out about eh:
(1.6) ((clears throat))
(1.3) mm well ehm mm
(1.6) ((sniffs)) ehm eh
(5.5) h (.) (g)hhh (Wilkinson, 2007, p. 548)

Paul forgets the word for what the doctor was trying to find out and then processed to produce a series of empty and filled pauses which culminates with the short laughter burst after the 5.5 seconds pause, when he gives up. Amy simply provides the completion: "What you have been doing at home" without any laughter. Paul's laughter may be interpreted as laughter of embarrassment, or as an attempt to dismiss as trivial his problem.

A different type of phenomenon is a "humorous noticing" defined by Wilkinson as consisting "of the highlighting of an error by either repeating it or noting its similarity to another word which would be incongruous in the context. As such, humorous noticings are a kind of small joke produced by the aphasic speaker" (2007, p. 556). The speakers produce laughter within the noticings. This kind of laughter is reciprocated by the hearers. The difference between the two situations described by Williams is striking: in the case of embarrassed laughter, much like in trouble talk laughter, joining in the non-humorous laughter could be interpreted as mockery. In the case of noticings, the speaker successfully keys the situation as humorous (either by laughing prior to repeating the error, and/or smiling), and thus laughter by the hearer is seen as supporting the humor (see Section 11.3.1.2). Wilkinson et al. (2003, p. 63) further document "embarrassed" laughter by aphasic subjects about "the exposure of their linguistic non-competence."

Dionigi & Canestrari (2018) report patient laughter to repair disagreements between therapist and patient, mitigate "overt resistance" (p. 7), self-deprecation, and positive assessment of the therapist. The therapist does not reciprocate in any of these instances, as there is no assumption of mirthful laughter.

Lavin & Maynard report "apologetic" laughter (2001, p. 460) initiated by respondents in telephone interviews, They compare it to Jefferson's examples of non-invitational laughter in troubles talk. Holt (2017) shows that callers to a public utility company use laughter to shift from serious business, such as complaining for a large bill, to less-serious (or partially serious) complaints, such that the computer system is slow. Despite the presence of laughter, Holt claims, "serious actions are performed" (p. 96).[8]

Clift (2016) "incredulous" disaffiliative laughter consists in framing the situation as laughable despite no such intention of the speaker: "a party to interaction constructs a prior action as risible or preposterous by means of laughter – as literally 'laughable'; the practice of laughing in such contexts does an emphatic display of incredulity or disbelief" (p. 86); "the laughter does a display of incredulity" (p. 80) and not of mirth.[9] Importantly, Clift (2016) notes that this sort of disaffiliative laughter may occur at any point in the conversation (i.e., is not limited to adjacency pairs) and may be produced by any of the participants. Also, while being disaffiliative to the person being mocked, the laughter is affiliative with (and may be joined by) a third person with whom the speaker producing the disaffiliative laughter "sides" against the person being laughed at.

Haugh (2017c) also discusses disaffiliative language play in jocular mockery. So does Romaniuk (2013) in the context of broadcast interviews. Günther (2003, p. 194) reports a much higher incidence of affiliative laughter than disaffiliative (finding in her corpora only 8 instances of disaffiliative laughter, contrasted with 45 affiliative instances). However, these results should be assessed carefully. The category of affiliative includes Supportive and invited laughter, but excludes what Günther labels "contextualizing" laughter, which would include all contextualizing cues. Furthermore, not all instances of laughter are taken into account. Nonetheless, Günther's data show that disaffiliative humor in conversation does exist, although it is infrequent.

Adelswärd (1989) considering laughter in institutional settings, broadens the perspective and comes to distinguish between reciprocated ("mutual") laughter, a sign of "rapport and consensus," and

---

[8] To be precise, it is unclear if Holt is claiming that there is no humor present when, for example, a speaker says that he/she "nearly had a heart attack" when they received the very large bill, which seems a humorous exaggeration, or that the presence of the humor is overwhelmed by the serious nature of the task surrounding it, or that the speaker is using humor to save the negative face of the employee, by downgrading the complaint, turning it into a merely laughable error. It is also unclear why Holt seems to think that there should be a "simple relationship between incongruity and laugh responses" (p. 115) since at this point it is a pretty safe conclusion (see Attardo, 1994) that there is no direct relationship between the two, incongruity being a proxy for humor, in this context. Regardless, some of the examples show non-humorous laughter in a serious context.

[9] The analysis is complex, as it involves the speaker producing the laughter pretending to be amused by what they consider the absurdity of the targeted other speaker's remarks. It remains that the situation is different from someone being genuinely amused by someone's remarks (say, a child making a clearly incorrect statement).

unreciprocated laughter: "We often laugh alone and not always at things considered particularly funny." For example, she reports that successful job interviews showed more reciprocated laughter than unsuccessful ones.

In conclusion, both non-humorous laughter and disaffiliative humorous laughter have been well-documented in a variety of contexts, including conversational ones. Neither type is usually responded to with laughter. The preferred response to mirthful laughter is humor support, the preferred response to non-mirthful laughter is ignoring it, either by attending to the source of the embarrassment, discomfort, etc. or by expressing support for the speaker. This is presumably because laughter carries a connotation of mirth (by association with it). This is what allows it to be a mitigator and to downgrade utterances to (partially) non-serious mode. When both parties in the conversation orient to the laughable (in the Glenn & Holt sense) as appropriate for laughter, they do orient to humor.

11.4.3 Is humor a test of understanding?

The term "understanding test" is used verbatim by Sacks (Sacks, 1974, p. 346) and defined as follows: "Not everyone supposably 'gets' each joke, the getting involving achievement of its understanding, a failure to get being supposable as involving a failure to understand. Asserting understanding failures can then reveal, e.g., recipients' lack of sophistication, a matter that an appropriately place laugh can otherwise conceal" (p. 346). As is well known, Sacks' example (the only example of joke he analyzed in this context) is an obscene joke which refers obliquely to fellatio. Since the teller is a 16–17 year old in the 1960s or early 1970s, it is credible that not all the hearers may have been familiar with the practice of fellatio, or at least the 12-year-old sister who originally told the joke (the brother is repeating it to his friends). However, it seems extremely unlikely that a joke such as

(117)   How to do tell if an elephant was in the fridge?
        Paw prints in the butter.

is testing anything in the knowledge of the audience. What factual knowledge could possibly be tested in the example above? The knowledge of the relative size of elephants and refrigerators? Thus at best, Sacks' understanding test could apply to *some* jokes, but not to all jokes.

Despite its prima facie implausibility, the idea of a test has taken hold in conversation analysis (Sherzer 1985; Norrick 1993, 2003). To be fair, Norrick's position is much more hedged than others, when he notes that rather than testing knowledge, jokes presuppose it for in-group solidarity building. In fact, in 2003, he states clearly that "Far from testing for background knowledge with jokes, tellers commonly fill the audience in on any information the joke presupposes in the interest of ensuring understanding and enjoyment, and hence the success of the performance" (pp. 1342–1343). In Attardo (1994), several issues with Sacks original discussion of the "test of understanding" hypothesis, as well as some issues with the analysis itself, are discussed.

Glenn (2003, pp. 115–117) provides an example of how a participant to a conversation may be mocked if they do not "get" the joke. Glenn reconceptualizes the test of understanding as a test of participation to the social event, since it seems unlikely that the speaker would not understand what "getting an F [= lowest possible grade] in sex" could mean. Indeed, the speaker himself in subsequent turns explains that he failed to hear the words of the reply. In this sense, there is a test of participation, as a competent speaker would have easily faked understanding, for example by snorting in (fake) dismay at the poor quality of the joke. In this sense, but only in this sense, we can accept the idea of a test of understanding. In the original sense, i.e., whether the hearer is familiar with the referent alluded or mentioned in the joke, the idea of a test can only be a rare exception.

A related idea, also presented by Sacks, but that has gotten virtually no recognition in the field, unlike the very popular understanding test, is the "recipient comparative wit assessment device" (Sacks, 1974, p. 349–350) which consists of the idea that since laughter is a display of understanding, delaying laughter may be interpreted as lack of understanding, which therefore would motivate speakers to laugh as soon as possible, despite the option of delayed laughter (i.e., laughing after a pause). The advantage of delayed laughter being that it allows one to assess how the other recipients react to the telling before committing to laughter.

11.4.4 Tellability

Norrick's application of the concept of tellability to humor in discourse is one of his most significant contributions to humor studies. Tellability is the term introduced by Sacks (1992), whereas Labov (1972, p. 366) speaks of "reportable" narratives. The concept is the same: a story, narrative, or just an extended turn, needs to be justified ("evaluated") by the narrator to his/her audience, least the narrator be accused of wasting his/her audience's time. A narrative is tellable if it is newsworthy or particularly relevant to its audience. So, Labov's famous "near-death" stories are tellable by definition. Surprising, unexpected, or novel events are also tellable. Another aspect of tellability is that the story needs to have a point, not in the senses of the "pointe" or punch line, but in the sense of making a point, having a coherent narrative arc that delivers a bit of information significant enough to justify the telling of the story. Labov notes that pointless stories are met with "a withering" "so what?" to indicate that the audience has not seen the point of the story.

Norrick (2004) notes that the humorous nature of a story may be enough to warrant its tellability: "an orientation toward the humor of a story replaces" its tellability (p. 86). Norrick speculates that what makes a story tellable is the same kind of thing (incongruity) that makes a story funny (p. 87).

Norrick (2005, 2010) elaborates the notion of tellability, not limited to the lower boundary of being worth telling, but also in terms of the appropriateness of telling the story in a given context, and shows that speakers actively negotiate both aspects of tellability. Canned jokes inherently have a certain degree of tellability, since somebody bothered to repeat the text, but for personal anecdotes and worse yet for puns, which may be disruptive of the conversation, since they are most often off the current topic, the tellability has to be negotiated. Norrick notes that both meaningfulness and appropriateness in context are negotiated by the participants. Furthermore, in settings with high degrees of intimacy, such as family or friends gatherings, familiar[10] humorous stories may be retold, not so much for their novelty or newsworthiness, but rather because the process of collectively re-creating the story reinforces the social bond: "Humor makes any story more tellable, even familiar stories, and humorous stories have characteristic patterns of participation: in particular, co-narration is acceptable whenever it creates humor" (Norrick 2010, p. 238). Telling the humorous anecdote becomes more of a shared performance, than just the telling of a story.

---

[10] No pun intended, but note that etymological source of the word "familiar" (i.e., belonging to the family).

11.5 Conclusions

One of the main conclusions that we can draw from this review of the field is that it has reached a certain maturity. At this point, the list of settings (speech events) that have been covered, often by multiple studies, is truly impressive (see Glenn & Holt, 2013, p. 18, for a list). Researchers have now available a broad range of descriptive studies which offer minutious, in depth analysis of significant amounts of naturally occurring speech acts, mostly conversational data. I think it is fair to say that it is unlikely that we will see any major novel configurations heretofore unexamined by scholars in terms of humorous speech acts and speech events, as far as English goes. The situation is different for other languages, which have a lot of catching up to do. In terms of speech situations, the broader setting postulated by Hymes (1972), we still have a ways to go, in terms of a truly representative set of situations, but at least for conversations among friends, workplace talk, medical encounters, and stand-up comedy, there are already sufficient data. The field still shows an over-emphasis on the positive, affiliative aspects of humor (see Attardo, 2015 for discussion), but new research is correcting this imbalance.

There seems to be some confusion between mirthful (humorous) laughter and non-mirthful laughter, as defined above. When mirthful laughter is reciprocated we have humor support (see above, Section 11.3.1.2). Non-mirthful laughter, as in trouble talk (Jefferson, 1984), does not generally get reciprocated. So what happens when we have reciprocated non-mirthful laughter? We can offer a conjecture: assume ex hypothesis that reciprocated laughter generally occurs only with mirthful laughter. The preferred response to non-mirthful laughter is serious bona-fide relevant communication. Then, reciprocated non-mirthful laughter is, or is perceived as, a highly disaffiliative (as in the examples reported by Clift, 2016) or aggressive move. Thus in Zayts & Schnurr (2017, p. 134) we see an example of reciprocated non-mirthful laughter, in which the nurse comments on the refusal of the testing by the patient (I paraphrase and gloss the complex transcription):

(118) N: You don't want the test? [within utterance and post utterance laughter]
P: [laughter overlapping with the previous turn] I am sure (I do not want it) [within utterance laughter]

N: You don't want it [within utterance laughter]
P: I don't want to (do it) [within utterance laughter]

I would suggest that rather than describing this as reciprocated laughter, we consider it as antagonistic laughter (i.e., as an attempt to "laugh off," to use Zayts & Schnurr evocative wording, each others' objections).

At the same time, it is quite possible that, as Zayts & Schnurr say, the laughter mitigates the dispreferred choices of both speakers, by marking the antagonistic conversation as not-that-serious (Holt, 2017). This is somewhat paradoxical, as laughter would be both affiliative (mitigating) and disaffiliative (antagonistic), but it is not incompatible with the indeterminacy of laughter: it is not clear (and probably not really knowable) what the nurse and the patient are laughing at (each other? what they said? their attitudes? their expressions?) and of course it is not clear what the function of the laughter is (mitigation, disaffiliation, or just trying to bring the exchange to a close), whereas it is relatively clear that there is no mirth involved in the exchange above.

11.6 Further readings

Due to its methodological stance against generalizations, CA tends not to produce overviews of the field. A review of the place of CA approaches to humor and laughter can be found in Attardo (2015). A full discussion of the CA notation system can be found in Atkinson and Heritage (1984).

On bracketing and its origins and definitions, see Tufford and Newman (2010). On bracketing in CA/DA, see Ten Have (2007). The clearest statement of the methodological bracketing of CA/DA in humor research is found in Glenn and Holt (2017), which is an indispensable collection of papers. Norrick (1993) is now dated, but it is a classic in the field as is Glenn (2003). The "antiphonal laughter" term is introduced in Smoski and Bachorowski (2003).

The indeterminacy of humor is discussed in Mulkay (1988: 70–71), Attardo (2002a), and Priego-Valverde (2003) while the indeterminacy of irony, in Sperber and Wilson (1986) and Gibbs (2012). On humor support and mode adoption, see Whalen and Pexman (2017) and Coolidge (2019).

12
Discourse analysis: humor in conversation II

12.1	Functional DA	264
12.2	Conversational humor in various settings	280
12.3	Corpus-based discourse analysis	286
12.4	Some issues in the DA of humor	289
12.5	Conclusions	297
12.6	Further readings	298

In this chapter, we will consider the discourse analysis (DA) of humor. As we said in the previous chapter, there is considerable methodological overlap between conversation analysis (CA) and DA: both emphasize ecologically valid data and both look in a very detailed way to the texts, for example. However, there are some differences as well: the first one is that DA has a broader outlook, in terms of data: CA is more focused on conversations, whereas DA admits more or less any kind of text, including written ones. DA is also more open toward quantification and has moved more readily toward using large corpora (see Attardo, 2015, for a review). Last but not least, DA is more interested in the functional aspect of the interactions, i.e., what interactional goals are the speakers achieving through the exchanges.

While by now it should be clear that any attempt at drawing a sharp line dividing CA from DA is impossible, I feel like I should repeat the warning not to attach any particular significance in a given article or book appearing in this or the previous chapter (or any other, for that matter). My primary choice in grouping studies has been subject matter

The Linguistics of Humor: An Introduction. Salvatore Attardo, Oxford University Press (2020). © Salvatore Attardo.
DOI: 10.1093/oso/9780198791270.001.0001

regardless of methodology: for example, Hay's work is probably best characterized as DA, but it is discussed in the previous chapter because it fit better in the development of the discussion there.

12.1 Functional DA

Moving away from the emphasis on the sequential organization of humorous discourse of classical CA, DA focuses more on the conversational goals of the speakers, or to put it differently what the speakers are trying to achieve by using humor. Here there is a logical problem: as Holmes (2000) notes "all utterances are multifunctional (...) Hence, a humorous utterance may, and typically does, serve several functions at once" (p. 166). Furthermore, Holmes warns of a potentially infinite regress: "the most general or basic function of humor is to amuse. But one can ask why does the speaker wish to amuse the audience" (2000, p. 166). Holmes is of course right to point out these problems. To ask "why do speakers do X?" is a question potentially impossible to answer. For example, let us say that a speaker produces a humorous turn and we establish that he/she intended to amuse his/her audience with the further intention of showing off his/her wit and thus reinforce his/her social status in the group. Surely, we may believe that our analysis is over. But what of unconscious goals, of which by definition the speaker will not be aware of? And what of the ideological and cultural norms that force upon the speaker the social roles that he/she worked so hard at reinforcing?

One final point: humorous utterances (i.e., the production of humor of any kind in conversation and/or communication) are indeterminate, "ambivalent" (Holt, 2017, p. 94), or as Kotthoff (2007, p. 287) has it: "Humorous intentions can seldom be pinned down exactly."

Consider the following example:

(119) A is the 80-year-old grandmother of B, a 30-year-old female.
B had just run up over a curb driving out of a store.

A: They just built that while you were in the store.
B: I know. (Attardo, 2002b, p. 171)

As I said in my original analysis, it is fairly clear that A is being ironical, as the claim that the curb was built while her grand-daughter was in the store is patently false. B has no reason to think that her grandmother has become intellectually incapacitated, etc. However, I asked in 2002 "But is A being funny? Is A teasing B? Is A exaggerating? Is A being metaphorical?" We may add: why is the grandmother saying this? Is she trying to get her grand-daughter to drive more carefully? Is she mocking her? Is she showing solidarity? Is she critiquing capitalist exploitation of natural resources for the sake of short term profit of the corporations that built the store? As I answered myself in 2002: "Any attempt at disentangling this cluster of implicatures would be quixotic, as the completely noncommittal answer of B seems to imply" (p. 171). Needless to say, I acknowledged then and repeat now, that we have no way of knowing what B meant, anymore than we may know what A meant.[1] For the exchange, we only can deduce that B is "going along" with A, i.e., she is adopting the ironical mode of communication, but in fact her response may be masking the fact that she has no idea what her grandmother meant. So, the ironical response that supports her grandmother's quip may be driven by her desire to avoid knowing exactly what grandma meant, because B may not like what A meant.

So, should we conclude that it is pointless to try to describe the functions of humor? To begin with, we must consider two facts:

1. Each interpretation of the function(s) of the exchange is subjective and, in my opinion, this involves the interpretations of the researcher, whether they are participants to the interaction or not.
2. Interpretations of the participants, especially if they agree, must be prioritized over other interpretations.

So, if all goes well, i.e., all the participants in the overall situation (speaker, hearer, and researcher) are in agreement, there is no problem. But what if one of the participants intended an utterance as serious, for example, but upon the reaction of their audience (say, laughter) decides to "go along" and pretend he/she meant it as humorous all along? There is no methodological prophylaxis against this. Consider the following example from the show Top Gear in which James May makes an unintended obscene pun, while talking about seating in a car

---

[1] Just in case anyone is wondering, I am not denying the possibility of linguistic communication. However, it would be too complicated to explain the differences between bona-fide and non-bona-fide inferential processes in this context.

(120) 1 May: She's effectively saying, "You've given me the baby, now get in the back."
2 Hammond: Yeah.
3 Clarkson: (Laughter; the audience joins in the laughter)
4 May: (pointing his finger) No.
6 (extended laughter from the audience and the show hosts)
7 Clarkson: That concludes the News
(https://www.youtube.com/watch?v=abX_qoYdtuw)

While the footage does not show May's facial expression while Clarkson starts laughing, it is clear from his denial in line 4 that he did not intend the utterance as being an obscene double entendre. However, when the camera returns to him, during 6, he is producing an open-mouth smile having apparently accepted the reframing of the situation as humorous.

In this case, it is fairly clear what happened, but in other cases it may not be clear and no methodology can prevent that, since even a direct question to the speaker would be vitiated by the fact that whatever motivation the speaker would have to reframe the intention post hoc would also presumably lead them to deny that any reframing took place. Having said this, in a sense the argument developed in Chapter 10 of the negotiated nature of the keying for humor of a situation makes the question moot: the initial intention of the speaker may be interesting but it is not the end all of the analysis. If we take seriously the methodological stance that all interactional keying is negotiated, then what the speaker initially may have meant is not that significant anymore. Thus, while retaining a healthy dose of skepticism toward any interpretation, and acknowledging that the inner mental states of the participants may not be available, even through interviews, since speakers may lie about their motives, we can nonetheless move forward with considering the functions of humor in conversation.

In the following sections we will review some of the foundational and exemplar studies in the DA of humor. Tannen's work is well known, albeit surprisingly not utilized to its fullest potential in the field. Davies' and Priego-Valverde's are less known, but just as deserving of attention, as they anticipated significantly several issues and results of the field.

12.1.1 Tannen's Thanksgiving dinner

Tannen's first book (Tannen, 1984), which is essentially a revised version of her dissertation, contains a full chapter on the humor used by the participants to the Thanksgiving dinner she analyzes. Surprisingly, and despite a very prominent mention in Attardo (1994), it has been largely overlooked by scholars; for example, it does not appear in the references of Glenn and Holt (2013); for an exception, see Norrick (1993).

This is all the more remarkable because Tannen's contribution is quite significant in several areas. First, Tannen was the first scholar to quantify the number of humorous turns produced by each participant and provide a ratio of humorous turns to overall turns, which shows a range of between 2% and 11% and a mean of roughly 7%. Second, Tannen introduces the idea of individual conversational humor style,[2] noting that the participant with the lowest number of humorous turns had appeared to be less involved in the conversation, whereas in terms of turns he was not the one who had contributed less to the conversation. Hence Tannen's conclusion that "humor makes one's presence felt" (1984, p. 165). The idea of conversational humor style is applied to a family setting by Everts (2003). Third, Tannen describes "extended [humor] routines" in which speakers "pick up" on the humorous elements of the situation and carry on extended humorous exchanges (pp. 176–177).

Tannen's analyses are squarely in the Gumperz-Hymes approach we have described in the previous chapters and focuses on the contextual cues that allow the participants to "pick up" on the humorous intentions of the other speakers. Another factor of interest is that Tannen did follow up interviews with the participants which show that considerable misunderstanding and lack of syntony existed at the time of the exchange: for example, Tannen reports that one participant (David) believed that another (Steve) was "truly angry" at Tannen's placing her tape recorder on the table, whereas, Tannen reports, Steve "was speechless" at the suggestion that he was truly angry (p. 168).

12.1.2 Catherine Davies' joint construction of humor

This article too, despite its very visible place of publication in the Proceedings of the Berkeley Linguistics Society, has been largely overlooked by later researchers, despite its having introduced many of the themes of the ethnomethodological approach to the discourse analysis of humor, including the joint construction of humor, the function of solidarity

---

[2] Not to be confused with the idea of humor styles in psychology (Martin et al., 2003).

enhancement, and the interactive ongoing definition of humor keying ("footing").

The following short passage from Davies' article will illustrate the nature of the joint construction of the humor. The situation is that of faculty members who meet in the staff lounge and argue as to who should pay for the coffee.

(121) Dyadic conversation among faculty members.
01   Ed: I'll pay for it.
02   Joyce: No, I already got it.
03   Ed: You shouldn't pay for my coffee.
04   Joyce: Oh, that's OK... you're worth every penny.
05   Ed: (laughs) I see your opinion of me has gone up.
06   Joyce: Not really. I'm coming back later to take fifteen cents out again.
07   Both: (laugh) (Davies, 1984, p. 361)

In turn 4, Joyce humorously demeans Ed by using a back-handed compliment: Ed is worth every penny of a cup of coffee, and since coffee is cheap, then Ed is not worth much. Ed reacts in turn 5, first by laughing, thus accepting the humorous framing of the situation and also not taking offense, and elaborates on Joyce's put down, by one-upping her: if Joyce is saying that Ed is worth only 25 cents, Ed remarks that the figure is an improvement over an imaginary previous figure that was even lower, or, in other words, that Joyce's opinion of him has improved. Joyce responds by denying the improvement and claiming, also fantastically, that she will later retrieve some of the money she has currently paid (15 cents) thus bringing her evaluation of Ed down to a figure of ten cents, which is coherent with Ed's remark about a figure lower than 25 cents.

This example nicely illustrates the collaborative, joint nature of the construction of the humorous footing of the exchange, as Ed and Joyce humorously spar in a fantasy environment spun off from the literal interpretation of the cliché "you are worth every penny" applied to a human being. The joint laughter in turn 7 sanctions the framing of the exchange as humorous, but the whole exchange (turns 4–7) consists of humor support (see Section 11.3.1.2). For another example of joint construction of humor, see example (122) below.

Davies notes that non-verbal cues (contextualization cues) may be used to signal the humorous footing/keying, but that also a deadpan delivery ("a straight face") may be used (p. 361). Among other strategies to jointly construct humor footing, Davies notes, building on what others have said (p. 363), elaborating (p. 364), and empathizing (p. 366). Davies distinguishes "a style oriented towards empathy more typical of women, and a style oriented towards solidarity (through the use of a version of 'ritual insult' joking) more typical of men" (Davies, 2017, p. 476).

Davies interestingly also recognizes the presence of incongruity ("bisociation") in all of her examples of humor (p. 368–369) which makes it one of the few articles to blend discourse analysis and incongruity. Other exceptions include Norrick (2003), Antonopoulou & Sifianou (2003), Archakis & Tsakona (2005, 2012), and Alvarado Ortega (2013).

12.1.3 Priego-Valverde's dialogic model

Priego-Valverde's (2003) book on humor has many reasons to be featured prominently in any review of the field of functional discourse analysis of humor (see Attardo, 2006, for a full list). Just to mention two, she was one of the very first authors to discuss failed humor (see Section 12.4.3), now a significant area of research and likewise she has an extended discussion of the co-construction of humor (pp. 203–226). However, another reason for its inclusion is the relative lack of impact it has had on the field,[3] no doubt due to its being written in French. Hopefully, by summarizing some of its main findings, more scholars will benefit from it.

Priego-Valverde analyzes a corpus of 33 hours and 20 minutes of conversations among friends, ranging from four to seven participants and lasting between 2h15m to 7h30m. The age range is very homogeneous (25–30 years) as is the socio-economic status (upper-middle class) and education (most of the participants are professionals or students). It is possible that the large size of her corpus (it was larger than the entire Wellington Workplace Corpus, in 2001; see below) allowed her to discern a wider variety of functions or phenomena, but whatever the reason, Priego-Valverde's is one of the most wide-ranging studies of humor in conversation.

---

[3] Exceptions to this neglect are the always well-informed N. Bell, W. Chafe, M. Haugh, and A. Viana.

Priego-Valverde raises a few methodological significant points, often overlooked in discussion about conversational humor: the first is that laughter cannot be used to identify humor, due to the lack of correlation between humor and laughter. Priego-Valverde is very clear about the connection with failed humor, which would be excluded a priori from analysis if laughter were used to identify humor (2003, p. 15). Her answer is to rely on the intention of the speaker (p. 15), which may be a controversial stance, but is alleviated by her role as participant-observer (p. 63). However, Priego-Valverde takes the line of reasoning further: she notes that it is a commonly assumed point that humor builds intimacy. However, Priego-Valverde notes, some degree of connivence (tacit assent) is necessary for humor. This presupposes an interlocutor, who must share "a certain amount of knowledge, of values upon which humor will rest" (p. 37). As Priego-Valverde notes: "it is this sharing of a common referent, which both creates a connivence between the interlocutors and can only exist if this connivence is already present" (p. 37). In other words: there must be a minimal common ground shared between the interlocutors (the speaker and the hearer) for the humor to function. This implies that a third party observer may not be able to assess the humorous nature of the text (p. 67). This common ground exists also among people who do not know each other, such as the audience of a theater play and its author, for example. The common ground consists of the language, at a minimum, shared cultural references, social values, and the like.

Her theoretical stance includes the idea that humor is the result of multiple voices, real or imaginary, that coexist in the speaker's utterance. The source for this idea is Bakhtin (1981), mediated by Ducrot (1984). Using Bakhtin's "dialogism" is not uncommon in European scholarship, for example it is also quoted in Kotthoff (2003). However, the idea acquires a special relevance in the context of humor because, as Priego-Valverde argues, the multiple voices in a humorous utterance account for

- the distancing between the speaker and the content or the form of his/her utterance, which goes hand in hand with the non-bona-fide nature of the utterance;
- the incongruity between the serious and the humorous mode of communication as well as the humorous incongruity within the text itself (as in "incongruity and resolution");

- the ambivalence of the text: by introducing a duality of intention, multiple interpretations can be justified within the text; and
- its playfulness: the distancing and the playful nature of deliberately producing an ambiguous utterance, explain the *goodwill* ("*bienveillance*") of humor.   (2003, p. 70)

Priego-Valverde finds that conversational humor exploits the same linguistic mechanisms that have been analyzed in the semantics and pragmatics of humor. Priego-Valverde presents a non-exhaustive list of mechanisms, including script opposition (pp. 82–83), play on ambiguity (p. 85), register humor (pp. 88–89), faulty logic (pp. 91–92), allusion (pp. 95–98), intertextuality (pp. 99–100), insinuation (p. 98), and value judgements (pp. 105–111). I will examine an example of the insinuation mechanism, because it is short and exemplifies a sort of aggressive, hedgy humor that is not found very often in studies about humor.

The conversation is between two couples of friends: F1 and M1 and F2 and M2.[4] The second couple is getting married (F2 and M2) and M1 is upset because F1 knew the details of where the wedding was going to take place, whereas he did not. The reason for his indignation is that he has long been friends with M2 and F2, whereas F1 only knows them through him.

```
1 M1: wait seriously you did not tell me (long pause)
2 How did you know?
3 F2: [smiling voice] they call each other on the
  phone\\
4 (general laughter)
5 M2: early enough that you're not back from work
6 M1: you didn't tell me anything, you know
7 F1: we have our times
8 (general laughter)
```

I have translated and will provide a few glosses for clarity: turn 1 is addressed to F1; turn 2 is addressed to F1. Turns 3 and 5 are addressed to M1.

Priego-Valverde glosses that F2 starts a game of "insinuations" which then gets picked up by M2 and eventually by F1, to the general amusement. Essentially, F2 by informing M1 that F1 and M2 talk on the phone,

---

[4] Priego-Valverde indicates by the initial the gender of the speaker and by a progressive numeral different speakers.

triggers the script for LOVERS' ASSIGNATION (lovers need to plan their rendez-vous). M2 plays along and provides a fictitious detail explaining why M1 could have been unaware of the calls (they happened before he was home from work) and finally F1 confirms that they have "set times" to call each other, thus confirming indirectly that they do call each other. Priego-Valverde comments on the hedgy, transgressive nature of the insinuation (that F1 and M2 are having an affair, to which F2 would be privy and would condone) and also that by diverting to a completely implausible and false accusation the potentially face threatening accusation that F1 neglected or forgot to tell M1 about the wedding it defuses any potential conflict between the friends. (Priego-Valverde, 2003, pp. 98–99). I would like to point out another aspect, which Priego-Valverde does not pursue, i.e., that F2, M2, and F1 "gang up" on M1, despite his attempt, in his second remark, at redirecting the conversation toward the serious issue of not having been told about the wedding. In fact, it is F1's "betrayal" of her loyalties that finally caps the exchange. F1 does not "stand by her man." The sexually charged nature of the allusion and the aggressive nature of the humor (insinuating that one is being cuckolded by one's best friend) are quite unusual for academic discussions of humor in conversation, but are representative of much humor that occurs casually.

This example also lends itself to two other themes found in Priego-Valverde's discussion: humor is often used for negotiating face demands, as in the example above, where the potential threat to M1 and F1 negative faces[5] is resolved humorously, as seen above. The other topic is the cooperative or competitive nature of the exchanges. Cooperation and competition should not be understood in a Gricean sense (Chapter 8) but rather as benevolent and aggressive, respectively (2003, p. 179). In another terminology, the create an in-group and an out-group (see below, Section 12.1.4).

Finally, let us mention that Priego-Valverde dedicates a significant part of her book to the discussion of the functions of humor. She presents several examples of communicative rituals that are performed through humor. One example (pp. 122–123) concerns the common practice, at least in some European cultures, to give guests a tour of the house on

---

[5] Negative face is "the right to be left alone": M1 has been humiliated by being in the dark about the wedding and F1 presumably forgot to tell him and if confronted about it will be embarrassed as well.

their first visit. Other examples include lightening up the mood of a conversation (pp. 130–131), averting conflict (pp. 132–136), and many others. Her general conclusion is that humor can be both cooperative (goodwill) and competitive, i.e., aggressive (p. 179).

12.1.4 Functions of humor in conversation

In Attardo (1994), based on work done in sociology, I classified the functions of humor in three main categories:

1. Social management: this is the fundamental group affiliation/disaffiliation mechanism of humor. By creating an in-group, those that "laugh together," i.e., share the experience of mirth or engage in overt displays of it with the group, and an out-group, those that do not participate in the mirth or are the target of the humor, the production of humor automatically creates a bonding experience, for the in-group participants which is, at least in part, based on the exclusion of the out-group. This has been variously characterized, with a very successful term in DA as "bonding" or "biting" (Boxer & Cortès-Conde, 1997; cf. also Priego-Valverde, 2003, p. 179, "cooperative" vs. "competitive" humor.)
2. Decommitment: this aspect of the humorous exchange is tied to the "this is play" metamessage (see Section 3.3.1). Because humorous messages are labeled as "play" the speaker is not fully committed to the bona fide nature of the utterance (i.e., its truth, relevance, etc.). This affords the opportunity of "taking back" any of the implicatures and even inferences that would normally be carried by said utterance in context. Likewise, the retractability of humor allows speakers to bring up uncomfortable or taboo topics (for example, death, in a hospital environment).
3. Defunctionalization: one of the central functions of language is to convey meaning. In puns, but also in other ludic uses of language, this function is partially or completely set aside. This is a deeper kind of decommitment than what is produced by the characterization of the message as play. Defunctionalization eliminates the semantic-referential basic aspect of language. If someone asks "when is a door not a door?" and provides the answer "when it's ajar," decommitment would be saying "I was just kidding, I did not

really want to know." Defunctionalization is the fact that no jars are really intended at all (or doors, for that matter). All that matters is the play on words and that the two strings sound alike (ajar vs. a jar). A fuller treatment of these topics is found in Chapter 9.

These three basic functions find numerous applications in social exchanges. We will now review some of them. An interesting aspect of the various uses of humor is that often speakers react to the literal message (the criticism in the tease, the said in irony). This is a sign of the fact that the speakers "see through" the social function of the humor and treat the message as serious.

12.1.4.1 Mediation

Because humor allows the speakers to claim that they did not mean what they said or implied or at least to have said it with the purpose of amusing their audience, humor may be used to broach difficult or touchy topics. Likewise potentially embarrassing or aggressive topics may be couched in humor to "soften" the sting. In this sense, humor is very close to some forms of politeness (and in fact, humor is listed as a form of politeness, see below).

12.1.4.2 Politeness

Brown and Levinson's seminal work on politeness included humor as one of the strategies of politeness. Essentially, by claiming common ground, the joint performance of humor is a form of positive politeness (Brown and Levinson, 1978/1987, pp. 103–104). Establishing jointly membership to the in-group also boosts common ground. Zajdman (1995) considers humorous Face Threatening Acts, i.e., a joking FTA, as another politeness strategy. Norrick (1993) also characterizes humor as positive politeness.

Holmes (2000), as part of the Language in the Workplace Project (see below, Section 12.2.3, conceptualizes humor as both a form of politeness serving both the positive face of the hearer (by expressing/enacting solidarity) and also the positive face of the speaker (self-deprecating humor). Holmes shows also that humor works for negative politeness as well, by reducing FTAs. So, overall in Holmes' application of politeness theory to humor discourse analysis we have the following:

12.1 FUNCTIONAL DA

- Humor as positive politeness
  - humor addresses the hearer's positive face needs (common ground, in group solidarity)
  - humor addresses the speaker's positive face needs (self deprecation)
- Humor as negative politeness
  - humor attenuates FTA to the hearer's negative face (e.g., hedging a directive)
  - humor attenuates FTA to the hearer's positive face (e.g., hedging a criticism) (Holmes, 2000, p. 167)

Holmes also shows that humor can be used as a way to negotiate power in asymmetrical encounters: both from the perspective of the powerful agent and of the subordinate one: "humor is also a very effective way of 'doing power' less explicitly, and hence some uses of humor are most illuminatingly analyzed as instances of coercive or repressive discourse" (p. 165). Essentially, by joking the person in a position of power can achieve their goals while on the surface not violating explicitly the negative face of the subordinate(s): if the boss asks his/her secretary for a cup of coffee while joking, he/she still expects and gets the cup of coffee. Conversely, humor can be used "by the subordinate in an unequal power relationship to subvert the overt power structure. Humor provides a socially acceptable means of signaling lack of agreement, registering a protest, or even a challenge to more powerful participants" (p. 165).

The research on politeness has seen a significant shift in focus and considerable methodological discussion in the past two decades. This is not the place to review, let alone address these, although see below for mention of some alternative approaches to Brown and Levinson's used by scholars. Holmes herself, in a co-authored paper (Holmes & Schnurr, 2005), moves away from the term politeness, which is "fraught with problems" (p. 142), and uses instead the term "relational practice" or "other-oriented behavior" (p. 142).

Holmes and Schnurr (2005) note that different ways of using humor help constitute "communities of practice." The following citation, is worth examining in full, despite its length, for the subtle and nuanced way it presents their conclusions. Holmes and Schnurr observe the emergence of preferred ways of using humor to construct and negotiate RP [Relational Practices] in workplace interaction in different project teams. We are not, of course, claiming that every team or every individual in any particular team uses a consistently similar amount or type of humor throughout our recordings. Rather, what we have identified is interesting indications of favored patterns of humor, both in relation to the amount of humor and the kind of humor used in the different project teams we have studied.

(p. 146)

Thus, the amount of humor used in different workplaces varies significantly, contributing to the establishment of different workplace cultures. Likewise, the different number of supportive and contestive (aggressive) instances of humor contributes to the differences among the communities of practice. Holmes and Schnurr conclude that some communities of practice end up having a more "feminine" (supportive) use of humor and others a more "masculine" (contestive) (p. 154). Mullany (2004) also applies the communities of practice approach and extends Holmes' work.

The following two examples will serve well to exemplify the supportive (122) and contestive (123) modes:

(122) Cla = Clara; [...] indicates overlaps
    1 Cla: deferred means [put it on hold]
    2 Tess: [mm   ] deferred yeah
    3 Cla: [(laughs)]
    4 Tess: [means that you're not going to]
    5   think about it just now
    6 Cla: we'll do it some other time
    7   (general laughter) ...
    8 Rob: deferred deferred means it
    9   might get done one day if it's lucky

(Holmes and Schnurr, 2005, p. 148; the notation was adapted, SA)

Example (123) needs a little background information: the discussion revolves around a file, sent by Callum to Barry. Callum failed to update the header, which led Barry, the manager, to think he has sent the wrong file. Note that Callum on line 7–8 mode adopts, but does not align *with* Eric, but rather against him.

(123) Call = Callum; Barr = Barry
    1 Call: I definitely sent you the
    2   right one

3	Barr:	(laughs)
4	Eric:	yep Callum did fail his office
5		management (laugh) word processing
6		lesson
7	Call:	I find it really hard being
8		perfect at everything

(Holmes and Schnurr, 2005, p. 149; the notation was adapted, SA)

While humor research has tended to be biased toward the positive aspects of humor, humor scholars have recognized that humor may have a negative tone. As we saw above, this would be characterized as a "biting" aspect of humor. If looked through the lens of the social management function of humor, it becomes immediately apparent that while positive humor, humor that creates an in-group perception for the speaker and the addressee(s), may be an effective strategy to mitigate an FTA, negative humor that creates an out-group division between the speaker and (some members of) the audience will be perceived as impolite and aggressive. Since the 1990s, politeness theory has turned toward an inclusion of impoliteness in the discussion, and thus we are now fully equipped to explore the complex relationships between humor and (im)politeness.

Kotthoff (1996) already anticipated the extension of humor beyond positive politeness to negative politeness, but she also makes a fundamental point: humor "can be located at all points on a scale from politeness to impoliteness" (p. 306). As she points out, not all affiliative practices are polite. Kotthoff lists jocular aggression and "playing" with politeness. She draws a profound alignment between Batesonian play as mock-aggression and "humorous provocations" such as mock impoliteness and jocular mockery (p. 309). This discussion anticipates Haugh's work on Australian jocular mockery, briefly discussed below.

Haugh (2010) presents an alternative view of the connection between humor and politeness, based on Arundale's Face Constituting Theory (Arundale, 1999) which allows him to see jocular mockery as "a non-aligning response" (Haugh, 2010, p. 2111) which solves the "paradox' (Tannen, 1986, pp. 94–95; Norrick, 1993, p. 75) of teasing displaying both power and solidarity, being both affiliative and disaffiliative at the same time, "simultaneously face threatening and face supportive" (Haugh, 2010, p. 2111). This is not the place to discuss the definition of "face," but in a nutshell, Arundale's Face Constituting Theory sees "face" as emerging from the co-constructed interaction of the participants, and not as something "owned" by an individual. In this sense, since the humorous framing is also co-constructed (Davies, 1984) Face Constituting Theory aligns well with humor studies.

Haugh sums up the analysis of jocular mockery in light of Face Constituting Theory thus:

> Within the context of FCT, then, jocular mockery is an action that is evaluated as face threatening because it involves interpretings of a particular utterance/act as mockery, but it is also evaluated as face supportive, since it involves interpretings of the utterance/act as non-serious in that particular local context. (2010, p. 2112)

which is strikingly reminiscent of the function of "decommitment" of humor (Attardo 1994, pp. 325–326) which is precisely based on the simultaneously serious *and* non-serious stance of the speaker toward his/her utterance.

12.1.4.3 Teasing

The literature on teasing is now remarkably large. One of the classical studies is Drew (1987) who introduced as a term of art "po-faced"[6] (serious) response and showed that the recipient of the tease may orient to the humorous aspect of the tease, and so react with laughter, humor support, etc., or to the critical aspect (po-faced).

Haugh (2017b) presents a synthesis of the research. Teasing may range over the whole gamut of pro-social to anti-social behaviors (p. 205). The various conceptualizations of teasing involve a serious/non-serious dichotomy (the tease must be presented as non-serious) and an evaluative aspect, both of the person teased and of the tease itself (p. 207). Plainly, teasing is a social action, as it involves at least two participants. Teasing may have many interactional functions, ranging from sanctioning (minor) transgressions, to romantic courting (p. 210). Culturally, teasing and the reactions to teasing show significant variation, both in what is acceptable to tease about. and in the ways people react to teases.

Haugh and Pillet-Shore (2017, p. 4) provide a useful three-part sequencing for the act of teasing

---

[6] The somewhat bizarre expression is related to the faces painted on chamber pots, according to Drew.

1. **Teasable**: a triggering action by the tease target that affords the tease
2. **Tease**: a teasing action directed at the tease target
3. **Affiliation**: mutual ratification of the non-seriousness of the tease

As is easy to see, the non-seriousness of the tease, pointed out in the third phase of the sequence, lies in its humorous nature.

12.1.4.4 Flirting

Glenn and Holt (2017, p. 301) summarize effectively the connection between humor, impropriety, and flirting:

> there is longstanding recognition that the use of improprieties and sexual references can draw laughter and foster intimacy. Routinely in conversation, a speaker will say or do something that might be considered a breach of tact or courtesy, perhaps of a sexual nature. These improprieties can generate sequences of action. Similar to teasing sequences, a range of recipient responses may occur, from overt disaffiliation to disattention, affiliation, and even escalation (Jefferson, Sacks, & Schegloff, 1987). Laughter represents a midpoint on this continuum: on its own, it recognizes the impropriety but does not necessarily affiliate with it. More overtly, if the recipient laughs and produces a next impropriety, that person is then co-implicated in the potentially offensive mentality. When this happens, the participants display conversational intimacy: "That is, the introduction of such talk can be seen as a display that speaker takes it that the current interaction is one in which he may produce such talk, i.e., is informal/intimate" (Jefferson, Sacks, & Schegloff, 1987, p. 160). Similarly, talk laced with sexual innuendo may be treated as a particular kind of impropriety that ambiguously raises the possibility of a romantic/sexual relationship between participants – that is, as flirtation.
> (Glenn, 2003, pp. 131–141)

To paraphrase, if a speaker produces a turn that is "improper," often sexual in nature, acceptance of this "breach of courtesy," by not censoring it, signifies its approval and hence establishes de facto intimacy between the speakers. The use of humor, in particular because of its decommitment function, which allows one to back off from full responsibility for what one has said, by claiming to not have been serious ("I was just kidding!"), facilitates the "testing of the waters" of the flirtation process. A good example of this is found in the strategies used by customers trying to pick up waitresses in a diner: they would couch their offer to go out as a joke, which allowed them, if they were turned down, to claim they had not been serious and thus to save face, to some extent (Walle, 1976).

12.1.4.5 Multifunctionality of humor

Summing up your discussion of some of the functions of humor, one of the clearest and best documented conclusions of humor studies is that, ultimately, humor is multifunctional (i.e., many goals may be achieved by interactants who produce humor at the same time). Priego-Valverde (2003) comes to the conclusion that humor may be "everything and its contrary" (p. 233), i.e., both aggressive and benevolent, face saving and face-threatening, "virulent" and "convivial." There are no limits to what functions humor may achieve in conversation, beyond those of contextual appropriateness. One cannot sentence a convicted criminal to death humorously because the context prevents the use of humor, not because one couldn't in principle do so. So, we can come to a final generalization about humor, and namely that any function that can be achieved communicatively can be achieved humorously, modulo contextual appropriateness.[7]

12.2 Conversational humor in various settings

Given that humor is multifunctional and indetermined, a natural way of organizing the research is by setting or situation in which the exchanges occur (i.e., Hymes' Setting in the "SPEAKING" acronym, discussed in Section 10.2).

12.2.1 Conversation among friends

Within discourse analysis, there is a long tradition of using conversations among friends as the source of data, so much so that, at least as far as humor goes, this is one of the most common categories. Tannen (1984), Davies (1984), Norrick (1993), Priego-Valverde (2003), Kotthoff (1996, 2007) are all examples of studies of conversations among friends.

---

[7] This rule cuts both ways: when a situation is socially coded for seriousness, humor is not acceptable; when a situation is coded for humor, seriousness is not acceptable. It would be very difficult for a stand-up comedian, in the middle of delivering his/her act, to pivot to a serious discussion. Comedians may intercalate isolated serious comments, but the point of a comedy act is to make people laugh.

12.2.2 Medical

In this section, we are concerned with the uses of humor and non-mirthful laughter in interactions in a medical setting (or with a medical topic). There exists a vast literature on the effects of humor on health (see Martin, 2007) but we will not address this aspect of humor research, which is too far afield from the perspective of the linguistics of humor.

Coser (1959) and Emerson (1969) are widely credited as the first studies on the use of humor in a medical setting. Coser (1959, 1962) shows that humor is used to reassure patients and relieve stress. Emerson (1969) shows how patients and medical staff use humor to negotiate sensitive (taboo) topics, such as death. Her focus is on the negotiations for admitting or rejecting the taboo topic.

West (1984) studies the power imbalance of the medical service situation. She found that patients laugh more than doctors but, in percentage, doctor's laughter is reciprocated more often. Ragan examines laughter and humor in gynecological exams, a situation which presents "special threats" to the face of *both* the patient and the medical personnel, "because of the parts of the body to be examined and the positioning of the body necessary for the examination" (1990, p. 68). The exam is "uniquely anxiety-provoking to both participants" (p. 69). Therefore Ragan conceptualizes the entire exam as a FTA (p. 70). Unsurprisingly then humor is seen as a way to redress the FTA, by finding a joint stance between the patient and the doctor *away* from the task at hand: in one example, the doctor asks how the weather is like outside and upon being told it's nice, engages in a playful interaction with the patient by noting that he/she hasn't been outside all day and that the patient could have lied and told him the weather was unpleasant. The patient obliges and playfully lies and the doctor thanks her in an exaggerated manner (pp. 75–76). Needless to say, after a short pause, the doctor returns to the serious mode of the medical exam. Pizzini (1991) finds that status is a very significant factor, and that very few instances of humor are directed upward (i.e., toward the physicians). Generally speaking, she found that the higher status participants (doctors) produced most of the humor. Nurses joke more when doctors are not present. The difference vis-à-vis other studies may be explained by the fact that Pizzini is considering Italian doctors and Italian culture is much more overtly hierarchical than the American culture.

Mallett and A'hern (1996) find that humor is used to highlight anxieties, avoid conflict, and that different patients use humor differently. Some humor occurs randomly as accidents happen, such as a nurse spilling rinsing fluid on the floor (p. 540).

Marci et al. (2004) also show that patients laugh much more than therapists: more than 70% of laughter is produced by patients and patients initiate laughter much more frequently than the therapists do. However, some studies show that patients use laughter to resist therapists' characterizations (Dionigi & Canestrari, 2018) or doctor's questioning (Ticca, 2013). Rees and Monrouxe (2010) consider triadic conversations involving a doctor, a patient, and a student, in a teaching hospital. They report that most laugher occurs around teases and that the mode is competitive (disaffiliative) rather than cooperative, as tends to be the case in other studies.

In a series of studies on Finnish doctor–patient encounters, Haakana (2001, 2002, 2010) shows that patients laugh mostly alone at delicate or embarrassing topics (such as financial matters). Zayts and Schnurr (2011, 2017) examine nurse–patient interactions in prenatal counseling. They find that nurses laugh more than the patients and that the nurses' laughter is responded to more. This results goes against Haakana's finding that doctors laugh less. However, Zayts and Schnurr note that this may be just a factor of the different situations (in doctor–patient interactions, patients talk more, whereas in prenatal counseling, the nurses do most of the talking). The nurses' laughter is used to "reassure and [...] put [...] at ease" the patients (2017, p. 126). For example, in one case laughter follows the statement that the mother is worried.

Chimbwete-Phiri & Schnurr (2017) study AIDS/HIV counseling sessions for pregnant women in Malawi. Humor is used to establish solidarity and to make the attendees feel comfortable, to facilitate the discussion of sensitive topics, and as a means to criticize the participants who are not engaged. More broadly, we have uses of humor as a coping mechanism by those facing devastating diseases, such as cancer (e.g., Beach & Prickett, 2016; Demjén, 2016; Semino & Demjén, 2017) or more generally (Åstedt-Kurki & Isola, 2001).

Overal, the picture that emerges from these studies (and many others that cannot be reviewed due to space limitations) is that humor is used to cope with a stressful job and inherently difficult, stressful topics and situations. The medical profession is very hierarchical and the power differential is felt in the use of humor, but humor can be used to carve out some spaces for the patients to express their feelings and attitudes. See for example Schnurr and Rowe's (2008) analysis of subversive[8] humor in emails.

12.2.3 Workplace

This section is primarily dedicated to presenting Janet Holmes' and her associates' Language in the Workplace Project, due to its significance and centrality in the literature. The project begun in 1996 at Victoria University of Wellington, in New Zealand. The corpus consists of about 1500 interactions, produced by 450 different people, in 20 different workplaces, and consists of about 150 hours of recordings.[9] As Holmes (2000) notes, most of the research on humor in the workplace focuses on the benefits that humor provides to management (e.g., increased productivity), the employees (e.g., increased well-being), or both. This aspect will not concern us presently.

We saw above, in Section 12.1.4.2, that humor can be used to enact politeness or relational practices in the workplace. We also saw that humor can be used both as a tool to control the subordinates, by catering to their face while still imposing the superior's will and conversely, it can be used by the subordinates to subtly undermine their superior's stance, for example by criticizing them.

Two main theoretical lenses through which the Language in the Workplace Project sees this setting are:

The social construction of identity (on social construction of humor, see Section 13.3). Essentially, workers construct an identity at work, through their interactions. Language and humor play a significant part in the identity they project. Holmes and Marra (2002, p. 380) show that subjects build multiple identities at work.

---

[8] I have always been bothered by the use of the word "subversive" in this sort of context: to me subversion is not the same thing as criticism: one can make fun of one's boss without subverting the hierarchical organization of the company; one can criticize the government's policy on taxation without being a subversive. In order to be a subversive you have to actively undermine the authority of the boss/government, for example by mounting a campaign to get the boss fired or by raising a militia and fighting the king, or some such activity likely to get you fired or sentenced to death. Nonetheless, I too bow to common usage and use subversive as a synonym of "mild criticism."

[9] The web site of the project is particularly useful and can be accessed at https://www.victoria.ac.nz/lals/centres-and-institutes/language-in-the-workplace.

The Communities of Practice approach. As the term itself states, communities of practice coalesce around ways of doing things (practices): "The development of a negotiated linguistic repertoire is perhaps the most crucial aspect of a community of practice from a sociolinguistic point of view" (Schnurr, 2009, p. 14). Specifically, members of a community develop ways of "doing humor" that are particular to their community and that help define it as such (Holmes & Marra, 2002). Ultimately, each workplace may develop a distinct culture (Schnurr, 2009). This idea could be usefully compared to the family humor styles (Everts, 2003) seen above.

Power is clearly a major factor, for example Holmes notes that "the chair [of a meeting] makes a disproportionately high contribution to the humour in most meetings" (Holmes et al., 2001, p. 96) This is of course consonant with the findings from other workplace settings that show that the power structure of the workplace is reflected in the discursive practices that occur within it. However, Holmes notes also that "in work contexts humour can be used by subordinates as a subtle (or not so subtle) license to challenge the power structure, as well as by those in power to achieve the speaker's goal while apparently de-emphasizing the power differential" (2000, 176). As we saw already above, in Section 12.1.4.2, humor has a Janus-like nature, being both supportive (i.e., affiliative) or "contestive" (i.e., disaffiliative), it can foster collegiality or assert power. This "subversive" aspect coexists with positive politeness (e.g., Holmes & Marra, 2002).

Schnurr (2009) is focused on "leadership" (a polite term for "management") and in particular their use of humor to both achieve "transactional goals" (getting the job done) and "relational" goals (making people feel good). The following is an example of interaction in which humor is used to achieve the purposes of the workplace (I significantly shortened the example; for a full transcription and analysis, see Schnurr, 2009, pp. 28–29):

(124) Donald = CEO of the company; Ann = project manager; notation edited for clarity

    Donald: yep+okay alright
                   do you wanna write up a letter of offer
    Ann: no [laughter]

12.2 CONVERSATIONAL HUMOR IN VARIOUS SETTINGS

>   Donald: [laughter]
>   are you the project manager
>   [laughter]
>   Ann: [how do I] do that
>   Donald: eh? (laughs)
>   there's standard templates

In example (124) Donald achieves the goal of instructing his project manager, who was relatively new to the position, without threatening her face by couching his "order" of writing the letter of offer for a new hire in a non-bona-fide question (he knows perfectly well that Ann is the project manager). By asking a self-evident question, he can both express the intention to be humorous (consider that Donald could have said "You have to write the letter" so his turn is clearly facetious) and invite a separate inference that since project managers write letters of offer and Ann is the project manager, it follows she should write the letter. Indeed, Ann, after acknowledging the humorous nature of the turn by laughing, takes the inference exactly as an order and asks how to perform the task she has been assigned. It should be noted that Ann herself had initially framed the situation as humorous by uttering a flat denial to the indirect (polite) request by Donald to write the letter, in her first turn. Schnurr notes that the example illustrates both transactional and relational goals: "By convincing Ann to write the letter of offer Donald achieves his transactional objectives; and by [...] expressing a request as non-threatening[ly] as possible, he also takes into account [the] relational aspects" (2009, p. 29).

Other contributions of the Language in the Workplace project include an emphasis on quantifiable results (see Section 12.3 below); another, perhaps the most surprising, result to emerge from the project is that women produce more humor than men. This will be taken up in more detail in Section 13.2.1.

Needless to say, the settings we have discussed have been picked almost at random. Another setting we will examine is the classroom, which will be discussed in more detail in Chapter 16. Many other workplace settings have been explored, such as for example, humor in a professional kitchen (Lynch, 2009, 2010), or factory work (Collinson, 1988), etc. but often in a sociological context.

285

12.3 Corpus-based discourse analysis

While corpus-based[10] discourse analysis has produced a smaller number of articles and books, the very significant results that they have produced promise to change the way we look at humor in discourse, and have already done so in a few cases, but also raise new questions and issues.

Corpus-based discourse analysis is distinguished by the use of large corpora (unlike the smaller corpora, usually collected personally by the researcher, often as a participant observer, which characterize conversation analysis) and the use of statistical analyses and descriptions. Needless to say, humor scholars had used corpora of jokes and puns for decades, but here we are referring to discursive data (mostly conversations). When looking at corpora of discursive data which have not been assembled by humor scholars, we are faced with the problem of identifying the humor. There are essentially two ways to go about it: one is to study what data are readily available, so for example, if a corpus is marked for laughter, to study laughter and not humor. The other is to categorize, manually, all instances of humor for the aspects one is interested in. Both approaches have been followed in the literature (Partington, 2017, p. 323).

Another point to remember is that most of the studies below find significant variability within their corpora. For example, Holmes et al. (2001) report a range of zero to 121 instances of humor per conversation. Nesi (2012) reports that 24 out of 160 university lectures contained no laughter. Lee (2006) found that in the MICASE corpus, 8 out of 152 "events" contained no laughter. He notes that the bottom 20, in terms of scarcity of laughter, were all lectures, but that 3 lectures made it into the top 20.[11] Günther found that more than half of the examples of jokes in her corpus came from *one* speaker (2003, p. 95). So, even when data come from the same activity type and the same setting (Hymes, 1972; see Section 10.2) there is nonetheless significant variation, due to individual preferences, for example.

---

[10] Corpus linguistics distinguishes between corpus-based, corpus-driven, and corpus-assisted methodologies. Corpus-based studies test linguistic hypotheses on a corpus, corpus-driven studies are inductive and the categories emerge from the study of the corpus (Biber, 2009). Corpus-assisted studies blend corpus analysis and discourse analysis (Partington, 2017). I use corpus-based as an umbrella term in this context.

[11] More discussion of humor in lectures can be found in Chapter 16.

12.3 CORPUS-BASED DISCOURSE ANALYSIS

Holmes et al. (2001) is one of the first large-scale corpus-based studies that considers the gender variable. In 2001, it was based on 22 workplace meetings spanning 1342 minutes (more than 22 hours) of interaction and involving 157 participants, 70 females and 87 males. An exact breakdown of each meeting's participants, duration, etc. is provided in Holmes et al. (2001, p. 87). The size of the corpus is such that it is probably representative of the population it describes. Within the corpus, 396 instances of humor occurred. Failed humor was not considered. Sustained humor sequences are counted as one instance of humor.

A very significant point is driven home by Holmes et al. (2001): there is a great degree of variability in the ratio of instances of humor per minute, with range from a low of zero to a high of 1.21 (121 instance of humor in 100 minutes; this was a shorter meeting) and likewise there is great variability in the number of collaborative (sustained) humor exchanges. Thus any generalizations should be extremely careful, as there are significant differences even within activity types and across activity types: conversations among friends have about 10 times the amount of humor of workplace meetings (Holmes et al., 2001, p. 93).

Günther (2003) considers humor, laughter and joke performances in conversations from two British corpora: the Conversational Corpus of the British National Corpus (BNC) and The Bergen corpus of London teenage language (COLT). Günther then characterizes all instances of humor in the corpus according to several categories. It is impossible to summarize all her results in this context, so I will focus on the most interesting ones. Contrary to expectations, she finds that men do not tell more canned jokes than women (p. 59); the two groups tell about the same number of canned jokes. Younger people told more canned jokes (p. 63), which are however relatively rare in the corpus. It would be interesting to compare this datum to contemporary corpora to see if this is still the case, since tastes in humor have shifted away from canned jokes lately.

In her analysis of the corpora, females speak more and laugh more than males. Both results are statistically significant (p. 129). Age-wise those in the 25–34 group laugh the most, whereas the younger group (0–14) laugh the least. Laughter and humor tend to occur more frequently in single-sex settings, especially among women; "multi-party, mixed-sex conversations trigger fewer laughter and humorous contributions" (p. 181). However, her sample ignores turns that consist only of laughter, which may skew the data. Günther also finds no support for the hypothesis that women are more supportive of men's humor (p. 200) but finds that men prefer "fantasy" humor (p. 209)

Partington is probably the name most associated with corpus-based linguistics if humor. In Partington (2006), he circumscribes the analysis to laughter, or "laughter-talk," i.e., "talk preceding and provoking, intentionally or otherwise, a bout of laughter" (Partington, 2006, p. 1). He considers White House press briefings, which come pre-annotated for laughter. In Partington (2007), he examines irony that is explicitly labeled as such in the discourse in which it occurs. In Partington (2011) he considers "phrasal irony," i.e., irony produced by combining phrasal expressions with contrasting evaluative polarity, as in "bent on self-improvement" where "bent" has a negative connotation (e.g., "bent on destruction"), whereas self-improvement has a positive valence.

Koester (2010) considers also workplace conversations. She gathers as a corpus of 60 humorous exchanges from the Corpus of American and British Office Talk and analyzes it according to five functions: building a positive identity; defending one's positive face; showing convergence; showing divergence; and negative politeness. She finds no differences between American and British speakers in terms of quantity of humor produced (p. 115). She finds that men produce more teasing humor and women more self-deprecating humor. Koester also reports that managers and subordinates initiate humor in comparable numbers.

The most significant trend in the discourse analysis of humor to emerge in the past 10 years has been a move toward the use of corpora for the gathering of large bodies of data. In a sense, even from its origins in conversation analysis, discourse analysis always relied on a corpus, except that the corpus was very small, and possibly consisted on a single instance of the phenomenon. So, the emergence of studies such as Günther (2003), which mined for data (i.e., humorous interactions) two corpora assembled completely independently of the intention to study humor, leads directly to Haugh (2014, 2016, 2017c) which are based on a number of corpora of Australian English, which have been scanned to find instances of jocular mockery, which are then analyzed in the papers. Likewise, Demjén (2016) uses corpus analysis to extract humorous instances to analyze.

12.4 Some issues in the DA of humor

12.4.1 Establishing the humorous intention

Given the multifunctional and indeterminate nature of humor, a relevant question is how do the speakers establish the intention to be funny. Clearly, the speakers do not have access directly to each others' intentions, but this is not a problem unique to humor. When I walk into a coffee shop and ask for a cup of coffee, the coffee shop clerk does not have access to my intentionality either; however, it is an easy inference from my utterance of "may I have a cup of coffee?" that I intend to have coffee (assuming of course rational bona-fide behavior, i.e., I do not secretly want tea or plan to rob the store). So, in this sense the ascription of humorous intention is not different from the problem of ascribing intention to speakers in general.

One strategy is to signal (intentionally or not) one's intention by exhibiting one of several contextualization cues typical of humor, such as laughter, increased smiling intensity, smiling voice, marked prosody, etc. This is the kind of cue that has been studied in conversation and discourse analysis. The problem with the signaling strategy is that it is itself ambiguous: one may be laughing *at* someone (i.e., one may be mocking them), or one may smile contemptuously, or just politely, and one's marked prosody may have other reasons (for example, emotional).

Thus another strategy is to explicitly state that one means one's utterance as humorous. There are a number of conventionalized such expressions, the most famous being "just kidding" (Skalicky et al., 2015; Haugh, 2016). Finnish apparently uses a reduplicated expression which translates as "joke joke." Another expression with the same function that is now used in colloquial American English is "I am just saying" often shortened to "just sayin'" (Margolies, 2016). "Just sayin'" is broader than "just kidding" in that it denies accountability for any sort of potentially antagonistic speech, not just humor. Haugh (2016, p. 127, 2017) examines the case of "jocular pretense" ("a form of teasing accomplished through the tease being delivered without any cues to non-seriousness") in which the deadpan delivery pre-empts the use of any of the usual markers of humor (smiling, etc.) and thus the occurrence of the "just kidding/joking" is the only clue to the humorous intention of the speaker. The functions of "just kidding" include wrapping up a humorous exchange, and thus returning to serious talk, revealing that a sequence was in fact humorous, if for example, humor fails, disclaiming the intention to offend or being "improper" ("inoculation," Skalicky et al., 2015). and expressing disapproval of a non-humorous response ("po-faced," Drew, 1987). The disclaimer of offense and the disapproval functions go back to the retractability function of humor (Attardo, 1994). The inoculation function, or disclaimer, is the most frequently found in a corpus of 1200 instances of the expressions (Skalicky et al., 2015, p. 23). Returning to serious discourse was the function of only 8% of the instances of "just kidding." Skalicky et al. (2015) note that this use of "just kidding" is similar to the use of "no" following a joke, to return to serious discourse, discussed by Schegloff (2001).

Let us return to the so-called "deadpan" strategy of delivery of humor, which is the exact opposite of the signaling strategy, i.e., it consists of *not* producing any signal of one's humorous intention. This should not be confused with the "blank face" (Attardo et al., 2003) which is a differential signal (i.e., producing an expressionless facial expression when one would expect some display of emotion). Deadpan delivery is by definition devoid of any markings. The idea here is that contextual pressure is so strong that even if one does not indicate one's non-serious intention, the audience will be able to extrapolate the correct implicature. Consider for example if I were to utter (125):

(125)   I cannot believe anyone would waste their time writing a book on humor.

anyone who encounters (125) in the above context will be aware of the fact that I have just done precisely that and, reasoning that one generally does not engage in activities one considers to be a waste of time, will work out the implicature that I do not mean what I just said and that therefore presumably the utterance is ironical. At this point my hypothetical reader-cum-interlocutor would still have to figure out *why* I am saying ironically (125), but we may safely abandon the example here.

The issue of signaling or marking the humorous intention is far from trivial, because since there is a general agreement that "humorous and serious discourse operate according to fundamentally different principles" (Mulkay 1988, p. 7), it becomes important to be able to tell in which mode of communication we find ourselves.

There is also a generally accepted idea that humor must be marked. In its most naive form, it assumes that speakers signal the humorous nature of the turns they intend to be humorous by using some paralinguistic feature, such as a special tone of voice ("some changes in the speaker's normal voice pattern," Mulkay, 1984, p. 47) or gestures, such as winking, etc.[12] The hearers, conversely, would react with laughter, thus validating the humor and signaling the understanding thereof. Mulkay stated very clearly the latter aspect "each humorous contribution has to be marked by recipients in a rather special way: that is by laughter, smiling, or some related token of appreciation" (Mulkay 1988, p. 46). Mulkay continues that "If this is not done continually, humorous interaction lapses and participants return to the serious mode" (p. 46). See also Fine's (1984, p. 85) point that if silence or a serious remark follow a humorous turn, "the humorous remark has failed."

Unfortunately, the idea that humor keying must be signaled "continuously" is incorrect, as has been shown by several empirical studies, reviewed in Section 10.3. Mulkay and Fine are correct that eventually the humorous keying/framing lapses, but its "half-life," to borrow a metaphor from nuclear physics, is longer than they think. The point is not that speakers never mark their departure from the serious mode, but rather that the "marking" is not compulsory and in fact much less frequent than generally assumed. It is definitely not the case that, as Fine maintains: "jocular remarks are typically accompanied by paraverbal and nonverbal cues which suggest that the remark should not be accepted on face value" (Fine 1984, p. 91). At most, there is a correlation between some paraverbal behaviors and humor but there are no consistent "cues" of humorous intent. Furthermore, as seen in Section 10.3, speakers generally produce much less obvious cues to their humorous intention than exaggerated prosody. The one reliable pattern that emerged was an increase in the intensity of smiling. Note that the increase is not of the frequency, but in the intensity of the smiling: people do not necessarily smile more, they smile more broadly.

12.4.2 How do speakers identify humor?

Glenn and Holt (2017, p. 298) address the issue of identifying humor, or rather, the referent of laughables. They summarize Ford and Fox's (2010) discussion of the "interrelated semiotic resources" for constructing

---

[12] Kotthoff (1996, p. 311), "*Laughter particles, atypical lexies* [=words], *cliche* [sic] *prosody and such formulae function as indicators of the contextualization of a humorous modality.*" (Emphasis in the original.)

laughables, including 1) various phonetic "practices," a) "long and loud aspiration after a word-initial voiceless stop, lengthening of fricatives, high pitch, laryngeal constriction, voicelessness at the beginning of vowels, breathiness, and modulations of loudness" (Glenn & Holt, 2017, p. 298); b) the smiling voice; 2) "nonvocal resources" such as "lip-spreading (interpreted as smiling), leaning and/or throwing back the head, covering the face with hands, lowering and raising shoulders, shaking torso and shoulders, clapping hands or slapping a surface, and tensing neck and facial muscles" (p. 298); and 3) Glen and Holt even list "incongruity." However, they argue that "The presence of one or more of these attributes – laughter, vocal features, visual features, and/or incongruity – does not necessarily mean that a turn will be treated as laughable" (p. 300) and finally conclude that "orienting to a contribution as laughable is dependent not only aspects of the turn itself but on the trajectory of subsequent contributions."

This nuanced position is a far cry from the use of laughter as the sole identifier of humor (as we saw in Section 11.2) or worse, canned laughter. Incidentally, the use of canned laughter is not a straw man: Pelsmaekers & Van Besien (2002, p. 247) is an example of using the canned laughter of the soundtrack of a sitcom to identify humor (irony, in this case). There is nothing wrong with the list in Glenn and Holt (2017). However, there are three issues with the idea that one can identify humor (or laughables associated with humor) "externally," so to speak. The first issue is that there is mounting evidence, reviewed in Section 10.3, that speakers do not necessarily mark or signal their humorous intention or that the markings are relational and not substantive, so that there is no ironical tone of voice per se or any special volume or pitch associated with humor. Rather, it is the incongruity between the expected, unmarked delivery and the unexpected, marked delivery that signals not the humor, but the presence of a notable phenomenon, which then the speaker will infer is humor. Therefore any attempt at producing a list of markers of humor is a losing battle, as any linguistic feature may, under the right circumstances, be used to cue the presence of the humorous intention. The second issue is that by definition the deadpan delivery of humor, or the delivery in contextually poor environments, such as writing, are without these markers. The third issue is failed humor, which we will review below, in Section 12.4.3.

Archakis and Tsakona noted that "the combination of incongruity and laughter is a relatively safe criterion for identifying humor"

(2012, pp. 77–78). In Attardo (2012) I presented a triangulation method for the identification of humor (see also Section 2.5), which consists of taking opportunistically advantage of all available textual and paratextual cues *and* of a full semantic and pragmatic analysis, using the General Theory of Verbal Humor. A preponderance of evidence is then used to adjudicate questionable cases. Thus cues may include, but are not limited to:

- intonational and prosodic cues
- laughter, smiling voice, and other expressions of mirth
- metalinguistic comments (such as "I was joking")
- facial expressions and other gestural markers
- paralinguistic cues (e.g., a text being included in a collection of jokes or a meme being included in a web page of funny memes)
- semantic and pragmatic analysis, as per the General Theory of Verbal Humor

Burgers et al. (2011) present a method to identify irony, the Verbal Irony Procedure (VIP). VIP is too complex to describe here, but it essentially consists of a full-fledged semantic and pragmatic analysis of the text, looking for the traditional components of irony (lack of congruence between the literal meaning and the implied meaning, evaluative scale, etc.). The analysis is to be performed by trained coders. VIP has a lot to recommend it, for example part of the protocol is to consider the entire text, a point made forcefully in Attardo (2017b) under the warning against cherry-picking of data (see Section 7.2.3). On the other hand, it seems to rely exclusively on internal (textual) evidence and to pay insufficient attention to the external evidence listed above.

12.4.3 Failed humor

The repertoire of humor responses has largely focused on humor support (Hay, 2001) and rightfully so, given the groundbreaking nature of Hay's contribution. It would not be until Bell (2009, 2015) that a full treatment of the negative side of the responses to humor, the unsupportive reaction, or "unlaughter," as Billig (2005, p. 192–194) calls it, would receive a full treatment. Bell sees failed humor as a form of miscommunication. Her definition of failed humor includes the intention to elicit mirth or amusement (2015, pp. 3–4) but she notes that failure may occur due to "any type of communicative disruption" (p. 4).

It would be impossible to do justice to Bell's book with the limited space within this context, so I will content myself with noting that Bell's mixed method approach which blends discourse analysis and elicitation[13] was particularly successful in eliciting a variety of reactions and behaviors that are not normally accessible to the DA scholar (or may be so only under accidental circumstances). For example, one of the reactions to the telling of a particularly bad joke was the hearer bursting into tears (p. 2) because she felt "inferior and humiliated" at not getting the joke. Another reaction was punching the speaker in the arm (playfully). This alone tells us that we need to broaden significantly any idea of repertoire of reactions to humor we may have held. Bell lists (p. 121) the types of responses to failed humor, which range broadly from non-verbal responses (rolling of the eyes, grimacing, etc.) to flat out admissions of not understanding the joke (a surprisingly frequent reaction), complete silence (also surprisingly frequent), to requests for more time to think about the joke and providing their own interpretation of the joke (Bell does not say so, but these may be cases of "mansplaining," i.e., the obnoxious providing of unrequested explanations by a man, who often has less expertise in the subject than the woman he is addressing).

Generally speaking, what strikes me as quite notable in the repertoire of failure managements is how willing to aggressively deny the humorousness of the would-be joke the audience is. Bell reports the following example: a husband and wife (probably Bell herself, given the humorous footnote) are discussing the shopping list. The wife suggests that the husband purchase some butter.

(126) (adapted from Bell, 2015, p. 108)

    Husband: do we really need it?
    Wife: yeah. we're in butter desperation (.)
          *b*utter desperation, get it?
    Husband: yeah not funny at all

Even factoring in intimacy and possibly the playful nature of the husband's comment, it is a far cry from hedging and politeness.

Priego-Valverde (2003) dedicates a significant discussion of failed humor, with several types of failures examined. An example is a failure

---

[13] The complete set of data is listed on pp. 38–39: direct observations from the researcher, self-reports from other parties, published data, corpora, television and film discourse, and elicitation.

of the humor because the targeted interlocutor fails to acknowledge it because they want to revert to the serious mode of communication (pp. 184–188). Another example shows one speaker left speechless by a mock callous remark and reacting with a surprised expression, while others laugh. In another example, one of the speakers simply ignores the humorous side sequence and continues his serious discussion of his army experience (p. 194). In yet another, two friends gang up on a third one mocking her humorously for using the wrong word while the latter friend changes the topic to a hairdresser's appointment (p. 198). Priego-Valverde notes that in the conflict between taking a serious or a humorous direction, the serious mode always wins out (p. 202), but there seems to be no reason to believe that it is impossible to have the opposite happen (and I am not saying that Priego-Valverde believes it either).

CA and DA have been long reluctant to engage with failed humor: see for example, Holmes' (2000, p. 163) definition of humor which deliberately leaves out failed humor, discussed in Attardo (2015). However, Mullany (2004) and Schnurr (2009) finally consider failed and unintentional humor in their discussion. The reason for the reluctance is probably that failed humor requires necessarily two steps, both of which CA and DA are reluctant to take: 1) accepting the distinction between a competence and a performance levels of analysis, and 2) accepting that failure requires logically the intentionality of at least one of the participants to be taken into account. While DA practitioners may be open to (or at least tolerant of) these, as are Bell and Priego-Valverde, for CA analysts they may be too big a pill to swallow. The problem of not including failed humor, or including only a subset thereof, is that, if our goal is to provide as complete as possible a picture of the phenomena surrounding humor and laughter in discourse, by refusing to engage with part of the phenomena, we condemn ourselves to failure.

12.4.4 Sustained humor turns

Sustained humor turns are extended stretches of conversation in which the exchange is framed/keyed for humor. They may consists of a single speaker producing a series of humorous turns while other speakers support the humor or in two or more speakers collaborating in the production of the humor and mutually supporting each other. "When humorous interchange is maintained over a period of time, the interpretative work that it requires generates a distinctive group atmosphere which is quite different from serious discourse" (Mulkay, 1988, p. 51). However, Mulkay adds, "the humorous mode can be sustained only by means of a continual production of appropriate cues, signals and responses" (p. 51). This is correct, generally speaking, except for the fact that the cues need not be continuous.

Tannen's (1984) "humor routines," "Norrick's "jointly produced narratives" (1993, pp. 57–58), Hay "fantasy sequences" (1995, pp. 68–70), Kotthoff's "joint fantasizing" (Kotthoff, 2007, 2009), and Winchatz & Kozin's (2008) "comical hypothetical" describe interactions in which in which speakers sustain a co-constructed humorous improvisation of various length. The longest sustained humorous interaction I am aware of lasts up to 13 turns (Kotthoff, 2007). As we have seen, mode adoption, one of the forms of humor support, consists precisely of "playing along" with the speaker who has produced a joking or ironical utterance. I used the term "mental space" (Attardo 2001b), after Fauconnier (1984/1985) who introduced it, to describe the pragmatic inferential processes necessary to build these co-constructed mental spaces in which two or more speakers develop a fleeting shared alternate mental space in which they explore the humorous possibilities of a situation. Most significantly, I address the emergent properties of mental spaces (Attardo, 2001b, p. 177), i.e., the fact that one may "discover" unanticipated consequences of what one has postulated in a mental space. In the paper, I also address the technical reasons why speakers do not become confused if different mental spaces have contradictory features.

A related, but slightly different, phenomenon are laughter "clusters" (Glenn, 2003, pp. 78–83): "[p]articipants can create additional laughables that cohere thematically or structurally with a preceding one" (p. 78; cf. Norrick, 1993, p. 117) but that need not be as collaborative as the examples above, as they may just be related instances of humor. Glenn notes that not all the instances of humor (laughables) "get shared laughter, but several do, and the cumulative effect creates and extended cluster of shared laughs" (p. 80). According to Glenn, the speakers' "focus moves sequentially to the next laughable" (p. 83) but Thonus (2008) suggests that speakers are "no longer responding to laughables but constructing laughter itself as a laughable" (p. 336).

Whether clusters of laughter or more organized co-constructions of humorous mental spaces, these extended bouts of mirth seem to be self-sustaining. I have made the suggestion that to some extent, there may be a "virtuous circle" at work, whereby the occurrence of humor feeds back into the situation and generates more desire to produce humor (Attardo, 2019). Be that as it may, "shared laughter naturally reaches termination points rather quickly. Conversationalists must actively renew shared laughter" (Glenn, 2003, p. 82) or to put it differently, the Least Disruption Principle is at work, enjoying the speakers to return to the serious mode, as soon as they are done with the humorous interlude (see Section 8.2.2).

Sustained co-constructed mental spaces require that at least two ("joint") speakers collaborate in the production of humor, but of course sustained humor turns need not require active collaboration of the speakers, but merely acceptance, support, and presumably enjoyment (appreciation). It is also possible, of course, that the hearer being subjected to social constraints, needs to pretend appreciation, while in fact not enjoying the humor at all. Acceptance and support of humor, presuppose (Hay, 2001) appreciation (or the pretense thereof).

12.5 Conclusions

The last two chapters have presented an interactional view on the performance of humor as part of the ethnomethodological approach introduced in Chapter 10, specifically on conversation and discourse analysis. Before we turn to the variationist approach, which will conclude the discussion of the performance of humor, it seems useful to draw some overall conclusions on this fast moving part of humor studies.

Indeed, the first observation is that the research in conversation and discourse analysis is by far the most active area of the linguistics of humor and, with the exception of psychology, probably of all of humor studies. This makes the relative lack of interest and cross-fertilization between conversation/discourse analysis and humor studies all the more disappointing. It is all too common to see decades of research in the linguistics of humor summarized as a vague mention of incongruity and the relative lack of influence of those scholars such as Neal Norrick, Béatrice Priego-Valverde, and Nancy Bell who *have* been influenced by humor studies. To be fair, more recent work seems to be more broadly accepting of interdisciplinary insights into humor. In the sense, the flurry of very recent work in conversation and discourse analysis, within which Haugh's contributions stand out, is to be welcomed.

The second trend that stands out is that the field is now broadly orienting itself toward corpus-assisted studies. What was a relatively new trend in my review of the field (Attardo, 2015), and had its roots in the more functionally oriented discourse analysis, has now become the more or less accepted norm, even within conversation analysis. This is a very positive development, if for no other reason that it moves away from what I still consider the most problematic aspect of the early conversation analytical studies of humor that proposed generalizations based on one instance of a phenomenon (see for example, in Section 11.4.3, the idea of humor as a test, Sacks, 1974).

The third tendency that I have observed is a slow but perceptible move away from the borderline neo-behaviorist idea of studying laughter in itself toward studying laughter (and smiling) as markers or contextualization cues, and eventually socially as an expression of mirth, with the corresponding reintroduction of the intentionality of the speakers in the picture (anathema to the original conversation analysis methodology).

12.6 Further readings

The overviews by Glenn and Holt (2017), Schnurr and Plester (2017), Attardo (2015) and Bell (2015) are the best sources to get started, in general. More speciifc problems are examined by Whalen and Pexman (2017), on humor support, and Burgers and van Mulken (2017), on humor markers. The works of Tannen, Davies, Hay, Priego-Valverde, and Holmes are fundamental. Schnurr (2009) is the only book from the Wellington Language in the Workplace project specifically focused on humor. A list of articles on humor by members of the project is available online: https://www.victoria.ac.nz/lals/centres-and-institutes/language-in-the-workplace/docs/biblios/humour.pdf. Many of their articles are readily available.

13

Sociolinguistics of humor

13.1 Universality of humor 299
13.2 Variationist humor theory 304
13.3 The social construction of humor 313
13.4 Conclusions 315
13.5 Further readings 315

This chapter will not deal with the sociology of humor. To do so would require a monograph of its own.[1] Another area that we will not cover, for the same reason, is verbal art and speech play (see Scherzer, 2002). The focus of the chapter is the sociolinguistics of humor, and specifically variationist sociolinguistics (the previous chapters have dealt primarily with interactionist sociolinguistics).

13.1 Universality of humor

One of the questions that a humor researcher gets asked most often is "is humor universal?" often in a slightly different form along the lines of "is humor from, say China, or from any other 'exotic' culture, different from ours?" The answer, as is the case for most interesting questions, is: "it depends." In a sense, this chapter addresses the issue of whether men and women, young people and old people, people from Japan, Namibia, France, and people from the USA laugh or appreciate as humorous the same things.

[1] Those interested should consult the work of Christie Davies, Giselinde Kuipers, Mulkay (1988), Koller (1988), Davis (1993), and Zijderveld (1983).

A good starting point is to recall that as a result of our discussion in chapters (2), (4), and (6) we are studying humor as a competence of the speakers, as Raskin's theory explicitly states.[2] Competence is usually assumed to be innate (i.e., genetically encoded in the DNA of the speakers) and would therefore have been selected for evolutionarily by some advantage in reproductive chances (Porteous, 1988; Vaid, 1999, 2002; Gervais & Wilson, 2005; Chafe 1987, 2007). Another possibility is that having a sense of humor is a completely neutral feature, reproductively speaking, that emerged as a by-product of other characteristics with reproductive advantages (for example, the capacity to experience surprise and inferential processes). Humor competence may also be merely a social abstraction of behaviors sanctioned by social practice. If humor competence is innate this means that logically all human beings share the same humor competence since they share the same DNA. If humor competence is merely a social construct, the argument is much weakened, or defeated as it would be conceivable that some culture do not have a humor competence at all or have a radically different one (one that is inaccessible to other cultures).[3]

The available evidence leans toward the universality of humor and hence to its genetic foundation. There have been no claims of cultures that do not have humor or laughter. There have been isolated claims of cultures lacking irony (Haiman, 1998) and lacking puns (in the sense of intentional manipulation of ambiguity/homonymy, etc. for amusement; cf. Sherzer, 1996), but at most this would show that those cultures lack some genres of humor, not that they lack humor. So, if humor occurs in all cultures it becomes likely to assume that it is part of the genetic make up of humanity. Another potential explanation of the universality of humor would be that it had already developed when the first hominids left the African savannah and therefore that it spread with them to all inhabited lands. In either case, be it genetically determined, or culturally inherited, humor competence is common to all cultures.

More compellingly, there have been no claims of radical untranslatability of humor across cultures. Most cross-cultural studies show the exact opposite, and namely that jokes and humorous themes travel freely across linguistic and cultural borders. For example, Essex girl jokes from England crossed the ocean and became blonde and sorority girl jokes.

[2] It should go without saying that we are not *only* studying competence.
[3] This footnote should be read only by trained linguists/philosophers: an anthropologist sees a rabbit run by, he shouts "Gavagai!" and all the tribe starts laughing.

American stupidity jokes about Poles correspond to jokes all over the world about "stupid" groups (for example, in Italy the same jokes are told about the police, and in Ancient Greece they were told about professors).

What are we to make then of claims such as those that some kinds of comedy "do not work" in a different culture? Usually what these mean is that the humor is not appreciated very much, not that it is not perceived as humorous. In other words, that the performance of the humor is not very successful (for example, TV audiences may not react well to it) and not the much more radical and significant claim that the audience fails to perceive that a give action or expression is intended to be humorous. The closest such mis-perception I am aware of is Regina Barreca's treatment of Benny Hill's comedy. Barreca (1991, pp. 146–148) fails to be amused by Benny Hill and thus denies the humorous status of the text(s), regardless of the fact that it ran in England between 1955 and 1989, albeit not always continuously. Had it been the case that BBC and Thames TV broadcast an unfunny comedy show, it would presumably not have lasted over forty years.

Why is it the case, then, that some types of humor are more or less popular in a given culture? Or how can Barreca and millions of British television viewers disagree? This can be due to two factors:

- lack of a given script (information) necessary for the humor to function
- social differences in the cultures.

Consider the following joke:

(127)   There are 10 kinds of people: those who know binary and those who don't.

The joke is completely opaque unless one knows that in binary mathematical notation 10 equals base-ten two. Once one is provided with the relevant information, the joke may fire (although the element of surprise is lost, thus considerably weakening the humor). The same goes for didgeridoo jokes (which my Australian informants assure me exist and are hilarious). Unless one knows what a didgeridoo is, one cannot really grasp the humor.[4] Most of the failures of humor to transfer from

---

[4] I met this bloke with a didgeridoo and he was playing Dancing Queen on it. I thought, "That's Aboriginal." http://nomadsrus.blogspot.com/2007/09/jokes.html

one culture to another can be explained very straightforwardly by simple lack of a script (information) about a given topic. For example, Morain (1991) describes a study contrasting ESL students' and American students' ratings of New Yorker's cartoons and underscores the necessity to possess a given cultural script to be able to understand the humor, let alone appreciate it.

A completely different situation is the observation, for example, that Germans enjoy scatological humor more than French or Italian people, or that puns are more frequent in English joke collections than in Italian ones. These differences can be explained by showing that different cultural backgrounds make this or that topic of humor more accessible for appreciation or more enjoyable. So, presumably, the fascination for sausage-related humor in German folklore is given by an interest in the subject matter (Hempelmann, personal communication). Other differences have more mundane explanations: for example, English is much richer in monosyllabic words than Italian (most Italian words are polysyllabic) and thus homophones and paronyms are much more frequent and therefore easier to exploit for humor.

Relatedly, we can note that there exist differences across cultures in the social acceptability of the use of humor. Different cultures codify differently the times/spaces available to speakers for the production and appreciation of humor. It is a well-documented fact that Americans start public speeches with a joke, whereas this practice was unknown in Europe. Needless to say, much cross-cultural trouble can ensue. I personally was astonished to hear a priest joke from the pulpit when I first attended a Catholic mass in the USA.

Moreover, different cultures may have different sets of scripts available for humor. Consider the following passage from an anthropologists' memoirs of her work among the Tiv, in Nigeria:

> Ngun was a nice old man who bore his blindness bravely (...).
>
> "Well," Accident [a native friend of the anthropologist] told his story with zest, "I was out hunting birds with my slingshot, and I met him. He was all alone, shuffling along because the path was so slippery with mud. He was about to fall anyhow. So I yelled, 'Watch out, Ngun. A snake!'" Accident hugged himself with mirth, and Ikpoom [another native friend] howled with laughter. Only Lucia [a madwoman] and I didn't get the point.
>
> "Well," I prompted. "Go on. Tell me what was funny."

13.1 UNIVERSALITY OF HUMOR

>Ikpoom (...) gave me the explanation, his usually monotonous voice lively with amusement. "Ngun is blind. He can't see. He wouldn't know which way to jump." He begun to laugh again. "There's nothing funnier than yelling 'Snake!' at a blind man."
>
>"Funny!" I looked at Ikpoom as though I were seeing him for the first time.
>
>"Yes," Accident put in. "He can't know where it is."
>
>Ikpoom saw that I was not amused. He was a sensitive man and a kind one; he thought he knew what disturbed me, and he tried to set my mind at rest. "If there's really a snake there, you mean to tell him where it is. Only people get so excited when they see snakes that they don't remember. They just yell. So of course a blind man can't be sure."
>
>(Smith Bowen [Bohannan] 1954: 228)

Clearly, to Smith Bowen, and presumably to most of the readers of this book, playing a practical joke on a blind man is unacceptable, whereas to the Tiv it was. Before we jump to conclusions about the relative sophistication of the Tiv culture and of Western culture, let us recall that during the Middle Ages people with physical handicaps were employed as court jesters and that until recently, if not still, freak shows made money by exhibiting people with physical deformities. So, what the example of the blind Tiv man shows is that there are differences between what the members of an African culture and the members of some parts of Western culture consider appropriate subjects for practical joking, but that the practical joke is recognizable as such (for example, Smith Bowen would probably have seen the humor if the butt of the joke (Ngun) had not been blind). To put it differently, the Tiv and Smith Bowen do not have a different competence of humor they merely differ at the performance level of which individuals are acceptable targets for humor (for example, presumably, a dying person would not be targeted for the snake joke by the Tiv).

The availability of scripts for humor will also change according to circumstances. For example, Gilbert Gottfried was booed for performing a joke about the Twin Towers "too soon" after the event (see Attardo, 2017a for discussion). Kuipers had collected over 800 jokes on the subject by 2005 (Kuipers, 2005). A wikipedia web page (https://en.wikipedia.org/wiki/Humor_based_on_the_September_11_attacks) lists jokes in sitcoms, etc. based on the attack. Clearly, the sensitivity to the event has changed significantly over time. Interestingly, some of Kuipers' examples appeared mere days after the event, in Dutch web sites. So, clearly, the Dutch and the American cultures differed in availability of those scripts for humor.

Recapitulating, humor is universal, either because genetically encoded in all humans or because it is part of the shared heritage of the first cultures. Different cultures may have different clusters of information or may have different attitudes toward certain kinds of humor which may facilitate or impeded the appreciation of given forms/examples of humor, but no humor is in principle inaccessible to any member of a different culture who would be given all the necessary information. Finally, different cultures may partition differently the social spaces available or not available for humor.

13.2 Variationist humor theory

In the following sections, I will briefly review some of the areas of in which variation in humor has been seen to occur and has generated some scholarship. The reader is advised to keep the universality of humor among humans firmly in mind, while reading the sections below, for perspective.

13.2.1 Humor and gender

Among the best-investigated topics in variationist sociolinguistics of humor is certainly humor and gender. Specifically researchers have been trying to answer the central question: do males and females sense of humor differ? Do the social circumstances in which speakers use humor and/or its function change according to gender? These questions have attracted significant research, in many disciplines, ranging from gender studies to psychology and passing by linguistics of course. A comprehensive review would require a monograph of its own. For these reasons, I will sketch out only in the most general terms the debate and will rely on overviews of the field to provide broad representation.

13.2.1.1 The feminist awakening

It is possible that one of the reasons for the very large body of research on the subject is that humor is a very visible sociolinguistic variable and as such it would have attracted the attention of scholars. Another, less flattering hypothesis, is that the existence of countless stereotypes on humor and gender may have fueled the interest of the scholarly community. Be that as it may, we can start our review with Robin Lakoff's provocation in the seminal paper-turned-booklet *Language and Woman's Place* (1975, p. 43) that women "have no sense of humor." It is fair to say that the first phase of the research is the awareness that there are gender-based differences in the type of humor and humor performance, in the broad sense we have been pursuing in this book, that people say and enjoy (or not enjoy).

Early feminist studies, reviewed in Crawford (2003) and Kotthoff (2006), emphasized the differences between male (competitive) and female (supportive) humor as well as the subservient role of women who did the laughing while men did the telling of humor. Jenkins (1985) seems to be the acknowledged source of much of the polar characterization of the differences between women's and men's humor: women's humor is "cooperative, inclusive, supportive, integrated, spontaneous and self-healing. In contrast men's [...] is more likely to be competitive, exclusive, challenging, segmented, preformulated, and self-aggrandizing" (p. 135). Interestingly, Davies (1984) had proposed a much more sophisticated approach, which characterized women's humor as directed toward empathy and men's humor as more oriented toward solidarity (for example, using banter or ritual insults).

13.2.1.2 Post-feminist research

Holmes et al. (2001) present particularly significant results because they go counter to most of the claims we have just reviewed. For example, Holmes et al. find that women produce more humor than men, regardless of the power status (Holmes et al., 2001, p. 93). Furthermore, women produce more humor regardless of being in single or mixed gender settings (p. 96). Contrary to the claims of Jenkins (1985), there was no difference in the number of collaborative humorous exchanges initiated by men and women, when they were in the chair position. When women were *not* in the position of chair they initiated *more* collaborative humor (p. 101). Holmes et al. conclude "the quantitative data contradicts the negative stereotype" that women "have no sense of humor" (p. 101). A full description of their methodology will be found in Section 12.3.

Günther (2003) found that women laugh significantly more than men, but don't produce more humor support (p. 200), thus contradicting the assumption that women are more supportive of humor. Laughter and humor have a higher frequency of occurrence in single-sex interactions, but women deliver more humor in women-only polyadic (more than two participants) settings (p. 181). So, once more, the humorless woman myth is laid to rest.

13.2.1.3 Empirical synthesis

The title of Martin's meta-analysis (Martin, 2014) is (modestly) restricted to psychological research, but Martin's wide-ranging scholarship covers far more than that and comes to a somewhat startling conclusion that "we find more similarities than differences between men and women" (p. 144) or as he puts it quoting Dindia's (2006) quip: "men are from North Dakota, women are from South Dakota" (p. 144). In light of the remarkable convergence of work from the New Zealand group around Janet Holmes, from the corpus-based work of Günther and Martin's authoritative results, the field of humor and gender is in need of a serious re-evaluation. Let me highlight two directions that strike me as particularly fruitful: 1) Holmes (1995), in the context of hedging by women and men, suggests that "women's subordinate social status may account not so much for the way women talk, as for the way their talk is perceived and interpreted" (p. 111); to my mind, this can be extended to the discussion of the gender differences in humor and describes pretty accurately the situation. 2) Increasingly researchers are problematizing the duality of the male/female opposition in favor of a "performative" approach to the study of gender, i.e., the way in which speakers define themselves in relation to each other through the category of gender and its stereotypes (Crawford, 2003) Again, I think that the gendered social practices of humor will have much to learn from such an approach. For example, the fact that a parodic genre such as "drag" contributes to the definition of gender seems to be quite significant (Butler, 1990, p. 174).

13.2.2 Social class

Davies (2017) provides a telling summary of the state of the art on the topic of social class and humor:

Whereas many studies implicitly relate to social class – for example, in that white- or blue collar workplaces may be assumed to have certain class characteristics, there has been little specifically on sociolinguistic variation in relation to class. The notable exception is the 2010 special issue of [*HUMOR: International Journal of Humor Studies*] edited by Attardo (2010). In his introduction, Attardo makes an important distinction between a sociolinguistic phenomenon and its mediatic representation. He defines working-class humor as "humor produced by members of the working class for other members of the working class" (p. 122), and points out that because mass media represents middle-class values, we are unlikely to get a full and accurate representation of humor embodying antagonism to those values. (p. 480)

The long extract is worth quoting in full because it highlights both the lack of research in the field and the problem that what little research there is on social class is focused on the media representation thereof, which is biased at best.

Davies herself in a paper for the special issue provided one of the most cogent discussion of class and humor in American society. Davies (2010) is dedicated to show that the popular

"You might be a redneck" joke cycle is appropriated to designate a lower social category within the Southern working class in Alabama (including imitation of the voices of the characters using exaggerated Southern features), and to negotiate the boundaries between the good old boy working class "red neck" [...] and the lower category of "white trash" [...]. This term, a slur that manages to combine both race and class, emerged in the racial caste society of the nineteenth century American South, and continues as a way of designating the bottom of the white social hierarchy. (p. 180)

Davies' conclusion is that the goal of the performance is "to convey social distinctions within the white Southern American working class" (p. 197) specifically pitting the relatively better off "red necks" against the impoverished "white trash."

The "You might be a redneck" joke cycle was popularized by comedian Jeff Foxworty, who released an album called *You Might be a Redneck' If...* According to Wikipedia, the album sold more than 2 million copies. Foxworthy's stand-up comedy act consisted in part of a list of statements beginning with the formula "You might be a redneck' if..." and completed by a statement, such as "You own a home that is mobile and 5 cars that aren't." In the show that Davies examines, the two hosts, Jack and Bubba, replace the expression "a redneck" with "white trash."

Davies provides a sophisticated analysis of the phonology of the dialect of the show hosts, as well as other features of their speech. For example, toothlessness, "a classic indicator of social class" (Davies, 2010, p. 187) is used as a defining feature of "white trash." Overall, the image of the "white trash" person that emerges from the analysis of the text is summarized as poor, stupid, reckless, dirty, toothless, homophobic, alcoholic, addicted to tobacco in various forms, [...] violent, drunk [...] a bad parent, sees no particular value in education, and thinks that procreation should start at puberty (possibly through marrying close relatives). He lives in a trailer with a refrigerator on the front porch, drives a truck that is a heap of junk, plays pool (which may imply gambling), and is a NASCAR fan. (Davies, 2010, p. 195)

Davies notes that many of these features are directly connected to poverty. When it comes to the interpretation of the material in a broad sociological sense, Davies notes that by characterizing "white trash" people as they do, the self-proclaimed "red necks" establish themselves as having some social respectability, for example, "He is not rich, but he is not poor in the way that the W[hite] T[rash] characters are. [...] Marriage and family are important to him, but he understands the appropriate kin relationships for these purposes" (p. 196).

Porcu (2005) is an eye-opening account of humor in a working-class Sardinian fish market. Unlike the Bowdlerized forms of working-class humor that appear in the media (which reflect middle- to upper-class values) that humor of the workers at the fish market is very physical, often violent, involving hitting people, sticking fish in their clothing, etc. It is needless to say rich in obscenity, homophobic, and above all extremely aggressive.

13.2.3 Age

As Coupland (2004) notes, there is a lack of research on aging in sociolinguistics at large. So, it will not come as a surprise that very little has been written on age grading and humor (but see Nahemow et al., 1986). There is a lot of research on the acquisition of humor in children, but that area has developed on its own and the focus is on cognitive development. Here we are interested in how children's humor may differ from teenagers, and the latter from adults and seniors.

Apte (1985, pp. 50–51) reports on "age-sets" that is joking that is limited to persons of the same age, in various cultures. Apte likens age sets to young people attending high school or college together. To use a familiar example, children and pre-adolescents in Western culture go through a period of telling and enjoying sexual and scatological jokes (Apte, 1985, p. 94). Interest in these topics wanes with age.

Apte (1985, pp. 79–80) notes that in a variety of cultures, older (post-menopausal) women are freer to engage in humor, often sexual, and even "obscene." Kotthoff (2006) notes an interplay of age and class in the behavior of women: younger women show "the greatest reserve" in dealing with aggressive and sexual humor, whereas older lower-class women are freer to address taboo topics (Kotthoff, 2006, p. 14). Nardini (2000) reports on an extended joking session among older women in an Italian-American club. The topic is what to do after widowhood and the suggestions undergo a crescendo of outrageousness which culminates in taking the deceased husband on a cruise in a box—without having had him cremated first. So, we can agree that older women may be indeed freer to express taboo topics.

This area is one where there is a particularly pressing need for research. With the advent of the internet and new media, I suspect that age grading will be particularly significant between generations.[5]

13.2.4 Dialects as humorous languages

As we saw, Hymes (1972) SPEAKING mode (Section 10.2) considers dialects, registers, etc. "instrumentalities" of the situation. We discussed briefly code-switching in Section 10.2.4. Here we focus primarily on diglossic situations.

There is a widespread understanding that non-standard dialects are used for humorous effect (Apte, 1985). Fry (1963, pp. 32, 144) mentions dialect as a contextualization cue (although Fry does not use this terminology). Siegel (1995) mentions dialectal humor. Papapavlou (1998) examines Greek Cypriot humor. Apte (1985) has a review of studies on the subject: in Tamil movies the buffoons speak in the spoken variety, whereas the heroes speak in the literary variety (p. 190); among the Burundi, joking is done with the "least degree" of formality (p. 191). In Zinacantecan Indian, "joking occurs in the informal style" (p. 191). The Chamula consider frivolous talk (which includes joking) as inappropriate for a ritual setting, the latter requiring "much formality." Apte notes that "certain dialect or languages are perceived as more suitable media for humor than others" (p. 191). In Paraguay, where Spanish and Guaraní coexist in a diglossic situation, speakers consider

---

[5] The difference between age sets and age grades is that one belongs to an age set throughout their life, whereas one passes through age grades as they age. Again, the example of classmates or college friends is enlightening: one will always have the same high school or college friends, but one will pass through a series of grades, childhood, adolescence, adulthood, middle age, etc.

Guaranì as "more suitable for humor." (p. 192). Davies reviews the scarce literature on the subject as well (2017, p. 477).

I would like to present as a hypothesis the idea that dialects, as subordinate lectal varieties of their respective acrolectal[6] languages, serve as the locus of humor because of the implicit devaluation of the subject matter ("non-serious matter") or the explicit presence of "low" (corporeal, scatological) subject matter. In this sense dialects are both a marker of the humor and the target of the humor, in the sense that humor is a debasing activity that must take place in a bounded environment and so the dialect provides the perfect place for both asserting the underprivileged nature of the activity (engaging in humor) and providing a natural "limit" to the social violations of humor. Needless to say, humor can occur in the standard varieties as well, but I hypothesize that the tendency of dialect to be associated with humor is tied to the factors discussed above. Apte claims that "Humor and joking exchanges need a familiar setting in which such barriers of communication as age, rank, and social status are considerably reduced" (p. 195). I would argue, that on the contrary, the awareness of the status differences between the lectal varieties is enhanced and that the very differences are emphasized.

I will now exemplify this suggestion, with an example of a 17-second skit that circulated in 2018 on various online fora in Sicily. It was brought to my attention by Totò Panzeca, who also contributed to its explanation. It is transcribed below. The bolded text is the original in the skit; a translation in English is provided in italics. When the text is in Sicilian an interlinear gloss in Italian has been provided.

The skit is recited by two unidentified male voices. The first line opens with the typical phone call greeting and by the identification of the recipient of the call as the Hospital in Catania (the second largest city in Sicily). This frames the situation as both a phone call and as a healthcare service call.

(128) 1. **Pronto, Ospedale Civile di Catania?**

'*Hello. Catania Civil Hospital.*'

---

[6] A dialect ("lect") has different levels of formality: the basilect is the lower form, also known as the vernacular, used in the most informal settings. The acrolect is the highest, most formal variety, used in formal or official settings; often a standard language will be the acrolect, especially in a diglossic situation. The mesolect is an intermediate form. Acrolect, mesolect, and basilect form a continuum.

2. **Eh, bongiorno. Scusi, peccasu pozzu prenotare una visita**
   Eh, buongiorno. Scusi, per caso posso prenotare una visita
   cu' pacchiologo?
   con il pacchiologo?

'Eh, good morning. Excuse me, could I book a visit with the vaginologist?

3. **Non ho capito, scusi, il pacchiologo?**

I did not understand, sorry, the vaginolologist?

4. **Se, se, u' pacchiologo**
   Si, si, il pacchiologo.

'Yes, yes, the vaginologist.'

5. **Forse voleva dire: il ginecologo**

'Perhaps you meant: the gynecologist.'

6. **Aspittassi un attimu. Sasà chi tti fa mmali, u' pacchio o u**
   Aspetti   un attimo. Sasà che ti fa male,   il pacchio o il
   ginocchiu?
   ginocchio?

'Wait a second. Sasà what hurts? Your genitals or your knee?'

    The humor in the skit revolves around the use of the term "pacchiu" (vagina) with the suffix "-ologo" (doctor of). The caller asks to make an appointment with the "vagina doctor" (line 2). The hospital receptionist is confused and guesses that perhaps the caller meant "gynecologist" (lines 3–5). The caller misunderstands based on a folk-etymology of "ginecologo" derived from the similarity between "ginocchio" (knee) and Greek "gunaikos" ('women) [whence the root "gineco" in Italian] (line 6). I translated "pacchiologo" (which obviously has no direct translation in Italian since it is not a word) with "vaginologist" because of the morphemic resemblance between "vaginologist" and "gynecologist." "Sasà" (diminutive of Rosa) is presumably the wife of the caller.

    What is particularly remarkable about this text is that it alternates between Standard Italian and Sicilian (Catanese). The turns of the telephone operator at the hospital are all in Standard Italian, whereas the caller uses a basilectal variety, mildly tempered by some mesolectal touches ("Bongiorno," "fa mmali" rather than "doli") and the suffix

"-ologo." This is a perfect example of the use of dialectal varieties to mark (or provide a contextualization cue for) the humor in the text. The caller is immediately characterized as less educated, which then helps justify the misunderstanding ginocchio/ginecologo predicated on the presumed ignorance of the word "ginecologo." It is no coincidence that the punch line (in turn 6) is delivered in Sicilian, precisely because the use of the dialect marks the orientation toward the lower class, and we might say in a nod to Bakhtin, the body. "Pacchio" is a vulgar expression, and in this sense my translation as "vaginologist" is not correct, and a better translation would have been "pussylogist."

Rising intonation is indicated with a question mark in 1 and 3. In both cases it indicates a request for information: in the opening turn, it is a request of a reason for the call, while in the third turn it is a request for an explanation. Lengthening of the vowel in turn 5, indicated with a ":" following the syllable, may indicate hesitation or embarrassment.

Gasquet-Cyrus (2004) discusses the status of the regional French variety of Marseilles (Southern France), which has a stereotypical humorous value in France. For example, Gasquet-Cyrus reports a local singer, who, while waiting on stage between songs, says, "Eh, i(l) va venir" [it's coming (referring to an instrument that was being brought to him)] with a strong Marseilles accent. Gasquet-Cyrus notes that there is nothing incongruous in the fact of waiting for an instrument and neither is the use by a local person in front of a mostly local audience of the local dialect, but nonetheless the remark was greeted with laughter, because of the stereotypes attached to the performer and his dialect (pp. 142–143). There is much more to Gasquet-Cyrus' work, especially his urban dialectological study of humor in Marseilles, but in this context we can only hint at the rich material in this dissertation, which unfortunately remained unpublished.

Another, related, way of looking at this is the idea of metaphorical code switching. The idea behind metaphorical code switching is that its purpose is to convey an inferential meaning, signaled by the change to a different code. This is in opposition to situational code switching, in which one shifts languages or varieties simply to accommodate the various speakers or because a given situation requires or favors a given variety. Essentially, whereas situational code switching is determined by the situation, metaphorical code switching is a choice by the speakers. As such, it generates an implicature. For example, my daughter who is essentially English monolingual but knows some Italian, speaks English with her son. However, I recently observed that when he gets too rambunctious she tells him to stop by saying "Basta!" [Enough!, in Italian]. The four-year-old knows exactly what the code switching means, i.e., you are about to get in trouble, and stops his behavior.

The difference between situational and metaphorical code switching was introduced by Blom and Gumperz (1972). The use of a particular code may serve as a contextualization cue (Gumperz, 1982, p. 131; see Section 10.2.4). Therefore, "a switch to the code appropriate for humor can be a signal that the content is not serious" (Siegel, 1995, p. 101). Archakis et al. (2014) is a review of studies on stylistic humor in modern Greek, both in a mass-mediatic environment, which reveals that "in mass culture genres, stylistic humour is employed as a crucial means for characterisation: characters in media genres are more often than not denigrated and laughed at for their 'unconventional', 'non-standard', and/or 'heterogenous' stylistic choices" (p. 49). The authors list also a few studies of stylistic humor in Greek sociolinguistics.

13.3 The social construction of humor

As Berger (1997) argues, the key to understanding the relationship between humor and society is to realize that social life exists becasue the people who share a social space/group have a large set of conventions, rules, received ways of doing things, habits, connections, etc. that define and constitute the "hanging together" of a social group. Think for example, how much the location where a group gathers determines what the group will do and how they will interact, so that if they decided to change the place where they gather, for example, that would change significantly how the group interacts (for example, think of students in class and outside of it).

These rules and conventions for a "reality" which, because it is so commonplace and taken for granted, becomes "transparent" to its members (i.e., they are no longer aware of it).

Berger argues that humor is the intrusion of another reality in the everyday reality of a social group. Other examples of alternate "realities" would be religion and magic. (Berger, 1997, p. 65). For example, both humor and the sacred are contained in time and place. "Church time" is constrained in terms of location (one must go to a special building, or designate a location to serve as such) and special behaviors (rituals) and language (formulas, prayers) are allocated to this time (ceremonial). In Western society, at least until recently, one would wear special clothing (one's best) for such occasions. Humor is not so much constrained in terms of place (although there are prescribed comic locations, such as comedy clubs, the stage, etc.) but it is more limited in terms of times or situations. All societies will have a more or less specific list of times when it is inappropriate to joke (for example, funerals), but more importantly, there are signals, known[7] to the entire social group, that introduce and delimit the humorous "reality." Typically, we think of formulas such as "do you know the joke about…" but other markers may be present as well, such as the familiar smiling, laughing, etc. but also face painting (clowns), special dress, such as carnival costumes or the practice of dressing like the opposite sex in the Caribbean carnival, documented in Sherzer (2002, pp. 145–146).

The social conventions about humor form that society's "comic culture," defined by Berger as "the definitions of comic situations, roles, and acceptable contents in any social group or society" (1997, p. 68). Needless to say, social groups may be as small as a couple and as large as a (trans-)national entity (e.g., Chinese humor, European humor).

However, the process of defining a situation as comic has another side, or as Berger puts it: "As the comic situation is socially defined, it is at the same time contained" (1997, p. 68). The process of delimiting, of containing the "alternate reality" reflects at the cultural level the same idea behind the principle of least disruption at the conversational level (see Section 8.2.2). In other words, an alternate reality is fine, but it cannot take over the "real" reality." The carnival, for example, works because it is limited to Mardi Gras. If one tried to have 365 days of carnival, the society would collapse, as no productive work would get done. As the proverb widely attributed to Seneca and Horace goes, *Semel in anno licet insanire* (Once a year, you may go crazy). Once the party is over, we all go back to our regular lives, work, and obligations.

---

[7] The knowledge need not be explicit: this is the kind of implicit knowledge of competence. Just like speakers of a language know how to speak without being able to articulate the grammatical rules that govern their behavior.

13.4 Conclusions

This chapter wraps up the third part of the book on the performance of humor. While the previous chapters have been mostly interactionist in their perspective, this chapter was more oriented toward variation, i.e., how the humorous practices of the speakers are affected by such factors such as gender, age, social class, and dialectal repertoire. The final part of the chapter deals with the ultimate form of variation, the cultural construction of humor at large. It is fair to say that less research is available, generally speaking, on these subjects, perhaps with the exclusion of the gender variable. This may explain the somewhat tentative nature of some of the treatments.

13.5 Further readings

Davies (2017) is an excellent synthesis of the subject. Good overviews of the research on gender and humor can be found in Crawford (2003); Kotthoff (2006); and the already mentioned Davies (2017). Apte (1985) remains a good synthesis of work on the social aspects of humor, but is now out of date.

Part IV
Applications

The final part of the book consists of three applications of the theories we have examined so far, to the fields of literary humor, translation, and teaching. On the one hand, I have selected these applications because of their relative vicinity to the rest of the field, but on the other hand my reasons for choosing these and not others (such as computational humor) is that in these areas a critical mass of research has been reached, which allows us to make some mature assessments of the nature of the application. In many ways, this is also the part of the book where I feel less at ease, in the sense that my credentials are mostly in theoretical linguistics and sociolinguistics: translation and pedagogy are in some ways rather new to me. Working on these chapters was a learning experience for me as well.

14

Humor in literature

14.1 Script-based theory of humorous texts	321
14.2 Other approaches	328
14.3 Narratology	330
14.4 Stylistics	332
14.5 Some examples of literary constructs	336
14.6 Further readings	339

This chapter deals with humor in literature but not with literary works per se. This stance deserves some clarification: I do not have a negative opinion of the study of literature in and of itself: my first undergraduate degree is in French literature. Literary studies is a perfectly fine field and scholars have done a fine job of studying the various aspects of literary works that happen to be humorous, such as comedies, picaresque novels, parodies, pastiches, etc. ad libitum. For example, within humor studies, Triezenberg (2008) provides a short historical overview and a glossary of terms. Nilsen & Nilsen (2008) consists of a long list of genres[1] and authors that are relevant to literary humor, without any attempt at integration. The terminology of literary studies is plagued by the problem, already discussed in Chapter 1, of first- and second-order constructs. While few native speakers will have a first-order construct of romantic comedy or of picaresque, authors, critics, and scholars argue extensively on the nature and coverage of the second-order concepts.

---

[1] Among the genres quoted are comedy, humor, satire, irony, fantasy, parody, picaresque, and farce. Each term has many subdivisions.

The Linguistics of Humor: An Introduction. Salvatore Attardo, Oxford University Press (2020). © Salvatore Attardo.
DOI: 10.1093/oso/9780198791270.001.0001

We will not attempt to summarize these discussions, but we will provide two examples, in Section 14.5, namely *farce* and *satire* to show how literary scholars engage these constructs. Individual entries in the *Encyclopedia of Humor Studies* may also provide more details about individual literary terms of interest.

However, our focus here is on the humor, not on the literary aspects of humorous genres. In a sense, we are interested in humorous literary works because they contain humor and not because they are literary works. Needless to say, this distinction is easier stated than respected, as various scholars and approaches we will review may "color outside the lines" we have just marked out, or completely disagree with our view and advocate an approach more oriented toward literature. Regardless of which position will turn out to be preferable, it would be impossible to even pretend to summarize all that has been said in literary studies about humor, so our survey will only concern itself with linguistically oriented works. Further, it will be concerned with those studies that are theoretically oriented. This is an important limitation, because most of the works that I have classified as no-theory theories, in Chapter 3, are from within literature-based approaches. So, in a sense, this chapter will not deal with mainstream literary studies involving humor because what is truly mainstream in the study of literature has little or nothing to do with linguistics.

Nilsen and Nilsen (2008), displaying a wonderful sense of humor, open their almost-40-pages-long chapter with a review of arguments that the analysis of literary humor is a bad idea. My favorite is Bernard Shaw's: "There is no more dangerous literary symptom than a temptation to write about wit and humor. It indicates a total loss of both" (Nilsen & Nilsen, 2008, p. 243). Nilsen and Nilsen note also that "The study of literary humor is in some ways as broad as the whole field of humor research, plus the whole field of literary criticism" (p. 246). Plainly, it would be impossible to account for all of this in one chapter, hence, again, the need to restrict our concerns with linguistically-related work. We will start out with the applications of the Semantic Script Theory of Humor and the General Theory of Verbal Humor to the study of literary texts and then move on to other linguistically-oriented approaches, including narratologically-oriented and stylistics approaches. We will wrap up the chapter with a brief look at a few exemplar literary studies that are less linguistically oriented, just to show off the power of literary analysis per se.

A different approach at delimiting the boundary between stylistics, broadly defined, and literary theory is proposed by Simpson and Bousfield (2017):

> In the absence of robust justification within a framework of language and discourse, it is simply not enough for the critic-analyst to decree that a passage of writing is humorous

in other words, the burden of determining the humorousness of the text is on the linguistic theory and not on the literary scholar's intuition.

14.1 Script-based theory of humorous texts

We start out by considering the application of Raskin's Semantic Script Theory of Humor to longer humorous texts. The Semantic Script Theory of Humor has a well-defined purview and namely jokes expressed verbally or in writing. How does it fare when applied to another kind of text? This is our concern in this section.

The Semantic Script Theory of Humor is very abstract. As such it does not address, in principle, various issues. For example, the script theory "flattens" any text onto a script opposition. This is not a criticism of the theory, it is merely a refection of its semantic nature, which leads it to abstract away from the chronological presentation of the scripts in the opposition, for example. To go from the SEX script to the NO SEX script is indistinguishable, in terms of semantic opposition, from going from the NO SEX to the SEX script. In both cases, the opposition is between sex and no sex. This is not to say that one could not handle the order of presentation of the scripts in the Semantic Script Theory of Humor with the introduction of an ad-hoc apparatus, such as a chronological labeling of the various scripts, but the point is precisely that in its abstraction, the Semantic Script Theory of Humor does not concern itself with the order of activation of the scripts.

Another issue that the Semantic Script Theory of Humor is unable to address is whether the source of the opposed scripts involves the phonological form of the utterance, or to put it more plainly, whether the joke is based on a pun or not. Once more, this is not necessarily a criticism: the Semantic Script Theory of Humor is interested in script oppositions and overlaps. The source of said opposition is not part of the purview of the theory and as such it coherently ignores the difference between puns, in which two senses are opposed, based in part on the sound resemblance between two strings, and other jokes in which the opposition is not based on any aspect of the string, except its semantics. So, if one is interested in distinguishing between puns and non-puns (referential humor), one has to either add to the theory or come up with a broader theory. The latter strategy is what Raskin and myself did, in Attardo & Raskin (1991).

There are two approaches to the application of the Semantic Script Theory of Humor to longer literary humorous texts: one can either apply the theory as is to longer texts and add ad hoc mechanisms to handle phenomena not covered in the original Semantic Script Theory of Humor, or one can build a broader theory, In Attardo (1994), I labeled these approaches the expansionist approach and the revisionist approach, respectively. We will address both in that order below.

14.1.1 The expansionist approach

There are two major proposals that fall under the expansionist approach. We will consider them in chronological order.

14.1.2 Chłopicki

Chłopicki's early work (1987) essentially assumed that the Semantic Script Theory of Humor as stated originally could be applied to non-joke texts. In a sense, it is a minimalist approach to a theory of literature which essentially denies that literary texts have features that are significantly different from jokes or that those features are relevant in assessing their humorous aspects. Chłopicki is essentially saying, we don't need a theory of literary humor, if we have a theory of humor. As such, and because it was the very first application of the Semantic Script Theory of Humor to longer texts, it deserves a full treatment.

Chłopicki (1987) considers some Polish short stories. He sees the major difference between a joke and a short story as one of length: he begins by identifying and analyzing all the script oppositions in the short story. This is the first difference between a joke and a short story: many jokes have only one script opposition, but a short story has tens of scripts oppositions (66, in one example). He finds that some script extend across stretches of text and in some cases across the entire text. He labels these "main scripts." Some script oppositions also stretch across large parts of the text or its entirety and are called "shadow oppositions." The shadow oppositions overlap with the main scripts and thus Chłopicki considers to have successfully applied the semantic script theory of humor to short stories. In the process of producing this analysis, Chłopicki also adds to the list of basic oppositions identified in Raskin (1985): the new oppositions Chłopicki adds are ABSENCE/PRESENCE, NECESSARY/UNNECESSARY, and MUCH/LITTLE (Chłopicki, 1987, p. 18).

It should be noted that Chłopicki's approach essentially "flattens" (Attardo 1994, p. 210) the text of the short story onto a script opposition, albeit a shadow opposition. What is missing is that the text of the short story is developed over time, it has a linear aspect. So does the text of a joke, but a joke is by definition short and thus issues involved to the linearity of the text are ignored more easily. Let me add that Chłopicki's approach is not the only one to do this. For example, a Greimasian semiotic analysis (Greimas, 1966) would flatten a text onto a semiotic square (two oppositions).

The expansionist approach was so labeled in Attardo (1994) because it expanded the reach of the semantic script theory of humor. Chłopicki was not the only one to advocate expansionist ideas. Other proposals are reviewed in Attardo (1994, pp. 221–222). More recently, Chłopicki has developed an approach based on character frames (Chłopicki, 2017) in which the readers builds macro-scripts accumulating all the pertinent information about each character as it is developed. See Chłopicki (2017) for a summary and examples.

14.1.3 Holcomb

Holcomb (1992) introduces the concept of humor "nodal points" which are defined as follows: "Nodal points of humor are locations in the narrative where humor is perceptibly more concentrated than in the immediately surrounding text. Although they can be isolated as funny instances in the story, the nodal points remain semantically tied to the entire narrative" (p. 234). A nodal point, "will contain one or several script oppositions – oppositions that occur within the node itself or that involve an allusion to some other region in the narrative" (p. 236). The first part of this definition is meant to reprise Raskin's Semantic Script Theory of Humor, while the second is meant to broaden it, by "find[ing] a means of incorporating those instances into the whole of the narrative" (p. 236). Ermida (2008, pp. 107–108) finds that Holcomb contribution is a significant one, but faults it for being vague on the specifics of how to connect the nodal points to the rest of the narrative (p. 108).

Vagueness is indeed a problem: Holcomb lists a series of excerpts from a Mark Twain story, in which violence is perpetrated on the narrator, who reacts with unflappable calm. Holcomb then notes that the excerpts are not jokes (which is to be expected since they are not self-contained narratives) but "joke-like" constructions. He distinguishes between "local" and "distant" script oppositions (p. 240) which are however left undefined, except for the mention of "script oppositions that are not mentioned explicitly in the quoted excerpts but must be retrieved from other parts of the text" (p. 241), but no explanation is given on how this takes place.

Holcomb generalizes thus:

At the beginning of each [story], several major scripts are evoked. These are held in suspension as the discourse proceeds and then appear in opposition at nodal points, those regions in the text where the humor seems especially concentrated. In the nodes, the mere mention of any element of an already established script sufficiently evokes the full script.

So, according to Holcomb, "major" oppositions occur at the beginning of the narrative, whereas local ones in the nodal points. However, while that may be true of the two stories he analyzes in his article, it seems hardly likely that this pattern will hold true of all or most humorous stories. It is definitely not true of the *Lord Arthur Savile's Crime* story, analyzed in Attardo (2001a), in which the main character is not introduced until after 25 instances of humor having very little to do with the main theme of the story. Despite the definitional problems just listed (see also Attardo, 2001a, pp. 41–42), Holcomb's nodal points anticipate the idea of jab lines, without the technical detail. These will be discussed below.

14.1.4 The revisionist approach

The reader will recall, from Chapter 7, that one of the purposes of the General Theory of Verbal Humor was to extend the coverage of the Semantic Script Theory of Humor to all texts, thus overcoming the limitation of a theory of jokes. Our discussion of the revisionist approach starts out with the General Theory of Verbal Humor which is directly predicated on the assumption that different kinds of texts may have different textual organizations, as captured by the Narrative Strategy Knowledge Resource (Section 7.1.2). Attardo (2001a) presented a much more elaborated application of the General Theory of Verbal Humor to long texts, analyzing a variety of samples and in one case providing a complete analysis of a short story by Oscar Wilde. In so doing, a number of new concepts and tools were introduced, which will be reviewed below.

14.1.4.1 Jab line and punch lines

Probably the most widely adopted distinction introduced in Attardo (2001a) is that between punch lines, which end a text and in so doing reveal the presence of a second script, forcing the reinterpretation of the text itself, and jab lines which occur in the text in any other position (i.e., they do not occur at the end of the text) and do not disrupt the overall interpretation of the text. Semantically speaking, jab lines and punch lines do not differ: they both have script oppositions, so their difference is purely due to their different functions within the text. Tsakona (2003) showed that many jokes are compound jokes (Raskin 1985, p. 134), i.e., incorporate more than one script opposition, and that in those jokes that are complex, the script oppositions that occur before the punch line are jab lines and that these are unrelated to the final script opposition of the punch line.

A long text such as a novel or a novella will not necessarily end in a punch line, nor will any of its component parts (e.g., chapters). Some texts do so (I mentioned Katherine Mansfield's *Feuille d'album* short story in Chapter 1) and I analyzed another example in Attardo, 1994) but the vast majority does not. In fact, in most cases, humor is "superimposed" to an essentially serious narrative, that can be summarized without any mention of humor.[2] This led the way to considering the position of humor in the text and its distribution.

14.1.4.2 Organization of humor in the text

Any text is a vector, i.e., is organized linearly and there is a direction to the line (left to right in English). One can imagine a really long sheet of paper in which the whole of *War and Peace* is written as one very

---

[2] The 2001a version of the General Theory of Verbal Humor accounts both for the humor in texts that are humorous overall and for the presence of humor in texts that are otherwise serious. For example, Attardo (2001a) examines some onomastic jokes in Umberto Eco's *The Name of the Rose*, which is hardly a humorous novel, but nonetheless contains some humor.

long line. This is a function of a very fundamental principle of language, i.e., the linearity of the signifier. Already Saussure observed that one can only produce one sign at a time (let's say, the French phoneme /o/ (=*eaux*, waters)) and attendant prosodic marks. While the meaning of an utterance may not be entirely linearly derived, the utterance itself is necessarily so. Writing introduces complications, to be sure, but the principle remains. We know from eye tracking research, that readers do not by and large "peek ahead," that fixations follow the linearity of the printed line, and that any advanced awareness (both semantic and formal) does not go beyond the limit of a line of printed text. Obviously, in the case of a printed text, or with the recording of an oral utterance, a hearer can go back and re-examine previous parts of the text, but it remains that the way the text is first perceived is necessarily linear, i.e., one thing after another.

Once we consider this principle, it becomes clear that the organization of the humor along the vector may be significant. Indeed, Attardo (2001a) identifies several significant patterns: certain jab lines (or punch lines) may be related because for example, they all have the same Target (say, Lord Arthur Savile). If several (three or more) instances of jab line are related either thematically, as in the Target example, or formally (for example, because they all include a pun in the Language knowledge resource), they are said to constitute a strand. Stacks are strands of strands: for example, all the witticisms uttered by a character in a sitcom may be a strand, since they will share the commonality of having been uttered by the character. All groups of memes produced from a single image also constitute a stack. Tsakona (2017) speaks of "recontextualization" of the image or of other components of the meme. Shifman et al. (2014, p. 41) defines memes as items "sharing content, form and/or stance."

Attardo (2001a) also introduced various specific configurations, such as for two related jokes that occur at a certain distance (called in stand-up comedy, a "call back") and for repeated use of a given feature in a restricted area of text. The terminology, bridges and combs, respectively, was inspired by a visual representation introduced also in Attardo (2001a). Despite having been put to very good use on some studies, see for example Vincent (2010), the terminology has not been widely accepted.

What all these structures have in common is the phenomenon of repetition. Whereas in jokes repetition plays a small part, the repetition of humor or of some of its features, as seen above, plays a significant part in the structuring of longer humorous text (or in the humor within longer texts). This is a significant difference between jokes and longer texts.

14.1.4.3 The distribution of humor in the text

Beyond the way the humor is organized vis-à-vis other instances of humor, it is possible to consider the overall distribution of the humor in the text, regardless of its content. Corduas et al. (2008) applied sophisticated statistical analysis, based on time series, to investigate the null hypothesis of the distribution of humor in the text, i.e., that the position of humor in the text of a short story was random. Their findings indicated very clearly that the distribution of the humor is not random, i.e., it has some underlying motivation. The statistical techniques and the General Theory themselves cannot tell us what these factors or motivations are. It is however, possible to guess that one possibility is that more humor occurs at the beginning of the text to establish the humorous frame of the text itself. In a sense, the author would be signaling to the audience: this will be a funny text. Another possibility is that the author modulates the amount of humor for esthetic effect. Attardo (2001a, p. 89) dubbed "serious relief" passages with few or no humor in an otherwise humorous text (see below, Section 14.4).

Despite the promising and original results of the application of the General Theory of Verbal Humor to long texts, it has been met with rejection (e.g., Ermida, 2008, p. 109) or with lack of interest. This is doubly disappointing, because the methodology presented affords asking questions that wouldn't even be intelligible in traditional literary criticism (there is no conception of counting the amount of humor in a humorous text, let alone analyzing its distribution) and the few studies that have been conducted using the methodology yield good results. Perhaps the fact that one of the goals of Attardo (2001a) was to put the General Theory of Verbal Humor on a sound psycholinguistic processing footing, with its inherent technical aspects, or perhaps simply the labor-intensive nature of the analysis, have discouraged its use.

The revisionist approach and the expansionist share more than our exposition might reveal. For example, both are based on the complete analysis of the text and on locating and analyzing *all* the script oppositions in the text. In this they are directly opposed to the traditional approaches that rely perforce on sampling based on the intuition of the analyst. When a literary scholar decides to focus his/her attention on a given passage of the text, as opposed to another one, randomly chosen, he/she does it on the basis of their intuition which tells them that that particular passage is more meaningful or more significant, or simply more appropriate for exemplification, than another one. Of course, this practice introduces an element of subjectivity. Both the expansionist and the revisionist approach, by analyzing the entire text are exempt from this problem.

One may argue, as some actually have, that the actual analysis of the script oppositions is still subjective. This charge is simply misguided and completely ignores the difference between a semantic analysis, constrained by very specific techniques and mechanisms, and the more or less free for all of literary criticism. If one wanted to produce a Marxist analysis of Lennon and McCartney's Yellow Submarine one is only limited by one's imagination: take the line "everyone of us has all we need." Is that because socialism has been realized, thus distributing the means of production according to everyone's need? Did the Beatles intend to tell us that socialism would eventually fail in the USSR because they failed to "live beneath the waves"? Well, why not? Realistically, probably because one's career in literary criticism would end therewith, but sillier ideas have been proposed entirely seriously.[3] Conversely, semantic analysis is done in an extremely regimented way: one starts from the actual words in the text, and works one's way up (see Chapter 6). To claim that semantic analysis is subjective is simply not to understand how it is done.[4]

14.2 Other approaches

We now turn to other approaches that, while informed by linguistics, are more oriented toward the literary side. The best known such approach is arguably Ermida (2008). Her book starts out with a broad review of the

---

[3] My personal favorite: that analyzing Shakespeare's works reveals that Shakespeare had a Christ-like personality.

[4] To be fair, since no full-blown automatic semantic analyzer actually exists, one really has to do the analysis by hand, which is both time consuming and inevitably subjective, but it is a different kind of subjectivity. One can compare it to the subjectivity of a parent deciding how much allowance to give to their child and the subjectivity of an insurer pricing an insurance policy. Both are subjective, but differently so: an insurer uses actuarial tables, competitor's rates, and the likes to determine a price, whereas parents essentially determine their child's allowance based on hunches and possibly the example of other parents. It is obvious that an insurance company's leeway in pricing is much more limited than the parents'.

theories we have just surveyed. Ermida also addresses the narratological approaches to literary/narrative texts (113–130) without, however, bringing them to bear on humor.

Ermida (2008) contains some errors of interpretation: for example, she equates bona-fide in Raskin with truthfulness (Ermida, 2008, pp. 87–88), whereas one can violate *any* of the four maxims and be non-bona-fine. However she provides a discussion of several proposal dealing with literary humor, including, among others, a sympathetic summary of Nash (1985) (Ermida, 2008, pp. 101–102) and one of Chłopicki's work (pp. 103–105).

A very strange (pp. 109–110) decision by Ermida is to declare that texts that are not "(integrally) humorous" fall outside the purview of a "model of humorous text" (p. 110). As far as I can reconstruct her argument (presented on p. 172), the reason is that her model would not work if it tried to integrate the humor that occurs in text that are not entirely humorous. However, this decision leaves us with, at best, a partial theory of humorous texts, since by definition it can only handle a certain type of text and not others. This is a clear weakness.

As for Ermida's central hypothesis, the following quote from Chłopicki's (2017) will suffice:

In her central hypothesis she puts forward five defining principles of humorous narratives: opposition, hierarchy, recurrence, informativeness, and cooperation (Ermida, 2008, p. 172). On the one hand, the theory seems to be too powerful and would apply to many literary and non-literary narratives deprived of humor, while on the other hand some humorous stories would not display all the principles she predicts.

(Chłopicki, 2017, p. 147)

Triezenberg (2008) introduces the concept of humor "enhancer" which is defined as a "narrative technique [which] helps an audience to understand that the text is supposed to be funny, that warms them up to the author and to the text so that they will be more receptive to humor, and that magnifies their experience of humor in the text" (pp. 537–538). An example of what is intended is the use of legal jargon in a joke about lawyers. The joke would function also without legal terminology (assuming, for the sake of the argument, that the joke is not predicated on the knowledge of some specific legal term) but adding a few legal terms will make the joke a little funnier.

An interesting emerging trend is corpus-based or corpus-assisted studies. For a broad discussion, see Partington (2017). Here, we will mention Duguid (2009), who studies a corpus of journalistic humorous pieces and finds that phraseological units (idioms, constructions, and other lexical "ready-made" units) are evoked as "an expectation raised up only to be disappointed" (p. 312): "The unexpected shifting of fixed or frozen wording of idioms creates a collocational shock (for instance *drunk as a sock, a rabble-soothing speech*) just as the incongruous juxtaposition of register creates a shift in narrative" (p. 313). "Collocational shock" (as the phenomenon gets dubbed) is not the only technique found in the corpus, which includes also the use of hyperbole, irony, and other figurative modes. Partington et al. (2013, pp. 165–186), considers the writing of P. G. Wodehouse.

The work by Burgers et al. (2011) on irony identification has been discussed in Section 12.4.2. It is likely to yield significant results.

14.3 Narratology

The expansion of the General Theory of Verbal Humor is very clearly extraneous to narratology (Attardo, 2001a, pp. 32–33) on two grounds: 1) it focuses deliberately and exclusively on humor; and, 2) it rejects the intuitive nature of most narratological work. See the discussion of cherry-picking of evidence, in Section 7.2.3, for the significance of this point.

Larkin Galiñanes (2005) is a narratological look at humor. She claims that humorous novels' "typical narrative structure is heavily conditioned by the sort of pragmatic processing attendant on the appreciation of humor in jokes" (p. 80). Larkin Galiñanes (2005) further claims that there is a "striking degree of coincidence" between Relevance theory and Raskin's Semantic Script Theory of Humor (p. 83) because she characterizes humor as a mode that deliberately enhance the ambiguities found in any text and thus she claims the two theories are equivalent. Likewise, she reframes incongruity resolution as the search for relevance. Regardless of the validity of such equations, which I suspect would be rejected by *both* Relevance theorists and by Raskin, Larkin Galiñanes (2005) presents some very interesting ideas.

First, she points out that the caricatural aspect of many characters in comic novels functions along the same lines as the well-known ethnic stereotypes function in jokes: much like when we are told that a Scottish character is involved we activate the mythical joke script for STINGY, or in her example LOVE OF WHISKEY, the characters in a comic novel are *not* well-rounded and complex, i.e., they are caricatural, because "the narrator's descriptions, or the character's own words, however widely and frequently scattered over the text, all point in a specific direction, generating a limited number of implicatures and making the character easy to assimilate" (p. 89) since "If the character 'scripts' were complex, the reader would find them more difficult to englobe and grasp, an effect which would inhibit the creation of humor" (p. 89). This is particularly interesting in that it militates against Chłopicki's most recent work (summarized in Chłopicki, 2017) which is dedicated to creating complex scripts for each character (see Section 14.1.2 above).

Second, she describes what she calls "strong implicatures," i.e., an accumulation of connotative aspects of metaphorical constructs that end up creating an overall impression or characterization of the individual described. In her example, an old professor in Kingsley Amis' *Lucky Jim* is described as changing his facial features like "a squadron of slow old battleships" (p. 89) this giving, especially in concert with other similar descriptors, the effect of "a slow-minded individual" (p. 90).

Larkin Galiñanes (2005) claims that an extended text at a macro-level develops two opposed scripts

always potentially present in parallel, humorous effects (the equivalent to the punch line) being caused at certain points in the plot when the two scripts are simultaneously brought strongly into evidence. (pp. 98–99)

These points correspond to Holcomb's (1992) nodal points and to Attardo (2001a) jab lines.

Another work that incorporates narratological insights and uses the General Theory of Verbal Humor, to some extent, is Hamilton (2013) which analyzes medieval stories (fabliaux). A discussion of the narratology of humor would be incomplete without mention of the extensive discussion of the analysis of jokes in three narrative functions (Morin, 1966), promoted by numerous, mostly European, scholars. The discussion is summarized in Attardo, 1994, pp. 85–91; see a short discussion in Section 4.3.1.

14.4 Stylistics

Stylistic approaches have been applied to humor. A broad review can be found in Simpson & Bousfield (2017). The boundaries between stylistics and other approaches to literary studies of humor are not always easy to define. Under some definitions, it matches the entirety of this chapter. Under this broad definition of stylistics, the entire domain of stylistics is literary humor: Simpson & Bousfield (2017) make this very clear:

> the first principle [of the stylistics of humor] is that humor requires some form of stylistic incongruity. [...] The second principle is that the incongruity can be situated in any layer of linguistic structure. (p. 159)

In this section, we will limit ourselves to a narrower scope for stylistics, limited to issues of style.

An important contribution to stylistics comes from Cognitive Linguistics and more specifically the work of Antonopoulou (2002; Antonopoulou & Nikiforidou, 2009; Antonopoulou et al. 2015); for more on Cognitive Linguistics and humor, see Brône et al. (2015). The general idea is that in literary texts puns may not be the only source of verbal humor. Authors may play with "the relative compositionality and transparency of linguistic expressions which may be more or less fixed for the ordinary language user, but allow inventive decomposition of their fixedness" (Antonopoulou & Nikiforidou, 2009, pp. 305–306).

Antonopoulou (2002) utilizes concepts from cognitive grammar (metaphors, constructions, etc.) as well as the GTVH, enriched by the notion of idiomaticity, drawn from cognitive grammar, to explicate a variety of instances of humor in Raymond Chandler's (1888–1959) noir novels. Idiomaticity is defined as

> The conventional/idiomatic aspect of meaning of a construction is, therefore, what is left unexplained after the contribution of the meaning of each word has been computed.
> (Antonopoulou, 2002, p. 200)

Consider the example, discussed by Antonopoulou, of the construction "What's X doing Y?" The non-idiomatic meaning is the compositional sum of the constituents: let us consider now an instance of the construction, where X = toothbrush and Y = the fridge:

(129) What's your toothbrush doing in the fridge?

The compositional meaning of the construction is the sum of the meanings of the lexical items, plus the syntactic information that the toothbrush is in the fridge and not vice versa, etc. The idiomatic/conventional aspect is the "implication of disapproval" (Antonopoulou, 2002, p. 200) of the construction.

The violation of idomaticity in puns and register humor was previously known (see Attardo, 1994, for discussion); however Antonopoulou significantly broadens the scope of applicability of this facet of humor theory and at the same time proposes a revision of the GTVH's knowledge resource Language:

> The GTVH acknowledges the importance of the Language KR in the case of puns. My point here is that actual wording may play a decisive role in humour appreciation, not only in cases of (lexical or syntactic) ambiguity, but also in cases of idiomaticity (as described above). (Antonopoulou, 2002, p. 203)

The following example gives an idea of the subtlety of her argument:

(130)   She was smoking a cigarette in a black holder that was not quite as long as a rolled umbrella.

In example (130), the comparison is between a cigarette holder and an umbrella. Normally, we would expect the comparison to be that the cigarette holder is shorter than the umbrella, or vice versa, the umbrella is longer than the cigarette holder. Our knowledge of umbrellas and cigarette holders is such that we know that umbrellas are much longer than cigarette holders or conversely that cigarette holders are much shorter than umbrellas. By couching the simile as Chandler does, he asks his readers to consider as plausible the fact that the cigarette holder is almost as long as the umbrella, which is an exaggeration. However, by couching it in the "not quite as long" construal, rather than the "slightly shorter" alternative option, "the narrator pretends that they are in fact so close in this respect that someone else might consider them identical in length" (p. 203).

Another example is the "count-mass noun reversal" (p. 204) exemplified as follows:

(131)   Anna Halsey was about two hundred and forty pounds of middle-aged putty-faced woman in a black tailor-made suit.

Here the non-idiomaticity of the construction is fairly easy to see, but Antonopoulou provides again a sophisticated analysis, summed up as

Although (...) [an] incongruity seems to be encoded in the second half of the sentence starting with of, in fact its resolution depends on the reader realizing the reason motivating the switch, i.e. that she is so fat that she is ?more mass than count?.

(p. 204)

Antonopoulou and Nikiforidou (2009) is focused on *coercion* defined as

the clash between the syntactic and/or semantic properties of a word with those of the construction in which the word is embedded and the principles that guide coherent, consistent interpretations in such cases of conflict. (2009, p. 290)

For example, in (132) below

(132) It wasn't that big an office, but the walls dripped modern art (Ian Rankin, *Set in Darkness*, 2000, quoted in Antonopoulou & Nikiforidou, 2009, p. 296)

the verb "drip" coerces a feature [+liquid] onto the normally [+solid] noun "art". One may argue that liquid art is conceivable, and it certainly is, but it would not be hung on walls (or would need to be in solid containers).

As Antonopoulou & Nikiforidou (2009, p. 300) note

coercion, by definition, foregrounds the linguistic incongruity per se, which may in turn be exploited in the creation of a superordinate, text-global opposition.

So, in other words, coercion causes an incongruity and the repetition of the same form of coercion in the text creates a strand (14.1.4.2).

Overall, Antonopoulou's argument that the GTVH can be usefully augmented by attention to the sort of linguistic manipulation such as idiomaticity, coercion, and more broadly stylistic choices (Antonopoulu et al., 2015) is a welcome corrective to what is an oversimplification in the GTVH due to its origins in the analysis of jokes, as Antonopoulou and Nikiforidou perceptively note (2009, p. 294, note 4). However, the GTVH was not entirely uninterested in these matters, as the discussion of register humor below will show.

14.4.1 Register humor

One of the most relevant topics in the stylistics of humor is register humor. Register humor is created by an incongruity between the register used to describe them and the facts, or between an expected register and an observed one. Registers are "language varieties associated with a given situation, role, or social aspect of the speakers' experience" (Attardo, 1994, p. 230). They are pretty standardly organized in high and low varieties, with formal, sophisticated registers in the high strata of the model and with informal, scatological, and other forms associated with low-income, poorly-educated folk in the low strata.

Attardo (1994, pp. 262–265) examines several examples from T. L. Peacock, a nineteenth-century humorist. These are often longish stretches of text, as a register is usually identified by accretion and not by a single lexical item of grammatical feature. However, an example such as (133) should give a feel for the phenomenon. The set up of the scene is that a certain character is exasperated and starts throwing things at his servants; this is described as follows:

(133) by converting some newly unpacked article, such as a book, a bottle, a ham, or a fiddle into a missile against the head of some unfortunate servant (T. L. Peacock (1815), *Headlong Hall*, p. 6).

"converting [an object] into a missile" is obviously a high register variant for "throw," so it is precisely the discrepancy between the expected word "throw" and the unexpected, non-idiomatic "convert into a missile" that causes the incongruity.

The theory of register humor had been prefigured by Bally, one of De Saussure's students who edited the *Cours de Linguistique Générale* (Bally, 1909). His approach, described in some detail in Attardo (1994, pp. 231–235) has had little impact on the contemporary treatments of the subject. Among contemporary scholars dealing with register humor, the most significant is Alexander's treatment (1997). Alexander presents register humor as the "comical confusion" of two registers defined as "selecting a lexeme or phraseological unit from a different style level than the context would predict" (Alexander, 1984, p. 60). As can be plainly seen, this fits perfectly the Peacock example above (133). Haiman (1990, pp. 199–202) claims that register clashes are an indicator of sarcasm. Attardo (1994, pp. 230–253) presents an approach based on script-theory and spreading activation, a psycholinguistic phenomenon. A more recent overview is found in Simpson & Bousfield (2017, pp. 160–161). Related but different from register humor, in that it involves two different linguistic varieties, is the practice of dialectal humor, i.e., the use of a dialectal variety of a language for the purpose of humor (see Section 13.2.4).

Register humor tends to develop over relatively large stretches of text in which individual features end up adding up to a strong enough "marker" of the presence of a given register. Register humor is considered a diffuse disjunctor humorous phenomenon in Attardo (2001a). A diffuse disjunctor is a disjunctor that is not necessarily embodied in a single lexical item or syntactic feature. Example (95), in Chapter 9, is a good example of diffuse disjunctor, albeit not a register-based one.

Attardo (2001a) introduced the idea of serious relief, i.e., that the author of a long humorous text would introduce passages deliberately less humorous for effect. In Attardo (2001b), some differences between the use of adjectives in the serious relief passages are found:

the distribution between humorous parts and serious relief of some adjectives is clearly not random. It seems to be the case that Wilde is deliberately, or if not deliberately, unconsciously, marking the serious relief passage by using a different 'palette' of adjectives. As we saw, not all adjectives are used in this marking function and in fact a significant number of high frequency adjectives is used randomly across the text.

(p. 28)

14.5 Some examples of literary constructs

It should be made clear at the offset, that trying to summarize the sophisticated, erudite, and stylistically gratifying works of the scholars I will describe in this section is like trying to produce a dehydrated version of your mother's coq-au-vin. The ersatz version will not taste anywhere as good as the original and much of the point of having it in the first place will be lost. My point here is to show that high-quality, theoretically sound studies that are not merely descriptive can be done, if largely outside of linguistics.

Davis (2003; originally published in 1978, but the 2003 edition has a very extensive introduction that throws significant light on the material) is dedicated to the description of "farce." According to Davis it "delights in taboo-violation, but [...] avoids implied moral comment or social criticism and [...] tends to debar empathy for its victims"; it treads "a fine line between offence and entertainment [...] farce-plots tend to be short and [...] peopled [...] by simplified comic types" (p. 2). Farce favors "direct, visual, and physical jokes;" it is aggressive, violent, politically conservative (p. 3). This sort of generalization over a vast number of texts is a spectacular feat of scholarship, but linguistically there is little that needs to be added, except that one would need a very sophisticated theory of context and discourse to be able to account for these categories in a work of linguistics. Likewise, the four plot types Davis identifies:

- Humiliation or deception farce: linear narrative someone is humiliated or deceived
- Reversal farce: as above, but the victim retaliates
- Equilibrium farce: two opposing forces confront each other but remain in balance
- Snowball or Circular farce: all the characters are caught into a mechanism

are very abstract and clearly define most farces, but would be hard to account for linguistically.

In the lack of strong moral stance, farce contrasts with satire, which has an element of "censoriousness" (Condren, 2012, p. 378) combined with humor. However, Condren argues that a general definition of satire may be impossible, because the various varieties of satire produced across the centuries and in different societies (the Greeks, the Romans, Renaissance Italy, etc.) are so great that it becomes impractical to provide such a definition. Ultimately the themes and the entities targeted can provide us with some definition based on "family resemblances" (à la Wittgenstein) (p. 386) but Condren notes immediately that such a definition is insufficiently restrictive (p. 387). Finally, he comes to the conclusion that an essentialist definition of satire may be impossible or pointless (p. 390) and goes back to "moral seriousness" (p. 391) i.e., censoriousness.

Simpson (2003) presents a linguistically sophisticated discussion of satire as a discursive genre (i.e., inclusive in the definition of discourse features). The argument is too complex to describe in detail here, so I will offer a "taste" of it, through a quote from Simpson's own summary:

Whereas the model of satire postulates that both prime [the antecedent of the satire, its object] and dialectic [the opposition, the antithesis] elements be present in a text, it further stipulates that the lack of congruence between these elements be recognized by a reader or listener, In other words, it is the dissonance between the domains of prime and dialectic which creates an interpretive pragmatic framework for satire and brings about the style-shift necessary to place the reader-listener on a *satirical footing*.

(Simpson, 2003, p. 10; emphasis in the original)

The reader will recognize the familiar script opposition (the relationship between prime and dialectic) and the incongruity of the connection ("lack of congruence"). Simpson's contribution is to place this dialectic (to borrow the Hegelian terminology) in the discursive domain, reminiscent (or at least compatible with) the Gumperz-Hymes ethnomethodological framework discussed in previous chapters.

Caputi (1978) represents a different type of study: while he does identify and define a "genre" called *buffo*, which corresponds to "vulgar comedy" (overlapping largely with farce), his focus is not on defining or creating boundaries, but rather in showing the uninterrupted continuity of transmission starting from the very early Greek comedies (Doric mimes, satyr plays, and *phlyax* farces) all the way to contemporary comics, clowns, and performers. Caputi's erudition is remarkable and his capacity to bring to bear to the argument sources of vastly different domains, such as six or seven national literatures, literary criticism, humor theory, anthropology, folklore, make his book worth reading even if one is not particularly interested in the overall thesis.

Literary studies has its own methodologies, tools of analysis, and in short "questions." For example, the question of biographical criticism is "how does the work reflect the life of the writer and vice versa"? The question of gender-based theorists are along the lines of "how does this work reflect and enact the patterns of gender dominance/identification that are found elsewhere in the society"?

Most literary analyses of humorous texts simply ignore the fact that the texts are or were meant to be humorous. While this claim may seem prima facie outrageous and presumably false, it is in fact an accurate description of the state of affairs in literary scholarship. Skowron (2003) analyzed some literary analyses of Oscar Wilde's humor and found not only the above statement to be factual but that, in fact, many scholars treated passages from, say, *The Importance of Being Ernest* as if they were accurate representations of Wilde's beliefs. What little attention was given to the humorous nature of Wilde's production consisted largely in reproducing his bon mots and in platitudes about wit. Clearly there are exceptions, and probably some humorists have been analyzed qua humorists (Wodehouse comes to mind), but by and large it has to be acknowledged that the initial claim remains true.

The above should not be interpreted as meaning that no analyses of literary humor exist. That is far from true. For example, Swift's *Modest Proposal* is a very well-known text and many discussions have focused on its irony. However, it is fair to say that the analyses of Shakespeare's comedies, for example, focus more on what they reveal about Shakespeare's beliefs, Elizabethan ideology, etc. than on how funny they are. In short, while literary texts that are funny have been analyzed, they are analyzed because they are part of the literary production of an author. Their being funny is often ignored, dismissed, or dealt with marginally.

This seems potentially very wrong, since we would expect that the fact that the author wrote the text with the apparent intention to amuse, entertain, or divert his/her audience should be significant to the understanding of the nature of functioning of the text itself (not to mention of its relationships with the audience, etc.).

14.6 Further readings

There are no introductory works on the applications of linguistics to humor in literature. Good but more advanced introductions to aspects of humor and literature are Chłopicki (2017) and, on stylistics, Simpson & Bousfield (2017). Chłopicki's early work is summarized in Attardo (1994) and in Ermida (2008). Attardo (2001a) is probably the best resource for a full understanding of the application of the General Theory of Verbal Humor to literary texts. On Cognitive Linguistics and humor, see Brône et al. (2015).

15
Humor and translation

15.1 A few definitions	343
15.2 Theories of humor translation	344
15.3 Audiovisual translation	355
15.4 Translating puns	359
15.5 Conclusions	365
15.6 Further readings	366

Speakers of other languages than the one in which a particular instance of humor was created may want to enjoy it too. Enter translation. Jokes, humorous texts, films, cartoons, advertising, and all sorts of other humorous materials (such as video games, cf. Iaia, 2014) are frequently conveyed in one or more languages different from the one in which they originated.

This chapter deals with the translation of humor. The magnitude of the phenomenon of the translation of humor is hard to assess. It is safe to say that a lot of humor gets routinely translated: consider American and British sitcoms, often broadcast, and hence translated, world-wide. I have found an unsubstantiated claims that *Friends* was broadcast in more than 100 countries[1] and the French cartoon *Astérix* translated into more than 110 languages.[2] Regardless of the details, this is a significant issue that affects millions of people and a multi-million business. The translation of humorous literature is likewise a huge segment in the

---

[1] Wikipedia: en.wikipedia.org/w/index.php?title=Friends&oldid=164835768
[2] The page is constantly updated. As of August 2019, the count stood at 116 languages and dialects: www.asterix-obelix.nl

The Linguistics of Humor: An Introduction. Salvatore Attardo, Oxford University Press (2020). © Salvatore Attardo.
DOI: 10.1093/oso/9780198791270.001.0001

publishing industry. Bucaria and Chiaro (2007) claim that on a week of programming in Italy in 2005, 562 hours of dubbed programming was broadcast (presumably not all humorous).

This chapter addresses only some of the aspects of the translation of humor, out of necessity. An entire book could not hope to address all the issues in the field, let alone a mere chapter. Nonetheless, a wide range of issues will be considered including some basic tenets of translation theory, audiovisual translation (subtitling, dubbing, captioning, etc.), translation from one semiotic system to another, and much more. Not all issues can be addressed. For example, all the previous chapters, and in fact most of the literature on humor, have implicitly assumed that humor comes in one language. Needless to say, this is not the case. While there obviously are monolingual texts, many texts use more than one language; large texts are often multilingual. We will not be concerned here with humorous texts that exploit multilingualism for humorous purposes, but see Valdeón (2005) for a discussion of multilingualism in the sitcom *Frasier* and the articles in the special issue of the *European Journal of Humour Research* guest-edited by Dore (2019).

I would also like to stress that I am concerned here with the theoretical issues concerning the translation of humor. By this, I simply mean that I will not consider the practical issues faced by translators. For example, many people professionally engaged in translation have told me that they are chronically underpaid. I am sure this is true and it is a serious issue well worth discussing, but a book about the linguistics of humor is not the proper place for such a discussion. I do not wish to make light of the issue, and of the many others that translators face when exercising their profession: for example, it is often true that the deadlines for the production of the translation are unrealistically short. This is especially true in subtitling and dubbing and particularly so in interpreting (see Section 15.3 below). It is often also the case that the translator does not have the time and/or energy to dedicate to finding an optimal solution due to overwork/overload, which forces him/her to "settle" for a given translation and stop searching for a better one. The astute reader will have recognized the competence/performance distinction once more: we are concerned with the competence of translation (i.e., an idealized situation in which time, energy, cost, etc. constraints are not relevant) and not with the performance of translation (i.e., the actual practice that actual translators engage in actual situations and subject to time, cost, energy, etc. limitations).

Another observation that Martinez Sierra and Zabalbeascoa (2017, p. 16) make is worth stressing: the field of translation studies has shifted its focus from textual (or verbal) humor to multimodal, audiovisual[3] humor. Here the distinction, popularized by Chiaro (2005), between verbally expressed humor and humor expressed by non-verbal means (i.e., visual, auditory, musical, etc.)[4] is worth remembering: in a multimodal event, such as a film or sitcom, but also a play or a conversation between two people, there are many "channels" active at the same time: people or characters say something (verbal channel) but at the same time they may grimace (visual) or other things may happen on stage or in the visual field (or even in a different location, in a split-screen shot), or the soundtrack may be incongruous. For example, a recent (June 4, 2017) video on YouTube shows members of the English Defence League, an Islamophobic movement (Wikipedia https://en.wikipedia.org/wiki/English_Defence_League), being "chased out of Liverpool to the Benny Hill tune" (as the caption of the video reads). Indeed, one can clearly hear the music, and several people in the video laugh and dance to it. It is not clear what the source of the music is. The YouTube caption reads also "Hilarious!" Thus it is clear that, while there is no discernible verbally expressed humor, the situation and the video are humorous (at least to some participants) due to the juxtaposition of the situation (a political rally) and the music.

Here the reader will do well to recall that while linguistic theories in their formulation do not concern themselves with extra-linguistic matters, their underlying principles apply to all semiotic systems (see Chapter 5) and hence to multimodal and audiovisual texts. It is one thing to eliminate some aspects of a phenomenon to narrow down one's purview to simplify the analysis, as linguistics has done, and it is another to be unable to handle a given subject, in principle. In other words, linguistics has chosen to simplify its analyses by limiting itself to the verbal channel, but there is no reason in principle, that it could not handle other channels (and it has done so, on occasion). While from the standpoint of the theory of translation, and even from the standpoint of some approaches to linguistics, it may make perfect sense to distinguish between humor in the verbal channel and humor that is not verbalized,

---

[3] I am here using multimodal and audiovisual as synonyms. Needless to say, they are not the same thing.

[4] The earliest mention of verbally expressed humor I am aware of is Eastmond (1992); see also Ritchie (2000).

from a semiotic perspective the distinction is unnecessary and even confusing. The text as a whole is humorous and all its parts need to be taken into account. To put it differently: it is a perfectly fine methodological choice to limit one's analysis to a given channel (verbal or visual or music, or montage, etc.) but that does not entail that the other channels are unimportant or cannot be analyzed (separately or in conjunction with the verbal). Finally, there is potential confusion here between verbally expressed humor (as in linguistically expressed) and verbal humor (as in humor that relies of the form of the signifier, puns for short; see Chapter 9). The two should not be confused.

The field of translation studies of humor is very active, as compared to other fields of the linguistics of humor. Thus it is somewhat surprising to see a recent survey of the field (Martinez Sierra and Zabalbeascoa, 2017, p. 13) describe the literature as "scarce." However, the assessment makes perfect sense when one notes that translation studies is a very fragmented field, and that a significant part of the literature falls on the "art" of translation, rather than on the "science" side (Steiner, 1975, p. 295). We will only be concerned with scientific approaches to translation, so we will more or less ignore the plethora of studies about translating an individual author or work in any given pair of languages.[5]

15.1 A few definitions

15.1.1 Source text and target text language

It is common in the field of translation studies to refer to the text that is translated as the *source text* (ST) and the resulting translation as the *target text* (TT). Correspondingly, the language in which the source text is worded is referred to as the source language (SL) and the language of the target text as the target language (TL). As we will see, translation may take place within varieties of a language, for example, dialects, but also high and low forms of a language (formal vs. colloquial varieties). Regardless, we will use the terms source/target text and language in all cases of translation. In fact, the picture is even more complex.

---

[5] Chiaro (2005, p. 136) rightly reminds us that the translation of humor is not only, or even not primarily, a translation between languages as it is between cultures. We will not address this issue in this context, but see Davies (2005).

15.1.2 Intra- and inter-semiotic translation

Following Jakobson (1987; originally published in 1960) we distinguish three types of translations:

- intralingual (paraphrase): translating within one language. An example would be paraphrasing or rewording a sentence, for example to make it easier to understand.
- interlinguistic: translating from one language (i.e., the SL) to another (TL). An example would be translating an English play into French.
- intersemiotic: translating from one semiotic system to another. An example, would be the film adaptation of a book (Jakobson, 1987, p. 429).

Usually, when we speak of translation, without further qualifying, we mean inter-linguistic translation. We adopt this usage in this book as well. We will also use the term source/target text regardless of the semiotic system in which it is expressed. For further discussion of the distinction, see Chiaro (2017).

15.2 Theories of humor translation

The Italian saying *traduttore, traditore* is a fitting place to start our discussion. But of what is the translator a traitor, precisely? The glib answer is "meaning." However, meaning is about the only thing that a skilled translator is pretty much guaranteed to be able to transpose from one language into another. Another suggestive idea is the title of Umberto Eco's collection of essays on translation (2003b): "dire quasi la stessa cosa" (*saying almost the same thing*), with the emphasis on *almost*. Again, the question boils down to the nature of this "almost": what gets lost or replaced? This section then discusses the question of what gets translated.

15.2.1 Faithfulness

Roman Jakobson points out that meaning itself is only understood through translation, as the meaning of a sign is simply its translation

15.2 THEORIES OF HUMOR TRANSLATION

in other signs, i.e., it exists only within the system of the language, as claimed by Saussure (1916) and Peirce (1960). Translation then reduces to equivalence: if a source text sign can be replaced with a target sign that is equivalent (i.e., has he same value) we have an ideal translation. However, since languages, varieties and semiotic systems are different, their signs have different values and hence one needs to substitute different signs. As Jakobson puts it, "equivalence in difference is the cardinal problem of language" (1987, p. 430). Jakobson also states some basic points: anything that can be said in any language can be translated into any other. It may be hard to do so, as languages differ "in what they *must* convey and not in what they *can* convey" (Jakobson, 1987, p. 433; emphasis in the original) but it can ultimately be done. Poetry is impossible to fully translate, only "creative transposition" is possible (p. 434), and this is especially valid for the pun, in which "Phonemic similarity is sensed as semantic relationship" (p. 434). Summing up, for Jakobson, translation ideally should reproduce the value of the signs in the source text or the target text. Since this is impossible, as languages differ, equivalence must be sought, while staying as close as possible (faithfulness) to the source text. In cases in which the signifier is involved (such as poetry and puns), since by definition the signifier will not be translatable in the target text, translation is strictly speaking impossible, but transposition (functional translation) should be sought.

Low (2011, p. 60) notes that within a "verbal process" view of translation "translating a joke means creating an amusing target text (TT) that is *nearly identical* to the source text (ST)." However, Low himself, states that such a goal is "unreasonable" and that the translator should instead aim at delivering "broadly speaking, the same joke" (p. 60). This brings to mind, whether Low intended this or not, the GTVH, whose stated purpose is to determine when two jokes are the same (and when they are not).

15.2.1.1 The GTVH as a tool to evaluate difference

Attardo (2002a) takes as his starting point Jakobson's equivalence and proposes using the GTVH's built-in metric of difference between humorous texts to determine how different a source text is from its translation, humor-wise. This is stated, in a nod to Grice's maxims, as another maxim:

if possible, respect all six Knowledge Resources in your translation, but if necessary, let your translation differ at the lowest level necessary for your pragmatic purposes.

No prescriptive intention is present, just as no prescriptive intention is meant in Grice's maxims. Essentially, the idea is that, if the translator determines that he/she needs to reproduce the humor of the original ST as faithfully as possible, then the rational (most efficient) way to do so is to follow the maxim above. Obviously, if the translator determines that the best choice is not to reproduce the humor (faithfully, or at all) then the maxim is of no use to him/her. The method is applied to translation as a set of binary choices in Zabalbeascoa (2005, pp. 202–204). According to an empirical study by Williamson & Ricoy (2014) translators do follow the proposed maxim, to some extent (p. 186). Shipley (2006) adopts the proposal and supplements it with a checklist of external factors to be considered as well. Asimakoulas (2004) also applies the General Theory of Verbal Humor to the translation of humorous films in Greek.

15.2.2 Literal vs. functional translation

Raphaelson-West's (1989) approach is based in Nida and Taber (1969). The focus is on semantics first and style second. As Nida and Taber put it, "anything that can be said in one language can be said in another, unless the form is an essential element of the message" (1969, p. 4). Implicit in this definition is that puns and poetry are untranslatable in principle. Raphaelson-West (1989) is more optimistic and notes that linguistic jokes are "most difficult to translate" (p. 131).

Raphaelson-West (1989) introduced a tripartite taxonomy of jokes, which became very influential in the field, distinguishing:

1. Puns: their translatability is "very unlikely" (p. 130)
2. Cultural (ethnic jokes): more translatable, but the two cultures must share the stereotype
3. Universal jokes: jokes based on universal semantic features, such as child vs adult, or the unexpected (p. 131)

Raphaelson-West (1989, p. 131) notes that the existence of universal jokes is questionable, but likely. Universal jokes correspond to Zabalbeascoa's (1996b, p. 251) "international joke [in which] (…) the

15.2 THEORIES OF HUMOR TRANSLATION

comic effect does not depend on either language-specific wordplay or familiarity with unknown specific aspects the source culture."

As Chiaro (2017, p. 420) notes, translation scholars have proposed several dichotomies revolving around the idea of equivalence: e.g., "formal vs. dynamic/functional" (Nida, 1964). Functional translation, in the case of humor, boils down to reproducing the perlocutionary goals of the ST. This has been clearly stated, for example, by Fuentes Luque (2004, p. 77) as "conseguir en el texto término el mismo efecto humorístico (en forma de sonrisa o risa) en la cultura y la lengua término que en las originales" [to achieve in the TT the same humorous effect (in the form of smile or laughter) in the target culture and language than in the originals; my translation SA]

Chiaro (2017, p. 421) argues that for theorists such as Toury (1985) and Vermeer (1989; see below), who reduce equivalence to function, the translator may "insert a completely new instance of verbal humor" to replace an otherwise untranslatable joke. Nida and Taber's own definition of dynamic translation, later changed to functional, allows this interpretation, since it is based on the idea of "response" of the audience (see Fuentes Luque's point above).

15.2.3 Zabalbeascoa's priority scales and solution types

Zabalbeascoa locates the practice of translation squarely within performance, which he calls "contingency" (2005, p. 186). He identifies ten "most obvious" factors that affect the context in which translation is performed. These include the languages and cultures involved, the medium of the texts, the purpose of the translation, the nature of the text, the intended recipients, the sponsors of the translation, the translator's skills and limitations, and the conditions in which the translation is performed.

Because of this significant level of contextual variability, Zabalbeascoa advocates for the practice of mapping and prioritizing before translating. Mapping consists of locating in the text significant items (e.g., the instances of humor; Zabalbeascoa, 2005, p. 187). On the problem of identifying humor, see Section 12.4.2. Prioritizing is more complex. Zabalbeascoa argues that each translation has a set of priorities and restrictions. The priorities are the goals of the translation and the restrictions are the "obstacles and problems" that motivate the priorities and "the solutions adopted in the translation" (1996b, p. 243).

Furthermore, Zabalbeascoa argues that the priorities are arranged on a scale of importance (p. 243), so that a top priority is also a restriction for the priorities below it. Thus different types of texts will have different priorities for humor. A TV comedy will place a higher priority on humor than a TV quiz show or a drama (p. 244).

A second scale is that of global/local relevance to the text. According to this scale, humor may be a local priority in the text (i.e., there is a joke in the ST), but a low priority globally (i.e., the goal of the text is not merely to have that particular instance of humor) and hence it may be omitted or substituted with another instance of humor elsewhere. After a priority scale and a global/local scale, the third scale of priorities is that of equivalence. It may range from "absolute identity" to "slight resemblance" (p. 247). So equivalence may or may not be a high priority, locally or globally, in the text.

As an example of a set of priorities for translating a sitcom, Zabalbeascoa mentions the following:

do well in popularity ratings, be funny, aim for immediate response in the form of entertainment and laughter, integrate the words of the translation with the other constituent parts of the audiovisual text, or use language and textual structures deemed appropriate to the channel of communication.   (p. 245)

We are now in the position to be able to understand Zabalbeascoa's sophisticated argument:

Translating comedy in order to produce comedy entails that *intended* comic effect is a priority that is both very high on the scale of importance and a global one, i.e. relevant to the text as a whole. It is moreover an equivalence priority, requiring near-absolute identity. The insistence on the word *intended* means that equivalence is here seen as a characteristic of an intention to be funny, regardless of the final outcome. What matters in this case is the perception of the source text's humour as a basis for the decision to make the translation a humorous text. The translation can then be judged according to exactly how funny it is in its own right. From this perspective, there is little point in comparing source and target texts in terms of the exact amount and type of humour they contain; if anything, it would be desirable for the translation to be even funnier than the source text.   (p. 247)

In other words, since the overall purpose of the text ("intended comic effect") is high on the scale of priority and on the global side of the scale, it is crucial to be faithful to that goal ("near-absolute identity"), i.e., the TT should be above all funny. Conversely, local equivalence is a low priority, to the point that, as Zabalbeascoa implies, a translator may choose to add humor to the TT, if there is an opportunity for it. Zabalbeascoa continues to point out that there may be cases in which non-equivalence is the goal (for example, a pedagogical setting in which the linguistic features of the text are significant, and thus it would be unadvisable to replace the joke with a different, albeit funny, joke).

15.2.3.1 Solution types

Zabalbeascoa (2000) sees the translation process as determined by methods, strategies, solutions, and solution types. Translation methods are identified based on "the formal and functional characteristics of a TT and its ST" (2000, p. 119). Examples of methods are word-by-word translation and adaptation. Strategies are defined as "conscious action(s) intended to enhance a translator's performance" (p. 120). Strategies include, for example, consulting dictionaries, writing a draft, etc. Solutions are then the results of strategies, i.e., concrete instances of TT arrived at from a ST. Translation techniques consist of parsing the ST into the "smallest constituents parts (...) for the purpose of translation (...) and then considering the most convenient way (technique) of rendering each unit" (p. 122). Zabalbeascoa notes that the implicit measure of the solution types is against the ideal of literal translation (p. 122) and later that it relies on the notion of "equivalence" (p. 123). A solution type is thus defined as "the shared characteristic of a number of different solutions" (p. 122). The results of Díaz Perez' (2017) study show that the solution-types most frequently used are those based on the source culture (p. 72).

15.2.3.2 Translation techniques

A certain consensus is found concerning translation techniques. Fuentes Luque (1998) sums up four techniques for the translation of humor:

1. Addition or compensation: inserting a joke where none was present to compensate for not translating another one;
2. Substitution: replacing a joke with another one (presumably easier to incorporate in the TT)
3. Metalinguistic commentary: explanations, paraphrases, footnotes, etc.
4. Omission: uncompensated lack of translation (1998, p. 667)

The proposal has been widely adopted: Chiaro (2005, 2010); Fuentes Luque (2010); Low (2011), who adds to the list a "dilution" strategy (translating only a few puns in a passage rife with them) and "explicitation" (i.e., a partial explanation of the otherwise untranslatable joke).

Techniques for translating puns will be discussed in Section 15.4 below. Cuéllar Irala and Garcia-Falces (2004), in the brilliantly titled article: "Cultura y humor: traductores al borde de un ataque de nervios" [Culture and Humor: Translators on the verge of a nervous breakdown] enumerate several strategies for translating cultural references that may not always exist in both cultures:

1. Maintain the reference (e.g., reference to Starbucks, which will be understood equally well in Spanish or in English).
2. Explicitation: explain the reference.
3. Generalization (hyperonymy): instead of using a specific reference use an hyperonym (for example, instead of "Ford F150" use "pickup truck").
4. Adaptation or naturalization: use a referent better known in the TL. This has three sub-cases, according to Cuéllar Irala and García-Falces (2004); it is unclear if there is a real difference between them:
   (a) Change the referent to retain connotations;
   (b) Naturalization due to the desire to avoid references extraneous to the TL (example: a reference to a rabbi is translated as "dentist" to avoid bringing in extraneous religious connotations);
   (c) Naturalization with an accepted cultural reference to create a more natural TT (as above, but with a purpose of creating a more familiar TT).
5. Over-translation: "in its most radical cases (…) the result is a completely free rewriting, independent from the original" (Cuéllar Irala & García-Falces, 2004, p. 14; my translation, SA). Cuéllar Irala and García-Falces attribute to commercialization this "strategy." López González (2017, p. 290) notes that Cuéllar Irala and García-Falces are "quite critical" of this "translation method."

López González (2017) finds that in a corpus of 14 DreamWorks movies, literal translation is the dominant strategy, which she attributes, credibly, to the dominant position of US culture vis-à-vis Spanish. Another possibility is that the movies are deliberately built using widespread, common referents that will easily translate globally.

15.2 THEORIES OF HUMOR TRANSLATION

15.2.4 Eco's translation-as-negotiation

Eco (2003a/b) presents a negotiation-based view of translation. Eco notes that the translator must determine the intention of the text (i.e., what is the text trying to accomplish, or as Eco has it: "the effect aimed at" (Eco, 2003a, p. 56)) and translate based on that. However, as Eco points out, "Many hypotheses can be made about the intention of a text, so that the decision about what a translation should reproduce becomes *negotiable*" (Eco, 2003, p. 56).

By "negotiable," Eco means the kind of intersubjective agreement whereby two individual speakers agree that a given small animal they both see is a mouse, despite the fact that one of them may be a biologist who knows that the given mouse is a *mus spretus* and not the more common *mus musculus domesticus*. The point is that, for the purposes of the exchange, it is not necessary to distinguish between the two.

For Eco, translating is never or at least rarely absolutely lossless. Much like in a negotiation both sides need to give something up to reach an agreement, the translator has to make choices (an "interpretative hypothesis," 2003a, p. 56) and give something up to achieve the intention of the text in the new setting (i.e., the new language in which it is translated).

Eco's remarks on translation are not a full-fledged theory. They are more like observations (the Italian subtitle has "experiences of translation") that are connected, post hoc, by a theory of translation based, at least in part, on skopos theory. Eco discusses many example of translation, many from translators of his own books, which is very interesting for the insiders' viewpoint, documenting precisely the (literal) negotiations between the author and the translators. Eco also addresses the translatability of puns, see more discussion below (Section 15.4).

15.2.5 Skopos theory

Skopos theory originates in the work of Hans Vermeer (1989; Reiss and Vermeer, 2014). As evident from the name, it foregrounds the purpose or goal (skopos) of the text, rather than the equivalence between source text and target text. Texts have purposes, they are written or spoken for a reason. According to skopos theory, translation is best achieved when the target text is adequate to the function or the purpose required by the recipients of the target text or established by the person or entity that commissioned the translation. One of the main contributions of skopos theory has indeed been to help differentiate the notions of author vs. translator of the text, by introducing the idea of the client who commissions the translation, and by focusing on the audience from whom the translation is meant.

When the skopos of the source and target text coincide we have "functional constancy" ("Funktionskonstanz," Vermeer, 2004, p. 233). In the case of humor, then since the main perlocutionary goal of a humorous text is to elicit mirth, skopos theory predicts that a good translation will be one that elicits mirth in the target language audience. Nord, a promiment proponent of skopos theory, puts it very clearly: "if the purpose is to amuse, then the text should actually make its readers laugh or at least smile" (Nord, 2006, p. 31). Chiaro (2017, p. 421) puts it similarly, "In the case of humor, as long as recipients recognize the text as being non-serious in scope, then its Skopos, its purpose, has been achieved." In general, there is little to argue with. Indeed, the definition of humor as having a perlocutionary goal (in Austin's 1962 sense) of eliciting (the recognition of the intention to elicit) mirth and thereby laughter/smiling is fundamentally correct.

However, this formulation seems too restrictive to me. Vermeer makes it clear that "the skopos theory merely states that the translator should be aware that *some* goal exists, and that any given goal is only one among many possible ones" (Vermeer, 1989, p. 234). For example, one may tell a joke with the intention to offend one of the hearers or to show off one's knowledge. In that case, recognition of non-serious intention or elicitation of mirth are no longer the skopos of the joke and hence of its translation. According to Vermeer then, jokes may involve "reformulation" (2004, p. 229), i.e., the ST and TT may differ from each other significantly, because the target culture may "verbalize a different phenomenon in a different way" (p. 229). To put it differently, the translator must choose a skopos and formulate a text, humorous or not, that achieves that skopos.

This raises an interesting question, that skopos theory has not addressed, to the best of my knowledge: each text has multiple skopoi that coexists in the text. Thus for example, a joke about fellatio (see Chapter 10, Sacks' 1974 joke) achieves several different skopoi: establishing non-serious mode, showing off one's knowledge of sexual practices (a significant goal if one is a teenager), showing that one is comfortable dealing with sexual matters, amusing one's audience, etc.

15.2 THEORIES OF HUMOR TRANSLATION

So, if the translator decides to replace the joke (for example because it involves a pun) with another joke that does not involve sexual practices, while some skopoi may be maintained (non-serious mode, amusement, etc.) other skopoi will be neglected (showing off one's sexual knowledge, showing that one is comfortable dealing with sexual matters, etc.). This is far from a trivial objection, because this line of reasoning reintroduces the need for faithfulness, if no longer to the ST, but to the skopoi of the ST: if the ST contains a joke, we have to assume that the ST had a reason, a skopos, for that joke to be there. So, the only way to guarantee "constancy" between the ST and TT is to reproduce the skopoi of the ST in the TT. Zabalbeascoa also points out (2005, p. 244) that different functions of humor (entertainment, social criticism, moralizing, etc.) need to be accounted for. See also Martin de León (2008, pp. 13–14) for the same criticism of skopos theory, in a general context.

Variants of skopos theory are widely accepted in the translation of humor. Popa (2005) is an application of skopos theory to the translation of jokes, based on a bilingual corpus of Romanian and English jokes. She notes that a perfectly literal translation between two referential jokes does not achieve functional equivalence ("constancy" p. 50) because the functions of the jokes in the SL is different from that in the TL. She further discusses the difficulty of achieving equivalence while respecting the genre and register variables of the respective languages. Amirian & Dameneh (2014) is an application to Persian. The study of humor translation using skopos theory seems very popular in China. Han (2011) documents 16 studies on humor translation. His thesis is that skopos theory broadens what counts as "translation" and thus allows more translations. Yin and Wu (2014) document that Chinese translators of the *Big Bang Theory* try to respect the ST humor in the subtitles.

15.2.6 Relevance Theoretic approaches

Translation, from the standpoint of Relevance Theory, can be defined as follows:

Translation, from a cognitive pragmatics perspective, can be explained as an inferential gap-filling activity in which the translator has to infer the intended interpretation, context accessibility and predictions of mutuality between the source-language communicator and the source-language addressee, all that framed in the source- language culture, and then transfer all this information to a target audience with a different language and a more or less different way of coding information, and possibly different social values, norms and stereotypes. (Yus, 2013, p. 125)

Relevance Theory then squarely places translation in the inferential domain and is in this regard even more radical than skopos theory in moving away from linguistic similarity as the criterion for translation. Yus (2013) concludes that there are three types of joke translations:

1. transferrable jokes, i.e., jokes that can be translated easily because they rely on shared stereotypes or "linguistic strategies for humour generation" that are common to both languages
2. replaceable jokes, i.e., jokes for which, in the absence of correspondences, "alternatives can be found in the target language achieving similar balances of cognitive effects and mental effort" and finally,
3. challenging jokes, i.e., jokes that are difficult to translate because they rely on "very specific intra-cultural referents, [and] linguistic resources that have no counterpart in the target language"

somewhat unexpectedly, given the radically different theoretical starting points, supporting Raphaelson-West's (1989) conclusions seen above.

Díaz Pérez (2017) notes that translation, from a Relevance Theoretic standpoint, is an interpretive use of language, similar in this to quoting or reported speech, rather than an "interpretive" use (i.e., when language is used to say something about the world). In the interpretive use of language there is a "relation of interpretive resemblance" (p. 52) between, say, what was originally said and its reported form. Díaz Pérez concludes then that the relationship between the ST and the TT is one of "interpretive resemblance." (p. 53). Furthermore, translation involves a meta-representation (since it is the use of language about language).

Díaz Pérez discusses culture-specific items (i.e., items that are not shared by both languages). Translation strategies ("solutions") can be arranged on a continuum between exoticism (which favors the source culture), as in the famous "kugel" joke quoted by Raskin (1985, p. 215; originally from Novak and Waldoks, 1981, p. 7) in which the word "kugel" is not translated at all,

(134) Somebody once asked Motke Chabad, the legendary wit: "Tell me, Motke, you're a smart fellow. Why is *kugel* called *kugel*?"

Motke lost no time in responding. "What kind of silly question is that? It's sweet like *kugel*, isn't it? It's thick like *kugel*, isn't it? And it tastes like *kugel*, doesn't it? So why *shouldn't* it be called *kugel*?

and, on the other end of the continuum, cultural transplantation, which favors the target culture, as in the case (Ferrari, 2011) of the dubbing of Fran Drescher's Jewish-American accent into an Italian-American accent for Italian audiences, which completely erases the Jewish identity of the character, aided by the remarkable similarities between Jewish and Italian-American stereotypes. A different example, reported by Zabalbeascoa (1996a, p. 249) concerns a character in the show *Fawlty Towers*, Manuel, whose recurring misunderstandings are attributed to his being from Barcelona. In the Catalan dubbing, Manuel comes from Mexico.

Díaz Pérez finds that in his corpus (two seasons of a sitcom), there is a tendency for translators to gravitate toward the source culture (p. 72) and he speculates that this may be due to the desire on the translator part to avoid alienating the audience who is aware of the foreign nature of the ST. This is also the conclusion reached by Martìnez-Sierra (2006). who fears that an over familiarized translation (i.e., adapted to the target culture) may be perceived as "artificial" (pp. 221–222). Already Zabalbeascoa (1993, p. 263) had warned the translator against excessive adaptation toward the target culture in an example involving town names in England which would not be familiar to a Spanish speaker.

15.3 Audiovisual translation

If translation were not an issue complex enough, the presence of multimodal texts, such as films and TV series, but also YouTube videos, animated GIFs, etc. entails the possibility and in some cases necessity of translating texts that contain both a linguistic and a visual component. Chiaro puts it clearly,

The main setback regarding translating for film is the fact that screen products are polysemiotic: that is, they transmit messages by means of diverse codes (...) When a joke, a gag, or a line is linked to the visuals translation becomes especially difficult.

(Chiaro, 2010, pp. 4–5)

Zabalbeascoa speaks of "constrained translation" (2008). The mixed modality (auditory and visual) or multimodality of audiovisual humor presents unique challenges, which have begun to be addressed by such authors as Di Pietro (2012, 2014, 2015, 2016) and Balirano (2013) with complex semiotic analyses that are one of the most interesting current trends of humor research. However, Martìnez-Sierra (2009) argues that the visual aspects of audiovisual translation may actually facilitate dubbing, in some cases, as the visual signifiers may be humorous in themselves and carry over.

Audiovisual translation extends to any audiovisual work that is translated, but generally speaking, given the inherent costs of producing a translation, mostly mass-market products are translated. Within television and cinema, two practices have drawn most attention: dubbing and subtitling. In dubbing, the part of the soundtrack of a film or TV program that comprises the voices of the actors in the ST is replaced by a TT recording of the voices of actors performing the lines anew. The rest of the soundtrack is generally not altered. In subtitling, the soundtrack is not affected, but a translation of the lines spoken by the actors, and possibly of other text appearing in the video track, is superimposed on the original video, generally at the bottom of the screen. For a general overview of audiovisual translation, see Bucaria (2017).

Translation of audiovisual humor produces generally some loss of the humor (Antonini et al., 2001; Bucaria, 2005). Williamson and Ricoy (2014) find that about a quarter of the puns are eliminated from the subtitling of a movie. Gottlieb (1997) and Chiaro (2007) find that the loss is minimal.

15.3.1 Dubbing

Because of its nature, dubbing has a set of issues that are unique to it. For example, if the face of the actors is visible on the screen when they speak, lip movements and opening of the mouth on screen must match reasonably well the movements of the mouth that would be produced if the TT were being produced by the character on screen. Zabalbeascoa reports that variation greater than 200 ms does not produce "satisfactory results" (1993, p. 250). Zabalbescoa (1993, pp. 248–253) provides an excellent review of these issues, which include intonation, pauses, gestures, and extend to non-linguistic issues as well.

An important issue in the dubbing of humor is the position of the punch line:

> due to the very nature of some of the Factors of dubbing, it will often be difficult or even impossible to change the position of the punch-line in the translation, and the translator will have to write a TT joke that will find its climax at exactly the same time as the original ST joke. (Zabalbeascoa, 1993, pp. 263–264)

Finally, dubbing, by its oral nature, has a special set of challenges that are unique to it, as a form of translation, i.e., the necessity to replicate or adapt the prosodic delivery of the humor from the ST (Zabalbeascoa, 1993, p. 292). This includes timing, the delivery of the joke, emphasis, pauses, timbre, and the likes. On timing and prosodic issues, see Chapter 10.

15.3.2 Subtitling

As we saw above, subtitling refers to the practice of translating the SL material in the original audiovisual text into written TL which is added (superimposed) onto the screen. Subtitling is quite popular in many countries, such as Scandinavian countries, the Netherlands, Belgium, and Israel. It is not common in many countries, such as the US and Italy, for example. The disadvantage of subtitling is that the viewers have to read the translation on screen, which is distracting, and since speakers read slower than they process spoken language, constrains the translation, for example by shortening the ST. The advantage is that subtitling is much less expensive than dubbing and in smaller linguistic markets (e.g., Dutch) the only financially feasible option. Subtitling presents a set of challenges that are unique to this practice. For example, subtitles remain visible in screen between one and six seconds, so a "screenful" of subtitles can only contain what is readable in up to 6 seconds. A good review of these constraints can be found in Williamson & Ricoy (2014, pp. 165–166)

There is some evidence that subtitling translation causes meaningful loss of the humor. Pelsmaekers & Van Besien (2002) find that most cases of irony in their corpus are translated directly, but that the cues to the ironical intention (irony markers) may change. Example or markers are hyperboles, intensifiers, diminutives, etc. In numerous cases, the markers were deleted altogether, producing deadpan irony (p. 263).

Interestingly, the simplification of the text due to the constraints of subtitling produced also more explicitly critical irony. Yetkin (2011) claims that in difficult cases (subtitling *The Simpsons* in Turkish, with significant mismatch between the two cultures) a full 70% of irony and satire is not translated in the subtitles. Harrison (2013) presents examples from the *Little Britain* show translated in Spanish.

Fan subtitling is a relatively new phenomenon, in which fans of a given show, translate and subtitle the show, which is then made available on the internet. The practice originated with Japanese anime fans, but has since spread widely (Díaz-Cintas & Muñoz Sánchez, 2006). This practice, of course, violates copyright laws, but their enforcement is rare, in this area. An interesting detail of fansubbing is that often the translator "translates" not the original text, but a prior English translation.

15.3.3 Interpreting

Interpreting (a.k.a. simultaneous translation) is the practice of translating a speech on the fly, as it is being delivered. It is generally performed at conferences or in multilingual bodies such as the United Nations, or the European Union. Because interpreting is done either simultaneously (i.e., as the speaker is delivering their remarks) or consecutively, i.e., immediately following the end of a short stretch of speech, all the limitations and difficulties already present in translation are exacerbated. If the interpreter has not been provided with the contents of the speech beforehand there is literally no preparation and no possibility of research. To make things even more complex, the interpreter cannot laugh at the humor or at least cannot interrupt the interpreting to laugh.

Under those circumstances, translating humor is particularly complex, and translating verbal humor is virtually impossible. Yet, as documented by Pavlicek and Pöchhacker (2002), humor occurs relatively consistently in the type of texts that interpreters have to translate. Irony, sarcasm, and generally speaking referential humor do not seem to present a particular challenge for interpreting, beyond the challenges inherent to interpretation, in and of itself. Conversely, Viaggio (1996) calls interpreting puns a "formidable challenge." Pöchhacker (1995, p. 45) concurs, "Jokes and funny stories embedded in a speech are among the challenges most dreaded by simultaneous interpreters." He provides an example of an English-to-German interpreter who translates a joke until the punch line (which turns out to be an untranslatable pun) and replaces the punch line with "Das ist ein Wortspiel im Englishen" (This is a pun in English) in "documentary-style" translation. Pavlicek & Pöchhacker (2002, p. 386) and Chiaro (2010, p. 21) discuss a similar example, presented in Bertone (1989) of an interpreter who asks the audience to laugh, for the sake of the speaker, thus achieving the perlocutionary goal of eliciting laughter, at the cost, however, of turning the joke from one by the speaker to one about the speaker, which Chiaro calls evidence that "skopos [theory] can be taken too far." Pavlicek & Pöchhacker (2002, p. 399) document the inverse situation, i.e., a speaker who deliberately produces and un-translatable text, as a prank on the translators, whom he explicitly calls out. Much as in the rest of audiovisual translation, a lot of humor gets lost in simultaneous translation. Antonini (2010) documents significant loss of humor in the simultaneous interpretation of the Oscars' ceremony in Italian.

15.4 Translating puns

The reader will recall the somewhat laborious definition of "pun" discussed in Chapter 9 and the related definition of "language play." Here, as many do, e.g., Vandaele (2011), we treat the two as synonymous. When venturing in this area we will do well to heed Zabalbeascoa's warning: "The question of the translatability of verbal humor [= puns] will tend to elude blanket assessments or universalistic claims" (Zabalbeascoa 1996b, p. 239).

As Chiaro (2017, pp. 415–416) reminds us, linguistic analysis has long used translation as a tool. In fact, this tradition goes as far back as Cicero's distinction between referential humor ("de re") and verbal humor ("de dicto") for which he proposes a surprisingly modern method of "changing the words" (endo-linguistic translation) to check the nature of the humor (verbal humor cannot be paraphrased arbitrarily); see Attardo (1994, p. 28) for references and discussion. This is because translation has an extreme case in the translation of poetry and puns. The connection is not accidental, as in both cases there is significant importance attributed to the form of the signifier, which is almost always different in another language or in a paraphrase.

15.4.1 Are puns untranslatable?

There is a vast literature on the untranslatability of puns, usefully reviewed by Henry (2003), who dedicates an entire chapter (pp. 69–110) to reviewing many claims of untranslatability of puns and refutes them one by one. Her thesis is simply that all puns can be translated, although some may require more work. Regattin (2015, pp. 132–133), also provides a review of similar claims, which are, needless to say, merrily refuted by the practice of translation on a daily basis and by many well meaning authors: Regattin himself, of course, Henry (2003), Eco (2003), and many others. I will focus on the latter two authors because, with wonderful self-aware irony, they conclude their discussion of the translatability of puns with an example (each) on untranslatable pun.

Eco (2003b, pp. 94–95) provides an example of an untranslatable joke:

(135) Un direttore d'azienda scopre che l'impiegato Rossi da qualche mese si assenta ogni giorno dalle tre alle quattro. Chiama l'impiegato Bianchi e lo prega di seguirlo discretamente, per capire dove va e per quali ragioni. Bianchi pedina Rossi per qualche giorno e poi fa il suo rapporto al direttore: "Ogni giorno Rossi esce di qui e compera una bottiglia di spumante, va a casa sua e si intrattiene in affettuosi rapporti con sua moglie. Poi torna qui". Il direttore non capisce perché Rossi debba fare di pomeriggio quello che potrebbe fare benissimo di sera, sempre a casa propria; Bianchi cerca di spiegarsi, ma non riesce che a ripetere il suo rapporto, al massimo insistendo su quel sua. Alla fine, di fronte all'impossibilità di chiarire la faccenda, dice: "Scusi, posso darle del tu?".

translated literally below

(136) A CEO finds out that one of his employee Rossi in the past few months is absent every day from three to four pm. He summons another employee, Bianchi, and asks him to follow Rossi discretely, to understand where he goes and for what purpose. Bianchi follows Rossi for a few days and then presents a report to the CEO: "Every day Rossi leaves and buys a bottle of sparkling wine, goes to his[/your] house and he engages in affectionate exchanges with his[/your] wife. The he comes back

15.4 TRANSLATING PUNS

her to work." The CEO does not understand why Rossi should do in the afternoon what he could very well do in the evening, always at his house. Bianchi tries to explain but only manages to repeat his report, at best insisting on that "sua" [his/your]. In the end, faced with the impossibility of clarifying the issue, he says: "May I address you with the [informal] 'tu' pronoun?"

The original is based on the referential ambiguity of the Italian possessive pronoun "sua" (= his/your[respectful]). However, the ambiguity is resolved, in the joke, by switching to the familiar form of address which allows the speaker in the joke to word the sentence as "tua" (your[familiar]). This detail is untranslatable in English, or French (which have different pronouns). The untranslatability derives from the enmeshing of the linguistic form and of the narration.

However, a simple adaptation of the text would resolve the problem and produce a joke very close to the original:

(137) A CEO is suspicious of one of his employees, Smith, who leaves work everyday from 3:00 to 4:00 pm. He asks the foreman to hire another employee to follow Smith. The employee returns after a few days and reports to the foreman about the CEO's suspicions: "I found that, as the CEO suspected, Smith every day at 3:00 pm goes to a motel and has sex with his wife until 4:00." The foreman thinks it is odd that Smith cannot just wait a couple of hours and go home to have sex, but overall is relieved and reports to the CEO that all is fine and he'll have a chat with Smith about excessive absenteeism.

I have shifted the puzzlement about why the employee wouldn't just wait until after work to the foreman rather than to the CEO, to allow me to stay with the third person and I have eliminated the final twist of the employee saying to the boss, "Excuse me, can I address you with the 'tu' pronoun"? which as the Italian reader will understand inferentially will remove the ambiguity of "si intrattiene in affettuosi rapporti con sua moglie." Nonetheless, since the Script Opposition, the Logical Mechanism, and the Target are the same, while the Situation and the Narrative Strategy have minimal and overall insignificant changes, the only significant differences are in the Language, and since this is a translation, most speakers would probably be inclined to find the two jokes (Eco's original and my translation/adaptation) to be more or less equivalent. Certainly they are equally funny (not very much).[6]

As usual, a clear definition will help understand the nature of the problem. The question "are puns translatable?" can be interpreted in two radically different ways: one is, can any arbitrary pun be translated with a feature-by-feature correspondence between the ST and the TT?, the other is, can any text that contains some punning elements be translated so that a reasonable amount of the features of the ST are also present in the TT, albeit not necessarily in the same position? Once stated clearly, as I just have, the two questions have almost obvious and opposite answers: feature-by-feature correspondence translation is axiomatically impossible, since I have shown (Attardo, 2002a) that any text in language L_1, when translated in language L_2 (and L_1 and L_2 are not the same), differs by definition in one feature: that of no longer being worded in L_1. Conversely, since among the strategies for the translation of an individual pun most authors include omitting the pun entirely, then any pun can be "translated" if *all* the translator needs to do is delete the pun and come up with another bit of humor to insert somewhere in the text. Note that this is far from easy, since it requires a creative step, but it is theoretically possible in any case, since what the translator needs to do is produce a new, different text.

What of Henry's untranslatable pun? I reproduce it below. It occurs in *Le cabinet noir* [The Black Cabinet] (1922) by Max Jacob, a French writer and painter who died in the Nazi concentration camps.

(138)   Tout enfant, je fus élevé dans une chambre à nourrice dessinée par Steinlen, c'est pourquoi j'adore les chats (jeu de mots intraduisible)

Henry tells us (2003, p. 110) "several specialists of this facetious author have considered this text and they are still looking for this enigmatic pun, which, as long as it will not have been discovered, will remain doubtlessly untranslatable" (my translation, SA).

I don't know what to make of this. Is the author pulling our leg, with a straight face? Or is she really thinking that there is a pun to be found? It seems to me that Jacob was mocking translators and there is no pun at all.

---

[6] It should also be noted that in my version the boss will not find out about the cheating wife.

15.4.2 The practice of translating puns

Delabastita (1996, p. 128) lists the following strategies for the translation of puns, which have been widely adopted (e.g., Chiaro, 2003; Low, 2011; Williamson & Ricoy, 2014)

ST pun to TT pun

ST pun to TT non pun

ST pun to TT related rhetorical device

ST pun to TT omission

ST non pun to TT compensatory pun

ST non pun to TT pun not present in ST (also compensatory)

Editorial techniques: footnotes, endnotes, translators' forewords, presentation of several options, etc.

Low (2011) offers additionally an original technique for translating puns that consists in looking for synonyms of the words or strings in the ST and then produce a new pun in the TT.

Formulated within the Interpretive Theory of Translation (Seleskovitch et al., 1984), Henry (2003) presents a remarkable amount of examples worked out in detail, but her most significant contribution to the translation of puns is a tripartite continuum of levels of functional significance, in regards to the text in which the puns occur. The puns, vis-à-vis the text may be

1. Not very important (punctual puns; p. 52);
2. Important: puns are one element of the textual organization (p. 54); and
3. Essential: pure are the writing system (p. 56).

Despite the rhetorical exaggeration, given that puns by themselves cannot constitute an entire text (say, a novel), since other factors are necessarily present, such as an array of para-textual factors such as titles, colophon, copyright page, etc., the subdivision is interesting. In the last case, puns are the main driving force of the text. Let us apply Henry's idea to an example she did not analyze. Consider the following poem, by American poet Aram Saroyan, which has the advantage of brevity:

(139)   My arms are warm
        Aram Saroyan

(*Complete Minimal Poems* (includes Aram Saroyan, Pages, and The Rest), Ugly Duckling Presse (Brooklyn, NY), 2007.)

It is clear, and this is Henry's point, that the assonances and alliterations of the poem, taken together with the signature of its author, are the point of the poem, as a literal translation in Italian, for example, would immediately prove:

(140) Le mie braccia sono calde.
    Aram Saroyan

(my translation, SA). Of course, a real translator would try to compensate by creating other assonances or alliterations, but that's not the point. If you translate literally example (139) the text, its raison-d'être is obliterated: "there is no text if there is no pun" (Henry, 2003, p. 56; my translation, SA). Conversely, at the other end of the continuum, are punctual puns: these are texts that contain puns somewhere in the text, but that if we removed the puns, we would only minimally alter the text (it would be less funny, of course). Therefore, if we replace the puns with other puns, since the puns are not an important aspect of the text, the text will not be altered significantly. Consider now another possible translation of (139) below,

(141) Saremo soriani.
    Aram Saroyan

(my translation, SA) which in back-translation corresponds to "we will be tabby cats" and clearly completely replaces the semantics of the line, but preserves some of the assonances and alliterations. Needless to say, the reader may object that there are no cats or feline feelings in the original and that the arms and the warmth are gone. I would object that the warmth is there by connotation with the cat, but my hypothetical critic is nonetheless correct: in a very clear sense, this is not the same poem.

Finally, the intermediate case in Henry's continuum, is a text in which the puns in and of themselves matter, but are not the main point of the text. A good example here are the translators' creative renderings of the various linguistic plays in Eco's own novels, for example, with medieval dialects, Baroque terminology, etc., discussed in Eco (2003b).

The Interpretive Theory of Translation has many similarities with skopos theory and with Zabalbeascoa's approach: they all recognize the importance of the participants in the translation, the situation in which it is performed, the purpose it serves, the importance of the cognitive context (i.e., how the text and its translation are inscribe in their respective cultures), and finally, they share a focus on textual equivalence, rather than linguistic similarity (Henry, 2003, pp. 66–67).

15.5 Conclusions

There seems to be a consensus (e.g., Raphaelson-West, 1989; Zabalbeascoa, 2005; Low, 2011; Yus, 2013) on the following points: The process of translation is highly contextualized: each translation has several goals or purposes which are negotiated (Eco 2003; Zabalbeascoa, 2005) among the participants to the act of translation and with the context and setting of the texts. Humor is, generally speaking, translatable. Some forms of humor are harder to translate than others. There is a scale of difficulty of translation, with the easiest being general jokes that do not rely of punning or culture specific jokes, followed by culture specific jokes (hard to translate) and "language-restricted jokes" (Zabalbeascoa, 2005), which are hardest to translate, or may be untranslatable. Mallafrè (1991, p. 119); Zabalbeascoa, 1993; Chiaro (1992, p. 87); Low (2011). The most significant problem areas are puns (language-specific structures, usually tied to the signifier) and cultural issues (such as the impossibility of talking about a referent unknown in the target culture: penguin jokes will not fare well in the Amazon).

Individual instances of humor (jab lines or punch lines) may be untranslatable, but the overall text in which the jab line or punch line occurs generally can be translated so as to respect the perlocutionary goal of eliciting amusement or the perception of the intention of humor. Translators may use a variety of strategies to effect the translation of difficult cases, which may reach the point where the translator has to give up trying to translate the specific instance of humor and use compensatory strategies, such as replacing the joke or omitting it entirely (and replacing it with something else), or just give up on the translation (i.e., omit the joke and not replace it). Audiovisual translation has its own specific challenges, related to the multimodal nature of the texts.

15.6 Further readings

Martinez-Sierra and Zabalbeascoa (2017) gives a very good view of the most recent work on translation. Chiaro (2017) and Bucaria (2017) are good surveys of their respective fields. De Rosa et al. (2014) contains several very interesting papers. The work of Zabalbeascoa, starting with his 1993 dissertation is foundational, as is Chiaro (2005). Delabastita's work and edited collections (1987, 1993, 1996, 1997) on the translation of puns remain classics.

16
Humor in the classroom

16.1 The pioneers — 368
16.2 The apologists — 371
16.3 The realists — 372
16.4 Classroom discourse analysis — 377
16.5 Conclusions — 379
16.6 Further readings — 380

This chapter needs to start with a major caveat. There exists a small cottage industry of publications on how to improve teaching through humor. I will provide a list of a few examples below. However, there is little empirical evidence that using humor while teaching actually improves learning and/or retention (Martin, 2007, p. 350). Some assessments are more stark: Halula (2013) concludes pessimistically that the literature "about humor and education [is] typically anecdotal and prescriptive in nature with little or no research backing" (p. 118). This is very similar to the situation that psychologists see with the humor and health movement. Again, lots of claims and anecdotal evidence, but a damning scarcity of empirical studies showing that laughing or having a sense of humor actually improves your health. This "split personality" leads to some awkward situations, as noted by Bryant and Zillmann (1989) who call it, a "curious contradiction" between claims that humor is "highly useful and extremely effective teaching tool" (p. 49) and the empirical results which are "decidedly mixed" (p. 50). The tongue-in-cheek understatement is followed by a short but effective review of "questionable strategies" used by some authors of popular works on the benefits of humor in the classroom, which include, ignoring the negative evidence and oversimplifying ambiguous results. In what follows I will focus primarily on the empirical research, and then with a bias toward applied linguistics, but of course most of the research in this area has been done in education and psychology.

The Holy Grail of the application of humor studies to education is the proof that humor facilitates or enhances learning in a classroom setting. The impact of humor on teaching, if any, may occur at different levels/moments of the learning process: humor may a) facilitate learning, i.e., make it easier to acquire the new information, or b) improve retention, i.e., hold on to the new information, or c) improve the pedagogical experience of either the student (e.g., by reducing stress) or the teacher (e.g., by avoiding burnout). It is important to remember that an effect in one aspect does not imply similar effects in another aspect. So, for example, we could find that humor improves the experience of the teacher but not of the students, or that it facilitates learning but not retention. This requires then to keep each hypothesis and claim separate, to avoid confusion.

The chapter is organized as follows: we will begin by reviewing a few pioneering studies, some of which showed some promising results and probably are the proximate cause for the existence of the books on how to improve teaching and leaning using humor. Then I will provide a sample of books touting the use of humor in the classroom, mostly just to document the size of the phenomenon, and then I will review the field using three meta-analyses and some recent publications that provide overviews of the field. The chapter is capped off by a final section which reviews an emerging area of interest, i.e., ethnographic studies of humorous behavior in the classroom (classroom discourse analysis).

16.1 The pioneers

One of the first studies to test empirically the idea that humor facilitates learning idea is Markiewicz (1974) who reviews the literature up to that point, which she finds riddled "with severe methodological problems." She provides a very useful chart with a meta-analysis of about 25 studies (p. 409) starting the tradition of really depressing findings in the field: only very few studies show significant positive differences with the use of humor. Markiewicz considers possible effects for humor and persuasion, humor and retention, and evaluation of the source (i.e., the idea that the audience of humor will assess more positively a speaker who uses humor than one that does not), and assessment of the interesting nature of the material. Only the last hypothesis is found to have some positive effect (p. 413). The degree of relevance of the humor might also be a factor: Markiewicz considers relevant (i.e., on topic) and irrelevant humor, but finds no differences. Her methodological discussion is still quite valid.

Another study is Kaplan and Pascoe (1977). They ran a large (n = 508) study involving four versions of a 20 minutes lecture on Freud. One version of the lecture was without humor. Of the three humorous versions, one contained humorous material related to the subject matter, one contained unrelated humor, and one a mix of related and unrelated material. The students were tested immediately after the lecture and then 6 weeks later. The results are mixed: there was no significant difference in the immediate understanding of concepts but the concepts introduced humorously were retained significantly better (p. 64). The students' performance on the tests was not significantly improved by humor (p. 64), even in the re-test condition, when their performance improved due to better recall. The authors conclude that the benefit of using humor is increased recall of the examples.

Ziv (1979a) explains learning through humor with the observation that humor attracts attention which leads to memorization and retention of the material. Students enjoy humor (1979a, p. 46). In (1979a/b) he further elaborates that a "positive teacher," who among other features uses humor, creates a better atmosphere in the classroom, and lowers anxiety which is conducive to learning (1979a, pp. 60–61; 1979b, p. 22). In fact, enjoying humor on the teacher's part has a significant correlation with teachers having a positive attitude in the classroom (1979a, p. 59). Ziv's name is usually linked with the idea that humor improves creativity. He finds a strong correlation between humor and creativity, particularly around the trait of originality (p. 109). In an experiment he shows that a single exposure to humor enhances creativity (p. 116). In a semester-long study he found enhanced creativity from continued exposure to humor (pp. 120–122).

Ziv (1988) describes the first semester-long study of the effects of humor on learning. Two intact statistics classes taught by the same instructor were taught, one with 3 instances of humor per 90 minutes lecture (1979a, p. 80)[1] and one without humor. The final multiple-choice exam was used as the assessment tool. The section taught with the humor scored significantly better on the final test. The same experiment was then replicated in a psychology class, with the same significant positive results for the section taught with humor. Ziv cautions that the amount of humor had to be calibrated exactly to 3 instances of humor per class (as he had found in pilot tests that that is an appropriate amount of humor). Moreover, the humor has to be directly relevant to the content of the course and varied in its format/presentation. Finally, negative/aggressive humor was avoided (such as sarcasm). Because of the clear cut results, which are unequivocally positive, and of the extended duration of the study, i.e., an entire 14 weeks semester, whereas most experimental treatments are at most 50 minutes long, this study has been vastly influential and is considered a classic.

Bryant et al. (1979) look at college lectures. They start out by noting that humor was being increasingly introduced in college lectures and that there already were some advocates for its use, but "without sound empirical evidence" (p. 111). The authors had students tape (apparently surreptitiously)[2] 70 lectures and assess the number of humorous incidents (inter-rater reliability was at 91%). The coders found 234 instances of humor which yields an average of one instance of humor every 15 minutes or so. There was a significant range: 20% of classes had zero occurrences of humor; conversely, 5% of the teachers used humor more than 10 times per class (every 5 minutes, on average) (p. 114). Female professors used significantly less humor but used surprisingly more sexual humor, more aggressive humor, and were rated as using more improvised humor (p. 116). Most of the humor was closely related to the subject matter, and here too, more so for women's humor. Also, surprisingly, male professors used more self-disparaging humor. More discussion on humor in lectures will be found below in Section 16.4.

Humor increases the students' positive perception of the textbook, but does not increase interest, learning, or persuasiveness (Klein et al., 1982). It does however negatively impact author's credibility. Bryant et al. (1981) shows that adding cartoons to a textbook does not improve

---

[1] This is actually on the low end of the scale; see the studies below in Section 16.4.1 that attempt to quantify the amount of humor produced by teachers in a lecture. Ziv's rate of humor in his experiment is equal to 1.6 instances of humor per 50 minute lecture, or 0.03 instances of humor per minute.

[2] This would be considered ethically unacceptable nowadays.

learning but the students enjoy them. Kaplan and Pascoe's (1977) found increased memorability of humorous examples. Davies and Apter (1980) also found greater recall for humorous materials.

Bryant and Zillmann (1989) report that teachers use humor in lectures and activities from elementary school to college, with males doing so more than females (p. 56). Humor can get the attention of the students (pp. 59–60) but does not improve the classroom environment, at least in the college classroom (p. 61); nonetheless, students enjoy it. Age and setting (elementary/high school vs. college) may be the key factors in these findings. For younger children, if they lack motivation, humor, and especially humor unrelated to the content, improved learning. If the students were already motivated, no improvement was found (p. 66). Bryant and Zillmann find no evidence that humor included in test improves performance or attitude toward the test and in fact report that it can hurt students with high test anxiety (p. 69). They conclude on a moderately optimistic note that "judicious use of humor" (p. 74) increases attention, improves enjoyment, promotes creativity, and "under some conditions" improves "information acquisition and retention" (p. 74). This sounds actually quite good, until they specify what "judicious" means: "success in teaching with humor [...] depends on employing the right type of humor, under the proper conditions, at the right time, and with properly motivated and receptive students" (p. 74).

Javidi et al. (1988) find that award-winning teachers use significantly more humor than non-award winning teachers. More on this study below. Buckman (2010) also finds a correlation between university teachers' performance and their use of humor.

16.2 The apologists

By the mid-1980s, Powell and Andresen (1985) could set out to review more than 50 articles on the benefits of using humor in the classroom and some empirical studies. Things did not stop here. Soon there were significant numbers of publications advocating teaching with humor. Nowadays, there exists a largish number of publications that advocate for the use of humor in educational settings. Most of these have scant evidence, gathered from the few studies that show positive effects of humor, but generally speaking the mode is not that of scientific argument, but rather of apology, in the classical sense, or of advocacy. The author is convinced of the effectiveness of humor and wants to proselytize or simply assumes that using humor is a good thing and provides advice on how to use humor in teaching. Rather than discussing the merits of these I will quote the titles of some of the best known books on the subject.

- Berk (2002) *Humor as an instructional defibrillator: Evidence-based techniques in teaching and assessment.*
- Berk (2003) *Professors are from Mars, students are from snickers*
- Shade (1996) *License to laugh: Humor in the classroom*
- Lundberg and Thurston (1992) *If they are laughing they just may be listening.*
- Loomans and Kolberg (2002) *The laughing classroom.*
- Medgyes (2002) *Laughing matters: Humour in the language classroom.*

A list of scholars advocating the use of humor in the classroom can be found in Bryant and Zillmann (1989) and in Banas et al. (2011). Banas et al. note that "the overwhelming majority of instructional communication research on humor has focused on the positive consequences of classroom humor" (p. 116). A search on Google will easily add hundreds of tiles. A search for "humor, teaching, advantages" produced 109,000 hits. The search "humor, teaching, disadvantages" produced 18,000 hits. Banas et al. do list four (!) authors who have considered the negative effects of humor in the classroom (p. 116).

Even national associations, such as the National Education Association contribute to the apology of humor, see McNeely (2002). As I said, this reminds one of the claims about the health benefits of humor, where anecdotal evidence reigns supreme. This is not to say that these books are without merits. They can be very useful if one wants to start using humor in the classroom and doesn't quite know how to do so.

16.3 The realists

Given the significant interest in the application of humor to teaching, with the possibility of improving teaching, learning, student attitudes, and even teachers' evaluations, a significant literature has developed, primarily in the fields of education and communication, and also of course in psychology. Linguistics has lagged, generally speaking, but recently some significant studies have appeared. We will review the field using primarily three excellent meta-analyses, which also provide effective summaries of the field.

McMorris et al. (1997) review 11 studies on college testing. Their conclusion is that there is insufficient evidence that use of humor in testing reduces stress and humor does not improves performance. However, the students report that they like it (p. 285). The authors conclude that test-writers may want to include humor in their tests.[3] McMorris et al. list the following issues that need to be addressed: the types of humor, the purpose of the humor (e.g., inclusive vs. distancing humor), the degree of incorporation of the humor, i.e., whether it is a) relevant to the material or unrelated to it, and b) presented in the test items, in the instructions, separate from the test, etc.

Martin et al. (2006) review 20 studies, They set out to answer the question "does humor in the "educational messages [...] result in understanding and learning?" (p. 18). They distinguish between three types of effect:

1. Cognitive: the learning was tested, for example, by a multiple choice test;
2. Affective: the respondents were asked if they enjoyed learning; and
3. Perceived: the respondents were asked how much they felt they had learned.

Their overall conclusion is that "Although students report enjoying learning and they report that they believe they have learned course material, objective measurements of the recall associated with humorous lectures are rather minuscule" (Martin et al., 2006, p. 305).

After an extensive review of the various types of humor and their classroom effects, Banas et al. (2011) conclude that "the relationship between instructional humor and educational [sic] cannot be understood without taking into account the type of humor used,

---

[3] The following is my personal opinion and I have no evidence for it except for my personal (anecdotal) practice. I'd think twice about doing what McMorris et al. advise. Most of the students I have taught in my career lost all sense of humor at test time. Any attempt at humor backfired in the most depressing way. Even my instructions to read the questions *before* answering them were met with concerned questions.

particularly regarding appropriateness and offensiveness" (p. 125). Generally speaking aggressive and denigrating humor is inappropriate in the classroom (and yet nonetheless they occur, we might add). They also report differences in gender usage, for example, male professors use more self-deprecating humor and female professors use humor to gain back control of the class after a disruption, but note that the statistical significance of the results in this area is not very reliable due to small samples. To complicate things, the teachers themselves are a variable, being more or less "humor oriented" (p. 127), i.e., funny. If a teacher is more humor-oriented, he/she produces more humor, which correlates with producing more inappropriate humor as well.

Use of positive humor improves teacher evaluations (p. 129) but "overuse" is rated negatively. "[A]ppropriate instructional humor [is] related positively to an enjoyable learning environment" (p. 130) but, again, aggressive humor may create an uncomfortable environment. Likewise, credibility is boosted by the use of appropriate humor (p. 131) and decreased by inappropriate or excessive humor. By and large, they conclude that positive and appropriate humor correlates with desirable instructional outcomes, such as "relaxed learning environment, higher instructor evaluations, greater perceived motivation to learn, and enjoyment of the course" and inappropriate humor with the opposite outcomes. So, their conclusion is positive as far as the learning environment goes. However, Banas et al. (2011) find that the "the empirical evidence for the effects of humor on learning is considerably more mixed, with some scholars finding that humor enhances learning [...] and others finding no relationship between learning [and] humor" (p. 131). The question of whether relevant humor performs better than irrelevant humor remains open, even though Machlev and Karlin (2016) found no correlation between relevant humor and learning.

Wanzer et al. (2010) proposed the Instructional Humor Processing Theory to explain why some types of humor produce increased learning and some do not. The Instructional Humor Processing Theory predicts that humor related to the subject matter of instruction would be positively correlated with learning. On the humor studies side, the Instructional Humor Processing Theory incorporates the incongruity theory framework, with the disposition theory, a variant of the superiority theory approach, which claims that one appreciates as humorous humor that targets something one is negatively disposed toward (see Chapter 3). So, humor related to the subject matter is appreciated by the students because it does not target students (which would violate the disposition theory, which assumes that students are well-disposed toward themselves), likewise, self-disparaging humor by the teacher may backfire, if the students are well disposed toward the teacher. The authors' study showed that students judged teachers to be humorous if they produced relevant humor; surprisingly, also self disparaging humor produced increased self-reported learning. Finally, "Professors that were perceived as humorous used significantly more related, unrelated, self-disparaging, other-disparaging, and offensive types of humor than less humorous professors" (Wanzer et al., 2010, p. 14).

Another wide-open topic is cross-cultural variation. For example, Zhang (2005) reports that humor made Chinese students *more* anxious. Heidari-Shahreza (2018) reports the use of humor in Iranian L2 classroom. Other non-Western contexts are Taiwanese Chinese (Liao, 2005), Mainland Chinese (Chen, 2013), Thai (Forman, 2011), Vietnamese (Petraki & Pham Nguyen, 2016), Japanese (Neff & Rucynski, 2017). The field is vast and there is no good overview.

Another area of interest, is the use of humor in the foreign language classroom, where humor has the potential to reduce anxiety above and beyond all the usual positive effects claimed for it. Studies focusing on foreign language teaching and humor include Deneire (1995); Schmitz (2002); Wagner & Urios-Aparisi (2011). Wagner and Urios-Aparisi (2011) couch the problem in terms of "immediacy," i.e., "the degree of directness and intensity of interaction between the communicator and the referent of communication" (Mehrabian, 1966, p. 34), or to put it differently the degree of involvement and closeness that the speakers communicates, both verbally and non-verbally. Wagner and Urios-Aparisi note that in both modalities humor figures prominently in the definitions in the literature on immediacy (Wagner & Urios-Aparisi, 2011, p. 403). So humor would have a positive effect on classroom activities mediated by the immediacy of the teacher. Wanzer (2002) also addresses immediacy, but within the broader context of "humor orientation," i.e., the general disposition of a teacher to produce humor. In particular she focuses on appropriate and inappropriate humor (Wanzer et al. 2006).

Bell (2011) presents the most sophisticated framework for applying humor studies to the second language classroom. The point is not so much to teach the students how to be funny (p. 150), but, as she puts it, the "cultural norms of humor usage" (p. 135) which consist of how humor "is contextualized, how and with whom joking relationships may be formed, and common responses to various types of humor" (p. 135). Topics that second language learners need to be aware of are available scripts for humor (i.e., what is appropriate for joking and what isn't), contextualization cues, which may vary across cultures, genres of humor, the pragmatic and social functions of humor, and the repertoire of responses to humor, which again may vary from culture to culture.

This brings up the idea of the existence of a specific separate humor competence as Vega (1989) claimed, to be placed alongside the other four communicative competences (grammatical; sociolinguistic, i.e., contextually appropriate; discursive, i.e., coherent and cohesive; and strategic, i.e., capable of solving communicative problems; Canale & Swain, 1980). Hodson (2014) shows that teaching unsuspecting students about humor theory doesn't particularly affect their capacity to understand humor and Bell tongue-in-cheek tells us the benefits of teaching humor theory to students "remain an empirical question." This is not surprising, since I have argued (Attardo, 1994, pp. 211–213) that there is nothing unique about humor competence except a) scripts that are available for humor (humorous stereotypes); b) scripts that are not available for humor (topics about which it is socially unacceptable to be humorous); c) contextual information on when and in what situations it appropriate to use humor; and d) a few genres that are culture specific (such as knock-knock jokes, unknown outside of the Anglo-Saxon world). So, if we were to compare the sheer size of knowledge involved in each of the four competences to the reductive size of the purported fifth one, it would seem obvious to argue that how to produce and use humor would be part of the other four competences, without the need to postulate a separate competence. Undeterred by these arguments, Wulf (2010) presents a curriculum for humor competence.

Bell and Pomerantz (2016) is primarily focused on the students' use of humor (and so will be examined in more detail below in Section 16.4), but it is also a very complete discussion of the literature, including the research on the benefits of using humor in the teaching environment. So, it is telling to see them conclude that "it has been difficult to connect the use of humor to increased learning" (p. 101) and so that "the most robust argument for using humor in education is affective" (p. 101).

16.4 Classroom discourse analysis

A major contribution to the analysis of classroom humor is Davies (2003) which is explicitly based on the ethnomethodological approach described in Chapter 10. It can be seen as an extension of Davies (1984), discussed in Chapter 12. Davies argues that students in a second language classroom "are able to exploit the limited gamut of sociolinguistic resources available to them within a discourse context in which the native speaker provides important support" which establishes the fundamentally collaborative nature of the situation. Davies shows that both students and teachers initiate humorous exchanges. The native speakers and the students themselves use a "scaffolding" mechanism to build jointly the humorous exchange, despite their limited proficiency. See also Davies (2015).

Bell and Pomeranz (2016, p. 78) view humor as a "safe house" for the students in the classroom. The concept of "safe house" comes from Canagarajah (2004) who identifies a variety of ways in which students carve small places for themselves within the broader context of school. Examples of safe houses would be passing notes, writing in the margins of books, or talking to other students off task. Considering humor as a safe house is not a stretch, given the function of deniability which has long been associated with humor ("Just kidding!"), but what is original is seeing humor as a play space, which is connected to the consideration of language play, a broader category than humor. Bell and Pomerantz note that humor is "normal" in the classroom (p. 73) and so it should be expected, as it would in any "normal" situation. It is possible that the impression of relative scarcity of humor in the classroom is due to the focus on the teacher and the "covert" nature of most of the humor, which occurs in a safe house, away from the eyes of the teacher (and of any researcher). Humor conversely can also be seen as a face-saving opportunity, of particular importance in the teaching setting, if we consider that the very act of teaching is inherently a face-threatening act: in order for you to teach me, I need to admit, more or less openly, that you know more than I do on the subject. So humor allows both teacher and student a way out of the inherently hierarchical setting. Relatedly, a student may elect to be the "class clown" and thus cultivate a "cool" identity (p. 80). For example, Damico and Purkey (1978) and Norrick and Klein (2008) consider disruptive humor in the elementary classroom ("class clowns"). Reddington (2015) and Reddington and

Waring (2015) are applications of conversation analysis to classroom interactions and provides some examples of the phenomena discussed above.

16.4.1 How much humor do teachers produce in class?

We have seen that students produce plenty of humor (Bell and Pomerantz, 2016). We turn now to the question of how much humor do the teachers produce. Javidi et al. (1988) report on a study in which award-winning college and high-school teachers were compared to non-award-winning teachers.[4] A sample of 50 minutes of lecturing was annotated for each teacher. The results show that award-winning teachers incorporated 7.20 instances of humor in a 50 minute lecture (roughly one instance of humor every 7 minutes). The humor "played off" the content of the course and was often used to clarify the content. In contrast, award-winning high-school teachers only produced humor 2.8 times in 50 minutes (about once every 18 minutes). Like college teachers, the humor was used to clarify content. Middle-school teachers scored even lower (2.33 per 50 minutes of lecture; once every 21.45 minutes). The non-award-winning teachers used a very small amount of humor: 0.26 instances per 50 minutes, or a remarkable once every 192 minutes).

Downs et al. (1988) report on a study of 57 college teachers. The college professors produced an average of 13.33 instances of humor per lecture (once every 3.75 minutes). Most of the humor was relevant to the class (only 12% was coded as non-relevant). Downs et al. also considered nine award-winning college teachers and found that they produced an average of 7.44 instances of humor per lecture (i.e., once every 6.72 minutes). This is a significant difference from the study by Javidi et al. Downs et al. provide a breakdown by week in the semester, which shows that teachers on average produced humor 9.3 times per lecture in the second week, 8.1 times in the 6th week, and 5.6 times in the 10th week. In other words, the variable of when the lecture is collected may be relevant. Most of the humor was relevant to the lecture in all cases.

Lee (2006) has a slightly wider scope, in the sense that it is not limited to classroom interactions, as it is based on the Michigan Corpus of

---

[4] The fifteen non-award-winning teachers consisted of five college teachers, five high-school teachers, and five middle-school teachers. Javidi et al. (188) do not explain why they chose not to differentiate between the three groups. They do, however, note this limitation in their discussion.

Academic Spoken English (MICASE). Lee considers the occurrences of laughter (which he takes to correlate with humor; see 11 for a discussion of the problematic nature of this assumption). He finds a wide range of variation, with events having zero laughter and an undergraduate social science thesis study group a whopping 179 laughter instances in 64 minutes, i.e., a ratio of 2.8 laughs per minute (Lee, 2006, p. 53). Lectures tend to have a low ratio of laughs per minute, but as Lee notes, some of the lectures are among the events with most laughter. Overall, lectures have 0.21 laughs per minute, whereas tutorials and study groups have more than one laugh per minute (1.35 and 1.12, respectively; Lee, 2006, p. 54). Lee speculates that distance of social status and intimacy of the event might be the causal factors behind these findings (p. 55).

Nesi (2012) considers laughter in university lectures taken from the British Academic Spoken English corpus (BASE). The BASE academic events are more limited in scope than the MICASE and include only lectures and seminars. 24 out of 160 lectures contained no laughter and four contained only one instance of laughter. Nesi compares her data to Lee's (2006) and finds that while the percentage of lectures containing laughter was roughly the same across countries, British lectures contain one laugh every 1.4 minutes, whereas American lectures contain only one laugh every 5 minutes. Nesi speculates that the cause is that British lectures are more formal and so the lecturers prepare the humor. An alternative explanation is that British lecturers are just funnier than Americans. Neuliep (1991) presents self-reports from high school teachers who claim to attempt humor roughly twice per class period. He notes that this figure is significantly less than other studies having as subjects college teachers.

Both Lee and Nesi list more or less impressionistic functions of the use of laughter, which include the usual suspects: building rapport, getting the attention of the students, criticizing behavior, self-deprecation, etc. In short, there seems to be no special function of laughter in lectures.

16.5 Conclusions

What conclusions can we draw from the literature on using humor in the classroom? The first one, is that by doing so, we probably will not do any serious damage to our students. The second one is that we should lower our expectations: using humor is not going to be the silver bullet of education and will not lead to massive improvements of learning and retention. It may improve the students' attitude and perception of the learning experience and that's obviously a good thing. The third conclusion is an obvious one: further study of these matters is to be recommended, especially in the direction of separating the various kinds of humor and of activities. Humor in banter with the students is not the same thing as humor in the lecture or humor in the test. Finally, we need to remember that a successful humorous exchange is a joint activity: the speaker and the hearer need to agree to the framing of the situation as humorous. This entails both that the teacher must relinquish some control of the situation and that he or she and the students must find a common ground to enjoy the humor. As Powell and Andresen had remarked in 1985, humor ages and one always runs the risk of "asking students to laugh at something that would have appealed to a previous generation" (p. 88). This observation is all the more true today, when memes, tweets, and instagram posts have replaced the jokes and cartoons of yore. If teachers want to be funny to their students, they will need to work at knowing why, at what, when, and where their students laugh.

16.6 Further readings

Martin (2007) is a very good broad review of the pedagogy of humor, even if it is skewed toward psychology, having been written by a prominent psychologist. Bell (2011) is squarely focused on applied linguistics. The meta-analyses discussed in the text are the best overviews of the pedagogical aspects of humor, McMorris et al. (1997); Martin et al. (2006); and Banas et al. (2011). Reddinton (2015) and Bell and Pomerantz (2015) provide overviews of humor in the classroom from the perspective of TESOL.

17

Conclusion

It is traditional to conclude a book like this with a look at the future. In the past, I have done so with results so amusingly off base, as when I predicted in 1994 a renaissance of studies on puns, only to see the field go dormant for 20 years, that I have decided to do so in the future only for entertainment purposes. No doubt more research will be done in all, or most, of the areas I have described in the book. Will the trends I have discerned, or think I have discerned, continue in the near future? Perhaps, or perhaps not. I have learned my lesson. However, I think we need to look a little farther out, as well.

I think it is fair to say that if any reader has made it this far in reading this book (skipping ahead does not count) they will readily agree that the study of humor, much like the study of language itself, is a complex problem. By this I mean to invoke, almost but not completely metaphorically, the idea of complex systems and complexity theory.[1] In a nutshell, the idea behind complex systems is that large, complicated, non-linear systems, such as, say, the weather cannot be understood and modeled by a simple, linear theory.

Consider an example: in Chomsky's standard model (Chomsky, 1965) there is no reason for language to change. Assume that you modeled perfectly your object (in other words, you achieved descriptive adequacy) and that you understood how the system worked (explanatory adequacy). You would have a set of transformations, a set of generative rules and a set of lexical items to insert at some point or another in your generation process. Assume, as we said, for the sake of the argument, that your system does produce all the sentences that native speakers judge

---

[1] See, for example, the Five Graces Group (2009) position paper; Larsen-Freeman & Cameron (2008); Ortega & Han (2017). I do not (only) mean complexity as in complication (as in Derks, 2014). A complex system is not just complicated.

The Linguistics of Humor: An Introduction. Salvatore Attardo, Oxford University Press (2020). © Salvatore Attardo.
DOI: 10.1093/oso/9780198791270.001.0001

to be grammatical and none of those they judge ungrammatical. The resulting system would be static, in the sense that there would be no reason or possibility for change. Why would a passive transformation change? It does exactly what it is supposed to do and so the speakers would have no reason or need to change their behavior which would be reflected in a change in the rule.

To pursue the example further, let us add another facet to our system: let us assume that speakers will follow a principle of least effort, i.e., that they will try to minimize the effort required to produce utterances. The simple addition of this principle will now cause our perfect (and static) system of syntax to lose some of its perfect descriptive adequacy (for example, through contractions, irregular dropping of frequently used morphological markers, but not of extremely high frequency ones, etc.) and thus eventually to have some asymmetry in the system (i.e., the speakers will sense that there's something wrong with the system) that will need to be corrected through change. If you think this sounds crazy, consider the fact that many speakers are, at the time of this writing, using the word "irregardless" with a double privative morpheme, thus showing that /-less/ was perceived to be too "weak" or somehow insufficiently negative. However, you do not hear "unhomeless," or "unjobless," i.e., the change is not (yet?) systematic.

Needless to say, none of this is novel to a historical linguist and my point is not that I have a novel explanation for language change. My point is much more banal: you cannot understand change without a different perspective/theory. This does not mean that the syntactic model is not good, on the contrary, by the stipulation of our example, the model is better than any linguistic model has ever performed. It just means that the syntactic model is not designed to account for change, or to put it differently, that change is outside the purview of the model/theory.

Let me be clear: I am not naive and I know all too well that often the proponents of one theory have explicitly or implicitly declared the phenomena that fell outside of the purview of their theory to be irrelevant, marginal, uninteresting, and so forth. Having been scorned and marginalized, or having perceived to be so, the proponents of other theories needless to say strike back declaring the theories to be irrelevant, uninteresting, etc. All of that is true and probably inevitable, as long as science is done by humans and not by artificial intelligences devoid of any emotions.

However, I see in the complex systems approach an opportunity to abandon the zero-sum mindset of many scholars (if your theory is right that makes my theory less right, somehow) and to embrace instead a collaborative mindset where the goal is to describe, understand, and explain the phenomena. All of them, not just those that one's theory works well for.

If I am correct in claiming that humor is a complex system, it follows that no single approach, no single discipline will ever succeed in explaining all the phenomena that humor encompasses. Conversely, the only way to make progress toward that goal is to embrace a trans-disciplinary approach, to supersede the interdisciplinary approach humor studies has long boasted of and in some ways pioneered. In a trans-disciplinary approach, all theories, all models can contribute something to the understanding of the problems at hand. All theories describe one or more facets of the phenomena and the goal is not to fulfill the disciplinary goals of one field or of two of them, as in interdisciplinarity, where one theory provides the methodology and another the questions to be answered, but rather to answer all the questions with information coming from every discipline. When you are building a house you need plumbers, carpenters, electricians, masons, and eventually a decorator. No one trade is the "owner" of the process, not even the architect, whose drawings would languish as unbuilt idealizations, but without the contribution of any of the trades, you would not want to live in the house.[2]

There are indications that a transdisciplinary approach to humor studies may be on the way. Demjén (2018) considers a set of jokes in an online community in a framework explicitly invoking complexity theory. While the article itself seems more programmatic on the complexity side of things, it is unquestionably a start. Bell's (2015) remarkably broad methodological approach is as transdisciplinary as it gets, blending discourse analysis, elicitations, corpora, self-reports, observations, and media samples. Brock (2017) seems to be advocating for something fairly close to that I am proposing, albeit with a much more limited scope. With all due modesty, Chapter 10 in this book also considers a broad range of disciplines. I hope that my friends and colleagues will see my prodding of conversation and discourse analysis here and there

---

[2] In many places, many people would be quite happy to trade their current living space for a house without plumbing or without electricity. Metaphors have limits and embody privilege.

as attempts to get a transdisciplinary (or at least trans-methodological) perspective going.

I harbor no illusion to have accomplished the task of creating a transdisciplinary approach to humor studies in this book. This was not my goal. My goal in this book was, so to speak, to look backward and see where we are, what we have learned that is useful, and set it out clearly in as comprehensive a framework as possible. The future, however, will require a much broader approach, which I think will incorporate a complex system approach.

Glossary

The glossary is provided as a resource for beginning researchers. The glossary does not include linguistic terms that are assumed to be known (e.g., phoneme) or terms for which a definition is provided in the text, unless they are central to humor studies (e.g., smile). No claim of completeness is made.

Ambiguity: For a linguistic sign, the property to have more than one meaning. Words, sentences, and texts may be ambiguous. See also: monosemy, disambiguation.

Antonymy: A lexical relation between two words in a semantic relation of oppositeness. For example, hot and cold are antonyms and so are dead and alive and smart and stupid.

Backchannel: In conversation and discourse analysis, the uttering of supportive turns that may overlap with the turn of the speaker but cause no interruption. Backchannel may range from a simple "uhuh" or nodding, to more elaborate turns such as "I cannot believe what you are telling me!"

Bona-fide: A mode of communication committed to the observance of the Cooperative Principle (see CP). Bona-fide discourse is truthful, clear, relevant and "just right" insofar as the amount of information is concerned (i.e., not too little and not too much). Non-bona-fide communication is communication that violates the CP but does not do so for the purpose of generating implicatures.

Character frame: A frame or script tied to the description of a character in a story/narrative. All the information available in the text about the character is gathered in the character frame.

Coercion: a semantic process whereby contextual pressure forces a marked, salient, unusual use of a lexical form. For example, in the sentence; "Bob bought too much car for him" the lexical item "car" normally a count noun, is coerced into a mass reading thereby generating an implicature, such as that the car is too powerful or too expensive for Bob.

Commutation, principle of: In linguistics, the methodological principle whereby is a change in the form of a sign results in a change in the meaning, the difference is systemic, i.e., it is part of the emic units at the linguistic level being considered. So, at the level of sounds a difference in one sound that results in a difference in meaning helps determine that the two sounds involved are phonemes and not allophonic variants. At the level of morphemes, likewise, if a change in the morphemes results in a change in meaning, the difference is morphemic. In humor studies, the principle of commutation helps determine what components of a joke text are essential and which are not.

Contextualization cue: In Gumperz sociolinguistic model, any prosodic, paralinguistic, repertoire or lexical choice that affects the way a given utterance is understood. For example, using an exaggerated high pitch and broad smiling may signal to the hearer that the utterance is not meant seriously.

Cooperative Principle: A set of strategies for optimizing communication. Originally stated as a preamble and maxims by H. P. Grice, it directs speakers to contribute to the conversation as is expected of them, i.e., truthfully, clearly, to the point, and in the appropriate amount, i.e., not too little and not too much.

Dialect: A variety of language. Dialects lie on a continuum ranging from an acrolect (formal, upper class), a set of intermediate varieties (mesolect) and a basilect (informal, lower class). Sometime the form "lect" is used to indicate a given variety. It should be remembered that dialects are functionally languages. The difference between a language and a dialect are not linguistic, but socio-economic.

Disambiguation: the process of removal of ambiguity, through contextual information. Thus the word "club" is ambiguous (social organizations vs. sticks) in the first sentence of this old joke "Do you believe in clubs for your men?" is disambiguated by the reply "Only when kindness fails." which contextually forces/selects the meaning "stick."

Disposition theory of humor: an approach to humor that claims that one appreciates more humor directed against things that one is disposed negatively toward, and vice versa. The disposition theory of humor is a type of superiority theory.

Exhilaration: The emotion tied to humor (see mirth).

Figure/Ground: An opposition, introduced by Gestalt theory and adopted by Cognitive Linguistics in which the field of attention of the speaker is divided in a salient core (figure) and a non-salient background (ground). Thus in the word "thief" the figure is [stealing]; in the construction a baby thief the figure is shifted to [-adult].

Ground: see Figure.

GTVH: General Theory of Verbal Humor. Presented by Attardo and Raskin in 1991, it accounts for jokes qua texts using six knowledge resources: the Script Opposition (SO), the Logical Mechanism (LM), the Situation (SI), the Target (TA), the Narrative Strategy (NS), and the Language (LA). The Language knowledge resource is merely the linguistic specification of the text. Later versions of the GTVh expand the Language to any semiotic system.

Heterophonic pun: Puns in which the two strings involved in the pun do not match exactly (a.k.a. imperfect or paronymic puns). Opposed to Homonymic (or perfect) puns.

Homography: A relationship between two (or more) words that are spelled the same way: "read" (present tense) and "read" (past tense) are homographs. "Fit" (a relation in which two things are of a shape and size such that one can be placed inside the other) and "fit" (attack, conniption) are also homographs.

Homonym(y): a sign that is identical to another sign, see Paronym(y).

Homophony: a relationship between words or strings that are identical in sound, but may differ in spelling: "red" (color) and "read" (past tense). "There," "their," and "they're" all sound the same. The same goes for "two," "too," and "to."

Humor competence: 1) According to Raskin's SSTH, speakers have a competence, comparable to Chomsky's grammatical competence, that lets them tell apart humor from non-humor. 2) In parallel to communicative competence, humor competence would be a fifth competence alongside the other four competencies that constitute communicative competence: grammatical, in the Chomskian sense, sociolinguistic, i.e., pertaining to contextual appropriateness, discursive, i.e., concerned with the coherence and cohesion of the text, and finally, strategic, i.e., when to apply all of the above to solve communicative problems (for example, when to repair an exchange gone awry).

Hyponymy: a lexical relation between words, in which one word (hyperonym) is a kind of or an example of the hyponym. For example, apples and oranges are a kind of fruit, and hence "fruit" is the hyperonym of both "apple" and "orange."

Immediacy: in communication studies, immediacy describes the quantity and nature of the interaction between subjects. Greater immediacy is tied to direct involvement in communication. Lesser immediacy is tied to distance, lack of expressiveness, lack of gestures, and generally to lack of involvement.

Implicature: an inference from the meaning of an utterance or text that is not part of what is explicitly stated in the utterance or text. Implicatures are produced by following or flouting the principle of cooperation. In the sentence, "Mary has a PhD" an implicature is that "Mary is smart." Implicatures are not logically necessary, so one could say "Mary has a PhD but she is not smart" without a logical contradiction. Contrast this to inferences, which are logically necessary, and trigger a contradiction: "Mary is married" implied "Mary is not single." "Mary is married but she is single" is a contradiction.

Incongruity: A violation of expectations. Not all incongruity is humorous. For example, cognitive dissonance is perceived negatively by subjects.

Incongruity, backgrounded/foregrounded: In a joke, the punch line foregrounds the incongruity it consists of by definition. However, there may be other incongruities in the text that are not foregrounded. Those incongruities that are not foregrounded in the punch line are said to be backgrounded. For example, in the joke: "A skeleton walks into a bar and orders a beer and a mop" the lack of stomach/aesophagus of the drinking skeleton is foregrounded, but that fact that it manages to order a beer (which is equally if not more incongruous) is not addressed and hence backgrounded.

Irony: a form of implicature (see) in which the speaker utters a sentence or text "X" while implying something different, often opposite ("not-X") to what the statement's meaning is. A prototypical example is uttering "That was smart!" when someone spills coffee on your coat. Clearly, the speaker does not mean that spilling coffee on his/her coat was smart. Hence the hearer is forced to seek another interpretation, using the principle of cooperation. In the example of the coffee spill, the irony is negative (it praises to express a negative judgement). However, irony can also be positive, i.e., it expresses a negative judgement to imply a positive one. This form of irony, called asteism, is rarer. An example would be your stock broker calling to tell you of a massive windfall and saying "I am sorry to bother you..." fully knowing that he is not sorry at all and that being called to be informed of positive financial news is not being "bothered."

Isotopy: is structural semantics, the repetition of semantic features across lexical items in a sentence responsible for the selection of the overall meaning of the sentence. For example, the word "coffee" may have either option of the feature [+/- liquid]. However, in the utterance "May I have a cup of coffee?" the word cup will have a semantic description that includes the information that it is a container for [+liquid] content. Hence the recurrence of [+ liquid] establishes an isotopy. The definition of "isotopy" changed significantly and eventually was taken to mean the repetition of any feature.

Jab line: An instance of humor within a text that does not occur in final position and does not interrupt the development of the text. It is opposed to punch lines.

Joke: A short humorous text ending in a punch line.

Joke cycle: A set of jokes that shares common features, usually thematic (e.g., lightbulb jokes, elephant jokes, dead baby jokes).

Keying: in Dell Hymes' terminology (Hymes, 1972, p. 62) a key is a cue that establishes the tone or mood of a linguistic event (speech act). An important key is serious vs. playful; other keys are formal vs. informal, use of profanity, etc. Keys are closely tied to the situation in which a speech act takes place. A synonym is "framing" in Goffman's terminology.

Latching: In conversation and discourse analysis, a turn that immediately follows another turn, without any perceptible pause is considered a latch.

Laughable: The referent of an instance of laughter. The thing laughed at.

Laughter: A pattern of breathing which include rhythmical aspirated syllables. It is associated with the expression of mirth.

Lexical Function: In Mel'čuk's Meaning-Text theory, any semantic relationship between lexical items. Some lexical functions are similar to well-known ones such as synonymy and antonymy, but others are more "exotic" and include, for example, the "Able" function which indicates that "capacity of being/doing something" hence the Able function describes the relationship between the following pairs of words: prove and provable, believe and believable, cry and tearful, trust and trustworthy, drink and potable.

Logical Mechanism: One of the Knowledge Resources of the GTVH. Equivalent to the resolution phase of the incongruity/resolution model.

Meronymy: See Partonymy.

Meta-humor: Humor that is based on the violation of the hearer's expectations for humor. For example, delivering a text that the hearer expects to be a joke but without a discernible punch line. (see)

Mirth: The emotion tied to humor (see exhilaration)

Modality: The mode of communication (visual, aural, spatial, linguistic, etc.) used in a text. Many non-linguistic texts are in fact multimodal, i.e., they utilize more than one modality at a time, for example, cinema (film) utilizes both the visual and aural modalities as well as the linguistic one (e.g., titles, credits).

Mode adoption: A response to a humorous turn by adopting the same humorous mode, for example responding to irony with irony, or to a tease with a counter-tease.

Monosemy: the property of having a single meaning. The opposite of ambiguity and polysemy.

Multimodality: see Modality.

Overlap: In conversation and discourse analysis the simultaneous occurrence of two turns by different speakers. Not to be confused with "script overlap."

Paradigmatic: Related to or coming from the options a speaker has at any given point in the production of a text. In the theory of puns, a pun in which one of the senses is not present in the text and has to be inferred (see syntagmatic).

Paratelic: non-goal directed. Usually said of an activity or a mode of activity that does not have a clearly identifiable practical goal (telos), such as play or humor.

Paronym(y): a paronym is a verbal sign that is similar but not identical in pronunciation to another sign. So, for example: "blue and "glue" are paronyms. Homonymy (identity between two signs) can be considered a limit case of paronymy i.e., two strings with a difference of zero between them.

Partonomy: A lexical relation in which a word is a part of the other word. For example, "motor" and "steering wheel" are partonyms of "car."

Phonemic distance: The degree in which two strings may differ from each other and still be considered paronyms for the purposes of a pun.

Polysemy: The property for a sign or word to have more than one meaning.

Prosody: The suprasegmental (i.e., not part of the segments, i.e., the individual sounds) properties of syllables and utterances. Stress, tone, intonation, and rhythm are all part of prosody. In literary theory, prosody considers the rhythm of verse.

Reanalysis: A word formation process in which a given word is interpreted as consisting of a sequence of morphemes inconsistent with its etymology. For example in "If it's feasible, let's fease it" the word "feasible" is humorously re-analyzed as "fease+able" whereas its etymology is from Old French "faisible" which itself comes from Latin "facere." There is no "fease" morpheme in English (although there was one, unrelated etymologically, in Middle English).

Referential: Humor based exclusively on the meaning of the text. See Verbal humor.

Register: A variety of language defined primarily by subject matter (stamp collecting), a given situation (recipes), activity (e.g., playing chess), or practice (newspaper headlines).

Relevant humor: In pedagogical research, humor that is related to the subject matter of the lecture. Not to be confused with Relevance theory.

Resolution: In the incongruity/resolution (INC/RES) psychological model, the second phase of the cognitive processing of the humorous stimulus in which the incongruity of the first phase is integrated into a cognitive model (resolved). There is considerable debate whether the resolution is complete or partial and to what extent it is fictional.

Script: a complex, organized set of information generally associated with a lexical item, but that can be associated with non-verbal procedures, situations, and settings containing linguistic and extra-linguistic (encyclopedic) information about the lexical item or situation, etc. Scripts are hierarchically organized in an ontology and non-hierarchically in a semantic network. The term "script" is used by Raskin (1985) and a generic umbrella term to encompass all quasi-synonyms, such as frame, schema, MOP, etc.

Script Opposition: A relationship of negation between two scripts. Two scripts are opposite if they are incompatible in a given context. For example, the script BIRTHDAY PARTY is opposed to the script INTERVENTION even though both involve a gathering of family and friends, surprise, and the focus on an individual. The purpose of the gathering is clearly different and thus, in that respect, the two scripts are opposite.

Semantic shift: a change in the meaning or denotation of a given word or sign.

Semiotics: The science that studies signs. Language is considered to be a special type of sign. Semiotics is concerned with the use of any system (visual, auditory, gustative, etc.) to convey meaning.

Sign: Generally speaking something that stands for (i.e., refers to) something else. A sign consists of a physical support (sound, letters, image, etc.), called the signifier, and a mental representation of its meaning, called the signified. The definition was introduced by De Saussure.

Signified: The meaning of a sign, the representation of its referent.

Signifier: The physical support of a sign.

Smiling: A facial expression involving the raising of the corners of the mouth and the wrinkling of the corners of the eyes. It is associated with the expression of mirth.

Stack: In the 2001 version of the GTVH, a set of strands that share some features (for example, all the versions of a given meme).

Strand: In the 2001 version of the GTVH, a set of jab or punch lines that share one or more identical or related knowledge resources (for example, the same target).

String: An ordered contiguous sequence of sounds or letters. abcd is a string of letters, for example. Strings stands in opposition to word or morpheme, which are linguistic units endowed with meaning. Thus, for example in the pun "Be alert, we need more lerts" "lert" is a meaningless string. String is also opposed to a sequence of sounds, which involve non-contiguous sounds.

Synonymy: A lexical relation in which two words have similar or identical meanings. Freedom and liberty and big and large are synonyms. Synonymy is always partial (i.e., no two words are exactly identical in meaning and collocation.

Syntagmatic: Related to or part of the syntagm, i.e., the sequence of linguistic units in a text. The syntagmatic ordering of the choices in the paradigm produces the text. In the theory of puns, a pun in which both forms involve din the opposition are present in the text, at different places along the syntagm (see Paradigm).

Target: The butt of the joke. A person, group, or institution that is made fun of in a humorous text.

Unlimited semiosis: (a.k.a. infinite semiosis) in Peircian semiotics, a sign consist of three components: a vehicle, and object, and in interpretant. Speaking very generally, the vehicle is akin to the signifier in Saussurean semiotics and the object can be considered the referent. The main difference between Saussurean semiotics and Peirce's version is that in Peirce the sign includes a third component, the interpretant: the sign has an effect on someone who produces an interpretation of the sign. In other words, the sign must mean something to someone. However, the interpretant is itself another sign, which will now require another interpretant, ad infinitum.

Verbal: Humor based on the meaning of the text and on some formal aspect (phonology, morphology, syntax, etc.) of the signs. Verbal humor is best exemplified with puns (see Referential humor).

References

Abrahams, R. D. (1962). Playing the dozens. *Journal of American Folklore, 75*(297), 209–220.

Adams, A. C. (2012). *Humor markers in computer-mediated communication.* (Unpublished master's thesis). Texas A&M University-Commerce, Commerce, TX.

Adelswärd, V. (1989). Laughter and dialogue: The social significance of laughter in institutional discourse. *Nordic Journal of Linguistics, 12,* 107–136.

Aiello, J. R., Thompson, D. E., & Brodzinsky, D. M. (1983). How funny is crowding anyway? Effects of room size, group size and the introduction of humor. *Basic and Applied Social Psychology, 4*(2), 193–207.

Aitchison, J. (1987). *Words in the mind: An introduction to the mental lexicon.* Oxford: Blackwell.

Alexander, R. J. (1997). *Aspects of verbal humour in English.* Tubingen, Germany: Günter Narr Verlag.

Aljared, A. (2017). The Isotopy-Disjunction Model. In S. Attardo (Ed.), *The Routledge handbook of language and humor* (pp. 64–79). New York: Routledge.

Al-Khatib, M. A. (1999). Joke-telling in Jordanian society: A sociolinguistic perspective. *Humor-International Journal of Humor Research, 12*(3), 261–288.

Alvarado Ortega, B. M. (2013). An approach to verbal humor in interaction. *Procedia: Social and Behavioral Sciences, 95,* 594–603. Retrieved from http://dx.doi.org/10.1016/j.sbspro.2013.10.687

Amirian, Z. & S. S. Dameneh (2014). Microstrategies employed for translation of english humor subtitled into Persian: a case study of the Simpsons' movie. *Journal of Intercultural Communication, 34,* n.p.

Anderson, R. C. & Pearson, P. D. (1984). A schema-theoretic view of basic processes in reading comprehension. In P. D. Person (ed.) *Handbook of reading research* (pp. 255–291). Mawah, NJ: Lawrence Earlbaum.

Andor, J. (1985). On the psychological relevance of frames. *Quaderni di Semantica. 6*(2), 212–221.

Andrus, T. D. (1946). A study of laugh patterns in the theatre. *Speech Monographs, 13,*(114), 183–200.

Antonini, R. (2010). And the Oscar goes to?: A study of the simultaneous interpretation of humour at the Academy Awards Ceremony. In D. Chiaro (Ed.), *Translation, Humor and the Media* (pp. 53–69). London: Continuum.

Antonini, R., Bucaria, C., & Senzani, A. (2001). It's a priest thing, you wouldn't understand: Father Ted goes to Italy. *Antares, 6*, 26–30.

Antonopoulou, E. (2002). A cognitive approach to literary humor devices: Translating Raymond Chandler. *Translator, 8*(2), 235–257.

Antonopoulou, E. & Nikiforidou, K. (2009). Deconstructing verbal humour with construction grammar. In G. Brône & J. Vandaele (Eds.), *Cognitive poetics: Goals, gains and gaps* (pp. 289–314). Berlin: Mouton de Gruyter.

Antonopoulou, E. & Nikiforidou, K. (2011). Construction grammar and conventional discourse: A construction-based approach to discoursal incongruity. *Journal of Pragmatics, 43*(10), 2594–2609.

Antonopoulou, E., Nikiforidou, K., & Tsakona, V. (2015). Construction grammar and discoursal incongruity. In G. Brône, K. Feyaerts, & T. Veale (Eds.), *Cognitive linguistics and humor research* (pp. 13–48). Berlin: Mouton de Gruyter.

Antonopoulou, E. & Sifianou, M. (2003). Conversational dynamics of humour: the telephone game in Greek. *Journal of Pragmatics, 35*(5), 741–769.

Apte, M. (1985). *Humor and laughter*. Ithaca/ London: Cornell University Press.

Apter, M. J. (1982). Fawlty Towers: A reversal theory analysis of a popular television comedy series. *The Journal of Popular Culture, 16*(3), 128–138.

Apter, M. J. (1989). *Reversal theory: Motivation, emotion and personality*. London–New York: Routledge.

Archakis, A., Giakoumelou, M. Papazachariou, D., & Tsakona, V. (2010). The prosodic framing of humour in conversational narratives: Evidence from Greek data. *Journal of Greek Linguistics, 10*(2), 187–212.

Archakis, A., Lampropoulou, S., Tsakona, V., & Tsami, V. (2014). Linguistic varieties in style: Humorous representations in Greek mass culture texts. *Discourse, Context & Media, 3*, 46–55.

Archakis, A. & Tsakona, V. (2005). Analyzing conversational data in GTVH terms: A new approach to the issue of identity construction via humor. *HUMOR: International Journal of Humor Research, 18*(1), 41–68.

Archakis, A. & Tsakona, V. (2012). *The narrative construction of identities in critical education*. New York, NY: Palgrave Macmillan.

Arieti, S. (1967). *The intrapsychic self*. New York–London: Basic Books.

Asimakoulas, D. (2004). Towards a model of describing humour translation: A case study of the Greek subtitled versions of *Airplane!* and *Naked Gun*. *Meta: journal des traducteurs /Meta: Translators' Journal, 49*(4), 822–842.

Åstedt-Kurki, P. & Isola, A. (2001). Humour between nurse and patient, and among staff: Analysis of nurses'. diaries. *Journal of Advanced Nursing, 35*(3), 452–458.

REFERENCES

Atkin, A. (2013). Peirce's Theory of Signs, The Stanford Encyclopedia of Philosophy (Summer 2013 Edition), Edward N. Zalta (ed.), URL = https://plato.stanford.edu/archives/sum2013/entries/peirce-semiotics/

Atkinson, J. M. (1984). Public speaking and audience responses: Some techniques for inviting applause. In J. M. Atkinson & J. C. Heritage (Eds.), *Structures of social action: Studies in conversation analysis* (pp. 370–409). Cambridge: Cambridge University Press.

Atkinson, J. M., & Heritage, J. (1984). Transcription notation (pp. ix–xiv). *Structures of social action.* New York: Cambridge University Press.

Atkinson, J. M. & Heritage, J. (1999). Transcript notation-structures of social action: Studies in conversation analysis. *Aphasiology, 13*(4–5), 243–249.

Attardo, S. (1988). Trends in European humor research: Towards a text model. *HUMOR: International Journal of Humor Studies, 1*(4), 349–369.

Attardo, S. (1993). Violation of conversational maxims and cooperation: The Case of Jokes. *Journal of Pragmatics, 19*(1), 537–558.

Attardo, S. (1994). *Linguistic theories of humor.* Berlin: Mouton De Gruyter.

Attardo, S. (1997). The semantic foundations of cognitive theories of humor. *HUMOR: International Journal of Humor Research, 10*(4), 395–420.

Attardo, S. (1998). The analysis of humorous narratives. *HUMOR: International Journal of Humor Research, 11*(3), 231–260.

Attardo, S. (1999). The place of cooperation in cognition. In Proceedings from ECCS99: *European Conference of Cognitive Science* (pp. 459–464). Siena, Italy.

Attardo, S. (2000a). Irony as relevant inappropriateness. *Journal of Pragmatics, 32,* 793–826.

Attardo, S. (2000b). Irony markers and functions: Towards a goal-oriented theory of irony and its processing. *Rask, 12*(1), 3–20.

Attardo, S. (2001a). *Humorous texts.* Berlin: Mouton De Gruyter.

Attardo, S. (2001b). Stylistic markers of 'serious relief' in Wilde's Lord Arthur Savile's crime. *Stylistika, X,* 19–31.

Attardo, S. (2002a). Translation and humor: A GTVH-based approach. *The Translator, 8*(2), 173–194.

Attardo, S. (2002b). Humor, irony and their communication: From mode adoption to failure of detection. In Luigi Anolli, Rita Ciceri, Giuseppe Riva (Eds.), *Say not to say: New perspectives on miscommunication* (pp. 159–179). Amsterdam: IOS Press.

Attardo, S. (2002c). Cognitive stylistics of humorous texts. In E. Semino & J. Culpeper (Eds.), Cognitive stylistics (pp. 231–250). Amsterdam, Netherlands: John Benjamins.

Attardo, S. (2002d, July). *Beyond humor competence and toward a theory of humor performance.* Paper presented at the ISHS conference, Bertinoro, Italy.

Attardo, S. (2003). The myth of unintentional humor. In Vladimir Karasik & Gennady Slyshkin (Eds.), *Aksiologicheskaya Linguistika: Igrovoe i Komicheskoe v Yazyke* (pp. 4–14). Volgograd.

Attardo, S. (2006, April). [Review of the book *L'humour dans la conversation familière*, by B. Priego-Valverde]. *Journal of Pragmatics, 38*(4), 605–609.

Attardo, S. (2008). Semantics and pragmatics of humor. *Language and Linguistics Compass, 2*(6), 1203–1215.

Attardo, S. (2008a). Fiction and deception: How cooperative is literature? In K. Korta & J. Garmendia (Eds.), *Meanings, intentions, and argumentation* (pp. 41–60). Stanford: CSLI.

Attardo, S. (2008b). A primer of the linguistics of humor. In V. Raskin (Ed.) *The Primer of humor research.* (pp. 101–155). Berlin: Mouton De Gruyter.

Attardo, S. (2009). Salience of incongruities in humorous texts and their resolution. In E. Chrzanowska-Kluczewska and G. Szpila (Eds.), *In search of (non)ense* (pp. 164–178). Newcastle upon Tyne: Cambridge Scholars Publishing.

Attardo, S. (2010). Preface: Working class humor. *HUMOR: International Journal of Humor Research, 23*(2), 121–126.

Attardo, S. (2012). Smiling, laughter and humor. In P. Santarcangelo (Ed.). *Laughing in Chinese.* (pp. 421–436.) Rome: Aracne.

Attardo, S. (ed.) (2014). *The Encyclopedia of humor studies.* Los Angeles: Sage.

Attardo, S. (2015). Humor and laughter. In Tannen, D., Hamilton, H. E., & Schiffrin, D. (Eds.), *The handbook of discourse analysis* (pp. 166–188). Chichester: John Wiley & Sons.

Attardo, S. (2017a). The GTVH and humorous discourse. In Chlopicki, W., & Brzozowska, D. (Eds.), *Humorous discourse* (pp. 93–105). Berlin: Mouton de Gruyter.

Attardo, S. (2017b). The General Theory of Verbal Humor. In S. Attardo (Ed.) *The Routledge handbook of language and humor.* (pp. 126–142). New York: Routledge.

Attardo, S. (2017c). Humor and pragmatics. In S. Attardo (Ed.) *The Routledge handbook of language and humor.* (pp. 174–188). New York: Routledge.

Attardo, S. (Ed.) (2017d). *The Routledge handbook of language and humor.* New York: Routledge.

Attardo, S. (2018). Universals in puns and humorous wordplay. In Winter-Froemel, E. & Thaler, V. (Eds.) *Cultures and traditions of wordplay and wordplay research* (pp. 1–20). Berlin: Mouton De Gruyter.

Attardo, S. (2019). Humor and mirth: Emotions, embodied cognition, and sustained humor. In MacKenzie, L., & Alba, L. (Ed.) *Emotions in discourse* (pp. 189–211). Amsterdam: Benjamins.

Attardo, S. (2020). Scripts, frames, and other semantic objects. In S. Attardo (ed.) *Script-based semantics: foundations and applications. A Festschrift for Victor Raskin.* (pp. 11–41) Berlin: Mouton De Gruyter.

Attardo, S., D. H. Attardo, P. Baltes, & M. J. Petray (1994). The linear organization of jokes: Statistical analysis of two thousands texts. *HUMOR: International Journal of Humor Research, 7*(1), 27–54.

Attardo, S. & Chabanne, J. C. (1992). Jokes as a text type. *HUMOR: International Journal of Humor Research, 5*(1–2), 165–176.

Attardo, S., Eisterhold, J., Hay, J., & Poggi, I. (2003). Multimodal markers of irony and sarcasm. *HUMOR: International Journal of Humor Studies, 16*(2), 243–260.

Attardo, S., Hempelmann, C., & Di Maio, S. (2002). Script oppositions and logical mechanisms: Modeling incongruities and their resolutions. *HUMOR: International Journal of Humor Research, 15*(1), 3–46.

Attardo, S. & Pickering, L. (2011). Timing in the performance of jokes. *HUMOR: International Journal of Humor Research, 24*(2), 233–250.

Attardo, S., Pickering, L., Lomotey, F., & Menjo, S. (2013). Multimodality in conversational humor. *Review of Cognitive Linguistics, 11*(2), 402–416.

Attardo, S. & Raskin, V. (1991). Script theory revis(it)ed: joke similarity and joke representation model. *HUMOR: International Journal of Humor Research, 4*(3–4), 293–347.

Attardo, S. & Raskin, V. (2017). Linguistics and humor theory. In S. Attardo (Ed.) *The Routledge Handbook of Language and Humor.* (pp. 49–63). New York: Routledge.

Attardo, S., Wagner, M. M., & Urios-Aparisi, E. (2013). *Prosody and Humor.* Amsterdam/Philadelpha: Benjamins.

Aubouin, E. (1948). *Technique et psychologie du comique.* Marseilles: OFEP.

Austin, J. L. (1962). *How to do things with words.* Oxford/New York: Oxford University Press.

Bakhtin, M. (1981). *The dialogic imagination.* Austin: University of Texas Press.

Balirano, G. (2013). The strange case of The Big Bang Theory and its extraordinary Italian audiovisual translation: A multimodal corpus-based analysis. *Perspectives, 21*(4), 563–576.

Bally, Charles. (1909). *Traité de stylistique française.* Heidelberg: Winter. 2nd ed. 1921.

Banas, J. A., Dunbar, N., Rodriguez, D., & Liu, S. J. (2011). A review of humor in educational settings: Four decades of research. *Communication Education, 60*(1), 115–144.

Barreca, R. (1991). *They used to call me Snow White – but I drifted: women's strategic use of humor.* New York: Viking.

REFERENCES

Bartlett, F. C. (1932). *Remembering*. Cambridge: Cambridge University Press. Reprint 1977.

Bauman, R. (1986). *Story, performance, and event. Contextual studies of oral narrative*. Cambridge, England: Cambridge University Press.

Bauman, R. & Sherzer, J. (1975). The ethnography of speaking. *Annual Review of Anthropology, 4*, 95–119.

Bateson, G. (1972). *Steps to an ecology of mind* (pp. 177–193). New York: Ballantine. (Reprinted from G. Bateson (1955), A theory of play and fantasy, *A.P.A. Psychiatric Research Reports, 2*, pp. 39–51.

Beach, W. A. & Prickett, E. (2017). Laughter, humor, and cancer: Delicate moments and poignant interactional circumstances. *Health Communication, 32*(7), 791–802.

Becker, A. B. (2014). Humiliate my enemies or mock my friends? Applying disposition theory of humor to the study of political parody appreciation and attitudes toward candidates. *Human Communication Research, 40*(2), 137–160.

Bekinschtein, T. A., Davis, M. H., Rodd, J. M., & Owen, A. M. (2011). Why clowns taste funny: The relationship between humor and semantic ambiguity. *The Journal of Neuroscience, 31*(26), 9665–9671.

Bell, N. D. (2009). Responses to failed humor. *Journal of Pragmatics, 41*, 1825–1836.

Bell, N. D. (2011). Humor scholarship and TESOL: Applying findings and establishing a research agenda. *TESOL Quarterly, 45*(1), 134–159.

Bell, N. D. (2015). *We are not amused. Failed humor in interaction*. Berlin: Mouton De Gruyter.

Bell, N. D. & Pomerantz, A. (2016). *Humor in the classroom: a guide for language teachers and educational researchers*. London/New York: Routledge.

Berger, A. A. (1993). *An anatomy of humor*. New Brunswick, NJ: Transaction.

Berger, A. A. (1995). *Blind men and elephants*. New Brunswick, NJ: Transaction.

Berger, P. L. (1997). *Redeeming laughter. The comic dimension of human experience*. Berlin: Mouton De Gruyter.

Bergler, E. (1956). *Laughter and the sense of humor*. New York: Intercontinental Medical Book Corporation.

Bergson, H. (1901). *Le rire. Essai sur la signification du comique*. Paris: Presses Universitaires de France. 203rd ed. 1964.

Berk, R. A. (2002). *Humor as an instructional defibrillator: Evidence-based techniques in teaching and assessment*. Sterling, VA: Stylus Publishing.

Berk, R. A. (2003). *Professors are from Mars, Students are from Snickers*. Sterling, VA: Stylus Publishing.

Berkowitz, L. (Ed.). (1969). *Roots of aggression: A re-examination of the frustration-aggression hypothesis*. New York, NY: Atherton Press.

Berlyne, D. E. (1960). *Conflict, arousal, and curiosity.* New York, NY: McGraw-Hill.

Bertone, L. (1989). *En torno de Babel: estrategias de la interpretación simultánea.* Paris: Hachette.

Bevis, M. (2013). *Comedy: A very short introduction.* Oxford: Oxford University Press.

Biber, D. (1988). *Variation across speech and writing.* Cambridge: Cambridge University Press.

Biber, D. (2009). Corpus-based and corpus-driven analyses of language variation and use. In B. Heine and H. Narrog (Eds.), *The Oxford handbook of linguistic analysis* (pp. 193–224). Oxford: Oxford University Press.

Bickle, J. (2006). Reducing mind to molecular pathways: Explicating the reductionism implicit in current cellular and molecular neuroscience. *Synthese, 151*, 411–434.

Billig, M. (2005). *Laughter and ridicule: Towards a social critique of humor.* London: Sage.

Bird, C. (2011). Formulaic jokes in interaction: The prosody of riddle openings. *Pragmatics & Cognition, 19*(2), 268–290. Reprinted in Attardo et al. (2013, pp. 81–102).

Blackwell, K. (2011). The wit and humour of Principia Mathematica. *Russell: the Journal of Bertrand Russell Studies n.s. 31*, 151–160.

Blake, B. (2007). *Playing with words. Humour in the English language.* London: Equinox.

Blom, J.-P. & Gumperz, J. (1972). Social meaning in linguistic structures: Code-switching in Norway. In J. Gumperz & D. Hymes (Eds.), *Directions in sociolinguistics* (pp. 407–434). New York: Holt, Rinehart & Winston.

Boxer, D. & Cortès-Conde, F. (1997). From bonding to biting: Conversational joking and identity display. *Journal of Pragmatics, 27*(3), 275–294.

Brock, A. (2017). Modelling the complexity of humour? Insights from linguistics. *Lingua, 197*, 5–15.

Brodie, I. (2015). Stand-up comedy. In S. Attardo (Ed.), *Encyclopedia of humor studies* (pp. 732–737). Los Angeles: Sage.

Brône, G., Feyaerts, K., & Veale, T. (2006). Introduction: Cognitive linguistic approaches to humor. *HUMOR: International Journal of Humor Research, 19*(3), 203–228.

Brône, G., K. Feyaerts, & T. Veale (Eds.) (2015). *Cognitive linguistics and humor research.* Berlin: Mouton de Gruyter.

Brown, G. E., Dixon, P. A. & Hudson, J. D. (1982). Effects of peer pressure on imitation of humor response in college students. *Psychological Reports, 51*, 1111–1117.

Brown, P. & Levinson, S. C. (1978). *Politeness. Some universals in language usage.* Cambridge: Cambridge University Press. 2nd ed. 1987.

REFERENCES

Brown, S. & S. Attardo (2000). *Understanding language structure, interaction, and variation.* Ann Arbor, MI: Michigan University Press. 3rd ed. 2015.

Bryant, G. A. (2010). Prosodic contrasts in ironic speech. *Discourse Processes, 47*(7), 545–566.

Bryant, G. A., & Fox Tree, J. E. (2005). Is there an ironic tone of voice? *Language and Speech, 48* (3), 257–277.

Bryant, J., Alan, D. B., Silberberg, R., & Elliott, S. M. (1981). Effects of humorous illustrations in college textbooks. *Human Communication Research, 8*(1), 43–57.

Bryant, J., Comisky, P., & Zillmann, D. (1979). Teachers? Humor in the college classroom. *Communication Education, 28*(2), 110–118.

Bryant, J. & Zillmann, D. (1989). Using humor to promote learning in the classroom. In P. McGhee & M. Frank (Eds.), *Humor and children's development* (pp. 49–78). New York: Routledge.

Bubel, C. M. (2008). Film audiences as overhearers. *Journal of Pragmatics, 40*(1), 55–71.

Bucaria, C. (2004). Lexical and syntactic ambiguity as a source of humor: The case of newspaper headlines. *HUMOR: International Journal of Humor Research, 17*(3), 279–309.

Bucaria, C. (2005). The perception of humour in dubbing vs subtitling: The case of 'Six Feet Under. *ESP Across Cultures, 2,* 34–46.

Bucaria, C. (2017). Audiovisual Translation of Humor. In S. Attardo (Ed.), *The Routledge Handbook of Language and Humor.* (pp. 430–443). New York: Routledge.

Bucaria, C. & Chiaro, D. (2007). End-user perception of screen translation: the case of Italian dubbing. *Tradterm, 13,* 91–118.

Buck, R. (1980). Nonverbal behavior and the theory of emotion: The facial feedback hypothesis. *Journal of personality and social psychology, 38*(5), 811–824.

Buck, R. (1994). Social and emotional functions in facial expression and communication: The readout hypothesis. *Biological Psychology, 38*(2), 95–115.

Buckman, K. H. (2010). *Why did the professor cross the road? How and why college professors intentionally use humor in their teaching* (Unpublished doctoral dissertation). Texas A&M University: College Station, TX.

Buján, M. (2019). The function of face gestures and head movements in spontaneous humorous communication. *The European Journal of Humour Research, 7*(2), 1–29.

Bull, P. E. (2006). Invited and uninvited applause in political speeches. *British Journal of social psychology, 45*(3), 563–578.

Bull, P. & Wells, P. (2002). By invitation only? An analysis of invited and uninvited applause. *Journal of Language and Social Psychology, 21,* 230–244.

Burgers, C. & van Mulken, M. (2017). Humor markers. In S. Attardo (Ed.), *The Routledge handbook of language and humor* (pp. 385–399). New York: Taylor and Francis.

Burgers, C., Van Mulken, M., & Schellens, P. J. (2011). Finding irony: An introduction of the verbal irony procedure (VIP). Metaphor and Symbol, 26(3), 186–205.

Butcher, J. & Whissell C. (1984). Laughter as a function of audience size, sex of the audience, and segments of the short film Duck Soup. *Perceptual and Motor Skills, 59,* 949–950.

Butler, J. (1990). *Gender trouble and the subversion of identity.* New York/London: Routledge.

Bybee, J. L. (1998). The emergent lexicon. *Chicago Linguistic Society, 34*(2), 421–435.

Bybee, J. L. & Moder, C. L. (1983). Morphological classes as natural categories. *Language, 59*(2), 251–270.

Canagarajah, S. (2004). Subversive identities, pedagogical safe houses, and critical learning. In B. Norton & K. Toohey (Eds.), *Critical pedagogies and language learning* (pp. 116–137). Cambridge: Cambridge University Press.

Canale, M. & Swain, M. (1980). Theoretical bases of communicative approaches to second language teaching and testing. *Applied Linguistics, 1*(1), 1–47.

Canestrari, C. (2010). Meta-communicative signals and humorous verbal interchanges: A case study. *HUMOR: International Journal of Humor Studies, 23*(3), 327–349.

Canestrari, C. & Attardo, S. (2008). Humorous syntony as a metacommunicative language game. *Gestalt Theory, 30*(3), 377–347.

Caputi, A. (1978). *Buffo. The genius of vulgar comedy.* Detroit: Wayne State University Press.

Carrell, A. (1993). *Audience/community, situation, and language: A linguistic/rhetorical theory of verbal humor.* (Unpublished Ph.D. dissertation). West Lafayette, IN. Purdue University.

Carrell, A. (1997a). Humor communities. *HUMOR: International Journal of Humor Research, 10*(1), 11–24.

Carrell, A. (1997b). Joke competence and humor competence, *HUMOR: International Journal of Humor Research, 10*(2), 173–185.

Carrell, A. (2008). Historical views of humor. In V. Raskin (Ed.), *The primer of humor research.* (pp. 303–332). Berlin: Mouton De Gruyter.

Cashion, J. L., M. J. Cody, & K. V. Erickson. (1986). 'You'll love this one...': an exploration into joke-prefacing devices. *Journal of Language and Social Psychology, 5*(4), 303–310.

Chafe, W. L. (1975). Some thoughts on schemata. In R. Schank and B. L. Nash-Webber (eds.), *Theoretical issues in natural language processing* (pp. 89–91). Cambridge, MA: MIT Press.

Chafe, W. L. (1987). Humor as a disabling mechanism. *American Behavioral Scientist, 30*(1), 16–25.

Chafe, W. L. (1994). *Discourse, consciousness, and time. The flow and displacement of conscious experience in speaking and writing.* Chicago: University of Chicago Press.

Chafe, W. L. (2007). *The importance of not being earnest: The feeling behind laughter and humor.* Amsterdam: Benjamins.

Chan, Y. C. & Lavallee, J. P. (2015). Temporo-parietal and fronto-parietal lobe contributions to theory of mind and executive control: An fMRI study of verbal jokes. *Frontiers in Psychology, 6*(1285), 1–13.

Chapman, A. J. (1976). Social aspects of humorous laughter. In Chapman, A. J. and Foot, H. C. (Eds.), *Humor and laughter: theory, research, and applications.* (pp. 155–185.) New York, NY: Wiley.

Chapman, A. J. & Chapman, W. A. (1974). Responsiveness to humor: its dependency upon a companion's humorous smiling and laughter. *Journal of Psychology, 88*(2), 245–252.

Chapman, A. J. and Foot, H. C. (Eds.) (1976). *Humour and laughter: Theory, research and applications.* London: Wiley.

Chapman, A. J. and Foot, H. C. (Eds.) (1977). *It's a funny thing, Humor.* Oxford: Pergamon.

Chapman, A. J. & Wright, D. S. (1976). Socially facilitated laughter: an experimental analysis of some companion variables. *Journal of experimental child psychology, 21,* 201–218.

Chen, G.-H. (2013). Chinese concepts of humour and the role of humour in teaching. In Davis, J. M, & Chey, J. (Eds.), *Humour in Chinese life and culture* (pp. 193–213). Hong Kong: Hong Kong University Press.

Chen, H.-C., Chan, Y.-C., Dai, R.-H., Liao, Y.-J., & Tu, C.-H. (2017). Neurolinguistics of humor. In S. Attardo (Ed.), *The Routledge handbook of language and humor* (pp. 282–294). New York: Taylor & Francis.

Chiaro, D. (2003). The implications of the quality of translated verbally expressed humour and the success of big screen comedy. *Antares, VI,* 14–20.

Chiaro, D. (2005). Verbally expressed humor and translation: An overview of a neglected field. *Humor International Journal of Humor Research,18*(2), 135–145.

Chiaro, D. (2007). The effect of translation on humour response. In Y. Gambier, M. Shlesinger, & R. Stolze (Eds.), *Doubts and directions in translation studies* (pp. 137–152). Amsterdam: Benjamins.

Chiaro, D. (2010). Translating humor in the media. Translation, humour and the media: *Translation, humour and the media: Translation and humour,* vol. 2, 1–16.

Chiaro, D. (2017). Humor and translation. In S. Attardo (Ed.), *The Routledge handbook of language and humor*, New York: Routledge, 414–429.

Chimbwete-Phiri, R. & Schnurr, S. (2017). Negotiating knowledge and creating solidarity: Humour in antenatal counselling sessions at a rural hospital in Malawi. *Lingua, 197*, 68–82.

Chłopicki, W. (1987). *An application of the script theory of semantics to the analysis of selected polish humorous short stories.* Unpublished M.A. Thesis. Purdue University, West Lafayette, IN.

Chłopicki, W. (2017). Humor and Narrative. In S. Attardo (Ed.), *The Routledge handbook of language and humor.* (pp. 143–157). New York: Routledge.

Chomsky, N. (1965). *Aspects of the theory of syntax.* Cambridge, MA: MIT Press.

Chovanec, J. (2018). Laughter and non-humorous situations in TV documentaries. In V. Tsakona & J. Chovanec (Eds.), *The dynamics of interactional discourse.* Amsterdam/Philadelphia: Benjamins, 155–179.

Chukwumah, I. (Ed.) (2018). *Joke-performance in Africa: Mode, media and meaning.* London: Routledge.

Clark, H. H. & van der Wege M. M. (2015). Imagination in narrative. In Tannen, D., Hamilton, H. E., & Schiffrin, D. (Eds.), *The handbook of discourse analysis* (pp. 406–421). Chichester: John Wiley & Sons.

Clift, R. (2012). Identifying action: Laughter in non-humorous reported speech. *Journal of Pragmatics, 44*(10), 1303–1312.

Clift, R. (2013). No laughing matter: Laughter and resistance in the construction of identity. In P. Glenn & E. Holt (Eds.), *On laughing: Studies of laughter in interaction.* London/New York: Bloomsbury.

Clift, R. (2016). Don't make me laugh: Responsive laughter in (dis) affiliation. *Journal of Pragmatics, 100*, 73–88.

Collinson, D. L. (1988). 'Engineering humour': Masculinity, joking and conflict in shop-floor relations. *Organization Studies, 9*(2), 181–199.

Colston, H. (2017). Irony and sarcasm. In S. Attardo (Ed.), *The Routledge handbook of language and humor.* (pp. 234–249). New York: Routledge.

Condren, C. (2012). Satire and definition. *HUMOR: International Journal of Humor Research, 25*(4), 375–399.

Consalvo, C. M. (1989). Humor in management: No laughing matter. *HUMOR: International Journal of Humor Research, 2*(3), 285–297.

Coolidge, A. (2019). Commit to the bit: Familiarity and mode adoption responses to conversational humor. Paper presented at the International Society for Humor Studies conference. Austin, TX.

Cooper, J. (2007). *Cognitive dissonance: 50 years of a classic theory.* Los Angeles: Sage.

Copi, I. M. (2011). *The theory of logical types* (Routledge Revivals). London: Routledge.

Corduas, M., Attardo, S., & Eggleston, A. (2008). The Distribution of Humour in Literary Texts is not Random: A statistical analysis. *Language and Literature, 17*(3), 253–270.

Coser, R. L. (1959). Some social functions of laughter: A study of humor in a hospital setting. *Human relations, 12*(2), 171–182.

Coser, R. L. (1962). *Life in the ward.* East Lansing: Michigan State University Press.

Coulson, S. (2001). *Semantic leaps: Frame-shifting and conceptual blending in meaning construction.* Cambridge: Cambridge University Press.

Coulson, S. & Kutas, M. (1998). Frame-shifting and sentential integration (UCSD Cognitive Science Technical Report, 98-03). Retrieved from http://www.cogsci.ucsd.edu/~coulson/papers.htm.

Coulson, S. & Kutas, M. (2001). Getting it: Human event-related brain response to jokes in good and poor comprehenders. *Neuroscience Letters, 316,* 71–74.

Coupland, N. (2004). Age in social and sociolinguistic theory. In J. F. Nussbaum & J. Coupland (Eds.) *Handbook of communication and aging research* (pp. 89–110). New York/London: Routledge.

Crawford, M. (2003). Gender and humor in social context. *Journal of Pragmatics, 35*(9), 1413–1430.

Creswell, J. W. & Miller, D. L. (2000). Determining validity in qualitative inquiry. *Theory into Practice, 39*(3), 124–130.

Cuéllar Irala, J. & García-Falces Fernàndez, A. (2004). Cultura y humor: traductores al borde de un ataque de nervios. *LINGUAX. Revista de Lenguas Aplicadas,* https//www.uax.es/publicaciones/linguax/lintei004-04.

Culpeper, J. (1996). Towards an anatomy of impoliteness. *Journal of Pragmatics, 25*(3), 349–367.

Curran, W., McKeown, G. J., Rychlowska, M., André, E., Wagner, J., & Lingenfelser, F. (2018). Social context disambiguates the interpretation of laughter. *Frontiers in Psychology, 8,* 2342, 1–12.

Dale, J. A., Hudak M.A., and Wasikowski, P. (1991). Effects of dyadic participation and awareness of being monitored on facial action during exposure to humor. *Perceptual and motor skills, 73,* 984–986.

Damico, S. B. & Purkey, W. W. (1978). Class clowns: A study of middle school students. *American Educational Research Journal, 15*(3), 391–398.

Darwin, C. (1872). *The expression of the emotions in man and animals.* New York: D. Appleton & Company.

Davidson, D. (1984). *Inquiries into truth and interpretation.* Oxford: Oxford University Press.

Davies, A. P. & Apter, M. J. (1980). Humour and its effect on learning in children. In P. E. McGhee & A. J. Chapman (Eds.), *Children's humour* (pp. 237–253). Chichester: Wiley.

Davies, C. (1990). *Ethnic humor around the world: A comparative analysis.* Bloomington: Indiana University Press.

Davies, C. (2004). Victor Raskin on jokes. *HUMOR: International Journal of Humor Research, 17*(4), 373–380.

Davies, C. (2005). European ethnic scripts and the translation and switching of jokes. *HUMOR: International Journal of Humor Research,18*(2), 147–160.

Davies, C. E. (1984). Joint joking: Improvisational humorous episodes in conversation. In C. Brugman, M. Macaulay, A. Dahlstrom, M. Emanatian, B. M/. O'Connor (Eds.), *Proceedings of the Tenth Annual Meeting of the Berkeley Linguistics Society* (pp. 360–371). Berkeley: University of California.

Davies, C. E. (2003). How English-learners joke with native speakers: An interactional sociolinguistic perspective on humor as collaborative discourse across cultures. *Journal of Pragmatics, 35*(9), 1361–1385.

Davies, C. E. (2010). Joking as boundary negotiation among "good old boys": "White trash" as a social category at the bottom of the southern working class in Alabama. *HUMOR: International Journal of Humor Research, 23*(2), 179–200.

Davies, C. E. (2015). Humor in intercultural interaction as both content and process in the classroom. *HUMOR: International Journal of Humor Research, 28*(3), 375–395.

Davies, C. E. (2017). Sociolinguistic approaches to humor. In S. Attardo (Ed.), *The Routledge handbook of language and humor* (pp. 472–488). New York/London: Routledge.

Davis, J. M. (2003). *Farce.* New Brunswick/London: Transaction.

Davis, M. S. (1993). *What's so funny? The comic conception of culture and society.* Chicago: University of Chicago Press.

De Beaugrande, R. A. & Dressler, W. U. (1981). *Einführung im die Textlinguistik.* Tübingen: Max Niemeyer.

de León, C. M. (2008). Skopos and beyond: A critical study of functionalism. *Target. International Journal of Translation Studies, 20*(1), 1–28.

De Mey, T. (2005). Tales of the unexpected. Incongruity-resolution in humor comprehension, scientific discovery and thought experimentation. *Logic and Logical Philosophy, 14*(1), 69–88.

De Rosa, G. L., Bianchi, F., de Laurentiis, A., & Perego, E. (Eds.). (2014). *Translating Humour in Audiovisual Texts.* Bern: Peter Lang,

DeCamp, E. (2015). Humoring the audience: Performance strategies and persuasion in Midwestern American stand-up comedy. *HUMOR: International Journal of Humor Studies, 28*(3), 449–467.

Deckers, L. (1993). On the validity of a weight-judging paradigm for the study of humor. *HUMOR: International Journal of Humor Research, 6*(1), 43–56.

Deckers, L. & Kizer, P. (1975). Humor and the incongruity hypothesis. *The Journal of Psychology, 90*(2), 215–218.

Deckers, L., Thayer Buttram, R., & Winsted, D. (1989). The sensitization of humor responses to cartoons. *Motivation and Emotion, 13*(1), 71–81.

Deckers, L. & Winters, J. A. (1986). Surprise and humor in response to discrepantly short and/or heavy stimuli in a psychophysical task. *The Journal of General Psychology, 113*(1), 57–63.

Delabastita, D. (1987). Translating puns: Possibilities and restraints. *New Comparison, 3.* 143–159.

Delabastita, D. (1993). *There's a double tongue. An investigation into the translation of Shakespeare's wordplay.* Amsterdam/Atlanta: Rodopi.

Delabastita, D. (1996). Introduction. In D. Delabastita (Ed.), *Wordplay and translation,* special issue of *The Translator* 2(2), Manchester: St Jerome.

Delabastita, D. (1997). (Ed.), *Traductio. Essays on punning and translation.* Manchester: St. Jerome and Namur: Presses Universitaires de Namur.

Demjén, Z. (2016). Laughing at cancer: Humour, empowerment, solidarity and coping online. *Journal of Pragmatics, 101,* 18–30.

Demjén, Z. (2018). Complexity theory and conversational humour: Tracing the birth and decline of a running joke in an online cancer support community. *Journal of Pragmatics, 133,* 93–104.

Deneire, M. (1995). Humor and foreign language teaching. *HUMOR: International Journal of Humor Research, 8*(3), 285–298.

Derks, P. (1996). Twenty years of research on humor: A view from the edge. In A. J. Chapman & H. C. Foot (Eds.), *Humor and laughter: Theory, research, and applications* (pp. vii–xxv). New Brunswick: Transaction.

Derks, P. (2014). Complexity. In S. Attardo (Ed.) *Encyclopedia of humor studies.* (pp. 164–165) Los Angeles: Sage.

Derks, P., Gillikin, L. S., Bartolome-Rull, D. S., & Bogart, E. H. (1997). Laughter and electroencephalographic activity. *HUMOR: International Journal of Humor Research, 10*(3), 285–300.

Devereux, P. G. & Ginsburg, G. P. (2001). Sociality effects on the production of laughter. *The Journal of General Psychology, 128*(2), 227–240.

Díaz Perez, F. J. (2017). The translation of humour based on culture-bound terms in modern family. A cognitive-pragmatic approach. In J. J. Martiŋnez-Sierra & P. Zabalbeascoa (Eds.), *The translation of humour. Monografias de Traducción e interpretación, 9,* 49–75.

Díaz-Cintas, J., & Muñoz Sánchez, P. (2006). Fansubs: Audiovisual translation in an amateur environment. *Jostrans: The Journal of Specialised Translation, 6,* 37–52.

Di Maio, S. (2000). *A structured resource for computational humor.* Unpublished Doctoral dissertation. Siena, Italy: University of Siena.

Dindia, K. (2006). Men are from North Dakota, women are from South Dakota. In K. Dindia & D. J. Canary (Eds.), *Sex differences and similarities in communication* (pp. 3–20). Mahwah, NJ: Lawrence Erlbaum.

Di Pietro, G. (2012). More than words: A study of paralinguistic and kinesic features of humour in dubbed sitcoms. In B. Fisher & M. N. Jensen (Eds.) *Translation and the reconfiguration of power relations: Revisiting role and context of translation and interpreting* (pp. 167–190). Zurich: LIT Verlag.

Di Pietro, G. (2014). It don't mean a thing if you ain't got that sync—An analysis of word order, kinesic synchrony and comic timing in dubbed humor. In G. L. De Rosa, F. Bianchi, A. De Laurentiis, & E. Perego (Eds.), *Translating humour in audiovisual texts* (pp. 333–358). Bern: Lang.

Di Pietro, G. (2015). Show me the funny: A multimodal analysis of (non) verbal humour in dubbed sitcoms. In Cintas, J. D., & Neves, J. (Eds.), *Audiovisual translation: Taking stock* (pp. 87–123). Newcastle upon Tyne: Cambridge Scholars Publishing.

Di Pietro, G. (2016). Locating plurisemiotic features of humor in dubbing. In A. Bączkowska (Ed.), *Perspectives on translation* (pp. 181–210). Newcastle upon Tyne: Cambridge Scholars Publications.

Dionigi, A. & Canestrari, C. (2018). The role of laughter in cognitive-behavioral therapy: Case studies. *Discourse Studies*, 20(3), 323–339.

Dollard, J. (1939). The dozens: The dialect of insult. *American Imago, 1,* 3–24.

Dore, M. (Ed.) (2019). Humour in multimodal translation. *European Journal of Humor Research, 7*(1). 1–143. Special issue.

Downing, H. R. & Recuero, S. I. (2008). Humor e ironìa: una relaciòn compleja. [Humor and irony: a complex relationship]. In L. Ruiz Gurillo and X. A. Padilla Garcìa (Eds.), *Dime còmo ironizas y te dirò quièn eres: Una aproximacion pragmàtica a la ironìa* (pp. 423–455). Frankfurt: Peter Lang.

Downs, V. C., Javidi, M., & Nussbaum, J. F. (1988). An analysis of teachers' verbal communication within the college classroom: Use of humor, self-disclosure and narratives. *Communication and Education (37)*(2), 127–141.

Drew, Paul. (1987). Po-faced receipts of teases. *Linguistics, 25,* 219–253.

Ducrot, O. (1984). *Le dire et le dit.* Paris: Editions de Minuit.

Duguid, A. (2009). Loud signatures: Comparing evaluative discourse styles and patterns in rants and riffs. In U. Romer & R. Schulze (Eds.), *Exploring the lexis-grammar interface* (pp. 289–315). Amsterdam: John Benjamins.

Dundes, A. (1973). *Mother Wit from Laughing Barrel.* Jackson. MS/London: University Press of Mississippi.

Dundes, A. (1987). *Cracking jokes: Studies of sick humor cycles and stereotypes.* Berkeley, CA: Ten Speed Press.

Dundes, A., Leach, J. W., & Özkök, B. (1970). The strategy of Turkish boys' verbal dueling rhymes. *The Journal of American Folklore, 83*(329), 325–349. (Reprinted in *Directions in sociolinguistics,* pp. 130-160, by Gumperz, J. & Hymes, D. (Eds.), *Directions in Sociolinguistics.* New York: Holt, 1972.)

Duruaku, T. (2015). Animated graphic film for the rejuvenation of a fading culture: The case of an African oral heritage. *African Journal of History and Culture, 7*(6), 123–132.

Dynel, M. (2009a). Beyond a joke: Types of conversational humour. *Language and Linguistics Compass, 3*(5), 1284–1299.

Dynel, M. (2009b). *Humorous garden-paths*. Newcastle upon Tyne: Cambridge Scholars.

Eastmond, J. N. Jr. (1992). Probing project humor for insights in ethnography: A case study. ERIC ED353322. 1–12. https://eric.ed.gov/?id=ED353322

Ebeogu, A. (1991). Njakiri, the quintessence of the traditional Igbo sense of satire. In G. Benneth (Ed.), *Spoken in jest.* (pp. 29–46). Sheffield, UK: Sheffield Academic Press.

Eco, U. (1979). *Lector in fabula*. Milan: Bompiani.

Eco, U. (2003a). *Mouse or Rat. Translation as negotiation*. London: Phoenix.

Eco, U. (2003b). *Dire quasi la stessa cosa*. Esperienze di traduzione. Milan: Bompiani.

Edge, J. & Richards, K. (1998). May I see your warrant, please?: Justifying outcomes in qualitative research. *Applied linguistics, 19*(3), 334–356.

Edwards, C. L. (1984). "Stop me if you've heard this one": Narrative disclaimers as breakthrough into performance. *Fabula. Zeitschrift für Erzählforschung.* 25(3–4), 214–228.

Edwards, D. (2005). Moaning, whinging and laughing: The subjective side of complaints. *Discourse Studies 7*(1), 5–29.

Eisterhold, Jodi, Attardo, S., & Boxer, D. (2006). Reactions to irony in discourse: Evidence for the least disruption principle. *Journal of Pragmatics, 38*(8), 1239–1256.

Ekman, P. & Friesen, W. V. (1969). Nonverbal leakage and clues to deception. *Psychiatry, 32*(1), 88–106.

Ekman, P. & Friesen, W. V. (1978). *Facial action coding system*. Palo Alto, CA: Consulting Psychologists Press.

Ekman, P., Levenson, R.W., & Friesen, W. V. (1983). Autonomic nervous system activity distinguishes among emotions. *Science, 221*, 1208–1210.

El-Arousy, N. A. (2007). Towards a functional approach to the translation of Egyptian cartoons. *Humor: International Journal of Humor Research, 20*(3), 297–321.

Emerson, J. P. (1969). Negotiating the serious import of humor. *Sociometry, 32* (2), 169–181.

Empson, William. (1947). *Seven types of ambiguity* (US edition). New York: New Direction.

Ermida, I. (2008). *The Language of Comic Narratives: Humor construction in short stories*. Berlin: Mouton de Gruyter.

Everts, E. (2003). Identifying a particular family humor style: A sociolinguistic discourse analysis. *HUMOR: International Journal of Humor Studies, 16*(4), 369–412.

Eysenck, H. J. (1942). The appreciation of humour: An experimental and theoretical study. *British Journal of Psychology, 32,* 295–309.

Fatigante, M. & Orletti, F. (2013). Laughter and smiling in a three-party medical encounter: Negotiating participants? Alignment in delicate moments. In P. Glenn & E. Holt (Eds.), *Studies of laughter in interaction* (pp. 161–183). London: Bloomsbury.

Fauconnier, G. (1985). *Les espaces mentaux.* Paris: Editions de Minuit. Engl. trans. Mental Spaces. Cambridge: MIT Press. (Original work published 1984)

Ferrari, C. F. (2011). *Since when is Fran Drescher Jewish?: Dubbing stereotypes in The Nanny, The Simpsons, and The Sopranos.* Austin, TX: University of Texas Press.

Ferro-Luzzi, G. E. (1990). Tamil jokes and the polythetic-prototype approach to humor. *HUMOR: International Journal of Humor Studies, 3*(2), 147–158.

Festinger, L. (1957). *A theory of cognitive dissonance.* Stanford, CA: Stanford University Press.

Filkuková, P. & Klempe, S. H. (2013). Rhyme as reason in commercial and social advertising. *Scandinavian Journal of Psychology, 54*(5), 423–431.

Fillmore, C. J. (1981). Pragmatics and the description of discourse. In P. Cole (Ed.), *Radical pragmatics* (pp. 143–166), New York: Academic Press.

Fillmore, C. J. (1982). Frame semantics. In The Linguistic Society of Korea (Ed.), *Linguistics in the morning calm* (pp. 111–137). Seoul, Korea: Hanshin.

Fillmore, C. J. (1985). Frames and the semantics of understanding. *Quaderni di Semantica, 6*(2), 222–254.

Fitzpatrick, T. (2013). Word associations. In C. A. Chapelle (Ed.), *Encyclopedia of applied linguistics* (pp. 6193–6199). Oxford: Wiley-Blackwell.

"Five Graces Group", Beckner, C., Blythe, R., Bybee, J., Christiansen, M. H., Croft, W.,... & Schoenemann, T. (2009). Language is a complex adaptive system: Position paper. *Language learning, 59,* 1–26.

Flamson, T., Bryant, G. A., & Barrett, H. C. (2011). Prosody in spontaneous humor: Evidence for encryption. *Pragmatics & Cognition, 19*(2), 248–267.

Foot H. C., Chapman A. J., and Smith J. R. (1977). Friendship and social responsiveness in boys and girls. *Journal of Personality and Social Psychology, 35,* 401–411.

Forabosco, G. (1992). Cognitive aspects of the humor process: the concept of incongruity. *HUMOR: International Journal of Humor Research, 5*(1), 45–68.

Forabosco, G. (1994). Seriality and appreciation of jokes. *HUMOR: International Journal of Humor Research, 7*(4), 351–375.

Ford, C. E. & Fox, B. A. (2010). Multiple practices for constructing laughables. In D. Barth-Weingarten, E. Reber, & M. Selting (Eds.), *Prosody in interaction* (pp. 339–368). Amsterdam, Netherlands: John Benjamins.

Ford, T. (2014). Humor mindset. In S. Attardo (Ed.), *Encyclopedia of Humor Studies* (pp. 361–362), Los Angeles: Sage.

Forman, R. (2011). Humorous language play in a Thai EFL classroom. *Applied Linguistics, 32*(5), 541–565.

Frank, M. G. & Ekman, P. (1993). Not all smiles are created equal: The differences between enjoyment and nonenjoyment smiles. *HUMOR: International Journal of Humor Research, 6*(1), 9–26.

Frank, M. G., Ekman, P., & Friesen, W. V. (1993). Behavioral markers and recognizability of the smile of enjoyment. *Journal of Personality and Social Psychology, 64*(1), 83. Reprinted in P. Ekman & E. L. Rosenberg (Eds.), *What the face reveals: Basic and applied studies of spontaneous expression using the Facial Action Coding System (FACS)* Oxford: Oxford University Press.

Freud, S. (1905). *Der Witz und seine Beziehung zum Unbewussten*. Leipzig: Deuticke. (Original work published 1905) Engl. Tr. *Jokes and their relation to the unconscious*. New York: Norton. 1960.

Fridlund, A. J. (1991). Sociality of solitary smiling: Potentiation by an implicit audience. *Journal of Personal and Social Psychology, 60*, 229–240.

Fridlund, A. J. (1994). *Human facial expression: An evolutionary view*. San Diego, CA: Academic Press.

Fry, W. F., Jr. (1963). *Sweet madness: A study of humor*. Palo Alto, CA: Pacific Books Publishers.

Fuentes Luque, A. F. (1998). Humor, cine y traducción?, In Leandro Fèlix y Emilio Ortega (Eds.), *II Estudios sobre traducción e interpretación (Actas de las II Jornadas Internacionales de Traducción e Interpretación de la Universidad de Málaga)* (Vol. II) (pp. 665–672). Málaga: Diputación de Málaga.

Fuentes Luque, A. F. (2004). Reír o no reír, esa es la cuestión: La traducción del humor verbal audiovisual. Estudio descriptivo de un fragmento de Duck Soup, de los Hermanos Marx. *Puentes, 3*, 77–85.

Fuentes Luque, A. F. (2010). On the (mis/over/under) translation of the Marx Brothers' Humour. In Chiaro, D. (Ed.) *Translating humor in the media. Translation, humour and the media: Translation and Humour, Volume 2*, 175–192.

Garmendia, J. (2010). Irony is critical. *Pragmatics and Cognition, 18*(2), 379–421.

Gasquet-Cyrus, M. (2004). *Pratiques et représentations de l'humour verbal. Étude sociolinguistique du cas marseillais* (Unpublished doctoral dissertation). Université de Aix-Marseille I, Marseille, France. OCLC Number 491429888.

REFERENCES

Gavanski, I. (1986). Differential sensitivity of humor ratings and mirth responses to cognitive and affective components of the humor response. *Journal of Personality and Social Psychology, 51*, 209–214.

Gavioli, L. (1995). Turn-initial versus turn-final laughter: Two techniques for initiating remedy in English/Italian bookshop service encounters. *Discourse Processes, 19*(3), 369–384.

Gerber, W. S. & Routh, D. K. (1975). Humor response as related to violation of expectancies and to stimulus intensity in a weight-judgment task. *Perceptual and Motor Skills, 41*(2), 673–674.

Gervais, M. & Wilson, D. S. (2005). The evolution and functions of laughter and humor: A synthetic approach. *The Quarterly Review of Biology, 80*, 395–430.

Gibbs, R. W. Jr. (2000). Irony in talk among friends. *Metaphor & Symbol, 15*, 5–27.

Gibbs, R. W. (2012). Are ironic acts deliberate? *Journal of Pragmatics, 44*, 104–115.

Gibbs, R. W. & Colston, H. (Eds.) (2007). *Irony in language and thought: A cognitive science reader.* Lawrence Erlbaum.

Giles, H. & Oxford, G. S. (1970). Towards a Multidimensional Theory of Laughter Causation and its Social Implications. *Bulletin of British Psychology Society, 23*, 97–105.

Giora, R. (2003). *On our mind: Salience, context and figurative language.* Oxford: Oxford University Press.

Gironzetti, E. (2017a). Prosodic and multimodal markers of humor. In Attardo, S (Ed.), *The Routledge Handbook of Language and Humor.* (pp. 400–413). London and New York: Routledge.

Gironzetti, E. (2017b). *Multimodal and eye-tracking evidence in the negotiation of pragmatic intentions in dyadic conversations: The case of humorous discourse.* Texas A&M University-Commerce. Commerce, TX. Unpublished PhD Dissertation.

Gironzetti, E., Attardo, S., & Pickering, L. (2016). Smiling, gaze, and humor in conversation. In Ruiz-Gurillo, L. (Ed.), *Metapragmatics of Humor: Current research trends* (pp. 235–254). Amsterdam/Philadelphia: Benjamins.

Gironzetti, E., Pickering, L., Huang, M., Zhang, Y., Menjo, S., & Attardo, S. (2016). Smiling synchronicity and gaze patterns in dyadic humorous conversations. *HUMOR: International Journal of Humor Studies, 29*(2), 301–324.

Glenn, P. (1989). Initiating shared laughter. *Western Journal of Speech Communication, 53*(2), 127–149.

Glenn, P. (2003). *Laughter in interaction.* Cambridge: Cambridge University Press.

Glenn, P. & Holt, E. (Eds.) (2013). *Studies of laughter in interaction.* London: Bloomsbury.

Glenn, P. & Holt, E. (2017). Conversation analysis of humor. In Attardo, S (Ed.), *The Routledge handbook of language and humor.* (pp. 295–308.) London and New York: Routledge.

Goatly, A. (2012). *Meaning and humor.* Cambridge: Cambridge University Press.

Goel, V. & Dolan, R. J. (2001). The functional anatomy of humor: Segregating cognitive and affective components. *Nature Neuroscience, 4*(3), 237–238.

Goffman, E. (1974). *Frame analysis. An essay on the organization of experience.* Cambridge, MA: Harvard University Press.

Goffman, E. (1981). *Forms of talk.* Philadelphia: University of Pennsylvania Press.

Goldstein, J. H. & McGhee, P. E. (Eds.) (1972). *The psychology of humor.* London/New York: Academic Press.

Goldstein, J. H. & Ruch, W. (2018). Paul McGhee and humor research. *HUMOR: International Journal of Humor Research, 31*(2), 169–181.

Gottlieb, H. (1997). You got the picture? In D. Delabastita (Ed.), *Traductio. Essays on punning and translation* (pp. 207–232). London/New York: Routledge.

Graesser, A. C., Long, D. L., & Mio, J. S. (1989). What are the cognitive and conceptual components of humorous text? *Poetics, 18,* 143–163.

Grant, M. A. (1924). *The ancient rhetorical theories of the laughable: the Greek rhetoricians and Cicero.* Madison: University of Wisconsin.

Greimas, A. J. (1966). *Sémantique structurale.* Paris: Larousse. Engl. Tr. *Structural Semantics.* Lincoln: U. of Nebraska P. 1983.

Grice, H. P. (1957). Meaning. *The Philosophical Review, 66*(3), 377–388.

Grice, H. P. (1975). Logic and conversation. In Peter Cole, and Jerry Morgan (eds.), *Syntax and semantics.* Vol. 3. *Speech Acts.* New York: Academic. 41–59.

Grice, H. P. (1989). *Studies in the way of words.* Harvard University Press.

Groos, K. (1898). *The play of animals.* (E. L. Baldwin, Trans.) New York: Appleton. (Original work published 1896.)

Gruner, C. R. (1978). *Understanding laughter.* Chicago: Nelson Hall.

Gruner, C. R. (1997). *The game of humor: A comprehensive theory of why we laugh.* New Brunswick, NJ: Transaction Publishers.

Guagnano, D. (2013). *L'umorismo e l'implicito.* Rome: Aracne.

Guidi, A. (2012a). *Il gioco di parole e le lingue: Dalla semantica alla pragmatica.* Perugia: Guerra.

Guidi, A. (2012b). Are pun mechanisms universal? A comparative analysis across language families. *HUMOR: International Journal of Humor Research, 25,* 339–366.

Guiraud, P. (1979). *Les jeux de mots* (2nd ed.). Paris: Presses Universitaires de France.

Gumperz, J. J. (1964). Linguistic and social interaction in two communities. *American Anthropologist, 66*(6), 137–153.

Gumperz, J. J. (1972). Introduction In Gumperz, J. J. & D. Hymes (1972).

Gumperz, J. J. (1977). Sociocultural knowledge in conversational inference, *28tn Annual Roundtable on Languages and Linguistics*. Washington, DC: Georgetown UP.

Gumperz, J. J. (1992). Contextualization and understanding. In A. Duranti. & C. Goodwin (Eds.), *Rethinking context: Language as an interactive phenomenon* (pp. 229–252). Cambridge: Cambridge University Press.

Gumperz, J. J. (2015). Interactional sociolinguistics: a personal perspective. In Tannen, D., Hamilton, H. E., & Schiffrin, D. (Eds.), *The handbook of discourse analysis* (pp. 309–323). Chichester: John Wiley & Sons.

Gumperz, J. J. & Hymes, D. H. (Eds.) (1972). *Directions in sociolinguistics: The ethnography of communication*. New York: Holt, Rinehart and Winston.

Günther, U. (2003). What's in a laugh? Humour, jokes and laughter in the conversational corpus of the BNC (Unpublished doctoral dissertation). University of Freiburg, Freiburg, Germany.

Haakana, M. (2001). Laughter as a patient's resource: dealing with delicate aspects of medical interaction. *Text, 21*, 187–219.

Haakana, M. (2002). Laughter in medical interaction: From quantification to analysis, and back. *Journal of Sociolinguistics, 6*, 207–235.

Haakana, M. (2010). Laughter and smiling: Notes on co-occurrences. *Journal of Pragmatics, 42*(6), 1499–1512.

Haiman, J. (1990). Sarcasm as theater. *Cognitive Linguistics, 1*(2), 181–205.

Haiman, J. (1998). *Talk is cheap: Sarcasm, alienation, and the evolution of language*. New York: Oxford University.

Halula, S. P. (2013). What role does humor in the higher education classroom play in student-perceived instructor effectiveness? (Unpublished doctoral dissertation.) Marquette University.

Hamilton, T. (2013). *Humorous structures of English narratives, 1200–1600*. Newcastle-upon-Tyne: Cambridge Scholars Publishing.

Hamrick, P. (2007). Notes on some cognitive mechanisms of humor. In D. Popa & S. Attardo (Eds.), *New approaches to the linguistics of humor* (pp. 140–150). Galati, Rumenia: Editura Academica.

Han, Q. (2011). On untranslatability of English linguistic humor. *Theory and Practice in Language Studies, 1*(2), 149–152.

Harmon-Jones, E. (1999). *Cognitive Dissonance: Progress on a Pivotal Theory in Social Psychology*. Washington, DC: APA Books.

Harrison, C. (2013). *Difficulties of translating humour: From English into Spanish using the subtitled British comedy sketch show "Little Britain" as a case study*. Hamburg: Anchor Academic Publisher.

Haugh, M. (2010). Jocular mockery, (dis)affiliation, and face. *Journal of Pragmatics, 42*(8), 2106–2119.

Haugh, M. (2014). Jocular mockery as interactional practice in everyday Anglo-Australian conversation. *Australian Journal of Linguistics, 34*(1), 76–99.

Haugh, M. (2016). "Just kidding": Teasing and claims to non-serious intent. *Journal of Pragmatics, 95*, 120–136.

Haugh, M. (2017a). Mocking and (non-)seriousness in initial interactions amongst American and Australian speakers of English. In D. Carbaugh (Ed.), *Handbook of communication in cross-cultural perspective* (pp. 104–117). New York/London: Routledge.

Haugh, M. (2017b). Teasing. In S. Attardo (Ed.), *The Routledge handbook of language and humor* (pp. 204–218), New York/London: Routledge.

Haugh, M. (2017c). Jocular language play, social action and (dis)affiliation in conversational interaction. In Bell, N. (Ed.), *Multiple perspectives on language play* (pp. 143–168). Berlin: Mouton De Gruyter.

Haugh, M. & Bousfield, D. (2012). Mock impoliteness, jocular mockery and jocular abuse in Australian and British English. *Journal of Pragmatics, 44*(9), 1099–1114.

Haugh, M. & Pillet-Shore, D. (2017). Getting to know you: Teasing as an invitation to intimacy in initial interactions. *Discourse Studies, 20*(2), 246–269.

Hausmann, F. J. (1974). *Studien zu einer Linguistik des Wortspiels. Das Wortspiel im Canard Enchaîné.* Tübingen: Niemeyer.

Hay, J. (1994). Jocular abuse patterns in mixed-group interaction. *Wellington Working Papers in Linguistics, 6*, 26–55.

Hay, J. (1995). *Gender and humour: Beyond a joke.* (Unpublished MA Thesis.) Wellington: Victoria University of Wellington.

Hay, J. (2000). Functions of humor in the conversations of women and men. *Journal of Pragmatics, 32*, 709–742.

Hay, J. (2001). The pragmatics of humor support. *HUMOR: International Journal of Humor Research, 14*(1), 55–82.

Heath, C. (1988). Embarrassment and interactional organisation. In P. Drew & A. Wootton (Eds.), *Erving Goffman: Exploring the interactional order* (pp.136–160). Cambridge: Polity.

Heidari-Shahreza, M. A. (2018). A cross-sectional analysis of teacher-initiated verbal humor and ludic language play in an English as a foreign language (EFL) context. *Cogent Education, 5*(1). 1430474.

Hempelmann, C. (2003). *Paronomasic puns: Target recoverability towards automatic generation* (Unpublished doctoral dissertation). Purdue University, West Lafayette, Indiana.

Hempelmann, C. F. (2017). Key terms in the field of humor. In S. Attardo (Ed.), *The Routledge handbook of language and humor* (pp. 34–48). New York/London: Routledge.

Hempelmann, C. F. & Attardo, S. (2011). Resolutions and their incongruities: Further thoughts on logical mechanisms. *HUMOR: International Journal of Humor Research*, 24(2), 125–149.

Hempelmann, C. F. & Miller, T. (2017). Puns: Taxonomy and phonology. In S. Attardo (Ed.), *The Routledge handbook of language and humor* (pp. 95–108). New York: Taylor and Francis.

Hempelmann, C. F. & Ruch, W. (2005). 3 WD meets GTVH: Breaking the ground for interdisciplinary humor research. *HUMOR: International Journal of Humor Research*, 18(4), 353–387.

Hempelmann, C. F. & Samson, A. (2007). Visual puns and verbal puns: Descriptive analogy or false analogy. In D. Popa & S. Attardo (Eds.), *New Approaches to the linguistics of humour* (pp. 180–196). Galati: Editura Academica.

Hempelmann, C. F. & Samson, A. (2008). Cartoons: Drawn jokes? In Victor Raskin (ed.), *The primer of humor research.* (pp. 609–640). Berlin, New York: Mouton de Gruyter.

Henry, J. (2003). *La traduction des jeux de mots.* Paris: Presses Sorbonne Nouvelle.

Hepburn, A. & Varney, S. (2013). Beyond ((laughter)): Some notes on transcription. In Glenn, P. and Holt, E. (Eds.). *Studies of laughter in interaction.* (pp. 25–38.) London: Bloomsbury.

Heritage, J. (1984). *Garfinkel and ethnomethodology.* Cambridge: Polity Press.

Herrick, M. T. (1949). The theory of the laughable in the sixteenth century. *Quarterly Journal of Speech*, 35(1), 1–16.

Hjelmslev, L. (1953). *Prolegomena to a theory of language.* 2nd ed. Madison, WI: University of Wisconsin.

Hockett, C. F. (1973). Jokes. In M. E. Smith (ed.), *Studies in linguistics in honor of George L. Trager.* (pp. 153–178.) The Hague: Mouton. Reprinted in Hockett, C. F. (1977). *The view from the language* (pp. 257–289). Athens: University of Georgia.

Hodson, R. J. (2014). Teaching 'humour competence'. Knowledge, skills and competencies in foreign language education. Proceeding of CLaSIC (pp. 149–161).

Hofstadter, D. & Gabora, L. (1989). Synopsis of the workshop on humor and cognition. *HUMOR: International Journal of Humor Research*, 2(4), 417–440.

Hoicka, E. & Butcher, J. (2016). Parents produce explicit cues that help toddlers distinguish joking and pretending. *Cognitive Science*, 40(4), 941–971.

Hoicka, E. & Gattis, M. (2012). Acoustic differences between humorous and sincere communicative intentions. *British Journal of Developmental Psychology, 30*(4), 531–549.

Holcomb, C. (1992). Nodal humor in comic narrative: a semantic analysis of two stories by Twain and Wodehouse. *HUMOR: International Journal of Humor Research, 5*(3), 233–250.

Holcomb, C. (1997). A class of clowns: Spontaneous joking in computer-assisted discussions. *Computers and Composition, 14*(1), 3–18.

Holmes, J. (1995). *Women, Men and Politeness.* London: Longman.

Holmes, J. (2000). Politeness, power and provocation: how humor functions in the workplace. *Discourse Studies, 2*(2), 159–185.

Holmes, J. & Marra, M. (2002). Having a laugh at work: How humour contributes to workplace culture. *Journal of Pragmatics, 34*(12), 1683–1710.

Holmes, J., Marra, M., & Burns, L. (2001). Women's humour in the workplace: A quantitative analysis. *Australian Journal of Communication, 28*(1), 83–108.

Holmes, J. & Schnurr, S. (2005). Politeness, humor and gender in the workplace: negotiating norms and identifying contestation. *Journal of Politeness Research, 1*(1), 121–149.

Holt, E. (2011). On the nature of 'laughables': Laughter as a response to overdone figurative phrases. *Pragmatics, 21*(3), 393–410.

Holt, E. (2017). "This system's so slow": Negotiating sequences of laughter and laughables in call-centre interaction. In Bell, N. (Ed.), *Multiple perspectives on language play (language play and creativity)* (pp. 93–118). Berlin: Mouton De Gruyter.

Huang, C. R., N. Calzolari, A. Gangemi, A. Lenci, A. Oltramari, & L. Prévot (Eds.) (2010). *Ontology and the lexicon: A natural language processing perspective.* Cambridge University Press.

Hurley, M. M., Dennett, D. C., & Adams, R. B., Jr. (2011). *Inside jokes.* Cambridge, MA: MIT Press.

Hymes, D. (1964). Introduction: Toward Ethnographies of Communication. *American anthropologist, 66*(6), 1–34.

Hymes, D. (1972a). Models of the interaction of language and social life. In J. J. Gumperz & D. Hymes (Eds.), *Directions in sociolinguistics: The ethnography of communication* (pp. 35–71). New York: Holt, Rinehart & Winston.

Hymes, D. (1972b). Toward ethnographies of communication. In Giglioli, P.(ed.) *Language and social context.*

Iaia, P. L. (2014). Transcreating humor in video games: The use of Italian diatopic varieties and their effects on target audiences. In G. L. De Rosa, F. Bianchi, A. De Laurentiis, & E. Perego (Eds.). *Translating humour in audiovisual texts.* (pp. 517–533). Bern, Switzerland: Peter Lang.

Ikeda, K. & Bysouth, D. (2013). Laughter and turn-taking: Warranting next speakership in multiparty interactions. In P. Glenn & E. Holt (Eds.), *Studies of laughter in interaction* (pp. 39–64). London: Bloomsbury.

Iwase, M., Y. Ouchi, H. Okada, C. Yokoyama, S. Nobezawa, E. Yoshikawa, et al. (2002). Neural substrates of human facial expression of pleasant emotion induced by comic films: a PET study. *Neuroimage 17*, 758–768.

Jackman, H. (2003). Charity, self-interpretation, and belief. *Journal of Philosophical Research, 28*, 143–168.

Jakobson, R. (1960). Linguistics and poetics. In T. A. Sebeok (ed.), *Style in Language* (pp. 350–377). Cambridge: MIT Press.

Jakobson, R. (1987). *Language in literature*. Cambridge, MA/London: Belknap-Harvard.

Janko, R. (1984). *Aristotle on comedy. Towards a reconstruction of poetics II*. Berkeley/Los Angeles: University of California Press.

Jared, D. & Bainbridge, S. (2017). Reading homophone puns: Evidence from eye tracking. *Canadian Journal of Experimental Psychology, 71*(1), 2–13.

Javidi, M. M., Downs, V. C., & Nussbaum, J. F. (1988). A comparative analysis of teachers' use of dramatic style behaviors at higher and secondary educational levels. *Communication Education, 37*, 278–288.

Jefferson, G. (1972). Side sequences. In D. Sudnow (Ed.), *Studies in social interaction* (pp. 294–338). New York–London: The Free Press–Collier-Macmillan.

Jefferson, G. (1979). A technique for inviting laughter and its subsequent acceptance declination. In G. Psathas (Ed.), *Everyday language. Studies in ethnomethodology* (pp. 79–96). New York: Irvington.

Jefferson, G. (1984). On the organization of laughter in talk about troubles. In J. M. Atkinson, & J. Heritage (Eds.), *Structures of social action* (pp. 356–369). Cambridge: Cambridge University.

Jefferson, G. (1985). An exercise in the transcription and analysis of laughter. In T. A. Van Dijk (Ed.), *Handbook of discourse analysis* (Vol. 3). London: Academic. 25–34.

Jefferson, G. H. Sacks & Schegloff, E. (1977). Some notes on laughing together. *Pragmatics Microfiche*. 1:8.

Jefferson, G., Sacks, H., & Schegloff, E. (1987). Notes on laughter in pursuit of intimacy. In G. Button, & J. Lee (Eds.), *Talk and social organization* (pp. 152–205). Clevedon, England: Multilingual Matters.

Jenkins, M. (1985). What's so funny? Joking among women. In S. Bremner, S., N. Caskey, & B. Moonwomon (Eds.), *Proceedings of the First Berkeley Women and Language Conference* (pp. 135–151). Berkeley, CA: Berkeley Women and Language Group.

Jessen, F., Erb, M., Klose, U., Lotze, M., Grodd, W., & Heun, R. (1999). Activation of human language processing brain regions after the presentation of random letter strings demonstrated with event-related functional magnetic resonance imaging. *Neuroscience Letters, 270*(1), 13–16.

Just, M. A. & Carpenter, P. A. (1980). A theory of reading: From eye fixations to comprehension. *Psychological review, 87*(4), 329–354.

Kaplan, R. M. & Pascoe, G. C. (1977). Humorous lectures and humorous examples: Some effects upon comprehension and retention. *Journal of Educational Psychology, 69*(1), 61–65.

Karman, Barbara. (1998). Postmodern Power Plays: A Linguistic Analysis of Postmodern Comedy. Unpublished M.A. thesis. Youngstown, OH: Youngstown State University

Kaukomaa, T., Peräkylä, A., & Ruusuvuori, J. (2013). Turn-opening smiles: Facial expression constructing emotional transition in conversation. *Journal of Pragmatics, 55*, 21–42.

Keith-Spiegel, P. (1972). Early conception of humor: varieties and issues. In Goldstein, J. H., & McGhee, P. E. (Eds.), *The psychology of humor* (pp. 3–39). London/New York: Academic Press.

Kihara, C. P. (2015). Mchongoano and the Ethnography of Communication. *University of Nairobi Journal of Language and Linguistics, 4*, 1–19.

Kintsch, W. (1998). *Comprehension: A paradigm for cognition.* Cambridge: Cambridge University Press.

Klein, D. M., Bryant, J., & Zillmann, D. (1982). Relationship between humor in introductory textbooks and students' evaluations of the texts' appeal and effectiveness. *Psychological Reports, 50*(1), 235–241.

Klungervik-Greenall, A. J. (2003). Lecture 13: Jokes. Unpublished paper.

Kochman, T. (1983). The boundary between play and nonplay in black verbal dueling. *Language in Society, 12*(3), 329–337.

Koester, A. (2010). *Workplace discourse.* London/New York: Continuum.

Koestler, A. (1964). *The act of creation.* London: Hutchinson.

Koller, M. R. (1988). *Humor and society: Explorations in the sociology of humor.* Houston, TX: Cap and Gown.

Kotthoff, H. (1996). Impoliteness and conversational joking: On relational politics. *Folia Linguistica, 30*(3-4), 299–326.

Kotthoff, H. (1999). Coherent keying in conversational humour: Contextualising joint fictionalisation. In W. Bublitz, U. Lenk, & E. Ventola (Eds.), *Coherence in spoken and written discourse.* (pp. 125–150). Amsterdam: Benjamins.

Kotthoff, H. (2000). Gender and joking: On the complexities of women's image politics in humorous narratives. *Journal of Pragmatics, 32*(1), 55–80.

Kotthoff, H. (2003). Responding to irony in different contexts: On cognition in conversation. *Journal of Pragmatics, 35*(9), 1387–1411.

Kotthoff, H. (2006). Gender and humor: The state of the art. *Journal of Pragmatics, 38*(1), 4–25.

Kotthoff, H. (2007). Oral genres of humour: On the dialectic of genre knowledge and creative authoring. *Pragmatics, 17,* 263–296.

Kotthoff, H. (2009). Joint construction of humorous fictions in conversation. An unnamed narrative activity in a playful keying. *Journal of Literary Theory, 3*(2), 195–217.

Krikmann, A. (2014). Bisociation. In S. Attardo (Ed.), *Encyclopedia of humor studies* (pp. 83–84). Los Angeles: Sage.

Kruger, J., & Dunning, D. (1999). Unskilled and unaware of it: How difficulties in recognizing one's own incompetence lead to inflated self-assessments. *Journal of Personality and Social Psychology, 77*(6), 1121–1134.

Kuhn, T. S. (1962). *The structure of scientific revolutions.* Chicago: University of Chicago Press.

Kuipers, G. (2005). "Where was King Kong when we needed him?" Public discourse, digital disaster jokes, and the functions of laughter after 9/11. *The Journal of American Culture, 28*(1), 70–84.

Labov, W. (1972). *Language in the inner city.* Philadelphia: University of Pennsylvania Press.

Lakoff, R. (1975). *Language and woman's place.* New York: Harper.

Landheer, R. (1989). L'ambiguïté: Un défi traductologique. *Meta: Journal des traducteurs/Meta: Translators' Journal, 34*(1), 33–43.

Larkin Galiñanes, C. L. (2005). Funny fiction; or, jokes and their relation to the humorous novel. *Poetics Today, 26*(1), 79–111.

Larkin Galiñanes, C. L. (2017). An overview of humor theory. In S. Attardo (Ed.) *The Routledge handbook of language and humor.* (pp. 4–16). New York: Routledge.

Larsen-Freeman, D. & Cameron, L. (2008). *Complex systems and applied linguistics.* Oxford: Oxford University Press

Latta, R. L. (1998). *The basic humor process: A cognitive-shift theory and the case against incongruity.* Berlin/New York: Mouton de Gruyter.

Lavin, D. & Maynard, D. W. (2001). Standardization vs. rapport: Respondent laughter and interviewer reaction during telephone surveys. *American Sociological Review, 66,* 453–479.

Lawson, T. J., Downing, B., & Cetola, H. (1998). An attributional explanation for the effect of audience laughter on perceived funniness. *Basic and Applied Social Psychology, 20,* 243–249.

Lee, D. (2006). Humor in spoken academic discourse. *NUCB journal of language culture and communication, 8*(1), 49–68.

Leech, G. N. (1983). *Principles of pragmatics.* London: Longman.

Lefort, B. (1986). Des problèmes pour rire. A propos de quelques approches cognitivistes de l'humour et la drôlerie. *Bulletin de Psychologie, 40,* 183-195.

Lehrer, Adrienne. (1974). *Semantic fields and lexical structure.* Amsterdam: Benjamins.

Lehrer, A. & Kittay, E. F. (1992). *Frames, fields, and contrasts: New essays in semantic and lexical organization.* Hillsdale, NJ: Lawrence Erlbaum.

Lessard, D. (1991). Calembours et dessins d'humour. *Semiotica, 85*(1–2), 73–89.

Leventhal, H. & Cupchik, G. C. (1976). A process model of humor judgment. *Journal of Communication, 26,* 190–204.

Leventhal H. & Mace, W. (1970). The effect of laughter on evaluation of a slapstick movie. *Journal of Personality, 38,* 16–30.

Levinson, S. C. (2003). Contextualizing 'contextualization cues'. In Eerdmans, S. L., Prevignano, C. L., & Thibault, P. J. (Eds.), *Language and interaction: Discussions with John J. Gumperz* (pp. 31–39). Amsterdam: Benjamins.

Lew, R. (1996). *An ambiguity-based theory of the linguistic verbal joke in English* (Unpublished doctoral dissertation). Adam Mickiewicz University. Poznań.

Liao, C.-C. (2005). *Jokes, humor and good teachers.* Taipei: Crane.

Lipps, T. (1898). *Komik und Humor. Eine psychologish-ästhetische Untersuchung.* Hamburg/Leipzig: Voss.

Loewenstein, J. & Heath, C. (2009). The repetition-break plot structure: A cognitive influence on selection in the marketplace of ideas. *Cognitive Science, 33*(1), 1–19.

Loewenstein, J., Raghunathan, R., & Heath, C. (2011). The repetition-shift plot structure makes effective television advertisements. *Journal of Marketing, 75*(5), 105–119.

Loomans, D. & Kolberg, K. (2002). *The laughing classroom.* Tiburon: CA: H. J. Kramer.

Lopez, B. G. & J. Vaid (2017). Psycholinguistic approaches to humor. In S. Attardo (Ed.), *The Routledge handbook of language and humor* (pp. 267–281). New York: Taylor & Francis.

López González, C.R. (2017). Humorous elements and translation in animated feature films: DreamWorks (2001–2012). *MonTI. Monografías de Traducción e Interpretación, 9,* 279–305.

Lorini, E. & Castelfranchi, C. (2007). The cognitive structure of surprise: Looking for basic principles. *Topoi, 26*(1), 133–149.

Lotman, J. M. (1975). On the metalanguage of a typological description of culture. *Semiotica, 14*(2), 97–123.

Low, P. A. (2011). Translating jokes and puns. *Perspectives: Studies in Translatology, 19*(1), 59–70.

Lundberg, E. & Thurston, C. M. (1992). *If they are laughing they just may be listening.* Fort Collins, CO: Cottonwood Press.

Lynch, O. H. (2009). Kitchen antics: The importance of humor and maintaining professionalism at work. *Journal of Applied Communication Research, 37*(4), 444–464.

Lynch, O. H. (2010). Cooking with humor: In-group humor as social organization. *HUMOR: International Journal of Humor Research, 23*(2), 127–159.

Macaulay, R. K. (1987). The social significance of Scottish dialect humor. *International Journal of the Sociology of Language, 65,* 53–64.

Machlev, M. & Karlin, N. J. (2016). Understanding the relationship between different types of instructional humor and student learning. *SAGE Open, 6*(3), 2158244016670200.

Maier, N. R. F. (1932). A gestalt theory of humour. *British Journal of Psychology. 23.* 69–74.

Mallafrè, J. (1991). *Llengua de Tribu i Llengua de Polis: Bases d'una Traducció,* Barcelona: Quaderns Crema, Assaig.

Mallett, J. & A'hern, R. (1996). Comparative distribution and use of humour within nurse–patient communication. *International Journal of Nursing Studies, 33*(5), 530–550.

Malpass, L. F. & Fitzpatrick, E. D. (1959). Social facilitation as a factor in reaction to humor. *The Journal of Social Psychology, 50,* 295–303.

Mandelbrot, B. (1977). *The fractal geometry of nature.* New York: Freeman.

Mandler, J. M. (1984). *Stories, scripts, and scenes: Aspects of schema theory.* Hillsdale, NJ: Lawrence Earlbaum.

Marci, C. D., Moran, E. K., & Orr, S. P. (2004). Physiologic evidence for the interpersonal role of laughter during psychotherapy. *The Journal of Nervous and Mental Disease, 192*(10), 689–695.

Margolies, L. (2016). *Defending against "I'm just saying" and other verbal annoyances.* Retrieved from https://psychcentral.com/lib/defending-against-im-just-saying-and-other-verbal-annoyances/

Markiewicz, D. (1974). Effects of humor on persuasion. *Sociometry, 37*(3), 407–422.

Martin, D. M., Preiss, R. W., Gayle, B. M., & Allen, M. (2006). A meta-analytic assessment of the effect of humorous lectures on learning. In B. M., Gayle, R. W. Preiss, N. Burrell, & M. Allen (Eds.), *Classroom communication and instructional processes: Advances through meta-analysis* (pp. 295–313). Mahwah, NJ: L. Earlbaum.

Martin, G. N. & Gray, C. D. (1996). The effect of audience laughter on men's and women's response to humor. *The Journal of Social Psychology, 136,* 221–231.

Martin, G. N., Sadler, S. J., Barrett, C. E., & Beaven, A. (2008). Measuring responses to humor: How the testing context affects individuals' reaction to comedy. *HUMOR: International Journal of Humor Research, 2*(2), 143–155.

Martin, R. A. (2007). *The psychology of humor: An integrative approach.* Burlington, MA: Elsevier Academic.

Martin, R. A. (2014). Humor and gender: An overview of psychological research. In D. Chiaro & R. Baccolini (Eds.), *Gender and Humor: Interdisciplinary and international perspectives.* (pp. 123–146). New York: Routledge.

Martin, R. A., Puhlik-Doris, P., Larsen, G., Gray, J., & Weir, K. (2003). Individual differences in uses of humor and their relation to psychological well-being: Development of the Humor Styles Questionnaire. *Journal of research in personality, 37*(1), 48–75.

Martín de León, C. (2008). Skopos and beyond. A critical study of functionalism. *Target, 20*(1), 1–28.

Martìnez-Sierra, J. J. (2006). Translating audiovisual humour. A case study. *Perspectives: Studies in Translatology, 13*(4), 289–296.

Martìnez-Sierra, J. J. (2009). El papel del elemento visual en la traducción del humor en textos audiovisuales: ¿un problema o una ayuda? *TRANS, 13,* 139–148.

Martìnez-Sierra, J. J. & Zabalbeascoa, P. (Eds.) (2017). The translation of humour. *Monografias de Traducción e interpretación, 9.*

McGhee, P. E. (1972). On the cognitive origins of incongruity humor: Fantasy assimilation versus reality assimilation. In J. H. Goldstein & P. E. McGhee (Eds.), *The psychology of humor.* (pp. 61–79). New York, NY: Academic Press.

McGhee, P. E. & Goldstein, J. H. (Eds.). (1983). *Handbook of humor research.* New York/Berlin: Springer.

McGlone, M. S. & Tofighbakhsh, J. (1999). The Keats heuristic: Rhyme as reason in aphorism interpretation. *Poetics, 26*(4), 235–244.

McGraw, A. P. & Warren, C. (2010). Benign violations: Making immoral behavior funny. *Psychological Science, 21*(8), 1141–1149.

McIlvenny, P., Mettovaara, S., & Tapio, R. (1993). 'I really wanna make you laugh': Stand-up comedy and audience response. *Tampereen yliopiston Suomen kielen ja yleisen kielitieteen laitoksen julkaisuja.* [Folia, fennistica and linguistica: Proceedings of the Annual Finnish Linguistics Symposium, 16, May 1992. Tampere, Finland: Tampere University Finnish and General Linguistics Department Publications.] 16, 225–245.

McMorris, R. F., Boothroyd, R. A., & Pietrangelo, D. J. (1997). Humor in educational testing: A review and discussion. *Applied Measurement in Education, 10*(3), 269–297.

McNeely, R. (2002). Using humor in the classroom. Retrieved from http://www.nea.org/tools/52165.htm

Meany, M. M., Clark, T., & Laineste, L. (2014). Comedy, creativity, and culture: A metamodern perspective. *International Journal of Literary Humanities, 11*(4), 1–15.

Meara, P. (2009). *Connected words: Word associations and second language vocabulary acquisition* (Vol. 24). New York: Benjamins.

Medgyes, P. (2002). *Laughing matters: Humour in the language classroom.* Cambridge: Cambridge University Press.

Mehrabian, A. (1966). Immediacy: An indicator of attitudes in linguistic communication. *Journal of Personality, 34*(1), 26–34.

Mel'čuk, I. A. (1981). Meaning-Text Models: A recent trend in Soviet linguistics. *Annual Review of Anthropology, 10,* 27–62.

Metz, R. (2018). Subcutaneous Fitbits? These cows are modeling the tracking technology of the future. Retrieved from https://www.technologyreview.com/s/611144/cyborg-cows-are-coming-to-a-farm-near-you/

Meyers, M. & Knapp, J. (1980). *5600 Jokes for All Occasions.* New York: Avenel.

Milner, G. B. 1972. Homo ridens. Toward a semiotic theory of humor and laughter. *Semiotica,. 5,* 1–30.

Minsky, M. (1974). A framework for representing knowledge. MIT technical report. http://hdl.handle.net/1721.1/6089

Mitchell, A. (2007). Ancient Greek visual puns: A case study in visual humor. In D. Popa & S. Attardo (Eds.), *New approaches to the linguistics of humour* (pp. 197–216). Galati, Romania: Editura Academica.

Mitchell-Kernan, C. (1971). *Language behavior in a black urban community* (Technical Report No. 2). University of California, Language-Behavior Research Laboratory.

Mitchell-Kernan, C. (1972). Signifying and marking: Two Afro-American speech acts. In J. J. Gumperz & D. Hymes (Eds.), *Directions in sociolinguistics: The ethnography of communication* (pp. 161–179). Oxford: Blackwell.

Mobbs, D., M. Grecious, A.-A. Eiman, V. Menon, & A. Reiss. (2003). Humor modulates the mesolimbic rewards centers. *Neuron, 40,* 1041–1048.

Monro, D. H. (1951). *Argument of laughter.* Victoria: Melbourne University Press.

Mooney, A. (2004). Cooperation, violations and making sense. *Journal of Pragmatics, 36*(5), 899–920.

Morain, G. G. (1991). X-raying the international funny bone: A study exploring differences in the perception of humor across cultures. In J. A. Alatis (Ed.) *Georgetown University Round Table on Language and Linguistics.* (pp. 397–408.) Washington, DC: Georgetown University Press.

Moran, J. M., Wig, G. S., Adams, R. B. Jr., Janata, P., & M. Kelley (2004). Neural correlates of humor detection and appreciation. *NeuroImage, 21,* 1055–1060.

Morin, V. (1966). L'histoire drôle. *Communications, 8,* 102–119.

Morreall, J. (1987). *The philosophy of laughter and humor.* Albany, NY: State University of New York.

Morreall, J. (2009). *Comic relief. A comprehensive philosophy of humor.* Chichester: Wiley.

Morrison, J. (1940). A note concerning investigations on the constancy of audience laughter. *Sociometry, 3*(2), 179–185.

Mulkay, M. (1988). *On humor: Its nature and its place in modern society.* Cambridge: Blackwell.

Mullany, L. (2004). Gender, politeness and institutional power roles: Humour as a tactic to gain compliance in workplace business meetings. *Multilingua, 23,* 13–37.

Murphy, B. & Pollio, H. R. (1975). The many faces of humor. *The Psychological Record, 25*(4), 545–558.

Nahemow, L., McCluskey-Fawcett, K. A., & McGhee, P. E. (Eds.). (1986). *Humor and aging.* Orlando, FL: Academic Press..

Nardini, G. (2000). When husbands die: Joke telling in an Italian ladies? club in Chicago. *Pragmatics, 10*(1), 87–97.

Nash, W. (1985). *The language of humor.* London/New York: Longman.

Neff, P. & Rucynski, J. (2017). Japanese perceptions of humor in the English language classroom. *HUMOR: International Journal of Humor Research, 30*(3), 279–302.

Nelms, J. L. (2001). *A descriptive analysis of the uses and functions of sarcasm in the classroom discourse of higher education* (Unpublished doctoral dissertation). University of Florida.Gainesville, FL.

Nerhardt, G. (1970). Humor and inclination to laugh: Emotional reactions to stimuli of different divergence from a range of expectancy. *Scandinavian Journal of Psychology, 11*(1), 185–195.

Nerhardt, G. (1975). Rated funniness and dissimilarity of figures: Divergence from expectancy. *Scandinavian Journal of Psychology, 16*(1), 156–166.

Nesi, H. (2012). Laughter in university lectures. *Journal of English for Academic Purposes, 11*(2), 79–89.

Neuliep, J. W. (1991). An examination of the content of high school teachers' humor in the classroom and the development of an inductively derived taxonomy of classroom humor. *Communication education, 40*(4), 343–355.

Nida, E. A. (1964). *Toward a science of translation.* Leiden: Brill.

Nida, E. A. & Taber, C. R. (1969). *The theory and practice of translation.* Leiden: E.J. Brill.

Nilsen, A. & Nilsen, D. (2008). Literature and Humor. In V. Raskin (Ed.), *The Primer of Humor Research.* (pp. 243–280). Berlin: Mouton De Gruyter.

Nirenburg, S. & Raskin, V. (2004). *Ontological semantics.* Cambridge, MA: MIT Press.

Nord, C. (2006). Loyalty and fidelity in specialized translation. *Confluencias, 4,* 29–41.

Norrick, N. R. (1993). *Conversational Joking: Humor in Everyday Talk.* Bloomington: Indiana University Press.

Norrick, N. R. (2001). On the conversational performance of narrative jokes: Toward an account of timing. *HUMOR: International Journal of Humor Research, 14,* 255–274.

REFERENCES

Norrick, N. R. (2003). Issues in conversational joking. *Journal of Pragmatics, 35*(9), 1333–1359.

Norrick, N. R. (2004). Humor, tellability, and conarration in conversational storytelling. *Text & Talk: An Interdisciplinary Journal of Language, Discourse & Communication Studies, 24*(1), 79–112.

Norrick, N. R. (2005). The dark side of tellability. *Narrative Inquiry, 15*(2), 323–343.

Norrick, N. R. (2010). Humor in interaction. *Language and Linguistics Compass, 4*(4), 232–244.

Norrick, N. & Klein, J. (2008). Class clowns: Talking out of turn with an orientation toward humor. *Lodz Papers in Pragmatics, 4*(1), 83–107.

Novak, W. & Waldoks, M. (Eds.). (1981). *The big book of Jewish humor.* New York: Harper and Row.

Nuolijärvi, P. & Tiittula, L. (2011). Irony in political television debates. *Journal of Pragmatics, 43*(2), 572–587.

Nwachukwu-Agbada, J. (2006). Ezenwa-Ohaeto: Poet of the Njakiri genre. *Matatu, 33,* 153–177.

Nwachukwu-Agbada, J. (2014). Igbo Humor. In S. Attardo (Ed.), *Encyclopedia of Humor Studies* (pp. 378–381). Los Angeles: Sage. 378–381.

Nwokah, E. E., Hsu, H. C., Davies, P., & Fogel, A. (1999). The integration of laughter and speech in vocal communication: A dynamic systems perspective. *Journal of Speech, Language, and Hearing Research, 42*(4), 880–894.

Oaks, D. (2010). *Structural ambiguity in English.* London/New York: Continuum.

Olbrechts-Tyteca, L. (1974). *Le comique du discours.* Bruxelles: Editions de l'Université de Bruxelles.

Oring, E. (1989). Between jokes and tales: on the nature of punch lines. *HUMOR: International Journal of Humor Research, 2*(4), 349–364.

Oring, E. (1992). *Jokes and their Relations.* Lexington: University Press of Kentucky.

Oring, E. (1999). Review of Latta, R. L. (1998). *The basic humor process: A cognitive-shift theory and the case against incongruity.* Berlin/New York: Mouton de Gruyter. *HUMOR: International Journal of Humor Research, 12*(4), 457–464.

Oring, E. (2003). *Engaging humor.* Urbana and Chicago: University of Illinois Press.

Ortega, L. & Han, Z. (Eds.) (2017). *Complexity Theory and Language Development.* Amsterdam: Benjamins.

Ozawa, F., K. Matsuo, C. Kato, T. Nakai, H. Isoda, Y. Takehara, & T. Moriya (2000). The effects of listening comprehension of various genres of literature on response in the linguistic area: an fMRI study. *Neuroreport, 11,* 1141–1143.

Paolillo, J. C. (1998). Gary Larson's *Far Side*: Nonsense? Nonsense! *HUMOR: International Journal of Humor Research,11*(3), 261–290.

Papapavlou, A. N. (1998). Attitudes toward the Greek Cypriot dialect: Sociocultural implications. *International Journal of the Sociology of Language, 134*(1), 15–28.

Partington, A. (2006). *The linguistics of laughter: A corpus-assisted study of laughter-talk*. New York: Routledge.

Partington, A. (2007). Irony and reversal of evaluation. *Journal of Pragmatics, 39*(9), 1547–1569.

Partington, A. (2011). Phrasal irony: Its form, function and exploitation. *Journal of Pragmatics, 43*, 1786–1800.

Partington, A. (2017). Corpus-assisted studies of humor and laughter-talk. In S. Attardo (Ed.), *The Routledge handbook of language and humor* (pp. 322–339). New York: Routledge.

Partington, A., Duguid, A., & Taylor, C. (2013). *Patterns and meanings in discourse*. Amsterdam: Benjamins.

Paulos, J. A. (1980). *Mathematics and Humor*. Chicago: University of Chicago Press.

Pavlicek, M. & Pöchhacker, F. (2002). Humour in simultaneous conference interpreting. *The Translator, 8*(2), 385–400.

Peace Love (2017, June 4). The EDL getting chased out of Liverpool to the Benny Hill tune! Hilarious!! [video file] Retrieved from: https://www.youtube.com/watch?v=1RX43xpy9ok

Peirce, C. S. (1931–36). *Collected papers*. Cambridge: Cambridge University Press.

Pelsmaekers, K. & Van Besien, F. (2002). Subtitling irony. *The Translator, 8*(2), 241–266.

Pepicello, W. J. & Green, T. A. (1984). *The Language of Riddles*. Columbus: Ohio State University Press.

Pepicello, W. J. & Weisberg, R. W. (1983). Linguistics and humor. In McGhee and Goldstein (Eds.), *Handbook of humor research* (pp. 59–83). Vol. 1. New York: Springer.

Peräkylä, A. & Ruusuvuori, J. (2006). Facial expression in an assessment. In H. Knoblauch, B. Schnettler, J. Raab & H.-G. Soeffner (Eds.), *Video analysis methodology and methods: Qualitative audiovisual data analysis in sociology* (pp. 127–142). Frankfurt: Lang.

Perlmutter, D. D. (2002). On incongruities and logical inconsistencies in humor: The delicate balance. *HUMOR: International Journal of Humor Studies, 15*(2), 155–168.

Petraki, E. & Pham Nguyen, H. H. (2016). Do Asian EFL teachers use humor in the classroom? A case study of Vietnamese EFL university teachers. *System, 61*, 98–109. Retrieved from https//doi.org/10.1016/j.system.2016.08.002

Petruck, M. (1996). Frame Semantics. In J. Verschueren, J.-O. Östman, J. Blommaert, and C. Bulcaen (eds.). *Handbook of Pragmatics.* (pp. 1–13.) Philadelphia: Benjamins.

Pexman, P. M., Zdrazilova, L., McConnachie, D., Deater-Deckard, K., & Petrill, S. A. (2009). 'That was smooth, Mom': Children's production of verbal and gestural irony. *Metaphor and Symbol, 24,* 237–248.

Pickering, L., Corduas, M., Eisterhold, J., Seifried, B., Eggleston, A., & Attardo, S. (2009). Prosodic markers of saliency in humorous narratives. *Discourse Processes, 46,* 517–540.

Piddington, R. (1933). *The psychology of laughter: A study in social adaptation.* London: Figurehead.

Pirandello, L. (1908). *L'umorismo.* Milan: Mondadori.

Pizzini, F. (1991). Communication hierarchies in humour: gender differences in the obstetrical/gynaecological setting. *Discourse & Society, 2*(4), 477–488.

Platow, M. J., Haslam, S., Both, A., Chew, I., Cuddon, M., Goharpey, N., Maurer, J., Rosini, S., Tsekouras, A., & Grace, D. M. (2005). 'It's not funny if they're laughing': Self-categorization, social influence, and responses to canned laughter. *Journal of Experimental Social Psychology, 41*(5), 542–550.

Platt, J. T. & Platt, H. K. (1975). *The social significance of speech: an introduction to and workbook in sociolinguistics.* Amsterdam: North-Holland.

Platt, T. & Ruch, W. (2014). Smiling and laughter: Expressive patterns. In S. Attardo (Ed.), *Encyclopedia of humor studies* (pp. 702–705), Los Angeles: Sage.

Pöchhacker, F. (1995). Simultaneous interpreting: A functionalist perspective. *HERMES-Journal of Language and Communication in Business, 8*(14), 31–53.

Poli, R., Healy, M., & Kameas, A. (Eds.) (2010). *Theory and applications of ontology: Computer applications.* New York: Springer.

Pollack, J. (2012). *The pun also rises: How the humble pun revolutionized language, changed history, and made wordplay more than some antics.* New York: Penguin.

Pollio, H. R. and Swanson C. (1995). A behavioral and phenomenological analysis of audience reactions to comic performance. *HUMOR: International Journal of Humor Research, 8*(1), 5–28.

Popa, D. E. (2005). Jokes and translation. *Perspectives: Studies in Translatology, 13*(1), 48–57.

Porcu, L. (2005). Fishy business: Humor in a Sardinian fish market. *HUMOR: International Journal of Humor Research, 18*(4), 69–102.

Porteous, J. (1988). Humor as a process of defense: The evolution of laughing. *HUMOR: International Journal of Humor Research, 1*(1). 63?80.

Potter, J. & Hepburn, A. (2010). Putting aspiration into words: 'Laugh particles,' managing descriptive trouble and modulating action. *Journal of Pragmatics, 42*, 1543–1555.

Powell, J. P. & Andresen, L. W. (1985). Humour and teaching in higher education. *Studies in Higher Education, 10*(1), 79–90.

Poyatos, F. (2002). *Nonverbal communication across disciplines: Culture, sensory interaction, speech, conversation.* Amsterdam/Philadelphia: Benjamins.

Prerost, F. J. (1977). Environmental conditions affecting the humour response: Developmental trends. In A. J. Chapman & H. C. Foot (Eds.), *It's a funny thing, humour* (pp. 4380–4441). Oxford, England: Pergamon Press.

Priego-Valverde, B. (2003). *L'humour dans la conversation familière: Description et analyse linguistiques.* Paris: L'Harmattan.

Priego-Valverde, B., Bigi, B., Attardo, S., Pickering L., and E. Gironzetti. (2018). Is smiling during humor so obvious? A cross-cultural comparison of smiling behavior in humorous sequences in American English and French interactions. Special Issue: Conversational humor: Forms, functions and practices across cultures. *Intercultural Pragmatics, 15*(4), pp. 563–591.

Propp, V. J. (1928). *Morfologija Skazki.* Leningrad: Akademia. Translation by L. Scott as Propp, V. J. Morphology of the folktale. *International Journal of American Linguistics. 24*(4). 1958. 2nd ed. Austin: University of Texas Press. 1968.

Provine, R. R. (2000). *Laughter. A scientific investigation.* New York, NY: Viking.

Quillian, M. R. (1967). Word concepts: a theory and simulation of some semantic capabilities. *Behavioral Science, 12*, 410–430.

Ragan, S. L. (1990). Verbal play and multiple goals in the gynaecological exam interaction. *Journal of Language and Social Psychology, 9*, 67–84.

Rahman, J. (2014). Verbal dueling. In S. Attardo (Ed.), *Encyclopedia of humor studies.* (pp. 786–789). Los Angeles: Sage.

Raphaelson-West, D. (1989). On the feasibility and strategies of translating humour. *Meta: Journal des traducteurs/Meta: Translators' Journal, 34*(1), 128–141.

Raskin, V. (1981). Script-based lexicon. *Quaderni di Semantica, 2*(1), 25–34.

Raskin, V. (1985). *Semantic mechanisms of humor.* Dordrecht: D. Reidel.

Raskin, V. (Ed.) (1985). Round Table Discussion on Frame/Script Semantics, Part 1 *Quaderni di Semantica , 6*(2),

Raskin, V. (Ed.) (1986). Round Table Discussion on Frame/Script Semantics, Part 2 *Quaderni di Semantica, 7*(1).

Raskin, V. (Ed.) (2008). *The primer of Humor Research.* Berlin: Mouton De Gruyter.

Raskin, V. (2017a). Humor theory: What is and what is not. In Chlopicki W. & D. Brzozowska (Eds.), *Humorous Discourse.* (pp. 11–22). Berlin: Mouton De Gruyter.

Raskin, V. (2017b). Script-based semantic and ontological semantic theories of humor. In S. Attardo (Ed.), *The Routledge Handbook of Language and Humor* (pp. 109-125). Routledge New York.

Raskin, V., Hempelmann, C. F., & Taylor, J. M. (2009). How to understand and assess a theory: The evolution of the SSTH into the GTVH and now into the OSTH. *Journal of Literary Theory, 3*(2), 285-311.

Reddington, E. (2015). Humor and play in language classroom interaction: A review of the literature. *Teachers College, Columbia University Working Papers in TESOL and Applied Linguistics, 15*(2), 22-38.

Reddington, E. & Waring, H. Z. (2015). Understanding the sequential resources for doing humor in the language classroom. *HUMOR: International Journal of Humor Research, 28*(1), 1-23.

Redfern, W. (1984). *Puns*. Oxford: Blackwell.

Rees, C. E. & Monrouxe, L. V. (2010). "I should be lucky ha ha ha ha": the construction of power, identity and gender through laughter within medical workplace learning encounters. *Journal of Pragmatics 42*(12), 3384-3399.

Regattin, F. (2015). Traduire les jeux de mots: une approche intègrèe, *Atelier de Traduction, 23*, 129-151.

Reiss, K. & Vermeer, H. J. (2014). *Towards a general theory of translational action: Skopos theory explained*. Abingdon/New York: Routledge.

Ritchie, G. (2000). Describing verbally expressed humour. Proceedings of AISB Symposium on Creative and Cultural Aspects and Applications of AI and Cognitive Science, Birmingham. Informatics Research Report EDI-INF-RR-0012. Retrieved from https://www.era.lib.ed.ac.uk/handle/1842/3403

Ritchie, G. (2004). *The linguistic analysis of jokes*. London: Routledge.

Rodden, F. (2018). The neurology and psychiatry of humor, smiling, and laughter. A tribute to Paul McGhee. Part II Neurological studies and brain imagining. *HUMOR: International Journal of Humor Research, 31*(2), 373-400.

Romaniuk, T. (2013). Interviewee laughter and disaffiliation in broadcast news interviews. In Glenn, P. & Holt, E. (Eds.), *Studies of Laughter in Interaction* (pp. 201-220). London, Bloomsbury.

Rosch, E. & Mervis, C. (1975). Family resemblances: studies in the internal structure of categories. *Cognitive Psychology, 7*, 573-605.

Ross, A. (1998). *The language of humour*. London/New York: Routledge.

Rothbart, M. K. & Pien, D. (1977). Elephants and marshmallows: A theoretical synthesis of incongruity resolution and arousal theories of humour. In A. J. Chapman & H. C. Foot (Eds.), *It's a funny thing, humour* (pp. 37-40). Elmsford, NY: Pergamon.

Rozin, P., Rozin, A., Appel, B., & Wachtel, C. (2006). Documenting and explaining the common AAB Pattern in music and humor: Establishing and breaking expectations. *Emotion, 6*(3), 349-355.

Ruch, W. (1992). Assessment of appreciation of humor: Studies with the 3 WD humor test. In C. D. Spielberger & J. N. Butcher (Eds.), *Advances in personality assessment* (pp. 27–75). Hillsdale, NJ: Lawrence Earlbaum.

Ruch, W. (1993). Exhilaration and humor. In M. Lewis & J. M. Haviland (Eds.), *The handbook of emotion* (pp. 605–616). New York, NY: Guilford Publications.

Ruch, W. (1995). Will the real relationship between facial expression and affective experience please stand up: The case of exhilaration. *Cognition & Emotion, 91*), 33–58. Reprinted in P. Ekman & E. L. Rosenberg (Eds.), *What the face reveals: Basic and applied studies of spontaneous expression using the Facial Action Coding System (FACS)*, 2dn ed. Oxford: Oxford University Press. 89–108.

Ruch, W. (Ed.) (1998). *The Sense of Humor*. Berlin: Mouton De Gruyter.

Ruch, W. (2008). Psychology of humor. In Raskin, V. (Ed.) (2008) *The primer of humor research* (pp. 17–100). Berlin: Mouton De Gruyter.

Ruch, W. & Ekman, P. (2001). The expressive pattern of laughter. In A. W. Kaszniak (Ed.), *Emotions, qualia, and consciousness* (pp. 426–443). Hackensack, NJ: World Scientific.

Ruiz Gurillo, L. (2009). ¿Como se gestiona la ironía en la conversación? [How is irony managed in conversation?] *Rilce: Revista de Filologia Hispanica, 25*(2), 363–377.

Ruiz-Gurillo, L. (2012). *La lingüìstica del humor en español.* [The linguistics of humor in Spanish] Madrid: Arco/Libros.

Ruiz-Gurillo, L. (2016a). Metapragmatics of humor. Variability, negotiability and adaptability in humorous monologues. In Ruiz-Gurillo, L. (Ed.), *Metapragmatics of humor: Current research trends* (Vol. 14) (79–101). Amsterdam: John Benjamins.

Ruiz-Gurillo, L. (Ed.) (2016b). *Metapragmatics of humor: Current research trends* (Vol. 14). Amsterdam: John Benjamins.

Ruiz-Madrid, M. N. & Fortanet-Gàmez, I. (2015). A multimodal discourse analysis approach to humour in conference presentations: The case of autobiographic references. *Procedia-Social and Behavioral Sciences, 173*, 246–251.

Rumelhart, D. E. (1980). Schemata: The building blocks of cognition. In R. J. Spiro, B. C. Bruce, & W. F. Brewer (Eds.) *Theoretical issues in reading comprehension* (pp. 33–58). New York: Routledge.

Ruppenhofer, J., Ellsworth, M., Petruck, M. R. L., Johnson, C. R., Baker, C. F., & Scheffczyk, J. (2016). *FrameNet II: Extended Theory and Practice.* https://framenet2.icsi.berkeley.edu/docs/r1.7/book.pdf.

Russell, B. (1908). Mathematical Logic as Based on the Theory of Types, *American Journal of Mathematics, 30*, 222–262; repr. in B. Russell, *Logic and Knowledge.* London: Allen and Unwin, 1956, 59–102.

Rutter, J. (1997). *Stand-up as interaction: Performance and audience in comedy venues* (Unpublished doctoral dissertation). University of Salford, Manchester.

Rutter, J. (2000). The stand-up introduction sequence: Comparing comedy compères. *Journal of Pragmatics, 32*(4), 463–483.

Rutter, J. (2001). Rhetoric in stand-up comedy: Exploring performer-audience interaction. *Stylistyka, 10*, 307–325.

Sacks, H. (1974). An analysis of the course of a joke's telling in conversation. In R. Bauman & J. Sherzer (Eds.), *Explorations in the ethnography of speaking* (2nd ed.). Cambridge: Cambridge University Press. 1989. 337–353, 467, 490.

Sacks, H. (1978). Some technical considerations of a dirty joke. In J. Schenkein (Ed.), *Studies in the organization of conversational interaction*. (pp. 249–275.) New York–San Francisco–London: Academic.

Sacks, H. (1992). Lecture 14. Paraphrasing; Alternative temporal sequences; Approximate and precise numbers; Laughter; Uhhuh. In: G. Jefferson (Ed.), *Lectures on conversation* (Vol. 2) (pp. 739–751). Blackwell: Oxford.

Sadie, S. (1965). *Mozart*. Grossman: New York.

Samson, A. C. & Hempelmann, C. F. (2011). Humor with backgrounded incongruity: Does more required suspension of disbelief affect humor perception?. *HUMOR: International Journal of Humor Research, 24*(2), 167–185.

Samson, A. C., Hempelmann, C. F., Huber, O., & Zysset, S. (2009). Neural substrates of incongruity-resolution and nonsense humor. *Neuropsychologia, 47*(4), 1023–1033.

Saussure, F. de (1916). *Cours de linguistique générale*. Paris: Payot.

Saville-Troike, M. (1982). *The ethnography of communication: An introduction*. Oxford/New York: Blackwell.

Scarpetta, F. & Spagnolli, A. (2009). The interactional context of humor in stand-up comedy. *Research on Language and Social Interaction, 42*(3), 210–230.

Schank, R. C. (1975). *Conceptual information processing*. Amsterdam: North Holland.

Schank, R. C. & Abelson, R. (1977). *Scripts, plans, goals and understanding*. New York: Wiley.

Schegloff, E. A. (1987). Some sources of misunderstanding in talk-in-interaction. *Linguistics, 25*(1), 201–218.

Schegloff, E. A. (1993). Reflections on quantification in the study of conversation. *Research on Language and Social Interaction, 26*(1), 99–128.

Schegloff, E. A. (2001). Getting serious: Joke! Serious 'no'. *Journal of Pragmatics, 33* (12), 1947–1955.

Scher, S. P. (1991). "Tutto nel mondo è burla": Humor in music? In R. Grimm & J. Hermand (Eds.) *Laughter unlimited: essays on humor, satire and the comic* (pp. 106–135). Madison, WI: University of Wisconsin Press.

Schmitz, J. R. (2002). Humor as a pedagogical tool in foreign language and translation courses. *HUMOR: International Journal of Humor Research,* 15(1), 89–114.

Schnurr, S. (2009). *Leadership discourse at work.* London: Palgrave.

Schnurr, S. & Rowe, C. (2008). The "dark side" of Humour. An analysis of subversive humour in workplace emails. *Lodz Papers in Pragmatics,* 4(1), 109–130.

Scholz, B. C., Pelletier, F. J., & Pullum, G. K. (2016). Philosophy of linguistics. In *The Stanford Encyclopedia of Philosophy.* Retrieved from https://plato.stanford.edu/archives/win2016/entries/linguistics/

Scogin Jr, F. R. & Pollio, H. R. (1980). Targeting and the humorous episode in group process. *Human Relations,* 33(11), 831–852.

Searle, J. R. (1969). *Speech acts: An essay in the philosophy of language.* Cambridge: Cambridge University Press.

Seewoester, S. (2009). *Linguistic ambiguity in language-based jokes* (Unpublished Master's thesis). DePaul University. Chicago, IL.

Seizer, S. (2011). On the uses of obscenity in live stand-up comedy. *Anthropological Quarterly,* 84(1), 209–234.

Seleskovitch, D., Lederer, M., & Ladmiral, J. R. (1984). *Interpréter pour traduire.* Paris: Didier.

Semino, E. & Demjén, Z. (2017). The Cancer Card: metaphor and humour in online interactions about the experience of cancer. In Hampe, B. (ed) *Metaphor: Embodied Cognition and Discourse* (pp. 181–199). Cambridge: Cambridge University Press.

Shade, R. A. (1996). *License to laugh: Humor in the classroom.* Westport, CT: Greenwood.

Shammi, P. & Stuss, D. T. (1999). Humor appreciation: A role of the right frontal lobe. *Brain,* 122, 657–666.

Sherzer, J. (1978). Oh! That's a pun and I didn't mean it. *Semiotica,* 22(3-4), 335–350.

Sherzer, J. (1985). Puns and jokes. In: T. A. van Dijk (Ed.), *Handbook of discourse analysis* (Vol. 3) (pp. 213–221). London: Academic Press.

Sherzer, J. (1996). Review of Attardo (1994). *Language* 72(1), 132–136.

Sherzer, J. (2002). *Speech play and verbal art.* Austin: University of Texas Press.

Shieber, S. M. (2003). *An introduction to unification-based approaches to grammar.* Brookline, Massachusetts: Microtome Publishing. Reissue of Shieber, S. M. (1986). *An introduction to unification-based approaches to grammar.* Stanford, California: CSLI Publications.

Schiffrin, D. (1994). *Approaches to discourse.* Blackwell: Cambridge, MA.

Shifman, L., Levy, H., & Thelwall, M. (2014). Internet jokes: The secret agents of globalization? *Journal of Computer-Mediated Communication,* 19, 727–743.

Shipley, T. Y. (2006). Towards a humour translation check-list for students of translation. *Interlingüística, 17*, 981–988.

Schultz, T. R. (1976). A cognitive-developmental analysis of humor. In Chapman, A. J., and H. C. Foot (Eds.) *Humour and laughter: Theory, research and applications* (pp. 11–36). London: Wiley.

Siegel, J. (1995). How to get a laugh in Fijian: Code-switching and humor. *Language in Society, 24*(1), 95–110.

Simon, R. K. (1985). *The labyrinth of the comic: Theory and practice from Fielding to Freud.* Tallahassee, FL: Florida State University Press.

Simpson, P. (2003). *On the discourse of satire: Towards a stylistic model of satirical humour.* Amsterdam: Benjamins.

Simpson, P. & Bousfield, D. (2017). Humor and Stylistics. In S. Attardo (Ed.), *The Routledge handbook of language and humor.* (pp. 158–173). New York: Routledge.

Skalicky, S., Berger, C. M., & Bell, N. D. (2015). The functions of "just kidding" in American English. *Journal of Pragmatics, 85*, 18–31.

Skowron, J. (2003). Inadequacy of literary analyses of humour in Oscar Wilde. In Csàbi, S. & J. Zerkowitz (eds.) 2003. *Textual secrets: The message of the medium. Proceedings of the 21st PALA Conference April 12-15, 2001.* (pp. 134–139). Budapest: School of English and American Studies. Eötvös Loránd University.

Smith, M. (2009). Humor, unlaughter, and boundary maintenance. *Journal of American Folklore, 122*(484), 148–171.

Smith Bowen, E. [L. Bohannan]. (1954). *Return to laughter.* New York: Doubleday. 2nd ed.

Smoski, M. J. & Bachorowski, J. A. (2003). Antiphonal laughter between friends and strangers. *Cognition and Emotion, 17*(2), 327–340.

Smuts, A. (n.d., but 2006). Humor. In *Internet encyclopedia of philosophy.* Retrieved from http://www.iep.utm.edu/humor/

Sobkowiak, W. (1991). *Metaphonology of English paronomasic puns.* Frankfurt-Bern-New York-Paris: Peter Lang.

Sowayan, S. A. (1989). 'Tonight my gun is loaded': Poetic dueling in Arabia. *Oral Tradition, 4*(1–2), 151–73.

Spencer, H. (1860). The physiology of laughter. *Macmillan's Magazine, 1,* 395–402.

Sperber, D. & Wilson, D. (1986). *Relevance.* Cambridge, MA: Harvard University Press.

Steiner, G. (1975). *After Babel: Aspects of language and translation.* Oxford: Oxford University Press.

Stokols, D., Rall, M., Pinner, B., & Schopler, J. (1973). Physical, social, and personal determinants of the perception of crowding. *Environment and Behavior, 5*(1), 87–115.

Straehle, C. A. (1993). "Samuel?" "Yes, dear?": Teasing and conversational rapport. In D. Tannen (Ed.), *Framing in discourse* (pp. 210–229). New York/Oxford: Oxford University Press.

Suls, J. (1972). A two-stage model for the appreciation of jokes and cartoons. In J. H. Goldstein & P. E. McGhee (Eds.) *The psychology of humor* (pp. 81–100). London-New York: Academic Press.

Suls, J. (1983). Cognitive processes in humor appreciation. In McGhee, P. E. & J. H. Goldstein (Eds.) (1983). *Handbook of humor research.* (Vol. I) (pp. 39–57). New York/Berlin: Springer.

Sutton-Spence, R. & Napoli, D. J. (2012). Deaf jokes and sign language humor. *HUMOR: International Journal of Humor Studies, 25*(3), 311–337.

Tabacaru, S. & Lemmens, M. (2014). Raised eyebrows as gestural triggers in humour: The case of sarcasm and hyper-understanding. *European Journal of Humour Research, 2*(2), 11–31.

Tannen, D. (1979). *Processes and consequences of conversational style* (Unpublished PhD dissertation.) University of Berkeley. Berkeley, CA.

Tannen, D. (1984). *Conversational style: Analyzing talk among friends.* Norwood, NJ: Ablex.

Tannen, D. (1986). *That's not what I meant!.* New York: Ballantine.

Tannen, D. (Ed.) (1993). *Framing in discourse.* Oxford: Oxford University Press.

Tannen, D., Hamilton, H. E., & Shiffrin, D. (Eds.) (2015). *The handbook of discourse analysis* (2nd ed.). Chichester, UK: Wiley-Blackwell.

Taylor, J. M. & Raskin, V. (2012). On the transdisciplinary field of humor research. *Journal of Integrated Design and Process Science, 16*(3), 133–148.

Ten Have, P. (2007). *Doing conversation analysis.* Los Angeles: Sage.

Thonus, T. (2008). Acquaintanceship, familiarity, and coordinated laughter in writing tutorials. *Linguistics and Education, 19*(4), 333–350.

Ticca, A. C. (2013). Laughter in bilingual medical interactions: Displaying resistance to doctor's talk in a Mexican village. In P. Glenn & E. Holt (Eds). *Studies of Laughter in Interaction* (pp.107–129), London/New York: Bloomsbury.

Tinholt, H. W. (2007). Computational humour. *Utilizing cross-reference ambiguity for conversational jokes* (Unpublished MA Thesis). University of Twente. Twente, Netherlands.

Titze, M. (1996). The Pinocchio complex: Overcoming the fear of laughter. *Humor and Health Journal, 5*, 1–11.

Toury, G. (1985). A rationale for descriptive translation studies. In T. Hermans (Ed.), *The manipulation of literature: Studies in literary translation* (pp. 16–41). London: Croom Helm.

Trier, J. (1931). *Der deutsche Wortschatz im Sinnbezirk des Verstandes.* PhD diss. Bonn.

Triezenberg, K. E. (2008). Humor in literature. In V. Raskin (Ed.) *The Primer of Humor Research* (pp. 523–543). Berlin: Mouton De Gruyter.

Trouvain, J. & Truong, K. P. (2017). Laughter. In S. Attardo (Ed.), *The Routledge handbook of language and humor* (pp. 340–355). New York: Routledge..

Tsakona, V. (2003). Jab lines in narrative jokes. *HUMOR: International Journal of Humor Research, 16*(3), 315–330.

Tsakona, V. (2009). Language and image interaction in cartoons: Towards a multimodal theory of humor. *Journal of Pragmatics, 41*(6), 1171–1188.

Tsakona, V. (2011). Irony beyond criticism: Evidence from Greek parliamentary discourse. *Pragmatics and Society, 2*, 57–86.

Tsakona, V. (2013). Okras and the metapragmatic stereotypes of humour: Towards an expansion of the GTVH. In M. Dynel (Ed.), *Developments in linguistic humour theory* (pp. 25–48). Amsterdam: Benjamins.

Tsakona, V. (2017). Genres of humor. In S. Attardo (Ed.), *The Routledge handbook of language and humor* (pp. 489–503). New York: Routledge.

Tsang, W. K. & Wong, M. (2004). Constructing a shared 'Hong Kong identity' in comic discourses. *Discourse and Society, 15*, 767–785.

Tufford, L. & Newman, P. (2010). Bracketing in qualitative research. *Qualitative Social Work, 11*(1), 80–96.

Turner, M. R. (2005). Signs of comedy: A semiotic approach to comedy in the arts (Unpublished doctoral dissertation), Ohio University. Athens, OH.

Vaid, J. (1999). The evolution of humor: Do those who laugh last? In D. H. Rosen & M. C. Luebbert (Eds.), *The Evolution of the Psyche* (pp. 123–138). Westport, CT/London: Praeger.

Vaid, J. (2002). Humor and laughter. In V. S. Ramachandran (Ed.), *Encyclopedia of the Human Brain* (pp. 505–516). New York: Elsevier.

Vaid, J. & Kobler, J. B. (2000). Laughing matters: Towards a structural and neural account. *Brain and Cognition 42*(1), 139–141.

Valdeón, R. A. (2005). Asymmetric representations of languages in contact: Uses and translations of French and Spanish in Frasier. *Linguistica Antverpiensia, New Series-Themes in Translation Studies, 4*, 279–294.

Vandaele, J. (2011). Wordplay in translation. *Handbook of translation studies, 2*, 180–183.

Vandergriff, I., & Fuchs, C. (2012). Humor support in synchronous computer-mediated classroom discussions. *HUMOR: International Journal of Humor Research, 25*(4), 437–458.

Veale, T. (2004). Incongruity in humor: Root cause or epiphenomenon? *HUMOR: International Journal of Humor Research, 17*(4), 419–428.

Veale, T., Feyaerts, K., & Brône, G. (2006). The cognitive mechanisms of adversarial humor. *HUMOR: International Journal of Humor Research, 19*(3), 305–338.

Vega, G. (1989). *Humor competence: The fifth component* (Unpublished master's thesis) West Lafayette, Purdue University.

Vermeer, H. J. (1989). Skopos and commission in translational action. In Venuti, L. (2012). *The translation studies reader* (pp. 227–238). New York/London: Routledge.

Vermeer, Hans J. (2004). Skopos and Commission in translational action. In Venuti, L. *The translation studies reader* (pp. 227–238). Oxon: Routledge

Viaggio, S. (1996). The pitfalls of metalingual use in simultaneous interpreting. *The Translator,* 2(2), 179–198.

Vincent, H. (2010). Roman satire and the general theory of verbal humor. In C. V. Garces (Ed.), *Dimensions of humor: Explorations in linguistics, literature, cultural studies and translation* (pp. 419–451). Valencia, Spain: University of Valencia Press.

Vrticka, P., Black, J. M., & Reiss, A. L. (2013). The neural basis of humour processing. *Nature Reviews Neuroscience,* 14(12), 860–868.

Wagner, H. L. & Smith, J. (1991). Social influence and expressiveness. *Journal of Nonverbal Behavior,* 15, 201–214.

Wagner, M. M. & Urios-Aparisi, E. (2011). The use of humor in the foreign language classroom: Funny and effective? *HUMOR: International Journal of Humor Research,* 24(4), 399–434.

Walle, A. H. (1976). Getting picked up without being put down: Jokes and the bar rush. *Journal of the Folklore Institute,* 13(2), 201–217.

Wanzer, M. B. (2002). Use of humor in the classroom: The good, the bad, and the not-so-funny things that teachers say and do. Chesebro, J. L. & McCroskey, J. C. (Eds.), *Communication for teachers* (pp. 116–125). Boston: Allyn & Bacon.

Wanzer, M. B., Frymier, A. B., & Irwin, J. (2010). An explanation of the relationship between instructor humor and student learning: Instructional humor processing theory. *Communication Education,* 59(1), 1–18.

Wanzer, M. B., Frymier, A. B., Wojtaszczyk, A. M., & Smith, T. (2006). Appropriate and inappropriate uses of humor by teachers. *Communication Education,* 55(2), 178–196.

Wells, P., & Bull, P. (2007). From politics to comedy: A comparative analysis of affiliative audience responses. *Journal of Language and Social Psychology,* 26, 321–342.

Wennerstrom, A. (2011). Rich pitch: The humorous effects of deaccent and L+ H* pitch accent. *Pragmatics & Cognition,* 19(2), 310–332.

West, C. (1984). *Routine complications: Troubles with talk between doctors and patients.* Bloomington: Indiana University Press

Whalen, J. M. & Pexman, P. M. (2010). How do children respond to verbal irony in face-to-face communication? The development of mode adoption across middle childhood. *Discourse Processes,* 47, 363–387.

Whalen, J. M. & Pexman, P. (2017). Humor support and mode adoption. In S. Attardo (Ed.), *The Routledge handbook of language and humor* (pp. 371–384). New York: Routledge.

Wilkinson, R. (2007). Managing linguistic incompetence as a delicate issue in aphasic talk-in-interaction: On the use of laughter in prolonged repair sequences. *Journal of Pragmatics, 39*(3), 542–569.

Wilkinson, R., Beeke, S., & Maxim, J. (2003). Adapting to conversation: On the use of linguistic resources by speakers with fluent aphasia in the construction of turns at talk. In C. Goodwin (Ed.), *Conversation and brain damage* (pp. 59–89). Oxford University Press: New York.

Williams, J. A., Burns, E. L., & Harmon, E. A. (2009). Insincere utterances and gaze: Eye contact during sarcastic statements. *Perceptual and Motor Skills, 108*, 565–572.

Williamson, L. & Ricoy, R. D. P. (2014). The translation of wordplay in interlingual subtitling: A study of 'Bienvenue chez les Ch'tis' and its English subtitles. *Babel, 60*(2), 164–192.

Winchatz, M. R. & Kozin, A. (2008). Comical hypothetical: Arguing for a conversational phenomenon. *Discourse Studies, 10*(3), 383–405.

Wittgenstein, L. (1953). *Philosophical investigations.* New York: Macmillan.

Wooffitt, R. (2005). *Conversation analysis and discourse analysis.* London: Sage.

Wulf, D. (2010). A humor competence curriculum. *TESOL Quarterly, 44*(1), 155–169.

Wycoff, E. B. (1999). Humor in academia: An international survey of humor instruction. *HUMOR: International Journal of Humor Research, 12*(4), 437–456.

Yetkin, N. (2011). A case study on the humourous load differences and cognitive effects of satirically/ironically humourous elements in subtitling from English into Turkish. *The Journal of Linguistic and Intercultural Education, 4*, 239–253.

Yin, P. A. & Wu, Q. (2014). On the translation of subtitles based on Skopos Theory? A case study of The Big Bang Theory. *Journal of Southwest Petroleum University (Social Sciences Edition), 1*, n.p.

Young, R. D. and Frye, M. (1966). Some are laughing; some are not: why? *Psychological Reports, 18*, 747–754.

Yus, F. (2013). Relevance, humour and translation. In E. Walaszewska, & A. Piskorska (Eds.), *Relevance theory: More than understanding* (pp. 117–146). Newcastle Upon Tyne: Cambridge Scholars Publishing.

Yus, F. (2017). *Humour and Relevance.* Amsterdam and Philadelphia: John Benjamins.

Zabalbeascoa, P. (1993). *Developing translation studies to better account for audiovisual texts and other new forms of text production* (Unpublished doctoral dissertation), University of Lleida. Lleida.

Zabalbeascoa, P. (1996a). La traducción de la comedia televisiva: Implicaciones teóricas. In P. F. Nistal & J. M. Bravo (Eds.) *A spectrum of translation studies* (pp. 173–201). Valladolid: Universidad de Valladolid.

Zabalbeascoa, P. (1996b). Translating jokes for dubbed television situation comedies. *The Translator*, 2(2), 235–257.

Zabalbeascoa, P. (2000). From techniques of translation to types of solutions. In Beeby, A. et al. (Eds.) *Investigating translation*. (pp. 117–127.) Amsterdam: Benjamins.

Zabalbeascoa, P. (2005). Humor and translation – an interdiscipline. *HUMOR: International Journal of Humor Research*, 18(2), 185–207.

Zabalbeascoa, P. (2008). The nature of the audiovisual text and its parameters. In G. D. Cintas (Ed.), *The didactics of audiovisual translation* (pp. 21–37.) Amsterdam: Benjamins.

Zadjman, A. (1991). Contextualization of canned jokes in discourse. *HUMOR: International Journal of Humor Research*, 4(1), 23–40.

Zajdman, A. (1995). Humorous face-threatening acts: Humor as strategy. *Journal of Pragmatics*, 23(3), 325–339.

Zayts, O. & Schnurr, S. (2011). Laughter as medical providers' resource: Negotiating informed choice in prenatal genetic counseling. *Research on Language and Social Interaction*, 44(1), 1–20.

Zayts, O. & Schnurr, S. (2017). Laughter as a 'serious business': Clients' Laughter in prenatal screening for Down's Syndrome. In N. Bell (Ed.), *multiple perspectives on language Play* (pp. 119–141). Berlin: Mouton De Gruyter.

Zhang, Q. (2005). Immediacy, humor, power distance, and classroom communication apprehension in Chinese college classrooms. *Communication Quarterly*, 53, 109–124.

Zhang, Y. & Attardo, S. (2015). Sustained Humor in Chinese Dyadic Conversation. Paper presented at the 2015 ISHS conference, Holy Names College, Oakland, CA.

Zhao, X., Zhu, F., Qian, W., & Zhou, A. (2013). Impact of multimedia in Sina Weibo: Popularity and Life Span. (2012). Joint Conference of the Sixth Chinese Semantic Web Symposium and the First Chinese Web Science Conference (CSWS & CWSC '12). Research Collection School Of Information Systems. (pp. 55–65). Springer, New York, NY.

Zijderveld, A. C. (1983). Introduction: The sociology of humour and laughter: An outstanding debt. *Current Sociology*, 31(3), 1–6.

Zillmann, D. (1983). Disparagement humor. In McGhee, P. E. & J. H. Goldstein (eds.), 1983. *Handbook of Humor Research*. (pp. 85–107). Vol I. New York-Berlin-Heidelberg-Tokyo: Springer.

Ziv, A. (1979a). *L'humour en éducation: Approche psychologique*. Paris: Editions Sociales Françaises.

Ziv, A. (1979b). The teacher's sense of humour and the atmosphere in the classroom. *School Psychology International, 1*(2), 21–23.

Ziv, A. (1984). *Personality and Sense of Humor.* New York, NY: Springer.

Ziv, A. (1988). Teaching and learning with humor: Experiment and replication. *Journal of Experimental Education, 57,* 5–15.

Author index

A'hern, R. 282, 421
Abelson, R. 114, 121, 431
Abrahams, R. D. 224, 393
Adams, A. C. 228, 393, 416, 423
Adams, R. B. Jr. 228, 393, 416, 423
Adelswärd, V. 257, 393
Aiello, J. R. 45, 203, 393
Aitchison, J. 195, 393
Al-Khatib, M. A. 154, 393
Alan, D. B. xvi, 169, 224, 400
Alatis, J. A. 423
Alba, L. 396
Alexander, R. J. 140, 335, 393
AlJared, A. 94, 393
Allen, M. 421, 430
Alvarado Ortega, B. M. 154, 269, 393
Amirian, Z. 353, 393
Anderson, R. C. 114, 393
Andor, J. 115, 135, 393
André, E. 404
Andresen, L. W. 371, 380, 427
Andrus, T. D. 45, 393
Anolli, L. 395
Antonini, R. 356, 359, 393–394
Antonopoulou, E. 140, 153, 269, 332–334, 394
Appel, B. 429
Apte, M. xiii, 227, 308–310, 315, 394
Apter, M. J. 63, 65, 86, 101, 371, 394, 404
Archakis, A. 153, 232, 269, 292, 313, 394
Arieti, S. 86, 394
Asimakoulas, D. 346, 394
Atkin, A. 116, 395
Atkinson, J. M. 142, 206, 238, 262, 395, 417
Attardo, D. H. 397
Attardo, S. iii–iv, xiii, xx–1, 3, 7–8, 13, 15–16, 18–19, 25–26, 28–30, 42, 52, 56–57, 59–60, 62, 70, 73, 75–79, 82–84, 87–95, 98, 103, 109, 111, 113, 115, 117, 121–122, 124, 126, 128–129, 131, 135–142, 144–145, 148, 150–151, 153–154, 156–158, 160, 163, 166–167, 169–170, 175–177, 180, 187–188, 190–191, 194, 198–199, 201, 206–207, 209, 214–215, 221–222, 227–232, 234–235, 240–241, 245, 251, 257, 259, 261–264, 267, 269, 273, 278, 290, 293, 295–299, 303, 307, 317, 319, 322–327, 330–331, 333, 335–336, 339–340, 345, 359, 362, 367, 376, 381, 386, 393, 395–397, 399–406, 408, 410–415, 419–420, 423, 425–428, 432–433, 435, 437–438
Aubouin, E. 9, 43, 82–84, 397
Austin, J. L. 158, 175, 215, 220, 352, 397, 403, 409, 428, 432

Baccolini, R. 421
Bachorowski, J. A. 41, 248, 262, 433
Bainbridge, S. 197, 417
Baker, C. F. 430
Bakhtin, M. 270, 312, 397
Balirano, G. 356, 397
Bally, C. 32, 212, 335, 397
Baltes, P. 397
Banas, J. A. 372–374, 380, 397
Barreca, R. 301, 397
Barrett, C. E. 45, 409, 421
Barrett, H. C. 409
Barth-Weingarten, D. 410
Bartlett, F. C. 114, 398
Bartolome-Rull, D. S. 406
Bateson, G. xiv, 27, 61–62, 67, 102, 218–220, 398

Bauman, R. 213, 218–219, 221, 229, 398, 431
Beach, W. A. 282, 398
Beaven, A. 45, 421
Becker, A. B. 65, 398
Beckner, C. 409
Beeke, S. 437
Bekinschtein, T. A. 196, 398
Bell, N. D. 85, 215, 229, 250, 269, 293–295, 297–298, 375–378, 380, 383, 398, 414, 416, 433, 438
Benneth, G. 408
Berger, A. A. 26, 72, 398
Berger, C. M. 313–314, 398,
Berger, P. L. 433
Bergler, E. 59, 77, 398
Bergson, H. 18, 21, 70, 82, 219, 398
Berk, R. A. 372, 398
Berkowitz, L. 50, 398
Berlyne, D. E. 50, 399
Bertone, L. 359, 399
Bevis, M. 70, 399
Bianchi, F. 360–361, 405, 407, 416
Biber, D. 221, 286, 399
Bickle, J. 68, 399
Bigi, B. 428
Billig, M. 65, 209–210, 222, 293, 399
Bird, C. 85, 231, 302, 399
Black, J. M. 19–20, 119, 143, 333, 362, 418, 423, 436
Blackwell, K. 27, 393, 399, 409, 423, 429, 431–432, 434
Blake, B. 70, 399
Blom, J. P. 313, 399
Blythe, R. 409
Bogart, E. H. 406
Boothroyd, R. A. 422
Bousfield, D. 140, 224–225, 321, 332, 335, 339, 414, 433
Boxer, D. 222, 273, 399, 408
Bravo, J. M. 438
Bremner, S. 417
Brewer, W. F. 430
Brock, A. 383, 399
Brodie, I. 234, 399

Brodzinsky, D. M. 393
Brône, G. 76, 114, 332, 339, 394, 399, 435
Brown, G. E. 14–15
Brown, P. 45, 49, 274–275, 399–400
Brown, S. xiii
Bruce, B. C. 430
Brugman, C. 405
Bryant, G. A. 228, 367, 370–372, 400, 409, 418
Bryant, J. A. 228, 367, 370–372, 400, 409, 418
Brzozowska, D. 154, 396, 428
Bubel, C. M. 5, 400
Bucaria, C. 92–93, 139, 182, 191, 341, 356, 366, 394, 400
Buck, R. 39, 400
Buckman, K. H. 371, 400
Buján, M. 232, 400
Bull, P. E. 206, 400, 436
Burgers, C. 228, 293, 298, 330, 401
Burns, E. L. 437
Burns, L. 231, 416
Butcher, J. N. 44, 232, 401, 415, 429
Butler, J. 88, 306, 401
Button, G. 417
Bybee, J. L. 195, 401, 409
Bysouth, D. 232, 241, 248, 416

Calzolari, N. 416
Cameron, L. 381, 419
Canagarajah, S. 377, 401
Canale, M. 376, 401
Canary, D. J. 406
Canestrari, C. 207, 221, 256, 282, 401, 407
Caputi, A. 338, 401
Carpenter, P. A. 115, 383, 417
Carrell, A. ix, xvi, 29, 203–204, 401
Cashion, J. L. 247, 401
Caskey, N. 417
Castelfranchi, C. 80, 420
Cetola, H. 419
Chabanne, J. C. 16, 98, 158, 221, 245, 397

Chafe, W. L. 41–43, 56, 69, 114, 227, 229, 240, 245, 248, 269, 300, 401–402
Chan, Y. C. 196, 402
Chapman, A. J. 19, 21, 29, 44–45, 402, 404, 406, 409, 428–429, 433
Chapman, W. A. 45, 402
Chen, G. -H. 375, 402
Chen, H. -C. 69, 77, 153, 196, 375, 402
Chew, I. 427
Chey, J. 402
Chiaro, D. xvi, 341–344, 347, 350, 352, 355–356, 359, 363, 365–366, 393, 400, 402–403, 410, 421
Chimbwete-Phiri, R. 282, 403
Chomsky, N. xv, 11, 32–33, 74, 202, 212, 381, 387, 403
Chovanec, J. 242, 403
Christiansen, M. H. 409
Chrzanowska-Kluczewska, E. 396
Chukwumah, I. 209, 403
Chlopicki, W. xi, 121, 322–323, 329, 331, 339, 403
Ciceri, R. 395
Clark, H. H. 149, 403, 422
Clark, T. 149, 403, 422
Clift, R. 239, 245, 253, 255, 257, 261, 403
Cody, M. J. 401
Cole, P. 409, 412
Collinson, D. L. 285, 403
Colston, H. 68, 175, 403, 411
Comisky, P. 400
Condren, C. 337, 403
Consalvo, C. M. 239, 403
Coolidge, A. 262, 403
Cooper, J. 50, 403
Copi, I. M. 27, 403
Corduas, M. 327, 404, 427
Cortès-Conde, F. 273, 399
Coser, R. L. 281, 404
Coulson, S. 68–69, 404
Coupland, J. 404
Coupland, N. 308, 404
Crawford, M. 305–306, 315, 404
Creswell, J. W. 37, 404
Croft, W. 409

Cuddon, M. 427
Cuéllar Irala, J. 350, 404
Culpeper, J. 224, 395, 404
Cupchik, G. C. 44, 419
Curran, W. 231, 245, 404

Dahlstrom, A. 405
Dai, R. H. 402
Dale, J. A. 45, 404
Dameneh, S. S. 353, 393
Damico, S. B. 377, 404
Darwin, C. 20, 41, 404
Davidson, D. 117, 404
Davies, A. P. 371, 404, 425
Davies, C. xvi, 147, 153, 204, 343, 405, 425
Davies, C. E. x, 209, 266–269, 278, 280, 298–299, 305–308, 310, 315, 377, 405, 425
Davies, P. 425
Davis, J. M. 336–337, 402, 405
Davis, M. H. 398,
Davis, M. S. 77, 299, 405
De Beaugrande, R. A. 405
de Laurentiis, A. 405, 407, 416
de León, C. M. 353, 405, 421
De Mey, T. 82, 405
De Rosa, G. L. 366, 405, 407, 416
Deater-Deckard, K. 426
DeCamp, E. 205, 405
Deckers, L. 45, 80–81, 405–406
Delabastita, D. 178, 363, 366, 406, 412
Demjèn, Z. 282, 288, 432
Deneire, M. 375, 406
Dennett, D. C. 416
Derks, P. 29, 68–69, 381, 406
Devereux, P. G. 406
Di Maio, S. 151, 397, 406
Di Pietro, G. 356, 407
Díaz Perez, F. J. 349, 406
Díaz-Cintas, J. 358, 406
Dindia, K. 306, 406
Dionigi, A. 256, 282, 407
Dixon, P. A. 399
Dolan, R. J. 47, 68–69, 196, 412

Dollard, J. 224, 407
Dore, M. xvi, 341, 407
Downing, B. 13, 175, 407, 419
Downing, H. R. 13, 175, 407, 419
Downs, V. C. 378, 407, 417
Dressler, W. U. 221, 405
Drew, P. 169, 209, 252, 278, 290, 407, 414
Ducrot, O. 270, 407
Duguid, A. 330, 407, 426
Dunbar, N. 397
Dundes, A. 66, 224, 407
Dunning, D. 55, 419
Duranti, A. 413
Duruaku, T. 225, 408
Dynel, M. 163, 222, 408, 435

Eastmond, J. N. Jr. 342, 408
Ebeogu, A. 225, 408
Eco, U. xi, 116, 122, 325, 344, 351, 360–361, 364–365, 408
Edge, J. Richards, K. xiv, 56, 70, 406, 408
Edwards, C. L. 247, 254, 408
Edwards, D. 247, 254, 408
Eerdmans, S. L. 420
Eggleston, A. 404, 427
Eiman, A.-A. 423
Eisterhold, J. 166, 175, 252, 397, 408, 427
Ekman, P. 39–41, 80, 408, 410, 430
El-Arousy, N. A. 154, 408
Elliott, S. M. xvi, 82, 86, 400
Ellsworth, M. 430
Emanatian, M. 405
Emerson, J. P. 221, 281, 408
Empson, W. 181, 408
Erb, M. 417
Erickson, K. V. 401
Ermida, I. 323, 327–329, 339, 408
Everts, E. 227, 267, 284, 409
Eysenck, H. J. 80, 409

Fatigante, M. 232, 255, 409
Fauconnier, G. 296, 409
Ferrari, C. F. 355, 409
Ferro-Luzzi, G. E. 70, 82, 409

Festinger, L. 50, 409
Feyaerts, K. 394, 399, 435
Filkuková, P. 195, 409
Fillmore, C. J. 114–115, 135, 221, 409
Fisher, B. 407
Fitzpatrick, E. D. 44, 421
Fitzpatrick, T. 195, 409,
Flamson, T. 232, 409
Fogel, A. 425
Foot, H. C. 21, 29, 45, 104, 402, 406, 409, 428–429, 433
Forabosco, G. 45, 62, 64, 77, 79, 82, 86, 94, 409
Ford, C. E. 242, 291, 410
Ford, T. 52, 77, 410
Forman, R. 375, 410
Fortanet-Gàmez, I. 430
Fox Tree, J. E. 228, 400
Fox, B. A. 242, 291, 400, 410
Frank, M. G. 15, 41–42, 400, 410
Freud, S. 6, 21, 60, 63, 65, 70–71, 79, 82–83, 140, 145, 171, 173–174, 220, 369, 410, 433
Fridlund, A. J. 39, 44–45, 410
Friesen, W. V. 39–40, 408, 410
Fry, W. F. Jr. 28, 61–62, 147, 220, 309, 410
Frye, M. 44, 437
Frymier, A. B. 436
Fuchs, C. 251, 435
Fuentes Luque, A. F. 347, 349–350, 410

Gabora, L. 77, 415
Gambier, Y. 402
Gangemi, A. 416
Garces, C. V. 436
García-Falces Fernàndez, A. 350, 404
Garmendia, J. 11, 396, 410
Gasquet-Cyrus, M. 209, 312, 410
Gattis, M. 232, 416
Gavanski, I. 45, 47, 411
Gavioli, L. 250, 411
Gayle, B. M. 421
Gerber, W. S. 80, 411

Gervais, M. 69, 300, 411
Giakoumelou, M. 394
Gibbs, R. W. Jr. 175, 252, 262, 411
Giles, H. 43, 411
Gillikin, L. S. 406
Ginsburg, G. P. 44, 406
Giora, R. 71, 168, 192, 411
Gironzetti, E. xvi, 40, 231–232, 411, 428
Glenn, P. 43, 239–245, 248, 252, 258–259, 261–262, 267, 279, 291–292, 296–298, 403, 409, 411–412, 415–416, 429, 434
Goatly, A. 163, 165, 184, 412
Goel, V. 47, 68–69, 196, 412
Goffman, E. xiv, 5, 40, 51, 167, 216–221, 234, 388, 412, 414
Goharpey, N. 427
Goldstein, J. H. 21, 29, 412, 418, 422, 426, 434, 438
Goodwin, C. 413, 437
Gottlieb, H. 356, 412
Grace, D. M. 381, 409, 427
Graesser, A. C. 248, 412
Grant, M. A. 35, 101, 242, 412
Gray, C. D. 45, 421
Gray, J. 421
Grecious, M. 423
Green, T. A. 198, 426
Greimas, A. J. 91–92, 323, 412
Grice, H. P. 61, 63, 81, 133, 159, 161, 165, 174–175, 179, 345–346, 386, 412
Grimm, R. 431
Grodd, W. 417
Groos, K. 21, 220, 412
Gruner, C. R. 65, 222, 412
Guagnano, D. 163, 412
Guidi, A. 190, 198, 412
Guiraud, P. 61, 76, 100, 191, 196, 198, 412
Gumperz, J. J. ix, xiv, 201, 211–217, 219, 221, 223–227, 234–235, 267, 313, 338, 385, 399, 407, 413, 416, 420, 423

Günther, U. 239, 254, 257, 286–288, 305–306, 413

Haakana, M. 255, 282, 413
Haiman, J. 300, 335, 413
Halula, S. P. 367, 413
Hamilton, H. E. 396, 403, 413, 434
Hamilton, T. 331, 413,
Hamrick, P. 72, 413
Han, Q. 353, 413
Han, Z. 381, 425,
Harmon, E. A. 50, 231, 413, 437
Harmon-Jones, E. 50, 413
Harrison, C. 358, 413
Haslam, S. 427
Haugh, M. 224–225, 257, 269, 277–278, 288–289, 297, 414
Hausmann, F. J. 189, 198, 414
Haviland, J. M. 429
Hay, J. xix, 47, 56, 167, 179, 224, 244, 249–250, 253, 264, 293, 296–298, 397, 414
Healy, M. 427
Heath, C. 142, 255, 414, 420
Heidari-Shahreza, M. A. 375, 414
Heine, B. 399
Hempelmann, C. F. xvi, 20, 26, 29, 87–90, 109, 134, 148, 150, 152–153, 188–190, 198, 302, 397, 414–415, 428, 431
Henry, J. 190, 360, 362–365, 415
Hepburn, A. 239, 253–254, 415, 427
Heritage, J. 238, 241, 262, 304, 395, 408, 415, 417
Hermand, J. 431
Hermans, T. 434
Herrick, M. T. 242, 415
Heun, R. 417
Hjelmslev, L. 97, 415
Hockett, C. F. 143, 152, 415
Hodson, R. J. 376, 415
Hofstadter, D. 77, 415
Hoicka, E. 232, 415–416
Holcomb, C. xi, 253, 323–324, 331, 416

Holmes, J. 63, 167, 236, 264, 274–277, 283–284, 286–287, 295, 298, 305–306, 416
Holt, E. 43, 239–244, 252, 256–258, 261–262, 264, 267, 279, 291–292, 298, 399, 403, 407, 409, 411–413, 415–416, 429, 434
Holt, J. 43, 239–244, 252, 256–258, 261–262, 264, 267, 279, 291–292, 298, 399, 403, 407, 409, 411–413, 415–416, 429, 434
Hsu, H. C. 425
Huang, C. R. 134, 416
Huang, M. 411
Huber, O. 431
Hudak, M. A. 404
Hudson, J. D. 399
Hurley, M. M. 60, 416
Hymes, D. ix, xiv, 51, 167, 201, 211–219, 221–225, 227, 234–235, 261, 267, 280, 286, 309, 338, 388, 399, 407, 413, 416, 423

Iaia, P. L. 340, 416
Ikeda, K. 232, 241, 248, 416
Irwin, J. 436
Isoda, T. 425
Isola, A. 282, 394
Iwase, M. Y. 68, 417

Jackman, H. 175, 417
Jakobson, R. 27, 101, 103, 344–345, 417
Janata P. M. 423
Janko, R. 19, 417
Jared, D. 197, 417
Javidi, M. M. 371, 378, 407, 417
Jefferson, G. xx, 46, 215, 222, 237–239, 241, 247–248, 252, 254, 256, 261, 279, 417, 431
Jenkins, M. 305, 417
Jensen, M. N. 407
Jessen, F. 191, 417
Johnson, C. R. 19, 430
Just, M. A. xvi, 3–4, 6–7, 12, 14, 25–26, 31, 35, 39, 46, 48, 59, 62–63, 66, 81, 86, 92, 97–99, 103, 105, 115, 119, 135, 138, 146, 152, 158–159, 173, 177, 179, 189, 193, 205, 209, 222, 233, 236, 239, 245, 260, 262, 264–266, 269, 273, 276, 279, 282, 289–290, 296, 303, 305, 314, 320, 324, 329–330, 346, 361–362, 365, 368, 372, 377, 379, 381–383, 385, 414, 417, 420–421, 433

Kameas, A. 427
Kaplan, R. M. 369, 371, 418
Karasik, V. 396
Karlin, N. J. 374, 420
Karman, B. 145, 418
Kaszniak, A. W. 430
Kato, C. 425
Kaukomaa, T. 233, 418
Keith-Spiegel, P. 59, 418
Kelley, W. 423
Kihara, C. P. 224, 418
Kintsch, W. 115, 124, 418
Kittay, E. F. 114, 135, 419
Kizer, P. 80, 405
Klein, D. M. 370, 377, 418, 425
Klein, J. 370, 377, 418, 425
Klempe, S. H. 195, 409
Klose, U. 417
Klungervik-Greenall, A. J. 163, 418
Knapp, J. 187, 423
Knoblauch, H. 426
Kobler, J. B. 69, 435
Kochman, T. 223, 418
Koester, A. 288, 418
Kolberg, K. 372, 420
Koller, M. R. 299, 418
Korta, K. 396
Kotthoff, H. 167, 221–222, 227, 239, 264, 270, 277, 280, 291, 296, 305, 308–309, 315, 418
Kozin, A. 296, 437
Krikmann, A. 77, 419
Kruger, J. 55, 419
Kuhn, T. S. 17, 23–24, 69, 419

Kuipers, G. 299, 303–304, 419
Kutas, M. 68–69, 404

Labov, W. 222–223, 259–260, 419
Ladmiral, J. R. 432
Laineste, L. 422
Lakoff, R. 227, 305, 419
Lampropoulou, S. 394
Landheer, R. 192, 419
Larkin Galiñanes, C. L. 330–331, 419
Larsen, G. 381, 419, 421
Larsen-Freeman, D. 381, 419
Latta, R. L. 77, 82, 419, 425
Lavallee, J. P. 196, 402
Lavin, D. 215, 256, 419
Lawson, T. J. 45, 419
Leach, J. W. 407
Leandro, F. 410
Lederer, M. 432
Lee, D. 286, 378–379, 419
Lee, J. 417
Leech, G. N. 11, 161, 175, 419
Lefort, B. 28, 419
Lehrer, A. 114, 135, 419
Lemmens, M. 233, 434
Lenci, A. 416
Lessard, D. 26, 107, 419
Levenson, R. W. 408
Leventhal, H. 44, 47, 419–420
Levinson, S. C. 226, 274–275, 399, 420
Levy, H. 432
Lew, R. 198, 420
Lewis, M. 429
Liao, C.-C. 375, 420
Liao, Y.-J. 402
Lingenfelser, F. 404
Lipps, T. 83, 420
Liu, S. J. 397
Loewenstein, J. 142, 420
Lomotey, F. 397
Long, D. L. xiii, 1, 6, 8, 36, 40, 42–43, 86, 98–99, 107, 139, 142, 147, 161, 167, 194, 203, 221, 229, 240, 243, 247, 271, 280, 292, 295, 307, 319–320, 325–327, 333, 336, 352, 359, 362, 369–370, 377, 382–383, 412
Loomans, D. 372, 420
López González, C. R. 350, 420
Lopez, B. G. 196, 420
Lorini, E. 80, 420
Lotman, J. M. 81, 95, 420
Lotze, M. 417
Low, P. A. xvi, 33, 52, 132, 287, 310, 335, 343, 345, 348, 350, 363, 365, 370, 379, 420
Luebbert, M. C. 435
Lundberg, E. 372, 420
Lynch, O. H. 285, 420

Macaulay, M. 405,
Macaulay, R. K. 420
Mace, W. 47, 420
Machlev, M. 374, 420
MacKenzie, L. 396
Maier, N. R. F. 73, 83, 421
Mallafrè, J. 365, 421
Mallett, J. 282, 421
Malpass, L. F. 44, 421
Mandelbrot, B. 122, 421
Mandler, J. M. 120–121, 421
Marci, C. D. 282, 421
Margolies, L. 289, 421
Markiewicz, D. 368–369, 421
Marra, M. 167, 283–284, 416
Martín de León, C. 421
Martin, D. M. 373, 380, 421
Martin, G. N. 45, 421
Martin, R. A. 17, 39, 56, 60, 62, 77, 80, 82, 94, 267, 281, 306, 367, 380, 421
Martínez-Sierra, J. J. 355–356, 422
Matsuo, K. 425
Maurer, J. 427
Maxim, J. 133–135, 159–161, 163, 166–170, 175, 329, 345–346, 386, 395, 437
Maynard, D. W. 215, 256, 419
McCluskey-Fawcett, K. A. 424

McConnachie, D. 426
McGhee, P. E. 21, 29, 52, 86, 400, 404, 412, 418, 422, 424, 426, 429, 434, 438
McGlone, M. S. 195, 422
McGraw, A. P. 20, 422
McIlvenny, P. 206, 422
McKeown, G. J. 404
McMorris, R. F. 373, 380, 422
McNeely, R. 372, 422
Meany, M. M. 204, 422
Meara, P. 195, 422
Medgyes, P. 372, 422
Mehrabian, A. 375, 422
Menjo, S. 397, 411
Menon, V. 423
Mervis, C. 115, 429
Mettovaara, S. 422
Metz, R. 84, 422
Meyers, M. 423
Miller, D. L. 37, 404
Miller, T. 188–190, 198, 415
Milner, G. B. 186, 188, 423
Minsky, M. 114, 423
Mio, J. S. 412
Mitchell, A. 26, 224, 423
Mitchell-Kernan, C. 224, 423
Mobbs, D. 68, 423
Moder, C. L. 195, 401
Monro, D. H. 59, 77, 423
Monrouxe, L. V. 282, 429
Mooney, A. 163, 423
Moonwomon, B. 417
Morain, G. G. 302, 423
Moran, E. K. 421
Moran, J. M. 47, 423
Morin, V. 92, 331, 423
Moriya, T. 425
Morreall, J. 7, 77–78, 94–95, 423
Morrison, J. 44–45, 203, 423
Mulkay, M. 89, 262, 290–291, 296, 299, 423
Mullany, L. 276, 295, 423
Muñoz Sánchez, P. 358, 406
Murphy, B. 45, 423

Nahemow, L. 308, 424
Nakai, H. 425
Napoli, D. J. 5, 434
Nardini, G. 309, 424
Narrog, H. 399
Nash, W. 70, 329, 424
Neff, P. 375, 424
Nelms, J. L. 12, 424
Nerhardt, G. 79–80, 149, 424
Nesi, H. 286, 379, 424
Neuliep, J. W. 379, 424
Neves, J. 407
Newman, P. 262, 435
Nida, E. A. 346–347, 424
Nikiforidou, K. 140, 332, 334, 394
Nilsen, A. 21, 319–320, 424
Nilsen, D. 21, 319–320, 424
Nirenburg, S. 115, 134, 424
Nistal, P. F. 438
Nobezawa, E. 417
Nord, C. 352, 424
Norrick, N. R. 152, 206, 221–222, 227, 229, 253, 259–260, 262, 267, 269, 274, 277, 280, 296–297, 377, 424–425
Norton, B. 401, 410
Novak, W. 354, 425
Nuolijärvi, P. 167, 425
Nussbaum, J. F. 404, 407, 417
Nwachukwu-Agbada, J. 225, 425
Nwokah, E. E. 240, 425

O'Connor, B. M. 405
Oaks, D. 181, 425
Okada, C. 417
Olbrechts-Tyteca, L. 43, 425
Oltramari, A. 416
Oring, E. xvi, 82, 86–90, 94, 114, 141, 144, 184, 425
Orletti, F. 232, 255, 409
Orr, S. P. 421
Ortega, E. 154, 269, 381, 393, 410, 425
Ortega, L. 154, 269, 381, 393, 410, 425

Ouchi, H. 417
Owen, A. M. 398
Oxford, G. S. iv, 1, 3, 30, 43, 57, 78, 95, 111, 113, 116, 136, 157, 176, 199, 201, 235, 263, 299, 317, 319, 340, 367, 381, 393, 397, 399, 402, 404, 409–411, 413, 419, 423, 428–431, 433–434, 437
Ozawa, F. 68, 425
Özkök, B. 407

Padilla Garcìa, X. A. 407
Paolillo, J. C. 141, 154, 425
Papapavlou, A. N. 309, 425
Papazachariou, D. 394
Partington, A. xvi, 169, 286, 288, 329–330, 425–426
Pascoe, G. C. 369, 371, 418
Paulos, J. A. 77, 82, 426
Pavlicek, M. 358–359, 426
Pearson, P. D. 114, 393
Peirce, C. S. 116, 122, 345, 392, 395, 426
Pelletier, F. J. 432
Pelsmaekers, K. 292, 357, 426
Pepicello, W. J. 113, 198, 426
Peräkylä, A. 233, 418, 426
Perego, E. 405, 407, 416
Perlmutter, D. D. 63, 82, 426
Petraki, E. 375, 426
Petray, M. J. 397
Petrill, S. A. 426
Petruck, M. R. L. 120, 126, 135, 426, 430
Pexman, P. M. 251–252, 262, 298, 426, 436–437
Pham Nguyen, H. H. 375, 426
Pickering, L. xvii, 211, 229–231, 240, 397, 411, 427–428
Piddington, R. 59, 77, 427
Pien, D. 88, 429
Pietrangelo, D. J. 422
Pillet-Shore, D. 278, 414
Pinner, B. 433
Pirandello, L. 21, 427
Piskorska, A. 437
Pizzini, F. 281, 427

Platow, M. J. 45, 427
Platt, H. K. 213, 427
Platt, J. T. 213, 427
Platt, T. 40–41, 56, 427
Pöchhacker, F. 358–359, 426–427
Poggi, I. 397
Poli, R. 134, 421, 427
Pollack, J. 180, 427
Pollio, H. R. 44–45, 147, 203, 423, 427, 432
Pomerantz, A. 376–378, 380, 398
Popa, D. E. 353, 413, 415, 423, 427
Porcu, L. 308, 427
Porteous, J. 69, 300, 427
Potter, J. 169, 253–254, 427
Powell, J. P. 371, 380, 427
Poyatos, F. 43, 427
Preiss, R. W. 421
Prerost, F. J. 45, 203, 428
Prevignano, C. L. 420
Prickett, E. 282, 398
Priego-Valverde, B. x, xvi, 145, 222, 262, 266, 269–273, 280, 294–295, 297, 396, 428
Propp, V. J. 92, 428
Provine, R. R. 240, 428
Psathas, G. 417
Puhlik-Doris, P. 421
Pullum, G. K. 432
Purkey, W. W. 377, 404

Qian, W. 438
Quillian, M. R. 116, 428

Raab, J. 426
Ragan, S. L. 281, 428
Raghunathan, R. 420
Rahman, J. 224–225, 428
Rall, M. 433
Raphaelson-West, D. 346, 354, 365, 428
Raskin, V. xvi, xix, 7, 17, 21–22, 36, 56, 59, 62, 71, 77, 84, 87, 89, 111, 114–118, 120, 122, 127–130, 132–135, 137–138, 142, 144, 150–152, 156, 163, 177, 202, 204,

Raskin, V. (*Cont.*)
 220, 300, 321–323, 325, 329–330, 354, 386–387, 390, 396–397, 401, 405, 415, 424, 428, 430, 434–435
Reber, E. 410
Recuero, S. I. 13, 175, 407
Reddington, E. 377, 429
Redfern, W. 70, 429
Rees, C. E. 282, 429
Regattin, F. 177, 360, 429
Reiss, A. L. 351, 436
Reiss, K. 423, 429
Ricoy, R. D. P. 346, 356–357, 363, 437
Ritchie, G. 198, 342, 429
Riva, G. 395
Rodd, J. M. 398
Rodden, F. 77, 429
Rodriguez, D. 397
Romaniuk, T. 257, 429
Romer, U. 407
Rosch, E. 115, 429
Rosen, D. H. 435
Rosini, S. 427
Ross, A. 70, 429
Rothbart, M. K. 88, 429
Routh, D. K. 80, 411
Rowe, C. 283, 432
Rozin, A. 142, 429
Rozin, P. 142, 429
Ruch, W. xvi, 7, 13–14, 17, 29, 38–42, 56, 79, 88, 90, 137, 412, 415, 427, 429–430
Rucynski, J. 375, 424
Ruiz Gurillo, L. 167, 407, 430
Ruiz-Madrid, M. N. 232, 430
Rumelhart, D. E. 115, 430
Ruppenhofer, J. 115, 430
Russell, B. 23, 27–28, 61–62, 399, 430
Rutter, J. 114, 204–206, 217, 232, 430–431
Ruusuvuori, J. 233, 418, 426
Rychlowska, M. 404

Sacks, H. ix, 89, 142, 206, 222, 236, 239, 241, 243, 246–250, 252–253, 258–259, 279, 298, 352, 417, 431
Sadie, S. 108, 431
Sadler, S. J. 45, 421
Samson, A. C. 26, 88, 90, 109, 415, 431
Santarcangelo, P. 396
Saussure, F. de 21, 31–32, 97, 116, 193, 195, 201, 211–212, 326, 335, 345, 391, 431
Saville-Troike, M. 234, 431
Scarpetta, F. 205, 431
Schank, R. C. 114, 121, 401, 431
Scheffczyk, J. 430
Schegloff, E. A. 236, 241, 252–253, 279, 290, 417, 431
Schellens, P. J. 401
Schenkein, J. 431
Scher, S. P. 108, 431
Schiffrin, D. 234, 396, 403, 413, 432
Schmitz, J. R. 375, 431
Schnettler, B. 426
Schnurr, S. 255, 261–262, 275–277, 282–285, 295, 298, 403, 416, 432, 438
Schoenemann, T. 409
Scholz, B. C. 58, 432
Schopler, J. 433
Schultz, T. R. 433
Schulze, R. 407
Scogin, F. R. Jr. 147, 432
Searle, J. R. 158, 175, 179, 215, 432
Seewoester, S. 182, 432
Seifried, B. 427
Seizer, S. 140, 206, 218, 432
Seleskovitch, D. 363, 432
Selting, M. 410
Semino, E. 282, 395, 432
Senzani, A. 394
Shade, R. A. 372, 432
Shammi, P. 48, 432
Sherzer, J. 171, 213, 218–219, 221, 225, 234, 259, 300, 314, 398, 431–432

Shieber, S. M. 126, 432
Shiffrin, D. 434
Shifman, L. 326, 432
Shipley, T. Y. 346, 432
Shlesinger, M. 402
Siegel, J. 227, 309, 313, 433
Sifianou, M. 153, 269, 394
Silberberg, R. 400
Simon, R. K. 20–21, 169, 433
Simpson, P. 140, 321, 332, 335, 337–339, 358, 393, 409, 433
Skalicky, S. 289–290, 433
Skowron, J. 338, 433
Slyshkin, G. 396
Smith Bowen, E. 303, 433
Smith J. R. 45, 409
Smith, J. 45, 436
Smith, M. 114, 209–211, 433
Smith, M. E., 415
Smith, T. 436
Smoski, M. J. 41, 248, 262, 433
Smuts, A. 59, 61, 77, 433
Sobkowiak, W. 433
Soeffner, H. G. 426
Sowayan, S. A. 224, 433
Spagnolli, A. 205, 431
Spencer, H. 20, 60, 433
Sperber, D. 262, 433
Spielberger, C. D. 429
Spiro, R. J. 430
Steiner, G. 343, 433
Stokols, D. 44, 203, 433
Stolze, R. 402
Straehle, C. A. 221, 434
Stuss, D. T. 48, 432
Sudnow, D. 417
Suls, J. 28, 64, 79, 434
Sutton-Spence, R. 5, 434
Swain, M. 376, 401
Swanson, C. 44–45, 203, 427
Szpila, G. 396

Tabacaru, S. 233, 434
Taber, C. R. 346–347, 424
Takehara, Y. 425

Tannen, D. x, 185, 218, 227, 234, 266–267, 277, 280, 296, 298, 396, 403, 413, 434
Tapio, R. 422
Taylor, C. 426
Taylor, J. M. 134–135, 428, 434
Ten Have, P. 262, 434
Thaler, V. 396
Thayer Buttram, R. 406
Thelwall, M. 432
Thibault, P. J. 420
Thompson, D. E. 393
Thonus, T. 253, 296, 434
Thurston, C. M. 372, 420
Ticca, A. C. 282, 434
Tiittula, L. 167, 425
Tinholt, H. W. 128, 434
Titze, M. 13, 434
Tofighbakhsh, J. 195, 422
Toohey, K. 401
Toury, G. 347, 434
Trier, J. 114, 434
Triezenberg, K. E. 319, 329, 435
Trouvain, J. 41–43, 56, 435
Truong, K. P. 41–43, 56, 435
Tsakona, V. xvi, 26, 88–90, 93, 141, 152–154, 167, 207, 222, 269, 292, 325–326, 394, 403, 435
Tsami, V. 394
Tsang, W. K. 206, 435
Tsekouras, A. 427
Tu, C.-H. 360–361, 402
Tufford, L. 262, 435
Turner, M. R. 26, 435

Urios-Aparisi, E. 375, 397, 436

Vaid, J. 69, 73, 196, 300, 420, 435
Valdeón, R. A. 341, 435
Van Besien, F. 292, 357, 426
van der Wege, M. M. 149, 403
Van Dijk, T. A. 417, 432
van Mulken, M. 228, 298, 401
Vandaele, J. 359, 394, 435
Vandergriff, I. 251, 435

Varney, S. 239, 415
Veale, T. 72, 82, 394, 399, 435
Vega, G. 376, 436
Vermeer, H. J. 347, 351–352, 429, 436
Viaggio, S. 358, 436
Vincent, H. 154, 326, 436
Vrticka, P. 77, 436

Wachtel, C. 429
Wagner, H. L. 45, 436
Wagner, J. 404
Wagner, M. M. xvi, 375, 397, 436
Walaszewska, E. 437
Waldoks, M. 354, 425
Walle, A. H. 279, 436
Wanzer, M. B. 374–375, 436
Waring, H. Z. 378, 429
Warren, C. 20, 422
Weir, K. 421
Weisberg, R. W. 113, 426
Wells, P. 206, 400, 436
Wennerstrom, A. 232, 436
West, C. 194, 255, 281, 346, 354, 365, 401, 403, 414, 428, 436
Whalen, J. M. 251–252, 262, 298, 436–437
Whissell C. 401
Wilkinson, R. 255–256, 437
Williams, J. A. 231, 256, 437
Williamson, L. 346, 356–357, 363, 437
Wilson, D. 69, 262, 300, 411, 433
Wilson, D. S. 69, 262, 300, 411, 433
Winchatz, M. R. 296, 437

Winsted, D. 406
Winters, J. A. 80–81, 406
Wittgenstein, L. 23, 69, 96, 337, 437
Wojtaszczyk, A. M. 436
Wong, M. 206, 435
Wooffitt, R. 237, 437
Wu, Q. 353, 437
Wulf, D. 376, 437
Wycoff, E. B. 22–23, 437

Yetkin, N. 358, 437
Yin, P. A. 353, 437
Yokoyama, S. 417
Yoshikawa. 417
Yus, F. 76, 175, 354, 365, 437

Zabalbeascoa, P. xi, xvi, 342–343, 346–349, 353, 355–357, 359, 364–366, 406, 422, 437–438
Zadjman, A. 438
Zayts, O. 255, 261–262, 282, 438
Zdrazilova, L. 426
Zhang, Q. 167, 375, 411, 438
Zhang, Y. 167, 375, 411, 438
Zhao, X. 204, 438
Zhou, A. 438
Zhu, F. 438
Zijderveld, A. C. 299, 438
Zillmann, D. 25, 65, 367, 371–372, 400, 418, 438
Ziv, A. 43, 53, 59, 82, 85–86, 369–370, 438–439
Zysset, S. 431

Subject index

A

absurd xv, 85, 99, 106, 125, 150
absurdities 69, 99
absurdity 84, 87, 89, 257
acrolect 310, 386
acronym 22, 280
addressee 179, 210, 216, 277, 353
affiliation 65, 206, 222, 224, 232, 249, 252, 257, 261–262, 273, 277, 279, 284, 403, 414, 436
Africa 66, 132, 209, 222, 224, 300, 303, 403, 408
aggression vi, xix, 1, 7, 9–10, 12, 20, 57, 59–60, 62–67, 71–72, 76, 99, 144–147, 168, 210, 218, 224–225, 261, 271–274, 276–277, 280, 294, 308–309, 336, 370, 374, 398
AI 114, 116, 429
alliteration 70, 139, 187, 364
ambiguity viii, 33, 70, 72, 107–108, 139, 160, 171, 181–182, 184–187, 196–197, 240, 245, 271, 300, 330, 333, 361, 386, 389, 398, 400, 408, 419–420, 425, 432, 434
ambiguous 7, 16, 93, 127, 146, 160, 171–172, 174, 186, 190, 192, 224, 241, 245, 271, 279, 289, 368, 385–386
American xiv–xv, 12–13, 16, 20, 66, 82, 99, 189, 203, 222, 281, 288–289, 301–302, 304, 307, 309, 340, 355, 363, 379, 393, 402, 404–405, 407, 413–414, 416, 419, 423, 428, 430, 433
anagrams 177
analogy 60, 85, 138, 415
anecdotes xvi, 9, 141, 144, 163, 221, 260
Anthropology 12, 21, 75, 300, 302, 338, 398, 413, 416, 422, 432

anthropomorphic 105, 184
antiphonal laughter 41, 248, 262, 433
antonymy 117–118, 128, 385, 389
aphorism 195, 422
appropriate incongruity 85–87, 1
appropriateness 87, 126, 166, 175, 215, 247, 260, 280, 374, 387
arousal 399, 429
asteism 11, 388
Astérix 340
audience 5–6, 31, 39, 42, 44–45, 48, 51, 55, 66, 98, 100, 102, 111, 131, 143, 158, 166, 171, 173–174, 179, 198, 203–206, 208–209, 216, 223, 237, 244, 246–249, 258–260, 264–266, 270, 274, 277, 290, 294, 301, 312, 327, 329, 339, 347, 352–353, 355, 359, 369, 395, 400–401, 405, 410, 416, 419, 421–423, 427, 430–431, 436
audiovisual xi, 340–342, 348, 355–357, 359, 365, 397, 400, 405–407, 410, 416, 422, 426, 437–438
Australian 225, 277, 288, 301, 414, 416

B

backgrounded vi, 83, 88, 90, 93, 98, 109, 148–149, 152, 388, 431
banter 11–12, 52, 167, 224–225, 305, 380
Bantu 224
basilect 310–311, 386
Beatles 328
behavioral 49, 81, 212, 393, 402, 407, 410,, 427–428, 430
behaviorist 298
behaviors 214, 278, 291, 294, 300, 313, 417
Belgium 147–148, 357

benign violation 20, 60, 422
bilingual 16, 353, 434
Biology 58–59, 351, 400, 411
bisociation vi, 60, 73–74, 77, 82, 269, 419
blank face 290
BNC 287, 413
bona-fide (non) vii, 72, 89, 113, 133–135, 153, 163, 165–167, 170, 174, 209, 220, 223, 261, 265, 270, 273, 285, 289, 329, 385
bracketing ix, 236–237, 262, 435
brain 31, 39–41, 68–69, 71, 88, 191–192, 196, 404, 417, 429, 432, 435, 437
British iv, 12–13, 20, 159, 180 205, 225, 287–288, 301, 340, 358, 379, 400, 409, 411, 413–414, 416, 421
Broca 68
buccinator (muscle) 40
Buddhism 35
buffo 338, 401
burla 431
burlesque 13
Burundi 309

C

CA ix, 235–237, 239, 241, 243, 245–249, 251–253, 255, 257, 259, 262–264, 295, 407–410, 417, 420, 434, 438
California 405, 417, 423, 432
cancer 282, 398, 406, 432
canned joke ix, 14–17, 206, 229–231, 243, 246–247, 260, 287, 438
canned laughter 292, 427
Caribbean 314
caricature 45, 86, 330–331
carnival 13, 314
cartoon 5, 8, 26, 44–45, 51, 88, 90, 104–105, 141–142, 154, 209–211, 302, 340, 370, 380, 406, 408, 415, 434–435
Catalan 355
Catanese 310–311
catastrophe theory 60, 77, 82
Catholic 19, 53, 302

Chamula 309
character v, 4–6, 9, 18, 20, 35, 65, 121, 124, 147, 149, 151, 163, 184, 193, 202, 307–308, 313, 323–324, 326, 330–331, 335, 337, 342, 355–356, 385
Charity 151, 172, 174–175, 417
Chastushka 144
chiastic 188
child 4, 6, 45, 66–67, 86, 129, 143, 161, 164, 173–174, 203, 225, 232, 252, 255, 257, 308–309, 328, 346, 371, 400, 402, 404, 426, 436
China 299, 353
Chinese 99, 176, 228, 314, 353, 375, 396, 402, 438
Chomsky xv, 11, 32–33, 74, 182, 202, 212, 381, 387, 403
Christ 328
cinema 25–26, 202, 356, 389 (see film)
classemes 91
classroom xii, 12, 177, 215, 240, 251, 285, 309, 377–380, 398, 400, 405, 407, 410, 413, 420–422, 424, 426, 429, 432, 435–436, 438–439
clichè 268, 291
climax 62, 229, 357
clowns 25, 104, 314, 338, 377, 398, 404, 416, 425
coercion 334, 385
cognition 17–18, 39, 46–48, 50–53, 58, 60, 64, 68–69, 73, 76–78, 80–81, 83, 86, 115, 123, 125, 231, 245, 308, 332, 339, 353–354, 365, 373, 386–387, 390, 394–397, 399, 403–404, 406–407, 409–413, 415, 418–420, 422, 425, 429–430, 432–437
collocation 185, 330, 391
comedian 25, 204–206, 208, 229, 249, 280, 307
comedy xvii, 7, 13, 17–20, 52, 54, 56, 154, 202–204, 216–218, 221, 223, 234, 249, 261, 280, 301, 307, 314, 319, 326, 338–339, 348, 394, 399,

454

401–402, 405, 413, 417–418, 421–422, 430–432, 435–436, 438
comic 3, 7, 9, 10, 20, 22, 83, 203, 296, 314, 330–331, 335–336, 347–348, 397–398, 405, 407–408, 416–417, 423, 425, 427, 431, 433, 435, 437
community 5, 23, 203–204, 212–213, 219, 227, 284, 383, 401, 413
communities of practice 275–276, 284,
commutation (principle of) v, 30, 34–36, 56, 385–386
compères 49, 430
competence v, vii, xiv–xv, 1, 30–33, 37, 49–50, 54, 81, 100, 111, 131, 134, 156, 197, 202, 204, 207–208, 211–212, 256, 295, 300, 303, 314, 341, 376, 387, 395, 401, 415, 436–437
complaints 46, 120, 243, 254, 255–257, 408
complexity 50, 137, 215, 234, 381, 383, 399, 406, 425
computer (computational) 14, 27, 60, 75, 81, 85, 115, 120, 123, 134, 217, 228, 256, 317, 393, 406, 416, 427, 432, 434–435
connector 91–94, 190–191
contextualization ix, 15–16, 62, 72, 96, 102, 127, 171, 205, 211, 213, 216, 218, 226–228, 239, 257, 267–268, 280, 289–292, 298, 309, 312–313, 347, 376, 365, 385–387, 398, 413, 418, 420, 438
contrast 47, 52, 59–60, 71, 106, 155, 162, 165, 169, 205, 228, 305, 378, 387
conversation ix–x, xiii–xv, xvii, 14–17, 24, 38, 42, 45, 47, 54, 99, 102, 144, 153–155, 159–160, 166–168, 179, 199, 202–207, 209, 215, 217, 222, 226–227, 230–244, 246–254, 256–264, 266–273, 279–283, 285–289, 295, 297–298, 314, 342, 378, 383, 385–386, 389, 394–397, 399, 403, 405–406, 408, 411–414,

418, 424, 427–428, 430–431, 434, 437–438
cooperation viii, 61, 63, 66, 81, 133, 135, 159–160, 165–166, 172–175, 220, 272–273, 282, 305, 329, 385–388, 395–396, 423
CORHUM 22
corpus x, 13, 23–24, 36–38, 54, 76, 89, 131–132, 155, 167, 237, 240, 254, 257, 263, 269, 283, 286–288, 290, 294, 298, 306, 329–330, 350, 353, 355, 357, 378–379, 383, 397, 399, 413, 425–426
cortex 47–48, 68
CP viii, 157, 159–161, 163–167, 175, 385
Cratylistic ix, 176, 192–198
cue 195, 226–227, 239, 289, 292, 309, 312–313, 385, 388
contextualization cues ix, 54–55, 62, 216, 218, 221, 226–227, 232, 257, 267–268, 289, 291, 293, 296, 298, 357, 376,
Cyrus 209, 309, 312, 410, 425

D
DA (Discourse Analysis) x, 236–237, 241, 262–267, 269, 271, 273, 275, 277, 279, 289, 291, 293–295
Dakota 306, 406
deadpan (delivery) 51, 268, 289–290, 292, 357
deception 6, 159, 161, 166, 220, 337, 396, 408
decommitment 273, 278–279
defunctionalization 61–62, 76, 96, 99, 100–103, 109, 273–274
derision 43, 59–60
dialect x, 218, 227, 307, 309–310, 312, 315, 335–336, 340, 343, 364, 386, 407, 420, 425
dialogic x, 8, 141–142, 269–270, 397
disaffiliation 262, 273, 279, 429
disaffiliative 224, 232, 249–250, 257–258, 261–262, 277, 282, 284

discourse ix–x, xii, xiv–xv, 12, 17, 22, 46, 54, 56, 58, 61–62, 76, 102, 128, 153, 163, 166, 169, 199, 201–203, 206, 208–209, 212, 216, 218, 221, 234–237, 239, 248, 253, 259, 263–264, 266–270, 272, 274–276, 278, 280, 282, 284, 286–290, 292, 294–298, 321, 324, 337–338, 367–368, 376–377, 383, 385, 387, 389, 393–394, 396, 400, 402–403, 405, 407–409, 411, 413–414, 416–419, 424, 426–428, 430, 432–438

disjunction vi, viii, 73–74, 79, 90–94, 182, 190–192, 336, 393

disparagement 59–60, 64–65, 67, 225, 370, 375, 438

disposition 60, 65, 374–375, 386, 398

dispreferred 166, 249, 255, 262

dissonance 50–51, 81, 123, 337, 387, 403, 409, 413

dozens 217, 222, 224, 393, 407

dubbing xi, 116, 142, 179, 327, 330, 341, 355–357, 400, 407, 409, 438

E

EEG 196

Egyptian 18, 408

electroencephalographic 406

Elizabethan 221, 339

embarrassment 13, 18, 40, 42–43, 46, 143, 225, 241, 243, 255–256, 258, 272, 274, 282, 312, 414

emotion 3, 17–18, 20, 39–41, 45–46, 48–49, 80, 90, 105, 233, 245, 289–290, 382, 386, 389, 394, 396, 400, 404, 406, 408, 417–418, 424, 429–430, 433

empathy 269, 305, 336

encyclopedia 1, 22, 133–134, 147, 390, 395–396, 399, 406, 409–410, 419, 425, 427–428, 432–433, 435

England 12–13, 16, 19, 98–99, 116, 141, 169, 180–181, 189–190, 192, 195, 198, 211, 222, 228, 261, 288–289, 300–302, 310, 312, 325, 342, 344, 350, 353, 355, 358–359, 361, 379, 390, 393, 398–399, 405, 411, 413–414, 417, 420, 424–425, 428, 433, 437

equivalence 101, 107, 345, 347–349, 351, 353, 365

essentialism vi, 57–59, 63–64, 66, 69, 75–77, 114, 131, 135, 337

ethnic 148, 330, 346, 405

ethnography 201, 211–213, 215, 222, 368, 398, 408, 413, 416, 418, 423, 431

ethnomethodological xiv, 76, 199, 201, 233, 235, 267, 297, 338, 377, 415, 417

ethological 62

etiolated (use of language) 220

etiquette 30

etymology 10, 182, 194–195, 260, 311, 390

Europe 22, 92, 270, 272, 302, 314, 331, 341, 358, 395, 400, 405, 407, 434

evolution vi, 59, 69, 135, 300, 410–411, 413, 427–428, 435

exaggeration 168, 257, 333, 363

excrement 132, 151

exemplar vii, 17, 129, 266, 320

exhilaration 17–18, 20, 39, 41, 46, 56, 386, 389, 429–430

exoticism 299, 354, 389

expectations 28–29, 64, 78–81, 106, 108, 128, 142, 159, 187, 229, 243, 287, 330, 379, 387, 389, 429

expected 29, 53, 62, 70, 166, 217, 223, 225, 243, 292, 324, 335, 377, 386

eye 6, 40, 105, 167, 173, 193, 197, 217, 231, 236–237, 294, 308, 326, 377, 391, 411, 417, 437

eyebrows 62, 232–233, 434

eye tracking 196–197, 217, 231, 326, 417

F

fabliaux 331

fabrications 220

Fabula 408
face 5, 40, 47, 62, 86, 105, 168, 179, 209, 231, 241, 244, 257, 269, 272, 274–275, 277–281, 283, 285, 288, 290–292, 314, 341, 356, 362, 377, 400, 410, 414, 430, 436, 438
Facebook 4, 37
face saving 247, 377
facetious 154, 215, 217, 254, 285, 362
facezie 8
facial 20, 39–42, 55, 62, 106, 176, 227–228, 232–233, 249, 266, 290, 292–293, 331, 391, 400, 404, 408, 410, 417–418, 426, 430
FACS 40, 233, 410, 430
failed 7, 55, 66, 80, 92, 171, 210–211, 215, 221, 244–245, 247, 250, 259, 269–270, 276, 287, 291–295, 328, 398
failure 47, 108, 156, 215, 244–245, 258, 293–295, 301, 395
fansubbing 358, 406
fantasy 52, 62, 85, 90, 222, 268, 288, 296, 319, 398, 422
farce 7, 13, 319–320, 336–338, 504
female 28, 58, 134, 152, 154, 172, 264, 276, 287, 304–306, 370–317, 374
fiction x–xi, 51–52, 61–63, 91, 96, 99, 109, 133, 144, 158, 160–161, 164–166, 186, 236, 263–265, 267, 269, 271–273, 275, 277, 279, 345–347, 349, 352–353, 363, 390, 396, 408, 412, 417–419
figurative 78, 104, 106–107, 162, 184, 330, 411, 416
Fijian 227, 433
film (see cinema) 5, 25, 176, 221, 294, 340, 342, 344, 346, 355–356, 389, 400–401, 408, 417, 420
fixations 197, 326, 417
flirting 40, 279
flout viii, 163–165, 169–170, 175, 387
fMRI 196, 402, 425
folklore 82, 86, 148, 302, 338, 393, 407, 428, 433, 436

fractal 121–122, 421
frame 21, 51–52, 62, 68, 73, 80–82, 89, 92, 104–106, 114–115, 119–123, 134–135, 147, 175, 212, 218–219, 221, 224, 227, 231–233, 247, 251, 310, 323, 327, 385, 390, 393, 397, 404, 409, 412, 419, 426, 428,
FrameNet 115, 430
framing 62, 167, 216, 218–221, 224, 257, 268, 278, 291, 380, 388, 394, 434
France xv, 19, 194, 209, 299, 312, 397–398, 410, 412
Friends (sitcom) 203, 340
friends x, xvi, 4, 45, 114, 125, 154, 217, 244, 258, 260–261, 269, 271–272, 280, 287, 295, 309, 383, 391, 398, 409, 411, 433–434
FTA (face threatening act) 274–275, 277, 281
function xix, 27, 58, 100–102, 117–118, 142, 145–146, 206, 220, 226–227, 243, 246–247, 262, 264–265, 267, 270, 273–274, 277–280, 289–291, 301, 304, 326, 329, 331, 336, 347, 351, 377, 379, 389, 400–401, 426
functional xi, 34, 58, 62, 91, 96, 99, 109, 133, 144, 158, 186, 236, 263, 269, 298, 345–347, 349, 352–353, 363, 386, 405, 408, 412, 417, 421, 427
Funktionskonstanz 352

G
gag 141, 355
games 25–26, 58, 69, 164, 177, 221, 271 340, 401, 412, 416
gender x, 34, 45, 58, 147, 208, 225, 231, 271, 287, 304–306, 315, 338, 374, 401, 404, 414, 416, 418, 421, 423, 427, 429
genre ix, 28–29, 31, 88, 139, 144, 160, 207, 216, 218, 221–222, 224–225, 246–247, 249, 300, 306, 313, 319, 337–338, 353, 376, 418, 425, 435
Gestalt 62, 73, 106, 114, 386, 401, 421

SUBJECT INDEX

gesture xvi, 102–103, 176, 217–218, 232–233, 249, 291, 356, 387, 400
grammatical 33, 55, 117, 211–213, 226, 314, 335, 376, 382, 387
graph xix, 116, 118–119
grapheme 26, 178, 193
graphical 97, 106–107, 121, 408
Greek 10, 18, 20, 63, 74, 78, 99, 133, 153, 167, 193, 195, 232, 242, 309, 301, 311, 313, 337–338, 346, 394, 412, 423, 425, 435
group iv, 8, 23, 36, 44–45, 49–50, 59, 67, 72, 88, 116–117, 120, 133, 145, 147, 187, 203, 207, 209–210, 212–213, 222–223, 225, 236–237, 246, 263–264, 272–275, 277, 287, 296, 301, 306, 313–314, 326, 378–379, 381, 392–393, 409, 414, 417, 420, 432
GTVH ix, 87, 113–114, 153, 206–208, 332–334, 345, 386, 389, 391, 394–396, 415, 428, 435
Guaraní 309–310
gyrus 47

H

handle (lexematic) 117, 121–122, 124,
hearer xix, 3–6, 47, 49, 51–52, 54, 63, 65, 67, 83–84, 98, 101, 145–146, 158, 161, 165, 167, 170–175, 178, 190–191, 207, 209, 216, 241, 245, 247–248, 250, 253–256, 259, 265, 270, 274–275, 294, 297, 326, 380, 385, 388–389
heteronomy 188–189
heterophonic 188, 387
heuristic 73, 169, 195, 422
homographs 117, 180, 179, 193, 387
homonymy 117, 139, 179, 184–185, 188, 193, 300, 387, 390
homophony 117, 139, 179–180, 186, 192–193, 197, 302, 387, 417
hospital 120, 273, 282, 310–311, 403–404
hostility 59–60, 67, 76, 212

hyperbole 162, 228, 330, 357
hyperdetermined 131
hyperonymy 117, 119, 350, 387
hypertext xv
hyponymy 117–119, 119, 387

I

idiomatic 140, 330, 332–333, 335
Igbo 225, 408, 425
Illocutionary 158
immediacy 375, 387, 422, 438
implicature viii, 56, 124–125, 159, 161–165, 167–168, 173, 265, 273, 290, 312, 331, 385, 387–388
implicit viii, 1, 10, 28, 32, 61–62, 79, 81, 83, 87, 107, 124–126, 141–142, 163, 171, 181, 188, 306, 310, 314, 341, 346, 349, 382, 399, 410, 412
impoliteness 246, 277, 404, 414, 418
improvised 17, 217, 296, 370, 405
inappropriateness 44, 164, 167–170, 174–175, 250, 254, 309, 314, 374–375, 395, 436
INC/RES 79, 390
incongruity vi, xv, 1, 19, 26, 28–29, 46, 50–53, 57, 59–60, 62–66, 68, 70–71, 73–90, 92–94, 104–106, 108, 113, 128, 139–140, 143, 148–150, 152, 163–165, 174, 177, 184, 187, 191–193, 196–197, 256–257, 260, 269–270, 292, 297, 312, 330, 332, 334–335, 338, 342, 374, 387–390, 394, 396–397, 405, 409, 415, 419, 422, 425–426, 429, 431, 435
indexical ix, 239, 242–243
inference 74, 83, 87, 102, 104–106, 117, 124–126, 129, 147–148, 150, 152, 162–165, 170, 173, 188, 226, 265, 273, 285, 289, 292, 296, 300, 312, 353–354, 361, 387, 413
ingroup 259
innuendo 173, 179, 191, 244, 279
insult 58, 222–224, 237, 305, 269, 407

458

interaction 5, 24, 52, 66, 71, 102, 145, 166–167, 184, 198, 204–205, 208, 213–214, 217–219, 231, 235–236, 239, 241–242, 247–248, 251, 253, 255, 257, 263, 265–266, 268, 276, 278–284, 287–288, 291, 296–297, 299, 306, 313, 315, 375, 378, 387, 393, 398–400, 403, 405, 409–411, 413–417, 420, 425, 427–432, 434–435, 437–438
interactionist 214, 299, 315
intercultural 393, 405, 428, 437
interdisciplinary 21, 297, 383, 415, 421, 438
internet xvi, 5, 10, 16, 59, 116, 204, 221, 309, 358, 432–433
interruption 6, 173, 218, 247, 358, 385, 388
intertextuality 108, 271
intonation 185, 189, 205, 227–228, 230, 232, 238, 293, 312, 356, 390
involuntary 15, 39, 53, 171, 179, 229
Iran 375
Ireland 21, 251
irony viii, xvi, xix, 3, 6–7, 9–13, 21, 68, 70, 76, 154, 157, 162, 167–170, 175, 227–228, 231, 247, 250, 262, 274, 288, 292–293, 300, 319, 330, 339, 357–358, 360, 388–389, 395, 397, 401, 403, 407–408, 410–411, 418, 425–426, 430, 435–436
ISHS xvi, 22, 395, 438
islamic 224
Islamophobic 342
isotopy vi, xiv, 8, 73–74, 76, 79, 90–92, 94, 388, 393
Israel 357
Italy 22, 301, 337, 341, 357, 394–395, 406

J

jab line 93, 144, 152, 155, 216–217, 230, 250–251, 324–326, 331, 365, 388, 391, 435
Jewish 34, 355, 409, 425

K

keying vi, xx, 30, 50–53, 56, 62, 80, 167, 175, 216–221, 224, 231, 247, 256, 266, 268, 291, 295, 371, 388, 415, 418
kinesic 5, 95, 407

L

latching 226, 237–238, 389
Latin 19, 22, 78, 133, 154, 390
laughable ix, 7, 239, 241–245, 252–253, 257–258, 291–292, 296, 389, 410, 412, 415–416
leakage 39, 408
Least Disruption (principle of) 166, 175, 297, 314, 408
lexeme 93, 117, 122, 145, 147, 164, 171, 335
lexical xix, 70, 91–92, 107–108, 114, 117–118, 120–121, 124, 126, 129, 133–134, 139, 145, 172, 180, 182, 184–186, 189, 191, 194–195, 226, 330, 333, 335–336, 381, 385, 387–391, 400, 419
lexicon 92, 195–196, 393, 401, 416, 428
lexies 291, 407
liberation 59–61, 71, 76
lie 11, 15, 31, 133, 148, 159, 161, 163, 165–166, 174, 223, 266, 279, 281, 386
Limerick 143
limericks 221
linearity xiv, 90, 92, 106, 323, 326
listener 5–6, 63, 216, 251, 337
literature xi, 13–14, 18–21, 26, 42–43, 46, 51, 69, 100, 115, 135, 144, 163, 177, 180, 203, 213, 219, 221, 227–229, 237, 244, 248, 278, 281, 283, 286, 309–310, 317, 319–322, 324, 326–330, 332, 334, 336–341, 343, 360, 367–368, 372, 375–376, 379, 390, 394, 396, 404, 417–418, 422, 424–425, 428–429, 433–436
Liverpool 342, 426

local logic 71, 85–86, 94, 105–106,
ludic 94, 273, 414

M

macroscript 120–121
Malawi 282, 403
marker ix, 42–43, 54, 62, 102, 201, 207,
    214, 227–229, 231–233, 239, 242,
    289, 292–293, 298, 310, 314, 336,
    357, 382, 393, 395, 397, 401,
    410–411, 427
maxim (of cooperation) 133–135,
    159–161, 163, 166–170, 175, 329,
    345–346, 386, 395, 437
Mchongoano 224, 418
meme 5, 10, 25, 142, 204, 222, 293, 326,
    380, 391
meronymy 117, 389
mesolect 310–311, 386
mesolimbic 423
metacommunicative 61, 218–219, 221,
    227, 401
metalanguage 12, 27–28, 61–62, 97, 103,
    177, 209, 214, 219, 228, 293, 349,
    346, 420
metamessage 61–62, 67, 102–103,
    218–219, 273
metaphonology 433
metaphor 37, 60, 67, 73–74, 78, 88, 116,
    151, 162, 184, 236, 265, 291,
    312–313, 331–332, 381, 383, 401,
    411, 426, 432
metapragmatic 207, 411, 430, 435
metasemiotics 97, 102–103
metatextual 56
MICASE 286, 379
mirth v, xix, 3, 17–20, 30, 39, 41–47, 49,
    56, 80, 101, 178–179, 245,
    254–258, 261–262, 273, 293, 296,
    298, 302, 352, 386, 389, 391, 396,
    411
misunderstanding 82, 114–115, 131,
    174, 267, 311–312, 355, 431
mitigation 223, 255–256, 258,
    262, 277

mockery 10, 24, 99, 102, 108, 132, 217,
    224–225, 256–257, 259, 265,
    277–278, 288–289, 295, 362, 398,
    414
morpheme xiv–xv, 9, 17, 117, 139, 145,
    180, 182, 189, 382, 211, 311, 386,
    390–391
morphology 17, 108, 113, 122, 139, 189,
    382, 392, 401, 428
morphosyntactic 228
movie 124, 184, 309, 350, 356, 393, 420
multilingual 341, 358, 417
multimedia 176, 438
multimodal 5, 25–26, 141, 176, 232, 342,
    355–356, 365, 389, 397, 407, 411,
    430, 435

N

narrative vii, xvii, 8, 14, 16, 62, 80, 89,
    92, 138, 141–144, 148–149, 151,
    163, 216, 229–230, 247, 250, 260,
    296, 323–325, 329–331, 337, 361,
    385–386, 394–395, 398, 403,
    407–408, 413, 416, 418, 424, 427,
    435
narratological 319–320, 329–331
narrator 149, 260, 324, 331, 333
Netherlands 357, 395, 410, 434
network 5, 72, 116, 118–120, 122, 390
neural 68, 417, 423, 431, 435–436
neuroanatomical 68
neurolinguistic vi, 68, 71, 77, 196, 402
neurological 47, 57, 153, 191, 196, 429
neurology 68, 429
neuron 68, 71, 423
Njakiri 225, 408, 425
nonsense 33, 79, 83, 88, 90, 106, 144,
    178–179, 425, 431
nurse 255, 261–262, 281–282, 394, 421

O

obscene 140, 143–144, 155, 188, 206,
    258, 265–266, 308, 432
ontology vii, 113, 115, 119, 134–135,
    390, 416, 427–428

opposition vii–viii, xiv, xvii, 9, 11, 14, 25, 27, 30, 44, 50, 58, 64, 71–73, 82, 84, 88–89, 91, 93, 96, 100, 103, 105–106, 111, 120, 127–133, 135–138, 142, 149–152, 156, 168–169, 171, 176–177, 180, 197, 202, 221, 229, 271, 290, 295, 300, 306, 312, 314, 321–325, 327–329, 331, 334, 337–338, 361–362, 374, 385–389, 391, 397
optimality 189–190
orbicularis oculi (muscle) 40
orthography 176–177, 195, 237
OSTH 428

P

paradox 27–28, 61–62, 100, 262, 277
paralinguistic 215, 226–227, 249, 291, 293, 385, 407
paraphrase 61, 104–105, 139, 168, 178, 250–251, 261, 279, 344, 349, 359, 431
paratelic 86, 101, 389
paratone xvii, xix, 230
parody 12, 108, 222, 306, 319, 398
parole 31–33, 202, 211–212, 412
paronomasic 414, 433
paronymy 177, 179–180, 188, 197, 302, 387, 390
partonomy 117–118, 389–390
pedagogical xiii, xv, 91, 118, 199, 317, 349, 368, 380, 390, 401, 431
performance v, ix, xiv–xv, xix, 1, 30–33, 35, 37, 49–50, 55, 76, 81, 100, 111, 131, 141, 152–153, 156, 197, 199, 201–204, 206–212, 214–220, 222–224, 226–235, 247, 259–260, 274, 287, 295, 297, 301, 303, 305, 307, 315, 341, 347, 349, 369, 371, 373, 395, 397–398, 403, 405, 408, 424, 427, 430
perlocutionary 98–99, 101, 158, 165, 178–179, 245, 347, 352, 359, 365
personality 151, 328, 367, 394, 400, 409–411, 419–422, 439, 429

phenomenological 37, 235–237, 427
philosophy 18, 20–21, 58, 75, 159, 395, 405, 412, 417, 423, 432–433, 437
phlyax 338
phoneme xiv–xv, 12, 17, 26, 34, 70, 139–140, 176–177, 179, 188–190, 326, 345, 385, 390
phonetic xv, viii, 12, 56, 92, 177, 180, 188–189, 195, 230, 292
phonology 17, 34, 41, 68, 108, 113, 136, 139, 177, 182, 190, 195, 197, 321392, 415
phonotactic 189
phraseological 330, 335
physiological 19–20, 39, 48, 60, 421, 433
picaresque 319
Pinocchio 434
play vi, 14, 28, 50–51, 61, 63, 66–67, 72, 80–81, 85, 99, 101, 106, 125, 149–150, 164, 177, 188, 210, 217, 220, 224–225, 271, 277, 281, 294, 296, 301, 303, 388, 390, 393, 399, 418
plot 6, 124, 173, 196, 331, 336–337, 420
Poetics 18–19, 394, 412, 417, 419, 422
poetry 194, 345–346, 359
pointe 260
Polish 90, 154, 322, 403
politeness 12, 109, 132, 161, 175, 218, 225, 274–275, 277, 283–285, 288–289, 294, 399, 416, 423,
political 11, 65, 102, 208–209, 336, 342, 398, 400, 418, 425, 436
polysemiotic 355
polysemy 91, 389–390
polysyllabic 302
polythetic 409
power 88, 181, 213, 255, 275, 277, 281–282, 284, 305, 320, 407, 416, 418, 423, 429, 438
powerlessness 39
pragmatics viii, 11, 36, 48, 54, 66, 94, 96, 100, 103, 108–109, 111, 115, 126, 133–135, 157–159, 160–162, 164, 166, 168, 173, 175, 177, 182

pragmatics (Cont.)
    184–186, 197, 207, 245, 252, 271, 293, 296, 330, 337, 346, 353, 376, 396, 406–407, 409, 411–412, 414, 419
presupposition xix, 13, 124–125, 162–164, 170, 207, 250
pretense 28, 42, 149, 164, 175, 206, 224, 226, 257, 265, 289, 297, 320, 333, 415
profanity 206, 208, 218, 388
prominent 27, 60, 185, 187, 189, 195, 215, 238, 267, 269, 352, 375, 380
prosody 141, 226–228, 230–232, 289, 291, 237, 293, 326, 357, 385, 390, 394, 399, 400, 411, 427
prototypical 3–5, 7, 11, 39, 53, 58, 95, 115, 141–142, 145, 152, 186, 388, 409
psychiatry 145, 398, 408, 429
psychoanalytical 59, 82
psycholinguistics ix, 31, 115, 168, 176, 192, 196–197, 327, 335, 420
Psychology 13, 20, 31, 33, 38, 40, 44, 47–48, 50, 52, 55, 60, 62, 64, 68, 73, 75, 77, 79, 81–83, 86, 94, 114–115, 124–125, 153, 181, 203, 216, 243–244, 267, 297, 304, 306, 367–368, 370, 373, 380, 390, 393, 397, 399–402, 404–406, 408–413, 416–424, 427–430, 434, 436–439
psychophysical 406
psychotherapist 13
psychotherapy 421
pun viii–ix, xi, 9, 19, 21, 25–26, 61, 66, 68, 70, 76, 78, 101, 107–109, 111, 136–137, 139, 171–172, 176–182, 184, 186–193, 195–198, 221, 252–253, 260, 265, 273, 286, 300, 302, 321–322, 326, 332–333, 340, 343, 345–346, 350–351, 353, 356, 358–366, 381, 387, 389–392, 396, 406, 412, 414–415, 417, 420, 423, 427, 429, 432–433
punch line xix, 8–9, 14, 16, 28, 53, 56, 62, 64, 88–89, 91–93, 118, 139–144, 149, 151–152, 154–155, 164, 191, 196, 205–206, 216, 229–232, 247, 260, 312, 325–326, 331, 357, 359, 365, 388–389, 391, 425

R

ratified (participants) 5, 210, 216
reaction xix, 4, 38, 41–49, 54, 80–81, 115, 123, 130, 144, 155, 173, 203, 205–206, 209, 214–215, 223, 236, 242, 245, 248–250, 254–255, 259, 265, 268, 274, 278, 291, 293–295, 324 408, 419, 421, 424, 427
reductionism vi, 57–59, 68, 71, 76, 114, 135, 399
referent 108, 186, 239–245, 259, 270, 291, 350, 354, 365, 375, 389, 391–392
referential 19, 25–29, 62, 68, 136, 140, 176–177, 180–182, 184–185, 196, 273, 322, 353, 358–359, 361, 390, 392
register xi, 139–140, 207, 218, 228, 271, 309, 330, 333–336, 353, 390
reinterpretation 13, 72, 93, 185–186, 194, 325
Relevance xi, 76, 99, 101, 126, 159, 165, 169, 175, 222, 270, 273, 330, 348, 353–354, 369, 390, 393, 433, 437
relevant xiv, xvi, 5–6, 17, 22, 33, 36–37, 45, 49, 56, 83, 91, 108, 130, 147, 159–160, 164–165, 169–170, 180, 196, 201–202, 211, 216–217, 234–237, 242–243, 260–261, 289, 301, 319, 322, 334, 341, 348, 369–370, 373–375, 378, 385, 390, 395
relief 59–60, 281, 327, 336, 395, 423
Renaissance 8, 13, 19, 132, 337, 381
repertoire 65, 207, 213–215, 224, 226, 253, 284, 293–294, 315, 376, 385
repetition 45, 70, 91, 129, 140, 142, 187, 194, 227–228, 250, 252, 326, 334, 388, 420

resolution vi, ix, xv, 1, 28, 51-53, 64, 68, 71-72, 75, 78-80, 82-90, 92-94, 105-106, 108, 113, 123, 148-150, 163-165, 170, 176-177, 185, 187, 192-193, 195-197, 270, 272, 330, 334, 361, 389-390, 396-397, 405, 415, 429, 431

retractability 76, 83, 109, 273, 290

rhetorics 13, 19, 78, 203, 228, 242, 363, 401, 412, 431

rhyme 143, 194-195, 407, 409, 422

rhythm 41, 226-227, 389-390

riddle 8, 28, 65-66, 88, 142, 231, 399, 426

ridicule 3, 7, 9-10, 12, 65, 67, 75, 102, 145, 174, 399

risorius (muscle) 40

ritual 217, 222-224, 269, 272, 305, 309, 313

Romenian 353

routines 52, 216, 221, 267, 296

Russian 175, 213

S

salient 12, 60, 72, 93, 140, 181, 187, 189, 385-386, 396, 411

sarcasm xix, 3, 7, 10, 12-13, 168-169, 218, 225, 227, 231, 233, 238, 335, 358, 370, 397, 403, 413, 424, 434, 437

Sardinian 308, 427

satire 9, 70, 154, 225, 319-320, 337, 358, 403, 408, 431, 433, 436-437

Scandinavia 224, 357, 409, 424

scatological 140, 302, 308, 310, 335

schema 33, 52, 81-82, 115, 120, 124, 390, 393, 401, 421, 430

schizophrenia 27, 86

script vii-viii, xi, xiv-xv, xvii, xix-xx, 5, 13, 17, 50, 68, 72-74, 76, 79, 82, 88-89, 92-93, 100, 104-108, 111, 113-138, 141-142, 145, 147-153, 156-157, 163-164, 171-172, 177, 180, 202, 204, 232, 271-272, 301-304, 319-325, 327-328, 330-331, 335, 338, 361, 376, 385-386, 389-391, 397, 403, 405, 421, 428, 431

semiotics vii, xi, xix, 1, 25-26, 74, 82, 94-109, 111, 116, 118, 122, 141, 291, 323, 341-345, 356, 386, 391-392, 395, 419-420, 423, 432, 435

sex 25, 66, 79, 130, 132, 146, 151, 171-173, 179, 191, 208, 244-245, 259, 272, 279, 287, 306, 308-309, 314, 321, 352-353, 361, 370, 401, 406

signified 26, 97-98, 101-104, 116, 140, 194, 391

signifier 26, 97-98, 101-104, 107, 116, 136, 140, 176-178, 197, 326, 343, 345, 356, 359, 365, 391-392

sitcom 54-55, 141, 203, 292, 303, 326, 340-342, 348, 355, 407

Skopos xi, 351-354, 359, 364, 405, 421, 429, 436-437

slapstick 25, 176, 420

smiling v, 1, 3, 17-18, 30, 38-42, 44-46, 48, 54-56, 62, 80, 106, 150, 167, 208, 214, 230-233, 238-239, 243, 249, 256, 266, 271, 289, 291-293, 298, 314, 347, 352, 385, 391, 396, 402, 409-411, 413, 418, 427-429

Sociolinguistics ix-x, xiv, 31, 36, 51, 199, 201-203, 208-209, 211, 213, 215, 217, 219, 221-223, 225, 284, 299-300, 302, 304, 306-308, 310, 312-314, 376-377, 385, 387, 393, 399, 404-405, 407, 409-410, 413, 416, 423, 427

Sociology 33, 38, 44, 57, 114, 147, 203, 273, 285, 299, 308, 418-420, 425-426, 438

Spanish 203, 231, 309, 350, 355, 358, 413, 430, 435

SPEAKING (model) 212, 216, 224, 280, 309

speech viii–x, 3–6, 11–14, 28, 33, 36, 38–39, 41–42, 44, 46–49, 51–55, 58, 61, 69, 71, 76, 78, 81, 95, 98–100, 103, 107, 116, 118, 129, 135, 137, 140–143, 145, 154–155, 158–161, 164–172, 174–175, 177–179, 182, 185, 190–191, 193–196, 199, 201–202, 204–205, 207–223, 227–233, 236–238, 240, 242–245, 247–252, 254–267, 270–271, 273–275, 277–279, 284, 286, 288–292, 294–300, 302, 304, 306–307, 309, 312, 314–315, 319, 330, 335, 340, 351, 354–355, 357–359, 361, 369, 375, 377, 380–382, 385–389, 393, 399–400, 403, 405, 411–412, 414–415, 423, 425, 427, 432, 437

spreading activation 118, 125–126, 335

stance xiv, 58–59, 63, 72, 76, 198, 207–208, 233, 236, 262, 266, 270, 278, 281, 283, 319, 326, 337

stereotypes 28, 147–148, 152, 184, 207, 248, 254, 305–306, 312, 331, 346, 354–355, 376, 407, 409, 435

stress 141, 189, 191, 193, 205, 211, 213, 227, 238, 281, 341, 368, 373, 390

style xi, xv, 32, 139–140, 218, 237, 267, 269, 284, 309, 313, 319–321, 332–337, 339, 346, 359, 394–395, 407, 409, 417, 421, 433–434

subtitles xi, 54, 341, 351, 353, 357–358, 393–394, 400, 413, 426, 437

superiority 19–20, 59–60, 63, 67, 71, 82, 374, 386

suprasegmentals 226, 390

surprise vi, xv, 19–20, 53, 59, 80–81, 108, 148, 173, 196, 207, 300–301, 308, 391, 420, 406

synchronicity 226, 231, 233, 407, 411, 435

syntagmatic viii, 180–181, 186–188, 389, 391

syntax 32, 113, 185–186, 202, 382, 392, 403, 412

T

target vii, xi, xvii, xix, 28, 63, 65, 71, 76, 80, 132, 138, 143–147, 169, 179, 197, 210, 222, 225, 273, 279, 303, 310, 326, 343–345, 347–348, 351–355, 361, 365, 374–375, 386, 391–392, 405, 414, 416, 421

taxonomy 13, 47, 108, 177, 180–181, 184, 346, 415, 424

tease 12, 99, 220, 222, 224–225, 252, 265, 274, 277–279, 282, 288–289, 389, 407, 414, 434

telephone 153, 195, 215, 254, 256, 311, 394, 419

television 5, 25–26, 167, 176, 221, 294, 301, 356, 394, 420, 425, 438

tellability x, 208, 259–260, 424

theater 25, 176, 202–203, 270, 393, 413

transcription xv, xx, 54–55, 205, 237–238, 254–255, 261, 284, 395, 415, 417

translation xi, xv, 7, 83, 103–104, 109, 154, 175–176, 199, 204, 219, 271, 289, 310–312, 317, 340–366, 393–395, 397, 400, 402–408, 410, 412–413, 415–416, 419–422, 424, 426–429, 431–438

triangulation vi, 30, 37, 54–56, 293

U

unconscious 31, 66, 156, 159, 187, 264, 336, 410

understatement 162, 168, 228, 254, 367

unintentional vi, 39, 53–54, 95, 170–171, 174, 295, 396

unlaughter 209–210, 243, 249, 293, 433

untranslatability xi, 300, 346–347, 350, 359–362, 365, 413

utterance 5, 11, 13, 46, 48, 51, 54, 102–103, 124–125, 133, 136, 158, 161, 166–170, 173–174, 178, 185, 214–215, 217, 221, 228, 231–232,

241, 248, 255, 258, 261–262, 264–266, 270–271, 273, 278, 289–290, 296, 321, 326, 382, 385, 387–388, 390, 437

V

variation 33, 92, 103, 199, 213, 223, 278, 286, 304, 306, 315, 356, 375, 379, 399–400

variationist x, xiv, 36, 297, 299, 304–305, 307, 309, 311

verbal v, vii-viii, xv, 19, 25–26, 29, 62, 68, 76, 79, 87, 95, 104, 107, 111, 113–114, 136–142, 144–146, 148–150, 152–157, 176–178, 180–182, 184, 186–188, 190, 192, 194, 196, 198, 203, 213, 216, 221, 224–226, 232–233, 238, 248–249, 268, 293–294, 299, 320, 324–325, 327, 330–332, 339, 342–343, 345–347, 358–359, 386, 390, 392–394, 396, 401–402, 407, 410, 414–415, 418, 420–421, 426, 428, 432, 436

vernacular 222, 310

violation viii, 20, 60–61, 63, 66, 80, 108, 133, 157, 160–161, 163–168, 170, 175, 310, 333, 336, 387, 389, 395, 411, 422–423

visual 5, 25–26, 95, 107, 109, 118, 141–142, 149, 176, 184, 292, 326, 336, 342–343, 355–356, 389, 391, 415, 422–423

volume 41, 131, 154–155, 205, 215, 229–230, 232, 234, 292

W

warrant 74, 260, 408

WHIM 21–22

WHIMSY 22

wit 7, 16, 83, 253, 259, 264, 320, 338, 354, 399, 407

witticisms 16, 78, 326

Witz 410

women 38, 45, 148, 151–152, 155, 179, 188, 227, 244, 246, 269, 282, 285, 287–288, 294, 299, 305–306, 308–309, 311, 333, 370, 397, 406, 414, 416–419, 421

wordplay 177–178, 221, 347, 396, 406, 427, 435, 437

workplace x, 167, 261, 269, 274, 276, 283–285, 287–288, 298, 306, 416, 418, 423, 429, 432

Z

Zinacantecan 309

zygomatic (muscle) 40